Franchthi Neolithic Pottery

Excavations at Franchthi Cave, Greece

FASCICLE 10

Franchthi Neolithic Pottery

VOLUME 2
THE LATER NEOLITHIC CERAMIC PHASES 3 TO 5

KAREN D. VITELLI

with a Contribution on the Post-Neolithic Remains by
James A. Dengate

INDIANA UNIVERSITY PRESS
Bloomington & Indianapolis

Production editing by Anne and Christopher Chippindale
Typeset by Gary Reynolds
Manufactured in the United States of America

This book has been supported by a grant from the National Endowment for the Humanities, an independent federal agency

Library of Congress Cataloging-in-Publication Data

Vitelli, Karen D.
Franchthi Neolithic pottery.

p. cm. — (Excavations at Franchthi Cave, Greece; fasc. 8)
Includes bibliographical references and index.
Contents: v. 1. Classification and ceramic phases 1 and 2.
1 Franchthi Cave (Greece) 2. Paralia Site (Greece)
3. Neolithic period—Greece. 4. Pottery, Prehistoric—Greece.
I. Title. II. Series.
GN816.F73V58 1993 738.3´ 82´ 09388—dc20 92-43943

p. cm. — (Excavations at Franchthi Cave, Greece; fasc. 10)
Includes bibliographical references and index.
Contents: v. 2. The Later Neolithic Ceramic Phases 3 to 5.
ISBN 0-253-21306-1 (pbk.: v. 2)

1 2 3 4 5 04 03 02 01 00 99

CONTENTS

TABLES

In the text

at the end of the volume

PLANS

FIGURES

PLATES

PUBLISHING ACKNOWLEDGEMENTS

The research and compilation of the manuscript for this final publication were made possible through a generous grant from The Shelby White-Leon Levy Program for Archaeological Publications; a Research Leave Supplement Grant from the Vice President for Research at Indiana University; and, from the National Endowment for the Humanities, a grant for preparation of the manuscript as camera-ready copy.

PREFACE

I have long looked forward to writing the preface to this second volume on the Franchthi pottery, knowing that doing so would mean the weight of my obligation to publish would be lifting at last. I have also long suspected that by the time I finished the volume, I would be so engaged by the later Neolithic material that this "final" publication, as we generally refer to excavation reports, would be anything but my final word on the subject. Both are true. I feel a growing sense of relief and liberation as the light in this long tunnel grows brighter, accompanied by an eagerness to begin an array of new experimental projects and research directions to address questions raised in my mind by the present study.

This is also the place where I may acknowledge with sincere gratitude the extensive help of colleagues and institutions. My colleagues in the field were many—noted in volume one (Vitelli 1993a:xviii)—and instrumental in pointing the direction for my work. Tom Jacobsen launched me on this project. Catherine Perlès, Tracey Cullen, and Reg Heron have been patient, inspiring, and supportive colleagues and friends throughout its long course. Recently, many others have taken time from busy schedules to find and supply information on short notice. I thank, in particular, John Coleman, Della Cook, Bill Farrand, Mats Johnson, Ada Kalogirou, Don Keller, Steve Koob, Dan Pullen, Jerry Rutter, Anna Stroulia, and Nancy Wilkie. Mary Pirkl, Robert Green, and Tom Whitcomb provided timely and welcome assistance with preparation of the manuscript. Anne and Chris Chippindale, knowing from prior experience what they were getting into, still agreed to take on the chores of editing and production.

In 1993, the Franchthi Project was awarded a grant from the National Endowment for the Humanities (RK 2002-73) to provide funds for editing and production of camera-ready manuscripts of five new volumes in the Franchthi series, including this one. The award encouraged us, eliciting a renewed sense of commitment to the project, and promises from all the authors to produce manuscripts by deadlines that were, inevitably, overly optimistic. We each pecked away at our respective studies at a "normal" pace, i.e., between other obligations, a month in the summer, occasional weekends, preparing short portions of the study for conference papers and journal articles. None could, or did, arrange the stretch of relatively uninterrupted time necessary to compile and digest the masses of data each of us was responsible for, but each was "making progress."

In November 1996, we learned to our horror that our NEH grant had an absolute deadline, that on July 31, 1998, any unexpended funds would revert to the US Treasury. Not only would we forfeit the funds we were counting on to transform our manuscripts into camera-ready copy, but the funds would not even be returned to NEH for use on other archaeological projects. A year and a half's notice is not much with which to rearrange one's life, which is what each of the authors covered by the NEH grant has had to do. As I write, it is still not clear how many of us will meet the NEH deadline. I am the lucky one who was able to arrange on short notice a leave of absence from Indiana University to spend the year writing. I thank colleagues and students in the Anthropology Department and the few remaining students in the Program in Classical Archaeology for their patience during my unexpected absence that has had repercussions for their lives as well.

NEH's deadline has forced me to "just do it." Writing under this kind of pressure is hardly ideal, but there is no question that NEH provided the impetus to complete something I had been putting off for far too long. Most of us have every intention of completing the projects we undertake, but always other obligations compete for our time. Most of them do have absolute deadlines. Most require less concentrated and extended time, and thus they take priority.

Had I been forced, say ten years ago, to make time to finish Franchthi, I would have found a way to do it. The result would, no doubt, have been different. I have learned in the last ten years, have developed additional ideas and interests. Much has been added to the literature of Aegean prehistory that would not have been available to me then. Reg Heron has made a few more photographs for the volume. I have looked at some sherds again and taken more notes. But ten years ago I was closer to the fieldwork at Franchthi, and remembered each sherd far more vividly—how often in recent months I have gone searching through notes for a piece "clearly" remembered from Franchthi, only to find that it was actually from Lerna, or seen on that trip to Thessaly. And in the interim, colleagues working with their own later Neolithic material have not been able to incorporate Franchthi's contributions into their own work, or have used outdated information from preliminary reports. Besides, it feels really good to complete an undertaking like this one.

I think an absolute deadline, and perhaps other enticements—return of funds if the project is not completed as and when promised, withholding of permits and funds for future projects until past ones are published and the archives secure—should be adopted by all agencies and organizations that support fieldwork.

I would also express my gratitude to the Shelby White–Leon Levy Publications Program, and Indiana University's Research Leave Supplement Grant Program, whose funding enabled my year free from most teaching duties to concentrate on writing. The new White–Levy Publication Program, which provides funds for the publication of older excavations too long left unpublished and therefore incomplete, is a most welcome and needed source of support for archaeology. Obviously, if we are to require colleagues to produce reports on fieldwork promptly, there must be means to make the time available to do so. I applaud the establishment of the program, as well as their requirement of documentation of permission to publish from the country in which the materials were recovered, and the proviso that recipients may be required to return funds if the proposed project is not completed. These seem to me responsible and thoughtful conditions, designed, like the Program itself, to make archaeology more professional and responsible to its public.

I regret and find most contradictory that the individuals who established and fund this Program and other important archaeological undertakings are also significant collectors of ancient art. I shall continue to urge them and others to see the error of their ways, and to make clear to a larger public the damage done to the archaeological record and our understanding of the past by the collecting of undocumented antiquities.

The damage, of course, is the destruction of archaeological context and the associations among all the remains of ancient activities. I have made that point so many times in so many ways that, when my turn comes to work with excavated materials, as here, I feel an absolute obligation to examine the fine details of contextual evidence and to explore fully the association of materials. Otherwise, as the collectors and dealers are fond of saying, and with some truth, "archaeologists are no better than looters." My experience suggests that, when we do pay as close attention to recovering and analyzing contextual information as we say we do when we are decrying collecting and looting, the results are every bit as rewarding as we claim. I trust colleagues will feel in the ensuing pages the frustration that is engendered by recent disturbances within the cave and the loss of contextual information for the latest occupations that those disturbances have caused. Perhaps Shelby White and Leon Levy, who are doing so much good for archaeology, will also understand the losses engendered by their collecting.

Bloomington, Indiana
May 1998

CHAPTER ONE

Background for the Study

INTRODUCTION

Franchthi Cave is located in a limestone headland north of Kiladha Bay, in the southern Argolid of Greece. Today it is a coastal site, but at the beginning of the Neolithic period the cave mouth looked out across a plain cut by several streams to sandy beaches and coastal marshes a kilometer or two distant (Jameson et al. 1994:203; van Andel and Sutton 1987:Fig. 17). By the later Neolithic, subject of the present study, the ongoing rise in sea level had brought the shoreline to within 500 m of the cave and substantially decreased the extent of the coastal plain (Jameson et al. 1994:208, Fig. 3.32). Franchthi was the site of repeated activities by prehistoric peoples from the Upper Palaeolithic through the Neolithic periods.

From 1967 to 1976, usually in alternate summer seasons, Thomas W. Jacobsen directed excavations in the cave and along the modern shoreline, or Paralia, for Indiana University and the American School of Classical Studies at Athens, and with the permission and supervision of the Greek Archaeological Service and the Delta Ephoria in Nauplion. An international team of scholars worked, and continues working, on the publication of the vast and complex materials recovered from this long-lived and important archaeological site.[1]

Among the published volumes, Fascicle 8 (Vitelli 1993a) provides my report on the ceramics from Franchthi Ceramic Phases 1 and 2, equivalent to the Early and Middle Neolithic phases in Greece generally. A break in occupation separates these earlier Neolithic phases from the subsequent deposits. The present volume completes the report on the remaining ceramics from the excavations—the later Neolithic, comprising Franchthi Ceramic Phases 3 to 5, an inventory of the ceramic objects other than pottery and figurines (Document 1), and a report on the Post-Neolithic finds by James Dengate (Document 2).

The total amount of pottery from the later Neolithic deposits at Franchthi constitutes only about a fifth of that from the entire excavations. Unlike the earlier Neolithic occupations, which were documented in multiple sequences inside the cave and on Paralia, the stratified material from the later Neolithic activities derives almost exclusively from a single trench. The methods and theory that guided my work on the entire assemblage are spelled out in Fascicle 8 (Vitelli 1993a:Part 1). For the present study, I needed to apply these to the specifics of the later Neolithic assemblage and deposits. My field analyses were completed, the data collected by the mid 1980s. When I began work on this volume, it looked as though my job would be much easier than has, in fact, proved the case.

The quantity of material is much smaller, but it is a far more diverse collection than that from the earlier Neolithic. Each of the greater number of ceramic categories required definition and description, but each has fewer examples than earlier categories by which to make clear its characteristics and range of variation. The limited amount of pottery (ca. 400 kg, vs 1500 kg for the earlier Neolithic) to represent activities over such a long span of time—as much as several millennia (see Table 9)—raises questions by itself. The nature of the material and of the deposits from which it comes made it difficult to apply rigidly the approaches and standards that I developed for and from the more extensive and uniform material from the earlier Neolithic.

Since the stratified material comes largely from a single trench, I needed to digest and describe less contextual information than for the multiple sequences of the earlier Neolithic activities. On the other hand, a single stratigraphic column rarely, if ever, presents a straightforward record of sequential activities free of (potential) mixing among the strata. With a single sequence, I had nowhere to test the multiple hypotheses suggested by each deposit within the preserved column. The results of the phasing are, necessarily, more tentative than for the earlier Neolithic.

Nevertheless, it was clear from the beginning of this study that the social dynamics responsible for the later Neolithic deposits at Franchthi and elsewhere in the Peloponnese were very different than those that had obtained earlier. Whereas a single strong ceramic tradition was shared throughout southern Greece during the Middle Neolithic, and pieces made in that tradition rarely found their way beyond the region of production, the later Neolithic presents an almost dizzying array of ceramic stylistic traditions. Differences in social and economic organization between northern and southern Greece are more apparent than in the Middle Neolithic. The similarity between some northern and southern Greek ceramic styles is a sign that people in the later Neolithic participated in a larger world or sphere of interaction. Yet, in southern Greece, at the same time that we find signs of people acquiring goods and ideas from around the Aegean and beyond, we also find fewer and fewer signs of their activities at home, in the reasonably well surveyed eastern Peloponnese.

The substantial remains from Middle Neolithic activities in the eastern Peloponnese dwindle to but a few sites in the late Neolithic. Because most of these are cave sites many have seen an increase in pastoralism in the later Neolithic, although shepherds in the hills with their flocks seem unlikely to have spawned the increase in "international" exchange evidenced in their material remains. Nor is it clear what happened to the apparently thriving Middle Neolithic communities. These, then, are the questions that, in addition to more general goals of the entire study, informed my analyses of the later Neolithic ceramics from Franchthi.

CLASSIFICATION

The later Neolithic remains at Franchthi Cave span roughly two millennia, ca. 5700–3700 BC calibrated (Table 9). The ceramics are here assigned to two Franchthi Ceramic Phases (FCPs), FCP 3 and FCP 4, that form part of what is generally called the Late Neolithic (LN) in southern Greece, and to a third phase, FCP 5, that represents a portion of the very long Final Neolithic (FN) phase.

Discussions of most of the pottery included in the present study have appeared in preliminary reports by Jacobsen (1969, 1973b) and Diamant (1974). Only a limited quantity of FCP 5 material, from excavations on Paralia, was excavated subsequent to those reports. Nevertheless, my conclusions differ markedly from the earlier accounts, particularly in terms of continuity in occupation of the cave. The addition of radiocarbon dates from crucial parts of the sequence is partly responsible for the differing interpretations; the major differences follow from the approaches used in arriving at them. Mine are essentially those used in studying the earlier Neolithic remains at Franchthi and detailed in the first volume (Vitelli 1993a:Part 1); they are only summarized here.

From the outset of my studies, I have aimed to organize the study of the ceramics to provide insights into the human behavior that produced the remains. Ultimately, I want to use the potsherds—only a single complete pot (FP 197, Fig. 67i) was recovered from the later Neolithic deposits—to help understand how the people at Franchthi ordered their lives, how they interacted with others at the cave and beyond, how their environment contributed to their choices and directions.

Potsherds provide a most direct access to human behavior through the traces they carry of their manufacture, hence to decisions exercised by potters, most or all of whom were probably women (Vitelli 1993a:xx). A potter makes choices in every step of the production process (Vitelli 1993b:3–5). By selecting variables from the potting process, and ordering them hierarchically in the sequence imposed by the ceramic production process, I can use the resulting classification to address questions related to the potters' choices and motivations in exercising those choices (Hill and Evans 1972:252–255).

My classification process begins with a determination of whether a particular clay body included calcium carbonates, hereafter "Lime," determined by dipping water-soaked sherds in dilute hydrochloric acid, and looking for nonplastic inclusions that effervesce. This step determines the "class"—calcareous or noncalcareous. In the second hierarchical step in classification, again following the potter's sequence, I consider the additional raw materials used for the clay body. I looked at the nonplastic inclusions and, based on what I could observe with a 10x hand lens and by dipping in hydrochloric acid, determined the "ware" assignment based on clay body composition. After building a pot, the potter has numerous options for finishing the surfaces. I used these, i.e., any additional raw materials used as pigments, and the series of procedures used to finish the surface of a piece to distinguish "varieties" as subsets of a ware.

This, at least, is the ideal procedure for which I aimed. For the FCP 1 and 2 pottery, which derived from multiple stratified sequences and was represented in tens, even hundreds of thousands of sherds, the system worked exceptionally well. In retrospect, I suspect it also worked well because the FCP 1 and FCP 2 potters worked very consistently, following relatively precise recipes and rules. Their successors were less well regimented, and worked under more variable social rules for pottery production. For FCP 3 and FCP 4, I was able to identify reasonably consistent classes, wares, and their varieties. I occasionally noted unusual nonplastics in a sherd that, in surface finish, resembled other sherds from the same unit. The occasional unusual nonplastic could be an accidental inclusion picked up in the place where the potter worked the clay, it could be something I simply failed to notice in other sherds, or it could indicate a different source for the clay body, i.e., a different ware. When I encountered an unusual inclusion, I checked other sherds specifically for similar inclusions. If I could not establish a clear pattern for the occurrence of the unusual inclusion, I generally assigned the sherd to the ware it most closely resembled. I suspect my assignments include some sherds that were made from somewhat different clay bodies than the majority of the pieces, i.e., the wares encompass a wide range of variation.

Occasionally I found sherds that differed from most others in the assemblage in both fabric and surface finish. These sherds, few in number, are likely to have been brought to Franchthi from elsewhere. The examples are too few to provide a good sense of the component raw materials with the field techniques I had available. Not assigning them to specific wares, I have segregated them as distinctive varieties, of uncertain ware.

For FCP 5, the system of classification employed for earlier phases works poorly. I was unsuccessful in identifying consistent "wares" within this assemblage, for a variety of reasons detailed in the introduction to FCP 5 (Chapter 5). I have identified a number of "vari eties," reflecting the different surface finishes used for the pieces, but the varieties may be from one or more unidentified wares. Although frustrating from the perspective of the typologist, the variation evident in the FCP 5 ceramics is in itself significant; it is probably more informative about ceramic production and practices in the 4th millennium than a neater classification would have been.

TERMINOLOGY

Because the classification system developed for the Franchthi pottery differs from other systems used in the Aegean, I have chosen names for the resulting categories that acknowledge the differences. Each sherd is, at least in theory, a member of three hierarchically ranked categories—class, ware, variety—and requires its membership in each to be identified. Table 1.1 provides these labels, including a common or short name used throughout the text and an abbreviation used in tables, for the categories in FCP 3 and FCP 4. The terminology for FCP 5 categories is explained in Chapter 5.

CHARACTERIZATION STUDIES

Fourteen sherds of later Neolithic varieties were among the Franchthi sherds submitted to the Fitch Laboratory of the British School in Athens in 1975 (Vitelli 1993a:13–19, Table I, #40–53). The samples included three Lime plus Iron (#40–42), two Ungritted Manganese Painted (#43–44), one Gray Burnished (#45), two Low Lime Burnished (#46–47), one Andesite Burnished (#48), two with a thick white crust (#51, 53), one with red powder on both surfaces (#50), and two with traces of both red and white powder (#49, 52).[2]

All later Neolithic varieties were not represented in the sample. Those that were, were represented by few samples. The sampled sherds did not all receive the full range of analyses. Many of the analyses were, by today's standards, unsophisticated. With these and the other caveats about the larger Franchthi characterization project (Vitelli 1993a:13–19) in mind, all the later Neolithic samples tested fall well within the cluster identified by Jones as "local clays," which "are not greatly different from those of the central and southern

Table 1.1. Later Neolithic Franchthi ceramic categories

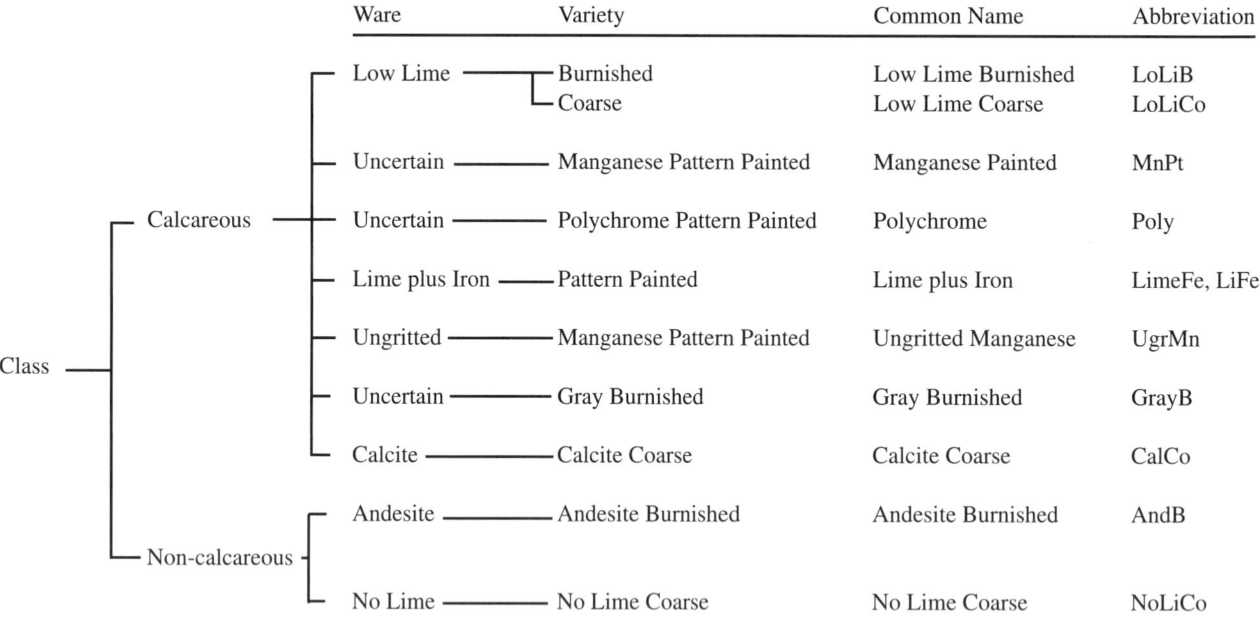

Class	Ware	Variety	Common Name	Abbreviation
Calcareous	Low Lime	Burnished	Low Lime Burnished	LoLiB
		Coarse	Low Lime Coarse	LoLiCo
	Uncertain	Manganese Pattern Painted	Manganese Painted	MnPt
	Uncertain	Polychrome Pattern Painted	Polychrome	Poly
	Lime plus Iron	Pattern Painted	Lime plus Iron	LimeFe, LiFe
	Ungritted	Manganese Pattern Painted	Ungritted Manganese	UgrMn
	Uncertain	Gray Burnished	Gray Burnished	GrayB
	Calcite	Calcite Coarse	Calcite Coarse	CalCo
Non-calcareous	Andesite	Andesite Burnished	Andesite Burnished	AndB
	No Lime	No Lime Coarse	No Lime Coarse	NoLiCo

Argolid" (Jones 1986:393, Fig. 4.3). Jones identified some pigments, by X-ray diffraction and fluorescence (1986: 770–771, Table 9.6a). These are referred to in the following text where relevant. A new program of study, with more specific questions, more thoughtful sampling, and more precise and appropriate analytical procedures, would be helpful in resolving some of the many remaining questions about Neolithic ceramic technology. It would be useful to include samples of southern Greek later Neolithic sherds in a larger program of characterization and other studies aimed at identifying sources of raw materials and pots but this will necessarily be a very large and long-term project.

THE CERAMIC PHASING

In phasing the later Neolithic sequence, I identified points of ceramic change within the stratigraphic sequence and evaluated the nature and magnitude of ceramic change at each point in the sequence. The excavation unit[3] (hereafter "unit") provides the closest temporal associations we can make among a number of objects. If a given unit removed (part of) a uniform sedimentological deposit, then we assume its constituent parts are in some sense contemporary. A series of superimposed excavation units, i.e., a stratigraphic column, through invocation of the law of superposition, records sequential events in one (limited) space.

The superposition of units implies only the relative sequence of their deposition. Nothing is implicit in their superposition about the rate of sediment accumulation, the continuity or completeness of accumulation in that space, or of the relation of units included in one columnar sequence to units in any other column. Such information must be inferred from the constituent parts of each unit. The ceramic phasing is a summary of correlations among units and sequences on the basis of their ceramic contents.

Procedures

Trench FA provides the only stratified deposits for Ceramic Phases 3 and 4. The trench was divided and excavated in north (FAN) and south (FAS) halves. Each half had four corners for which the complete sequence of superimposed units is recorded. FA, therefore, provides eight stratigraphic columns, if all from a small area. I began by sorting the ceramic contents of each FA unit into the categories noted above, and recorded the weight in grams of each category in each unit. I then converted the absolute weights to percentages to facilitate comparison of excavated units of different volumes. The resulting percentages for the entire Neolithic sequence are plotted in histograms for each of the eight stratigraphic columns in FA (Vitelli 1993a:Tables 4–11). The percentages are provided in Tables 1–8 in this volume. Each ceramic phase is defined

Table 1.2. Phases, subphases and assigned units

Note: Units in parentheses crosscut phase or subphase boundaries and may therefore be listed in more than one (sub)phase. Commas separate units in a sequence, semicolons separate sequences.

Early Late Neolithic	FCP 3	FAN: (121–119), 118–112, (111)
		FAS: (117–116), 115–114, (113)
Later Late Neolithic	FCP 4.1	FAN: (111), 110–100, 98, 96
		FAS: (113), 112–100, 98–97, (96)
	FCP 4.2	FAN: 99, 97, 95–94, 90–89
		FAS: 99, 95–87
	FCP 4.3	FAN: 87–84, 82–81 (very mixed)
		FAS: 86–82
Final Neolithic	FCP 5.1a	FAN: (84–83, 80), 77, 73
		FAS: (83–82), 81–75
	FCP 5.1b	FAN: 69, 67, 65–63
		FAS: 74–59
	FCP 5.1c	FAN: 61–59
	FCP 5.1	L5NE: 22, 16, 10, 5; 26–24, 14, 12, 8, 4; 32, 29, 23, 19–17, 13, 6; 21–20, 15, 11, 7–6, 3–2
		L5(NW): 98–95, 89–85; 68–63, 61–55
		L5(SE): 17–1 (pit: 14–13)
	FCP 5.2	FA 46–45, 39

by a set of varieties that represents the total ceramic production, use, and discard over one stretch of time.

Ceramic Phase Boundaries

The appearance in a given sequence of one or more new varieties marks a point of innovation, of cultural change. New varieties might be added to an ongoing tradition in the course of gradual change, as was apparently the case with Urf varieties at the beginning of the Middle Neolithic (Vitelli 1993a:53). Alternatively, they might represent an entirely new tradition that abruptly replaced an earlier one, even though the discarded sherds entered the archaeological record slowly at first and are found in low frequency with older varieties, through artificial mixing along the lithostratigraphic boundary. To examine these alternative explanations and evaluate the nature of the ceramic change, I assigned, at least initially, units in a sequence in which new varieties first occurred to a phase boundary.

Thus units in which the first examples of FCP 3 varieties occur were assigned to the FCP 2/FCP 3 boundary and examined for evidence relevant to the nature of the change. I did the same for units along the FCP 3/FCP 4 and FCP 4/FCP 5 boundaries. In each case, I considered all the variables of sherds from both sets of varieties and compared them with sherds from earlier and later deposits, looking for any features that suggested development or change between the examples in the boundary units and units above and below the boundary group. I also considered information in the field notebooks and other stratigraphic records, joins among sherds from different units, and the presence of human bone scatter for any suggestion of cross-cutting or other indications of artificial mixing of cultural materials along a stratigraphic interface. The weight of the evidence determined whether the units with combined variety sets pointed to gradual or abrupt change.

Because the total number of especially FCP 3 and FCP 4 sherds is relatively small, I found that dividing them into many subgroups produced statistically unconvincing differences among the groups and made it difficult to see any patterns at all. Thus, once I had established that a group of sherds from boundary units were found together because of artificial mixing along an interface that represented abrupt change (at least within FA), I reassigned sherds from the boundary units to the relevant larger phase group. For example, having determined that a hiatus separated the deposition of FCP 2 and FCP 3 ceramics and that sherds from FCP 2/FCP 3 boundary units were found together because of artificial mixing, I reassigned sherds of FCP 3 varieties to FCP 3. Similarly, FCP 4 sherds from FCP 3/FCP 4 boundary units were eventually reassigned to the first FCP 4 subphase.

Subphase Boundaries

The term "subphase" implies that each is part of a continuous ceramic tradition. For FCP 1 and FCP 2, I was able—in fact found it necessary—to consider spatial as well as temporal variation in evaluating differences in the ceramics of a single variety set from various locations (Vitelli 1993a:23–25). For FCP 3 and FCP

4, all the stratified ceramics derive from FA, so there is no opportunity to evaluate the potential role of spatial variation in the sample. Within FCP 4 I was able to identify an innovation (the addition of Calcite Coarse ware) within an ongoing tradition that was clearly located within a sequence of superimposed deposits. I have therefore assigned the units with the innovation to a later subphase within FCP 4. The subphase boundary, between the earlier FCP 4.1 and the later FCP 4.2, is drawn along the lower interface of units in which the innovation first appears (Vitelli 1993a:25). If we had had other sequences with which to compare the FCP 4 sequence in FA, the Calcite-tempered coarse ware and the other features noted in FCP 4.2 might have been seen to occur in earlier deposits. The apparent innovation in FA would then be an indication of differential use of space rather than an indicator of temporal change. Without other sequences, and given the lithostratigraphic change and the superposition of FCP 4.2 units above FCP 4.1, I elected to emphasize the temporal difference by creating a subphase.

I examined the pottery from units assigned to the FCP 4/ FCP 5 boundary in the same way, and again concluded the innovations probably marked abrupt change. Before reassigning the FCP 4 sherds from those units to the later subphase, I compared the two groups. Again, although a richer set of stratigraphic sequences might change the picture, I found sufficient innovations among the sherds from the boundary units, along with a lithostratigraphic difference, to justify the creation of a third subphase, FCP 4.3.

Stratified deposits with FCP 5 varieties occur both inside the cave in FA and on Paralia in L5, and might have provided opportunity for evaluating spatial versus temporal variation in the deposits. Unfortunately, the FCP 5 pottery is so variable, the quality of preservation between cave and Paralia sherds is so different, and documented ancient and modern reworking and mixing of deposits is so pervasive that this was not possible. One clear point of innovation within FCP 5 is documented within FA, and allows the designation of two subphases, FCP 5.1 and FCP 5.2. The Paralia deposits in L5 are closer to the earlier than the later subphase material in FA and thus are also assigned to FCP 5.1, but a more precise temporal relationship is not possible to extract.

Three superimposed strata recorded on the section drawing within the FCP 5.1 deposits in FA suggest sequential activities within the subphase in that area. I tried eliminating potentially cross-cut or reworked deposits from the initial phasing considerations, a practice that had been effective for earlier Neolithic deposits (Vitelli 1993a:24). Eliminating units from consideration on these grounds for the later Neolithic, however, left few if any units to consider. When it did prove possible, the sample size became so small that any observations of differences are far from compelling. The evidence was simply insufficient to justify the creation of a subphase for each of the strata. On the chance that future sites may recover a clearer stratigraphic sequence and find the hints at Franchthi helpful, I have kept the pottery from each FA stratum separate and designated each as a potential subset of FCP 5.1 by the addition of letters, i.e., FCP 5.1a–c.

NOTES

1. Nine volumes, or fascicles, in the series of specialist reports have appeared: Jacobsen and Farrand 1987, van Andel and Sutton 1987, Perlès 1987, Shackleton 1988, Perlès 1990, Wilkinson and Duhon 1990, Hansen 1991, Vitelli 1993a, and Talalay 1993. Four additional volumes, in addition to the present one, are, as I write, approaching the final manuscript stage (Whitney-Desautels, "Land and Freshwater Molluscs"; Farrand, "The Sedimentology"; Rose, "Fishing"; Cullen and Cook, "Mortuary Practices and Human Biology"), and another four are expected to follow within the next two to three years (Stroulia, "Ground Stone"; Miller, "Ornaments"; Perlès, "Neolithic Lithics"; Redding, "Macrofauna"). Preliminary work has begun on a "Level Two" volume that will synthesize the picture provided by the fascicles of specialist reports (see Jacobsen and Farrand 1987:9–10).

2. The specific analyses performed on each sample are indicated in Vitelli 1993a: Table I, the full results of the optical emission spectrography in Jones 1986:386–402, Fiches 510.040–053.

3. "Excavation units: Three-dimensional bodies of sediment removed sequentially by excavators within each trench. Details vary, but in general, excavation units are numbered serially from the top down for each trench. An excavation unit may comprise all the sediment through a given thickness (normally between 1 cm and 10 cm) across the whole trench, or across only a part of the trench, or of an individual feature (a hearth, burial pit, etc.). To the extent possible, excavation units were dug to conform to the lithostratigraphy. There may be more than one excavation unit, either vertically or horizontally (laterally) contiguous, within a given lithostratigraphic unit, if the latter is extensive" (Jacobsen and Farrand 1987:16).

CHAPTER TWO

The Later Neolithic Contexts

INTRODUCTION

The Late Neolithic pottery from FCP 3 and FCP 4 derives entirely from inside the cave, which also has substantial remains from FCP 5. Not a single Late Neolithic sherd, i.e. from FCP 3 or FCP 4, was identified from Paralia. After extensive use in FCP 2, Paralia was apparently abandoned; it saw no activity that produced ceramic remains until FCP 5.

Inside the cave the later Neolithic deposits were near the surface. They were largely excavated in the first seasons of work, before standard recording and other procedures were firmly established. The records for the relevant units are of variable quality and detail. Many of the units that produced later Neolithic pottery were reworked or redeposited and included post-Neolithic pottery. Some were rich in Palaeolithic and Mesolithic materials (Perlès, pers. comm.).

Unfortunately, the pottery from trenches excavated in 1967 (Trenches A–G) was lotted;[1] much was discarded immediately (Vitelli 1993a:32–33 and n.10). When excavation on Paralia began in earnest in 1973, additional discard of the majority of sherds from mixed deposits in the cave took place to make room in the cramped storage facilities in Navplion for the large amounts of new pottery coming from Paralia. Much of the pottery from the upper deposits in the cave is thus no longer available for study. For affected units, I have had to rely on often sketchy accounts in the notebooks, which frequently refer to categories of pottery (e.g., "slipped and burnished," "coarse/undiagnostic") that are too vague to assign to a phase, much less a ware.

Pottery from the reworked deposits includes occasional sherds from essentially all post-Neolithic phases, including relatively recent modern sherds, probably from within the last 50–60 years. Since some "hearths" within these disturbed levels produced fine examples of pottery and other objects from all phases of the Neolithic, they might represent the work of *arhaiokapili*, looters (Vitelli 1993a:34, n. 13). For several such hearths encountered within the reworked deposits of Trench A, the field notebook records: "other patches of orange clay . . . can be seen on the surface in the cave. . . . Workmen called hearth a bread oven for a Vlach (herd)" (notebook 501:6, 22/6/67). Immediately before our excavations began, and during winters between excavation seasons, shepherds used the cave to shelter flocks of goats, contained within *mandria*. According to various sources, locals used to mine dung from the cave for their agricultural fields (Jacobsen 1969:367 n. 29). Catherine Perlès was told that Mr. Livanos, who owns the small island in Kiladha harbor directly opposite the cave, had transported ferryboat-loads of cave sediment to the island to improve its soil (pers. comm. 7/97).

It seems unlikely that mining activities could be entirely responsible for the deep digging into Neolithic and the even deeper Palaeolithic deposits; the remaining reworked deposits are still quite rich in artifactual material, suggesting that the deposits were dug through and rearranged, but not removed. Mining activities would, logically, have been located near the mouth of the cave for relatively easy access. The trenches nearest the modern entrance, G, G1, and H2 (Plan 1), produced relatively undisturbed Middle Neolithic deposits very close to the modern surface. Any deposits of later Neolithic remains in those trenches may have been lost to mining. Whatever the occasions of the recent digging, they succeeded in destroying a substantial portion of the prehistoric record.

LATER NEOLITHIC DEPOSITS WITHIN THE CAVE (Plan 1)

Trenches in the Center of the Cave

Trench H1

The entire Neolithic deposit within Trench H1 was disturbed by massive post-Neolithic digging. Units that included FCP 3 and FCP 4 sherds (as well as FCP 5 and post-Neolithic pieces) produced more than 19,000 sherds (H1:1–71; J and F:Pl. 13).[2] Of these, only ca. 50 sherds can securely be assigned to FCP 3, and perhaps 350 to FCP 4. There is no assurance that even these sherds were found in the general area of the cave in which they were originally deposited. The evidence we have, however, is that no substantial discard took place in H1 during FCP 3 or FCP 4. A somewhat larger quantity of FCP 5 sherds (ca. 500–600), also thoroughly mixed with earlier and later material, came from H1 and from the shallow terrace to the east and south (Plan 1).

Trench H

In the area of Trench H, recent digging was less deep, and left a small area of earlier Neolithic deposits in situ (Vitelli 1993a:33, 44–45, 60–61), but any later Neolithic deposits were thoroughly disturbed. The reworked deposits that included FCP 3 and FCP 4 material, again, along with FCP 5 and post-Neolithic, produced nearly 17,000 sherds. The FCP 3 (ca. 60) and FCP 4 (ca. 75) sherds occur in such small numbers that they seem unlikely to represent any substantial FCP 3 or FCP 4 activity in the center of the cave. FCP 5 sherds were slightly more numerous. Joins among sherds from the reworked deposits within Trench H and sherds from similarly reworked deposits in Trenches FA and G point to possible lateral redistribution of sediments in modern times.

Trench H2

Trench H2 produced no undisturbed deposits with FCP 3 or FCP 4 material. Far less pottery was recovered from the upper H2 units (just over 2000 sherds) than from comparable levels in H and H1; again, fewer than 1% of those can be securely identified as coming from FCP 3 wares, and perhaps 3% as FCP 4 wares. A few units included one or two FCP 5 and no post-Neolithic sherds, but FCP 5 activity was minimal.

Very little deposition of Late Neolithic pottery took place in the center of the cave.

Trenches along the Western Wall of the Cave

Trenches along the western wall of the cave produced larger quantities of Late Neolithic pottery. Only FAN and FAS produced stratified material. In the other trenches (G, G1, F, F1, A), the later Neolithic deposits had been disturbed by recent digging and/or were excavated and recorded inadequately; much of the pottery had been discarded before my analyses began. Occasional examples of well-preserved pieces of Late Neolithic wares were saved and provide some useful information for the present study.

Trenches G and G1

No numbers were recorded for the amount of pottery recovered from Trench G in 1967. Estimating from my counts for G1 units (1968) and the notebook comments for 1967, there was rather more FCP 3 than FCP 4 pottery in this area, although the FCP 3 material consisted of only several hundred sherds. Fewer than 50 FCP 4 sherds were recovered in G and G1 units.[3]

Trenches F and FF1

Trench F was begun in 1967 as a 3x3 m trench, but only a few units were removed from the surface. In 1968, the area was extended to the east with another 3x3.5 m square (F-1). After a few surface units brought the new extension to the level of the 1967 work, the entire area was excavated as FF1 (see Farrand forthcoming).

Deep and relatively recent disturbances extended almost throughout the area, and well into EN deposits (J and F:Pl. 20).[4] From units 1–19, FF1 included substantial quantities of ceramics (ca. 14,000), of which perhaps 3% can be assigned to FCP 3, 5% to FCP 4; with the possible exception of FF1:19 the units include mixed Neolithic. Some crosscutting must have taken place, either through the obviously disturbed deposits evident on the west section (J and F:Pl. 20), or through pits in the interior of the trench, not recorded on the sections. No discrete deposits belonging to any later Neolithic phase can now be isolated in FF1. Pottery from the trench is illustrated and included in the discussions, but it cannot be used to answer questions about or determine phases, subphases, or phase boundaries.

Trench A

Trench A was the first one opened in 1967, in a dark back corner of the cave. The excavators frequently comment in the field notebooks, for this and other early trenches, on the difficulty of seeing stratigraphic differences until well after excavation when the scarps had dried.[5] The top 1.70 m in Trench A, removed in baskets (units) 1–21 and 40, consisted largely of loose rocky fill that included pottery from Early Neolithic through modern.[6] Once the upper loose stony fill was removed, no certain post-Neolithic pottery occurred; the deposits, from notebook descriptions, appear to have been relatively undisturbed and in a sequence comparable to that encountered in FAS, directly north of Trench A (Plan 1). Units were not tagged on the scarps, so it is difficult to correlate units in FAS with specific units excavated in A. The pottery from Trench A was lotted and the bulk of it discarded at the end of the season. I have never seen it, aside from the few inventoried and saved sherds. The latter are included in the illustrations here, as relevant, but generally the material from Trench A could not be used in the analyses. The notebooks record rough percentages of categories of pottery, but no counts or weights.

FA Balk

The excavation of Trench A in 1967 and Trench FF1 in 1968 exposed deep sections where the stratigraphy could be read fairly clearly, if only after the fact. It was decided, therefore, to take advantage of the possibility these sections offered to preview what was to be dug, by focusing further excavation on the area between the two trenches, dubbed FA Balk. The disturbed, loose, and very rocky upper sediments were removed in 1969, in FA units 1–58, dug variously in the West Balk (WB), the East Balk (EB), and the Southeast (QSE) and Southwest (QSW) Quadrants (Plan 2). These units were dug statigraphically, following as closely as possible the natural strata as diagnosed from the exposed scarps of Trenches A and FF1.

As in FF1 and A, the upper deposits in FA Balk had been disturbed by recent digging. They produced, nevertheless, large quantities of pottery, much of it Final Neolithic, mixed with post-Neolithic. Near the bottom of the mixed fill, three units removed undisturbed deposits; the pottery from them was saved in its entirety. Units FA:1–58 isolated an area of apparently undisturbed deposits that stood as a pedestal above the excavated areas on three sides: the north scarp exposed to a depth of 4.8 m by Trench FF1; the south scarp exposed to a depth of 5.88 m by Trench A; and the east end standing ca. 1.50 m above the terrace created by excavation of the EB and QSE (Farrand forthcoming). This pedestal, ca. 2x3.5 m, was divided into North (FAN) and South (FAS) halves, each excavated separately. Work began in FAN:59 through 119N, which took the north half of the balk down to roughly the level of the terrace on the east. The south section exposed by these units (J and F:Pl. 19) provided a preview of the north scarp of FAS, which was excavated next, with the removal of units 59S through 72S in the same 1969 season.

The next season of excavation was in 1971. Work resumed with FAS:73 through FAS:114. With the completion of the FAS:114, the south balk was at approximately the level of the north balk and the east terrace.[7] From this point on, excavation produced a standing east section (J and F:Pl. 8). The later Neolithic deposits, however, begin just below the level of the east terrace, so only a few units are recorded on the east section. The west scarp of FA is the only one standing after excavation, with unit tags to relate excavated units to specific deposits. With hindsight it is clear that we should have drawn the standing north and south sections prior to excavation and recorded unit numbers on them as the deposits were excavated.

Within the FA Balk the later Neolithic sediments generally slope downward from north to south (Fig. 86) and from east to west (J and F:Pl. 19). Numerous "hearths,"only a few of which touched the west section, were encountered throughout these deposits. Most had a depth of at least 0.20–0.30 m; i.e., they were dug into extant sediments. A pile of rocks is prominent in the scarp of FAS (Fig. 86, south of 98S tag), but did not extend into the excavated area. Such features and complexities made it difficult for the excavators to identify and follow the strata three-dimensionally in the upper portion of FA. Even where units appear from the tags on the west scarp to have cleanly removed a single stratigraphic layer, it is not certain that they did so throughout the area of the trench. Extensive cross-cutting, especially in the upper portion of FAN, is clear in many cases and likely in others. Many units did not abut the west scarp, or indeed, any scarp, so it is difficult to relate them securely to any other unit, especially in the absence of measured plans for each unit excavated (see also Farrand forthcoming).

FCP 1 and, in greater quantities, FCP 2 sherds are present throughout the later Neolithic deposits (Tables 1–8), if always in small and battered condition. Although their percentages tend to decrease from FCP 3 to FCP 5, as one would expect if they were being kicked up from contemporary surface sediments, the decrease is not steady. Units with jumps in the percentage of FCP 2 varieties (e.g., 76S, 71S, 66N, 83N) imply that the later Neolithic occupants dug into earlier deposits in areas other than FA and redeposited the sediments within FA. Substantial human bone scatter (Tables 1–8) may also point to reworking of deposits within the Neolithic.

Rear of Cave

A few FCP 5 sherds were recovered from the pool at the very rear of the cave (Fig. 75a ; see Document 2). Additionally, in 1974 Jacobsen and Payne conducted a brief exploration of sediments that underlie a large mass of rockfall from the "window" at the rear of the cave (J and F:Pl. 2, "1974;" see also Farrand forthcoming). Of the 180 sherds recovered, ten or eleven are of FCP 1 or

2 varieties: seven small fragments of monochrome Urf, two patterned Urf, and one or two very small pieces of Lime Burnished. The rest are FCP 5 in date. The earlier sherds are more worn and heavily encrusted than the FCP 5 sherds and could have been redeposited in the course of FCP 5 activities, as so many were in FCP 5 deposits in the front of the cave.

The sediments appear to be in situ and to pre-date the collapse of the roof, at least the final stages of collapse and the formation of the large window. The area would have been quite dark and dank if the window had not yet opened, and an unlikely choice for a living area.

The possibility that the large rockfall that today separates the front and back of the cave (J and F:Pl. 2) post-dates the Neolithic activities introduces another set of uncertainties to the analyses of prehistoric activities in the cave. If no window existed, the cave would have been a much darker, less pleasant place than it is today, without the fresh breezes that blow through in summer. It might have been warmer and more protected in the winter. If the large area now inaccessible because of the rockfall had been open and available for occupation, then we are probably missing a very substantial component of the activities from all periods. There is no assurance, however, that the window collapse occurred at one time. Portions of the cave may have been covered with rocks throughout the Neolithic and inaccessible to human occupation (see also Farrand, forthcoming). For the present analyses, I have assumed the latter.

LATER NEOLITHIC DEPOSITS ON PARALIA

No ceramic material from FCP 3 or FCP 4 was recognized from anywhere on Paralia. After intensive activities in FCP 1 and FCP 2, the Paralia was apparently unoccupied for nearly a millennium, although it must have been traversed repeatedly by those entering the cave. The FCP 2 terrace walls (Vitelli 1993a:Plan 3) would have collapsed and been overrun in many places, but some echo of the former terraces may have remained. The slopes were probably covered with maquis vegetation.[8] In FCP 5, activities resumed on Paralia. Occasional FCP 5 sherds occur in most surface units of the Paralia trenches. A number of FCP 5 burials testify to specific events. The only substantial deposit of FCP 5 material, however, occurred in the area of Trench L5, at the northernmost edge of our excavations (Plan 3).

The limited distribution and reduced frequency of ceramic remains from the later Neolithic signal from the outset that the nature of occupation at Franchthi, especially in FCP 3 and FCP 4, was different from that during earlier phases of the Neolithic. The remains suggest fewer occupants, staying for less extended stretches of time than in the earlier Neolithic. The activities themselves may have been different in kind, as well as duration.

FRANCHTHI CERAMIC PHASE 3 (FCP 3) CONTEXTS

The FCP 2/FCP 3 Boundary

The earliest stratified examples of FCP 3 varieties occur in FA units that removed the top of a rocky red stratum and the bottom of a dark yellowish brown stratum with few stones (Fig. 86; J and F:Pls. 8, 19).

Assigned Units

FAN: 121–119
FAS: 117–116

Unit tags on the East and West sections (Fig. 86; J and F:Pl. 8) are among the records that document crosscutting of strata along the boundary. Units that removed sediments primarily from the rocky red stratum produced less than 1% of FCP 3 varieties while units that were fully within the upper yellowish brown stratum included over 50% FCP 3 varieties, a dramatic increase that coincides with the sedimentological change. Most FCP 2 sherds from the upper units are small (2–4 cm maximum dimension) and battered. The FCP 2.5 sherds are indistinguishable from FCP 2.5 sherds found elsewhere at the site in deposits lacking FCP 3 varieties. There is no development to suggest that production of FCP 2.5 varieties continued within a stretch of time represented by the FCP 2/ FCP 3 boundary. Similarly, no differences are evident between the sherds of FCP 3 varieties found in the boundary units and those from superimposed deposits. Numerous joins between FCP 3 sherds found in the boundary units and sherds found in the upper deposits document that pieces of the same pots occur in both. Similarities between FCP 2 and FCP 3 varieties are superficial at best.

None of the ceramic evidence supports an interpretation of a gradual change in ceramic production and use between FCP 2 and FCP 3. All the ceramic evidence points to an abrupt change.

Contextual evidence supports this conclusion. A small number of FCP 1 and FCP 2 sherds (ca. 40–50) from boundary units were encased in—or coated on one face by—a calcareous film, probably cave drip. Another 40–50 sherds from the same units are weathered and eroded on one portion, well preserved on the other, as though partially buried and partially exposed to weathering. On Paralia, which had been the site of substantial activity throughout the earlier Neolithic, not a single FCP 3 sherd was recovered. At the end of FCP 2.5, the occupants abandoned the site and did not return. When people returned to the cave, they were bearers of a new ceramic tradition. The FCP 3 sherds contained in units that were excavated along the boundary are there as a result of artificial mixing. They are, therefore, included among the sherds discussed in FCP 3.[9]

A single C-14 date derives from an FCP 3 context in FAN:114 (P-1662. Table 9). The calibrated date, at two sigmas (6090–5420 calBC), falls within the range of FCP 2 dates. The hiatus in activity between FCP 2 and FCP 3 was probably not lengthy—perhaps a generation or less. The cave drip encasing the sherds may suggest that it was an unusually wet period. The large dripstone encountered in H1 (J and F:Pl. 14; Farrand forthcoming: Chapter 2) may have begun forming around the same time. The dripping and dampness in the center of the cave may explain the relative paucity of later Neolithic remains in that area.

Franchthi Ceramic Phase 3 (FCP 3)

FCP 3 deposits are those stratified above strata that produced exclusively sherds from FCP 2 variety sets, that include the full set of FCP 3 varieties, and are entirely lacking in FCP 4 varieties. FCP 3 varieties bear superficial resemblance to aspects of the Urf potting traditions—a few shapes and motifs, and possible aspects of production technology—that may signal some vague relationship, but the differences are more pronounced. The FCP 3 potters belonged to what must be considered, at Franchthi, a new ceramic tradition.

Assigned Units

Units in parentheses crosscut (sub)phase boundaries. Commas separate units within the sequence.

FAN: (121–119), 118–112, (111), 110–100, 98, 96
FAS: (117–116), 115–114, (113), 112–100, 98–97

A substantial number of FCP 2 and fewer FCP 1 sherds are present in units assigned to FCP 3 (Tables 1–8). The numbers are sufficiently high to suggest some reworking and redeposition of pre-existing sediments not necessarily derived from within FA, during FCP 3. Other evidence points in the same direction.

Units 118S–116S and 121N, 119N–117N, 115N and 112N each produced a handful of rounded water-worn sherds that seem likely to have been brought in, probably incidentally along with something else, from the coastline or stream bank (Jameson et al. 1994:208). The botanical remains from FCP 3 units included seeds from small wildflowers and herbs (e.g., Medicago sp., Echium sp., Cruciferae sp.: Hansen 1991:199) that might have grown on the slopes of Paralia. They may have been brought into the cave intentionally or incidentally along with sediments.

The quantity of human bone scatter, especially within FAS, is noteworthy (Tables 1–8). Nine single or related small groups of bones representing, minimally, an infant, two young children, and an adult (Cullen and Cook forthcoming) were recovered from units assigned to the FCP 2/3 boundary and FCP 3. They cannot be assigned securely to either FCP 2 or FCP 3; their presence is a likely indication of the reworking of sediments somewhere in the site (Cullen in prep.).

When the people responsible for the FCP 3 remains arrived at the cave, the area of FA, near the west wall (Plan 1), sloped downward from north to south and east to west.[10] Early activities included building a fire near the eastern end of FAN (J and F:Pl. 19, at tag 114N), at the high point of the slope in that area. Subsequent activity resulted in a 0.10–0.30 m accumulation of carbon-flecked sediments that follow the pre-existing slope, but no other features were encountered.

As noted above, some of the sediments may have been redeposited from elsewhere. There are also potential indications that some reworking of the sediments occurred after FCP 3. The very large unit FAS:116, with nearly 15 kg of pottery, included a small number of sherds that are unique in the Franchthi assemblage (Figs. 12b, h; 13a–b, d–e). A single, roughly finished FCP 5 horned handle fragment (not illustrated) occurs in FAS:117, and in FAN:119 a 1 cm square sherd of the FCP 4 Lime plus Iron painted variety is accompanied by roughly half a kilo of mostly thick, worn sherds that I could not securely identify. These are potential indications of minor contamination from at least FCP 5, if not later. The later sherds need not signal general contamination. The odd sherd can easily fall from a loose scarp or be returned to the wrong sherd bag.[11] Even if some small area of contamination was included in the later Neolithic deposits from FA, the overall sequence of FCP 3 and FCP 4 varieties is reasonably secure. The potential for contamination simply serves as a caution against drawing conclusions based on any single object from the upper deposits in FA.

The FCP 3/FCP 4 Boundary

In ceramic terms, the boundary between FCP 3 and FCP 4 is marked by a series of superimposed units above those assigned to FCP 3 and which include the first examples of FCP 4 varieties.

Assigned Units

FAN:111–106
FAS:113–110

The sedimentological interface between FCP 3 and FCP 4 is marked by a layer of sharp, angular cave rocks that covered the entire surface of FAN and extended 0.30–0.40 m along an east–west line into FAS. From the exposed south scarp of FF1, the excavators were able to note that the line of rocks extended only a "short way" beyond the western extent of FAN. The layer, in some places several rocks deep, sloped downward markedly from north to south (J and F:Pl. 8), but was relatively level from east to west (J and F:Pl. 19: below 106–107 tags; Pl. 20: the line of rocks at the top of the deep sounding on the south section, at roughly 7 m).

The rocks were first uncovered in FAN:108, 110 and FAS:112–113. Further clearing and removal of the rocks was accomplished in FAN:111–113 and FAS:114, although a few rocks were missed along the west edge and removed in FAS:115. The sediments that accumulated around and over the rocks included the first examples of FCP 4 varieties; they are considered, on the basis of the ceramics, to belong to the boundary. Units that removed the rocks included no FCP 4 varieties; they are assigned to FCP 3.

At the time of excavation there was much discussion about whether the rock layer was a built or a natural feature. Opinions were equally divided. The rocks are sharp, angular cave rocks of various sizes, and of the sort encountered everywhere within the cave. That, some argued, suggests a natural feature. Others were struck by the completeness with which they covered a limited area and, in particular, the fairly straight line their edge formed in FAS, which suggests a built feature. I am inclined to agree with the latter opinion. Another similar feature occurs just to the south in the FAS west scarp (Fig. 86, south of tags 98S and 102S), from a somewhat later date. The question of whether the rock layer, natural or artificial, is related to activities at the end of FCP 3 or the beginning of FCP 4 (or, if natural, accumulated during a hiatus in activities between the two) is difficult to settle with certainty. That it is part of the early FCP 4 activities is the most likely.

A comparison of the FCP 3 sherds from below the boundary with those in and above the boundary units, where they occur together with FCP 4 varieties, reveals no clearly significant differences; the sample from both contexts is small, and minor differences are hard to evaluate.[12] The same is true of FCP 4 varieties from within and directly above the boundary: the kinds of differences that might be noted are as likely to occur within a single unit as between superimposed units, so no conclusions about development are possible. I can point to no shared trait or tendency between FCP 3 and FCP 4 varieties that might suggest that the potters of either tradition learned from each other or shared information or practices while coexisting at the same site.

Inferences based on the patterns of joining sherds are also ambiguous. Several sherds from boundary units join sherds from well within FCP 3 deposits (e.g., 111N + 115N, 113S+112S+117N), while other sherds from the boundary units join sherds from further up the sequence (e.g., 110N+101N, 112S+103N).[13] A few scattered bones were found in boundary units, as well as in the FCP 3 units below the boundary (Tables 1–8). Joins and bone scatter signal possible crosscutting or disturbance, but prove neither.

The C-14 dates provide critical, if also somewhat ambiguous, evidence. The single date for FCP 3 falls within the range of Middle Neolithic dates. The next dates, all from late in the FCP 4 sequence, are 240–500 years later (Table 9). FCP 4 pottery shows relatively little development from one subphase to the next, suggesting relatively little passage of time between each of the sequential deposits of that phase (below, Chapter 4). The quantity of pottery and the nature of the deposits in FCP 4 point to short-lived occupations, unlikely to have spanned a full 200, much less 500 years. The cave must have been essentially unoccupied for one or more lengthy stretches of time. The most likely place for a long hiatus is between FCP 3 and FCP 4, rather than within FCP 4.

Because of this hiatus separating the occupations of FCP 3 and FCP 4, I assume that all the examples of FCP 3 varieties from the FCP 3/FCP 4 boundary units on up are redeposited and essentially contemporary with each other. All examples of FCP 3 varieties from FA, as well as from mixed deposits elsewhere in the cave, are combined for the ceramic analyses, regardless of their specific context.

FRANCHTHI CERAMIC PHASE 4 (FCP 4) CONTEXTS

Deposits assigned to FCP 4 occur stratified between deposits with FCP 3 varieties and later deposits with FCP 5 varieties. FCP 4 can be divided into three subphases, FCP 4.1, the earliest, through FCP 4.3, the latest. Units assigned to FCP 4.3 were originally examined as boundary units, as they include sherds from both FCP 4 and FCP 5 variety sets. The boundary, in this case, corresponds to a discrete stratigraphic layer. Once I had determined that the FCP 4/FCP 5 boundary represented an abrupt change, and that the combination of variety sets resulted from mixing along the interface, I looked for differences between the FCP 4 sherds within the boundary and below it. Several developments were evident, so the sherds from the boundary are assigned to a discrete subphase, FCP 4.3.

The suggestion of subphases within FCP 4 is evident from the Frequency Tables (Tables 1–8). In Table 2 for example, the cluster of FCP 4 varieties includes a series of units at the bottom of the FCP 4 sequence with five FCP 4 varieties, but lacking the sixth, Calcite Coarse. That variety first appears in the FAS SW sequence, in unit 94S; it is consistently present thereafter until the first appearance of FCP 5 varieties. The same pattern shows up in the other FA corner sequences (Tables 1–8), although it is less clear in FAN, where the relevant units crosscut strata that were probably also already disturbed.

FCP 4.1

Units assigned to FCP 4.1 are those that occur between the FCP 3/ FCP 4 boundary and the first unit above it with one or more sherds of the Calcite Coarse variety, the boundary drawn along the lower interface of the first unit with the innovation. The activities in the FA area in FCP 4.1 were probably different in nature from those of FCP 4.2 (see below), and some of the differences noted in the pottery may be related to differences of function. The deposits assigned to FCP 4.2 are, nevertheless, clearly stratified above those of FCP 4.1, which justifies the creation of separate subphases.

FCP 4.1 Assigned Units

Units in parentheses crosscut (sub)phase boundaries. Commas separate units within the sequence.

FAN: (111), 110–100, 98, 96
FAS: (113), 112–100, 98–97 (96)

Excavation within the strata assigned to FCP 4.1 proceeded in a number of units of limited horizontal extent, as the excavators attempted to follow the very complex and confusing sedimentological variations they encountered. This makes it difficult to follow the analyses; many of the units are not recorded on a section, several touched no scarp, and the sequential unit numbers do not provide an accurate sense of the vertical or horizontal relationships among units. Units that were actually superimposed in each of the corners provide the sequence used in the Tables 1–8, but precise relationships among units elsewhere in the trench are unclear. In spite of the best efforts of the excavators, considerable crosscutting of strata took place. Several sequential activities can be reconstructed from the sections (Fig. 86; J and F:Pl. 19), but they cannot be accurately associated with specific units or sherds.

When the Neolithic group responsible for the FCP 4.1 deposits arrived at the cave, they found the surface in the FA area sloping from the north and east down toward the wall of the cave, to the south and west (Fig. 86; J and F:Pl. 19, the line of rocks at ca. 7 m). It is likely they built the rock floor (above FCP 3), and perhaps a clay or carbonate-rich structure on top of it. Sediments removed in units FAN:102–107 were described by the excavators as virtually stone and carbon-free, and comprised an exceptionally sticky yellow "clay," unlike other sediments encountered in the trench.[14] An activity along the western edge of FAN, immediately above the rock layer, left behind a solid loaf-like object (Fig. 20g:FC 107) modeled from a carbonate-rich material with traces of red paint that was found sitting near a "clay patch" and small amounts of ash and charcoal in FAN:110. To the east of the "loaf" was the sticky yellow "clay" of FAN:102–107. Within this yellow clay, FAN:104 removed a lighter yellow clay lens (J and F:Pl. 19), and at the eastern tip of the trench, FAN:101 and FAS:110 removed an ash and charcoal lens. Generally, these units in the east of FA included a small amount of pottery, most of which is from earlier phases (FCP 1 through FCP 3), but each unit included a few FCP 4 sherds. The "clay" is possibly part of a structure, and presumably redeposited from a location that had been occupied in earlier times.

The accumulation of the yellow clay stratum above the rocks left the surface of the FA area with roughly the same slope as before (J and F:Pl. 19: top of Moderate Yellowish Brown stratum). The next series of activities filled in and leveled off the area. First, the northwestern part of FAS was the site of a large hearth (Fig. 86: charcoal lens below tag for 102S). The excavators identified the presence of a hearth at the top of FAS:98, where it appeared as a scatter of rocks and, along the northern edge of FAS, as a patch of "hearth clay." The "hearth" area was next excavated in FAS:102, when the rock scatter took on a more defined, almost circular arrangement, with a diameter of ca. 0.70 m. FAS:103 continued down in the hearth area and actually reached the carbon-rich lens shown on the section (Fig. 86), some 0.40 m below the top of the "hearth." Sitting in the very center of the circle of stones (although presumably well below their top), directly on the carbon layer, a Lime plus Iron painted female figurine (FC 118, Fig. 20f) lay balanced on its toes and neck. [15]

It is hard to rationalize the excavators' description of the deep "hearth," which would have been dug into existing strata, with the stratigraphy evident in the sections (Fig. 86; J and F:Pl. 19, Grayish Brown stratum) and the ceramic evidence from the deposits. Probably the carbon-rich lens marks the level of the actual fireplace. The figurine seems to have been placed in the ashes, at some point after they had cooled, since it shows no signs of soot from smoldering coals. The figurine and the hearth area were then covered, either gradually by ongoing activities, or quickly, with the intentional addition of sediments (which included some FCP 2 and a larger quantity of FCP 3 sherds, see Table 2.1) from elsewhere. A C-14 date from wood charcoal recovered in FAS:102 produced a date that is far too early (Table 9). The charcoal may have derived from redeposited sediment used as intentional filling or covering. The figurine may have been encircled with stones, perhaps as a protection, before being covered.[16]

Although the pile of large rocks evident in the west section of FAS (Fig. 86) did not extend into the excavated area of FAS, it must have been put in place around the same time, since the sediments removed in FAS:102 and FAS:98 built up against it. By the end of FCP 4.1, the former east–west slope in the FA area had leveled off (J and F:Pl. 17, top of Grayish Brown stratum).

FCP 4.2

Units assigned to FCP 4.2 are those stratified above FCP 4.1 that include the apparently new FCP 4 Calcite Coarse variety along with the rest of the FCP 4 variety set, and that have no FCP 5 varieties represented.

Assigned Units (see pp. 12, 13)

FAN: 99, 97, 95–94, 90–89
FAS: 99, 95–87

The FCP 4.2 deposit shows in the west scarp (Fig. 86) as a distinctive dark, carbon-rich stratum that slopes from north to south, above the FAS rock pile. On the section it appears as one of the clearest strata in the entire FA sequence. Unfortunately it was not as clear within the trench area, as implied by the numerous small units employed to remove the variable sediments. FAN presented the more serious challenge. Substantial crosscutting was one result. In the south section of FAN (J and F:Pl. 19) the surfaces are shown as level, but units appear to have crosscut parts of two strata ("dark" and "dusky yellowish brown" between tags 95N and 89N).

Sediments removed in FAN units 94–96 and 98N, tagged to the north of the rock pile in FAS (Fig. 86) in a reddish clay stratum moderately distinct from that below, probably accumulated as part of FCP 4.1 activities. They included only a few sherds of Calcite Coarse, probably the result of slight crosscutting along the undulating lower interface of the dark stratum. These sediments accumulated against, and eventually covered the rock pile to the south, and reintroduced the north–south slope in the area.

In FAN, only units 89–90N removed sediments entirely within the dark stratum or below it. The other units tagged within it (88N, 84N) crosscut upper deposits and included FCP 5 sherds.[17] In the northwest corner of FAN, the dark stratum is shown stopping abruptly against a rock (Fig. 86). Immediately north of and below the rock, FAN:87 removed a clay deposit that included FCP 5 sherds. Directly under unit 87N, unit 97N removed the carbon-rich patch (untagged). This lens of carbon provides the next C-14 date in the FA series, which lends particular significance to its stratigraphic context. Only 129 grams of pottery were recovered in 97N: 6 small pieces of Urf, a fragment of FCP 1 Lime ware, a Lime plus Iron and an Ungritted Manganese Painted, a Low Lime Burnished, and several small crumbs of a coarse fabric that cannot be securely identified. The relatively high percentage of FCP 2 and FCP 3 varieties is more characteristic of FCP 4.1 than later deposits. If nothing else, it suggests redeposited material. FAN:99, which extended under 97N, included Calcite Coarse sherds, intrusive from at least FCP 4.2. It appears as though that corner of FAN stepped down 20 cm or so, accumulating first FCP 4.2, then FCP 5 deposits comparable to those to the immediate south, but at a lower elevation. That is not impossible, but it seems more likely that a small FCP 5 pit in the corner cut through and redeposited material. The date (Table 9), which is very close to others from FCP 4.3, may have been obtained from redeposited charcoal. The context makes the date unreliable for determining the relationships between the FCP 4 and FCP 5 activities.

In FAS, the dark stratum was more uniform and appears to have been removed more cleanly. Units near the bottom of the stratum at the eastern tip found traces of burnt red "hearth clay" (FAS:99, 95). The main source of the carbon flecks throughout the stratum, however, was probably a large "three-burner" hearth (Plate 1a) located in the very center of FAS and removed in FAS:91. In addition to the scatter of carbon, the large percentage of fish bones (ca. 40% of the faunal remains in 91S, and generally high in units from 92S to 83S: Rose forthcoming) and a significant jump in the percentage of coarse varieties (Tables 1–4) make this "hearth" a more convincing example than some others.

FCP 4/FCP 5 Boundary (FCP 4.3)

From this point upward, FA Balk is stratigraphically much more complex and confusing than the single section drawing (Fig. 86) might suggest. The strata once again incline sharply, and deposits include numerous "hearths" and ashy deposits of limited horizontal extent. Substantial crosscutting, especially in FAN, is documented, even though our records for these deposits are not as full as one might have wished.

Units along the boundary between FCP 4 and FCP 5 removed deposits stratified above FCP 4.2, and include the first sherds of FCP 5 varieties. As usual, the boundary units are designated to facilitate analysis of whether the change between the phases was an abrupt or gradual and continuous one. Since this boundary has not previously been explored at sites in southern Greece, it seems particularly important to scrutinize the evidence preserved at Franchthi.

Assigned Units

FAN: 87–84, 82–81 (very mixed, clear crosscutting)
FAS: 86–82

The contextual evidence points toward discontinuity in occupation. The percentages of FCP 5 varieties in the boundary units are highly variable. In the southeast sequence of FAN (Table 8), the FCP 5 varieties are entirely absent in FAN:94 and 92N, but jump to 88% of the total in the next superimposed unit, FAN:83. Sequences in the other corners of FAN and FAS (Tables 1–7) show less dramatic jumps, but the increases are inconsistent from sequence to sequence. In FAS in particular, the substantial presence of human bone scatter (Tables 1–4) is an indication of possible prehistoric mixing along the interface, in addition to the documented modern mixing through crosscutting of the strata.

Farrand's sedimentological analyses (Farrand 1993; forthcoming) and four C-14 dates from the upper FA sequence contribute critical information to this discussion. Farrand recognizes a stratigraphic discontinuity between his lithostratigraphic phases Z and Y2 (Farrand 1993:88, 90)[18] corresponding to the interface between excavation units FAN:79 and FAN:81. These correspond in ceramic terms to the top interface of the FCP 4/FCP 5 boundary in the west of FAN. His sediment samples 1–2 and 1–3 are from sediments equivalent to excavation units FAN:81, 84, 88. These units, by their ceramic content, are located within the FCP 4/FCP 5 boundary. The soil samples show clear signs of weathering, indicating they were exposed at the surface for a period of time during which no additional sediments accumulated (see Farrand, forthcoming).[19] That weathered lithostratigraphic boundary, coinciding with a change in ceramic content, adds weight to the argument for discontinuity in occupation at the end of FCP 4.

Three C-14 dates, all from units tagged on the west section (Fig. 86; Table 9: P-1630 from 89N, P-1661 from 97N, P-1920 from 83S), are so close as to be statistically the same (ca. 5240–4805 calBC). One is from a unit assigned on the basis of ceramic content to FCP 4.2 (FAN:89). The others are from units that include a small percentage of FCP 5 varieties, hence considered boundary units. All three dates must apply to the end of the FCP 4 occupation.

The fourth date is from higher up the sequence, and from the eastern end of FAS, in FAS:72, a secure FCP 5 unit: 91% of the pottery is from FCP 5 varieties. This date is 500–850 years later than those from the end of FCP 4 where the weathering points to a hiatus in occupation. Although not from the earliest FCP 5 activity, the date, together with the signs of weathering within the FCP 4/5 boundary, argues for a lengthy hiatus between FCP 4 and FCP 5. Given the dominance of FCP 4 pottery in the units from the FCP4/ FCP 5 boundary and the evaluation that a hiatus occurred between the two phases, I consider the boundary units as a third subphase of FCP 4, and refer to them in the following discussions as representing FCP 4.3.

FRANCHTHI CERAMIC PHASE 5 (FCP 5): CAVE CONTEXTS

Strata illustrated along the south scarp of FAN (J and F:Pl. 19, from 81N tag to top of section) show the surfaces as relatively level from east to west, with two main strata evident. The earlier is shown as a dark yellow-brown layer with ash and charcoal. The later stratum comprises, at its lower interface in the east, a red clay lens (tag for 64N), covered by a grayish brown stratum and, to the west, light brown stony sediments. These two clearly defined strata did not, however, extend into the interior of the trench. The color and texture of the sediments were highly variable and patchy, suggesting reworking in prehistoric times. In their attempts to follow the natural stratigraphy and to isolate undisturbed deposits, the excavators removed the FCP 5 sediments in many small units; most are not recorded on a section drawing and are now difficult to relate to one other.

FCP 5.1

Units assigned to FCP 5.1 are stratified above units with the latest FCP 4 varieties and extend to the top of FAN and FAS. Several sequential activities are documented on the section, but crosscutting and other disturbances, probably from within FCP 5, make it impossible to define subphases within the sequence. Rather than treat the entire sequence as contemporary, however, I have grouped units that can reasonably be associated with each of the sequential deposits within FAN and FAS in an attempt to extract some sense of temporal change, and distinguish each group by a letter, i.e., FCP 5.1a–c. I omitted from consideration those units in FAN that are certainly mixed, crosscut, or otherwise difficult to relate to the main sequential deposits. Those units included few and quite small sherds, and no substantial profiles, so their omission from the ceramic analysis does not reduce the sample size significantly. Some amount of artificial mixing within FCP 5 is surely still present in each of the groups.

Assigned Units

Note: Units in parentheses crosscut, or may have, several deposits. Commas separate units within a sequence.

FCP 5.1a	FAN: (84–83, 80), 77, 73
	FAS: (83–82), 81–75
FCP 5.1b	FAN: 69, 67, 65–63
	FAS: 74–59
FCP 5.1c	FAN: 61–59

At the eastern tip of FAN, the excavators identified a small "hearth," or circle of stones ca. 0.35 m in exterior diameter, in FAN:60, near the top of the Balk and within the later stratum. All other FCP 5 sediments along the eastern tip of FAN were also removed in a series of quite small units that included only the eastern tip. From at least the level of FAN:76 (See J and F:Pl. 19), and possibly from as high as the red clay layer tagged above 67N (J and F:Pl. 32), those sediments came from within a pit that was visible in the scarp before excavation began and extended well into FCP 4 deposits.[20]

Other units of limited lateral extent removed sediments in the center and western portion of FAN. Only a few of those, all from the earlier FCP 5 stratum, are tagged on the west section (Fig. 86), because recent disturbance had extended into the top of FAN along its westernmost edge.

The west section for FAS is more complete (Fig. 86) and confirms the presence of at least two strata of FCP 5 deposits, sloping downward from north to south. Unit FAS:81, and perhaps 79S and 78S, removed most of the first, lower FCP 5 stratum seen also in FAN, although in FAS the sediments were reasonably uniform only in the western third of the trench. FAS:77–74, in the eastern portion of FAS, correspond in elevation to FAN:80, 76, 73–72, and 67 (J and F:Pl. 19), although the sediments are described as of variable color and texture.

FAS:73 (Fig. 86), in the southwest corner of FAS, removed another "hearth" with half a circle of stones ca. 0.70 m in diameter preserved within the trench area, the other half presumably within the west scarp. This "hearth" was dug into extant FCP 5 sediments, so must belong to the second stratum of occupation. The oddly shaped lens of stones tagged on the west section at 80S (Fig. 86) must have been originally deposited during the first stage of occupation; it had been dug up and redeposited in the course of digging the "hearth" in FAS:73.[21] To the east, FAS:72 should correspond to the red clay lens and ashy patch encountered in FAN:64 (J and F:Pl. 19), just above the interface with the first FCP 5 stratum. The C-14 date from this unit (Table 9) should date the beginning of the second FCP 5 occupation.

Above FAS:72 in the east and FAS:73 in the west, the sediments were again rather patchy and loose. A possible "hearth" was noted in FAS:66–64 to the east, but no clearly defined deposits were recognized. Numerous pieces of human bone scatter, especially within FAS (Tables 1–8), add weight to the impression that FCP 5 deposits were reworked in prehistoric times. It is also clear that these deposits were seriously crosscut during excavation (Farrand forthcoming), especially within FAN. Thus, while it is possible to reconstruct a sense of sequential activity from the sections, artificial mixing in both ancient and modern times seriously impedes our ability to separate ceramics and other remains into categories that might correspond to the different stages of occupation.

The weathering of the sediments along the upper interface of the FCP 4/5 deposits indicates a hiatus in activity in the cave following the latest FCP 4 activities. The next C-14 date in the sequence, some 500–850 years later than the latest FCP 4 date, comes from FAS:72, a unit that lies at the lower interface of the second occupation stratum. The date, then, does not apply to the earliest FCP 5 deposit after the hiatus in FA, but to an activity that took place somewhat later. The hiatus in occupation between FCP 4 and FCP 5 was somewhat shorter than the interval suggested by the C-14 dates, but, depending on the amount of time it took for the earliest FCP 5 stratum to accumulate, perhaps not significantly so.

A few units at the top of FAN (FAN 59–61) removed a deposit apparently missing in FAS (J and F:Pl. 19), and included a substantial amount of pottery and small finds. The deposit may represent a brief visit to the cave between the FCP 5.1b activities and those of FCP 5.2, or it may be a remnant of the latter.

FCP 5.2

A few units stratified above FAN:59 and FAS:59, i.e., above the point where the balk was divided into north and south halves, include a new variety, not represented in FCP 5 deposits in FAN and FAS. These units are the only stratified deposits assigned to FCP 5.2, but other examples of the new variety occur in upper mixed deposits within the cave and in a few units on Paralia.

Assigned Units

FA:46–45, 39

A small "hearth," excavated in several units above FAS and FAN, miraculously escaped disturbance by the deep recent digging. All the pottery from these units was saved and includes no post-Neolithic material. The units also include a few FCP 5 sherds of varieties that do not occur in the FAS and FAN deposits. Since the units are above the FA Pedestal and were surrounded by disturbed deposits, they are recorded on no section. The "hearth" itself appeared in FA:39 and consisted of a small circle of stones resting on a carbon-rich clay layer. Its location and appearance are recorded only in a very sketchy plan, but coordinates ("2.14 m from the western perimeter, and 3.83 m from the southern perimeter of FA") place it roughly in the center of what was to become FAN (Plan 2). A second unit, FA:45, removed the area directly under the stone circle, and the third, FA:46, a small ashy patch directly to the east. A C-14 date from FA:39 (Table 9) provides a date for this latest in situ deposit of FCP 5 in the cave.

Upper FA and other disturbed contexts

FA units 1–58 in the QSW+WB and QSE+EB (Plan 2) removed masses of earth and rock, following the stratigraphy, such as it was, in the areas between the already deep holes of Trench A to the south and FF1 to the north. Interestingly, colleagues inform me that early units (ca. FA:1–38) were, in terms of lithics, bone and shell, almost "pure" Palaeolithic, along with, in units FA:41–43, 35–36, 37–40A, definitely Mesolithic lithics. From units FA:39–58, this material is essentially "pure Neolithic." The same units, however, produced quantities of pottery, both Neolithic and, through most of the units above FAN and FAS: 59, post-Neolithic, including some decidedly modern sherds (probably from pots made within the last 50–60 years). The excavators also noted finding pieces of wood "in good condition"—so probably quite recent. Most of the pottery from these units was discarded before I had a chance to look at it (Vitelli 1993a:33 and 34 n. 12), but pottery notebooks provide some useful information. Occasional saved sherds from these upper units seem to be non-joining fragments of pots represented in similarly reworked deposits at the top of HH1 and H Terrace.

Thus in relatively recent times, substantial digging and redeposition of prehistoric sediments took place inside the cave. Somewhere, that digging reached Mesolithic and Palaeolithic deposits, which were removed and redeposited, along with other sediments that included Neolithic and later sherds, within the area of upper FA. How much of the prehistoric material, especially the FCP 5 material, from those sediments was originally deposited in the location where it was found, and how much was redeposited in the balk area from some other location of original deposition, is unclear.

That the recent digging just to the east of FAN and FAS, in QSE and EB, penetrated at least to the depth of the FCP 3 deposits is clear from the FA East section (J and F:Pl. 8). Units 46 to 55A, tagged on the east section, were excavated just to the east of FAN and FAS (J and F:Pl. 8: "Upper section set back to east 25 cm"). Some of the deepest units there included no post-Neolithic pottery (55A, 55D) but the range of Neolithic phases represented (FCP 1 through FCP 5) suggests those units either crosscut disturbed deposits or were themselves part of the reworked sediments; the absence of any modern ceramic material is fortuitous.

Fortunately, the pottery from the three undisturbed FCP 5.2 units includes at least one variety that does not occur in earlier FA, but does occur elsewhere in reworked deposits within the cave. The few FCP 5.2 units serve to connect the pieces from poor contexts to a subphase of FCP 5 later than any represented within the FA Balk.

Trench A

While recent disturbances appear to have destroyed the later Neolithic deposits, and in FF1 and H1, the earlier Neolithic as well, the disturbance within Trench A appears to have been less severe. Although the records are poor, and much of the pottery was discarded, some sense of the sequence and deposits represented can be reconstructed. These provide some assistance in understanding the activities within FA. At the beginning of excavation, the trench presented loose rocky sediments in the northeast and southwest corners, with compacted earth and few stones in between. Units A:1–16 removed stony fill. Unit A:17, in the NE corner adjacent to what would become FAS, removed stone fill; it revealed a series of two superimposed hearths, each consisting of a layer of fire-reddened clay with thick white ash and carbon above it. A semicircle of stones surrounded the hearth area (ca. 1.20 m diameter). The upper hearth was removed in unit A:18, the lower, in unit A:19. At a depth of 0.80–1.05 m below the modern surface of the cave, both hearths were well above the level of FA Balk (Fig. 86). While the finds associated with the hearths were dominantly Neolithic (including sherds from FCP 2, 4, and 5 at least), some modern sherds (a fragment of a classical cooking pot and a Medieval or modern glazed sherd) were also present and came from directly beneath the hearths.

Excavation continued in the northern two-thirds of Trench A through unit A:39. Modern sherds ceased to appear after unit A:22; indeed units A:23–25 seem, from the notebook descriptions, to have been "pure" FCP 5. Unit A:25 removed the contents of "2 clay-lined pits (bothroi?) near [the] east flank of [the] trench" (notebook 501:44), ca. 1 m south of FAS and 2.30 to 2.65 m below the surface, at roughly the same elevation as the hearth in FAS:73. Two more units around and below the pits, units A:26 and A:27, also produced substantial quantities of FCP 5 pottery, but mixed with FCP 3 and 4 sherds as well. Unfortunately, much of the pottery from these units was discarded, and units A:23–27 were lotted together in A Lot 13, although a few sherds have pencilled unit numbers on them. The rim illustrated in Fig. 75d, which may be Early Bronze Age in date, is from this lot, so the units may not have been entirely undisturbed. FCP 5 material is not included in the Lots of units below 27.

After unit A:39, unit A:40 returned to the southern portion, under unit A:10, again in the loose rocky fill of the reworked deposits. It produced a large quantity of pottery (no absolute count was recorded), including plentiful FCP 5, along with earlier and post-Neolithic sherds. It is the only unit in Lot 12, but ca. 50% of the pottery was discarded. Lot 11 includes pottery from Trench A units 11–22, all of which were quite mixed, with recent sherds present in all. Lot 10 includes pottery from units A:1–10, all of which included post-Neolithic material.

FRANCHTHI CERAMIC PHASE 5 (FCP 5): PARALIA CONTEXTS

While FCP 3 and FCP 4 activities were conducted inside the cave, Paralia was apparently used for nothing more than to provide access to the cave. No remains from those phases have been identified anywhere on Paralia. In FCP 5, after an hiatus of perhaps an entire millennium, the slopes of Paralia were once again the site of occasional human activity that produced material remains.

Pottery from the top 0.20–0.30 m—essentially surface—deposits on Paralia is all poorly preserved; soft weathered surfaces make it difficult to identify any variety securely. The very low-fired FCP 5 pottery scratches easily, breaks into small sherds, and may even dissolve when wet. It is particularly susceptible to weathering and especially difficult to identify securely when it derives from surface deposits that might include ceramics of any phase of the Neolithic or post-Neolithic. In many cases, the FN identification is, in fact, based largely on the degree of weathering, in addition to the bright red surfaces and black cores.

All the trenches on Paralia produced some sherds from surface units that fit that description (rounded, soft red lumps with black cores) and are probably Final Neolithic (Plan 3). Few units, however, included certain FCP 5 sherds (Table 10). O5NE included three FCP 5 burials, one with an intact pot (Fig. 67i). Q5N, Q6NE, and L5(NW) each included a single FCP 5 burial. Two burials in Q4 may be FCP5 in date.[22] Bone scatter potentially derived from FCP 5 activity is substantial (Cullen and Cook forthcoming). Few of the burial units or units immediately around them included FN sherds. The burials seem to have taken place without the breaking of pots and in places that were not occupied and used for other FN activities that might have resulted in a concentration of sherds.[23]

Only in L5 was there a substantial deposit that is certainly attributed to FCP 5 activities. The relevant units produced quantities of relatively well-preserved FCP 5 pottery, along with numerous artifacts, including 20 spindle whorls (Document 1), ground and flaked stone tools, sea shells and bones. While the topmost units (L5NE 2–3, 6–7, 11) comprised a dark brown sediment that may post-date the major FCP 5 activity, the bulk of the deposit is uniform and distinctive; it probably represents a short-term occupation devoted to a specific activity.

The FCP 5 deposits in L5 were cut into much earlier, FCP 2.1 levels (Vitelli 1993a:59); they are limited in extent. They are most clearly illustrated in the north section of L5 (J and F:Pl. 44), where they are indicated by stippling, just below topsoil.[24] The FCP 5 deposits were excavated over the course of three seasons, first in L5NE, then in L5(SE), and finally in L5(NW).

Assigned Units

Units in parentheses crosscut, or may have, several deposits. Commas separate units within a sequence, semicolons separate sequences.

Possibly later than main activity: L5NE:11, 7, 8, 6, 3–2

Main Activity
L5NE NW Corner: 21–20, 15, (11, 7)
NE Corner: 32, 29, 23, 19–17, 13, (6)
SE Corner: 26–24, 14, 12, 8, 4
SW Corner: 22, 16, 10, 5
L5 (NW): 98–95, 89– 85; 68–63; 61–55
L5 (SE): 17–1 (pit: 14–13)

In L5NE, the excavators followed what they considered related but slightly different deposits in each of the four corners of the trench. The sediments in all four areas were pale gray to white in color, with plentiful limestone cobbles. Clumps of very white calcium carbonate occurred in several units, while others included "lots of sea shells and sea pebbles." In the southeast corner, the pale gray sediments did not extend all the way to the east and south scarps, and so do not appear on the sections in that corner (J and F:Pls. 60–61). In the southwest corner the outline of a shallow pit is clear in the section (J and F:Pl. 60 "Light Gray"). That pit was recognized within L5(SE), where it was removed in units L5(SE):13–14. In the northeast corner of L5NE another depression or shallow pit is evident in the north sections (J and F:Pls. 44, 62), and contained on the southeast by Wall CC (Vitelli 1993a:Fig. 93). The fourth pit can be made out in the northwest corner (J and F:Pls. 62–63). It is not entirely clear (nor was it to the excavators) exactly how these four pits or depressions related to each other in the interior of the trench. None had clearly recognizable limits: the pale gray fill spread over the entire interior of the trench. The northeast and northwest areas are closely related by pottery joins (Vitelli 1993a:252). The northeast and southeast depressions may have formed a continuous trough (Plan 3, Structure BB; Wilkinson and Duhon 1990:143).

Apparently, the surface of L5NE, before the accumulation of the pale sediments, was dug down to an undulating surface, with slightly deeper depressions in the corners. The activity area was bounded at the southeast by Walls AA and CC (Plan 3; Vitelli 1993a, Fig. 93), which must have pre-dated the activity that produced the pale gray sediments. Since wall AA is bedded on deposits that include a few poorly preserved FCP 5 sherds, it is not much earlier and may have been specially constructed for the activity.

Aside from the pit removed in units 13–14, the pale gray sediment was absent in L5(SE). In that area, units 1–12, and 15–17, which removed Wall AA and the sediments immediately under and to the east and west of it, included a few very worn sherds of probable FCP 5 date, but nothing more. Deposits of the pale gray sediment in L5(NW) on the other hand, were substantial. There, too, an area had been prepared for the activity by digging into earlier sediments along the north and east scarps (Plan 3). Along the west edge of the trench area, the accumulating pale gray sediments were contained by earlier sediments, but the FCP 5 gray fill extended over the entire NE area of the trench.

Within the dug-out area in L5(NW), two deeper pits were also dug and filled in as part of the FCP 5 activity. One is evident in the north section (J and F:Pl. 44, above tag 98); the other was along the shared boundary with L5NE (J and F:Pl. 63 "white"; Pl. 59 "gray"). Both of these deeper pits had small clumps of very white calcium carbonate along their walls; it was not possible to determine whether they had been lined with, e.g., plaster, or whether the carbonate lumps were redeposited by water activity from the gray soils.

Whatever the nature of the activity responsible for the deposition of the pale gray sediments (see Chapter 5, Discussion), the purposeful digging and confinement of the sediments, and their uniformity suggest that it was an activity that took place over a relatively short period of time—perhaps only days or weeks. The ceramics and other remains from within the deposit, therefore, present an opportunity to examine material that was in use at one time, with little, if any, reworking by later occupants.

Having said that, a few units at the top of L5NE (L5NE:2–3, 6–7, 11) removed a brown sediment, immediately below topsoil, full of many rocks with only occasional traces of the pale gray from underneath. Several sherds from these units are unique in L5. If they are later, one may ponder why activity again occurred in precisely this spot and, indeed, why this spot had been selected for the earlier FN activity.

NOTES

1. In lotting, pottery from adjacent units that produced joining sherds and generally similar pottery was physically combined into a single "lot," a form of phasing of the material. From the "lot," a few interesting, large, well-preserved, or representative sherds were selected and saved. The rest of the sherds, perhaps as much as 90–95% of the total, were discarded in the Bay of Nauplion. After the first season, lotting was not practiced by the Franchthi project.

2. Most of the reworked deposits from trenches in the central area of the cave included at least 50% FCP 2 Urf sherds. Jacobsen and Farrand 1987 includes the section drawings and plans of the excavated areas, with the exception of that for L5 East, which is included in Vitelli (1993a:Fig. 93). References to sections in the Jacobsen and Farrand volume are abbreviated throughout the text as "J and F." Fig. 86 in the present volume reproduces the upper, Neolithic, portion of J and F:Pl. 7, the section for FA West, as it is frequently referred to in the following discussion.

3. FCP 2 deposits were close to the surface in G and G1; the later Neolithic material was mixed with it, rather than coming from actual deposits of later date.

4. The excavators isolated areas of apparently undisturbed deposits with FCP 3 through FCP 5, and without post-Neolithic pottery, in the western portion of the trench in units 18–20, 22, 24–25, 27. These should be the units that removed the strata evident in the western third of the south section (J and F:Pl. 20—roughly through the series of "hearths" at ca 8.50 m through the continuous line of rocks in "yellowish" soil at ca. 7.00 m). Units were not tagged in the scarps in 1968 so the relation of deposits shown on the sections with specific units is only approximate. To judge from the pottery, FF1:19 removed the equivalent of FAS:116–111 and FAN:118–112, i.e., an FCP 3 deposit, although there are a few clearly later sherds. FF1:18, from the pottery, appears to have removed an FCP 4 deposit, possibly without contamination from later phases.

5. This was one of the considerations that led to the isolation of the FA pedestal, where exposed scarps allowed the excavators to see the strata they were about to dig, thus greatly increasing their ability to follow strata precisely. Unfortunately, this approach left no standing scarps on north, east, and south sides of the trench after excavation, with which we might relate excavated units to lithostratigraphic units.

6. The notebooks mention Bronze Age, Archaic, Classical, Roman, Byzantine, Medieval, and very recent.

7. The excavators squared off the eastern end of the pedestal (producing the 0.25 m "setback" of the balk from the east terrace; see J and F:Pl. 8, at the 7.00 m mark, above FAN:120), before returning to the north half of the balk, and unit 120N.

8. In the twenty years since our excavations on Paralia, scrub and grasses have returned. The depressions of partially infilled trenches are barely detectable, even to one who knows where to look.

9. Unit numbers in which sherds were found are listed in the captions for all illustrated sherds, should anyone chose to compare those from boundary and later units.

10. The slope is evident in Fig. 86: the north–south slope in the 119N tag at ca. 7 m and 115S at ca. 6.60 m; J and F:Pl. 19: the east–west slope along the interface below tags 117N, 119N.

11. In some seasons, the unit number was written in india ink on all sherds larger than 1–2 cm, to avoid creating artificial contamination when a sherd was accidentally placed in the wrong unit. Numbering, however, an extremely labor-intensive undertaking, was not completed for all units. When I opened the sherd bag for FAS:119 in 1980 I found sherds with numbers from several other units, along with a collection of FCP 5 sherds with no numbers. The numbered sherds were returned to their correct units. I assume, in this case, that the unnumbered pieces had also mistakenly been returned to the 119S bag. The pottery notebook entries from the time of excavation make no mention of even the distinctive unnumbered pieces I found bagged with FAS:119. The FCP 5 handle from FAS:117 was noted in the original pottery notebook entry for that unit.

12. The reader may pursue this comparison with the illustrated fragments in Figs. 1–7, as unit numbers are provided for each sherd. Unillustrated pieces added no useful information.

13. See Vitelli 1993a:250–251 for the full list of cross-unit joins.

14. I was unable to locate soil samples from these units. Samples from FAS:103–102, which were similar in color and consistency to those described in the notebooks for the FCP 4.1 units, proved to foam and disappear in hydrochloric acid; i.e., they were highly calcareous.

15. Two large bags, labeled only as "clay samples" from FAS:102 and FAS:103, include chunks of pale "clay" up to 3x4x5 cm in size, that foam and dissolve completely in hydrochloric acid. Small chunks of charcoal and lighter-colored lumps of carbonate are embedded in the "clay."

16. From repeated experience, the excavators came to identify "hearths" by finding, first, a small collection of rocks next to, or sitting directly on "hearth clay," i.e., a thin layer of clay reddened by exposure to the heat of a fire. As they uncovered the group of rocks, they generally found a more ordered arrangement, usually defining one or more rough circles (or "burners", as they describe them in the notebooks) and plentiful carbon and ash. The depth of these "hearths" varied. Sometimes, as in this case, it was as much as 0.40 m. Since the traces of "hearth clay" were generally outside the area enclosed by the rock circles, and since fires burn poorly inside relatively deep and narrow pits

because of poor oxygen flow, the "hearths" may have been pits dug next to the fire itself. They may have been used for baking with hot coals, as discard pits, or for some other purpose.

Joins among sherds from these deposits are few (Vitelli 1993a:250) and unrevealing. A human tibia was recovered from FAS:98 (Fr 126), which also included a few sherds of FCP 2 and FCP 3 varieties. The bone could have come with sediments from elsewhere. If the sediments removed as the "hearth" accumulated after the remains of the fire and the figurine were in place, the "hearth" above FAS:103 would appear to be an intentional marking of their placement.

17. Contemporary deposits at the eastern tip of FAN were reworked by an FCP 5 pit, recognized and removed discretely in units 76N, 80N, 83N, 91N, and 93N.

18. Farrand's more recent analyses identify an additional stratum Y3, between Y2 and Z. The stratigraphic discontinuity falls between Y2 and Y3 (Farrand forthcoming).

19. I am very grateful to Bill Farrand for taking time to track down answers to my questions about this segment of the FA sequence. Without his help and results of his analyses, I would have been far less comfortable locating the hiatus in relation to the ceramics.

20.The pit was removed in FAN:76N, 80N, 83N, 91N, 93N. The excavators recognized the top at the level of 76N, shown in J and F:Pl. 19 as a lens of yellow clay and ash. The top of this pit was not unlike the many "hearths" recognized throughout the sequence, and in fact, most "hearths" proved to have been dug into extant sediments, i.e., they too were "pits." The main difference between this "pit" and the "hearths" is that the FCP 5 pit was evident in advance in the exposed scarp.

21. The excavators thought they removed the bottom of the 73S hearth in units 79S–78S, although the section drawing does not confirm the relationship.

22. The burials are: Fr 63 (O5NE:6, 11), Fr 62 (O5NE:5, 9, 10), Fr 61 (O5NE: 2, 3, 7, 10), Fr 19 (Q5N:19), Fr 18 (Q6NE:1, 6, 10), Fr 115 (L5:57), Fr 69 (Q4:10, 16, 25), and Fr 221 (Q4:9). See Cullen and Cook forthcoming.

23. But see also, below, Chapter 5, Discussion.

24. On J and F:Pl. 44, the NW corner of L5NE suggests a deep pit cutting through the stippled FCP 5 deposits and surmounted by a large boulder. The ceramic evidence does not support this interpretation, which may have been based on evidence in the scarp after it was scraped several centimeters for the final drawing of the scarp. Sections of the north and west scarps of L5NE drawn at the time of excavation (J and F:Pls. 62 and 63), especially when folded and joined at the corner, suggest a rocky "gray" pit (above tags 34NE and 39NE) that does not extend as deeply as that suggested by J and F:Pl. 44. This coincides neatly with the ceramic evidence for a relatively shallow FCP 5 deposit in that corner. Multiple joins of FCP 5 sherds from that shallow pit or depression and the similar shallow depression in the NE corner further point to contemporaneity of deposits in both areas.

CHAPTER THREE

Franchthi Ceramic Phase 3 (FCP 3): The Pottery

All FCP 3 pottery belongs to the calcareous class. One ware, Low Lime, accounts for most of the pots and was probably produced locally. The relative quantity, size, and perhaps even the specific nonplastics vary from sherd to sherd. The wide range of variation suggests that the potters followed the recipe loosely. The Low Lime Burnished variety occurs without further elaboration or with applied, impressed or incised, pattern burnished, or painted decoration, sometimes in combinations of several of these techniques. With a larger sample, each of these techniques for elaborating the surface would have been called a separate variety. The small sample size encourages their analysis as a single variety. Other varieties, the manganese painted and polychrome painted sherds, have diverse fabrics. They occur in too few examples to allow definition of the ware(s). Multiple varieties of each may also be present; I have grouped them because of the small size and number of sherds. A small group of unique sherds is described without attribution to ware or variety.

LOW LIME WARE (LoLi)

Fabric

The basic recipe called for a clay body that included Lime and other white nonplastics, usually under 1 mm in size, and rounded bits of iron-oxide-rich grit in the larger vessels, up to several mm in size, with the occasional piece up to 5 mm or more. The gray cores of the sherds from smaller vessels make it difficult to distinguish the nonplastics against the dark background. I occasionally noted the presence of iron-oxide-rich inclusions, but more often was unable to distinguish them, whether because of their small size against the dark background or because they were truly not present. White inclusions show up clearly, and most sherds have at least some of these, usually under 1 mm in size but sometimes larger. Sometimes the white is powdery, indicating that it is Lime that has been exposed to temperatures over ca. 800°C. Actual Lime "pops," where the carbonate inclusion has expanded and removed the surrounding surface with it, are rare. Powdery white Lime is obvious against the dark surfaces of the pot. The Lime in the breaks, which did not reach the same high temperatures, often remains hard and gray, and more difficult to see; the Lime content of sherds may well be higher than recorded.

Pits from dissolved Lime nonplastics are common, especially on unburnished surfaces. Some may have been formed during use or burial; some were certainly the result of heavy soaking in an acid bath just after excavation.[1] Not all the white or light-colored nonplastics are Lime: some react not at all to hydrochloric acid and are probably quartz or feldspar. Some sherds certainly feel more sandy and raspy along the breaks than others.[2]

In the larger vessels with thick-walled sherds and more frequently light-fired cores, rounded red, gray, and black (probably iron-oxide-rich) nonplastics are clear. These are usually ca. 1 mm in diameter, but sometimes in the 2–3 mm range, and occasionally a stray 4–

Table 3.1. FCP 3 Classes, Wares, and Varieties

Calcareous Class
- Low Lime Ware
  - Burnished variety (LoLiB)
  - Coarse variety (LiCo)
- Uncertain Ware(s)
  - Manganese Painted varieties (MnPt)
  - Polychrome Painted varieties (Poly)

5 mm pebble is present.[3] It appears that the FCP 3 potters adjusted the clay body for vessel size, as the FCP 2 potters had done for large Coarse Urf and cooking pots (Vitelli 1993a:162, 213).

On some sherds, especially those on which the surface has worn considerably, the glitter of silver mica (muscovite) attracts attention. On most sherds I noticed none. If a regular component of the clay body, the mica was covered by a slip and perhaps a layer of carbon soot from the firing (see below), so the glitter is noticeable only when the surface layer has worn away.

Low Lime Burnished Variety (LoLiB)

Building Procedures and Surface Finish

To judge from the evidence of breaks along joints that preserve the relatively smooth surface where two lumps of clay were joined (e.g., Fig. 7d), the pots were built up with coils or slabs. Many of the thicker sherds have broken in half, with only one intact surface on all or part of the sherd, suggesting that the coils (or slabs) on the larger vessels were overlapped. Within the breaks, rims often show evidence of having been folded to the interior or exterior, to level and finish the rim and expose potentially dangerous nonplastics while the clay was still plastic enough to remove them easily.

The potters may have built some pots entirely or in part upside down, starting at the rim or point of maximum diameter. The spreading shape on the lower part of many pots (e.g., Figs. 2b, 5g, 6e, 7a–b, e) would have been easier to build in that manner than by starting at the bottom and fighting gravity as the lower walls were built up. This procedure could have contributed to the occasionally marked lopsidedness (e.g., Fig. 5g). The thickened rims (Fig. 7a–b, e) could also be a consequence of building from the rim, a thicker coil being useful at the "bottom" or beginning of the process to support the upper walls and to prevent the rim from drying out before the piece was finished.

Most of the sherds from FCP 3 have irregular horizontal curvature, sometimes so much so that reliable diameter measurements are impossible. When enough of a pot is preserved to judge, the profile on one side is generally rather different than that on the other. However they approached the building process, the potters did not work with the rhythm of regular repetition of familiar motions that would have produced more symmetrical pots.

The even surfaces and, on unburnished interiors, shallow gouges from nonplastics dragged along the surface indicate that the potters scraped the finished pot to eliminate the irregularities of the building surface and to thin the walls, although they did not generally achieve a uniform thickness around the vessel. Scraping marks show that in this part of the process as well, potters had no standard working procedure. The marks go in all directions, sometimes parallel to the rim, sometimes at angles to it. The direction of scraping strokes is not, as it is for the work of FCP 2 Urf potters, a reliable indicator for orienting body sherds.

Additions to the basic pot body, such as pedestal bases, lugs, handles, relief pellets, and ribs, do not usually detach at the joint, as happened commonly in all earlier wares. That joints were not apparent weak points suggests that appendages were added at an early stage of building while the clay of the body was quite damp and a good seal could be made. The potter usually rubbed a wet hand over accessible surfaces on the finished pot, raising a self-slip while smoothing over the ridges and gouges of the scraping process.

In addition to relief decoration, the potters chose among a number of options for elaborating their pots. They could use: simple burnishing, repeated as the pot went through stages of drying; a coat or two of an iron-oxide-rich slip before a final burnishing; application of the same slip in patterns; selective pattern-burnishing, with or without the addition of the slip; impressed and incised patterns, with or without the addition of a white Lime powder in the depressions; painted decoration in a light-colored pigment; or a combination of several of these. The wide range of choices exercised in the small sample available make it difficult to describe any procedures as standard. Rather, the potters achieved—and perhaps aimed for—individuality within a broadly defined tradition.

Relief Decoration

All preserved fragments of shouldered bowls have a relief pellet or strip applied on the shoulder (Figs. 6a–d, 11c), and a shouldered jar fragment has an applied donut (Fig. 1j). A thicker-walled, red-fired carinated sherd (Fig. 4g) also has part of a low-relief pellet marking the carination. Such relief markings were applied and tooled onto the pot during building, as similar relief marks had been added to pots since the Early Neolithic. No examples are sufficiently preserved to indicate whether the marks were repeated around the pot or stood alone, although the fact that all the shouldered bowl rims include one may suggest that each pot carried several. A thick sherd from a large vessel (FAN:113, not illustrated) preserves three rows of pellets. Another form of relief decoration, ridges and grooves, occurs on several examples (Figs. 8h, 9d); in the latter, and on a smaller sherd possibly from the same pot (FAN:113, not illustrated), it is combined with "white" painted decoration. The relief ridges could have been created by using a burnishing tool on a damp surface to impress the grooves and push up ridges between them. A small worn sherd from FAN:95 has only the grooves left, separated by scars where the ridges have detached, so probably small strips of clay were added to create the ridges.

The lugs on these pots are so small that they, too, might be considered more decorative than functional (Fig.1g, where the right side of the pierced hole has been closed by subsequent burnishing; Figs. 5f–g, 11d).

Iron-Oxide-Rich Slip

It is clear from the occasional firing cloud at the rim that some pots were given a coating of iron-oxide-rich slip, usually over the exterior and just inside the rim. In oxidized areas, the slip has fired a clear red that contrasts with the paler clay ground. These pots tend to fire a deep black, rather than the dark blue-gray of unslipped pieces. Sometimes the slip was applied thickly, perhaps in several coats. The burnished surface then has a waxy quality, and is often flaking off.

On at least a few larger pots that were fired in an oxidizing atmosphere, the same slip was use to create a vague pattern (Fig. 3b–c). If other jars that fired black had similar patterns (Fig. 2a–b), the patterns were obliterated by the firing reactions. In oxidized areas of the jar in Fig. 2a, streaky red paint is visible, but it seems to cover the entire surface.

Pattern Burnishing

A few small pots were elaborated with pattern burnishing (Figs. 1m, 5g, 6k). For these, the potter burnished the whole pot while it was still leather-hard. As it dried further and additional shrinkage from evaporation dulled the sheen of the initial burnish, the potter added the selective pattern burnishing, which stands out in contrast with the compacted, but dull background. The pot in Fig. 1m may have been slipped before the final pattern burnishing, as the pattern lines are a deep black, against the lighter gray unburnished area. The bowl in Fig. 5g seems to have been slipped after pattern burnishing, and only between the burnished panels, then burnished again only in the newly slipped areas; these fired a deep black, while the pattern itself shows up as gray against a lighter gray. The little cup in Fig. 6k seems to have been slipped before burnishing, to judge from the dark band that extends for ca. 2 cm inside the rim; the pattern is barely visible because the contrast between burnished and unburnished areas is very low.

Impressed Decoration

Small pots were sometimes elaborated by impressing one or more rows of delicate ovals along the line of the carination (Figs.1h, 5b–c, 8b). The impressions, made after the pot had received an initial burnishing, were probably done with a seed or the tip of a small pebble, very carefully pressed into the damp vessel surface.

A few sherds, apparently from very small and very large jars, are decorated with a distinctive pattern of zigzags or triangles formed by small punctate impressions, usually outlined by impressed (rather than incised) lines, probably made with something like a bone point (Figs. 8e–g, 9a–c). The dots have a little hump in the center that suggests they were poked with a hollow tool while the clay was still relatively damp. The pot was burnished after the pattern was impressed, since some of the grooves and holes are nearly closed by the burnish. The troughs from the burnish are clear, so this must have been done while the pot was still damp enough to take the impression of the burnishing tool. At some point after the vessel dried, a Lime powder, little of which remains today, was rubbed into the depressions, probably after firing and presumably to make the decoration stand out against the black background.

That particular technique and even the motifs of decoration are commonly associated with the Final Neolithic in mainland Greece. Only one of the fragments from Franchthi (Fig. 8g) comes from a stratified context, FAS:116, a unit with other problematic sherds (see below). The other examples are from mixed contexts, in every case from a unit that also produced substantial amounts of FCP 3 Low Lime Burnished varieties. No example occurs in any stratified FCP 5 unit or in any mixed unit that is dominated by FCP 5 sherds. The fragments from large jars in particular (Fig. 9a–c) are similar in both fabric and shape to other Low Lime Burnished jars. It seems likely, therefore, that the technique was used in FCP 3, as one of several features characteristic of more than one Neolithic phase (see, e.g., shape discussion, below).

"White" Painted Decoration

The most common form of decoration on Low Lime Burnished pots is patterns painted in a "white" pigment (e.g., Fig. 1a–b, g, k, Pl. 1b), sometimes in combination with another technique (e.g., Figs. 5b, 9d). The paint is not a stark white, but a rather granular, dull gray that stands out against the dark burnished background of the pot both by color contrast and texture, for the paint is never burnished.

The pigment does not react to hydrochloric acid, so is not a calcium carbonate. What it is and when it was applied are more difficult to determine, and may not have been the same in all instances. The choices for pigment would have included talc, kaolin, or another clay with minimal iron oxide content, or some combination of these. In experimental work, my students and I have had no success in persuading a pure talc pigment to adhere to a clay body. Our only successes with talc have come when we mixed it with a clay slip, painted it on a pot that was just slightly damp, and then burnished it hard, forcing the pigment into the clay body. Unburnished talc mixtures, once dry, brushed off at the slightest touch. Since the Low Lime Burnished paint is never burnished, it seems unlikely that it was a talc or talc–clay mixture. Light-firing clays present fewer problems of bonding; they seem the more likely source of at least some of the Low Lime Burnished "white" paint. Other possibilities cannot, however, be entirely ruled out pending additional experimentation and analysis (see below).

The very large necked jar (Fig. 10) preserves evidence of the painter erasing a line to adjust the relationship of motifs above and below the neck joint. The dashed lines in Fig. 10 indicate a ghostly pale line on the pot where the potter wiped off the original painted line and reburnished the area over it. Pl. 2a shows the next group of lines to the right of those illustrated in the drawing. There, the potter wiped off four lines, reburnished the surface, and repainted four new lines to the left of the original group. This pot was clearly painted before firing, and while the pot was still damp enough to burnish after the first lines had been wiped off. The pigment could have been the same clay used for the body of the pot. It has fired to roughly the same light color as the subsurfaces. The streaky quality of the black color on the surface suggests that reduction of an iron-oxide-rich slip was responsible for the black background.

On some sherds, the extant pattern lines suggest strongly that part of the pattern has disappeared (e.g., Figs. 1a, 11a), yet where the missing lines should be, no trace of them remains. Pigment applied as paint has to be mixed with a liquid medium. Liquid applied to an unfired burnished surface should cause at least a minute amount of swelling of that surface, enough to destroy the gloss of the burnish, and create the dull "ghost" line that we normally see when pigment has worn from a burnished sherd. Even tilted at various angles to the light, however, no interruption in the burnish line is evident on the Low Lime Burnished pots with missing decoration. On these and other sherds with a thick grainy paint line, I have been able to scratch off parts of the painted line with my fingernail, and again, no trace is left to show the line had once been there. These observations suggest that the painted decoration was sometimes applied after firing.

A post-firing paint made from a clay slip or clay–talc mixture with water as the medium would, however, be soluble in water; the paint would dissolve when wet, so it would be unlikely to survive millennia of burial and—if it did—should wash off readily in water today. A glue-like medium, perhaps a resin or albumen mixture, might have provided a more durable paint. Alternately, the vessel might have been refired; this would necessarily have been a short firing at a low temperature not to affect the black background.[4]

I suspect all the "white" paint on Low Lime Burnished sherds is, in fact, a pre-firing application. Sherds from two carinated bowls (Fig. 5a–b) provide additional clues. The painted lines above the carination on those sherds are thick, with palpable relief. They can be scraped off easily, leaving no trace behind. Below the carination, the paint in the lines is thinner, although individual grains are still evident to the naked eye. These lines are more permanent. It seems unnecessarily complicated to posit pre-firing decoration on part of the pot, followed by post-firing decoration on another, followed in turn by a second firing. A simpler explanation would be that the potter began by painting the unfired, burnished, but still damp pot with the area below the carination. The paint pot—possibly a recycled ceramic container—held a fresh mix of paint, diluted with plenty of water and only the finest particles in suspension in the liquid. The painter dipped the brush, and painted on the first fluid lines. As she worked, the porous container absorbed liquid from the paint mixture, which became increasingly viscous. When she dipped her brush later, it collected a thick paint, including the large pigment particles that would have settled out of a runnier mix; the painted lines became correspondingly thicker. Since she was painting on a still damp, burnished (i.e., compacted) surface, the clay body did not absorb much if any liquid from the viscous paint. During firing, the larger particle pigment grains in the thick areas of paint allowed the atmosphere of the firing to reach the vessel surface under the paint and react, i.e., to become darkened. Their larger size also prevented bonding with the vessel surface at the temperatures reached; so they became fugitive after firing. Where the paint was thinner and composed of finer particles, the temperature was sufficient to achieve some bonding with the clay body, making the thinner lines more permanent.

Colors and Firing Practices

The potters who made the Low Lime Burnished pots generally fired with techniques that successfully produced dark-surfaced pots. Several techniques, however, may produce similar surface effects.[5] The simplest of these is smudging, which takes place at the end of a firing as the temperature drops and the pots begin to cool to less than ca. 400°C (Skibo 1992:160). If ready access to oxygen is cut off at this stage, e.g., by smothering the fire and completely covering the pots with something like earth, damp seaweed or dung, incomplete combustion will deposit carbon soot on exposed vessel surfaces. The presence of moisture contributes to a metallic-looking, shiny finish, probably carbonized resin (Skibo 1992:162), that actually enhances the sheen of a burnished surface (Vitelli 1994:143). If a potter overly anxious to see the results of her firing uncovers a pot while it is still hot (i.e., more than 400°C), the carbon has access to oxygen; it will burn off immediately, the color potentially changing from black to light faster than one can re-cover the piece. Potters quickly learn that it is wise to leave the covered, smoldering pile for several hours at least before uncovering the pots. That extended cooling period almost ensures that some soot will be absorbed into the porous clay body, so that, on a broken edge, the black color will extend for a millimeter or so into the subsurface. Surface carbon deposited by smudging will burn off at relatively low temperatures if the pot is re-exposed to any fire with plentiful oxygen available (Shepard 1968:220).[6]

A more complex technique for producing dark colored pots is reduction firing—more complex because it generally involves higher temperatures and greater control of atmosphere than does smudging.[7] In true reduction, insufficient oxygen is available in the firing atmosphere to support combustion, so oxygen is taken from the constituents of the clay, and the oxygen content of the clay body, including any slips or paints, is reduced (Shepard 1968:219; Grimshaw 1980:714). That process changes the color of the iron oxide from red to black or gray. The difficulty of reduction firing for the potter is to achieve and maintain temperatures sufficient for the reactions to take place, while also depriving the atmosphere around the pots of oxygen. The choice of fuel may be crucial. A kiln makes the process easier.[8]

Some pieces of Low Lime Burnished in the Franchthi assemblage were certainly exposed to a hot fire for an extended period at some point after the original firing, sufficient to alter the original color (see below). Some of the other variation in color, texture, and hardness among the Low Lime Burnished sherds may also be explained by secondary exposure to fire.

Firing circles never occur, nor are clouds located at points of maximum diameter that might suggest spots where vessels touched each other in the firing. The potters did not, then, stack pots inside one another or place them to touch each other during firing. They could have fired each pot separately.

The smaller, thin-walled vessels are consistently dark gray or black on the exterior (ca. 2.5 YR 3–4/0), lighter gray on the interior (ca. 10YR 5–6/1–2). Cores are lighter than the surfaces and are uniformly gray. This is equally true of upper and lower body sherds, including bottoms (e.g., Figs. 5g, 6e–g). On pedestals (Figs. 7c, f, 11f), the unburnished underside is darker gray than the interior of the bowl to which it was attached. The pattern of coloration indicates that the pots were fired upside down, on their rims; exterior and bottom surfaces were most directly exposed to the final atmosphere responsible for the dark color.

The hardness of sherds, tested by the Mohs' scratch test, ranges from 3, which usually scratches up a greasy black powder that could be slip or deposited soot, to 6, which leaves a clear scratch on the vessel surface. The softer sherds, usually with jagged and irregular breaks, seem unlikely to have been fired to temperatures sufficient for reduction. Their black color may be the result of smudging. The harder, thin-walled sherds often have glassy, melted-looking breaks, which are usually straight and sharp. These also have a greenish tinge to the gray color (ca. 10 YR 5–6/1) in the core and on unburnished surfaces—a color often associated with high-fired calcium-oxide-rich clays. Many of the harder sherds are a glossy black when wet, but dry quickly, with a creamy white bloom on the surface. Sherds that dry quickly suggest low porosity, one effect of temperatures high enough to initiate sintering. Together, the characteristics of the harder sherds suggest that the potters probably reached and sustained temperatures in excess of ca. 850°C on occasion, temperatures appropriate for reduction.

The cores of the dark-surfaced sherds are quite uniformly gray. No example has a deeper gray or black streak at the very center. Nor does the deep black surface color penetrate the subsurface. The gray core must come, not from incompletely oxidized organic material in the original clay body or from absorption of carbon soot during an extended period of smudging, but from exposure to a reducing or an incompletely oxidizing atmosphere.

Assuming the light-colored painted decoration was applied before firing (see above), its condition also contributes to an analysis of firing practices. It is never a pure chalky white, but a very pale gray. Individual pigment grains are evident to the naked eye. If the black background of the pot had been produced entirely by smudging, the carbon soot should have, at least occasionally, covered the paint lines as well as the background of the pot.[9] That this apparently never happened also points to reduction as the explanation for the black background.

The larger pots were probably fired in much the same way although their greater size may have made it more difficult to keep them entirely covered and deprived of access to oxygen. Some have large areas of oxidation on the surfaces, which could have been caused by subsequent exposure to a fire. The pots with painted patterns that have fired red may have been intentionally allowed access to oxygen, simply by not covering the fire at the end and allowing the vessels to cool while exposed to the air.

The potters apparently did not have complete control over temperature. When the temperatures they reached were high enough for reduction and they covered the fire at the right moment, they produced reduced pots. When temperatures were insufficient or they covered the fire as the temperature dropped markedly, smudging produced the black surfaces.

I doubt that the large vessels were used as firing enclosures for the small vessels, as I have suggested was true of the large Coarse Urf vessels in FCP 2 (Vitelli 1993a:184–185). They are less hard-fired than the smaller vessels, and the interiors tend to be a less deep gray than the exteriors. If they had been used to enclose the smaller pots during firing, they should be hard-fired, their interiors heavily reduced or blackened with soot, and the exteriors oxidized. For the reduction firings, an enclosure would have helped to hold the heat, to attain the necessary temperatures, and to keep the fuel away from the pots. Temporary enclosures might have been built for each firing, especially for the largest pots; if firings took place at Franchthi, we have found no trace of them.

Although the pots are lumpy and lopsided, they were scraped to quite thin walls. The very large vessels are not the work of timid potters. The lopsidedness, uneven wall thickness, inconsistent scraping directions, variable quality of the surface finish, and the variation in firing point to potters that practiced infrequently. Nevertheless, they put a substantial amount of time and effort into finishing their pots. Even undecorated, these are labor-intensive pieces.

Shapes

Jars: Figs. 1– 3; 8a–b, d–i; 9; 10; 11a
Bowls: Figs. 5; 6a–d; 8c; 11b–c
Basins: Figs. 7a–b, d–e; 11e
Varia: Figs. 4d–g; 6h, j–k; 11d
Pedestals: Figs. 4h; 7c, f; 11f
Bottoms: Figs. 2b; 3b, d; 5g; 6e–g, h?; 11d?

Diameter measurements vary markedly on even small rim or body sherds that join, and almost every substantial arc of sherd shows asymmetrical curvature. The irregularity of the curves is such that diameter readings are almost guesswork. I am not certain of the size of any of these pieces. For example, the rims in Figs. 6a–d, and 11c are clearly from a similar shape, and several or all could derive from the same vessel, but the diameter measurements vary from a small 0.14 m to a substantial 0.25 m. Drawn with the different diameter measurements, the profiles suggest rather different vessels. It is unclear if the rims represent the range of sizes drawn, or whether all pots with this rim profile were approximately the same size and simply had quite crooked rims.

We were able to reconstruct only a single complete profile (Fig. 5g). Furthermore, rims may be lumpy, and, lacking consistent scraping and burnishing directions, the angle of the rim is difficult to establish with certainty. Tilting the angle slightly can produce a very different-looking vessel. The restored drawings represent my best guess at the original shape, but I would not be surprised to find joining fragments or better-preserved examples from other sites that demonstrate that the fragments from Franchthi derive from rather different-looking vessels.

Four or five basic shapes make up the main repertoire in this ware, although the variations give the impression of many more. One substantial profile of a small necked jar was restored (Fig. 1a), with a carinated body and a single strap handle preserved from rim to shoulder. Restored on paper to an original height of ca. 0.10 m, it would have had a capacity of slightly under one liter if filled to the rim. Another carinated body (Fig. 1g), probably from a similar if slightly larger jar, has a small horizontal tubular lug at the carination. One side of the hole is burnished closed, suggesting the lug was more decorative or symbolic than functional, the piercing perhaps intended to ease the firing by lessening the thickness. Two other small carinated body sherds (Figs. 1h; 8b) may be from similar jars. Other body sherds with traces of a neck joint have a thickened shoulder rather than a carination (Fig. 1i–j), while another (Fig. 1k) has a faceted or doubly carinated shoulder. Rim sherds with smaller diameters (e.g., Figs. 1b–f: less than ca. 0.20 m) probably come from the necks of carinated or shouldered jars. That illustrated in Fig. 1f preserves the edge of a joint. The curves at the lower body of both carinated and shouldered jars suggest they tapered to flat bottoms.

Examples of necked jars with apparently rounded bodies, and potentially rounded bottoms, come from disturbed contexts (Figs. 8d, h–i), as do the two examples of quite small, constricted necks, both with incised and white filled decoration (Figs. 8e–f). The shallowly grooved piece (Fig. 8h), quite soft and worn, is now the pale gray color of later "Gray" ware (see below FCP 4), which has a similar fabric. The finger groove along the neck joint seems to relate it to FCP 3 Low Lime Burnished pieces (e.g., Fig. 2), which also made use of vertical ribbing (e.g., Fig. 9d); but it could be a later piece.

Larger necked jars (Figs. 2–3) have a convex or lightly carinated body (Figs. 2b; 3c) with a rounded (Fig. 2a) or flat bottom (Fig. 3b). The neck fragment in Fig. 3a provides an impression of the neck on a jar about the size of that in Fig. 2b. The finger groove along the joint is a distinctive feature of these jars. Using the summed cylinders method (Rice 1987:222), the capacities of the three well-preserved jars, if filled to the neck joint, were approximately 12.5 liters (Fig. 2a), 13.5 liters (Fig. 2b) and 9 liters (Fig. 3b).

The two larger jars in Fig. 2 show no signs of wear of the sorts Skibo describes (1992:110–173) on the interior bottoms or upper walls, although the round-bottomed one has three drill holes, presumably for mending, in its lower body. The slightly smaller, painted jar in Fig. 3b also has drilled holes in its lower body: two pairs, plus two whose adjoining sherd is not preserved. Its interior has a black soot stain on the bottom, slightly off center and with a patterning that suggests post-firing deposition. The carbon penetrates the subsurface more deeply and irregularly in some places than others, perhaps suggesting that coals or chunks of meat—rather than something like gruel, of fairly uniform consistency—burned inside it for some time. Unfortunately, it is not possible to determine if this happened before or after the vessel broke.

The potters also made necked jars in a very large size (Figs. 4a–c; 9; 10), with well-burnished surfaces and extensive surface elaboration in the full range of techniques used on the smaller vessels. The most fully preserved example, FP 55 (Fig. 10), restored on paper (Fig. 75) with a thick flat bottom like that in Fig. 3d, would have stood approximately 0.75 m tall and had a capacity, filled to the rim, of nearly 100 liters.[10] Very little of the body below the neck is preserved, and none of the body below that illustrated can be securely identified. The preserved portions are uniformly dark, without clouds or areas where the burnish has obviously been affected by, e.g., post-firing exposure to fire—even this is difficult to judge because of the massive plastering done in the original restoration work.[11] In short, no evidence clearly suggests what function a vessel of this impressive size and decoration might have served.

The thick, flat bottom fragment in Fig. 3d should have come from a vessel of the same general shape and size. It retains a good burnish sheen on the exterior and underside, comparable to that on the upper bodies of the very large necked jars, but it is oxidized to a reddish tan color (7.5 YR 6/6). Its interior surface is no longer discernible, as it is heavily charred and sooted. The carbon soot extends deep into the subsurface, more deeply on the preserved portion of the vessel wall than on the actual bottom, and extends over the breaks. Unfortunately for our attempts to understand vessel functions, since this sherd was found, inverted, on a pile of ash and carbon—a "hearth"—the charring is more probably to be attributed to secondary use over the fire than to original use when the vessel was intact.

A few rim sherds suggest a slightly piriform bowl or jar (Figs. 1l–n; 11a), with only minimal traces of burnishing on the interior. Open bowl shapes are of three basic kinds, carinated, shouldered, and pedestalled basins. The relatively shallow, carinated bowls (Figs. 5; 8c; 11c), probably all with a flat bottom (Fig. 5g), are similar in concept to some carinated bowls from the preceding FCP 2 phase (cf. e.g., Vitelli 1993a:Fig. 89, FCP 2.5 PB Urf), but they are far more irregular and lopsided than their predecessors. Some (e.g., Figs. 5c, e, h; 11b) may have been deeper than others. None shows evidence for a true base, nor have any base fragments, other than narrow pedestals (see below), been recognized in the ware. The lugs applied at the carination (Fig. 5f–g) are surely more decorative than functional, given their size. FP 240 (Fig. 5g) comprises roughly half of the pot, with a single lug preserved. Two carinated bowls have post-firing drill holes (Figs. 5f, 11b, Pl. 1b) below the rim, suggesting they were sufficiently prized to have warranted mending. The bowl in Fig. 5f also has a brown-black stain over much of the interior that looks as though something was burned inside it. The stain has not been analyzed. The interior bottom of the fragment in Fig. 5h is quite pitted and worn. These rare examples of interior stains or wear, however, are insufficient to distinguish the effects of primary use as whole pots from those of potential secondary use in sherd form.

Shouldered bowls with an offset rounded lip (Figs. 6a–d, 11c) are a shape unique to FCP 3. All have a thickened shoulder similar to the shouldered and necked jars (Figs. 1i–k), suggesting both shapes may have been the specialty of a particular potter. The rim tips were folded to the exterior, and a groove separates the rim from the shoulder. All shouldered bowls apparently had one or more relief marks on the shoulder. All probably had flat bottoms (Figs. 6e–g). Those bottoms are all well burnished on the exterior and interior, and show considerable pitting on the lower interior. That in Fig. 6g, which also has a drill hole, is so abraded on the interior bottom that the wall is noticeably thinned. The consistent pattern of pitting on the interior of these bowls begins to suggest wear related to use, perhaps involving acidic contents that dissolved the Lime inclusions. A sample of three, however, is hardly conclusive.

Spreading basins (Figs. 7a–b, d–e; 11e) that, by analogy with earlier and later basins, probably sat on narrow pedestals (Figs. 7c, f; 11f) are found in a number of examples in Low Lime Burnished. The characteristic "rolled rim" was not created by rolling, but by using a finger to depress a shallow groove along the interior. The rim in Fig. 7d, while conceivably from a broad pedestal, is burnished on the interior; it seems more likely to have been a basin rim that did not receive the final grooving. In that respect, it looks more like basins in other wares, earlier and later. The interiors of all the basin rims are very well burnished, with a well-compacted surface, although the exterior usually has the glossier appearance from the effects of firing the vessels upside down. The bowl interiors preserved on the pedestal fragments are darker than the rims, and all three are pitted; that shown in Fig. 11f is so worn that no original surface survives. Assuming the basins were attached to the pedestals, they seem to have received heavy use, comparable to that of basins in FCP 2 (Vitelli 1993:215). The small painted fragment in Fig. 4h may be a rim rather than a pedestal, although the interior was not finished beyond scraping. If a pedestal, it is unclear what shape it was attached to.

Only a single small cup occurs (Fig. 6k), surprisingly given their popularity in earlier phases. Another unique vessel small enough to cup in one hand (Fig. 6j) preserves the stump of a solid round horizontal protrusion that was apparently pierced vertically just at the point where it broke. It suggests a ladle, but a ladle, if intended for liquids, should be well burnished on the interior to decrease porosity, and this example has only a few strokes of burnishing. A more convincing ladle is that in Fig. 4e, with the handle extending vertically above the rim, but it, too, is unburnished on the interior. The small, thick-walled piece in Fig. 4d looks like a very small saucer, but could be another variant of the ladle-like shape. It is well burnished on all surfaces. A small curved fragment of a beautifully burnished, black handle, ca. 0.5 cm in diameter and broken at both ends, was found in FA:116S (not illustrated). No other sherd suggests the shape to which the delicate handle might have been attached.

Two other quite small pieces (Figs. 6h; 11d), while similar to each other, remain enigmatic. They are narrow (diam. 0.06–0.07 m) with flat "bottoms" (tops?) that are well burnished on the underside or resting surface (as drawn), as are other bottoms in Low Lime Burnished. The interior of Fig. 6h has a brown-black stain, similar to that in the carinated bowl (Fig 1f, see above). The entire interior surface is flaking away, as though it had been burned. The other piece (Fig. 11d) has one complete and one partial tiny horizontal lug pierced vertically preserved at the bottom edge, and spaced to suggest four on the complete piece. It is burnished on all surfaces, though worn, and partially oxidized. No wear patterns or stains are evident on the interior. No rims in the Low Lime Burnished assemblage have a small enough diameter to be associated with these (except perhaps the two incised white-filled rims in Figs. 8e–f, which do not appear appropriate). This appears to be a specialized shape, but the special function is obscure.

The remaining illustrated shapes (Figs. 4f–g; 8a) suggest simple slightly convex or carinated bowls. That in Fig. 8a includes the only example in Low Lime Burnished of a (small) horizontal strap handle at the belly. These simple bowls of medium size are the shape one might expect to find as the staple in any household cupboard. They, along with cups, are remarkable for their rarity in this assemblage.

Decorative Style

Few vessels are well enough preserved to convey much sense of the composition of the decoration. Those few show that motifs, regardless of technique, were sometimes repeated around the vessel, in continuous running groups (e.g., Figs. 5b, 9b), or as repeating panels (Figs. 5f, g; 9c; 10), with panels of alternating techniques as a variation on that theme (Fig. 9d). The indentations along a carination (Figs. 1h; 5b–c; 8b) and grooves and ridges (Fig. 8h) could be considered part of such a repeating scheme.

The erasures on the very large necked jar (Fig. 10) suggest a concern to coordinate decorative elements on different segments of a vessel. It is unclear from the small portions of decoration preserved on the lower segments of other pots whether this was always the case (e.g., Figs. 1a, g; 5a–b, f; 11b), and whether decoration was always provided on all segments, i.e., above and below carinations and necks.

At first glance, the design shown in Fig. 11b, executed entirely with broad brush strokes that float unconnected to another line or structural element, appears to be painted in a different style than the other pieces. But the broad brush was used for painting below the carination on several pieces (e.g., Figs. 1a; 5b) whose upper portions were painted entirely with a narrow brush; and floating lines occur elsewhere as well (Figs. 3b; 10). The jar in Fig. 11a appears to have floating elements and large undecorated areas, but this vessel in particular may have lost much of its original decoration. It is one of the pieces from which parts of lines have clearly disappeared without a trace.

The few pieces of pattern-burnished decoration also include examples with narrow lines (Fig. 5g) and broad ones (Figs. 1m; 6k). Most of the sherds with white-filled incisions have outlines around the punctate elements (Figs. 8e–g; 9a, c); one example (Fig. 9b) omits the outlines, using only closely spaced impressed dots. Several very small sherds with painted decoration use dots of paint to outline or elaborate a line (Fig. 6i). Aside from a partially preserved pellet at the carination of a simple bowl (Fig.4g), relief pellets and strips are confined to shouldered bowls (Figs. 6a–d; 11c); this shape apparently received no other form of decoration. Basins are the only shape to be given no surface elaboration beyond careful burnishing. Indeed, it is perhaps significant that the interiors of bowls, which would have presented the largest accessible surface areas for elaboration, receive none. The fugitive nature of the white/gray paint might have discouraged its use on a "working" surface, but the other techniques could have been used.

Whether looking at the decoration by individual technique or all techniques together, the impression is of considerable variety, with few "rules" other than to make each vessel distinctive. The decoration is usually intricate and delicate, quite carefully if not always skillfully executed, and labor-intensive. Some elements and placement of designs—e.g., the stacked running chevrons and other groups of parallel lines above carinations and on jar shoulders—are reminiscent of FCP 2 designs. Sherds of Urfirnis must have been visible around the cave and at other former Middle Neolithic sites in the Peloponnese, so this need not suggest continuity or any direct relationship between the two phases.

Low Lime Ware, Coarse Variety (LiCo)

Fabric

The potters used the same general recipe as for Low Lime Burnished: the raw materials are roughly the same, although the nonplastic inclusions are much larger. They include irregularly rounded lumps of Lime, in some examples up to 7–8 mm in size (Pl. 2b), but usually closer to 2–3 mm. At the surface of the vessel, the Lime is often white and powdery, but not popped. Within the breaks, the Lime inclusions are usually gray. They are accompanied by non-calcareous, rounded red, white, and gray grits, usually under 2 mm in size, in some examples up to 3–4 mm. The bowl from FF1:22 (Fig. 11g) includes red pebbles up to 5 mm that have the glitter of mica (muscovite), a nonplastic occasionally evident in Low Lime Burnished sherds.[12] The nonplastics are very irregularly distributed. Some sherds appear very heavily gritted, while joining fragments from the same pot appear to have few and much smaller grits (see Pl. 2b). The irregular distribution suggests the (larger) nonplastics were intentionally added, but the potters did not work or wedge the clay well before building.

Building Procedures and Surface Finish

A coil joint preserved in the break of the bowl in Fig. 11g suggests the building method for these pots. If the profiles of the jars sloped gradually to a flat bottom (e.g., Fig. 15e), as did the Low Lime Burnished shapes, they were probably relatively tall vessels. They would have been most easily built in sections, the lower portion begun at the point of maximum diameter and added to, upside down, then turned over and the upper body built up to the rim.

The pots were scraped as they were built, especially on the interior, probably with a quite convex scraping tool that contributed to the strong convex curve of the body walls, as well as to their reasonably uniform wall thickness. Some pots, not scraped on the exterior at all, were left with the building surface (e.g., Fig. 11g).

As in the Low Lime Burnished examples, no lugs have detached at the point of attachment to reveal the underlying surface. Probably they were added as soon as the vessel was built and while the clay was still quite damp, thus achieving a solid join. When the pot dried to leather hard, the potter rubbed the building surfaces, probably with her fingers, to smooth some of the roughness and compact the surface slightly. Some pots were given a perfunctory burnish while still leather-hard. Several examples (Figs. 15b–c) have traces of an oxidized red slip applied to the exterior and just inside the rim. One large jar body has red drips of slip on the interior (Fig. 15c). The pots are solidly built, but their surfaces retain the irregularities of building, and the rims are lumpy and uneven. Stress cracks along the rim (e.g., Fig. 15a) suggest that the carelessness in clay preparation sometimes caused problems, for example, when a large pebble ended up too close to the rim.

Colors and Firing Practices

The Lime Coarse pots were fired in a basically oxidizing atmosphere, probably in a direct open fire. All have fired to light reds on the exteriors (ca. 2.5YR 6/8), usually a more yellow-tan on the interior (ca. 7.5 YR 5–6/4), with gray firing clouds at variable locations on the exteriors. They were, like the Low Lime Burnished pieces, probably fired upside down. Core colors are generally uniformly light, but may be gray where the surface is clouded gray. Powdered Lime nonplastics at the surface of some sherds suggest firing temperatures reached ca. 800–850°C in parts of the fire, but those temperatures were not maintained sufficiently long to affect nonplastics buried within the walls.

Shapes

Deep jars: Figs. 15a–c
Large bowl: Fig. 15f
Shallow basins: Figs. 11g, 15d

Three shapes are represented: several examples of a (probably deep) jar with inleaning rim and solid ledge lug(s) at the point of maximum diameter (Figs. 15a–c), a single example of a large bowl (Fig. 15f), and two examples of a shallow basin (Figs. 15d; 11g). The jars probably had flat bottoms (Fig. 15e). The bowl and basins may have had rounded bottoms. No evidence for the number of lugs per jar is preserved; it seems likely that there were at least two.

The interior of the single base fragment (Fig. 15e) is worn down to a sandy subsurface, but that could have resulted from use in sherd form. The interior of the basin in Fig. 11g is quite smooth to the touch, perhaps the result of regular use, although no scratching is evident with a 10x lens. No other traces of wear are evident, e.g., on the interior shoulders (cf. Skibo 1992:142), nor do any sherds show soot or other traces of having sat on a fire. The coarse sherds represent only about 10% (20–26% in FAS:112, FAN:117) of the total FCP 3 assemblage, and the calculations based on sherd weight should exaggerate their frequency.

UNCERTAIN WARES, MANGANESE PAINTED (MnPt) AND POLYCHROME PAINTED (Poly) VARIETIES

A small collection of pots decorated and fired differently than the Low Lime Burnished variety also occurs within FCP 3 deposits. Their small numbers suggest they were not made locally. The fabric varies from one example to the next. In a few cases it may indicate they are local products, or at least made by the same potters who made the Low Lime Burnished variety.[13]

Three sherds from FAS:116 (Figs. 12b, 13a–b) and one from FAN:113 (Fig. 13c) stand out by virtue of shape and, to a lesser extent, fabric and surface finish, as unique in the entire Franchthi assemblage. They are discussed separately, and may be intrusive in FCP 3.

Almost every unit in FA that is assigned to FCP 3 produced a few, usually very small and worn, sherds with traces of one or more manganese-oxide painted lines, sometimes still thick and deep brown or black, more often only a pale gray or silver ghost. These same units also often produced equally small and worn sherds with traces of stripes in two colors, red (FeO) and black (MnO), although rarely well enough preserved to say more than that the piece was painted with two pigments. Similarly small bits of both Manganese Painted and Polychrome sherds, along with a few larger and better preserved sherds (Figs. 36–37), also occur in all the mixed deposits that include substantial quantities of Low Lime Burnished sherds. The consistent co-occurrence of Manganese Painted and Polychrome and Low Lime Burnished sherds reinforces the impression that, although few, the sherds are a legitimate part of the FCP 3 assemblage and not intrusive from FCP 4. They are slightly more common in FCP 3 contexts than in FCP 4 (Tables 1–8); it is unlikely that only these rare sherds would have intruded from FCP 4 while the far more common FCP 4 varieties did not.

A few sherds from Manganese Painted pots preserve enough of the vessel to suggest we are not missing fragments with additional iron-oxide-rich paint, i.e., that some pots received only manganese painted decoration, while others received both manganese and iron oxide. Six sherds, almost certainly from a single vessel, are true polychrome, with decoration applied in three pigments (Fig. 12h, Pl. 3a). There, in addition to the manganese-oxide- and iron-oxide-rich paints used for the chevrons, a true white pigment was used to add dots along the outer edge of the black lines.

It is not clear whether these painted patterned pieces represent separate wares or were made from the same raw materials as each other and as the Low Lime Burnished. Several are severely over-fired and oddly colored (e.g., Figs. 12c, f; 13d), whether from the original potters' fire or, more likely, subsequent exposure to a very hot fire. The sherds are too small and too few, without clearly exotic inclusions visible at 10x, to recognize a clear pattern or to establish the probable range of variation.

Fabric

In all but a few sherds (Figs. 12e; 14d) of both the plain manganese painted and the polychrome pieces, the fabric includes obvious Lime, usually well under 1 mm, but occasionally up to 2–3 mm where it has turned powdery and expanded. Along with the Lime are small (<1 mm) red and gray rounded nonplastics that have a tendency to fall out, leaving a rounded depression and sometimes the glitter of silver mica (muscovite). The bowl in Fig. 12g also has a few very small and inconspicuous flecks of gold mica (biotite), not noticed in the other examples.

Building Procedures and Surface Finish

These pots were probably built up with coils or slabs, but no clear direct evidence is preserved on the few examples. The potters scraped the surfaces well, producing thin walls (4–6 mm) and fairly regular surfaces that were probably smoothed with a damp finger before being burnished while leather-hard. Both red and black paint were applied to a probably still damp, burnished surface, thickly enough to have a tangible relief when well preserved. The iron-oxide-rich paint has usually fired to a dull, often crackling red that does not generally appear to have been burnished.

The manganese paint was probably always applied

thickly, and was burnished on to help the pigment adhere more firmly to the surface. Manganese oxides do not generally bond chemically with the pot surface in low temperature firings (Shepard 1968:41–42). Many of the manganese painted sherds today have only the faintest trace of silvery gray pigment left in what is now a ghost line. Shepard notes that some Mayan potters may have used a resin or lacquer-like coating derived from plants to hold their manganese-based pigments to the pots (Shepard 1968:42).[14] The famous Acoma potter, Lucy Lewis, and her daughters Emma and Dolores insist that, unless *guaco*, an organic substance made from the Rocky Mountain Bee plant, is mixed with their manganese pigment and water, the paint "will not stick" (pers. comm. 1991; Peterson 1984:132).[15] I have never scraped a "reddish material" such as Shepard describes from the surface of a well-preserved manganese painted line.[16] The Franchthi sherds may not retain an original surface, or any plant-based coating may have deteriorated over the many millennia of burial. If the manganese pigment was as fragile originally as it is today, the decoration would not have withstood much handling unless it had had a protective coating of some kind.

The white dots on Fig. 12h are a true white that does not react in hydrochloric acid and is therefore not a calcium carbonate. This material, too, is easily scratched off the surface; it has not bonded to the pot. It is hard to imagine that the small dots could have been burnished to improve adhesion without smearing them beyond recognition. They, like the manganese paint, may argue for the use of a protective post-firing coating.

Colors and Firing Practices

Unlike iron oxide pigments, manganese oxides retain their brown or black color regardless of firing atmosphere (Shepard 1968:40–42). This property made polychromy predictable for the prehistoric potter. Pots painted with iron-oxide- and manganese-oxide-rich pigments, and fired in an oxidizing atmosphere will produce reds from the iron and black from the manganese on a light-colored, oxidized clay ground. A pot painted with manganese pigment alone will produce black lines on a light ground from a simple oxidizing fire, without the need for a controlled three-stage firing that an iron-oxide-rich pigment requires for the same effect (Vitelli 1993a:201–203).

The body sherd in Fig. 14b has a gray cloud on the exterior; most sherds, other than the over-fired pieces, are uniformly oxidized. The Lime nonplastics are often powdery at the surface, suggesting exposure to temperatures of ca. 800–850°C, probably only briefly since nonplastics in the interior walls were not affected by heat. Many sherds have a narrow gray streak at the center of the core, also pointing to a relatively brief firing. The clear colors with rare clouds could have been achieved in a direct firing if the potters protected the pots from direct contact with fuel by covering them with sherds, or scraped coals away from the pots at the end of the firing while the pots were still hot enough to oxidize fully.

Shapes

Polychrome
Deep bowls or jars: Figs. 12c, 14a–b
Small necked jar: Fig. 12h
Carinated bowls: Figs. 12g, 37a–b
Pedestalled basin: Figs. 12d; 14c–d

Several medium-sized deep bowls or jars are represented—the interiors of all three are burnished, so that, if jars, the necks were wide enough for the potter's hand to reach inside easily (Figs. 12c, 14a–b).[17] The body sherds in Figs.12e–f, similarly finished on the interior, probably derive from similar shapes. Small fragments of the dotted polychrome piece (Fig. 12h) hint at a concave neck and a convex body, i.e., a small, necked jar with a maximum diameter of perhaps 0.22 m.

A carinated bowl is also represented (Fig. 12g), probably more shallow than it appears in the drawing. The upper and lower body sherds do not join; they may well come from overlapping portions of the bowl, making the shape closer to that of the carinated bowls in Low Lime Burnished (e.g., Fig. 5g). Two large fragments of basins that preserve the pedestal joint come from mixed, but probably FCP 3, contexts (Figs. 14c–d). The sherd in Fig. 12d is illustrated as a basin rim, largely because it is painted on the interior and exterior; unlike the Peloponnesian practice, pedestals in Thessaly were sometimes decorated even on the underside of the pedestal, so this example could be from a pedestal. Basin rims and pedestal fragments are recognizable in another seven or eight of the unillustrated fragments. The remaining unillustrated pieces are such small body fragments that nothing can safely be said about shape.

Shapes

Manganese Painted
Jars: Figs.13d–e, 37d
Pedestalled Basin: Figs. 37f–g; possibly FCP 3
Bowls: Figs. 37a–b

The jar neck in Fig.13d suggests a medium to large jar with a very narrow neck, closer in its proportions to the necks with white-filled incision in Figs. 8e–f than to the necked jars in Low Lime Burnished. The sherds from the manganese painted jar are over-fired; even allowing for the strange colors and quality caused by burning, the well-burnished pattern lines and the pattern itself are different from the other Manganese Painted pieces. This pot may be another of the unique pieces, intrusive into FCP 3. The shoulder fragment in Fig. 13e is closer in both proportions and decoration to Low Lime Burnished examples of necked jars. The rim in Fig. 37d may be from the neck of a similar jar.

Two examples of pedestalled basins (Fig. 37f–g) are probably to be assigned to FCP 3. They are quite similar to other examples of Manganese Painted in decoration and fabric. Two carinated bowls (Fig. 37a–b) are both from A Lot 16, which produced other examples of FCP 3 pots, as well as later material through modern. It is unclear whether they should be attributed to FCP 3. The profile of Fig. 37a looks reasonably close to examples in Low Lime Burnished, while that of Fig. 37b, with its thick carination, looks out of place. The mostly very small, unillustrated fragments include at least three pedestal joints; nothing else is securely assignable to a particular shape.

Decorative Style

Polychrome

Patterns were applied to all portions of the exterior, including the lower body below a carination, and on basins to the interior as well. Some lines are curving, probably to accommodate the curve of the vessel wall (Figs. 12d–e; 14c–d); most are straight. Motifs consist of stacked chevrons and loops, with alternating red and black lines or groups of one, usually red, outlined by the other, black. Individual lines and the negative spaces between them are of variable thickness, wobbly rather than sure. The tail ends of lines (e.g., Fig. 14c) and places where lines meet (e.g., Fig. 12g) also suggest inexperienced painters who did not plan or execute the painting with great precision.

Manganese Painted

Groups of narrow parallel lines, often arranged in chevrons (Figs. 13e; 37b, d, f, and probably g), with or without a broad outline are the standard motifs on the more securely identified pieces. Most sherds preserve only a segment of one or more parallel lines.

UNUSUAL AND POTENTIALLY INTRUSIVE PIECES

A few sherds distinctively different from others in the FCP 3 deposits at Franchthi, as well as from each other, derive from units along the FCP 2/ FCP 3 boundary. These units, coincidentally, removed sediments located directly adjacent to deposits in the East Balk that were certainly disturbed in relatively recent times (Chapter 2). None of these sherds has a close parallel elsewhere in the Franchthi sequence.

The context of the unusual sherds permits a number of explanations and chronological niches, none of which can be securely eliminated from consideration. The cave was apparently unoccupied for a brief time between FCP 2 and FCP 3. It is possible that one or more visitors, perhaps arriving by sea, stopped briefly at the abandoned cave—not long enough to register their stay in the archaeological record other than by the presence of a few sherds. In that case, the sherds would be earlier than FCP 3. Another possibility is that the sherds represent pieces brought from elsewhere to the cave during the FCP 3 occupation. A third possibility is that they derive from the disturbed deposits of the East Balk, accidentally included with FA units; then they could derive from any phase up to the present. I am unable to establish any one of these possibilities as more likely than another.

A small group, consisting of few sherds from not more than four pots (Figs. 12a–b, and unillustrated pieces from FAN:120 and FF1:23), is decorated in a manganese-rich pigment applied after the entire exterior surface had been coated with an iron-oxide-rich paint. The fabric includes large, 1–2 mm powdery or popped Lime at the surface, along with smaller Lime, red grits and the glitter of mica. The red coating, fired to a dull red, is crackling and flaking off. The black lines on the narrow-necked jar (Fig.12a) are ragged, as though the painter was having trouble with the viscosity and adherence of an unfamiliar pigment.[18] The narrow neck with two strap handles from rim to shoulder on opposite sides of the rim, a new shape at Franchthi, is unique in FCP 3.

The sharply carinated body fragment in Fig. 12b is also decorated with manganese-rich paint, by a more sure hand. The group of zigzags, with each leg painted with an independent stroke of the brush, suggests the style of FCP 4 Lime plus Iron (below, e.g. Fig. 24g), but the shape is unparalleled at Franchthi in any phase. It is probably not a local product[19] and may be intrusive in the FCP 3 context.

A single sherd with a heavy iron-oxide-rich coating and the ghost of pattern lines, probably once in a white pigment, occurs at Franchthi (Fig.13a). The clay body includes plentiful gray and white Lime, and bits of a soft red rock in sizes up to 2–3 mm, accompanied by a few minute flecks of biotite and a pink rock that includes silver mica—apparently the same rock noted occasionally in sherds of Low Lime Burnished and Lime Coarse, and in a few sherds of FCP 5 varieties (above, n. 12). If the sparkling pink rock is an indication of local manufacture, perhaps a foreign potter made this pot at Franchthi. If the rock is not local, its presence in this and other sherds may someday reveal their source.

Carinated bowls are a common shape from FCP 2 on at Franchthi. Nevertheless, this one stands out. The thickened area at the angle of the carination looks, in profile, more like an appendage than part of the body; it probably was made by adding a coil to the exterior of a basically rounded body. The lower body suggests a deep bowl, similar to FCP 4 Andesite Burnished bowls (e.g., Fig 35h) or even FCP 5 Heavy Burnished bowls (e.g. Figs.70f–g). Just at the carination (on the left edge of the sherd) is the edge of a scar where something was attached. Above, the rim turns out ever so slightly at the break, suggesting the possibility of a strap handle from rim to carination.

The interior and exterior surfaces have been completely coated with a thick iron-oxide-rich slip that has fired red. Over that red coating, a pattern was painted and then the whole pot was burnished. The faint ghost of the original pattern of repeated stacked chevrons remains only in the interruption of the burnish gloss where the pigment has disappeared. In spite of the complete absence of pigment, we have always thought of this pot as white-painted. Perhaps some pigment was still present when originally excavated; none remains today. The interior bottom of the bowl is worn free of paint, the fabric slightly gray at the center, although the rest of the pot is oxidized, if not particularly hard fired.

The piece has puzzled us since the day it came out of the ground. Cressida Ridley, who happened to be visiting at the time, suggested that it looked Macedonian (pers. comm. 1969). I have found no better suggestion since. The thick carination is generally similar to some from, e.g., Late Neolithic deposits at Megalo Nisi Galanis, carbon-dated to 6150±90 BP (Kalogirou 1994:31; Fig. 13b), which would be roughly contemporary with FCP 4.2 (Table 9); and to profiles of black-polished ware from Ayios Mamas (Heurtley 1939:Fig. 26b–c). The decoration and firing of the Franchthi piece are not matched at either site.[20]

Another carinated bowl fragment (Fig. 13c) has a carination more like other Franchthi FCP 3 examples, but with a drooping pair of small lugs or pellets at the carination. Like most of the other later Neolithic fine wares, the clay body includes plentiful Lime, red, and gray rounded nonplastics to 1–2 mm. Both surfaces were coated with slip, given painted decoration, and burnished. The firing—or perhaps exposure to a subsequent fire—has produced the unusual appearance of red painted decoration on a black ground. The background black is quite hard. I was unable to scratch up a powder, thus it is probably not a manganese oxide slip (nor am I aware of any ceramic tradition that makes use of a manganese-rich slip to coat an entire vessel). Reduction is probably responsible for the black background, but that should also have affected the red paint. Perhaps the pigment grains in the paint are sufficiently larger than those in the slip that they remained unchanged at the temperatures reached. The odd appearance could simply be the result of re-exposure to a fire with an unusual fuel. Were it not for the presence of other unusual pieces in neighboring units, it might have been unremarkable.

The small jar with a heavy semicircular pierced lug at the lip and applied vertical relief ridges is a polished piece that has fired the blue-gray of some burned examples of Low Lime Burnished (e.g., Fig. 9c) and of the FCP 4 Gray ware. The fabric includes tiny dark nonplastics, less than 1 mm in size, and essentially no Lime. The shape has no parallels at Franchthi.

SUMMARY AND DISCUSSION

The total weight of all FCP 3 varieties recovered from FA Balk is ca. 23 kg (ca. 2000 sherds). The Lime Coarse variety accounts for only ca. 5 kilos. Almost 80% (ca. 18 kilos) of FCP 3 sherds represent well-finished, often decorated pots. Since much of the pottery from other trenches was discarded without counts or weights being recorded, no actual measurement of the total amount of FCP 3 pottery recovered is possible. If we assume that the trenches adjacent to FA Balk, A and FF1, produced quantities roughly equal to those in FA, while the other trenches, for which extant records suggest minimal FCP 3 remains, would add only a small additional amount, we might posit a total sherd weight of 70–80 kg for FCP 3.

The Low Lime Burnished potters made some very large pots. The evidence suggests at least four very large pots in the cave (Figs. 9–10). Each probably weighed about 8–10 kg. Sherds from medium-sized jars (Figs. 2–3) again suggest a minimum of four, each weighing ca. 2 kg. It is more difficult to estimate the number of pots represented by sherds from smaller pots because of the variety of shapes and the uncertainty of diameter measurements and actual depth. The profiles illustrated (Figs. 1, 4–8, 11) suggest there may have been as many as 40–50 pots, averaging ca. 500 gr each. These estimates also produce a figure of ca. 70–75 kg.

Compared with the roughly 400 kg of sherds recovered for FCP 1 and 2 from undisturbed deposits in the cave alone—another 525 kg came from Paralia, and roughly that much again from mixed deposits in the cave—it is clear that FCP 3 was a relatively small and probably short-lived occupation, and the number of pots involved were few. Even if the total number of pots is adjusted to include unexcavated areas of the cave[21] it would have been possible for one or two potters to produce all of them in 3-4 weeks of steady work. It is curious that such a large percentage of the total is what we would consider "fine" ware, with very few coarse or cooking pots, and no evidence suggests that any pots were used on a fire. The high proportion of carefully finished, decorated pottery is very similar to that of the preceding Middle Neolithic phase.

The contextual evidence points to a hiatus between FCP 2 and FCP 3 (Chapter 2). Overlapping radiocarbon dates suggest the hiatus was not a long one (Table 9). The FCP 3 potters built with coils, scraped the walls carefully, added relief pellets, mixed and used iron-oxide-rich slips, burnished and pattern burnished surfaces, and fired in reduction fires—all techniques that were also used by earlier FCP 2 potters. Shallow carinated bowls and perhaps piriform bowls are similar in both phases. Potters in both phases made large open basins that sat on tall pedestals, although the details differ. Large round-bodied collared jars in Low Lime Burnished, apparently without handles, look more like FCP 2 jars than the taller, handled, FCP 4 versions. Both made large coarse jars with ledge lugs from a clay body similar to the more finely finished pots, but with nonplastics adjusted for the larger size and potentially different functions. Both made very large, carefully finished pots, although the shapes and, possibly, their functions were different. Some relationship between the potters of the two phases is likely.

Many differences, however, also exist between the work of FCP 2 and FCP 3 potters. FCP 3 potters chose to paint the decoration with light-colored pigments, low in, or free of iron oxides. Some of these light pigments may have been applied after firing. They used impressed and applied decoration, combined decorative techniques on a single piece, painted above and below carinations, but never the interiors of bowls or basins. They may have calcined Lime for the powder used to highlight impressed designs, another possible post-firing elaboration.[22] Many of their shapes, especially those with thickened shoulders, have no parallel within the FCP 2 repertoire, and if more complete profiles were preserved I suspect the differences among shapes would appear even greater. Flat bottoms on almost all shapes replaced the ring bases that were typical of the work of the earlier potters. They appear often to have supported relatively tall sloping walls that suggest parts of the pots in FCP 3 may have been built upside down. The reduction firings of FCP 3 were less complex than the three-stage firings used by the Urf potters, and judging from the results, less consistent in temperature and timing.

But the aspect of the FCP 3 potters' production that strikes me as most different is their work habits. They were less than thorough in working or wedging the clay bodies before they began work. The direction of scraping and burnishing marks varies around each pot and from pot to pot, reflecting inconsistent work patterns. Pots are unintentionally asymmetrical in all dimensions, again reflecting a lack of rhythm that comes from infrequent practice and irregular work habits. These fundamental aspects of production are so different from those of FCP 2 that the FCP 3 potters could not have been the same individuals who had once made Urf, and changed a few techniques, materials, and shapes. The FCP 3 potters might have been the daughters or granddaughters of FCP 2 Urf potters, who had perhaps observed but never practiced pottery-making under their supervision. More likely, I think, the FCP 3 potters had few, if any direct ties to the Urfirnis ceramic tradition.

Pots that look very much like the FCP 3 Low Lime Burnished examples are reported from Corinth (Lavezzi 1978:Pl. 108, nos. 20-33; Phelps 1975:Figs. 27, nos. 2–13; 28, no. 11), and Aria (Dousougli 1989, Hadzipouliou 1989:Pls. 64, 70b). None is present in the Lerna Neolithic collections (Vitelli forthcoming). The quantities at Peloponnesian sites are nowhere large, certainly nothing like the quantities of FCP 2 Urfirnis.

In much of Greece the Late Neolithic begins, in ceramic terms, with a "black burnished" phase, in (Eastern) Thessaly now called the Tsangli-Larissa Phase (Gallis 1987). Material from that phase at, e.g., Makri Chorion includes all the decorative techniques seen in the FCP 3 Low Lime Burnished assemblage. The shapes (e.g., Gallis 1987:148, Abb.1; Demoule et al. 1988:Fig. 12), however, are not particularly close to those of FCP 3. Additionally, not all features included in the Larissa Phase black burnished assemblages (e.g., Demoule et al. 1988:Fig. 13; Hauptmann 1981:Pl. 1), or in the Peloponnesian black burnished groups of Phelps (1975) and Lavezzi (1973, 1978) are present in FCP 3. Some of the material in those groups is more closely paralleled in FCP 4, in Andesite Burnished Ware, another of the black and burnished varieties at Franchthi, but made from a distinctively different clay body than the FCP 3 ware. Indeed, some of the pieces noted in the Larissa Phase assemblages, those with relief bead and rib, and scratch incised decoration (e.g., Hauptmann 1981:Pl. XII), find their closest parallels at Franchthi in FCP 2 (Vitelli 1993a:160-161). Thus, while the FCP 3 ceramics share some characteristics and point to a degree of interaction with groups within the Middle Neolithic Urfirnis sphere of the Peloponnese, as well as with others beyond that region, the nature and timing of those interactions are not clear.

NOTES

1. Most of the later Neolithic pottery was excavated in the first two to three seasons, when all pottery was put directly into concentrated acid baths when it was brought in from the field. From 1971 on, sherds were washed only in water. A dilute solution of hydrochloric acid was used only when necessary to reveal the surface of a heavily encrusted sherd or to test a portion of a sherd for the presence or absence of carbonate inclusions, and the sherd was subsequently rinsed in fresh water. Pottery bags were searched for crusted varieties before the remaining sherds were soaked in water, to avoid dissolving the crust or separating it from the sherd body.

2. Two Low Lime Burnished sherds were submitted to the British School at Athens Fitch Laboratory for analyses, samples #46–47 (Vitelli 1993a:Table I; Jones 1986:388). X-ray fluorescence identified the presence of "Fe" on the surface of #47. OES was the other analysis conducted. Both samples fell into Jones' "local" category (Jones 1986:391–393).

3. The rounded iron-oxide-rich grits have a tendency to fall out, leaving rounded depressions, especially obvious on interiors that were scraped but given no further finishing. I have wondered if these rounded red bits could be grog—bits of fired clay or ground sherds. None of the later Neolithic sherd samples submitted to Jones was subjected to petrographic analysis, but grog is notoriously difficult to identify (Whitbread 1986).

4. The question of how ancient potters achieved a somewhat fugitive "white" paint on a dark ground is not unique to Franchthi or to early Late Neolithic. Extensive studies of the Gournian EM III white slip concluded that it could have been applied before firing and fired once, applied post-firing and lightly re-fired at a much lower temperature, or applied post-firing without additional firing (Betancourt et al. 1984:73, with references to other related studies). I have painted patterns with an iron-oxide-rich slip on an already fired pot and re-fired it in an oxidizing atmosphere. The re-fired pigment is less fugitive than if unfired, but still scratches off easily and would not survive extensive handling or regular washing.

5. Shepard points out that gray pots may also have been produced "from a highly carbonaceous clay that was not oxidized in firing" (1968:219). While this must remain a possibility for the Low Lime Burnished variety and other gray varieties from Neolithic Greece, until adequate analyses and testing are conducted, the weight of the evidence at present points to reduction or smudging as the more likely explanations.

6. Techniques such as *raku* firing, where the potter removes a pot from an oxidizing firing while it is still very hot and plunges it directly into sawdust, leaves, or other organic mixture to produce black markings is a variation on the theme of smudging. Carbon soot is again responsible for the dark surface coloring.

7. Noble says that temperatures of ca. 950°C were used in producing Attic black glaze (Noble 1988:154–55). The temperatures required for reduction vary according with clay body composition and the nature of the fuel (Rice 1987:80–98; Shepard 1968:219–221). Grimshaw notes that "if Fe_2O_3 is heated in the presence of carbon and the supply of oxygen is limited—as it often is in the firing of clays—at temperatures above 260°C., there will be a tendency for reduction to Fe_3O_4. Above 570°C., further reduction to FeO is likely and at about 700°C complete reduction to metallic iron can occur" (1980:564).

8. In our numerous experimental attempts at reduction firings, the only successes have come using a climbing kiln, partly dug into the side of a hill, and stoked for nearly 12 hours to reach ca. 900°C. When that temperature was finally reached, we filled the firebox with fuel, closed all vents, covered the entire kiln with clods of earth, and left it to cool overnight. The high temperature and oxygen trapped within the kiln was sufficient for the fuel to continue burning long enough to use up the oxygen in the air around the pots and, finally, to reduce the oxygen content of the clay pots themselves.

9. My experimental attempts to reduce a white-painted pot have so far been unsuccessful. One, in which the white paint consists of a talc–clay mixture, heavily burnished, ended up with a large, shiny black cloud of carbon sooting. Along the edges of the cloud where the carbon deposit is relatively thin, the painted lines appear grayish-white against a dark gray background; where the sooting is heaviest, the painted lines are a dull black against the shiny black ground. That portion of the experimental pot looks very much like a burned example of "white" painted pottery from FCP 5 (Pl. 6b). I have not seen the same effect on any Low Lime Burnished example.

10. The volume was calculated using the summed cylinders method (Rice 1987:222). The volume for the preserved portion alone, filled to the rim, would have been about 54 liters. The preserved body portion alone, i.e., below the neck joint, holds just over 30 liters.

11. The sherds illustrated in Fig. 10 were excavated in the first season, 1967. Those that could be securely oriented were used to restore the upper portion of the vessel in plaster, but the large size of the vessel and the relatively few joining fragments meant that a great deal of plaster had to be slathered onto the interior surfaces to hold the piece together. Numerous other sherds that might derive from the same vessel were recovered that year, and subsequently, from the FA sequences, but it was not possible, because of the extensive plaster, to determine if any was certainly from this vessel. While the plastered restoration allowed us to appreciate the size and accomplishment of the Low Lime Burnished potters, it also resulted in a pot that was too large for the Navplion museum's exhibition case, or our excavation storage shelves. For years, the piece sat on the

floor in the back of our overcrowded storerom. By 1997, it had been moved or had things piled on it once too often. Many of the plastered joins have broken and the pot is again in many fragments, presenting a major cleaning and restoration challenge.

12. The same pink pebbles that glitter with muscovite occur in a few FCP 5 sherds, over a millennium later. They may indicate local manufacture.

13. Although geologists with the Franchthi project assured me that I should be able to find manganese in the Franchthi environs, I was never successful in doing so. The limited use of manganese oxides on pots at Franchthi suggests the Neolithic potters may have had the same problem. Perhaps it was a trade item, and used infrequently, on special pots, when and as available.

14. Barley, among others, notes the use of post-firing resins to waterproof and protect fugitive decoration, although he does not specifically mention the practices in the context of manganese paints (Barley1994:44–45).

15. In fact, even with the use of *guaco*, the manganese pigments on their pots may be soft after firing. I have a pot made by Lucy Lewis that has been passed around classes a number of times, with everyone rubbing it gently to see that the pigment comes off on the hands. The design is still quite clear and shows no ill effects, yet, of the rubbing, but it has received very limited handling and has never been washed.

16. Shepard implies it may require considerable magnification to observe.

17. The last two jars are from mixed deposits in G1 that also produced substantial pieces of Low Lime Burnished (e.g., Figs.8i; 9d) and relatively few and smaller fragments of later, mostly FCP 5 pottery. G1:5 also produced a manganese painted basin (Fig. 37g). In G Lot 8, a manganese painted sherd submitted for OES analysis (Jones 1986:388, 770 sample #43) looks very much like an unburned piece of the jar neck in Fig. 13d. Another pair of joining sherds between FA and G units is recorded for FAS:115 and G Lot 8. These cross-trench joins seem to point not only to contemporaneity of deposits in both areas, but to some activity that produced considerable horizontal movement of sherds.

18. In fact, if it is not an intrusive piece, this is the earliest example of manganese paint at Franchthi. If manganese oxide was mixed with an organic "glue," its consistency may have been unfamiliar and required some experience to apply consistently.

19. Phelps (1975:191–198) suggests that various Black on Red sherds from the Peloponnese derive from Central Greece, perhaps the Kephissos Valley, and that the "ware" is most probably a development from Urfirnis (1975:194). The Franchthi examples, other than bearing decoration in a black manganese oxide pigment on a red iron oxide slip, have no obvious similarity to the pieces he illustrates in either shape or decoration. Nor do I see any close relationship to Urfirnis in the Franchthi pieces. The Franchthi examples do not resemble, e.g., Arapi style black on red sherds (Hauptmann 1981:Pl. B), or those from Servia (Ridley and Wardle 1979:Fig. 13). Once manganese pigments were known and available to potters, apparently early in the LN, they might have been used in many areas, in a variety of combinations and styles. Many of our traditional names for Greek Neolithic pottery styles—e.g., black burnished, matte painted, red on black, polychrome—may be masking or confusing our understanding of both temporal and spatial variation in ceramic production. It is unfortunate that the few Franchthi examples come from potentially disturbed deposits.

20. I have seen sherds from Makri Chorion 2 with similarly pointed carinations, from a deposit (box 9) that also produced pattern burnished sherds with profiles close to those of the FCP 4 Andesite Burnished bowls with thickened rims.

21. Jacobsen estimates that our excavations explored about 10% of the cave (Chapter 1 in Farrand forthcoming). FCP 3 remains were concentrated along the western, rear portions, in front of the rockfall. Estimates of the total number of FCP 3 pots in the cave might range from 600 if the whole cave had been occupied evenly, to 100 if activities concentrated in the rear portion of the western third.

22. Barley notes that the Baganda potters of Uganda rub a paste of ground snail shells into surface indentations after firing (Barley 1994:44).

CHAPTER FOUR

Franchthi Ceramic Phase 4 (FCP 4): The Pottery

Franchthi Ceramic Phase 4 is subdivided into three subphases, FCP 4.1–4.3. Both Calcareous and Noncalcareous classes are represented, in at least five wares. Several varieties (Manganese Painted, Polychrome, Gray Burnished), which occur in low frequencies, cannot be assigned to a specific ware, and some may be out of context in FCP 4.

FRANCHTHI CERAMIC SUBPHASE 4.1 (FCP 4.1)

The first subphase of FCP 4.1 includes all varieties with the exception of Calcite Coarse.

ANDESITE WARE, BURNISHED VARIETY (AndB)

The clay body used for the Late Neolithic version of this ware is visually similar to that of the FCP 1 and FCP 2 Andesite varieties. These pots are made with what appear to be the same raw materials, but their production is separated by hundreds of years; which suggests a local source for the clay and mineral ingredients. This has yet to be demonstrated, however, by full characterization studies.

A single sample of FCP 4 Andesite ware was submitted to the Fitch Laboratory for analysis (Jones 1986:388, #48). Optical emission spectrography, the only analysis performed on it, suggests that it falls within the range of other Franchthi samples, all considered "local" by Jones (1986:393). The FCP 4 Andesite sherd in the small Franchthi study collection in Bloomington was thin-sectioned as part of Runnels' study of Aegean andesite sources (Runnels 1981); the andesite was identified as the same kind used at Franchthi for millstones. Cohen, the geologist who did the analyses for Runnels, also suggested that the size and angularity of the inclusions in the sherd implied that they had been intentionally added to the clay body (Runnels 1981:103).

Fabric

The most easily noted nonplastic is biotite (black or gold mica), in pieces up to 1–2 mm in diameter. Tiny (less than 1 mm in diameter) shiny black grits, probably hornblende or pyroxene, are often evident on a worn or unburnished surface. In the breaks, angular bits of a white, or occasionally colorless, mineral from 1–2 mm, are evident; these are probably feldspar or quartz. A single sherd (Fig. 16i) includes a 4 mm Lime pebble in the break, probably an accidental inclusion respon-

Table 4.1. FCP 4 Classes, Wares, and Varieties

Calcareous Class
- Lime plus Iron ware
  - Iron Oxide Pattern Painted variety (LimeFe or LiFe)
- Ungritted ware
  - Manganese Pattern Painted variety (UgrMn)
- Uncertain ware
  - Gray Burnished variety (Gray)
- Uncertain ware
  - Manganese Pattern Painted varieties (MnPt)
- Uncertain ware
  - Polychrome Pattern Painted varieties (Poly)
- Calcite ware
  - Calcite Coarse variety (CalCo)

Non-calcareous Class
- Andesite ware
  - Andesite Burnished variety (AndB)
- No Lime ware
  - Coarse variety (NoLiCo)

sible for breaking the pot. The other sherds show no reaction in hydrochloric acid. No fragments of the andesite matrix were certainly noted, but occasional small pinkish inclusions are suggestive.

Building Procedures and Surface Finish

The sherds from FCP 4.1 are generally small and worn. None preserves clear traces of building techniques.[1] The rather straight-sided walls below the carination on some bowls suggest they were shaped from the exterior, perhaps with a paddle. The potters achieved relatively even, thin walls (generally between 3–5 mm) with regular surfaces. While the pot was still damp, the potter coated the exterior, and the interior of open bowls, with an iron-oxide-rich slip, probably in several layers, given the waxy quality of the finished product. The slip effectively covers the nonplastic inclusions in the clay body. Although probably burnished repeatedly, even the last round was done with considerable pressure and while the surfaces were sufficiently yielding to take the impression of the burnishing tool: every stroke is visible. The direction of burnishing strokes reflects the way the potter held and moved the vessel around during the process. Unlike the FCP 2 Urf potters, the Andesite Burnished potters did not have a consistent pattern—or rhythm—but moved the vessel randomly. The direction of the strokes is not a reliable guide to the orientation of body sherds.

If the potter chose to add patterns by burnishing, she would wait until the pot had dried slightly after applying the first burnish. That additional drying caused enough shrinkage to dull the luster of the original burnish (Shepard 1968:124) so that additional selective burnishing stood out as a pattern (Pl. 3b). After burnishing, the potters occasionally added delicate patterns with a fine brush in a thin, granular paint. The paint fired to a pale grayish-white color. It does not react in hydrochloric acid, so is not carbonate-based. It may be a clay slip. If pattern burnished and pattern painted sherds had occurred in larger numbers, they would have been assigned to separate varieties; as their numbers are so small, I have included all the Andesite Burnished sherds in a single variety.

Color and Firing Practices

Exterior surfaces have generally fired to a glossy black, sometimes with reddish clouds. No firing circles are present. Interiors, even on open shapes, are less glossy and usually a dark gray. Even on black sherds, a red powder (2.5 YR 5/8) is often evident in depressions untouched by the burnishing tool. Cores tend to be reddish brown, only occasionally uniformly gray or with a thin central strip of gray. Hardness is usually 3, which scratches up a greasy black powder.

The pots were fired upside down, sitting on the rim, and were not in contact with one another during firing. The firing atmosphere was basically oxidizing until the final stages, when the potter cut off the oxygen supply. Reduction may have turned the original red slip to black, leaving the larger grains of unburnished red pigment, and the essentially iron-oxide-free "white" pigments unaffected. The softness of the surfaces and the greasy powder seem to argue that smudging is largely responsible for the black color. The sherds are generally quite scratched and worn; they tend to break into smaller pieces than other, harder-fired wares.

Shapes

Jars: Fig. 16d–e
Carinated bowls: Fig. 16a–c, m
Bowls with thickened rim: Fig. 16h–m
Shouldered bowl: Fig. 16g
Basin: Fig. 16n
Bottom: Fig. 16f
Rhyta, not illustrated

The horizontal curvature of Andesite Burnished sherds is less obviously irregular than on most other later Neolithic wares at Franchthi, but sherds are so small that this impression may be misleading. I do not have great confidence in the measured diameters for any of these pieces: the true size of the pots represented in the drawings may be slightly larger or smaller than the reconstructed drawings that are based on measurements from small segments of the curve.

On two small rim fragments with narrow diameters (Fig. 16d–e), the burnish extends only for a few centimeters inside the rim; by analogy with better-preserved later examples (Fig. 26e–k), these suggest small closed jars, probably with two strap handles from the rim to the shoulder. A small fragment of a strap was found in FAN:110 (not illustrated).

Several sherds suggest carinated bowls (Fig. 16a–c), although only one actually preserves the carination. From that small fragment it is not possible to say whether the bowl was shallow or deep. The fragment illustrated in Fig. 16g is probably a rim, from a shouldered bowl comparable to those in Lime plus Iron (e.g., Figs. 22c–d), although the actual tip of the sherd is broken; it is possible that a very thin-walled neck extended vertically above it (compare FCP 3, Fig. 1j).

The most common shape represented in these units is the deep open bowl with thickened rim (Fig. 16h–m). Although the exact profile of the rim varies, all have a carination more or less well defined on the exterior and a bulging curve on the interior, sometimes well articulated (Fig. 16j–k, m), sometimes gradually curving into the body wall (Fig. 16h–i, l). In addition to the bowl in Fig. 16h, five or six other sherds in FCP 4.1 have (the same) pattern burnished decoration on the interior. One bottom fragment (not illustrated) shows the crisscrossing lines extended across the interior bottom. Aside from the small bottom fragment in Fig. 16f, with pattern burnished bands on the exterior/underside, which could be from a similar bowl, this is the only shape to have been decorated in this technique. One example (Fig. 16j) was provided with a small horizontal lug pierced vertically on the exterior carination. The shape is similar to pattern-burnished Larissa style examples from Thessaly (e.g., Hauptmann 1981, Pl. 1.1–2; Demoule et al. 1988, Fig. 13), although they generally lack the bulge on the interior of the rim and the pattern burnished motifs are different.

Occasional fragments from flat bottoms, together with the absence of ring bases and other bottom forms, suggest all the above shapes had simple flat bottoms. The remaining shape, a large bell basin (Fig. 16n), seems a variation on the better-represented version in Lime plus Iron (Figs. 23–24). Although no pedestal fragments were recognized in Andesite Burnished, the shape seems to require one.

Two fragments, too small to illustrate meaningfully but probably from rhyta, were found in FCP 4.1 contexts (FAS:98, 103). Larger rhyta fragments are discussed below, under FCP 4.2.

Decorative Style

Besides the all-over crisscrossing net pattern on the interior of some bowls with thickened rims, a few Andesite Burnished pots from FCP 4.1 were given painted decoration (Fig. 16a, c, e) in a light paint on the dark burnished ground. The patterns were painted with a fine, thin-bristled brush, in a series of short, delicate strokes. The crow's foot pattern on Fig. 16a, c is unique to this ware, as are the two loops below the rim in Fig. 16e, although on that piece, the diamond is drawn in the fashion of the Lime plus Iron and Manganese Painted painters (e.g. Figs. 18c Manganese Painted; 20d, 22i Lime plus Iron.)

UNCERTAIN WARE, POLYCHROME VARIETY (Poly)

Two non-joining sherds from a collared jar (Fig. 18e) and one from a pedestal (Fig. 18f) are closely similar to FCP 3 Polychrome varieties in fabric, decoration, and shape (Fig. 12); they probably represent redeposited material from that earlier phase. Polychrome sherds with red and black painted decoration, extremely rare in FCP 4.1 deposits, are essentially confined to the lower units that also include substantial numbers of other FCP 3 varieties. Two non-joining sherds from the same pot came from FAN:101 and FAN:109 (not illustrated). They have a red, Lime-free fabric, a white coating on the exterior surface that does not react to hydrochloric acid, and several lines painted in a brownish-black manganese oxide pigment. They could be FCP 5 intrusions. All the Polychrome sherds in FCP 4 may be out of context. They were certainly not a major part of the FCP 4 assemblage; if not intrusive, they are probably exchange items.

UNCERTAIN WARES, MANGANESE PAINTED VARIETIES (MnPt)

At least two wares occur in FCP 4.1 contexts with painted decoration in manganese-oxide-rich pigments, the Ungritted Manganese Painted ware, and one or more uncertain wares. The painted decoration on both has fired to a dark brown or black, and when well preserved is so thick the lines stand out in relief. Scratched with a fingernail, these lines produce a velvety brown powder. More often, the powder has long since disappeared: the pattern now appears as a pale gray, ghostly line—if any pigment is preserved at all. These are characteristics of manganese-rich pigments (Shepard 1968:41–42), which seldom bond with the clay body at the relatively low temperatures of prehistoric firings.

The painted lines were burnished with substantial pressure to compact the pigment and force it into the surface. They may have been coated after firing with a protective resin (see above, FCP 3). Manganese has the virtue of firing black regardless of temperature and atmosphere of firing. Prehistoric potters may have been attracted by a pigment that would produce a black color—desirable for symbolic meanings or just because of the greater contrast with the clay ground—that could be achieved in a simple oxidizing firing.[2]

Black painted decoration on a light clay ground can also be accomplished with an iron-oxide-rich pigment, but that requires a more controlled, probably three-stage firing. A three-stage firing takes longer and uses considerably more fuel than a simple oxidizing fire. When a three-stage firing is successful, the appearance of an iron oxide black can be quite similar to a manganese black. The iron oxide pigment, however, usually bonds with the fabric and is too hard to produce a powder when scratched. Usually, a small spot of incompletely reduced, red or yellowish color also helps identify the black iron-oxide pigment.

UNGRITTED WARE, MANGANESE PAINTED VARIETY (UgrMn)

Fabric

The clay is, to judge from the colors, calcareous; the body quite compact, with few visible nonplastics. Occasional bits of Lime to 1 mm, rarely 2 mm, are present in most sherds, as well as tiny (<1 mm) dark red-brown grits. Both the Lime and dark inclusions are scattered irregularly throughout the clay body. They vary in number and size from sherd to sherd, and probably occurred naturally in the clay beds. While the superficial appearance is very similar to the FCP 1 Ungritted ware, the more frequent inclusions suggest that, if using the same clay, the FCP 4 potters dug it from a different (part of the) clay bed than had been used by the FCP 1 potters.

Building Procedures and Surface Finish

No direct evidence for building procedures was noted; coil or slab building is likely. The interiors of most sherds preserve clear marks of the scraping that produced the thin, regular walls. The exteriors and handles were wet smoothed, painted with a usually quite fine, delicate brush, using a viscous manganese-oxide-rich pigment that left the pattern, originally, in low relief. The painted designs were allowed to dry to just the right consistency before the entire exterior was burnished: the burnish rarely smeared the fine lines. Accessible surfaces feel quite smooth, and only occasionally show slight troughs from the burnishing tool. A high burnish gloss was not achieved with this clay. Today, few portions of the patterns remain in relief. More often, the manganese has powdered away, leaving only a faint brownish or sometimes silver trace.

Colors and Firing Practices

The cores are generally a light pink or yellow, rarely pale gray. Interior and exterior surfaces are generally a uniform pale yellow or green,[3] without clouds or circles. Hardness varies from Mohs' 3 to 5. Yellow and greenish hues are common in calcareous clays exposed to an incompletely oxidizing atmosphere (Grimshaw 1980:353). Probably these pots were fired in a fairly long, slow fire, that burned out any organic matter. They must have been protected from direct contact with the fuel, either by cover sherds, a saggar, or a true kiln (see Vitelli 1997:24–26).

Shapes

Jars: Fig. 17a–b, e–k
Bowl: Fig. 17c
Bottom: Fig. 17d

Only two sherds preserve traces of a carinated body (Fig. 17a–b), unburnished on the interior, so probably from a closed shape. One (Fig. 17a) preserves the edge of what was probably a handle attachment at the carination. The upper walls of the carination may have formed a continuous curve with a neck similar to those in Fig. 17e–i, in which case the handles would have extended from rim to carination. Alternatively, the shape may have resembled the carinated jar from FCP 3 (Fig. 1a, g).

Rim fragments, several with strap handles attached just below the rim, suggest slightly larger jars (Figs. 17e–h). A body sherd (Fig. 17i) provides no true guide to orientation; its curvature could suggest the continuous curve of the neck of a jar slightly larger than that in Fig. 17g. Two slightly convex body sherds (Figs. 17j–k), in the absence of rims or other body parts that might go with them to suggest another shape, might best be understood as coming from the body of a narrow-necked jar.

The only other shape represented in Ungritted Manganese sherds is a small bowl with a flat rim (Fig. 17c). Flat bottoms, one pictured in Fig. 17d, probably provided the resting surface for all shapes. No ring bases or rounded bottoms were found.

Decorative Style

All rim sherds preserve at least traces of a broad band of paint along the rim. The body sherd in Fig. 17j preserves a few broad diagonal stripes, perhaps part of a chevron motif. The carination in Fig. 17a is highlighted with a broad band, and an unillustrated body sherd from FAS:98 preserves a solid, roughly triangular patch of paint. Otherwise, the patterns are painted with a very fine brush. Each dip of the brush provided enough pigment for a line 1–2 cm long, at most. While delicate, the strokes are not terribly neat or precise: the beginning and end of each stroke within a continuous motif is evident, and parallel motifs are not entirely parallel or of the same thickness (e.g., Fig. 17f). Groups of, especially wavy, lines are favored. Some float in space (Fig. 17c, e), though most are connected to lines that mark structural points of the vessel (Fig. 17a–b, f–g); too little is preserved to say much about structure. Each sherd is different. The wavy line superimposed over a straight line (fig. 17h) is interesting for its similarity to the motif on the interior of Lime plus Iron basins (Fig.23a–b; 24b, d–e), although the execution of the motif is different in the two wares.[4]

In FCP 1, Ungritted is the one ware that seems unlikely to have been produced locally (Vitelli 1993a:209), in part because it occurs in much higher frequencies at other Peloponnesian sites to the north of Franchthi. It is hard to tell from published accounts how much material comparable to FCP 4 Ungritted Manganese occurs at LN sites in the Peloponnese, but the impression is that frequencies are similar to those at Franchthi, i.e., quite low. Four sherds are included in the Lerna collection. The variety seems to me to be most similar to oxidized sherds of Thessalian Gray on Gray ware that I saw in Thessaly (Wace and Thompson 1912:Fig. 54a–b: B3e ware from Tsangli).

UNCERTAIN WARE(S), MANGANESE PAINTED VARIETY (MnPt)

I feel reasonably confident in assigning some of the manganese painted sherds to Ungritted ware (above). Others are harder to identify. Some are close to the Lime plus Iron fabric, others seem different from everything else at Franchthi. Quite possibly they represent a number of different wares, coming from a variety of sources, but each exists in too small a sample and size to assign to a ware. I have grouped them here as Manganese Pattern Painted varieties, ware(s) uncertain.

Fig. 18a–d illustrates the best-preserved examples of manganese painted sherds in a fabric other than Ungritted. All have plentiful nonplastic inclusions, including Lime, along with other sandy grits and, usually, the glitter of mica, gold and/or silver. The fabric is not unlike that of some manganese painted and other sherds I saw from Plateia Magoula Zarkou in Thessaly.

The shapes are different than those represented in Ungritted Manganese ware. The lightly carinated bowl in Fig. 18a is very similar in shape to apparently contemporary examples in Lime plus Iron (e.g., Figs. 22e–f), also decorated with stacks of zigzagging lines, although the Lime plus Iron examples are decorated on the exterior only. The pedestal fragment in Fig. 18d is decorated with chains of diamonds that have a close parallel in Lime plus Iron (e.g., Fig. 20d), including on the figurine (Fig. 20e), but the very narrow pedestal is unparalleled in Lime plus Iron or any other contemporary ware at Franchthi.

UNCERTAIN WARE, GRAY BURNISHED VARIETY (Gray)

Fabric

One sherd (Fig. 19a) has Lime pops[5] up to 2 mm on the surfaces; the other examples have very fine Lime inclusions, well under 1 mm, along with equally small dark grits and the glitter of silver mica. The softer sherds feel silty and the clay body looks very compact. Several worn examples are quite pitted on the interior, which may suggest that more Lime is present than is visible with a 10x lens.

I spent considerable time in the field comparing the

Gray sherds with other wares to see if they could simply be misfired or refired pieces of another ware, particularly black Low Lime Burnished. The Gray sherds have no biotite, so cannot be misfired Andesite Burnished ware. They lack the rounded red and gray inclusions common to both FCP 3 Low Lime Burnished and FCP 4 Lime plus Iron, and the Lime nonplastics are much smaller and fewer than those in Lime plus Iron. No painted decoration occurs and the shapes are different from the various Manganese and Polychrome varieties. The Gray Burnished variety does not appear to be a misfired or burned version of another Franchthi ware.

Building Procedures and Surface Finish

No direct evidence is preserved for the construction techniques used. The potters scraped the walls to a uniform thickness, working primarily from the interior, but the direction of scraping is not necessarily parallel to the rim. Exteriors tend to be slightly lumpy. The self slip raised during that process seems to have been the only slip used. Even well-burnished surfaces never have a waxy quality. Burnishing troughs on the exteriors, and the interiors of open shapes, cover most of the surface.

Colors and Firing Practices

The sherds have fired to a light gray on the surfaces (ca. 10 YR 5–6/1–2), usually with a slightly lighter core. The edges of broken sherds are sharp and feel hard, although the Mohs' hardness on different examples varies from a soft 2–3, to quite hard 6. The bottom fragment in Fig. 19d has a large blister on the interior, probably caused by too rapid heating that trapped gases within the walls (Grimshaw 1980:419).

I have discussed elsewhere the difficulty of achieving a uniformly light gray color (Vitelli 1994). It requires achieving temperatures and an atmosphere to support intermediate reduction, as full reduction would have turned the vessels black. Some, probably highly calcareous clays may be more susceptible to such firings than others (Schneider et al. 1994:68, 147–48), but would still have required a fairly sophisticated control on the part of the potters to produce with any consistency. Saggars were probably used.[6]

Shapes

Bowls: Fig. 19b, e–f
Jars: Fig. 19a, c
Basins: Fig. 19g–i
Pedestal: Fig. 19j

Three shapes represented in Gray ware are unique for FCP 4.1 at Franchthi: a small carinated bowl with a rounded, offset rim and two small holes poked through the shoulder before firing (Fig. 19b); a small jar with a concave-convex profile and a small, non-functional handle at the point of maximum diameter (Fig. 19a); and a shouldered jar with a concave neck (Fig. 19c). All probably had flat bottoms similar to that in Fig. 19d.

Of equal interest are the shapes that closely parallel shapes in other wares at Franchthi: in particular, deep bowls with thickened rims (Fig. 19e–f), which, except for these two examples, occur only in Andesite Burnished ware (e.g., Fig. 16h–m). The basins (Fig. 19g–i) with pedestals (Fig. 19j) are similar in profile to those in contemporary Lime plus Iron (e.g., Figs. 23–24).

Sherds of the Gray Burnished variety are infrequent in the Franchthi assemblage. Some shapes occur only in this variety at Franchthi; others resemble those made by the Andesite Burnished and Lime plus Iron potters. The Gray variety is probably not a local product. Similar shapes occur in a gray ware at Corinth and Klenia (Phelps 1975:Figs. 30–34), where additional shapes not represented at Franchthi are also present. Western Thessaly is another potential source (e.g., Demoule et al. 1988:19). Substantial analytical work has been done on the western Thessalian Gray ware, which was apparently produced in a very limited geographical area, but was carried quite far afield (Schneider et al. 1994:67–68), some of it perhaps reaching Corinth (Lavezzi 1978:418). Comparable studies remain to be done on the later Neolithic Peloponnesian gray pottery.

LIME PLUS IRON WARE, PATTERN PAINTED VARIETY (LiFe)

Fabric

The clay body consistently includes Lime, rounded red and gray minerals, and the glitter of mica; the relative proportions of red and gray to Lime, and the size of the inclusions are quite variable. Some sherds have relatively few inclusions, all less than 1 mm. More commonly, the fabric is very gritty, with heat-expanded powdered Lime chunks from 1–3 mm breaking through the surfaces (Pl. 4a–b). In the breaks, the bits of Lime are smaller and generally not powdery. The rounded red and gray inclusions are usually smaller than the Lime, ca. 1 mm in size. Given the variability in size and proportions, both were probably prepared and added intentionally by the potters. The red/gray nonplastics might be grog made from an iron-rich clay. A single sample was submitted to petrographic analysis, which reported "pelitic sediments," which could be grog (Jones 1986:397, sample #40). In some sherds the nonplastics are quite evenly distributed, in others quite unevenly. The amount of working or wedging of the clay body apparently varied from batch to batch or from potter to potter.

Building Procedures and Surface Finish

Two or three examples of breaks along a coil (or slab) joint point to that as the probable method used for building. That such breaks are so rare probably means that potters worked with very moist clay, and quickly, rarely allowing a lower coil to dry too much before adding the next and firmly bonding the two. For the basins with their spreading rims (Figs. 23–24), this may indicate that the potters built from the rim to avoid fighting gravity. That might also have contributed to the strong S-curve of the profile, the lower (rim) walls sagging slightly as the weight of the upper walls was added. If the basins were built upside down, they were turned before drying to finish the interior. One large bowl (Fig. 21d) shows a poorly melded lip fold on the interior; it may indicate that the potters usually folded the rims before smoothing them between their fingers, to achieve the thinned lip evident on most pots.

While the interiors of many pots were not finished beyond scraping, they show fewer of the irregularities, the lumps and dents of building, than do the more visible exteriors. The potters must have worked and shaped the contours, especially of the larger pots, more carefully from the interior than the exterior, which is often quite irregular, in spite of having received more stages of finishing. Some interiors were scraped while the pot was still quite damp; the scraping tool dragged nonplastics along the moist clay, leaving short grooves in the surface. Other pots were scraped, perhaps for a second time, when sufficiently dry that the scraper dislodged the grits from the body, leaving shallow pits, rather than creating grooves. Scraping and other finishing stages were executed in random directions, as the potter moved the pot around to reach different parts. In spite of the lumpy exterior surface, the potters usually achieved a fairly uniform wall thickness. The direction of the marks on interiors or exteriors is not a reliable indicator of sherd orientation.

After scraping, the potters smoothed at least the exterior surface, with or without water and probably using their fingers, to level the ridges from scraping. Pots that were fired in an intermediate atmosphere often have a dirty greenish white color to the ground, as though they had been smoothed with dirty water. Salts from sea water may be responsible for this scum. A handle detached from a scraped and smoothed surface (Fig. 21a) shows that at least one potter added handles after initial finishing, but before the final burnishing and painting. This is also the likely stage at which pedestals would have been added to basins. One basin was probably turned over to rest on its pedestal too soon, before the pedestal clay had dried sufficiently to provide good support for the weight of the bowl (Fig. 24j). The pedestal has sagged; the interior is covered with stress cracks and traces of extra clay added to patch the cracks and to add support.

The potters usually burnished the exteriors, and the interiors of open shapes, before adding the painted decoration, sometimes while the body was moist enough to take a deep impression from the tool, sometimes when so dry the tool marks barely show. They were not always careful completely to cover the surface with burnish, although the interiors of basins usually received full attention. Large pots sometimes were left unburnished.

Painting

An iron-oxide-rich pigment that fired to the full range of colors from red to black was used for painting patterns. Most motifs left large portions of the surface unpainted. Some pots may have received no decoration. A unique example (Fig. 22g) was given a monochrome coat of paint over the entire surface. Sometimes the paint was applied so thickly that the pattern lines almost have relief and individual pigment grains are evident (e.g., Fig. 20f); on others, the paint was so diluted that the pattern appears as an interruption of the burnish with barely any color (e.g., Fig. 20e). Occasionally the painted lines have a slight luster; more often they are dull or matte. On some of the broader lines, most evident on those that have fired red, the pigment grains have collected along the edges of the line or at the overlap of brush strokes, leaving the center with little color or creating the effect of dots at the point of overlapping strokes, while the rest of the line is barely visible (Pl. 5a). The variation in the granularity of the paint suggests that it derived from a mineral pigment that had to be ground. It may have been mixed with clay slip to improve adhesion to the body.

The painters used short strokes, rarely more than a centimeter or two in length, and often produced blobs rather than neat lines (e.g., Pl. 4b, Figs. 22a, 23c). They sometimes seem to have lost track of their motif, forgetting lines or adding extras that break the repetition (e.g., Figs. 20a, c; 22i, j). Trailing lines from a stray bristle are often present (e.g., Fig. 22c). Occasional examples of neat lines painted with a well-made narrow brush also occur (e.g. Fig. 24e). A broad brush was used for striping rims and pedestals (e.g., Figs. 23–24), for the exterior of basin bowls, and for decorating larger pots (e.g., Fig. 21c–f).

Colors and Firing Practices

Inconsistencies in firing are evident as soon as a bag of sherds is emptied onto the table. Every color combination possible for a clay body with iron oxide is likely to occur in each unit. A minority of sherds is uniformly oxidized to a pinkish tan (ca. 5 YR 7/4–6), with a clear red-orange paint (10 R 5/8). A slightly more yellow tan (ca. 7.5 YR 7/4) is common on light-colored sherds, suggesting incomplete oxidation. The paint on these sherds has fired red, reddish-gray, or black. Cores may be uniformly the color of the surfaces, or may have a narrow gray center, or may be entirely gray, lightening only at the subsurface. Probably the majority of pieces,[7] if we include the dirty greenish-white sherds in this category, have fired to a shade of gray with gray cores and gray-black paint; sherds with a gray surface may also have reddish or yellow cores, with or without a central gray streak. A few examples are gray on the exterior and a more nearly oxidized brownish pink on the interior. On many sherds, most often the gray but also light-colored examples, the paint in the pattern has fired to a color so close to that of the clay ground that it is essentially invisible, except when the sherd is wet, when the painted patterns stand out more clearly.

A few examples of joining sherds with major color differences coinciding with the break point to prolonged post-firing (and post-breakage) exposure to a hot fire of at least one of those sherds (e.g., Figs. 21e, 24f). Nevertheless, the variation in color of the Lime plus Iron sherds is so consistent throughout the assemblage that it must reflect variation in the original firing. Occasional small firing clouds occur, but they are not common. No examples of firing circles were noted. Some, especially oxidized, sherds are soft enough to scratch with a fingernail (Mohs' 2–3). Most are harder (Mohs' 4–7). Quite a few of the hard gray pieces look glassy and must be sintered, if not fully vitrified.

Because the surfaces are marred by expanded powdery Lime grits 2–3 mm in diameter, many of the pieces look far less carefully made than is in fact the case (Pl. 4c). The Lime has expanded and turned to powder, but has not caused spalling.

Either individual potters used different firing regimes or the firings were all quite variable, with little control exercised by the potters. Some kind of enclosure was probably necessary to reach and maintain the temperatures responsible for the hardest pieces. Most pots must have been protected from direct exposure to fuel by using cover sherds around individual pots, by raising the pots above the fuel on a grate of some sort, or with a built kiln. Occasional clouds would be likely in any of those arrangements. A few very thick, sintered sherds in the same fabric (not illustrated) may have come from a containing structure comparable to what I proposed for FCP 2 Urf firings (Vitelli 1993a:185, 1997:30–38), although the evidence is minimal.

In a simple open firing, fuel is added until a desired temperature is reached—determined by some observation such as the glowing color of the pots within the fire (Rice 1987:157–158)—and then the fire is allowed to burn down and the pots to cool in the air. With this procedure, oxidized colors would be the norm, especially if the pots were protected from ash by surrounding cover sherds. Since most of the Lime plus Iron pieces are at least lightly reduced, some more complex firing regime must have prevailed. The clay body has never fired black, so smudging at the end of the firing is not responsible for the darker colors. Rather, a true reduction process must have been involved to produce the gray fabric colors and the darker gray and black paint colors. The relatively high temperatures (for prehistoric potters) needed for reduction fires, and providing and maintaining a reducing atmosphere took more fuel, more time, and more knowledge than the oxidizing fires used for the Manganese Painted varieties. The result was a harder-fired ware that would have stood up to regular use without the scratching and frequent breakage likely with softer wares. It also was responsible for the expanded Lime and the gray-on-gray colors that left the decoration barely visible.

I suspect that the potters were, at least initially, aiming for a dark-on-light effect, comparable to that achieved with manganese paints by potters in other parts of Greece at roughly the same time. If I am correct, that may imply that the Franchthi potters did not know the special properties of manganese paints that permit the black-on-light effect in a simple oxidizing fire. Perhaps the Franchthi potters could not find manganese pigments locally, but knew they could achieve the same effect with readily available iron oxide pigments. They were sometimes able to produce the effect with their pigments; more often they fell short. Either they did not know exactly what was responsible for those successful pieces, or they knew in principle but could not control the outcome in practice—a problem I share with them. I think the following evidence supports the latter interpretation.

The three-stage firing that the FCP 2 Urf potters had all but perfected to produce black on light with their iron-oxide-rich pigment (Vitelli 1997:30–38) is best known today through its use by Classical Greek potters who produced black- and red-figure pots. It calls for an initial oxidizing atmosphere to heat the vessel and burn out organic materials. The entire vessel, at the end of this stage, is light in color. When the potter judges that this first stage has progressed sufficiently, she needs to raise the temperature and adjust conditions so that the fire consumes all the oxygen in the atmosphere around the pots to keep burning. By claiming some of the oxygen within the iron oxide pigments and clay body, it literally "reduces" their oxygen content, and changes their color from light red to gray. The more finely divided particles in the pigment react more quickly and fully than those in the clay body and sinter, forming a nonporous glassy coating over the painted lines. Since pots have to be protected from the air to be in a reducing atmosphere, the potter cannot observe this change directly but has to have some indirect method for judging that the time is right. Once this has occurred, oxygen has to be reintroduced to the atmosphere while the pots are still hot enough for further reactions to take place. The renewed access to oxygen allows the iron oxides in the porous clay body to reabsorb the oxygen they had given up in the reducing stage, thus turning back to their lighter colors. The sintered coating on the painted lines prevents these from reoxidizing, so they remain black.

The process sounds simple, but is difficult to achieve in practice; it may not work with every clay body. In experimental work with my students, the most difficult parts are achieving high temperatures (ca. 900–950°C) and maintaining a reducing atmosphere at the same time.[8] We have usually accomplished this by sealing off the hot kiln with its burning fuel inside the stoking chamber—covering it with earth and clods of damp grass—when we had finally reached the desired temperatures, and leaving it overnight to cool in a reducing atmosphere. Had we come back in the middle of the night to open an air vent into the kiln before too much cooling had taken place, we would have established the third and final oxidizing stage.

The FCP 4 Lime plus Iron potters may have known that to achieve a dark-on-light effect, they needed long hot fires and needed to cover them with something airtight at the hottest stage. Sometimes they did not get them hot enough or sealed the fire too soon and incompletely—it takes only a small crack to admit enough oxygen to affect the colors—hence the soft, light-colored pieces. Sometimes they hit the temperature, sealing and uncovering just right, and produced the desired dark-on-light pots. Most often, they reached high temperatures, sealed the kiln effectively, and waited too long to uncover for the final oxidation stage, ending up with the gray-on-gray pieces.

Since they continued to fire in a way that produced pots with barely visible decoration (see below, FCP 4.2), they must have been satisfied with these results, because they could have achieved a better contrast between pattern and background with less effort and less fuel in a simple oxidizing fire. Perhaps they were aiming for the same effect as the Thessalian Gray-on-Gray pots. It is also possible that they were unconcerned about color, or were more interested in hard-fired pots or in the process of the firing itself. Once they found that their gray-on-gray pots had decoration that only became clearly visible when the pot held a liquid, they may have continued the firing procedures to capture that "magical" effect.

Whatever their original intent, the FCP 4 Lime plus Iron potters achieved very inconsistent results in every stage of their production, from mixing the clay body to final firing. They were not potters who worked with an established routine that involved going through the same steps in the same way, time after time, a rhythm that would have produced more similar products from each effort.

Shapes

Jars: Fig. 20a–c, possibly d–e, 21a–f
Bowls: Fig. 22
Basins: Figs. 23a–c, 24a–g
Bottom: Fig. 22b
Pedestals: Figs. 23d, 24h–j, possibly a

Although no example is well enough preserved to allow estimates of capacity, a necked or collared jar with strap handle(s) from rim to shoulder occurs in small (Fig. 20a, probably b–c) and large (Fig. 21a, probably b–c) sizes. Each probably had two handles, on opposite sides of the rim as did the jar in Fig. 21a, for which almost the entire collar is preserved. Most strap handle fragments are nearly flat in section; a small segment of a round handle, ca. 1 cm in diameter (not illustrated) could have come from such a jar. The handle attachment scars on the small fragments in Fig. 20b–c suggest slightly rounded handles. The pressure used in applying the handle in Fig. 20c distorted the curve too much to be able to get the diameter reading from it. It seems more likely to have come from a small, necked jar than from any other documented shape. The two rim fragments in Fig. 20d–e may also derive from small jars, perhaps with a continuously curving wall rather than an articulated neck. They could also come from simple round-bottomed cups, although that shape is not clearly documented in Lime plus Iron. Fragments that are probably from large, necked jars (Figs 21a–c) are not uncommon in the assemblage, although few preserve clear profiles. These, like all the Lime plus Iron pots other than basins, probably tapered to a flat bottom, of which a number of examples occur (unillustrated); rounded bottoms cannot be ruled out. No ring bases occur in the assemblage.

Large deep jars occur with a sinuous profile (Fig. 21e, probably f) and with a simple convex wall (Fig. 21d). The latter is uncommon, as is the solid ledge lug that accompanies it. A similar lug occurs in FAN:101, possibly from the same pot. From the same unit, a flat bottom fragment from a large thick-walled, unpainted jar preserves the attachment scar of a large lug or handle.

Very large jars, with walls over a centimeter thick, were also a part of the shape assemblage, although even relatively large pieces mended from a number of fragments provide little information about the actual shape. The body fragment in Fig. 21f suggests a sinuously curving jar. At least one mended fragment preserves the stump of a strap handle and the suggestion of a collar. It probably came from a very large collared jar with strap handles from the rim to the shoulder. Large, unpainted, flat strap handle fragments (FAS:107) probably come from similar jars, as do several large, thick, flat bottoms. Some of the thick fragments have nonplastics comparable to smaller thinner-walled vessels in Lime plus Iron, and are well burnished and hard fired. Other sherds have plentiful and large nonplastics, with expanded Lime up to 5 mm at the surfaces; these are poorly finished and soft-fired. Although especially in small fragments they look like a true coarse ware, these are probably best considered as yet another variation of Lime plus Iron.

Small open bowls occur with some frequency and in a number of variations. The best-preserved example from FCP 4.1 is a simple convex bowl with a flat bottom (Fig. 22a), with interior decoration. Shouldered bowls (Fig. 22c–h), with a sharply incurved rim and, in at least one example (Fig 22c) a thick hump, or with a carination below the shoulder (Fig. 22e–f), are more typical. In this subphase, they received decoration on the shoulder or entire exterior. A unique example (Fig. 22g) is coated with a monochrome wash on the interior and exterior. A carinated and a rounded body fragment (Fig. 22i, j) seem to come from deeper bowls; the orientation of body sherds can never be securely determined in this ware, and one or both might be tilted slightly to produce a shape closer to the shouldered bowls. Both are burnished on the interior, so are probably from bowls rather than jars. I suspect that the curve of the rim fragment in Fig. 22h exaggerates the actual diameter, and that it, too, comes from a bowl closer in size to the others. All the bowls probably had flat bottoms. The illustrated bottom (Fig. 22b) is, unusually, decorated on both the interior and exterior.

The best-preserved pots from FCP 4.1 are basins (Figs. 23a–c, 24a–g). They are also among the most carefully made and finished. While most share the concave-convex profile, a few have simple flaring walls (Fig. 24b, d); the relative depth, wall thickness, and even the lip of the rim vary with each example. Several (unillustrated) joint fragments preserve a painted stripe around the exterior of the joint and substantial abrasion on the interior bottom of the bowl. Almost certainly, all basins sat on pedestalled bases, although most of the illustrated pedestals (especially Fig. 24h–j) seem to have diameters too small to have supported the illustrated basins. Some of the pieces illustrated as rims (Fig. 24a, c) may in fact derive from pedestals that were painted on the underside, a practice not usual at Franchthi, although it occurs in Thessaly.

Decorative Style

In this earliest FCP 4 subphase, some of the motifs are very reminiscent of earlier FCP 1 and FCP 2 motifs, e.g., the running chevrons on carinated shouldered bowls (Fig. 22e–f) and the large jar in Fig. 21e, or the simple bands at rim and neck (Fig. 21c). But most of the motifs, even if derived from much older designs, are executed in a distinctive fashion. Where the painters of, e.g., the Ungritted Manganese variety (Fig. 17) created a zigzagging line with one dip of the brush, continuing the alternating line directions until the brush ran dry, the Lime plus Iron potters lifted the brush after each leg, using a separate stroke for the change of direction (e.g., Fig. 21a). Not all painters had a steady hand (e.g., Fig. 22a, j). Their net patterns (e.g., Fig. 20a) were created by rows of zigzags with touching apices, rather than by the simpler series of crosshatched lines, used by Urf potters. Their diamond chains sometimes received a fifth side (e.g., Fig. 20c, f), or sprouted appendages (Fig. 22i).

It may be significant that one variation on the zigzag line occurs in Lime plus Iron only on the interiors of basins, and on almost all basins. A single line encircles, or more probably spirals, around the interior of the basin bowl (Figs. 23a–c; 24b–e). Over this line runs a continuously zigzagging line, each leg created by a separate brush stroke. In one example, Fig. 23c, instead of a zigzagging line, the initial spiral is provided with fringes. The zigzag-over-line motif is the same as that on the neck of a jar in the Ungritted Manganese variety (Fig. 17h), although on the basins it is executed in typical multiple brush strokes of the Lime plus Iron style. Two bell basins that lack the guiding line of the former motif (Fig. 24f–g) still have running zigzags around the interior. Although the general idea of the motif is not exclusive to basins, its regular presence makes it tempting to consider that it carried some particular symbolic meaning particularly appropriate to that shape.

While some Lime plus Iron shapes are similar to Late Neolithic shapes from other sites, and occasional decorative parallels exist, the style of decoration, executed in the iron-oxide-rich pigment is essentially unique to Franchthi. Lime plus Iron dominates the FCP 4 assemblage (Tables 1–8). It was probably made locally.

NO LIME WARE, COARSE VARIETY (NoLiCo)

Throughout the FCP 4.1 units, small worn sherds of coarse wares are present. They may have plentiful or large non-plastics, or both, sometimes including Lime, sometimes not. Wall thickness ranges from 6 mm to over 1 cm. They have minimal surface finish, variable colors, and are generally soft fired. Some of these are certainly worn fragments from FCP 1 through FCP 3 pots. Some with large chunks of Lime and rounded red grits are probably from relatively low-fired, large pots of Lime plus Iron. Because FCP 5 includes such a large percentage of "coarse" pottery and the stratigraphy in the upper units of FA balk is so confusing, I could never be absolutely sure that the coarse lumps in units assigned to FCP 4 were not intrusive pieces of an FCP 5 coarse variety. One would expect that, if intrusive, an occasional example of one of the many characteristically FCP 5 features would show up. None did, so I assume that the units assigned to FCP 4.1 are essentially free of FCP 5 contamination.

Most of the coarse lumps were of a size that justified putting them with the residue for purposes of calculating frequencies (Tables 1–8). Within the general "coarse" category were a few larger sherds that did not react at all in hydrochloric acid, i.e., include no Lime nonplastics. The surfaces are finished differently from earlier no Lime varieties, so the sherds are apparently not kick-ups from earlier phases. Preserving a few profiles (Fig. 25), they probably are a local product of FCP 4.1. The sherds are not consistently present in every unit, and when present, make up a quite variable percentage (1–21%) of the unit total calculated by weight. The total number of small sherds, however, cannot represent a very large number of pots.

Occasional sherds are heavily charred on the interior surface and into the break for up to a third of the thickness; this could well have happened after breakage. Sherds of appropriate size and thickness may have been used as supports within fires. They were often found in association with carbon and ash, with no joining fragments in neighboring units to suggest their use as whole pots on the fire. No coarse sherd retains carbon soot on any exterior surfaces.

Fabric

Angular and rounded red, gray, and white nonplastics vary in size from 1–2 mm to as much as 7–8 mm in different examples. Mica glitter and tiny black flecks, well under 1 mm in size, are evident in some examples. No Lime is present.

Building Procedures and Surface Finish

The edges of the sherds, soft and worn, preserve no indication of coil joints, although coiling seems the most likely method of construction. The potters scraped the damp pots on both interior and exterior surfaces, probably in the course of building. Some pots were given no further surface finish. Most were at least smoothed with the potter's fingers, usually without water. One or two sherds have a few troughs from a scribbly burnish; none received a thorough going-over with the burnishing tool. Surfaces, in spite of the scraping, remain irregular and lumpy. Wall thickness varies from 6 to 10 mm, probably depending on the size and part of the vessel from which the sherd derives.

Colors and Firing Practices

Most sherds have brick red surfaces (2.5 YR 5/4–6), often with gray or black clouds on the exterior, especially on rims. Cores are sometimes uniformly red, sometimes gray to black. All sherds scratch easily with a fingernail. The pots were probably fired in a direct fire, in contact with the fuel, which was allowed to burn down to ash, leaving the pots to cool in the air. Temperatures probably did not exceed 700–800 °C, and the firing was probably short.

Shapes

Bowls: Fig. 25

Each of the six preserved rim sherds suggests a slightly different shape; all suggest simple variations on the theme of bowl, and all are reminiscent of Early Neolithic shapes. They are from small to medium-sized pots that required no great skill or experience to build. Three suggest deep bowls with slightly inleaning rims (Fig. 25a–b, d). The slight flare of the bowl in Fig. 25c, which might suggest a collar, seems equally likely to be a simple, even unintentional, variant of a deep bowl. The shallow bowl in Fig. 25e carries a heavy ledge lug just below the rim, a feature shared with the piriform bowl in Fig. 25f. Several additional lugs and another sherd with a lug scar also were found. A small sherd from FAS:98 in a red-fired fabric without Lime was pierced before firing with a series of small holes covering the preserved 2 cm of surface. The piece of a small strainer may be another fragment of the strainer found scattered throughout FCP 4.2 units (Fig. 32b).

FRANCHTHI CERAMIC SUBPHASE 4.2 (FCP 4.2)

The second subphase of FCP 4 includes all the wares and varieties of FCP 4.1 and a new ware, in a coarse variety, Calcite Coarse. Although FCP 4.2 is represented by only a relatively shallow deposit, sherds are more plentiful than those from FCP 4.1.

ANDESITE WARE, BURNISHED VARIETY (AndB)

Fabric

The fabric is essentially the same as in FCP 4.1. The biotite inclusions often seem smaller than in earlier sherds, while the feldspar or quartz minerals are sometimes as large as 2–3 mm. The broken edges tend to be crumbly, the sherds to break into small fragments.

Building Procedures and Surface Finish

The techniques used to build and finish the FCP 4.2 Andesite Burnished pots were generally similar to those used by potters in FCP 4.1. More profiles from the lower bodies of pots are preserved from FCP 4.2 contexts (compare Figs. 26–27 with Fig. 16). They present, almost uniformly, a lightly convex profile that was not evident in FCP 4.1 examples. If they were shaped with a paddle, as suggested for FCP 4.1, it was now a curved paddle, perhaps a large rib bone, rather than the straight-sided, probably wooden paddle used earlier. The same curvature might equally have been produced by a convex scraper working on the interior of the pot.

On the best-preserved lower body (Fig. 26h), slight irregularities in the wall thickness below the carination feel like the depressions that come from pinching that was not entirely evened out by subsequent scraping. Relief pellets, usually in groups of two or three, were added at the carination (Fig. 26f–h), or singly, on delicate flat strap handles (Fig. 26m–n), before the potters slipped and burnished the piece. Several rounded bottom fragments (not illustrated) appear to have once had pedestals or ring bases that apparently detached before firing. The attachment scar on the dried, unfired pot was scraped and burnished to minimize its traces, and the pot was apparently fired and used without a base.

Colors and Firing Practices

These appear to have been quite similar to those used in FCP 4.1; many more of the sherds have a reddish, generally oxidized core, which suggests the smoky stage of the firing was shorter. Occasional sherds (e.g., Fig. 26h) have a cream-colored bloom in areas untouched by the burnisher. These may reflect salts in the slip, possibly from slaking with brackish water.

Shapes

Jars: Fig. 26a–l
Bowls: Figs. 26o–p, 27a–b
Basins: Fig. 27 c–f
Bottom: Fig. 26h
Pedestals: Fig. 27g–i
Handles: Figs. 26i–n, 27a

The shapes represented in FCP 4.2 are more varied and generally different from those in the earlier subphase (compare Fig. 16). Most sherds that reveal shape information come from small carinated jars with a clearly articulated neck or collar (Fig. 26a–h). The capacity of the best-preserved example (Fig. 26h), calculated by the summed cylinders method (Rice 1987:222), was ca. 1.5 liters filled to the neck, with another half liter if filled to the brim of a 3 cm tall neck. Most examples were roughly the same size or slightly smaller.

The collar fragment in Fig. 26c has the beginnings of a handle that was attached directly over the lip. That in Fig. 26a preserves the edge of an attachment at the break, which suggests a handle attached just below the rim, the more typical location for the upper end of a handle in this ware (Figs. 26i–j; 35f). If the handles rising from carinations (Fig. 26k–l) are from vessels of the same shape, the handles on the carinated jars ran from rim to carination. The unstratified jar fragment in Fig. 35f shows the lower end of the handle attached just above the carination. That may suggest that the diameter of the sherds in Fig. 26j–k was not exaggerated by the pressure of attaching the handles and that the sherds are indeed, from different, wide-mouthed jars or bowls. The body fragments in Fig. 26k–l are smoothed but not burnished on the interior, as other open shapes are, so I suspect Fig. 26j–l are in fact from carinated collared jars, and that precise handle attachment location varied. Either way, the absence of any trace of a handle on the large fragment in Fig. 26h, assuming that all such jars (and bowls) had handles, suggests the carinated collared jars probably had only one or two handles total. Some, and possibly all, were given two or three relief pellets along the carination (Fig. 26e–h). The shape is similar to the jars in Low Lime Burnished from FCP 3 (Fig. 1a, g).

Body and collar fragments preserve joints that show the collar was essentially vertical (Figs. 26a, c, e, f–h; 33a–b; 35f). The neck fragment in Fig. 26i presents a slightly different, more angled and concave profile. It may have come from a shouldered jar like the unstratified example in Fig. 35a, and reminiscent of the Gray ware jar in FCP 4.1 (Fig. 19c). The relatively long handles on both kinds of jars are thin, flat straps that narrow like an hourglass in the middle.[9] A number of examples have a small, flattened pellet applied on the narrowest part of the handle just above the change in curvature. That pellet seems a precursor of FCP 5 horned handles.

Two body sherds, with burnished interior surfaces, suggest shouldered bowls (Fig. 26o–p), again quite similar to examples from FCP 3 (Fig. 1i–k), including one in each phase with a faceted shoulder (Figs. 26p,

1k). The FCP 4.2 faceted shoulder piece has, unusually, silver as well as gold mica inclusions; it may be of a fabric different from the other Andesite Burnished pieces. It cannot, however, be a Low Lime Burnished sherd, since the earlier black pieces are calcareous and have no gold mica.

Carinated bowls with a strap handle from rim to carination may be new in this subphase (Fig. 27a). Another carinated bowl sherd with the scar of a strap handle (not illustrated, FAS:92) may come from the same pot, on which two handles were originally present. Sherds from carinated bowls are not as common as those from closed jars.

The open bowls with thickened rims and carinated shoulders that dominated the FCP 4.1 Andesite Burnished assemblage are essentially absent in FCP 4.2. The single example (Fig. 27b), with perfunctory pattern-burnishing on the interior and exterior, is the same shape; the thinner, less well-articulated rim and shoulder suggest it may have been made differently, the potter re-creating a shape seen or remembered without entirely understanding how it was done. Possibly replacing those open bowls are straight-sided or lightly convex basins (Fig. 27c–f) of roughly the same size. The basins probably stood on pedestals (Fig. 27g–i), if their attachment survived the drying stage (see above, building). One small basin or shallow bowl was provided with two adjacent short tabs along the rim (Fig. 27c), another with an applied relief pellet along the exterior wall (Fig. 27d), possibly a horizontal strip like one on an unstratified example (Fig. 35j). A straight-sided basin fragment from FAS:90 has a hole 1 cm in diameter poked below the rim before firing. The complete bottom of a basin bowl, with a pedestal attached to a scraped surface (not illustrated, FAS:87), shows heavy wear on the interior bottom of the bowl. All shapes other than basins probably rested on flat bottoms.

Decorative Style

In addition to relief applications, which may have been primarily decorative, pots were occasionally embellished with painted designs (Fig. 26i) and pattern-burnishing (Figs. 26a, d, f, o; 27b, f, h). The paint is similar to that used on FCP 4.1 examples, a grainy dull "white," probably a clay slip. The motif is unique at Franchthi, but closer in style to Ungritted Manganese than to Lime plus Iron versions. Pattern-burnished motifs are uninspired groups of vertical lines, one or two (e.g., Fig. 26d, o) or more (Figs. 26a; 27b) strokes in width. The pattern on the basin (Fig. 27f) is less a real pattern than a reserved band below the rim on the interior and exterior.

At least two sherds (Fig. 26c, j) retain traces of a stark white Lime powder in the unburnished depressions around the joint, rim, and handle. If the powder is a remnant of a larger coating, rather than just rubbed off some other object, it must have been applied after firing. Similar white Lime powder is present on some of the rhyta (see below), a few of which are made in Andesite ware.

Rhyta

Franchthi produced thirteen very fragmentary pieces from rhyta, the four-legged bowls with a side opening and basket handle along the upper rim that are documented at sites from the Peloponnese well north into the Balkans (Fig. 28; Weinberg 1965:Figs. 4–6). Nine of the thirteen fragments are in Andesite ware, and probably local products. Of the other four, only one, which may be a Gray Burnished variety (Fig. 28j), can be related to other wares represented in FCP 4. The non-Andesite pieces were probably brought to Franchthi from elsewhere given their unusual fabrics.

Three fragments were found in units assigned to FCP 4.1. The smallest is from the "hearth" in FAS:103, a 1 cm length of an Andesite Burnished handle, burnished on what is probably the top, and with traces of a fugitive red powder on the unburnished underside (not illustrated). Another small, very battered fragment from FAS:98 (not illustrated) is also Andesite Burnished; it preserves a small portion of a "thigh" where a leg was joined to the bowl, a portion of the interior bowl, about half a centimeter of exterior surface, and the scar where a leg detached from the bowl. Like other Andesite Burnished pieces, it was slipped, burnished, and fired black on all preserved surfaces. The best preserved of the three, also from FAS:98 (Fig. 28i), is made from a clay body with plentiful angular red and gray inclusions up to 5–6 mm in size, and a few smaller Lime inclusions; at least one 5 mm Lime pebble is evident in a break. The fabric is not otherwise represented at Franchthi.

Only six of the fragments at Franchthi are from stratified deposits in FA, three from units assigned to FCP 4.1 (Fig. 28i and two unillustrated, from FAS:103 and FAS:98), three from FCP 4.2 (Fig. 28c, g, k). The rest were found in mixed deposits. The foreign rhyton from FAS:98 (Fig. 28i)—maybe the earliest example at Franchthi—may have served as the inspiration for the copies made in the Andesite Burnished variety. It preserves a section of the interior front and lip of the bowl and the front right (as drawn) leg. A pigment that has fired red was painted and burnished over the exterior and interior of the lip and the side of the leg before the incised decoration was added. Where the burnisher missed parts of the surface, the pigment is powdery; it does not slake or rub off in water, so was apparently fired with the pot. The piece is well fired, if soft. The core is brown, the exterior surfaces clouded red through black. The interior of the bowl is black, perhaps from carbon deposition.

The other examples from secure FCP 4.2 deposits include: a small segment of a round handle (Fig. 28c), presumably from above the bowl, in Andesite Burnished ware; a relatively delicate and shapely left leg modeled from a single lump of clay (Fig. 28g), also in Andesite Burnished ware; and a small piece from a left thigh in a non-calcareous clay with no biotite (Fig. 28k). The handle fragment retains traces of diagonal stripes in alternating red-orange and white Lime powder, both fugitive and probably post-firing additions. The front and side of the Andesite Burnished leg are painted with a stack of vertical white zigzags, each line executed with a separate brush stroke, in the manner of the Lime plus Iron painters. The white paint is partly Lime. After the fizzing reaction to hydrochloric acid, a dull, granular, whitish line remains; it too can be scratched off the surface with a fingernail, and leaves no mark or ghost on the clay. Along the outer thigh of this leg are traces of a fugitive red-orange powder. Both white and red pigments are probably post-firing additions. A neatly incised or impressed line marks one side of the leg joint.

The non-calcareous piece (Fig. 28k) has 1–2 mm dark and light nonplastics, but no Lime or biotite. It was also burnished on the exterior, but only smoothed on the interior. A careful groove was impressed along the left side of the leg joint, and crosshatched bands were incised along the leg when the piece was quite dry. Traces of a red-orange powder remain on the interior of the bowl and in some of the incisions on the side of the leg. The groove is filled with Lime powder.

The fragments from mixed deposits demonstrate considerable variation in the details of the rhyta. One handle fragment (Fig. 28h), in a foreign fabric, shows the shape usually associated with these rhyta (Weinberg 1965: 197, Fig. 4), along with fringed, Lime-filled incisions at its base, and a fugitive red powder along the upper exterior of the rim. A very small sherd of the Andesite Burnished variety (A Lot 16, not illustrated) has similarly incised, Lime-filled incisions. Delicate incised lines and dots, with traces of fugitive white and red powder, decorate the Gray Burnished leg (Fig. 28j).

Handles made in the Andesite Burnished variety (Fig. 28a–c) must be from rhyta: no other shape can be associated with them, and they share the fugitive red and white pigments of other rhyta. They suggest two types of handle, both apparently local variations. That in Fig. 28a was made from a coil joined at both ends into a circle (clearly visible in the breaks), whose lower half was incorporated into the wall of the bowl. It is not clear which side is the interior, and the complete object must have been unlike other examples. Another handle (Fig. 28b), preserving part of a joint on one end, was probably attached directly to the upper rim of the bowl. It is made from a rather thin coil; the joint appears not to have been reinforced with additional clay, but attached with a bit of pressure to smear over the joint. The resulting joint may have been too weak to support the weight of the rhyton, with its solid feet. That failure may explain the more elaborate attachment technique used for the circular handle.

Two leg fragments in Andesite Burnished (Fig. 28d–e) have so little modeling that they look like (and could be from) ladles, rather than rhyta. Traces of an incised line around the joint and fugitive paint suggest they are probably from rhyta. The best preserved example, also in Andesite Burnished (Fig. 28f), preserves the stumps of two legs and the indication of at least a third. The legs are painted in wavy lines, in the style of the Ungritted Manganese painters, in a granular whitish pigment that does not react to hydrochloric acid, scratches off easily with a fingernail, but leaves a ghost line in the burnish. This piece was apparently painted before firing. It has traces of fugitive red powder along the unburnished underside of the legs, and a drip of red paint on the interior of the bowl. A triangular area between each set of legs is marked off by an incised line, but on only one ("front") side are additional dots impressed within the triangle.

Whatever these unusual pots represented, they surely had some special meaning, some symbolic, ceremonial, or ritual function. Their specific meaning and use may have varied over the broad geographical area and many ceramic traditions of the places where they are found. Nevertheless, the rhyta seem to have struck a common chord, to have made manifest something understood by, and appealing to the diverse groups who exchanged and copied them, with or without modifications to suit local style and practice. They are a good indicator of the wide sphere of interaction engaged in by peoples of the later Neolithic in the Aegean and Adriatic.

UNGRITTED WARE, MANGANESE PAINTED VARIETY (UgrMn)

This variety accounts for 1% or less of the sample, except in FAN:94, where seven small sherds (Fig. 29c) represent 4% of that unit. It is entirely absent in a number of units (see Tables 1–8). Slight variations in shape and decoration from what was present in FCP 4.1 may suggest the pieces in FCP 4.2 are in situ, rather than kick-ups from the earlier deposit, although that remains a possibility.

Shapes

Jars: Fig. 29b–c
Bowl: Fig. 29a

Each of the three shapes represented, unique to this variety, presents a close analogy to contemporary shapes in other wares and varieties. The small open bowl in

Fig. 29a is very similar to one from FCP 4.1 (Fig.17c) and to another from a mixed deposit in FF1 (Fig. 36f). The shape seems analogous to small shouldered bowls in Lime plus Iron (Fig. 31a–b).

The small necked jug (Fig. 29b) is perhaps analogous to the small carinated necked jars in Andesite Burnished (Fig. 26e–f). The very thin walls of the jar shoulder in Fig. 29c suggest that the curve of the neck may be distorted and preserves a larger diameter than was actually the case. The shoulder directly below the joint is nearly flat, and traces of extra clay added on the interior around the joint and the bottom preserved edge show the potter's concern for stress at points where the curvature was fighting gravity. The angle of the neck cannot be determined from the edge of the joint. The collar could have been vertical (e.g., Fig. 17e–f), making it similar to Lime plus Iron collared jars (e.g., Fig. 30a–c); if it was more inleaning (e.g., Fig. 17g–i), it would have been similar to the Andesite Burnished shouldered jar (Fig. 35a).

Decorative Style

As is true of the earlier examples, the painting is done with a very thin bristled brush, for the delicate, if not terribly neat lines; and a broader brush for highlighting structural parts of the pot.

UNCERTAIN WARES, MANGANESE PAINTED AND POLYCHROME PAINTED VARIETIES (MnPt, Poly)

Other Manganese painted varieties are not represented in FCP 4.2 units. The rare, small and battered pieces of polychrome varieties are surely kickups.

GRAY WARE, BURNISHED VARIETY (GrayB)

The Gray Burnished variety is never present in large quantities, even in FCP 4.1, where it is most common. Few sherds from FCP 4.2 are other than featureless body sherds, and all are worn, making it difficult to be certain whether they are true examples of Gray Burnished or simply pieces of other wares that have fired or been burned to a light gray color. I counted only 33 sherds as Gray Burnished from these deposits. They include three fragments from flat bottoms (Fig. 29e, g), and four rims from open bowls with thickened rims (Fig. 29d, f). The rims are less well-articulated versions of the shape found in FCP 4.1 (Fig. 19e–f), a development also evident in the single example of the shape in Andesite Burnished (Fig. 27b) in this subphase. The Gray Burnished examples lack the carination on the exterior. One of the rims (Fig. 29f) has the beginning of a drill hole on the interior, through the thickest part of the rim. It was abandoned in favor of the thinner body area further from the rim; perhaps still too close to the original break, since the pressure seems to have broken the sherd again.

If the few sherds of the Ungritted Manganese and Gray Burnished varieties are in situ in FCP 4.2, their limited occurrence suggests that interactions with the groups responsible for their manufacture were less frequent and intense than they had been in FCP 4.1.

LIME PLUS IRON WARE, PATTERN PAINTED VARIETY (LiFe)

Lime plus Iron ware dominates the FCP 4.2 assemblage, as it did in the earlier subphase. It was probably produced locally.

Fabric

The fabric is generally the same as in FCP 4.1. Sherds show potters who were not consistent in preparing nonplastics or in the exact proportions and preparation of batches of clay. Some sherds include plentiful Lime, with fragments expanded to 2–3 mm or more; others have smaller Lime particles, unaffected by heat. The hard-fired sherds show very little, if any reaction in acid. The firing temperatures for those pieces were high enough for the calcium to liquify and combine into new chemical compounds (Rice 1987:98).

Building and Surface Finish

Potters, using essentially the same procedures as in the earlier subphase, made more very large vessels, which they smoothed with their fingers and painted. They sometimes omitted, or provided only minimal burnishing even on smaller vessels. A large fragment with a concave vertical curve, probably from the neck of a jar (FAS: 88, not illustrated), must have cracked in the early stages of drying. A clay slurry mixed with a substantial amount of Lime was smeared over the crack to mend it before the pot was painted. The pattern of the air pockets in the breaks of several fragments of large strap handles suggests they were made from coils or folded, flattened slabs, rather than by pulling. Several strap handle scars show that handles were attached to the scraped vessel body, before smoothing the entire vessel.

The consistency of the paint is as variable as in the earlier subphase. Sometimes individual pigment grains are clear. Parts of lines where the pigment is thick tend to be crackling and dull, while lines made with a dilute paint may show no grains and a slight luster. Line quality varies on a single sherd. Individual pigment grains are often large enough to be visible to the naked eye. Many were too large and heavy to stay in suspension in the medium for long; the painter had to stir the mixture frequently to incorporate enough pigment to color the line. If too many of the heavier grains settled out before the painter dipped her brush, the paint would produce a dilute, watery line. If she dipped into the settled sludge, or if too much water had evaporated or been absorbed by the container, she would find a viscous mixture, including the largest grains, that clumped on the brush and produced thick blobs of pigment when she touched brush to pot surface. These are not difficult problems to overcome. The painter could have ground the pigment more finely, or been more careful about stirring and waiting a few seconds for the largest grains to settle out before dipping the brush. That painters did not do this suggests lack of concern with the quality of a painted line, an attitude reflected in the execution of the painted designs as well.

Colors and Firing Practices

The colors of surfaces, paint, and cores, as well as the hardness of sherds, show the full range of variation evident in the earlier subphase. Some sherds, often the very thick ones (1–2 cm) with no traces of paint, are oxidized and quite soft and crumbly. In some units, most of the sherds are light colored. Other units are dominated by hard gray sherds that often appear glassy and are probably vitrified. Color and hardness, not correlated with shape or size, presumably reflect the practices of different potters or the results of different, poorly controlled firings.

Both oxidized and reduced pieces carry decoration that is barely visible unless the sherd is wet. Unlike the manganese and light painted varieties, the Lime plus Iron pattern lines have bonded with the fabric; they have probably not changed in appearance since they were fired. If the first Lime plus Iron potters were aiming for a dark-on-light effect (above, FCP 4.1), it seems unlikely that they would have continued to fire in the same way for generations, with the same low rate of success, if that continued to be their goal. The barely visible patterns they produced with their pigment and firing routine were satisfactory for their purposes. It would have been easier to fire differently or to use another pigment, such as a slip made from one of the red clays exposed everywhere in the southern Argolid, than to continue their high-temperature, fuel-consuming reduction firings. They may have liked the way water brought out the painted decoration on a pot which, when dry, looked undecorated.

Shapes

Jars: Fig. 30
Bowls Fig. 31a–d, g–h
Cup: Fig. 31f, i?
Basins (?): Fig. 31e, i–j
Pedestal: Fig. 31k

Two small collars (Fig. 30a–b) could be from small collared jars comparable to that from FCP 4.1 (Fig. 20a); neither is delicately modeled. Several unillustrated fragments preserve the shoulder and neck joint of larger collared jars, with shoulder and neck diameters around 0.30 m. The tall, narrow collar with concave walls (Fig. 30c) is suggestive of the contemporary necked jar in Andesite Burnished (Figs. 26i, 35a). A small handle fragment with traces of red paint and a delicate horn probably comes from a collared jar (not illustrated, but similar to Fig. 39c).

The most distinctive new feature—occurring on many shapes, small and large, open and closed—is the ridged shoulder (Figs. 30d–e; 31f–h). It was probably produced by running a finger around the still-damp shoulder of the vessel, marking the point of contour change with a subtle ridge. Although the feature was noted on many small, unillustrated sherds in these deposits, the total number of pots represented is not too large to represent the work of a single potter, and, indeed, it may be one potter's signature style.

The FCP 4.2 deposits include numerous sherds from very large pots with walls up to 2 cm thick. Rim sherds suggest some were jars with inleaning rims (Fig. 30f–i); at least some had heavy vertical strap handles from the rim. A thick flat bottom fragment probably comes from one of the very large pots. Measured rim diameters range from 0.26 to 0.50 m. Body sherds are generally too small to measure accurately from the minimal curvature preserved, but clearly some of the pots were quite large. If not firing chimneys (Vitelli 1993:184–185), they would have had capacities similar to the large FCP 3 Low Lime Burnished pot (Fig. 10). When decorated—and all may have been, since small sherds could come from unpainted areas between lines—they have broad horizontal bands at the rim and vertical or diagonal bands on the bodies.

Large open bowls painted with simple broad bands around the rim (Fig. 31e, i–j) may have replaced the bell-shaped basins of FCP 4.1. None preserves a joint, but several probable pedestal fragments in addition to the one illustrated (Fig. 31k) have no other rim shape with which to be associated. Three very small segments from rims of open bowls preserve a slight upward curve along the rim that suggests a tab, perhaps larger than those in Andesite Burnished (Fig. 27c). Many of the sherds from open bowls show extensive abrasive wear on the lower interiors, the only shape that does.

Two small shouldered bowls (Fig. 31a–b), one of which (Fig. 31b) looks as though it once had a collar that was too thin and broke off, are all that remain of the shape that was so common in FCP 4.1. The small sherds could be kickups. Simple open bowls, provided with small strap handles from the rim (Fig. 31c–d), may be their FCP 4.2 analogue, although the simple bowl was also represented in FCP 4.1 (Fig. 22a) and may have had a different function. It is tempting to see in the open shapes illustrated (Fig. 31) the work of two potters, one fond of simple bowls, the other who added a ridged shoulder to differentiate her work.

The small pinch pot in Fig. 31l is unique in FCP 4. It could have been a small cup (although that shape is not otherwise present), a beginner's trial piece, or a hollow figurine comparable to examples noted in FCP 2.5 (Vitelli 1993a:Figs. 82n; 84i–m). While the fabric is comparable to some of the finer pieces of Lime plus Iron, it is also possible that this object *is* one of the pieces of Urf in these deposits (Tables 1–8), redeposited from an FCP 2 context.

Decorative Style

Many more examples than illustrated continue the characteristic zigzag and net motifs (Figs. 30a–c, e; 31a–c) also favored in FCP 4.1. The exact patterns are difficult to reproduce. They show up poorly on the originals to begin with; the painted lines are often just blobs that blend into one another, and the painters themselves seem to have lost track of their motif, so that lines connect or not in almost random ways. The patterns with alternating wavy and straight lines (Figs. 30d, h; 31h, k) remind me of early examples of FCP 2 Urf pots (e.g., Vitelli 1993a: Figs. 29l; 32s–u), as do the triangles along the tip of the pedestal (Fig. 31k). While these motifs are not so complex that they could not have been arrived at independently, Urf sherds littered the cave; they were being dug up, for whatever reason, by the FCP 4.2 occupants, so would have been available to provide inspiration (cf. Bunzel 1972:52). The spirals below a handle (Fig. 31f) and other curvilinear motifs are also new in FCP 4.2.

NO LIME WARE, COARSE VARIETY (NoLiCo)

Fabric

Nonplastics include plentiful red and dark minerals up to 1–2 mm in size, along with smaller black grits, i.e., comparable to the No Lime Coarse variety of FCP 4.1, but in most sherds only the plentiful red nonplastics are noticeable. In the thickest sherds, the red rock fragments may be as large as 5 mm. It may be that two wares are represented here. Potters appear sometimes to have chosen a relatively flat and rounded red material that gives the fabric the texture of barely cooked oatmeal. In other sherds, the red inclusions are quite angular; these may be a different mineral from another source (see captions for Fig. 32a–g).

Building Procedures and Surface Finish

Sherd edges are too crumbly to preserve traces of coil or slab joints, but those are the likely methods of building. Potters scraped the walls to a fairly regular thickness, smoothed most surfaces, and often burnished the exteriors, although the surfaces remain lumpy. Quite a few of the sherds are only 5–6 mm thick, suggesting they derive from relatively small vessels.

Colors and Firing Practices

The majority of sherds are a deep brick red, often with dark clouds. A few pieces are soft and become muddy when wet, i.e., they are barely fired. Most are fired well beyond the slaking point, if still far from vitrified. Cores are more often red than gray. The potters probably fired rather quickly, in an open fire, with pots in direct contact with fuel that was allowed to burn to ash. The pots cooled with access to plentiful oxygen.

Shapes

Saucer: Fig. 32a
Strainer: Fig. 32b
Bowls: Fig. 32c–g
Lug: Fig. 32c

Small pots include a saucer, a small strainer with pre-firing holes poked randomly over the body to within a half centimeter of the rim, and a small bowl with sharply incurving rim and a cupped ledge lug that curves upward (Fig. 32a–c.) A medium-sized bowl (Fig. 32d) has almost vertical walls; the other bowl rims lean sharply inward at the rim, a profile that may reflect potters trying to avoid rim cracks in a heavily tempered clay body as much as functional requirements of the pot itself. More than half a dozen lugs, some large and with minimal cupping, several small and cupped like the one in Fig. 32c, occur in these deposits. No base or bottom sherds were recognized. Since flat bottoms necessarily create an angle between wall and bottom, their absence may point to rounded bottoms on these pots.

CALCITE TEMPERED WARE, COARSE VARIETY (CalCo)

The new and very distinctive coarsely tempered Calcite ware is the clearest marker of the FCP 4.2 deposits. Most of the sherds are quite crumbly and small, so few profiles were recognizable. The ware accounts for 20–30% of the assemblage in these units and in units assigned to the FCP 4/FCP 5 boundary (FCP 4.3).

Fabric

Freshly crushed crystals of calcite up to 3–4 mm in size fill the clay body of this ware. Occasionally the crystals are white, and a few may be rounded (possibly natural inclusions), but the calcite dominates and is unquestionably an intentionally prepared and added temper. It is never powdery.

Building Procedures and Surface Finish

One sherd preserves the concave impression of a coil joint in the break, a centimeter below the rim. Potters scraped the wet clay as they built up the pot, working primarily from the interior. They usually smoothed the surfaces, also while the clay was still quite damp; they may have applied a slip to all pots, since the nonplastics are barely visible at the surface. A number of sherds that probably derive from the same pot have a 1 mm thick, flaky, inclusion-free layer on the exterior surface that suggests a thick slip. The potters gave most, but not all pots at least a cursory burnish before the pot dried to leather-hard. Surfaces are still quite irregular; while the burnish compacted the surface slightly and depressed the nonplastics, subsequent drying removed any luster produced by the process.

Colors and Firing Practices

Colors are generally a deep brick red on the surfaces and through the core, with gray and black clouds on the exterior. Sherds are quite soft (Mohs' 2–3) and crumble easily. Those qualities, as well as the calcite crystals unaffected by heat, point to a short open firing, with temperatures under ca.700°C.

Shapes

Bowls: Fig. 32h–j
Lug: Fig. 32i

The preserved rims suggest deep bowls of various sizes with inleaning rims (Fig. 32h, j). Some sherds have wall thickness under one centimeter, but most are close to 2 cm. They may come from different parts of vessels of the same general size, with thick lower walls, or from vessels of various sizes. The presence of at least one large straight ledge lug (not illustrated), along with several additional examples of cupped lugs like the one in Fig. 32i, suggests the latter. One very thick sherd is lightly carinated with a handle or lug scar at the edge of the break, and a thin walled piece includes a segment of a handle with a bend like an elbow. A few sherds have charred interiors, but it is impossible to tell whether the charring occurred before or after breaking.

FRANCHTHI CERAMIC SUBPHASE 4.3 (FCP 4.3)

The FCP 4 sherds from units assigned to the FCP 4/FCP 5 boundary represent the latest FCP 4 material in the FA sequence. Some of the shapes found in the highest frequency in the underlying FCP 4.2 stratum are absent in the boundary units, while new shapes and features, absent in earlier deposits, occur. The weight of the evidence suggests that material from the boundary units represents a later activity, perhaps different in kind from that in FCP 4.2. The pottery has therefore been assigned to a separate subphase, FCP 4.3.

ANDESITE WARE, BURNISHED VARIETY (AndB)

Fabric

The nonplastic inclusions and general preparation of the clay body are indistinguishable from earlier examples of the ware.

Building Procedures and Surface Finish

Building procedures were, as far as it is possible to judge, unchanged from earlier subphases. A pedestal joint preserves, in the lower break, traces of cutouts, the first evidence for the use of these since FCP 2, when they were standard on most pedestals. The waxy burnished slip is flaking away from a smoothed surface on the carinated jar in Fig. 33b, suggesting the potter allowed the jar to dry too long before applying the slip. Slip was applied with a finger to the handle in Fig. 33c, evident from finger rills in the slip on the underside, which was left unburnished.

Colors and Firing Practices

Several sherds have a greenish tinge to the still basically black surface, while others have a creamy scum. These colors might be the result of some change in, e.g., the fuel, but the numbers are too few to draw firm conclusions. In other respects, the colors suggest firing practices were unchanged from FCP 4.2.

Shapes

Jars: Fig. 33a–b
Bowl: Fig. 33h
Basins: Fig. 33d–f
Pedestal: Figs. 33f–g
Handle: Fig. 33c

Carinated necked jars are present (Figs. 33a–b and several unillustrated). The neck in Fig. 33a, less vertical than in earlier examples, could be an accidental variation. The neck preserves, just below the rim, the edge of a handle, probably like the hourglass handle in Fig. 33c. The carinated body fragment (Fig. 33b) has two pellets on the carination rather than the three or four found on multiple examples from FCP 4.2 contexts (e.g., Figs. 26g–h); otherwise the shape is the same as earlier examples.

The basin rim in Fig. 33e, with part of an applied horizontal pellet, is comparable to the FCP 4.2 example in Fig. 27d, if smaller, but the rim in Fig. 33d is unique. From a small basin, it has a short tab added to the exterior of the rim, leaving a slight ridge along the interior lip. The cutouts in the pedestal below the joint (Fig. 33f) are new for the Andesite Burnished shape. The pedestal tip (Fig. 33g) has a larger diameter than earlier examples; if attached to one of the smaller basin rims, it would have presented an effect different from the slim pedestals on large basins of earlier subphases. The rim from a large deep bowl (Fig. 33h), unique in this ware, does not compare closely to FCP 1 or FCP 2 Andesite rims; this is probably an FCP 4 piece. The broad attachment scar 2 cm below the exterior rim may have carried a broad handle or a relief band.

Decorative Style

In addition to the illustrated examples, five or six small rim fragments preserve traces of vertical or diagonal pattern-burnished stripes. The tail ends of pattern-burnished lines on a basin bowl interior (Fig. 33f) suggest a pattern different from that recorded for earlier units, perhaps simple stripes from the rim, converging near the bottom of the bowl. A few very small sherds retain traces of white paint; not enough is preserved to indicate motifs.

FAS:81 is the latest context in which this ware occurs at Franchthi.

LIME PLUS IRON, PATTERN PAINTED VARIETY (LiFe)

Throughout FCP 4, sherds in the same fabric as the Lime plus Iron, but with no trace of painted decoration, are present in some quantity. The nature of the decorative style in Lime plus Iron makes it likely that some number of these unpainted sherds derive from unpainted areas of painted pots, so I did not create a separate variety for the unpainted examples. It is, however, possible that entirely unpainted pots are present throughout the FCP 4 sequence.

The quantity of sherds without painted decoration increases steadily through time, reaching more than 50% by units in FCP 4.3 (see Table 4.2). It is only in FCP 4.3 that profiles from pots that retain no trace of painted decoration were recovered (Figs. 34b–d, j).

Fabric

Many sherds from FCP 4.3 include fewer Lime and more red nonplastics than do pieces in earlier units. Several low-fired sherds, including the unpainted pot in Fig. 34b, react not at all to hydrochloric acid; these seem to have had no Lime nonplastics.

Building Procedures and Surface Finish

The same basic building procedures are likely to have prevailed, but the potters were even less careful about details than their predecessors. Most surfaces are quite lumpy and irregular, even if burnished. The burnish, rarely more than perfunctory, leaves many areas between troughs untouched. The cup in Fig. 34f cracked at the rim while drying, and the potter smeared a layer of clay slurry over the crack before painting the pot. The paint, especially over the mended area, is barely visible, even when wet. The collared jar in Fig. 34h is, besides pockmarked by the expanded lime nonplastics, extremely lumpy, with such variable wall thickness that the profile differs at every point on the sherd. Where traces of the handle attachment remain on the neck and shoulder, extra support clay was added on the interior

Table 4.2. Average percentage of unpainted Lime plus Iron, calculated by number and by weight, for all FCP 4 subphases.

Subphase	Percent by number	Percent by weight
FCP 4.1	37%	31%
FCP 4.2	46%	47%
FCP 4.3	55%	56%

and not scraped off when the handle had set. A few pots, such as the large collared jar in Fig. 34k, are as carefully finished as any earlier examples.

Colors and Firing Procedures

While some sherds look glassy and are covered with expanded Lime nonplastics, the majority were fired to lower temperatures. They may be marked with pits where the Lime has been dissolved (probably by the pot-menders' acid bath in the field), but they are less hard, less frequently (over)fired to a blue gray color. Most have been fired in an incompletely oxidizing fire that produced a grayish paint on a yellow-buff ground with an occasional lighter or darker cloud; the length of firing and the maximum temperatures reached were generally less than earlier. The lower-fired, softer sherds of Lime plus Iron are much closer to the coarse varieties, which increase in these units.

Shapes

Jars: Fig. 34 h, k, m
Saucer(?): Fig. 34a
Cups: Fig. 34d–f
Bowls: Fig. 34b, g, i
Double Bowl: Fig. 34c
Handles: Fig. 34j, l–m

The round-bodied collared jars (Fig. 34h, k) may be a new variation on the shape (or a return to an earlier, FCP 4.1 version, see Fig. 20a), not clearly attested in the previous subphase. The ridge-shouldered bowls (Fig. 34b, g, i), in the FCP 4.2 tradition, could be kickups. The unpainted strap-handle fragment with a small relief horn (Fig. 34j) is similar to a painted example from FCP 4.2, and the large jar with a strap handle (Fig. 34m) could come from a shape comparable to the large jars in FCP 4.2.

The remaining shapes—small cups (Fig. 34e–f); a slightly asymmetrical saucer, with two pre-firing holes poked just below the rim (Fig. 34a); a deep piriform cup (Fig. 34d) and joined double bowls (Fig. 34c)—are new shapes, not previously represented in this or other FCP 4 wares at Franchthi. A similar double bowl fragment, with painted decoration and a basket handle, was found at Corinth (Phelps 1975: Fig. 41.27). Simple open bowls and basins of various sizes, which made up a large proportion of earlier assemblages, are completely absent from this group.

Decorative Style

The most noteworthy aspect of the painted decoration is its absence on the four illustrated pieces (Fig. 34b–d, j). In other respects, the decoration is close to that of earlier subphases.

NO LIME WARE, COARSE VARIETY (NoLiCo)

Sherds of No Lime Coarse are plentiful, but few profiles are preserved. The illustrated examples (Fig. 33i–k) are comparable to earlier ones. Ledge and cupped lugs are present. Sherds as much as 2 cm thick may suggest the presence of very large pots.

CALCITE TEMPERED WARE, COARSE VARIETY (CalCo)

The Calcite Coarse variety is well represented by sherds; none is sufficiently large to provide a profile. Thick sherds from, presumably, large pots are rarely burnished. One short rim fragment preserves traces of a painted stripe along the tip.

FCP 4 VARIETIES FROM MIXED DEPOSITS

A corollary of Murphy's Law decrees that the best-preserved profiles and most intriguing sherds derive from disturbed contexts! Figs. 35–42 include the drawings of probable FCP 4 wares and varieties that fall into this category. Some are closely paralleled by examples from good FA Balk contexts; some which remain unique could be from subphases not represented within FA. Their probable relationships to FCP 4 examples are suggested below.

ANDESITE WARE, BURNISHED VARIETY (AndB)

An almost complete profile of an open bowl with thickened rim and flat bottom (Pl. 3b, Fig. 35h) fills in information for the many similar rim fragments from FCP 4.1 (Fig. 16h–m). The interior pattern burnished decoration consists of a series of crosshatched lines that cover the interior below the rim. The rim in Fig. 35d is a unique miniature version of this shape.

The open bowl is essentially absent in FCP 4.2, perhaps replaced by the basin (Fig. 35i–j), which first occurs then (Fig. 27d–e) and continues into FCP 4.3 (Fig. 33e). A horizontal relief strip below the rim (Fig. 35j) seems to have been a standard way of marking some of these vessels (Figs. 27d; 33e).

Abrasive wear has removed the surface and several millimeters of the subsurface on the lowest portion of the interior of one basin (Fig. 35i). Body fragments from FCP 4 deposits with similarly located heavy wear may well come from basins. The wear patterns are comparable to those on FCP 2 basins, although the small crisscrossing scratches evident on the Urf examples are not discernible with a 10x lens on the FCP 4 pieces (Vitelli 1993:215). Nevertheless, the similarity of shape and the fact of heavy wear confined to the lowest portion of basin interiors point to a degree of continuity in the use and meaning of pedestalled basins over a very long time, and in spite of significant changes in Neolithic societies.

The shouldered jar fragment in Fig. 35a would seem to belong with a rim like that in Fig. 26i, from FCP 4.2. A similar shouldered jar occurs earlier in the Gray Burnished variety (Fig. 19c); it may have inspired the Andesite potters.

The apparently substantial FCP 4 deposits in Trench A produced the collared carinated jar in Fig. 35f, with close parallels in FCP 4.2 (Fig. 26k–m), and an apparently unique fragment of a ring base (Fig. 35c). The resting tip of the base appears to have been ground or worn down after firing; probably it was originally a pedestal base that broke and continued to be used in its shorter form. In that case, it is comparable to examples from FCP 4.2 onward (Figs. 27g–i; 33f–g).

A small sherd in typical Andesite Burnished fabric suggests a shape that is unique at Franchthi (Fig. 35g), a nozzle. The carinated body to which the nozzle is attached has a small diameter (ca. 0.085 m). The nozzle was formed by attaching a conical pellet of clay at the carination and piercing both pellet and body wall. The exterior is well burnished. A roughly similar concept is illustrated from Sitagroi Phase I (Renfrew et al., eds. 1986: Fig. 11.8 #11, 12), there on apparently much larger vessels. Nozzles illustrated from Saliagos also are apparently from larger vessels than the Franchthi example (Evans and Renfrew 1968:Fig. 59). The Franchthi example, by its size, seems designed to provide small amounts of (a prized?) liquid, slowly. It may have been designed as an infant feeding bottle. The sherd was found in Trench A, Basket 30, for which 80% of the pottery was discarded; the notebook descriptions suggest nothing later than FCP 4, and ca. 30 other sherds of the Andesite Burnished variety are among the saved pieces. It is not impossible that the nozzle is intrusive, but all evidence suggests it is a legitimate FCP 4 piece.

UNGRITTED WARE, MANGANESE PAINTED VARIETY (UgrMn)

Some of the pieces of the Ungritted Manganese variety from mixed deposits have close parallels with FA Balk material. The bowl in Fig. 36f is similar to an example from FCP 4.1 (Fig. 17c), and closer still to an FCP 4.2 example (Fig. 29a), although the unstratified example is painted in the Lime plus Iron style of single-stroke zigzags. The collar rim with strap handle (Fig. 36d) compares closely with examples in FCP 4.1 (Fig. 17f–g). One sherd (Fig. 36e) probably comes from a neck of a vessel of the same shape. Its decoration, solid ovals with feet or fringe, is close to that on a rim (Fig. 36b), and similar to a Lime plus Iron handle from FCP 4.3 (Fig. 34l).

The other three rims (Fig. 36a–c) could represent

variations on the same jar shape, although the profiles are slightly different and the diameters a bit larger. That in Fig. 36c, with its deeply concave upper body profile, suggests a carinated bowl, a shape otherwise unattested in this ware. Three carinated fragments (Fig. 36h–j), like carinated body fragments from FCP 4.1 (Fig. 17a–b), are scraped without further finishing on the interior, suggesting closed rather than open shapes. The handle stump at the carination in Fig. 36i is repeated in an FCP 4.1 example (Fig. 17a). The motif on the upper (?) body of Fig. 36j is the same as that on an FCP 4.1 jar neck (Fig. 17h).

A collared or necked jar (Fig. 36g) is not closely matched, either in shape or decoration, by any stratified example. The shape is closest to the small jar from FCP 4.2 (Fig. 29b), the decoration has no match at Franchthi.

UNCERTAIN WARES, MANGANESE PAINTED VARIETY (MnPt)

Manganese painted varieties other than Ungritted are rare in FCP 4. Fig. 37 illustrates the Manganese painted sherds from contexts other than FA. Most (Fig. 37a–b, d, f–g) find their best parallels in FCP 3. Several, however, have greater affinities with FCP 4. A shouldered bowl (Fig. 37c) is similar to a manganese painted sherd from FCP 4.1 (Fig. 18a), but closer in shape and decoration to a Lime plus Iron example from FCP 4.1 (Fig. 22e). The painted lines in the unstratified piece appear to have the characteristics of manganese paint; conceivably it is a reduced iron oxide, and the bowl actually a piece of Lime plus Iron.

The carinated body sherd in Fig. 37e, well burnished on interior and exterior surfaces, is probably from an open shape. The zigzags of the pattern are painted in a manganese-rich pigment, but in the Lime plus Iron style, i.e., with the brush lifted after each leg; the small, relatively neat zigzags are matched in an unillustrated body sherd in Lime plus Iron from an FCP 4.1 context (FAN:110). Similarly, a body sherd from a large pot with the stump of a strap handle (Fig. 37h) is from a shape not exactly matched elsewhere at Franchthi. It is decorated in a manner reminiscent of the style of Ungritted Manganese variety painters, with a series of connected, short wavy lines (e.g., Fig.17f, g), a style that occurs in a Manganese Painted sherd from an FCP 4.1 context (Fig. 18c). Both unstratified body sherds are probably nonlocal products.

UNCERTAIN WARE, GRAY BURNISHED VARIETY (GrayB)

The Gray Burnished variety sherds from mixed deposits, like the FA examples, include no or very few Lime inclusions, usually well under 1 mm in size. Of the profiles, only a basin rim (Fig. 38f) has a good stratified parallel, from FCP 4.1 (Fig. 19i), and the latter lacks the impressed dents that line the interior of the rim from Trench A.[10] The remaining shapes are more or less similar to FCP 4 shapes in other wares, but without close matches.

The small collared jar in Fig. 38d, the most completely preserved example of the Gray Burnished variety from Franchthi, is the only one with traces of painted decoration. A narrow band of light paint encircles the neck joint, while the vertical stripes on the neck are visible only as ghost lines interrupting the burnish. The shoulder area is covered with high relief pellets arranged in roughly diagonal lines from the joint to the point of maximum diameter. The uppermost preserved edge turns out slightly, suggesting a rim type not otherwise known from FCP 4. A body sherd with a high relief pellet from FAN:102 (not illustrated) might have come from the same or a similar pot; this suggests an FCP 4.1 date for the pellet-studded jar. The jar shoulder in Fig. 38e comes from a similar, undecorated shape.

The potters who made Gray Burnished pots were fond of small handles (Fig. 38a–b, h; Fig. 19a). A handle below the rim (Fig. 38b) is the only horizontal handle in FCP 4, probably on the neck of a small collared jar. A large jar (Fig. 38h), with a more sharply inleaning rim than any other, may not have had an articulated neck joint. The small piriform jar (Fig. 38c), with a slight adjustment of the diameter, is not unlike the jar in FCP 4.1 (Fig 19a); it finds another local parallel in an early Lime plus Iron jar (Fig. 21e). The large shallow basin (Fig. 38g), unlike anything in FCP 4, may be post-Neolithic.

LIME PLUS IRON WARE, PATTERN PAINTED VARIETY (LiFe)

Several aspects of the jar in Fig. 39a suggest it is a late example, although the continuously curving profile is comparable to early FCP 4.1 examples (Fig. 21c, e–f). Late features include the relatively thick walls with slightly out-turned lip tip (Fig. 34d, k), the attempt to mend a pre-firing rim crack with a clay slurry (e.g., Fig. 34f), the handle attached to a surface still rough from the building stages, and the very perfunctory burnish. The rim mend was not entirely successful: a post-firing drill hole points to a later attempt to mend along the same line of weakness. The breaks on one side are worn down from abrasion, suggesting the piece served a useful purpose, not necessarily as an intact pot.

The large collared jar with a strap handle from the shoulder to somewhere on the neck (Fig. 39b) could come from any of the FCP 4 subphases. Another jar with a rounded bottom is probably from FCP 4.2 or later, since thick fragments decorated with broad brush strokes are especially common in the later subphases. Strap handles with a small relief horn (Figs. 39c; 40e) should also be FCP 4.2 or later in date. The example in Fig. 40e is from a smaller pot than the other examples, perhaps one of the ridge shouldered bowls (Fig. 40a–c), which are also from FCP 4.2 or later. The example in Fig. 40d lacks the ridge on the shoulder, also a feature of small, relatively deep bowls from FCP 4.3 (e.g., Fig. 34d–f).

The small "saucer" in Fig. 40f compares well in its size and in the two small tabs on the rim with an Andesite Burnished bowl from FCP 4.2 (Fig. 27c), which is not well enough preserved to tell whether or not it also had a base. The Lime plus Iron example is slightly asymmetrical, taller and with a slightly sharper curve on one side than the other, the attachment scar less than circular. Another sherd from the same lot (not illustrated) has two rim tabs, and a diameter that measures 0.14 m on one side, 0.16 m on the other; wall heights and carinations differ from one side of the sherd to the other. That we have two examples with the same asymmetries suggest the potter(s) made them intentionally, but what the intact piece looked like remains unclear. It seems unlikely they could be part of a "ladle," the shape suggested by another sherd with a shallow bowl (Fig. 40g); all may be related to the fragment in Fig. 34a, from FCP 4.3, with its two small pre-firing holes just below the lip.

A number of shouldered bowl fragments (Fig. 41a–e), one preserving almost the complete profile (Fig. 41e), derive from mixed deposits. Parallels for the general shape are most common in FCP 4.1 (Fig. 22c–h), but also occur in FCP 4.2 (Fig. 31a–b). Two bowls include relief pellets on the rim (Fig. 41d–e), along with the painted decoration. The small bowl in Fig. 41a, while similar in profile to the others, includes the stump of an attachment that was in higher relief than the pellets on the larger bowls; the outer edge of the rim curves outward just beyond the point of attachment. This bowl may be half of a double bowl, similar to that in Fig. 34c (FCP 4.3), the stump a part of the basket handle that spanned the connecting ridge.

Two small bowls (Fig. 41f–g), which preserve complete profiles, have no exact parallels from FA. While the potter scraped the interior of the one in Fig 41f fairly well, she painted the exterior directly on its lumpy building surface. The walls are thick for such a small pot and the bend at the rim was probably accidental, since it does not continue all around the pot. The sloppiness of the workmanship points to a late, probably FCP 4.3 date. If not one of the finest examples of a Lime plus Iron bowl, it nevertheless received heavy use. The interior, especially on the very bottom, is worn down below the original surface. Part of this pot burned after it broke. The paint, now completely invisible on the oxidized pieces, shows up as streaky red on the gray, reduced ones. The other bowl (Fig. 41g) is also rather sloppily made, its bottom neither flat nor centered.

One basin from a mixed deposit (Fig. 42c) is very close to examples from FCP 4.1 (Figs. 23a–b; 24b–g). The two larger fragments (Fig. 42a–b) are closer in concept to the simple bowls of FCP 4.2 (Fig. 31e, i–j). The differences may simply reflect the work of different potters. The narrow pedestals in Fig. 42d–e seem more likely to have carried the bell basins of FCP 4.1 (Fig. 24h–j).

Decorative Style

The painters were very fond of floating groups of zigzags (Figs, 40a–g; 41c–e, g; 42d). The motif may have had particular significance—it is a rare piece of Lime plus Iron that has none—or the choice may represent lack of imagination on the part of the painters. A shouldered bowl with a single snaky line on the interior (Fig. 41e), and the only basin at Franchthi decorated on the exterior of the bowl and pedestal (Fig. 42b), stand out as unusual pieces.

Table 4.3. FCP 4 pottery distribution by subphase

Subphase	Approximate Depth	Total grams without Residue	Total grams of FCP 4	Grams of Coarse Wares	% Coarse of Total FCP 4
FCP 4.1	0.40–0.50 m	25,229	12,933	2,204	17%
FCP 4.2	0.15–0.20 m	20,523	18,666	6,555	35%
FCP 4.3	ca. 0.10 m	14,043	11,566	3,880	34%

SUMMARY AND DISCUSSION

Of the ca. 400 kg of pottery excavated from undisturbed deposits inside the cave, FCP 4 wares and varieties account for only ca. 43 kg, or 11%. Very little was recovered from the disturbed deposits in the central trenches (H, H1, H2) or from the GG1 area. As they were in FCP 3, FCP 4 discard activities were largely confined to A, FA, and FF1.

FCP 4.1

In FCP 4.1 units, only 51% of the pottery recovered derives from FCP 4 wares and varieties. Nearly half is redeposited material from FCP 1 through 3. The relatively small amount of FCP 4 pottery (Table 4.3), however, includes considerable diversity. Seven varieties are present (Andesite Burnished, Ungritted Manganese Painted, other Manganese Painted, Polychrome, Gray Burnished, Lime plus Iron, No Lime Coarse), and the range of shapes is greater than in either of the following subphases (Figs. 77–79). Of the seven varieties, three—Andesite Burnished, Lime plus Iron, No Lime Coarse—are probably local products.

Andesite ware is present in FCP 1 and FCP 2, as well as FCP 4. While a minor ware in the FCP 4 assemblage, it is consistently present in low frequencies throughout the phase. The nonplastics were probably intentionally added by the potters rather than naturally occurring, so they could have come from some distance; yet the recurrence of a fabric that is not, to my knowledge, attested in any quantity elsewhere in the Peloponnese suggests a likely local origin.[11] It also suggests a relationship, however temporally distant, between the FCP 2 and FCP 4 occupants of the cave.

Lime plus Iron ware is arguably a local product: it dominates the FCP 4 assemblage; it includes very large vessels that would have been difficult to transport over long distances—and would have occupied substantial space on any sea-going vessel; and it includes shapes and decorative motifs that are essentially unattested elsewhere. The patterns are executed in an iron-oxide-rich paint, at a time when most potters at other sites were using manganese pigments. The clay body has inclusions similar to—if usually larger than—those in FCP 2 Urf ware, and very close to many of the FCP 5 varieties. That also suggests the use of locally available materials.[12]

The No Lime Coarse ware is also likely to be a local product because of the size of the pots. The raw materials were available locally—a Lime-free ware occurs throughout FCP 1 and FCP 2. The rough finishing and often thick, heavy shapes would not appear to make them appropriate as a trade item. Preliminary studies of coarse wares in Thessaly suggest that, unlike the more finely constructed and finished varieties, coarse wares rarely left the area of production (Schneider et al. 1994:69).

The other varieties in FCP 4—Gray Burnished, Ungritted Manganese Painted, Manganese Painted, Polychrome—occur in such small frequencies at Franchthi that they are likely to have been brought from elsewhere. Some ingredients also point to the use of non-local resources.[13] Only the Gray Burnished and Ungritted Manganese varieties survive into FCP 4.2; all are gone by FCP 4.3.

In addition to the diversity of varieties and shapes in FCP 4.1, the deposit is marked by a relatively large number of pedestalled basins, especially in Lime plus Iron, but represented also in Andesite Burnished, Gray Burnished, and Polychrome. Noteworthy too are shapes shared by several, but not all varieties (Fig. 77). The straight-sided, open bowl with thickened interior lip occurs in Andesite Burnished and Gray Burnished, but never in the other varieties. The small shouldered bowl in Andesite Burnished is quite close to examples in Lime plus Iron. The carinated bowl in Manganese Painted has a close match in Lime plus Iron. Larger collared jars with strap handles are similar, if varying in details, in Gray Burnished, Ungritted Manganese Painted, and Lime plus Iron. The small carinated, necked jar ocurs only in Ungritted Manganese in FCP 4.1. In FCP 4.2, it is the most common Andesite Burnished shape. Motifs and their execution are also shared occasionally between two or more varieties.

Shared elements are also evident with pottery of various traditions throughout the Peloponnese and well beyond; some pottery may have come from more distant sources than anything in FCP 2. For all the sharing, however, each variety at Franchthi has its own shapes and peculiarities of execution. Along with a discrete fabric, these features point to different potters as responsible for each variety, and to some other factor(s) that kept each tradition separate from the others, even if the potters practiced at the same site.

FCP 4.2

The much shallower FCP 4.2 deposit produced substantially more FCP 4 pottery (Table 4.3), and very little pottery from phases earlier than FCP 4. The heavy carbon flaking in the deposit, the high percentage of fish bones (Rose forthcoming), the near-doubling of the frequency of coarse varieties, and the almost complete absence of pedestalled basins point to a difference in the nature of the activities responsible for the deposit. The strange rhyta, in both the foreign and local Andesite Burnished varieties, seem most clearly associated with this deposit; but these may have appeared at the end of FCP 4.1. Gray Burnished is represented only by several of the bowls with thickened rims, a shape that has all but disappeared in Andesite Burnished, although that ware is represented by more shapes than previously. New shape features include a tab rim and small pellets on the top of strap handles. Generally, Andesite Burnished is the most carefully made and finished of the varieties in FCP 4, the potters more practiced, observant, and creative than others.

Manganese Painted examples in the Uncertain ware and Polychrome painted pieces are no longer present in FCP 4.2. Curiously, while the frequency of Ungritted Manganese Painted is lower than in FCP 4.1, the same three shapes are represented: a medium large collared jar, a small carinated necked jar, and a flat-rimmed bowl. Since these seem to have been brought to Franchthi from elsewhere, this trio may have been a meaningful set—perhaps the minimum required for a traveler's meals, a particular kind of exchange, or a specific ceremony.

Shared features among the varieties, within and among subphases, are again evident (Figs. 77–79). The impressive size of some Lime plus Iron pots is noteworthy, as is the diversity, in all subphases, of the simple shapes and sizes in the coarse varieties. A small sieve is among those shapes. The new Calcite tempered coarse ware is used to make the same shapes produced in No Lime Coarse ware.

FCP 4.3

FCP 4.3 is represented by a very shallow deposit that, nevertheless, produced nearly as much FCP 4 pottery, by weight, as the half meter deep FCP 4.1 deposit (Table 4.3), along with a substantial amount of earlier sherds. Only the local varieties of FCP 4 pots remain, however, and they produced very few profiles (Fig.79). Much of the assemblage is made up of small, crumbly fragments of coarse wares. While some of the pottery may be residual from FCP 4.2, some is surely new. Shapes such as open bowls in Lime plus Iron, common in the earlier subphase, are absent in FCP 4.3. New shapes appear, notably a double bowl and the cups which are the smallest pots in the entire FCP 4 assemblage. Unpainted pots are more common. Generally, the Lime plus Iron potters spent less time in FCP 4.3 building and finishing their pots, and less time and fuel firing them, practices also characteristic of the later FCP 5 potters.

The C-14 dates and general similarities in pottery suggest that little time elapsed between FCP 4.2 and FCP 4.3. Similarities in the pottery between FCP 4.1 and FCP 4.2 are close enough that no great amount of time is likely to have separated them—perhaps a generation, conceivably less. The duration of any subphase is difficult to estimate. The amount of pottery and its apparent confinement to one portion of the cave, rather than more evenly distributed as it was in FCP 2, may suggest a relatively short period of activity. Regular, ongoing occupation and traffic throughout the cave probably would have scattered material.

If the trenches adjacent to FA Balk had roughly the same quantity of FCP 4 pottery as FA, the total weight of sherds from the excavated area would be ca. 135–150 kg. Unexcavated areas might contribute another 250–300 kg. If we allow for ca. 10 large pots weighing up to 10 kg apiece, and consider 1 kg as an average weight for the remaining very small to medium large pieces, we arrive at a very rough estimate of 300–350 pots to represent all of the FCP 4 activity. For a group of roughly 100–300 (Jameson et al. 1994:542), that is a small number of pots for a stay of many seasons, assuming pottery was used in normal daily activities. The group at Franchthi may have been smaller during FCP 4. It may have been a large group staying for a brief time. Or it may be that pottery was used only in specific kinds of activities, and therefore not required in large quantities.

NOTES

1. I achieved one FCP 4 shape—a bowl with thickened rim (e.g., Figs. 16h–m)—by starting with a thick but slightly hollowed, cone-shaped lump of quite stiff clay and paddling upward around the perimeter to increase the height. After paddling the bottom flat, I inverted the bowl and found that the pressure from sitting on the rim as I paddled had produced a thickened rim. Smoothing it between my moistened fingers, with my thumb on the exterior, produced a profile quite like that of the Franchthi bowls.

2. Manganese is toxic to humans. Absorbed through the skin and by inhalation, it may, in large enough doses, bring on symptoms resembling Parkinson's disease. Prehistoric potters, and the users of the pots, may not have lived long enough to be affected by it (Stecher et al. 1968:642 "Manganese").

3. In the early field seasons, we referred to these distinctive sherds as "chocolate on pistachio," reflecting the common excavation obsession with food, as well as the colors.

4. The same motif is present on a number of sherds on exhibit in the Diros Neolithic Museum, executed in a black manganese pigment on what appears, through the glass case, to be a white slipped background. Several examples of the motif occur on the collars of large jars. I recognized no examples of specific FCP 4 wares and varieties in the Diros museum, but many general similarities with FCP 4 and FCP 5 shapes and decoration are visible.

5. At temperatures above ca. 800°C, calcium carbonate (Lime) decomposes into calcium oxide. After cooling, calcium oxide hydrates by combining with water in the atmosphere, and expands. The expansion can exert enough pressure within the vessel wall to force flakes, or spalls, off the surface, or even to crumble the pot (Shepard 1968:30; Grimshaw 1980:280). Small spalls removed by expanding Lime at the surface of a pot are called Lime "pops." In most of the FCP 4 examples, the Lime has expanded and become powdery, but true spalls around the inclusion are rare.

6. Several joining sherds from a large unstratified Low Lime Burnished jar (Fig. 9c) were exposed to a fire after the vessel broke and fired to the same light gray color as the sherds of the Gray Burnished variety. The waxy quality of the black burnished portions of the pot is absent from the gray-fired pieces, perhaps because of the higher temperatures to which they were exposed. The only fire other than a potter's that I can think of in an early prehistoric context that might have needed such high temperatures is a cremation fire. While cremation burials have been found at, e.g., Late Neolithic Plateia Magoula Zarkou, accompanied by Gray ware pots (Gallis 1982), no evidence for cremation burials in the later Neolithic has been found at Franchthi.

7. I did not count the sherds of each color and combination, but my impression and notes indicate the black-on-gray are in the majority.

8. These temperatures require an enclosure or kiln, which also has to be heated, along with the pots. In the four or five successful attempts we have made to reach such high temperatures, it has taken us 8–12 hours of constant stoking, using assorted hardwoods up to 7–8 cm in diameter. If we had a fast, hot-burning fuel such as good dry pine, I suspect that we could cut the time considerably; because pine burns quickly, substantial quantities, not readily available to us in Indiana, are needed.

9. A similarly shaped handle occurs in black burnished examples in Thessaly, e.g., at Tsangli, with white painted decoration (Wace and Thompson 1912: Fig. 55a), but without the pellet.

10. Phelps notes several Gray ware basins with "notched" rims from Corinth (Phelps 1975:Figs. 30.3, 30.14, 31.29). Notched and dented rims are common in Thessaly, in black burnished varieties.

11. The single sherd of this FCP 4 ware analyzed by Jones falls within his "local" group (Jones 1986: Fig. 4.3, #48).

12. Jones analyzed three samples by OES. The first two fall within his "local" group, the third, #42, just slightly outside it (Jones 1986: Fig. 4.3, #40-42).

13. Jones analyzed one sample of Ungritted Manganese Painted (#44), one Manganese Painted (#43), and one Gray Burnished (#45); all fall within his "local" group (Jones 1986: Fig. 4.3)

CHAPTER FIVE

Franchthi Ceramic Phase 5 (FCP 5): The Pottery

INTRODUCTION

Most FCP 5 pottery has generally been described as "coarse" (Jacobsen 1969:369, 1973b:271; Diamant 1974:65, 69). That is the result, more than any other single factor, of the firing practices—short firings that barely altered the clay body, so the resulting soft pots scratch and break easily into crumbly sherds, often very small. Some firings were less effective than others. In several trenches excavators noted rounded red lumps that dissolve in water. These probably were remnants of pieces of pottery, fired so quickly that chemical and physical transformation was sufficient to prevent them from slaking back to the plastic state, but not enough to prevent their later disintegration. Other firings, slightly longer or hotter, produced somewhat harder and more durable pots. These are the pieces that survive, often with little of the original surface intact.

Classes

The clay bodies are highly variable; indeed, they seem to have been prepared almost randomly. Both calcareous and non-calcareous clay bodies were used, with no consistent pattern or correlation apparent between clay body and any other feature. Most sherds show some reaction in hydrochloric acid, but the reaction can often be traced to one or two apparently stray lumps of carbonate.

Wares

The variation in clay body from pot to pot, even among sherds from the same pot, is so great that I have been unable to establish clear patterns that might distinguish particular wares. I describe here a "main" fabric that in a general way applies to the bulk of the pottery, especially the larger, apparently undecorated pieces. Brief descriptions of each sherd illustrated are included in the figure captions, and noteworthy deviations from the main fabric are mentioned in the text.

Most of the FCP 5 pots were made from a clay body whose preparation varied with the potter, the occasion, and, perhaps, the pot she set out to make. The clay itself most often fired to a deep red (2.5 YR 4–6/8); given the nature of the firing and the color of the minimally fired sherds, the clay was probably also a deep red when raw. Nonplastics generally are quite plentiful, but only up to 1 mm in size, with the occasional large pebble of 3–5 mm, usually evident in a break and the likely cause of the break. Most sherds include some Lime, but not in large quantities or sizes. Red and gray inclusions, sometimes angular, sometimes rounded, make up the majority. Some of these may be grog, ground-up bits of fired clay, possibly potsherds.[1] At least one FCP 5 sherd included a small retouched piece of obsidian.

Many sherds also have numerous small holes and depressions on the surfaces and in the breaks that look vaguely vegetal in origin, sometimes rounded like seeds, sometimes long and narrow, like bits of straw or grass.[2] They appear to have been made by something organic that burned out in firing, contributing to the light weight of many sherds.

The size, number, composition, and irregular distribution of nonplastics suggest that potters may have dug their red clay in several different locations, sometimes finding a clean clay, sometimes a gritty one.[3] They generally added temper, perhaps not always the same kind, and they worked in a place where other activities had already contributed plentiful small particles of all kinds that might accidentally be included as the potter worked the clay. Very thick sherds (over 2 cm) usually have more and larger nonplastics, suggesting that the potters were aware of the primary role of temper, but were not as particular as their predecessors about which temper they used.

Duhon analyzed, with X-ray diffraction techniques, one example of a melting red clay lump, presumably a sherd from a poorly fired pot, from Trench L5 on Paralia, in conjunction with her study of the Paralia soil samples (Wilkinson and Duhon 1990: 199 n. 1, and Fig. 23). She found that it included smectite, along with the other clay minerals illite and kaolinite. Interestingly, the sediments from the FCP 5 deposits in L5 were also distinguished from other sediments on Paralia by the presence of smectite (Wilkinson and Duhon 1990:36, 46), possibly derived from other disintegrated sherds, or from raw clay supplies intended for use in pottery-making.

The smectite or montmorillonite group of clays "tend to be common in recent sediments and are major components of soils in arid regions" (Rice 1987:48). They occur widely, with many different specific compositions and interesting properties that affect how they may be worked and the characteristics of the finished product. Some signs in the FCP 5 pots suggest that the potters intentionally chose clays with the properties of smectite.

Smectites tend to be very sticky, with high plasticity and strength in both wet and dry states (Rice 1987:49). The stickiness of the FCP 5 clays is often evident in the quality and texture of unsmoothed surfaces. The plasticity and wet strength would have made the clay relatively easy for inexperienced potters, which the FCP 5 potters seem to have been (below), to form into even large vessels. On the other hand, smectites tend to absorb large quantities of water with attendant swelling, and subsequent high shrinkage on drying and firing (Rice 1987:87), which would explain the higher numbers of sherds with shrinkage cracks and other shrinkage-related problems than in any previous phase. It might also explain the poor fit between clay body and the pigments used for surface elaboration. Smectites dehydrate at lower temperatures than other clays, ca. 100–200°C; they are particularly prone to cracking and explosion if heated too rapidly (Rice 1987:87), which may explain the low temperature firings used by the FCP 5 potters. Many of their pots may have broken during firing.

Some smectites have an unusual ability to absorb coloring agents (Grimshaw 1980:140). If this is true of the FCP 5 clays, it might explain why some sherds are very red throughout; some have a red glow on one surface yet retain no trace of pigment grains; and others are very pale, especially on the surfaces. The red glow and pale surfaces may be all that remains of a former surface coating.

Colors and Firing Practices

The firing practices of the FCP 5 potters had a major effect on the durability of their pots and on what has remained for us to analyze. Because firing influences so much of what we can now see, it is discussed before the procedures for building and surface finishing.

The vast majority of sherds scratch easily by Mohs' 3. Many have dark black cores and light, usually red surfaces; interiors are occasionally gray or black. A whitish bloom is not uncommon. Dark firing clouds are a regular feature. Sherds tend to break into fragments ca. 3–4 cm in maximum dimension. The central core of thick sherds sometimes appears minimally fired, with a tendency to dissolve in water. These features point to a short, relatively low temperature firing with the pots in direct contact with fuel. The deep black cores could indicate that pots were sometimes fired before they had been allowed to dry.[4] The fuel was allowed to burn down to ash, exposing the pots to a fully oxidizing atmosphere as they cooled. Accumulations of ash and bits of charcoal in contact with the cooling pot produced firing clouds. The white bloom is probably from salts, from clay that was dug near the coast, from slaking with salt water, or from the fuel.

Duhon's analysis of the single melting sherd from L5 noted the presence of kaolinite. From its presence she concluded: "prolonged heating at temperatures of 400°C or greater is ruled out. Brief heating (ca. 15 minutes) to the 400–500°C range, however, would not have destroyed the kaolinite" (Wilkinson and Duhon 1990:199 n. 1). The analysis appears to confirm a generally short, low-temperature firing. The sherds that have not disintegrated must have been fired somewhat longer, and to slightly higher temperatures. Pots with thicker walls take longer to heat up; if fired in the same fire with smaller, thin-walled pots, they would emerge less hard-fired than the smaller vessels—the pattern observed in the FCP 5 thick- and thin-walled sherds.[5]

Pots subjected to such brief firings are fragile and break easily. The FCP 5 pots could not have withstood frequent moving and heavy use. Large pots with thick walls (e.g., Figs. 47e, 55e) are the least well fired. They would have been heavy, even when empty, and fragile—functional if left in place for use, but unlikely to have been transported over any great distance. They were probably made locally.

The FCP 5 potters may have chosen their clay because it was easy to work, because it required only minimal firing time and fuel, because it was readily available, or for some other reason(s). Pots that would endure heavy, long-term use were not, apparently, the potters' priority. Executing the whole process quickly, from digging clay to finished pot, may have been their foremost goal.

Building Procedures

Regardless of the surface finish (the variety), all potters used much the same building procedures. Small cups were generally pinched from a solid lump of clay, the pinching depressions still palpable on many (e.g., Figs. 50b, 59a–b). Lugs, horns, handles, and other applied elements were also formed by pinching and modeling solid lumps or coils of clay (e.g., Figs. 47a–e, 55e).

The potters started larger vessels with a roughly formed disk and built up the walls with coils or slabs. Bottom disks, detached at the wall joint around the entire circumference, are not uncommon in the FCP 5 assemblage. Various bottom sherds show the walls were added either to the exterior edge of the initial disk (e.g., Fig. 73f), or to its upper surface. One bottom disk (Fig. 50k) still has a segment of wall attached to it, looking like a tab handle. It suggests the walls may have been built up with slabs of clay rather than coils.

Sometimes potters supported their work on a woven mat, which left an impression on the underside of the pot (Fig. 73e, Pl. 7a–c, Jacobsen 1973b:Pl. 51c).[6] Some potters appear to have used a flat, porous rock as a support,[7] judging from the irregular depressions and the slightly tacky surface on the underside of some bottom sherds. At least one pot (Pl. 7c, right) was built up on a bed of grasses, which left their impression. Bases with such impressions may have been from large, heavy pots that were finished in place and removed from their support only for the firing, if then. More often, the potters picked the pot up before it dried completely and scraped and smoothed the bottom, removing any traces of the support that had been used.

Potters were not always careful to apply pressure to secure the joints, but simply smeared a thin layer of clay over the cracks between two joined pieces. In consequence, many pots broke along coil or slab joints. At least some of the potters made another mistake common to beginners: in building up the walls with coils or slabs, they started each new addition in the same place, aligning the joints. This alignment created a vertical line of weakness, in addition to the horizontal lines of the joints between superimposed coils. Either the FCP 5 potters were not concerned about the longevity of their pots or they had so little experience that they did not connect the breakage with their own practices, which might easily have been adjusted. Perhaps both were true.

Scars on interior walls, where a spall of clay has detached from a smooth surface, indicate that potters added patches of clay to fill in depressions and to even out the wall thickness. Potters gave little attention to achieving vertical or horizontal symmetry: many sherds look warped or suggest asymmetrical vessels, although most are probably just from lop-sided pots. Large strap handles were generally formed from flattened coils, attached at the upper end, bent down to the lower attachment point and, using clay from the sides of the handle itself, joined by smearing over the joint. This produced a characteristic narrowing of the lower handle joint (e.g., Fig. 47e), which probably weakened the handle. Piecrust rims may have been developed as a technique to reduce cracking by introducing artificial, decorative cracks that could absorb the shrinkage along the rim.

Although the potters were not timid about building large pots, they avoided complex shapes. Their efforts at refinement are confined to visible surface elaborations (below), rather than to the less visible fundamentals of careful preparation of the clay body and building procedures that make for durable, functional pots. The building practices reflect a greater concern with appearances and quick results than with the durability of the pot.[8] Irregularities in wall thickness and curvatures, the direction and timing of building marks, and all other aspects of production preserved in the sherds point to potters working with an *ad hoc* plan, not with the consistent rhythm and patterns of working that potters who work regularly develop, if unconsciously. Although not lacking in what we call "talent," the FCP 5 potters appear to have been relatively inexperienced, practicing their craft infrequently.

Surface Finishes

For earlier phases, I used the surface finish given to pots made in a particular ware to identify varieties of that ware. Certainly the FCP 5 potters used many different techniques for finishing the surfaces of their pots; perhaps with a better-preserved sample of more certainly contemporaneous pots, my system would produce useful results. Unfortunately, the low firings and the circumstances of use, burial, and often redeposition have destroyed or altered many of the original surfaces. The condition of preservation makes secure identification of original surface treatments difficult at best.

I sorted the sherds from FCP 5 deposits on as many as five occasions. On each occasion I produced quite different categories, and quantities of each category. If I cannot come close to replicating my own categories, no other investigator is likely to be able to do better with them. Rather than identifying specific varieties and assigning each sherd to one of them, I present here the range of surface treatments present in the FCP 5 assemblage. For some sherds, the decorative technique is clear, but for many several options are possible—hence the different results of my various attempts at classifying the material. In the end, I have opted not to assign every sherd to a variety and to provide no quantification of "varieties"—because I could find no reason to prefer one set of my figures to another.

For the FA Frequency Tables (Tables 1–8) and histograms (Vitelli 1993a:Tables 4–11), I needed some form of quantification to record the transition from FCP

4 to FCP 5. I elected to record the FCP 5 material in two broad categories. FN Rough includes thick and thin sherds with minimal (preserved) surface finish, lacking elaboration with added pigments. FN Finished includes sherds that preserved some degree of finishing beyond simple smoothing and a few burnish strokes on the surface: complete burnishing, with or without the addition of a slip; pattern burnishing; decoration added in one or more pigments before or after firing; incision; or impression. The "Finished" pieces together account for a small minority (Tables 1–8). Each of the many "varieties" of "Finished" pottery obviously accounts for an even smaller percentage—probably no single Finished variety accounts for more than 1–5%

Surface Finishing

Most pots were scraped, primarily on the interior, which is usually more even and regular than the often rather lumpy exterior. Sometimes the scraping was done while the clay was so moist and plastic that scraping produced a very smooth surface, the texture resembling thick oil paint applied with a palette knife. Other times the clay was nearly dry, and scraping produced a crumbly texture. Some pots received no surface finish beyond that which occurred in the course of building. When the shaping was complete, the pot was finished. Most sherds in this category appear to be from special-function pots or from very near the bottoms of large pots, where the potter may have found it awkward to reach (e.g., Figs. 63d; 73a–b, d, f, but see Fig. 59g–h).

More often, the potters used their fingers to smooth the surface, at least the interior, and sometimes the exterior as well. Most of the larger roughly finished pots have traces of some burnishing strokes, done while the clay was still quite damp and yielding. The strokes rarely cover the surface completely, and have no luster. The potters generally gave more effort to burnishing the interiors. Their efforts on the less even exteriors were often perfunctory and had little effect. The direction of the burnishing strokes is essentially random, as the potter moved around a given portion of any pot. For these low-fired, minimally burnished pots, it is doubtful that the burnishing would have decreased porosity appreciably. If the pots were intended to hold liquids, they would have required post-firing treatment.

Plain Burnished

Thin-walled sherds (<7 mm), presumably from relatively small pots, sometimes have fully burnished surfaces, perhaps with the use of a self or applied slip, although the surface is never waxy. Pieces have fired to all colors, from black through deep red. A whitish bloom is common; it may point to the use of salt water for smoothing and raising a slip. Occasional sherds have dull areas of patterned lines, although it is unclear whether the lines are painted, the ghosts of painted lines, or unburnished areas. A few examples have a burnished red layer on the interior that turns powdery and more orange when scratched. Other examples have traces of a bluish-red powder, usually on the interior, rarely on the exterior over the burnish.

Red Slipped

At least when newly excavated, the exterior surface of some thicker sherds, probably from medium to large pots, retains flecks of a waxy red pigment; this is presumably the remnant of a thickly applied red slip that was well burnished and may have covered the entire exterior. The burnishing was done while the pot was still fairly damp, for the troughs of the burnishing tool are evident in the clay body even where the slip has completely flaked away. The slip was probably made from a clay different than that used for the body, one that did not react at the low temperatures used for firing the pots. With little or no bonding between slip and surface, the slip was held in place largely by the compaction of burnishing. It flakes away easily, leaving no trace or scar on the surface. Scratching with a fingernail can reduce the red flakes of slip to a red powder, usually brighter, indicating that it has been little affected by exposure to heat. The red powder is indistinguishable from that on some of the "crusted" pieces (below). Many more pots than now appears to be the case may have been coated with this red slip. A few sherds have remnants of patterns painted in a pigment that has fired red (e.g., Fig. 44d–e).

White Paint

Sherds with patterns painted in white occur in FCP 5.1 deposits in FA, in the Paralia L5 deposits, and in the FA FCP 5.2 deposit. In each case the pigment and the pattern style are slightly different. The details are elaborated in the discussion of the specific pieces. All are probably pre-firing applications.

Red on White Painted

Sherds with traces of a red paint on a whitish background, probably also a paint or slip, occur throughout FCP 5 deposits. Firing clouds that affected both red and white areas suggest these are pre-firing applications. The "white" background varies in color and thickness from sherd to sherd, and the pigment may have been prepared differently by different potters. In most examples, the white paint does not react to acid, so is apparently not Lime-based; in other examples, the pigment reacts, and is Lime-based. The "white" is rarely, if ever, a thick layer of pure white, but varies from a watery white that is not always convincingly a painted layer, to a more convincing layer of bluish-white, to a thick creamy or even pinkish color.

Iron-oxide-rich pigments were used for the red patterns, and the whole surface was burnished. Well-preserved examples (of which there are few) have a lovely glassy finish. Some examples lack any trace of burnishing over the pigments; in at least one case, an unburnished sherd joins a well-burnished one, so probably all were originally burnished. The paints tend to flake off the surface, leaving the earlier stages of finishing quite clearly exposed and unaffected. The paints were either applied to a leather-hard or drier surface, or to an already fired pot that was subsequently re-fired. The pigments were little affected by the firing: when scratched with a fingernail the red changes to a more orange color and a fugitive powder. In the powdery state, it looks like the red of some "crusted" pieces (below).

Manganese Oxide Paint

Manganese-oxide-rich pigments were known and used by FCP 5 potters for black paint on polychrome pieces (below). Whether the black was ever used alone to decorate a pot is unclear. Several sherds from mixed deposits (Fig. 72k–m) could be FCP 5 in date, or could be from an earlier, LN phase.

Polychrome Paint

Fragments from a large polychrome painted jar were found in the L5 FCP 5 deposits, where there is no question of them being intrusive from an FCP 3 or FCP 4 deposit (Fig. 66a). Other examples were found stratified in early FCP 5 deposits in FA (Fig. 45), and in mixed deposits inside the cave (Fig. 72h–j). The black lines must be from manganese-oxide-rich minerals, the red, from iron-oxide-rich ones. Although the black lines tend to be fugitive, which is generally true of manganese pigments, these pieces were certainly painted before the initial firing.

Crusted Decoration

White and red "crusted" decoration have long been considered a hallmark of the latest Neolithic in Greece. The white version is reasonably called crusted. Usually, a several-millimeter-thick, crust-like layer of crystalline white carbonate covers the exterior surface; it may carry painted decoration in other colors (e.g., Figs. 51; 64). Sherds with this white crust usually are coated on the interior with what is now a fugitive, red-orange or bluish-red powder that rubs off on the hands and may dissolve in water, although it does not react in acid (Jacobsen 1973b:273–74 and n. 49). There is nothing in fact crust-like about the red powdery coatings associated with the crusty white version.

Variations on the theme of pots with a true white crust on the exterior and powdery red pigment on the interior are numerous. Some pots (sherds) are coated entirely with a fugitive, red-orange powder, with no white crust; a few have traces of pattern lines in powdery white Lime applied over the red (e.g., Fig. 71j); others have alternating red and white stripes, both powdery. A few sherds appear to have repeated applications over the entire piece in alternating layers of powdery white on powdery red on white, etc. Others have a coat, perhaps in multiple layers, of only powdery white Lime. On all of these, the pigments were applied to an unburnished, sometimes smoothed surface.

Other sherds are well burnished, except for a reserved band around the exterior rim, which retains traces of red and white powder, once a painted design (e.g., Fig. 54a–b). One unusually well-preserved example has an intricate pattern painted in now-fugitive and powdery red and white pigments on a well-burnished surface that has fired black, providing a dramatic background for the bright pattern (Fig. 71e). Other combinations of the powdery, fugitive red and white pigments may also be present. Several kinds of red pigment may be involved, since the colors vary from the more common bright orange-red (ca. 10 R 6/8) to a red with a bluer tint. It should be clear that the term "crusted" covers a multitude of styles and, perhaps, of techniques and materials.

The "crusted" paints are generally assumed to be post-firing applications (few sophisticated analyses have been done).[9] Sherds with white crusts from Franchthi occasionally have dark firing clouds on the ceramic surface under the crust, which should mean that the original firing was done without the crust. When a crust detaches, it usually leaves no trace on the ceramic surface. Since the pots were apparently fired only briefly and to temperatures well under 800°C, the carbonate crust would not have been adversely affected by the firing; it is not impossible that the white crusting was added before the potters' original firing. I am inclined to think that the thick white crust was applied after firing, but that remains to be proved, and may have varied from place to place.

A primary motivation for the use of the crust—aside from any symbolic value of the color and material—may have been to provide a clear background for the brightly colored decoration it usually carried. Whether or not the crust itself was fired, decoration could have been added after firing; the bright colors of the red patterns suggest it was. Unfired clay slips, colored by various ochres, are much brighter and varied than when fired. The plaster-like crust would probably have absorbed the pigments better than a ceramic surface and held them more firmly. Many minerals that lose their color when subjected to even low-temperature firings, can be used for post-firing applications, as can vegetal dyes (e.g., Shepard 1968:43). The potential palette for post-firing paints, especially on a plaster-like crust, is far greater than for pigments that must withstand firing with the pot. If the painted decoration on the FCP 5 white crusted pots is a post-firing addition, it is curious that the only preserved colors are reds and black, colors that can be achieved with traditional ceramic pigments. The reds are brighter than fired reds, and the black could be a carbon black rather than the harder to obtain manganese, but we might wonder why, for example, greens and blues from copper-rich minerals, naturally occurring in the Franchthi area, were not used.[10]

It is unclear whether the white carbonate crusts were made from burned Lime, or from simple crushed calcite, limestone, or shell. Bullard suggested that the Kephala sample he examined was finely ground dolomite (Coleman 1977:37). Jones found that the "fine particulate form of the crusts hints at calcination" (Jones 1986:779). The thick white crusts at Franchthi have a granular, crystalline texture that could suggest finely ground rock, rather than a plaster-like mixture made from burned Lime. The more powdery white Lime coatings and that used for painted decoration, on the other hand, appear too fine to have been ground mechanically; they are almost certainly burned Lime (see also below, "whitewash"). If the crusts were made from ground calcite or other carbonate-rich rocks, some medium other than water would seem necessary to produce a paste that would adhere to the pot, and light firing may have been necessary to give it permanence.

Carefully designed experiments and examination with, *inter alia*, a scanning electron microscope should help resolve how the white crust was prepared, whether it was applied to an unfired or fired pot, and whether all examples of white crust were prepared in the same way (Gourdin and Kingery 1975:138–139). Burning carbonate rocks is a technology that was exploited little, if at all, in earlier phases of the Neolithic in southern Greece, although it was widely known at much earlier dates elsewhere (e.g., Frierman 1971). It represents an interesting opposition to the ceramic process, in that the raw material must be fired before it can be mixed with water and shaped, or made into paint. The addition of water to the quicklime created by calcination starts a chemical reaction that gives off heat sufficient to irritate skin, although a layer of fat or oil protects the hands. When dry, the mixture is hard and insoluble. The process of calcination needs temperatures in the range of 750–850°C sustained for eight hours or more. Small quantities, sufficient to coat a small pot or two, might have been burned in an open fire. Larger quantities probably required a kiln and would have consumed substantial amounts of fuel (Gourdin and Kingery 1975:149).

The nature of the red pigments and the timing of their application are equally uncertain. Jones' analyses of the red powdery pigment on several pieces of "crusted" pottery by X-ray fluorescence identified the red as "iron-rich"(Jones 1986:770, Table 9.6a).[11] Bullard, examininng a piece coated with red powdery pigment from Kephala, found that the red power was "the remnants of a paste (or slip) composed of finely ground hematite (Fe_2O_3) containing about 10% fine clay" (Coleman 1977:28). Matson re-fired a sherd from Kephala that had red pigment over the entire inside surface. Even at low temperatures, it turned a powdery white; he concluded that the red pigment "would not have stood up to firing" (Coleman 1977:10–11, 28; cited also by Jones 1986:779). Hematite, an iron-rich mineral, however, should not turn white and powdery when exposed to low temperatures. Cinnabar, the vivid vermilion-colored sulfide of mercury, on the other hand, might (Shepard 1968:389–90). Cinnabar, an "exotic and rare" red pigment (Jones 1986:779), is attested on prehistoric pottery at Hvar on the Dalmatian coast (Novak 1959); it was suggested long ago as a possible source of pigment on Neolithic pottery from Samos (cited in Jones: Heidenreich *AM* 1935–36:130), but has never been confirmed by analyses. If some of the powdery red pigments at Franchthi are cinnabar, we need to discover the potential sources and explore the implications. Cinnabar is, like manganese oxide, potentially toxic.[12] It vaporizes at relatively low temperatures, so if used as a ceramic pigment, was surely a post-firing application.

Some of the red pigments are probably derived from iron-rich minerals or clays. Those that occur on ceramic surfaces that have fired black are almost certainly post-firing applications, since the atmosphere that produced the black ceramic should have affected the iron-rich pigment as well. I think it likely that most of the powdery red pigments are post-firing applications, because of the vivid red colors that firing would have subdued. This conclusion, however, must also remain tentative, given the observations (above, red slipped, red on white painted) that burnished and apparently fired, darker red pigments yield up a bright red powder, when scratched, of the same color as the "crusted" reds.

The powdery red pigment, when used for painted decoration, was clearly applied in a fluid state. The thick red powders that cover larger surface areas were probably also applied in liquid, rather than dry or powdered form. A ground mineral mixed with water, applied to a fired ceramic body, would become powdery and quite fugitive as soon as the water evaporated. The same mixture with the addition of some clay, or a pure clay slip, would have somewhat more cohesion, especially on an unburnished, rough surface, but it would not survive much handling or washing.[13] If applications were made post-firing, the pigments may have been carried in a glue-like medium; or some form of lacquer coating may have been applied to help them adhere to the pot and to preserve them. It is unlikely that the now-powdery pigments were originally in that state. It is also unlikely that they could have withstood much handling. Pots with such fragile decoration may have held dry foods or goods, but they seem designed more to be looked at than handled. It is worth noting that the first appearance at Franchthi of fugitive powdery white and red pigments on ceramic vessels is on the rhyta of FCP 4.[14]

Post-firing applications to pottery, at least in theory, could have been added by anyone, at any time after the firing of the pots, and they could have been removed, altered, and renewed repeatedly. Decoration added after firing need not have been part of the potter's production process. Much remains to be learned about, and surely, from the Final Neolithic pots with "crusted" elaboration. Acknowledging the diverse forms that this elaboration took and the many questions related to its production is a small step toward that end.

Incised and Impressed Decoration

Fewer than a dozen sherds from FCP 5 include traces of incised decoration. A few come from each of the chronological groups, and together they appear to represent four or five styles or hands. Aside from applied rope bands with fingertip impressions, and piecrust rims, only three or four sherds have impressed decoration.

Pattern Burnished Decoration

Fewer than fifteen sherds preserve traces of patterns created by selective burnishing of a slipped surface. Three sherds from FCP 5.1 (Figs. 54i–j; 56i) differ from those from upper mixed deposits (Fig. 71a–d) in that the latter have reserved bands around the rim and on the interiors that preserve traces of fugitive red powder. Both groups have fired to a red color. Pieces of a unique, black carinated bowl with pattern burnishing on interior and exterior surfaces were found scattered through numerous units in L5 (Fig. 67j). The bowl looks out of place with the other FCP 5 material, but it is equally out of place in FCP 1 or 2, the only other phases represented in L5.

Details of individual pieces are provided in the captions to the illustrations, and in the analyses of the shapes represented. The following discussions of shapes cover, first, the FCP 5.1a–c material from FAN and FAS, and then FCP 5.1 from L5 on Paralia, since those deposits appear to pre-date the latest deposit within the cave. The discussion then moves to the material from FCP 5.2 contexts and the sherds that were saved from upper mixed deposits within the cave, followed by a review of the surface remains from the rest of Paralia.

THE POTTERY FROM FCP 5.1a IN FA BALK

Main Fabric

Shapes

Deep bowls or jars: Fig. 43
Cup: Fig. 44f
Open bowls: Figs. 44a–e, g–k
Rim tab: Fig. 45g
Cupped lugs: Figs. 45f, h
Handle: Fig. 45i
Base and bottoms: Figs. 45j–m

The sherds are mostly in small, crumbly pieces that rarely present obvious joining fragments. Their size is surely a result of the low firing, rather than or along with extensive trampling and reworking of the sediments from which they came. Their crumbly state also probably explains why fewer than ten pots in the entire FCP 5 assemblage were drilled with post-firing holes for mending. We had little more success than the hole-drillers did in putting pots together from the sherds, so the information about shapes, especially large ones, is sketchy. Articulated neck and shoulder joints are absent, as are carinations and other indications that might suggest the complex shapes of earlier phases. Jars and bowls of various sizes apparently had continuously curving profiles, and, with very few exceptions, sat on flat bottoms.

Truly closed shapes with small, restricted mouths are absent. The closest thing to closed pots is suggested by inleaning rims with medium (Fig. 43a–c), or very large (Fig. 43f) diameters. The shape, if not the finish, is similar to that of FCP 1 bowls; it may have been made for the same reason the earliest potters made it—a basic shape, relatively easy for an inexperienced potter to build. The narrowing rim helps to prevent the development of shrinkage cracks during drying and firing. Its function need not have been different from a similarly deep bowl with a slightly more open rim. The smaller examples are less well finished, with notably lumpy exteriors, than the very large one, which is carefully burnished on both surfaces. Very large vessels represent a substantial investment of materials and time, so it is not surprising that they often received more careful attention to the details of making a pot strong than did smaller pots.

More nearly vertical profiles are suggested for other large bowls or jars (Fig. 43d–e, g) all of which were provided with some surface elaboration. The largest fragment (Fig. 43d) had at least one vertical strap handle, with applied rope bands extending around the vessel and aligned with the attachment points of the handle. The bands were made from narrow coils, added while the pot was still quite damp, with pressure from a fingertip that left its impression. A larger pot received a similar applied rope decoration, but with the attachment depressions smoothed over (Fig. 43g). One large bowl has traces of painted decoration on a smoothed surface, in broad diagonal stripes that have fired to a dull, crackling red.

The relatively heavy, deep bowls were the likely bearers of the occasional solid, tilted lugs (Fig. 45f, h) and heavy strap handles in the deposits. The strap handle in Fig. 45i was heavily encrusted with cave Lime, which preserved a thin coating of red rusty pigment that dissolves in water. It is likely to have been a post-firing application.

A small bowl with a convex profile (Fig. 44d) may have had a double tab on the rim—only a crescent-shaped depression between the tabs is preserved. Traces of a deep red powder cling to the interior and, on the exterior, suggest diagonal pattern bands. A small tab, pierced before firing, may have come from a similar bowl (Fig. 45g).

A single rim sherd from a pot small enough to be considered a cup occurs in the main fabric (Fig. 44f). Its profile is similar to a number of other examples of spreading open bowls or basins (Fig. 44a–c,e, g–i, k) in varying sizes and surface finishes. The bowl in Fig. 44a is the only rim sherd, although a few body sherds occur in various deposits, in a fabric that has fired nearly white (10 Y/R 8/2), with crackling surfaces. Another of the bowls (Fig. 44b) has traces on both interior and exterior of a fugitive bluish-pink powder (a bit more blue than 7.5 R 5/8), but it is not possible to say whether the powder covered the entire pot or was applied in patterns. A larger bowl (Fig. 44e) has remnants of several horizontal bands painted in a crackling red pigment and a few red pigment grains in the depressions of the piecrust rim. A larger, less spreading bowl (Fig. 44j) has minimal surface finishing; it was given a piecrust rim by someone with quite long fingernails. An attachment scar on the edge of the break of another bowl (Fig. 44g) hints at a handle or lug low on the body, and a less spreading bowl (Fig. 44c) has a simple form of pattern-burnished decoration.

Although the general spreading shape is shared by these examples, each is executed differently and provided with different surface elaboration. This diversity of execution is generally true of FCP 5 pots, with the possible exception of the Heavy Burnished variety (below). It stands in contrast with the assemblages of earlier phases when pot shapes were both more complex and more consistently repeated, when potters adhered to some stricter sense of cultural norm.

Most pots probably sat on a flat bottom like the examples in Fig. 45l–m. The interior of the example in Fig. 45l is coated with a fugitive red powder (ca. 7.5 YR 4/8) that extends slightly over the breaks. It may have been used in broken form as a paint pot. A single example of a ring base occurs in this group (Fig. 45j). The tip of the base has been ground down after firing, so the base may have been a pedestal originally, and attached to a basin. The fabric is distinctive; the exterior coated with a dull red paint. The thick dimple bottom (Fig. 45k) is unique in the FCP 5 assemblage, although the fabric appears to be the local one.

Other Varieties

A small number of sherds with polychrome decoration occur in FCP 5.1a (e.g., Fig. 45a–c). They differ in style from earlier polychrome pieces, and are probably in situ. They are similar to sherds I have seen from Klenia, generally called LN (e.g., Phelps 1975:Fig. 45, no. 9) but which perhaps should also be re-dated to the Final Neolithic. Each example from Franchthi may be made from a different clay body; none is likely to be a local product. Similarly, two sherds with incised decoration (Fig. 45d–e) differ from each other in fabric, shape, and style of incision. Both were probably brought to Franchthi from elsewhere.

Plain Burnished sherds are common throughout the FCP 5.1 deposits, but they tend to break into quite small fragments. No profiles are illustrated; shapes seem to have included open and closed bowls of relatively small dimensions. Small body sherds with red on white painted decoration, thick white crust, white painted decoration, and a red slipped and burnished coat, along with a few sherds that have fired a creamy white throughout, are present in FCP 5.1a (not illustrated).

THE POTTERY FROM FCP 5.1b IN FA BALK

Main Fabric

Shapes

Deep bowls or jars: Figs. 46, 47c–e, 49b–h
Cups and small bowls: Figs. 48a–k, 49a, 50a–b
Basins: Fig. 50c–f
Rough plate: Fig. 50g
Lugs: Fig. 47a–b, d
Handles: Figs. 47c, e, 48d–i
Bottoms: Figs. 47f, 48k, 50h–k

Again, no rim or body sherds suggest a truly closed or complex shape. The body sherds shown in Fig. 47e suggest that bowls or jars may have been quite deep, with sharply sloping lower walls; the intact pots would have looked more different from FCP 1 bowls and jars than the rim fragments alone suggest (Fig. 81). Two rims (Figs. 46a–b) appear to be from small deep bowls with lightly convex walls like those so common in FCP 1; these they may have had deep bodies, and probably had flat bottoms, unlike the FCP 1 examples. The rim sherds in Fig. 46c–d suggest more open bowls, worked carefully from the interior. Those, as well as the more closed bowl in Fig. 46b, were left unfinished on the exterior, something FCP 1 potters never did. The other four rims (Figs. 46e–h) are from larger vessels, one with a piecrust finish (Fig. 46f), one with an applied horizontal band of fingertip-impressed rope decoration (Fig. 46g). Other (unillustrated) small body sherds, about 20 in number, from the same FCP 5.1b deposit include similar rope bands, running at various angles, and impressed with the tip of a finger while the clay was still quite wet.

The body fragment with a vertical strap handle and a small cone-shaped horn (Fig. 47e) provides the best impression of what many of the whole pots must have looked like. The big strap handle is—characteristically for FCP 5—narrower at the lower attachment point, indicating that the potter attached the handle at the top end first, bent it down, and smeared some of the clay from the handle into the vessel wall to attach it. The potter scraped to even, fairly thin walls (ca. 7 mm, except at the very bottom, where it thickens to ca. 1 cm) for such a large pot. She burnished the interior carefully, with strokes running roughly parallel to the rim, so she probably held it on her lap as she worked. On the exterior, the strokes run perpendicular to the rim, so she probably burnished the exterior while sitting next to, or leaning over the upright pot. When enough sherds are preserved to suggest this much of the shape, the impression is of far less "coarse" pottery than when one is confronted by the more usual small non-joining sherds.

Other large pots were equipped with solid lug handles (Figs. 47a–b, d), which probably tilted slightly upward, like their FCP 4 predecessors (e.g., Figs. 32c, i), although these are not cupped. The horizontal strap handle (Fig. 47c) is uncommon in FCP 5.

Cups and small bowls (Figs. 48; 49a; 50a–b) are less common than one would expect if they had served for individual portions dipped or served from a larger bowl or jar. The sherd drawn as a conical cup in Fig. 48a might equally derive from a tall ring base, perhaps on a vessel similar to that in Fig. 48c. The latter example has traces of five oval holes poked through the damp clay from the exterior. The curve of the interior bowl bottom suggests that the holes are in the upper body wall, not cutouts from a pedestal as we might expect from earlier Neolithic practice. Neither piece is well finished, although the conical cup/base may have had a light burnish on the exterior. The pierced pot preserves the building surface.

The small bowl in Fig. 48b was pierced all along the rim from the interior before firing, in the manner of the so-called "cheese pots." The pot seems to have cracked along the rim before firing; it was mended with a smear of clay that clogged the hole on the right edge (as drawn). In the break on the lower right is the edge of another hole that pierced the bottom of the bowl. The pot was finger smoothed on the interior; it may have been given a red slip on the exterior, followed by light burnishing.

A series of small bowls with vertical handles at (Fig. 48f–g), or looping above (Fig. 48d–e, h) the rim, seem intended to be the "same" shape, although each differs in details. All received little or no finishing beyond smoothing. The heavy attachment clay on the handle in Fig. 48d suggests a potter with little skill. The pot in Fig. 48h cracked along the rim, possibly before firing, and probably helped along by the weight of the handle. The broader and taller loop handle on a small cup (Fig. 48i) is, by contrast, almost elegant. Other rims suggest bowls of similar size (Figs. 48j; 49a–b; 50a), with more or less spreading walls. All may have had relatively deep walls and flat bottoms like that in Fig. 48k. The only cup with a nearly complete profile (Fig. 50b) is smaller than the others. It is a simple shallow pinch pot with a flat bottom and no surface finish beyond minimal wet smoothing. It reminds me of what a completely inexperienced person might produce with a first handful of clay.

Rim sherds from larger bowls, of unknown depth, are fairly common, and equally variable in their details (Fig. 49b–h). The potters sometimes slipped the surfaces (Fig. 49d–f, h), and gave most surfaces at least a light burnish, but they left some with a simple scraped (Fig. 49g) or smoothed (Fig. 49c) exterior. One (Fig. 49g) has traces of very fine white Lime powder clinging to the exterior surface. The potters had trouble building these larger bowls as well. The rims are lumpy, with irregular curves that make measuring diameters and determining angles difficult. The sherd in Fig. 49e preserves part of a rare drilled hole, presumably for mending the broken pot. In the interior, the beginning of another drill hole, intended to meet the first, but slightly off-center, was abandoned, perhaps when drilling broke the pot further.

The small open bowl or basin in Fig. 50c had a tab, or perhaps a handle, at the rim. It was slipped and burnished on the exterior and just inside the rim, and fired harder than most. The larger basin rim in Fig. 50d, with an unusual applied band just below the exterior rim, is also relatively hard-fired (Mohs' 4–5), with a crackling black exterior. The two largest examples (Figs. 50e–f) are more typically mottled and soft fired. None is well enough preserved to indicate the depth of the bowl or whether these sat on ring or pedestal bases, or, more likely in the absence of base joints from large vessels, on flat bottoms like most other pots.

A very lumpy shallow bowl or plate (Fig. 50g) was roughly shaped from a solid lump of clay, using a rough scraper on the interior. The thickness varies considerably. This might be considered an unfinished piece that was accidentally fired if it were not for traces of light burnishing on the very irregular exterior. An experienced potter, even if rushing and interested only in a minimal container, would have done better without trying. It could be the work of a child, certainly of a beginner.

With the exception of an occasional ring or pedestal on a small vessel (e.g., Fig. 48c), all the evidence points to simple flat bottoms for all pots (Figs. 47f; 48k; 50h–k), in most cases with a carefully articulated edge. The bottom in Fig. 50k is preserved in its entirety. It may have been built with slabs rather than coils, attached to the top edge of the disk. Most of the lower wall has detached at the joint with the bottom, leaving a tab-like piece of wall that might have served as a convenient handle for reuse of the bottom. The exterior is light with dark clouds, the interior surface and half of the core is deep black, perhaps from use, either as an intact pot or after its breaking.

Crusted White and Red Powdery Decoration

The fabric of the pots with a true white crust includes a substantial proportion of red, dark, and white nonplastics under 1 mm in size, but with an occasional pebble of iron oxide or Lime. In a few examples, the nonplastics are larger, many up to 2 mm in size.

The potters scraped the walls of these pots quite thin (3–4 mm), although the thickness varies around the circumference of the vessel. Most examples have a slight flip to the rim, formed by running a finger around the exterior edge of the rim, and probably intended to catch or hold the crust. The clay body has generally fired to a light tan color with a uniformly light core, although light gray streaks in the center of the core occur. Hardness ranges from Mohs' 2 to 4. Where the crust has detached, the underlying surface has a slightly roughened texture. These sherds occasionally have gray firing clouds on the exterior surface under the crust. That is the primary argument, at this point, for suggesting that the pot was fired without the crust.

Shapes

Small deep bowls: Fig. 51a–h
Basin: Fig. 51i
Bases: Fig. 51b, k–l

All but one of the sherds come from small deep bowls with lightly convex walls. The only other shape is the small basin in Fig. 51i, with thicker walls than the other bowls. The best-preserved bowl (Fig. 51a) has a thick white crust on the exterior, with no trace of additional colors. The interior has a red glow, but no pigment grains are evident with a 10x lens. Two bowls (Fig. 51c–d) have traces of red pattern lines on top of the white crust, and red powder along the interior of the lip. The other examples with thick white crust on the exterior (Fig. 51g–i) also have traces of red powder on the interiors.

All the bowls may have been provided with ring bases (Fig. 51b, k–l), although no fragments preserve the actual joint between bowl and base. A rare example of a low ring base in the later Neolithic (Fig. 51b) has detached at the joint, and preserves a thick layer of white crust. The taller base fragments are less certainly associated with the true crusted pots. One (Fig. 51k) seems to have successive layers of white and red and white and red pigments covering the exterior; none is a true crust. The other (Fig. 51l) has traces of a thick crust-like layer applied to the burnished exterior.

The rims in Figs. 51e–f, possibly from the same pot, show no traces of having been crusted, but in fabric and surface finish they closely resemble other true crusted pieces. One (Fig. 51f) has a 4–5 mm pebble in one break, an unusually large inclusion and one that could well have caused the pot to break during firing. Perhaps this happened, which is why the pot never received its intended post-firing elaboration. That would suggest that potters made these pots locally.

The fabric of three non-joining body fragments from a bowl (Fig. 51j) includes a few pieces of gold mica, along with red nonplastics and lime. The interior is coated with a fugitive red pigment (10R 6/8); the exterior appears to have had, first a layer of red pigment, then a white layer, and finally, pale gray lines painted on the white.

Unillustrated body sherds with traces of white crust or powder, other than the whitewashed and smeared sherds (see below), include a small piece of a round handle (?) ca. 5 mm in diameter, and numerous relatively thin walled (6–7 mm) sherds with or without a well-burnished surface under the white lime coat, with and without traces of red powder, with multiple layers of red and white, and with alternating red and white stripes. The fabric is usually light colored; some sherds are dark brown and burnished under the remnants of the powdery pigments. Some may represent other varieties of true crusting, as pots made specifically to receive crusting, but the sherds are small, with only minimal traces of the white and red pigments.

Another group of pots uses the powdery white lime and red pigments more sparingly than the true white crusted versions. The best-preserved example (Fig. 54a), not radically different in fabric from the others, is more carefully made and finished in ways that suggest it might be a non-local product, perhaps subsequently copied by local potters. It has well-scraped walls with very regular thickness and an even exterior surface that was burnished to a high sheen, except for a 3–4 cm reserved band along the rim. The pot was fired in a basically oxidizing atmosphere, producing a red-brown core, but the fire was smothered at the end and the pot emerged with a glossy black surface, with only a small red cloud on one side. After firing, since the colors were unaffected by the final smothering of the fire, white and red pigments, now fugitive, were added along the reserved band; not enough remains to determine the sequence of colors or any idea of the pattern. The interior of the bowl, as in related varieties, is covered with a fugitive red powder.

The more closed bowl in Fig. 54b is similar, except that the potter did not even the surface so well before burnishing; the burnish is less effective. Although fired in a manner that produced a uniformly dark gray fabric, the burnished surface has no luster. The reserved band along the rim has traces of white crusting; on the burnished area just below the reserved band is a bright orange (10 R 5/8) stripe. A reserved band with traces of crusting occurs on the rim of a small cup or jar (Fig. 54c)—possibly a truly closed shape—and along the bottom of a probable pedestal (Fig. 54d).

A miniature strap handle (Fig. 54e) and a pierced crescent lug (Fig. 54f) have traces of a fugitive orange powder that apparently once covered the surfaces on the interior and exterior. The surfaces under the powder are roughly finished, the pots oxidized, with deep black cores.

Two large bowl rims (Figs. 54g–h) have burnished surfaces on the interior and exterior, with traces of a pinkish-orange powder (ca 7.5 YR 6/6) clinging in the cracks of both surfaces. On the longer rim fragment (Fig. 54g), the powder is also evident inside the drill hole and on the breaks. The entire pot may have been coated after firing (and drilling the mend hole) with the now-powdery pigment, perhaps in the course of use. It is also possible, given the fugitive nature of the pigment, that the pigment was never intentionally added to the pot, but was redeposited on this (and other) sherds during burial.

White Painted Decoration

Sherds with traces of patterns painted in a runny whitish pigment on a light, usually unburnished ground, occur infrequently but consistently throughout the FCP 5.2 units. Fabric, building procedures, firing, and hardness are similar to that of sherds in the undecorated main ware. The patterns were painted with a broad brush using a dilute pigment that included Lime, but was not pure Lime: the painted lines effervesce slightly in hydrochloric acid, but the acid does not completely dissolve them. Lines that are clear on one part of a sherd may fade out suddenly and completely (e.g., Fig. 52g).

Shapes

Cups: Fig. 52a, c
Small bowls: Fig. 52b, d–f
Large bowl: Fig. 52g

A small cup (Fig. 52a) was probably pinched from a solid lump of clay. A slight bulge near the break may be part of the general lumpiness of the piece, or it may indicate there once was a handle near the rim. The sherds in Fig. 52c suggest a more conical cup. Horizontal band(s) at the rim, with vertical bands below are a combination repeated on a few unillustrated body fragments from slightly larger vessels, and possibly completed the decoration on the small bowls in Fig. 52d–e. The flaring bowl rim in Fig. 52b has the edge of an attachment scar along the break in the lower wall, suggesting a handle or lug. It preserves only a broad band of white paint along the exterior rim.

The large bowl (Fig. 52g) has the same pear-shaped profile as several of the small bowls (Fig. 52d–f); all may have been made by a single potter. The bowl in Fig. 52f is very red on the interior, although no pigment grains are evident with a 10x lens. It appears to have a thin white wash of paint over the entire exterior. An attempt was made to mend the large bowl in Fig. 52g. The bowl was exposed at some point to a fire hot enough to cause parts of the surface to shrink and crackle, and some sherds to warp. All its sherds have the consistency of cinders. Where reasonably well preserved, the painted pattern appears as rather randomly connected and enclosed blocks. In places the pattern disappears entirely, in others (e.g., far right as drawn) narrow lines and patches of white that seem to have no relationship to the pattern are all that remain.

Red on White Painted Decoration

Most sherds with red on white painted decoration are very small, with minimal traces of the pigments preserved. All may not be made from the same clay body. Most sherds have small dark and occasional white nonplastics, under 1 mm, but in some sherds many inclusions are 1–2 mm in size. Hardness and colors, including firing clouds that affect the pigments, suggest firing practices comparable to those used for the main fabric. Cores are often dark gray, but sometimes fully oxidized.

The pots were scraped to more even surfaces than

most other varieties, usually finger smoothed, and allowed to dry before the paint was applied. The paints tend to flake off the surface, leaving the earlier stages of finishing quite clearly exposed. The "white" background varies in color and thickness from sherd to sherd, and different pigments were used on different pieces. In most examples, the white paint does not react to acid, so is apparently not Lime-based; in other examples, the white effervesces in acid and must be Lime-rich. The "white" is rarely, if ever, a thick layer of pure white, but varies from a watery white that is not always convincingly a painted layer, to a more convincing layer of bluish-white, to a creamy, or even pinkish color.

Iron-oxide-rich pigments were used for the red patterns, and the whole surface was burnished. The few well-preserved examples have a lovely glassy finish. The pigments are soft and abrade easily. The red pigment, when scratched, turns to a fugitive powder, indistinguishable from the red powder on "crusted" varieties. Gray firing clouds are sometimes evident in the paints, which suggests they were fired. The clear evidence for prior stages of finishing on surfaces where paint has flaked off would be more easily explained if the burnished paints had been added to an already fired pot. The pots may have been fired once without paint, and again, too briefly to affect the lime-rich pigment, after painting.

Since the pigments become powdery when abraded, it is possible that some sherds that now have only traces of powdery pigments once had burnished red on white painted decoration. Of the sherds that still retain traces of these burnished pigments, not all were made with the same raw materials. The red on white painted and burnished, and the red on white "crusted" varieties are related in concept and, perhaps, in techniques. Both must have been visually striking when new. The diversity from pot to pot suggests that potters aimed for that striking appearance, achieving it in whatever way they knew how, with whatever materials were available, i.e., that they were reproducing an idea or visual effect rather than using a common recipe, long familiar and frequently followed. I suspect that the highly visible decorated pots are not the "local style" of a particular group; instead they represent kinds of decoration appropriate for particular occasions and specially produced by potters in many groups specifically for those occasions.

Shapes

Small open bowls: Fig. 53a–d
Deep bowls: Fig. 53e–f

The rim fragments suggest small open bowls with splaying walls (Fig. 53a–d). One (Fig. 53d) has a slight upturn at the edge of the lower break, perhaps indicating a handle or lug, similar to one with white painted decoration (Fig. 52b). Flecks of red on the interior of the sherd in Fig. 53f suggest it may also be from an open bowl, with decoration on the interior as well as the exterior. The body sherd in Fig. 53e has a thick coat of red paint on the interior, carefully burnished, so is probably also from an open shape.

White Paint on Red Slip

The large bowl rim in Fig. 53g has alternating unburnished red and white horizontal bands below the exterior rim. It is a unique example at Franchthi in which the white paint appears to have been added on top of a red slip. The interior is coated with a crackling, red-fired paint.

Incised Decoration

A single example of an incised sherd occurs in the deposits assigned to FCP 5.1b (Fig. 53h). The rim of the open bowl was folded out, creating a thickened band at the rim, which was well scraped and smoothed. Incisions were made in the damp clay with a double-pointed tool, perhaps a small split bone that incised a narrow double line with each stroke. The exterior of the bowl below the rim ridge was well burnished. Several very similar rim sherds were found in mixed deposits (Fig. 75a–b). All may be examples of the late Heavy Burnished variety, in which case the rim in FAS:74 is intrusive.

Pattern Burnished Decoration

Several sherds with pattern burnished decoration on a red-orange slip occur in FCP 5.1b. None has a reserved band around the rim or any trace of powdery pigment, as examples from later contexts do (Fig. 71a–c). The two rim sherds suggest bowls (Figs. 54i–j), although each has a very different profile and style of decoration.

"Smears" and Whitewash

Of particular interest in the FCP 5.1b deposits are a number of sherds with "smears" up to 5 mm thick of a gritty clay mixture applied over a portion of the finished pot's surface (Pl. 5b–c). One to ten sherds in this category were recovered in each unit from FAS:72–66 and FAN:70, 66, 64, 63, 61. Most are relatively thick, plain sherds from fairly large vessels; several are thinner walled and burnished, from relatively small pots. In several cases the fabric of the pot itself has no Lime, while the smear layer effervesces madly in hydrochloric acid, and is clearly a Lime-rich mixture. Other smears include fragments of Lime up to 2–3 mm in size, but otherwise do not react to acid. Some have no Lime at all. In several cases it is clear that "smears" cover a crack in the pot wall, or an impressed rope band and the edge of a handle (Pl. 5b, 5c, upper left). In one example, burnish marks around the joint show that the clay and Lime smear was used to glue a dry, unfired bottom slab back on to the body wall it had broken away from. In this case, the smear was clearly applied to a dry, unfired pot, which was then fired. The other "smears" are probably also fired: they do not slake in water. In the break, it is easy to see that the smear was applied to a finished surface: the layers are quite distinct. Some smears have bonded with the clay body. Others can be pried away from the pot, and leave behind a surface completely unaffected and indistinguishable from that of pots without smears. In the latter case, the pots may have broken after firing, been glued with a thick smear mixture, and re-fired. If the pot was not moved around much after the second firing, the clay smear glue might have held it together for a while. The smears that are mixtures of clay and substantial amounts of Lime may also have been reasonably waterproof.

The same units that produced the pots with "smears" also produced a number of sherds that appear to have been whitewashed—coated, in some cases repeatedly, with a layer of Lime-rich liquid. Many sherds, including some sherds of earlier FCP 1 through 4 wares, have traces of a thin watery layer of white Lime flaking off one or both surfaces. On some FCP 5 sherds, as many as seven or eight layers, each 1–2 mm thick, are clear. On some, the whitewash has become soft and powdery; on others it looks like a thin layer of white paint, although it dissolves completely in hydrochloric acid. The whitewash is certainly a post-firing application, probably made from burned limestone or calcite. The range of pots to which it was applied, including sherds from earlier phases, suggests it was painted on fired pots standing in situ, much as it is in modern Greek villages, and caught anything, including stray sherds, that happened to be in the vicinity.

THE POTTERY FROM FCP 5.1c IN FA BALK

Main Fabric

Shapes

Bowls: Fig. 55a–e
Bottom Fig. 55f

Figure 55 illustrates the profiles of pots in the main fabric from the few units in FAN that may be later than the FCP 5.1b deposit. Features of building, of finishing and of firing, as well as the shapes, are similar to examples from FCP 5.1b, but it is perhaps noteworthy that the four bowls (Fig. 55a–d) have minimal finishing. Body sherds from thin-walled pots include a number with a slipped and well-burnished, waxy surface, including several that have fired with completely black surfaces; those could be called "black burnished."

The large body fragment with a horned strap handle (Fig. 55e) has a more baggy profile than the jar from an earlier deposit (Fig. 47e), although it, too, may have had a deep, narrowing bottom. The horn on the handle has been flattened, so it looks like a crest. At the upper attachment end, the sides of the handle continue in relief bands. They may have been part of an applied rope band. The lower attachment joint narrows in the same manner as earlier examples.

White Painted Decoration

Shapes

Cup: Fig. 56a
Basin: Fig. 56b

Examples of white painted decoration include a small cup (Fig. 56a) and a basin (Fig. 56b) both with white painted bands along the exterior rim. Both were scraped and smoothed. The cup was burnished lightly on the interior; the basin was not. The white pigment on the cup does not react to acid; that on the basin does. The basin has traces of vertical lines below the rim band, which would seem to link it to earlier examples (e.g., Figs. 52a, c) decorated in a Lime-free pigment.

Polychrome Decoration

Shapes

Cup: Fig. 56c
Bowl: Fig. 56d

The small rim (or pedestal) in Fig. 56c is burnished on the inside and outside of the rim, but the surfaces below that were only scraped. The decoration is flaking off and only barely visible; it consists of a white, Lime-free band along the rim, with two vertical white lines below, flanked by two red verticals and then two black verticals—a rare example of decoration using three applied colors, all poorly bonded with the body.

The bowl in Fig. 56d resembles two bowls from earlier deposits (Figs. 54a–b) in fabric. Like the earlier examples, it has a well-burnished exterior that has fired black, a reserved band along the rim filled with a fugitive red (10R 5/8) pigment outlined with a Lime-rich white band, and bits of a grainy red powder clinging to the interior.

Crusted and Red Powdery Pigments

Shapes

Cups: Fig. 56e, g
Spout: Fig. 56f
Crescent lug: Fig. 56h
Ring base: Fig. 56j

The cup in Fig. 56e has the clay body and surface finish that should have received white crusting, but it retains no traces of pigment. A shallow, donut-shaped depression makes it look as if something was attached to it while damp, but detached before firing, probably when the piece was too dry to smooth over. The sherds in Figs. 56f, h, and j have, on the exterior, faint traces of white Lime crusting with red pigment on top of the crust and clinging to the interior surfaces. The rim in Fig. 56f suggests a spout. The body sherd with a doubly pierced crescent lug (Fig. 56h) could be from the same spouted vessel (see Fig. 82). The sherd in Fig. 56g has the dimensions of a pedestal or cup. Since it is burnished on both surfaces, the latter is more likely.

Rhyta: Fig. 57

Fragments of pots that must have been similar in concept to the FCP 4 rhyta (Fig. 28) come from FCP 5.1 deposits in FAS (Fig. 57a–c, h–i) and from upper mixed deposits in the cave. A very worn, small hollow foot similar to those in Fig. 57i and l was found in a surface unit on Paralia (Q5N:10, not illustrated).[15]

The fragment in Fig. 57c is probably from a strutted basket handle. Its well-smoothed, even, and burnished surface is decorated with incised outlines filled with punctate depressions, all with white Lime fill.[16] The handle is unique in FCP 5, except for a small body sherd from the joint with a base (perhaps a leg with the interior of the bowl) from FAS:71 and two even smaller body sherds from FAS:74, all of which are probably from the same vessel as the handle.

Fig. 57b may be from a similar—or possibly even the same—handle. It has no curvature, so may be from the straight upright part of the handle. It too is well burnished, but without trace of incised or other decoration. One complete drill hole, and two others started, but abandoned before they penetrated very deeply, suggest an effort to mend a presumably important pot. Although the fabric of these pieces is not distinctive, the quality of workmanship stands out from other sherds; it may point to the piece being a non-local product.

Three other handle fragments (Fig. 57a, f–g) suggest a similar concept, executed with less care. All were simply smoothed with wet fingers during building, without further surface finish. The piece in Fig. 57a has a central depression at one end, where it curves inward slightly; it may be from near the joint with the body. It has traces of fugitive orange powder on both surfaces. The small hollow foot in Fig. 57i is from the same unit; although retaining no trace of orange powder on its roughly finished surfaces, it could be from the same pot as the handle. A similar hollow leg (Fig. 57l) came from a mixed deposit. If the hollow legs were attached to the bottom of pot, they must have been pierced to allow steam to escape during firing, or they would have detached from the pressure of expanding gasses inside the leg. The rim fragment in Fig. 57h suggests, by its angled rim and attachment scar, the lower rim and body of a vessel that might have carried the handles and feet—although the greater quantity of red gritty nonplastics argue that it is not from the same pot. The interior was painted with a red slip that is neither powdery nor fugitive, but the surface finish is similar to the foot and handle.

The remaining fragments, two possibly from the same handle (Fig. 57d–e) and three solid legs (Figs. 57j, k, m), are from mixed deposits. As they have no close parallels from within the FA Balk, they may reasonably be considered later than anything within FA. A fragment almost identical to that in Fig. 57e was found in H1:61, also a reworked deposit that included modern material. All may point to a later development of the rhyton form. The impressed handle fragments may be from scoops.

Pattern Burnished Decoration

Shape

Pedestal: Fig. 56i

A pedestal or small bowl rim (Fig. 56i) has traces of red pigment on parts of the unfinished interior; on the exterior it was coated with a red paint and decorated with scribble burnishing. The paint is not powdery until scratched, when the red coating turns to an orange powder.

Red on White Painted

Shape

Bottom: Fig. 56k

A bottom fragment (Fig. 56k) retains the troughs of burnishing on both surfaces, along with faint traces of burnished red and white pigment, neither of which reacts in acid.

THE POTTERY FROM FCP5.1 IN L5

Deposits in L5 produced the only stratified FCP 5 material on Paralia. That material is assigned to FCP 5.1.

Main Fabric

Shapes

Cups: Figs. 58a–e, 59a, c–d, 60a, c
Small sieve: Fig. 59b
Small open bowls: Figs. 58f–i; 61a–d
Deep bowls or jars: Figs. 59e–h; 60b, d–g; 61 e–h; 62a–b
Large basins: Fig. 62c–d
Large jars: Figs. 63a–c
Small pan: Fig. 63d
Bottoms: Figs. 60h–i; 61b, f; 63 e–f
Tab rims: Figs. 58i, 59c
Handles: Figs. 59d, f; 61b, e, h

Small cups that could have been pinched and pulled from a single handful of clay are shallow and open (Figs. 58a–e; 59d), or relatively deep (Fig. 59a, c; 60a), some with strongly convex walls (Fig. 60c). Most have minimally finished surfaces; a few were burnished inside and out (Figs. 60a, c). A small tab was added to several (e.g., Fig. 59c), and one has a crooked and lumpy loop handle above the rim (Fig. 59d). The collection is roughly what is produced on the first day of a beginning ceramics class when everyone is given a handful of clay and told to pinch a small pot. The differences in shape in the FCP 5 examples may have been meaningful, but I think it more likely that all are just "little pots" and served a similar purpose. One piece made in the same way, but with rows of small holes poked before firing all around the body wall may have served a special function (Fig. 59b). The example in Fig. 58c preserves a single pre-firing hole below the rim.

Slightly larger, shallow open bowls also received minimal finishing (Fig. 58f–i), or a light burnish on the lumpy exterior and the more even interior (Fig. 61a–d). The wall thickness of the bowl in Fig. 61d varies markedly and the curvature is so irregular it may have been intentionally asymmetrical. One bowl has a large tab above the rim, with an oval hole cut before firing (Fig. 58i). Although the surface is quite rough on the exterior and only lightly burnished on the more even interior, someone felt the pot worth mending. The half drill hole in the break suggests that the mending attempt made matters worse, and the effort may have been abandoned. The bowls probably sat on flat bottoms (e.g., Fig. 61d).

Deep bowl rims also present diverse profiles; none is sufficiently preserved to suggest the actual depth. The larger examples with strongly inleaning rims (Figs. 59h; 60g) are, as in FA, the most nearly closed or restricted shape in the main fabric. Most of the rims suggest basic, multipurpose deep bowls. At least one has a piecrust rim (Fig. 62b). A handle at the rim (Fig. 59f) or on the upper body (Figs. 61e, h) may indicate a more specialized function for some, especially since the last two preserve faint traces of possible white paint on the exteriors. These are fairly large bowls that would have taken some effort from the potter to build and to fire, although little effort was expended on finishing the surfaces. A drill hole (Fig. 62a) indicates an attempt to repair one.

The FCP 5 potters may have worked infrequently, but they were not timid. They had difficulty with several large basins (Fig. 62c–d), a particularly challenging shape for any potter since the walls fight gravity, and shrinkage around the rim can be severe. These examples, with many non-joining sherds, are so irregular in curvature they appear warped, perhaps from being moved before they were sufficiently dry to maintain their shape. The rims are lumpy and uneven; although the interiors are evenly scraped, the exteriors were left unfinished, with bits of curled and smeared clay from working still evident.

Very large vessels with rim diameters around 0.40 m are also present (Fig. 63a–c).[17] If they had the tapering lower body suggested by the FA fragment (Fig. 47e), they would have stood close to a meter tall (see Fig.

83). It would have been easiest to build pots of this size in sections, perhaps using a braided hoop of twigs as a template to ensure the diameters would be closely similar at the points of attachment (Rye and Evans 1976:Pls. 7–8). The relief rope bands may have begun as a means of covering and reinforcing the joins between such sections. On several sherds from L5, a coil joint breaks directly under an applied rope band.

The large pots, like all the others, must have stood on flat bottoms. The flat bottom, one of the simplest kinds of support for a pot, is not without problems for the potter. That in Fig. 63f was made by forming a rounded clay disk that rested on the building platform, in this case probably a flat rock. To the edges of the disk, the potter attached a coil or slab to form the beginning of the lower walls. That first join is a critical one, since it must support the weight of the entire vessel. Surprisingly, the potters often made the joint poorly, relying on smearing a thin layer of clay over the crack between the two pieces rather than applying pressure to bond the joint. Multiple examples of bottom disks detached at the joint are present in the L5 deposits. A very large pot may have been too heavy and awkward to move while it was still damp, so the bottom disk held the impression of the surface on which it rested. If that was a nonporous surface, drying shrinkage in the walls would have contributed to cracking along the joint with the slower-drying bottom disk. Potters who used a woven mat as a building surface avoided that problem, since the mat allowed access of air to the underside of the disk.

A small "pan" (Fig. 63d) was made in the same way as the larger pots, but with a single coil attached around the exterior edge of the flattened clay disk. The maker smeared clay from the interior surface of the disk upward over the joint, thinning (and weakening) the bottom next to the joint. The underside of the pan retains the irregular impression of the working surface. The exterior and interior were only lightly smoothed. It is a very lumpy, irregular piece, that looks like a mistake—an intended bottom disk to which the potter added the first coil and, unintentionally, allowed it to dry too much before additional coils could be added. A second example from a mixed deposit in the cave (Fig. 73d), however, shows this was an intentional shape.

Decorated Pots

White "Crusted" Decoration with Fugitive Paints

Shapes

Small deep bowls: Fig. 64

Although one might have expected the crusted decoration in particular to suffer from the effects of weathering on Paralia, the examples from L5 are in better condition than are those from the cave. All rims suggest a rather small deep bowl (Fig. 64a–g), with a rim slightly everted to hold the 1–2 mm thick layer of crusting. One rim with only a small patch of thick crust preserved has considerably thicker walls than the others (Fig. 64g) and a smaller diameter. It may not have been made with the original intent to add crusting. It is probably from a smaller cup, but might be a neck from a closed shape. A large fragment preserves a flat or slightly dimpled bottom. The interior bottom bulges noticeably directly above the dimple, so the dimple may be the accidental effect of applying pressure to the bottom while it was still damp, rather than a true variant of the flat bottom. No fragments of pedestals with true crusting occur in L5. One sherd that has all the characteristics of the other crusted pieces has no trace of crust on the exterior, nor red powder on the interior (Fig. 67g). It may have been a pot intended to receive crusting that broke before the crust was added.

The interiors of the white crusted pots retain faint traces of a powdery red-orange pigment (10R 6/8) of the same color as the paint used for the patterns on the crusted exterior. The decoration on the white crust is, if fragmentary, sufficiently well preserved in a few cases to give an idea of how lively and vivid the pieces looked originally. Most of the pots have at least a trace of bright red-orange pigment on the white crust. Five pots preserve enough red pigment to hint at elaborate solid geometric patterns, different in each case, around the rim and lower body (Fig. 64a–e, h). Four of these (Fig. 64a, c–e, h) also have faint traces of black pigment lines outlining and elaborating the red patterns. The black lines are extremely faint: I noticed them only after several days of examining the sherds in various lights. In places where black pigment certainly once existed—e.g., Fig. 64a, the sherds to the left and right of the one shown with black lines—it has disappeared with no trace (Pl. 6a). It is possible that many more, and perhaps all of the crusted sherds once had bichrome decoration; conceivably there were even more varied colors in pigments and dyes even less durable than the red and black.

The bright colors and textures of these few sherds remind us of one of the inadequacies of the archaeological record. The durable remnants of Neolithic life tend to come in drab colors, which we repeat in the pictures we reconstruct. The busy bright surfaces of the crusted pots, along with the brightly whitewashed surfaces of pots within the cave (above), whatever their symbolic meaning, might remind us of the joy of bright colors against the blues of sea and sky on a sunny Aegean day—even in the Final Neolithic.

White Painted Decoration

Shapes

Cups: Figs. 65a–b
Bowls: Figs. 65c–f

Only the exteriors of bowls and cups were given white painted decoration. Complete profiles of two cups with flat bottoms came from the same pit in L5(NW) (Fig. 65a–b). One (Fig. 65a) is complete except for a short stretch of rim next to a pair of small tabs. The bottom of both cups sags slightly. That in Fig. 65b is so thin that it is unlikely to have survived firing intact. It is also extremely irregular in thickness, rim height, and profile at different points along the circumference.

A shallow open bowl is suggested by the fragments in Fig. 65c. The rim is warped or bent and gives diameter readings between 0.20 m (as drawn) and 0.27. The remaining rim sherds (Figs. 65d–f) suggest larger and deeper bowls, one with a small rim tab (Fig. 65d).

The painted lines were added after the surfaces had been burnished, with a white pigment that does not react in acid (with the exception of the sherds in Fig. 65e), but has largely disappeared, leaving a ghostly line. The pigment may have been a mixture of Lime and talc. The bowl in Fig. 65c was exposed to a hot, smoky fire, perhaps after the original potter's firing. It is warped and heavily fire clouded; the painted lines are black in places, crackling and crawling, probably from extreme heat (Pl. 6b). The narrow brush used to paint complex asymmetrical patterns on a burnished ground, as well as details of the shapes, distinguishes these white painted sherds from those found in FA (Fig. 52).

Red on White Painted Decoration

The sherds included here have at least a tiny speck of red paint on a Lime-free white paint, both well burnished, but the remains of the decoration are minimal and the sherds may belong in a different category. The pigments on one sherd (Fig. 66c) are well preserved, but difficult to decipher. It appears that broad areas of red paint were added after a full coating of white paint on the exterior, but the reverse is equally possible. The interior is also coated with red paint. The Paralia pieces show some general similarities to those with red on white painted decoration in the cave (Fig. 53a–f)), but they need not be closely related.

Shapes

Necked jar with shoulder handle: Fig. 66b
Bowls: Fig. 66c–d, f
Small basin: Fig. 66e
Pedestal: Fig. 66g
Bottom Fig. 66h

Three rims suggest convex-sided deep bowls with slight flips at the rim, similar to those on crusted bowls (Fig. 66c–d, f). They probably sat on flat bottoms (Fig. 66h). A small basin (Fig. 66e) may have rested on the pedestal (Fig. 66g), the only example of a base from L5. The only sherd to suggest a relatively large vessel with red on white painted decoration (Fig. 66b) has the stump of a strap handle and, on the interior, a well-defined angle marking a neck joint. The unusual profile and fabric are so similar to that of the polychrome jar in Fig. 66a that the sherd may well derive from the same pot.

Polychrome Decoration

A large jar, with a broad neck articulated at the interior joint, is the rare, and perhaps unique, jar in the FCP 5 assemblage. It is also a rare example in its clear, if fragmentary, traces of polychrome decoration without the use of crusting (Fig. 66a). Although very worn, the exterior appears to have been coated with a white, Lime-free paint, on which broad geometric shapes, both rectilinear and curving, were painted in red and outlined in black. A small body fragment with only a few flecks of red on white paint preserved (Fig. 66b) may be from the same pot, in which case the jar had one or more strap handles from the joint to the shoulder. Drill holes suggest an attempt to mend the broken pot, and that it was prized enough to be worth mending.

Red Painted Pots

A few of the sherds from L5 retain traces of a burnished red slip or paint covering one or both surfaces. All but one (Fig. 67a), which includes small flecks of biotite, appear to be made from the main fabric.

Shapes

Cups: Fig. 67a–b
Bowls: Fig. 67c–f, h

A cup with vertical walls and a small horizontal handle just below the rim (Fig. 67a) may be a non-local piece. The fabric includes small flecks of biotite. A more rounded cup has a small bead-like lug, pierced vertically, at the rim (Fig. 67b). Both handle and lug are unique in L5. The remaining red painted rims are from bowls; each is quite different in the details of the profile (Fig. 67c–f) and the quality of workmanship and finish. As a group, they have little in common other than the burnished red paint: were the surfaces better preserved, individual pieces might have been assigned to other varieties.

Pattern Burnished Decoration

Five non-joining sherds, from a single patterned burnished vessel (Fig. 67j), were found in a number of non-pit units in L5NW that included small amounts of FCP 5 pottery along with earlier FCP 1 and 2 sherds. The pattern burnished pieces suggest a small carinated bowl, with burnished decoration in broad lines on both interior and exterior. The surface has fired black, with a waxy quality and sheen to the burnished lines that indicates the use of a slip. The core has fired a deep red, and the whole is quite soft and worn. Several sherds appear to have broken along a coil joint. The piece is unique in the Franchthi assemblage. The shape is most similar to later FCP 2 Urf bowls; the fabric, construction, interior and exterior pattern, and soft firing seem more at home in FCP 5.

Incised Decoration

Two pots with incised decoration came from the uppermost units in L5NE. One (Fig. 67l) is from a deep bowl with a profile and fabric similar to several with red on white painted (e.g., Fig. 66c–d) and crusted decoration (e.g. Figs. 64a–b, d), although the edge of an attachment scar suggests the possibility of a lug or handle on the incised piece. The other (Fig. 67k) is probably also from a bowl, smaller and with thicker walls. The style of incision is different on each piece, and both are different from the examples from FAS (Fig. 45d–e) and from upper mixed deposits in the cave (Fig. 75 f–g). The unusual presence of mica (muscovite) in the fabric of the smaller bowl may suggest it is not a locally manufactured piece.

Uncertain Decoration

The sherds illustrated in Fig. 68 are probably from decorated pots, but the surfaces are so worn that little or no trace of pigment remains. Most have at least flecks of red pigment on one or both surfaces (Figs. 68c–i). The fabric is a pale pink color, the pink effect caused by minute red grains within the pale clay body. Several also have traces of a whitish encrustation or slip (Figs. 68d, h). The pale color of the sherds, similar to the surface color of the polychrome jar (Fig. 66a), suggests they once had a white coating. For whatever reason, they stand out from other sherds from the L5 deposits. As all are from units above the pits in L5NE, they could conceivably be later than the contents of the pits. They include several shape features not otherwise attested on Paralia.

Shapes

Cups: Fig. 68c–d, f (with horned lug), i (with two high, strutted loop handles)
Deep bowls: Fig. 68 a–b; Jar: Fig. 68g
Horned strap handles: Fig. 68e
Pierced elephant lug: Fig. 68h

Besides the simple cups in Figs. 68c–d, several cups have more or less elaborate appendages. Fig. 68f preserves a solid lug broken at the tip, probably a hook or horn that extended above the attachment joint. A more elaborate pair of handles was provided for the cup in Fig. 68i. No sherds from the rim area between the handles were found, but the two handles are surely from the same vessel. The walls of the body are extremely thin (2–3 mm) for the weight of the handles they supported. The handles must have been added while the clay of the cup was still fairly damp, and one has to wonder how the potter kept the weight of the large loop handles from pulling the cup apart. That the shape is not a one-time aberration by an overly adventuresome potter is suggested by a fragment from FAQSW+WB:31 (Fig. 71i), with very similar fabric and profile. The FA handle is painted in stunning bands of red and white (not Lime), and was sufficiently appreciated that mending was apparently attempted: it preserves three drill holes and the beginning of a fourth on the underside. The Paralia cup may also have been painted in vivid colors.

Two slightly inleaning bowls (Fig. 68a–b) retain no trace of pigment other than the very fine red grains within the clay body itself. Such bowls may have carried a pair of strap handles with small horns (Fig. 68e1–2), which are similar in fabric. No sherds with attachment scars were recovered from the L5 deposits. The elephant lug in Fig. 68h was attached to a deep bowl, judging from the curvature of the wall and traces of red pigment on the interior. The lug looks quite zoomorphic when the "trunk" is facing down and the horizontal piercing looks like eyes, but the curvature of the body wall suggests the reverse orientation. Another "elephant" lug was found in a mixed context inside the cave (Fig. 74e). The fabric looks different from that of the L5NE example, a difference which could reflect burial conditions. It, too, may have been oriented with the "trunk" above the horizontal piercing. As drawn (which reflects the way the piece was seen when the vessel was upside down), one can appreciate the playfully zoomorphic appearance of the "trunk" swung to one side, the pierced "eyes" looking out over the wrinkled snout.

A small body sherd suggests the neck of a large jar (Fig. 68g), similar to the polychrome jar (Figs. 66a–b), but without the articulated interior neck joint. With faint traces of red paint on the upper interior neck and on the exterior, it is similar enough in fabric to the polychrome piece to suggest that it, too, may have had polychrome decoration.

THE POTTERY FROM FCP 5.2

The three latest stratified units in FA, FA:46, 45, and 39, include a new variety, Heavy Burnished, along with examples of familiar FCP 5 varieties and a few battered examples of sherds from earlier phases (FCP 2 and FCP 4). The earlier sherds indicate that the late FCP 5 occupants, like their predecessors, dug into and redeposited sediments from elsewhere in the cave. Some of the familiar FCP 5 varieties may be redeposited, but others appear to be contemporary with the Heavy Burnished variety. The number and size of the sherds from the three stratified units is so small that I include unstratified examples in the documentation of the variety.

Heavy Burnished Variety

Fabric

The clay body is always heavily gritted with red, black, and white nonplastics; in some sherds, these are less than 1 mm in size, in others, as large as 2–3 mm. Roughly half the examples include a small number of Lime nonplastics, while the other half show no reaction in acid. The larger red and dark nonplastics are sometimes angular, sometimes rounded. Some may be grog. Several sherds have numerous tiny voids, possibly from rootlets or other organic materials in the clay. The nonplastics are usually well integrated with and evenly dispersed throughout the clay body.

Building and Surface Finish

The pots were built up with coils, as evident inside the neck of small collared jars (e.g., Fig.69a, c) where the joint between coils is not completely smeared over, and in the slits between overlapping coils visible in the breaks of several carinated bowls. A heavy vertical tubular lug was made by spiraling a very narrow coil into a tube, perhaps by wrapping it around a stick, and attaching it to the vessel wall (Fig. 70j). Other lugs of various sizes and shapes are common features (Figs. 69a, c, e; 70b,g–h). The potters scraped interiors and exteriors to produce even, regular surfaces, although they left the walls relatively thick (7–8 mm or more), even on small pots. After scraping and finger smoothing, they slipped accessible surfaces, probably with an iron-oxide-rich clay that is sometimes visible as a red or black stripe inside the neck of collared jars or in the unburnished areas between troughs. They burnished these surfaces well, using a tool that left fine striations within the trough—possibly a bone—often achieving a good sheen and waxy texture on the slipped surfaces.

White Painted Decoration

The potters add painted decoration to some Heavy Burnished pots, using a white pigment that does not react to acid and, today at least, often appears more black than white, or shows up only as a dull area against the sheen of the burnished surface. The painted lines were applied with a very narrow brush in multiple vertical or diagonal lines (Figs. 69d, f–g, i; 70e).

Incised Decoration

Several Heavy Burnished sherds from mixed contexts were decorated with incised or impressed lines. A bowl or lid has groups of parallel impressed or incised lines on its flat surface (Fig. 69j). Several basins with thickened, folded rims have similar lines along the exterior rim folds (Fig. 75a–b).

Colors and Firing Practices

Most examples have fired black or dark brown, with dark gray cores, but many are mottled with firing clouds from red through tan to greenish grays, especially on the exteriors. Sometimes the contrasting colors of the ground and firing clouds create a dramatic effect, as on the jar in Fig. 69c, deep black with a bright red cloud around the lug and a spot of the rim. A couple of otherwise dark fired sherds have tiny, 2 mm-round, red clouds, probably from something small and organic in the pot or the fuel that flared up at the end of the firing. A creamy bloom is sometimes evident on parts of the surface. Occasionally grains of red pigment in unburnished areas around lugs and between troughs, probably part of the original slip, give a reddish glow to the whole piece. Cores are usually dark, but not as black as the surfaces, and light subsurfaces occur. Most sherds have a hardness of Mohs' 4; they are harder than most other FCP 5 sherds, but considerably

Table 5.1. Relative frequencies of varieties in FCP 5.2.

Unit	Total #	Urf	LiFe	Powder	Crust	PB	RonW	Rslip	HB	FNCo	CalCo
FA:39											
#	137	13	•	3	5	2	•	•	11	103	•
%		10%	•	2%	4%	2%	•	•	8%	75%	•
FA:45											
#	236	8	5	6	4	1	3	1	22	185	1
%		3%	2%	3%	2%	•	1%	•	9%	78%	•
FA:46											
#	67	1	•	2	•	•	•	•	10	54	•
%		2%	•	3%	•	•	•	•	15%	81%	•

less hard than, e.g., the FCP 4 Lime plus Iron pots.

The Heavy Burnished pots were fired in direct contact with the fuel, as were other FCP 5 pots; these were probably fired more slowly, for a longer time, and covered at the end of the firing, to smother the fire and smudge the pots. A black surface may have been the desired effect, but the potters were not entirely successful in cutting off the oxygen supply while the pots were still hot, thus often ended up with clouded, mottled surfaces.

Shapes

Small necked jars: Fig. 69a–d, e
Convex bowls: Fig. 70i–j
Carinated bowls: Fig. 70a–e
Collared or shouldered bowls: Figs.69g, i, 70f–h
Open bowls with lips: Fig. 69f, h
Flat bottomed (topped) bowl?: Fig. 69j

The shapes are new for FCP 5, a complete departure from the earlier generic bowls and jars, and a return to more complex shapes with clearly articulated parts. Although rim curvature is usually irregular and coil joints were not always thoroughly sealed, the impression is that the makers of these pots worked more frequently than those responsible for the earlier FCP 5 pots. They also worked with a more clearly defined concept of pot shape, reproducing a set of specific shapes with some consistency. The cultural "rules" governing the creation of these pots were more rigid than had been the case earlier in the phase.

The small necked jars in the Heavy Burnished variety (Figs. 69a–d) are reminiscent of FCP 3 examples (e.g., Figs. 1a, g, h–j), although the Heavy Burnished pieces are less delicate and often equipped with lugs. The simple convex bowls (Figs. 70i–j) are made distinctive by additions: a neatly squared, applied pellet (Fig. 70i) or a spiraling tubular lug (Fig. 70j). Carinated bowls, a staple of the FCP 2 and FCP 3 potters, occurred rarely in FCP 4, and are absent earlier in FCP 5 (Figs. 70a–e).[18] They, too, could be equipped with substantial lugs (Fig. 70b), and they were probably deep, with steeply sloping lower walls resting on a flat bottom. Collared or shouldered bowls (Figs.69g; 70f–g, probably h) with heavy horizontal tubular (Fig. 70g) and trumpet (Fig. 70h) lugs probably also had deep lower bodies and flat bottoms. Sharply rounded bowls were given out-turned lips (Figs. 69f, h). It is not clear whether the "rim" on the fragment with incised or impressed decoration on its flat surface (Fig. 69j) is, in fact, a rim with wear along the very tip, or whether it has broken along a (very narrow) joint, and we are missing something from the profile. It shows traces of wear along the interior curve and on the interior bottom (as drawn), but nothing suggesting patterned wear on the decorated surface. The wear and location of the decoration suggest it may have been a lid. A small sherd (not illustrated) that preserves only the bottom joint has similar impressed decoration on the "bottom," and powdery red and white pigments in the depressions. It was found in the mixed deposits of H Terrace.

Similar heavy, dark, burnished pottery occurs from Argos (Touchais 1980:24) and Lerna (Vitelli forthcoming), from Sitagroi I (Keighley 1986:349), and throughout much of the Aegean area.

ADDITIONAL POTTERY FROM UPPER MIXED DEPOSITS

Most of the pottery recovered from upper mixed deposits in the cave was discarded, but a few well-preserved sherds were saved and are illustrated here. Most have no close parallels in the material from the FCP 5.1a–c deposits in FA, and, with the possible exception of the red on white painted examples, these are probably contemporary with, or later than the Heavy Burnished material from FA:39, 45–46.

Red on White Painted Decoration

The best-preserved examples of pieces with red painted decoration on a painted white, Lime-free background come from reworked or poorly documented contexts (Figs. 72a–f). Two, however, were found in clay-lined pits in Trench A:25 (Figs. 72b–c), which are probably to be associated with FCP 5.1b (see Chapter 2), where sherds of this variety are most common. The best-preserved profile (Fig. 72c) is a small bowl, not unlike crusted bowls, but with a small strap handle reaching up toward the rim from the belly. Tooling traces along the bottom suggest the bowl sat on a base. The surface is worn and without signs of burnishing, and the white background may be the natural ground of the clay or an accidental salt slip, rather than an applied coating: the pale color penetrates the subsurface along part of the break. The bowl was painted red on the interior.

A more closed bowl (Fig. 72a) has lost most of its decoration; the white background looks like an applied slip. Only flecks of red on the exterior and interior remain. The sherd illustrated in Fig. 72b suggests a neck, but the curvature may be accidental. The red and white pigments are well preserved, well burnished, and flaking away from a nicely smoothed ceramic surface.

The remaining examples (Fig. 72d–f) give no indication of shape or size, other than that two (Fig. 72d, f) are decorated on both surfaces and thus probably from open bowls. The pigments in Fig. 72d were applied to an already burnished surface and are themselves well burnished. The white pigment is not Lime; it can be turned to powder by scratching. The pigments in Fig. 72f were applied to a well-smoothed surface, from which they are flaking away. Red and white pigments were affected by fire—the red turning orange in the area where the white has a gray-black cloud. The sherd (or pot) might have been exposed to additional fires beyond that of the potter.

Powdery White Lime and Powdery Red Decoration

From a mixed cave deposit comes an example of stunning decoration added after firing to a small, well-burnished bowl that was fired to a deep black (Fig. 71e). The elaborate pattern was painted in what are now fugitive red-orange and white Lime pigments. The black surface of the pot shows through between double narrow white lines. The space around the white lines was filled in with bright red-orange (2.5 YR 6/8) pigment, and the interior of the bowl coated with what is now an equally fugitive, bluish-red (7.5 YR 3/8) pigment.[19]

A tab lug above a rim is similarly decorated (Fig. 71g). The lug itself is coated with a fugitive red powder, on top of which the painter used a white Lime paint to add small rectangles; these, deteriorated since excavation, are now almost impossible to make out. To the left of the lug (as drawn), a small area of black burnished pot surface was unpainted. The interior of the bowl has traces of a powdery red pigment. A similar lug (Fig. 71h) was burnished, but it retains no traces of painted decoration.

Pattern Burnished Decoration, with Reserved Rim Band

Sherds with pattern burnished decoration are associated with the Heavy Burnished variety in FA:39 and occur in upper mixed deposits. Three rims (Fig. 71a–c) and a flat bottom (Fig. 71d) are illustrated, all probably from medium-sized, deep bowls. The pattern burnishing stands out as a glossy red against a dull, lighter red ground. The rims have a reserved, unburnished band around the exterior that retains traces of red powder, and all but Fig. 71c have traces of a similar red pigment on the interior. In Fig. 71a, the broad burnished lines were created by burnishing first a vertical or two, then an abutting horizontal, then a vertical, and so on (Pl. 6c). The pattern produced resembles in style pieces from Kephala (Coleman 1977: Pl. 86), some of which also had red "crusting" on the interior (Coleman 1977:28) but not the reserved rim band coated with orange powder (Coleman 1977:11).

Other Combinations of Red and White Pigments

The odd fragment shown in Fig. 71l is coated on the exterior surface with a burnished yellowish-white pigment that retains traces of a powdery red-orange pigment. The piece reacts strongly to hydrochloric acid. The interior surface is very rough, with clumps of clay from the building process still clinging to it. The scar of a strut or other attachment is preserved on the interior near the upper, broken edge. The other end is finished with indentations that create six little "toes." If it was a handle above a rim, the unfinished inner surface would have been very evident. Probably it was a foot, perhaps something similar in concept and function to the Sitagroi tripods (Elster 1986:303) or the footed bowl from Aigina (Walter and Felten 1981:Fig. 72).

The remaining pieces in Fig. 71, from reworked deposits, are likely to be examples of late varieties. A simple open bowl (Fig. 71f) has lost most of its pattern since I drew it in the 1970s. At that time, the entire interior and the pattern along the exterior rim were covered with a powdery red-orange pigment, applied over a well-burnished surface. The clay ground between the pattern lines is a pale, near-white color, probably a white paint. Below the pattern, the piece has fired black, which suggests the pigments were applied after firing. The pigments do not react to hydrochloric acid.

The handle fragment in Fig. 71i is so similar in shape and fabric to the tall strutted loop handles from L5 (above, Fig. 68i) that it is difficult not to think they are contemporary. This small fragment, with three mend holes and the beginning of a fourth on the interior, is brightly painted in burnished red-orange and white pigments that seem to have been fired with the pot; they do not react in hydrochloric acid. It may be unrelated to the L5 pieces.

A small basin (Fig. 71k) and two narrow pedestals (Fig. 71m–n) have traces of red powder that once covered the interior or the bowls and the exteriors. One pedestal (Fig. 71n) preserves the edges of small, pre-firing cut-outs. The other has a very small, pre-firing pinhole piercing the pedestal just below the joint. Both techniques were used in FCP 2 to help even out the drying of bowl and pedestal, and to prevent the base from detaching during firing. Their reappearance here points to potters with some experience and concern for the details of successful building. A small, hole-mouthed jar (Fig. 71j) with a button lug on the upper shoulder is coated with what was once a thick pinkish (2.5 YR 6/6) powder that has faint traces of white powder on top of it. The closed shape is unusual for FCP 5; were it not for the powdery pigments and unburnished surface, it could be thought an Early Neolithic piece.

No sherds coated with fugitive red powdery pigment were found in the L5 deposit, perhaps confirming the suggestion from the FA sequence that such pieces are later than the true white crust. A nearly complete pot, coated on the exterior and just inside the rim with a fugitive orange pigment (2.5 YR 5/8),[20] was found with a burial of a middle-aged woman (Fr 63) in O5NE:11 (Fig. 67i, FP 197). Firing clouds are evident under the powdery coating, suggesting the pigment was added after the original firing.

Fig. 72g illustrates a small, unique, fragment of a "face pot" (FP 173) found in a deep, but reworked deposit in H1A. The interior of the sherd is scraped and curved as though it were a pot with a diameter of 5–6 cm—a very small pot. The fabric, with mixed nonplastics including Lime and a red mineral up to 2 mm in size, is comparable to that of many FCP 5 pieces. Along the interior of the preserved top of the sherd, which is broken, traces of a red stripe remain, suggesting that the "rim" was not far above the preserved edge. The face is carefully modeled, with depressions for eye sockets. The left is filled by a small round pellet for the eyeball. The right eyeball is missing. Above and behind the left eye, a bit high for an ear, is another deep spherical depression that may have penetrated the thickness of the sherd. Where parts of the brow are flaking away, one can see that the modeling was done by adding small bits of clay. The whole face was burnished before being entirely coated, including the eyeball, with a white Lime paint. Flecks of red paint remain from more extensive painting on the face. Both red and white paints were burnished on; both are now fugitive.

Talalay, in publishing the piece as early Middle Neolithic coarse Urfirnis (Talalay 1993:21), cited general parallels from Nea Nikomedeia, Thespiae, and Achilleion (p. 65); she noted that the findspot, H1A: 78, while including modern contamination, bordered a unit with predominantly early Middle Neolithic material (p. 94). She may be correct about the date, given other examples of faces on pots,[21] although the context is unreliable. The piece is certainly not a variety of Urfirinis, however, and characteristics of the pigment suggest an FCP 5 date.

Manganese Painted Decoration

Several sherds from what should be the earliest FCP 5 context at Franchthi have polychrome decoration that uses a black manganese-oxide-rich pigment (Fig. 45a–c). A well-preserved rim sherd (Fig. 72j) from FA:50 in the reworked deposits east and well below the top of FA Balk (see Jacobsen and Farrand 1987:Pl. 8) is very similar in decoration to the two rims from within the Balk. All could be kickups from FCP 3 or 4; since all the known examples at Franchthi occur in early FCP 5 contexts, it seems reasonable to assume they *are* FCP 5 products, probably foreign to Franchthi.

From another reworked context, FA QSW+WB:31, that included primarily late FCP 5 material, a body sherd with polychrome decoration on interior and exterior, including on a horizontal button lug (Fig. 72h), is probably another example of FCP 5 polychrome decoration. Broad red and narrow black lines were painted over a white Lime-free slip, and burnished on. The button lug helps establish this polychrome example as probably FCP 5. The remaining illustrated sherds (Figs. 72i, k–m) are less securely assigned to FCP 5 because they lack distinguishing features. All resemble earlier shapes and decoration, at least in the small fragments preserved, enough to raise the possibility that they predate FCP 5. The jar rim with manganese black decoration on a pale ground (Fig. 72m) is from A Lot 13; this, including no clear FCP 3 or 4 material, is probably to be associated with FCP 5.1b.

Coarse Varieties

The upper mixed deposits in the cave included large quantities of "coarse" pottery, most of it FCP 5 in date, and probably from a late stage of occupation. Most were body sherds, and most of those were discarded. Among the saved sherds are several with interesting features. Two small rims (Figs. 73a–b) have small pre-firing holes pierced along the rims and surfaces that are the unfinished, rough building surfaces. Although very little is preserved, the sherds are remarkably similar to the large "drums" at Lerna, which were found in association with sherds of the Heavy Burnished variety (Vitelli forthcoming). A miniature profile of these large pots from Lerna is reproduced in Fig. 73:1. The actual preserved length of the larger example at Lerna is 0.44 m, with the width at the mouth 0.49 m.

The flattened horns on the strap handles in Figs. 73c and 75e are closer to one in FCP 5.1c (Fig. 55e) than to the rounded or conical horn of the example in FCP 5.1b (Fig. 47e). The mat impressions on the bottoms of large pots (Fig. 73e, Pl. 7b; 7c left) from upper reworked deposits suggest more sophisticated basketry than does the example from L5 (Pl. 7a), and may be late features.

Small undecorated and minimally finished cups are common from at least FCP 5.1b on. A nearly complete example came from A Lot 13 (Fig. 74a). FCP 5 potters poked holes through a number of their small, damp pots, presumably to serve some particular purpose. The cup in Fig. 74b has holes poked through its bottom. A more likely cheese pot than those with holes along the rim, it is at any rate a potential strainer. The odd little pot in Fig. 74d is more likely a stand than a container: made by smearing clay around a flat disk, it was joined so poorly that a hole remains along the joint. It is pierced with two sets of three holes on opposite sides of the rim, aligned so that sticks can be run through two sets of opposed holes; the third set is not aligned. Although the rough shaping makes it look like something made on the spur of the moment to fill a specific need, it has traces of red and white lime powder that may suggest it was more than a casual creation.

Throughout the phase, FCP 5 potters frequently added handles, rim tabs, and lugs of all sorts to their pots. An elephant lug (Fig. 74e) and a thick lug or tab above a rim with two ears and a pierced hole that suggests eyes (Fig. 74h) are among the more fanciful, and probably late examples. A pierced crescent lug that seems to have been part of an applied rope band (Fig. 74k) is also probably a late example, as are the two pierced tabs with double tips (Fig. 74i–j). One (Fig. 74j) was coated with red-orange pigment that is now powdery.

The surface of a small body sherd is covered with applied worm-like bits of clay, several of which have detached (Fig. 74f, Jacobsen 1973b:Pl. 51b). The body curvature is uneven; the thick wall suggests a large pot. If the entire surface was covered with applied strips, the pot would represent an extremely labor-intensive piece of work. The sherd, unique at Franchthi, may not be Neolithic.

Folded-out, thickened rims with impressed or incised decoration (Fig. 75a–b) may be worn examples of the Heavy Burnished variety. If so, the very similar rim from FAS:74 (Fig. 53h) would represent an intrusive piece in that context. The rim in Fig. 75a was recovered by divers from the pool at the back of the cave (Jacobsen and Farrand 1987:Pl. 2; see Document 2). Large basins with similar profiles but different elaboration (Figs. 75c–d) could be from FCP 5 or later. The example from A Lot 13 (Fig. 75d) has a crispness to the indentations that is suspiciously Early Bronze Age.

Several incised sherds (Figs. 75f–g) from lots in Trench A that included primarily late FCP 5 material are different in style from the incised sherds from other FCP 5 cave deposits (Fig. 45d–e) and from Paralia (Figs. 67k–l). Roughly incised decoration is reported from many Final Neolithic sites in Greece (e.g., Tharrounia, Sampson 1993:Figs. 111–123; The Cave of the Lakes, Sampson 1997:235–249), in a wide range of styles. The Franchthi sequence suggests that incised decoration, like "crusting," rope bands, horned handles, mat impressed bottoms, and other "typical" FN features, may have been produced throughout the very long Final Neolithic phase. We shall have to be more precise in defining the technological and stylistic aspects of each of these features if we are to sort out the temporal and spatial complexities of the phase.

FCP 5 ON THE REST OF PARALIA

While the major FCP 5 deposit on Paralia was in L5, other areas produced some traces of FCP 5 activity. Sherds from the upper 20–30 cm of topsoil were universally in poor condition: heavily weathered, with surfaces largely gone and what remained quite soft, sometimes powdery, and rounded. To the extent that any sherds could be securely identified in the first three to four units from the surface, post-Neolithic material was generally present, although usually amounting to only a couple of pieces. Because of the predictable condition of sherds from uppermost units, I studied them only selectively. Everywhere that I did look, FCP 5 material was definitely or probably present (Plan 3, Table 10). When a feature such as a horned handle, an impressed rope band, a spindle whorl, or a trumpet lug was represented, I felt certain of the FCP 5 designation. Usually, all that suggested FCP 5 activity was a small pile of rounded red ceramic lumps, barely fired and with no surfaces or features preserved. These are probably the remains of low-fired FCP 5 pots, but identification is hardly certain. In no unit other than in L5 were FCP 5 (or potential FCP 5) sherds in the majority.

Burials

At least six FCP 5 burials were excavated from deposits very close to the surface on Paralia: Fr 115 (L5:57), Fr 61–63 (O5NE: 2–3, 5–7, 9–11), Fr 18 (Q6NE: 10), and Fr 19 (Q5N:19). Two additional burials in Q4 cannot be dated securely, but are potentially of FCP 5 origin: Fr 69 (Q4:10, 16, 25) and Fr 221 (Q4:9) (see Cullen and Cook forthcoming). The bones were so close to the modern surface that, unless very substantial erosion has taken place, they must have been in extremely shallow graves, perhaps even requiring mounded earth to cover them.

One of the O5NE burials (Fr 63) included a small cup coated with orange powder (FP 197, Fig. 67i) found sitting near the right hand, bent up next to the skull. Downslope from the O5NE burials, in O5:3-4, were a fragment of an elephant lug (cf. Fig. 68h from L5) and a Heavy Burnished lug; both units included post-Neolithic sherds. Q5N:19 included a spindle whorl (FC 121; Document 1) possibly associated with the burial (Fr 19). Upslope, to the east of the burial, and at roughly the same elevation, Q5N:10 included a fragment of a small hollow ceramic foot—similar to those in Fig. 57i, l—that may be related to the burial. No grave goods were found with the other burials, nor was FCP 5 pottery abundant in the units immediately above or around the burials, except for the one in L5, which was located at the top of, and between, the two deep carbonate-rich pits in the northwest quadrant (Plan 3).

Pottery from units in Q4 that included Fr 69 was coated with a Lime powder similar to that in the L5 pits; it included no securely identified FCP 5 sherds (see Table 10). Q4:9 (Fr 221), in terms of ceramics, is "pure" Early Neolithic; stratified above units with plentiful Middle Neolithic sherds, the sediments are necessarily redeposited. The redeposition may have occurred in FCP 5 in conjunction with the burial.[22]

Other FCP 5 Deposits

A slightly more substantial collection of FCP 5 sherds came from the center of P5, south of Wall K. P5:22, 29, and 30 produced a little more than a kilogram of FCP 5 sherds, including a fragment of a strutted loop handle (cf. Fig. 68i from L5), a bit of an impressed rope band, a thick sherd with traces of a pinkish Lime-rich smear on the exterior surface comparable to examples from FCP 5.1b in FA, and several lumps of white carbonate.

Another kilogram (just over 100 sherds) of FCP 5 sherds came from the upper 0.20–0.30 m of PQ5. In Q5S, a few FCP 5 sherds occur in units between Wall D and the south scarp. Surface units covering the whole of Q/R produced a few additional sherds. Had I examined the material from other surface units in Q5S and P5, I expect I would have found at least occasional FCP 5 sherds, since they occur everywhere I did look. Had quantities comparable to those in L5 been present, however, the excavators would have noted them in the field notebooks.

Q4 sits on the 4-m contour line, at the same elevation as L5 (Jacobsen and Farrand 1987:Pl. 2). The difference in the depth of the topsoil (Stratum XXXII) between Q4 and Q5N (Jacobsen and Farrand 1987:Pl. 56) suggests that Wall DD, probably constructed as a retaining wall in FCP 1 (Vitelli 1993a:43 and Plan 6), had maintained a reasonably level terrace downslope, in Q5N. By FCP 5, however, the fill behind Wall DD had accumulated sufficiently to be close to, if not actually overtopping it. The area of Q4, not a particularly attractive or useful activity area in FCP 1 and 2 (Vitelli 1993a:43), by FCP 5 had filled in and leveled off, and it may have been occupied. Wall T was probably built in FCP 5, perhaps to reinforce Wall DD and prevent more sediment from overtopping it. Some sediment directly below Wall DD, within Q5N may have been removed, to level off the old Upper Terrace again (Vitelli 1993: Plan 3).[23] Deposits on either side of Wall T include small amounts of FCP 5 pottery with, in Q4:38, a small fragment of the HB variety with a small trumpet lug (cf. Fig.70h from FA). Wall T would seem to be a late, FCP 5.2, addition, post-dating the FCP 5 activities in L5. The pottery from these units was coated with a fine gray caustic powder (Vitelli 1993a:82, n. 7) that suggests the sediments may have been rich in quicklime. Q4:10, 16, and 25, in the southwest corner, removed a burial (Fr 69). Sherds from these units were also coated with caustic Lime powder. Although securely identified FCP 5 sherds are lacking, the Lime coating and the shallow depth of the burial (ca. 20 cm below modern surface) argue that the burial was made in FCP 5. Another potential FCP 5 burial was encountered ca. 25 cm below the modern surface in the southeast quadrant (Q4:9, Fr 221; see Cullen and Cook forthcoming). An FCP 5 date is less certain for this burial. Whatever the specific activities of FCP 5 on Paralia, they left few sherds or other material remains behind.

Overall, the FCP 5 presence on Paralia is intriguing, but puzzling. The FCP 5 occupants used Paralia to bury at least six individuals. Two (Fr 61–62) were so closely spaced that they must have been buried together, and almost on top of a third (FR 63), the only one with a clearly associated grave gift.[24] Of the other three burials on Paralia, one may have been provided with a spindle whorl. No units around the burials include quantities of FCP 5 pots that might indicate extensive feasting or other ritual or ceremonial activity associated with the burial; at least, nothing produced any quantity of durable remains.

The burial of an eight-year-old child in L5 sat just at the top edge of one of the Lime-rich pits. It could be related to the activities that produced the pits, or it could post-date the filling of the pits. A notable feature of the L5 pits is the quantity of Lime, in clumps especially along the edges in two pits, and in the sediments in and around them in sufficient quantity to make the sediments appear white. If the source of the Lime had been quicklime applied to the corpse, either in some form of body painting or other ritual associated with the burial (whether intentionally or incidentally to speed decomposition of the flesh), the bones should show traces of corrosion. Cook reports no such traces are present. If the carbonates were quicklime that had, for example, been rained on or otherwise slaked, and then the burial took place, the Lime would not have had a corrosive effect on the bone, but would actually have improved bone preservation (Cook, pers. comm. 2/3/98). That sequence, fitting the contextual evidence, would appear to disassociate from the burial whatever activities were involved in digging and filling the pits and in producing the carbonates. The area was used for the pit-related activities; when they were over, it was chosen, perhaps coincidentally, as the location for a burial, although no great lapse of time necessarily separated the two.

WHORLS AND "WEIGHTS"

The FCP 5 ceramic repertoire included specially manufactured spindle whorls[25] in biconical, conical, and discoidal shapes (Document 1). Made in the main FCP 5 fabric, they could have been fired together with the pots. Minute flecks of red and white paint on a few examples suggest some or all of the whorls may once have carried decoration.[26] The very fugitive nature of the pigments suggests the decoration may have been added at some time after the brief firing the whorls received. The three basic shapes occur together in some of the same deposits,[27] so shapes are not chronologically distinct; they may have been a matter of personal preference. All can be made quite easily by rolling a small lump of clay between the hands to produce a biconical lump. Slight pressure on one or both points of the cone produces the other shapes, and a stick poked through the middle completes the whorl.

Whorls occur throughout the FCP 5 deposits in some quantity: 46 in FA; 19 in Trench A; 20 in L5; 2 from mixed deposits on Paralia; another 21 from mixed deposits inside the cave (see Document 1). The quantities, especially in the pit fill in L5, raise the possibility that whorls were used as a kind of votive.

A spherical ball of almost pure calcium carbonate, 8.5 cm in diameter and weighing ca. 600 g, came from FA:39, the FCP 5.2 hearth unit.[28] The ball is not unlike five objects[29] previously published as a group of "spherical weights" (Jacobsen 1969:372) and "loom weights" of fired clay (Jacobsen 1973b:277), and assigned to the Middle Neolithic. All are from mixed contexts in Trenches G, G1, and A, so their date is uncertain. The five examples are made, not from fired clay, but from almost pure calcium carbonate that foams and disappears in hydrochloric acid, leaving behind small chunks of carbon and rock. The spheres are mottled with dark fire clouds, so were apparently exposed briefly to fire. All are centrally perforated, unlike the FA:39 "ball," and are smaller (weighing ca. 100–120 g). They may or may not be related to the FCP 5.2 "ball." They could have been used in textile production, but other functions are possible.

SUMMARY AND DISCUSSION

Estimates of the total amount of FCP 5 pottery at Franchthi are extremely rough at best because no figures are available for many units and the pots are extremely fragmentary. Approximately 30 kg of FCP 5.1 sherds were recovered from FAS, another 17 kg from FAN, and perhaps 3 kg from the three FCP 5.2 units above the balk, for a total of ca. 50 kg. Sherds included in that 50 kg account for ca. 17% of the pottery recovered from FAS and FAN, twice as much as the FCP 3 pottery, just slightly more than the FCP 4 sample (Table 5.2).

An educated guess of the additional quantities rep-

Table 5.2. Weight of pottery by phase from FA deposits

	All	FCP 1+2	FCP 3	FCP 4	FCP 5
Total Weight (kg)	292	175	23	44	50
%		60	8	15	17

resented in mixed deposits in the cave, including the back of the cave, added to the material from FA, suggests that a total of 200–500 kg of FCP 5 pottery may have been recovered. L5 produced an additional 36 kg, the rest of Paralia probably less than 5 kg. Even if reasonably accurate, the weight estimates alone are a misleading guide to the intensity of occupation: many more FCP 5 sherds than in earlier phases are from thick-walled, often quite large pots that may have weighed 5–10 kg each.

The profile drawings, if interpreted generously, suggest 125–150 pots for FCP 5.1 in FA, 80–85 for the L5 deposits, and perhaps 50–60 from FCP 5.2, if examples from reworked deposits are included. But it is hard to evaluate such estimates. Whatever the actual quantity of pottery, FCP 5 activities took place over a wider portion of the front of the cave than in either FCP 3 or FCP 4, and extended into the depths of the cave and across Paralia. Our sense of the intensity of occupation represented by the quantity of pottery depends in large part on the length of time it took to accumulate.

C-14 Dates

Three closely spaced dates place the end of FCP 4 around 4160 calBC (Table 9). Signs of weathering within sediments removed in FAN:88, 84, and 81 (Farrand forthcoming: sample numbers 1–2, 1–3) point to a hiatus in activity in the cave following FCP 4. The earliest FCP 5 date, from FAS:72 (Table 9), is 500–850 years later than the FCP 4.3 dates, confirming a hiatus. FAS:72 is assigned to FCP 5.1b, so the date is not from the earliest FCP 5 deposit in FA. Apparent similarities in the ceramics of FCP 5.1a and 5.1b sets them probably close in time; the hiatus between FCP 4 and FCP 5 may not be much less than indicated by the C-14 dates.

The latest Neolithic C-14 date comes from FA:39 (Table 9), a unit that provides the stratified Heavy Burnished sherds that define FCP 5.2. The C-14 dates thus suggest that FCP 5 activity at Franchthi took place over the course of several hundred years, roughly in the middle of the long, 1500-year span of the Final Neolithic in Greece.

The Temporal Relationship between FCP 5.1 Activities in the Cave and L5

The temporal relationship between the FCP 5.1 deposits in the cave and those in L5 on Paralia is not easy to establish. Comparison of the pottery is difficult because the material is so fragmentary and preservation so variable. Complete profiles are lacking and examples of decoration preserve little of the composition. For FCP 1 and FCP 2, the pottery from Paralia is far less well preserved than that from the cave, presumably through greater exposure to the elements. Yet the FCP 5.1 pottery from L5, although quite soft, is in better condition than that from inside the cave. The Lime-rich sediment of the L5 deposit may have contributed to its preservation; more likely the good condition is the result of rapid burial without subsequent disturbance.[30] The material from inside the cave was protected from the weather, but it must have been exposed to more battering and traffic before being completely buried, and it suffered further when the sediments were reworked during the Neolithic.

The shapes from both deposits are, with few exceptions, simple bowls of various sizes and degrees of openness. Variation is as great within a single unit as among different units or areas. The rare shapes with more distinctive features are so rare that their absence from one of the deposits can be given little weight. Impressed rope bands, piecrust rims, and heavy strap handles occur in all FCP 5 contexts, early and late, inside the cave and on Paralia.

The more distinctive pieces from L5 find a few parallels inside the cave. A small pan (Fig. 63d) finds its closest match in A:23 (Fig. 73d), a unit that should be roughly equivalent to FAS:73 (FCP 5.1b), although the records are too poor to feel very secure on this point. The elephant lug (Fig. 68h) has a rough parallel from A:11 (Fig. 74e), a very mixed unit. The strutted loop handles (Fig. 68i) are very similar to a fragment from FA:31 (Fig. 71i), a thoroughly mixed unit. The necked jar (Figs. 66a–b, 68g) has no parallel in the cave deposits, unless a small dark, burnished fragment with a possible neck joint (not illustrated) from the exploration at the rear of the cave is an FCP 5 sherd. A lumpy loop handle above the rim (Fig.59d) is similar to several examples from FCP 5.1b (Fig. 48d–h). A cup with a pre-firing hole below the rim (Fig. 58c) shares that feature with a cup from FAS:73 (Fig. 48b), again from FCP 5.1b.

While some shape features suggest an affinity with FCP 5.1b, the specifics of surface elaboration raise new questions about the relationship of the two deposits. The best-preserved examples of white crusted pots come from FCP 5.1b (Fig. 51a–d) in the cave, and from L5 (Fig. 64a–i); the examples from the cave appear to have sat on crusted bases, while the Paralia examples had flat or dimpled bottoms. The Paralia examples, slightly smaller, preserve elaborate decoration in bright orange and black pigment. The cave examples may have had similar decoration—traces of red pigment are present—which has not survived. Alternatively, the differences in surface elaboration may have been real, and significant.

White painted decoration is another of the "typical FN" decorative techniques. In the cave the best-preserved examples come from FCP 5.1b (Fig. 52). A number of fragments also occur in L5 (Fig. 65), but their style of painting is quite different. Differences in execution between cave and Paralia examples exist for the polychrome, pattern burnished, incised, and perhaps for the red on white painted sherds as well. With the possible exception of white painted decoration, these varieties, as well as the white crusted, also occur in FCP 5.2, so the mere presence of similar techniques is not sufficient argument for contemporaneity.

Three varieties may be present in the FA Balk and missing entirely from L5: the dark, burnished sherds with a rim band reserved for crusting (Fig. 54a–b); the (usually) undecorated plain burnished sherds (e.g., Fig. 49d–f, h); and the variety that is now coated with a fugitive orange powder, sometimes with added white decoration (e.g., Figs. 54f, 56f, h, j). The comparisons between the two areas suggest that the Paralia L5 assemblage is closest to that from FCP 5.1b. The differences between the assemblages, however, suggest they are not entirely contemporary or the result of activities by the same group.

Nature of the L5 Activities

L5 is the northernmost area excavated on Paralia, the furthest from the cave. It produced the only substantial deposit of FCP 5 material on Paralia, including one burial. It may have been chosen because it presented a relatively level surface, because it caught the breeze better than more protected areas to the immediate south, because it provided a better view to the inland valley, or for reasons that completely escape us. Nothing particularly distinguishes the spot today from the rest of Paralia.

The FCP 5 occupants dug at least four relatively shallow depressions in the NE quadrant, perhaps adding a small section of stone wall to contain the area at the SE. They also dug two deeper pits within the area of the NW quadrant (Plan 3), and filled the whole with plentiful cultural debris and a Lime-rich sediment. Chunks of Lime up to 2–3 cm in diameter were found along the walls of the deep pits. A burial of an eight-year-old child was placed at the top of and between the deep pits in L5NW, and covered over. The burial may have been part of a later activity, separate from the filling of the pits. The material in the surface units may be contemporary with the burial, or it may represent yet another, still later activity.

When I first looked at the pottery from the L5 pits and depressions, as it was being excavated, I noticed in almost every large sherd some defect that could be attributed to a firing error: spalls; breaks along coil joints; large pebbles embedded within breaks; melting, minimally fired sherds. I was convinced the pits and depressions where these flawed sherds were found were the remains of a potters' firing area, the sherds representing wasters.

Subsequent observations make that interpretation less likely. Flaws are commonplace in all FCP 5.1 sherds. The potters must have lost many pots during the initial firing; some were mended and used, while others probably survived, at least briefly, in spite of the flaws. Charcoal and ash were not preserved anywhere on Paralia in any quantity, so their absence in L5 is not particularly troubling. Other evidence for a pottery firing is minimal, and the evidence against it substantial. In only one of the L5 pits did the excavators note minute flecks of carbon. That pit also produced two joining sherds, one of which had been burned after the two broke apart. That pit, as well as the others, included numerous sherds with post-firing decoration, which we would not expect to find as firing wasters. Sherds with drill holes also suggest pots that had been mended and used, rather than wasters never removed from the firing ashes. Some of the sherds appear to be made of nonlocal clay bodies, unlikely to have been brought to Franchthi for firing. The quantity of chipped and ground stone tools, shells, and pebbles recovered from the deposits hardly suggest a firing pit. Nor should a pottery firing produce the Lime-rich sediments that filled the area.

The Lime-rich sediments are the most distinctive element of the L5 deposits. The pits and depressions may have been dug initially to burn Lime. White Lime seems to have played an important role in FCP 5 activities. In addition to use as a pigment, perhaps for the thick crusts on pots, and definitely for some painted decoration, it was sometimes mixed with clay to make the "smear" mixture used to glue broken pots.[31] It was also used for whitewash, applied in multiple coats to pots of all sizes, apparently while they sat in a reasonably permanent place of use. Pottery from Q4:10, 16, 25, 117–120, which included a few possible FCP 5 sherds, was coated with a caustic dust, perhaps the remains of quicklime (Vitelli 1993:82 n.7).

If the L5 pits had been used for burning Lime, surely the Lime would have been removed for use once the burning was complete. Any remnants would have been at the bottom of the pits rather than mixed throughout sediments that subsequently filled in the depressions, as in L5 and perhaps in Q4.

Interestingly, a situation very similar to the one in L5 was found at Lerna, where large fragments of Final Neolithic pots were recovered from several neighboring pits that included substantial amounts of Lime (Vitelli forthcoming) and a burial in the vicinity. Whether or not the burials are related to the pits, the similarity of the pits and their contents at two open-air sites suggests they reflect a regular practice rather than an accidental or incidental occurrence. Neither Lerna nor Paralia produced any substantial number of FN sherds from the remainder of the site.

One possible explanation is that the occupants intentionally cleaned up after themselves. Rather than leave sherds and tools exposed around the site to bear testimony to their activities, they may have collected the debris, buried it in pits, and covered the pile with quicklime. The white Lime might have been a symbolic marker, or a practical move to kill odors and prevent wild animals from finding and disturbing the remains, or both.

FCP 5.2

Within the FA sequence, the Heavy Burnished variety (Figs. 69–70) defines FCP 5.2. Other examples of Heavy Burnished pottery were found in mixed deposits in the A–FA–FF1 area, and in smaller numbers in H, H1, G, and G1. One or two sherds from the rear of the cave may be Heavy Burnished. None is present in the L5 deposits. One or two Heavy Burnished sherds were found in surface units elsewhere on Paralia (see Table 10).

FCP 5.2 deposits also include small fragments of sherds with surfaces decorated in ways that otherwise occur only in mixed deposits in the cave; these are, therefore, also likely to be markers for the subphase. They include: pattern burnished sherds with a reserved area at the rim decorated with powdery red and white pigments (e.g., Fig. 71a–c); black burnished sherds with elaborate post-firing decoration in powdery red and white pigments (e.g., Fig. 71e, g); and sherds coated on the exterior or both (light fired) surfaces with a powdery red-orange pigment (e.g., Fig. 71j, n), with or without additional decoration in powdery white Lime. The burial pot from O5NE (Fig. 67i) is one of very few examples from Paralia of a late variety. Other FCP 5.2 sherds from Paralia include battered pieces of HB from QR5:6, QR5:8, Q4:38, O5:4, and possibly the hollow foot from Q5N:10 (see Table 10).

The activities of FCP 5.2, then, included much of the interior of the cave, with limited activity on Paralia, including at least the burials in O5NE. Estimates of the frequency of pottery remains for this occupation are relatively low, perhaps pointing to occupation by a small group for a limited time. After the FCP 5.2 occupation, sporadic, small-scale activities in later stages of the Final Neolithic and, possibly, the Early Bronze Age left behind only the occasional sherd.

The Potters

The FCP 5.1 potters show little concern for the fundamentals of potting. They gave minimal attention to preparing a uniform clay body, to sealing joints and eliminating air pockets between additions of clay, to building a strong body—the aspects of potting that take time if a potter is to build strong, durable pots. Their firings were very brief, at best producing soft friable pots that scratched and broke easily, and sometimes were so minimally fired that they slaked when wet. The potters made little, if any, effort to control the color of their pots by adjusting the firing atmosphere, something their predecessors had been doing since the beginning of pottery making.

The short firings may reflect a desire to conserve fuel, which, since they were also burning Lime, may have been in short supply in the immediate environs of the cave.[32] Their pots also suggest they were concerned, in all steps of the process, with making pots quickly. Their haste is evident in the minimal amount of time spent in evening surfaces, in smoothing and, most time-consuming of all, in burnishing carefully and completely at repeated stages of the drying process—all procedures their predecessors had developed to a fine art.

The FCP 5.1 potters rarely built any but the most simple of shapes—basic bowls without changes of wall angle, shoulders, or other distinctive, if risky curves. Every step of their work is so apparently random that the potters seem to be reinventing their production steps with each pot. They did not work regularly enough to develop an unconscious rhythm for the process. They were not without skill, daring, or imagination, but, except on the very large pots, they put those qualities to use only after they had built the basic pot.

They focused on superficial, visual effects: imaginative, if not convincingly functional, lugs and handles; rim tabs, which may have developed as a way to cover lumpy rims; applied bands and nicked rims, which cover and correct for sloppy clay preparation and building procedures. Incised decoration, although infrequent at Franchthi, is the fastest way to enliven the surface of a pot, and it hides cracks and surface imperfections as well. The potters were fascinated with color, far more so than is usually acknowledged in archaeological studies of ceramic assemblages, probably because color is rarely preserved intact. The low-fired red clay used for the majority of pieces was itself a brighter red than earlier, more fully-fired wares, and many more of the pieces than now preserve traces may have been coated with a red slip. The brightly colored and decorated pieces, a small minority of the total, made up in brightness and busyness of the patterning what they lacked in numbers. The choice of post-firing pigments may have been partly motivated by the brighter hues possible than when even the same pigments are fired. The extensive use of white Lime added to the striking effects.

Post-firing applications may also have been used to cover the flaws of building and firing. The clay smears were certainly used in this way. Thick crusts, whitewash, or a thick coat of the red pigments would have masked surface flaws and perhaps helped hold cracked or fragile pieces together. I think it likely that resins and other vegetal glues, long since disintegrated, were used as well, since many of the sherds point to pots that should not have survived drying and firing in one piece, yet received post-firing elaboration.

The number of pots that received no surface finish beyond that produced in the course of building are relatively few. Many of them—the small cups, lumpy pans, a few larger bowls—look so much like the work of beginners that perhaps that is what they are. Others, such as the big "drums," are certainly special-function pieces, and the function may have precluded further finishing. Cups and small bowls with holes poked through the walls before firing (Figs. 48b–c, 58c, 74b) may belong in this latter category, although Kalogirou and others are certainly correct in pointing out that all of these cannot have been intended for the same function (Kalogirou 1995, Sampson 1993: 293).

Although surfaces are rarely well preserved and few substantial profiles could be restored, it is curious that pots that are soft-fired and scratch easily retain no signs of a patterned scratching that might suggest wear from use. Nor have the soft-fired, porous pots absorbed carbon soot that would point to use on or over a fire. Those mended with Lime-rich smears (or other glue) would not have been appropriate for use on a fire, or for any function that involved regular handling and moving.

Most shapes, as noted, are simple bowls that allow easy access to and display their contents. The element of display may have been enhanced by the red coatings frequently applied to the interiors of smaller bowls; those coatings, probably unfired, were relatively fragile and would not have stood up to heavy use or repeated washing.

In fact, everything about the FCP 5.1 assemblage suggests pots that were made for limited use, and largely for display, of the pot and/or its contents. Most seem to have been manufactured locally, probably for special, ceremonial and ritual uses.

The great diversity of decorative finishes, each represented by few examples but consistently throughout the cave deposits and on Paralia, can be explained in several ways. Archaeologists generally assume, implicitly or explicitly, that each style and technique of decoration represents a particular group, producing in a specific, limited geographical area, whether or not we can identify the specific source. The rarely stated presumption is that any one human group at a certain place and at a certain time used only one decorative repertoire: if material from a certain place and time is more varied, then more than one human group must have been involved. If we apply that assumption to the FCP 5.1 assemblage, we might understand that the unpainted "coarse" pieces, which make up the majority of the finds, are the local Franchthi product, and that all or most of the decorated pieces are foreign. They would have been brought to Franchthi from other production centers and represent the interaction sphere of the FCP 5.1 community.

Certainly the varieties represented at Franchthi occur widely throughout the Aegean area and even beyond. No site, however, has yet produced such quantities of any one style as to be clearly identified as its production center. While the decorated pots are generally small, and without appendages that would have made them difficult to stack and more risky to transport, other factors are surely relevant for large-scale exchange of pots over long distances. The FCP 5 pots are soft and fragile. The seven, small, brightly decorated crusted pots from L5 (Fig. 64a–e, h–i)—for example—would have required careful packing for long-distance transport. They would have been bulky, if not heavy, to carry overland for any distance and would have taken up valuable space in the surely small seafaring craft of the time.[33] Franchthi is not the only site where they occur. If they were an item intended for exchange, a traveler might have had to carry many examples to exchange at sites all along his or her route. None of these obstacles is impossible to overcome, but long-distance exchange in pots would not have been as simple as exchange of obsidian, ornaments, or celts. More troubling for the assumption that many decorated pots at Franchthi came from distant production centers is that many of the pieces appear to be made of the same clay body as the supposedly local "coarse" pots.

Another explanation could be that it was not pots that traveled, but potters. By this model the group at

Franchthi would have included a number of foreign potters, perhaps "wives" acquired through exchange. Each of the foreign women continued, after joining the Franchthi group, to work in her native style, using locally available resources—and either passed her style on to her daughters, or was succeeded by another wife from the same foreign community in each successive generation.

A third possibility seems to me the most likely, although it would have grown out of a limited exchange in pots or in potters. The diversity of techniques and styles at Franchthi and other sites in FCP 5 suggests that all were widely known and practiced. Some may have developed in one place, others in another, but the amount of interaction throughout the area was such that most potters were familiar with a range of styles. Somewhere along the line certain decorative combinations could easily have become associated with particular kinds of events or occasions. When appropriate, the local potters, wherever they were, produced the best version they could muster of that decoration, using local materials and their knowledge of ceramic procedures. The occasional pots and potters were no doubt still exchanged over long distances, but the styles and techniques of decoration were basically shared and practiced by many individuals within the large geographical area in which all interacted.

The potters responsible for the FCP 5.2 Heavy Burnished pots were more practiced and consistent in their work, the shapes they created more daring and complex. They prepared their clay more carefully, built stronger walls, spent far more time in finishing the burnished surfaces, and exercised some control over the colors achieved during firings that lasted long enough to ensure a pot that would withstand use, although the few examples from Franchthi are not complete enough to reveal any signs of use. Curiously, the shapes they made are reminiscent of many FCP 3 shapes. The similarities may be a result of similar building procedures. Heavy shoulders and carinations above deep sloping walls may be features that follow from building the lower body upside down, beginning at the widest portion of the vessel, decreasing the diameter of each addition until the bottom disk is added, then inverting the pot to complete the rim.[34] Whatever the techniques used, the similarly heavy, burnished pots produced over a broad geographical region[35] point to a further homogenizing of the Aegean's ceramic traditions.

The FCP 5 occupation of Franchthi was more extensive and may have involved a greater variety of activities than did those of FCP 3 and FCP 4. The activities, like those in FCP 4, appear to have taken place in a series of relatively brief visits, separated by periods of limited, if any, occupation. Much of the ceramic evidence points to ceremony and ritual provided for by potters of varied backgrounds. The occupations fell within several centuries in roughly the middle of the long Final Neolithic phase.

NOTES

1. In at least two instances, I found within the fabric indisputable fragments of sherds, up to 5–6 mm in size, with recognizable burnished surfaces. One was almost certainly a fragment of FCP 1 Serpentine Ware. When I have ground (homemade) sherds and remnants of kilns for use as temper in experimental pots, however, most fragments are reduced to dust, and far too small to preserve a surface or to be recognizable as grog with the naked eye. The Acoma potters Emma and Dolores Lewis also reduce their sherd temper to a fine powder (personal observation).

2. Julie Hansen looked at a number of these and rejected them as grain or stalk impressions. A small number of probable FCP 5 sherds from Paralia have bits of a whitish fibrous material that resembles certain cigarette filters—possibly a form of asbestos or shell.

3. Clay I dug along the beach at Salandi Bay, just north of Paralia, was very pebbly in some places, cleaner in others. All of it included plentiful bits of reeds.

4. Riegger explains why this works (1972:58–59). I have added freshly formed, damp figurines to our experimental firings on several occasions, but they did not survive intact and, in the several-hour-long firings, did not emerge with black cores.

5. Many traditional potters today use similarly short firing regimens (e.g., Barbour and Wandibba 1989:96). The Acoma potters Emma and Dolores Lewis conducted a firing as part of a two-week workshop in Bloomington in 1990. They set their small pots on a bed of dry cattle dung (brought with them from New Mexico), covered the pots with sherds from previous firings, followed by a layer of dung patties, and lit the dung. The dung burned with a clean hot flame (temperatures climbed quickly to ca. 850°C), for a total of 20 minutes. After another 10 minutes, they began scraping away the loose ash and removing the pots. Peterson reports that Lucy Lewis' firings lasted less than 35 minutes (Peterson 1984:141).

6. See Jacobsen 1973b:271 n. 47 for Jill Carrington Smith's report on the details of the mat impression on FP 151. No further studies have yet been conducted on the three mat impressions. When I learned of the traces of woven fabric inside the walls of coarse Final Neolithic sherds from Kephala (Smith 1977:114–127), I looked closely for any trace of the same practice at Franchthi, but found none.

7. Potters regularly build their pots on some kind of moveable support, as it facilitates turning the pot during building so the potters can reach all surfaces from one position. The alternative is for the potter to move around the pot as she works. The support needs to be porous, so that air can reach the bottom surface and allow it to dry at roughly the same rate as the lower body walls. If the walls dry while the bottom remains wet, the shrinkage of drying will pull the walls away from the bottom.

8. The work habits of the FCP 5 potters remind me of beginning students in my experimental pottery classes, whose first concern is to make a pot, any pot, quickly. They love working with the local red clays in Bloomington, because they are easy to build with. Only after they experience the problems caused by the clay's excessive shrinkage, and have lost a few pots when drying and firing reveal the flaws in workmanship, do they begin to spend time on selection of raw materials, clay preparation, and careful building procedures.

9. Coleman reports that an example of true white crust was examined by R. G. Bullard, of the University of Cincinnati, Department of Geology. He said the crust was "very finely ground magnesium carbonate (probably derived from local magnesian dolomite or marble rock sources). The material contains less than 10% calcium. The material was added to the ceramic surface after the pottery was fired; post-firing abrasion on the ceramic surface occurs under the coating material" (Coleman 1977:37). Jones assumes the crusts were applied after firing, and identifies the crusts at Franchthi as "essentially calcite," while those from Kephala were dolomite (Jones 1986:778–779).

10. One might also explore whether vegetal dyes, if used to paint on the plaster-like crusts, would have survived and whether apparently unpainted white crusted sherds might once have carried decoration in dyes that have since vanished.

11. Jones analyzed samples #49–50, 52. Sample #49 from FAN:60 had a white powdery coating applied to the exterior black burnished surface, and a red powder on the burnished interior. Sample #50, from A:23, had a thick red powder applied to unburnished interior and exterior surfaces. Sample #52, from FAS:67, had red powder on the interior and exterior applied to a smoothed surface, with traces of powdery white painted lines on top of the red powder.

12. Bentley reports that cinnabar has "a cumulative morbid effect on health" but that a "sufficiently high intake of calcium would alleviate the toxic mercury" (1971:139). He also notes sources of "copper-cinnabar" along the Yugoslav coast (citing Novak 1959), as well as at Suplja Stena, to supply Vinca, and at Sisma to supply Çatal Hüyük, where he says cinnabar was used to paint skeletons.

13. The potters of Sawos village in New Guinea use many colors of clay slip for post-firing decoration of deeply incised exterior designs on their serving and eating bowls. The colors fade with use, and eventually, one assumes, disappear, although they could easily be renewed. The post-firing paints probably last longer than those on the Final Neolithic pots would have because the pigments are applied only on the exteriors, and within the grooves around deeply carved designs, where they are largely protected from handling and scrubbing (pers. comm. Jack Edler 2/98, and observation of Mathers Museum collection 1998).

14. Many pots decorated with post-firing paints in traditional African contexts have largely ceremonial or ritual functions (e.g., Barley 1994: 51, 54, 82, 104–5).

15. Hollow feet of a very similar sort are reported from Saliagos (Evans and Renfrew 1968:Fig. 59 nos. 21, 24).

16. A similar form of incised and white Lime-filled decoration occurs in FCP 3 (Figs. 8e–g; 9c) in Low Lime Burnished ware. Similar versions of incised and punctate decoration with white Lime fill occur from Crete to the Balkans throughout the later Neolithic. A sherd of similar shape to that in Fig. 57c, with different incised decoration, is published from Saliagos (Evans and Renfrew 1968:Fig. 59 no. 20).

17. The pot in Fig. 63a may have been even larger than drawn: the lower body fragment is drawn using the minimum diameter measurement (0.46 m) better to fit the dimensions of our page, but the sherd gives a maximum diameter reading of 0.55 m.

18. A carinated bowl from Trench A:24 (Fig. 70a) is like the Heavy Burnished examples in every way, except that it has much thinner walls. The shape is not documented in earlier FCP 5 varieties, and the even, regular walls are much closer to those of the Heavy Burnished variety than to anything earlier.

19. The piece was treated with PVA, probably several years after its excavation, but the decoration has already become less clear than when I first saw and drew it.

20. My notes indicate the pigment was powdery when first excavated. The pot was probably conserved with PVA soon after: the pigment is no longer soft and powdery.

21. Two pots with schematic representations of faces are reported from Final Neolithic deposits at Kum Tepe, although both are quite different from the Franchthi example (Sperling 1976:353, Pl. 79).

22. Scattered human bones occur in many of the units with FCP 5 pottery (see Cullen in prep.); since earlier pottery is also common in those units, we cannot securely associate the bones with a specific phase of occupation.

23. The latest in situ deposits in the northern portion of Q5N are of FCP 2.1. No further activity in the immediate area is documented after that until FCP 2.5 (see Vitelli 1993a:Plan 18) when the area just south of Q5N saw considerable deposition. FCP 2.5 material was found upslope, in the Q5/Q4 balk area and immediately west of Wall T; it was badly worn and probably redeposited (Vitelli 1993a:81). Perhaps it was dug and thrown up over Wall DD in FCP 5, to level off the Upper Terrace. Wall T would then have been a later addition, set back from the edge of Wall DD.

24. Two of the individuals remain in large part within the scarp.

25. Sherds with edges ground to a roughly circular shape, and with a hole drilled in the center occur in various sizes in FCP 1 and earlier subphases of FCP 2 (Vitelli 1993a:41, 53); they may have been used as spindle whorls (Jacobsen 1973b:276). Similarly rounded sherds without drill holes also occur in various sizes, including quite small ones (ca. 1 cm diameter). Jacobsen mentions two examples of whorls "that actually seem to have been created for that purpose" from Middle Neolithic contexts (1973b:276). I am unsure which specimens he refers to, but none recorded in the inventory (Document 1) comes from a secure Middle Neolithic/FCP 2 context. All the purpose-made whorls at Franchthi come from FCP 5 or mixed contexts.

26. I noted traces of paint, visible with a 10x lens on a few examples when I examined the whorls in the early 1980s. Unfortunately, I neglected to record inventory numbers for the relevant examples and later discovered that no mention of paint is included in the inventory books. The flecks of paint were not obvious, and could easily have been missed.

27. A biconical (FC 92), a conical (FC 94) and a discoidal (FC 91) whorl were found together in FAN:59 and 60N, and on Paralia in L5NE:17 and L5NE:11, conical (FC 152), biconical (FC 145, and discoidal (FC 146, 151) whorls occur together. See also Document 1.

28. The carbonate "ball" was not inventoried. It appears to preserve no original surface, and has broken into a number of chunks since excavation. It has no signs of a perforation. The carbonate mix includes plentiful 1–3 mm mixed sandy inclusions, along with clear bits of shell. It reduces to powder with pressure from a fingernail, and the powder foams away in hydrochloric acid.

29. See Document 1: FC 9, 10, 26, 39, 44.

30. Ironically, the harder-fired, near-vitreous Urf ware is more seriously affected by burial in basic soils than are the low-fired FCP5 varieties.

31. One sherd with a thick smear was found in the rear of the cave, and another on Paralia in P5:29. All other examples are confined to FA units assigned to FCP 5.1b.

32. Harriet Blitzer tells me that Lime burners in Greece around the turn of the century had Lime kilns in a number of locations. They used a three-year rotation because it took about that long for the brush used as fuel to grow back (pers. comm. 4/14/98).

33. Substantial numbers of pots, including large ones, are carried to market by a single individual over distances that seem unimaginable to many of us (e.g., using a tumpline backpack, Whitaker 1978:52, or a rope net, Edson1979:81). Exchange of pots within Thessaly is reasonably well documented (Demoule and Perlès 1993:395; Schneider et al. 1994) in the later Neolithic, but surely carrying pots from *magoula* to *magoula* on the Thessalian Plain is rather different from carrying the same load across the much more rugged terrain of the Peloponnese.

34. In my experimental ceramics classes over the last twenty years, most students, without prompting, start their first pot at the bottom and build up. Two or three individuals, however, have chosen to build upside down, starting at the rim or widest portion. The only explanation any of them could offer was "because it makes sense." For many shapes and with certain clays, the upside-down procedure is, in fact, easier to control and allows the potter to work more quickly. That experience with experimental potters suggests that, after the lengthy FCP 5.1 period when potters seemed to be making up their procedures as they worked, a few individuals might have happened on the upside-down approach. The ease of working that way could have caught on quickly, as it did in my classes, and resulted in the widespread use of the procedures.

35. Similar pots occur even at some distance from Franchthi, for example, at Emporio and Ayio Gala (Boardman 1981:59, 715), at Kum Tepe (Sperling 1976), and at Sitagroi in Phase 1 (Keighley 1986:349).

CHAPTER SIX

The Implications of the Pottery Analysis

THE MIDDLE NEOLITHIC BACKGROUND

During the earlier Neolithic the main settlement at Franchthi may have been along the now submerged riverbank, but groups of people were active inside the cave and along Paralia. On Paralia, they constructed extensive terrace walls, modifications to the site that imply a long-term commitment to place, even if occupation was not necessarily year round. Nearly one and a half metric tons of Middle Neolithic (MN) Urf ware testify to considerable intensity of occupation in that phase.

The potters who made FCP 2 Urf ware and its varieties worked regularly and adhered closely to a rather strict set of ceramic rules.[1] Their products are very consistent in all aspects of manufacture from preparation of the clay body to final firing. The choice of shapes and the kind and location of decoration were guided by rules whose rationale may be hidden from us, but whose existence is transparent. The vast majority of the FCP 2 pottery consists of elegant, well-made and hard-fired fine wares. Coarser pots, apparently specially designed for cooking, form only ca. 10% of the total assemblage. Large basins on tall pedestals are the only shape that shows signs of wear, on the bottom interior of the bowl.

Potters at Franchthi were guided by essentially the same rules as the potters at Lerna, Corinth, Asea and every other known Middle Neolithic site in the Peloponnese. Minor stylistic variations from site to site suggest that each site had its own potters, but all shared a common sense of what a pot should look like and how it should be made (see also Cullen 1985:339–351). The similarity of pots from one site to the next may inhibit our ability to document exchange in pots among settlements within the region, but the Urf ware is readily distinguished from contemporary wares produced in other regions. It is clear that few pots were exchanged among regions.

Developments within the production of Urf ware from the many stratified sequences at Franchthi suggest six subphases (Int 1/2, FCP 2.1–2.5: Vitelli 1993a). The same general sequence of developments appears at other sites. The particulars of the Franchthi sequence point to a series of departures and returns to the cave and Paralia during the Middle Neolithic. Abandonments after FCP 2.2 and FCP 2.4 may have lasted longer than the others, perhaps for a generation or two. Two other cave sites in the southern Argolid (Pullen 1995:6), and numerous other Middle Neolithic sites in the eastern Peloponnese may represent locations where (parts of) the group stayed when not at Franchthi. After the FCP 2.5 activities, the occupants left and did not return to Franchthi (Vitelli 1993a:218), nor is their presence elsewhere in the southern Argolid evident.

FRANCHTHI CERAMIC PHASE 3 (FCP 3)

The next group to occupy the cave, after a hiatus of perhaps no longer than those between subphases within FCP 2, used a new, Low Lime, ware. This group left no remains on Paralia, and only a small quantity of pottery in a limited area of the cave. Whatever the activity, it involved the reworking of sediments, and the resulting deposit included substantial human bone scatter. It is unclear whether the human remains are from earlier, disturbed burials, or contemporary with the FCP 3 activities.

Most of the pottery was apparently made locally, by potters who worked less frequently and with less control of the medium than had the Urf potters. While some rules of the style are evident, the pots are marked by considerable variation in detail. The majority of pieces, including some very large pots are finely finished, and often decorated with labor-intensive procedures. Coarse pots account for only 10–15% of the production, and they show less careful finishing and firing practices than do the FCP 2 coarse wares. A small number of highly decorated, polychrome pieces are probably not local products, although their likely sources remain unknown. While some general similarities with earlier Urf ware—including basins on pedestals—are evident, the similarities are only superficial. Most of the FCP 3 shapes, and the pigments, the building techniques, and the firing procedures are markedly different from those characteristics of Urf.

Pullen identifies a black burnished carinated bowl fragment from the Southern Argolid Survey as Late Neolithic (LN) (1995:7, Fig. 1 no. 6).[2] Further north, some similar material occurs at Aria and Corinth, but it is lacking at Lerna and Asea. I saw nothing comparable to FCP 3 varieties in the collection from Klenia. The quantities of FCP 3 pottery at Aria and Corinth, while not reported precisely, appear to have been small, suggesting small groups and/or brief visits at those sites as well.

For the first time in the Franchthi sequence, close similarities to material at sites beyond the Peloponnese occur. Similarities to material from Larissa phase sites in Thessaly are apparent, although the overall FCP 3 assemblage at Franchthi differs in many respects from Larissa phase assemblages, and it is difficult to evaluate the precise relationships (above, Chapter 3). It is clear, however, that whoever was responsible for the FCP 3 pots at Franchthi had a wider experience of the Greek mainland than had been true in the earlier Neolithic.

FRANCHTHI CERAMIC PHASE 4 (FCP 4)

After a relatively brief sojourn at the cave, the FCP 3 people also left, and the cave sat essentially empty for several hundred years before the arrival of another group with distinctively different pottery, marking the beginning of FCP 4. The FCP 4 group also confined its activities to the inside of the cave.

The first FCP 4 deposit in FA includes nearly 50% earlier pottery, apparently dug up and moved from somewhere else inside the cave. This rearrangement of the sediments may have been related to construction of a structure that rests on a rock floor and was built up with yellow clay-rich sediment brought from outside the cave. The deposit included a number of examples of basins on pedestals, all decorated with a similar motif.

Subsequent activities may have followed soon on the first or have been separated from it by short hiatuses. The relatively small quantity of pottery and its limited distribution inside the cave suggest that FCP 4 activities in each of the three subphases were short-lived. They included the use and discard of unusual items: a carbonate loaf-shaped object with painted decoration; a seated female figurine whose painted decoration suggests clothing hardly likely to have been that of daily wear; and four-legged rhyta elaborated with red and white pigments after their initial firing. Calcium carbonate lumps recovered near the figurine may be from a dissolved structure. Certainly they were brought into the cave, and perhaps manufactured, like the "loaf" in the earlier deposit, from burned Lime.[3]

Payne's preliminary analyses of the faunal remains indicate that sheep and goat dominate the assemblage, as they do throughout the Neolithic, but in FCP 3 and FCP 4 cow and red deer are quite scarce (Payne 1973:66, Phase F). Rose reports a peak in fish remains in the FCP 4 strata (Rose forthcoming). The not extensive botanical remains include wheat (*T. turgidum* ssp. *dicoccum*), barley (*H. vulgare* ssp. *distichum*), almond, and lentils (Hansen 1991:Figs. 53, 56a–c). Medicago, a wild herb whose seeds were used in antiquity for a poultice (Hansen 1991:66), as well as animal fodder, occurs in quantities equal to or greater than the foodstuffs.

The pottery assemblage for FCP 4 includes numerous varieties, most of which are decorated or well finished. At least four wares were probably manufactured locally: Lime plus Iron, Andesite Burnished, No Lime Coarse, Calcite Coarse. The coarse wares account for 17% by weight of the earliest, and 35% of the later subphase assemblages, a substantial increase over earlier phases. No coarse sherds, however, show signs of use, on a fire or otherwise. Only the interior bottom of basins in the earliest deposit, and shallow bowls in the later ones, show evidence of wear.

The ingredients and general recipes used for the Andesite Burnished ware, and perhaps the Lime plus Iron ware, are very similar to those used for similar locally produced wares in FCP 1 and FCP 2. The similarities may be coincidence, resulting from the local availability of the materials, or may suggest an element of cultural continuity. I have suggested that in FCP 1 and FCP 2 the specific ingredients used for each ware may have had symbolic significance (e.g., Vitelli 1993b: 254). Perhaps their meaning or associations outlived the Middle Neolithic. Spreading basins on tall pedestal bases, which occur throughout the Neolithic sequence, may be another symbolically charged element that survived larger ceramic and cultural changes.

Stylistic rules, discernible within each of the FCP 4 varieties, were certainly less strict or operated differently than those of FCP 2. Some aspects of production and decoration are reasonably consistent, but never to the extent of the FCP 2 products. Some of the inconsistencies are surely the result of potters who practiced the craft only infrequently. Much of the painted decoration is quite sloppy, and either unimaginative or restricted by symbolic associations. Decoration was increasingly omitted toward the end of the phase.

Relatively small vessels in Gray Burnished, Manganese Ungritted, and other manganese painted and polychrome varieties were probably brought to Franchthi from elsewhere in small numbers. Although precise sources cannot, at this stage, be identified for these foreign varieties, relative frequencies of occurrence and specific characteristics of the fabrics suggest that each region or limited geographical area may have developed its own signature style (e.g., Schneider et al. 1994, Demoule and Perlès 1993:392). Each of the varieties represented at Franchthi seems likely to have been made by a different set of potters; some, or all, may have been clearly associated with a specific group and place. Nevertheless, numerous examples exist at Franchthi of potters copying or imitating the shape and decorative elements of other groups' styles.

Parallels for individual pieces from the FCP 4 assemblage can be found at Corinth and the few other Peloponnesian sites known from the phase, as well as in Thessaly and beyond; the overall assemblage at each site is quite different, although local and foreign styles are represented at each. Pullen reports finding small numbers (14–15) of "definite" Late Neolithic sherds from four sites in the Southern Argolid Survey, but cautions that the presence of the phase remains "tenuous" (Pullen 1995:7). I agree that none of the six illustrated sherds is compellingly Late Neolithic.[4] Nor are truly diagnostic Late Neolithic sherds reported from surveys in the Berbati (Johnson 1996b:274–75), Nemea (Cherry et al. 1988:174–175), or Asea (Jeannette Forsèn, Eva Alram, pers. comm. 6/97) valleys. Even if all the possible Late Neolithic sherds are accepted as such, the quantity of ceramics and number of sites represented in the eastern Peloponnese in the Late Neolithic is very small. The evidence suggests several short-term visits to Franchthi, and long stretches of time when the cave was unoccupied and there is no sign of people anywhere else in the southern Argolid, and few anywhere in the larger region.

FRANCHTHI CERAMIC PHASE 5 (FCP 5)

The departure of the group responsible for the FCP 4.3 deposit was followed by another centuries-long hiatus in activity in and around the cave. When people returned, in unknown numbers, they left remains over a much larger portion of the cave, apparently including the dark rear and pool area. They eventually buried at least six individuals on Paralia, and an assortment of cultural debris in pits at the northern end of the slope. They appear to have used much of Paralia, but left very few remains anywhere except in the L5 pits. The activities seem to have taken place over a period of several hundred years, roughly in the middle of the long Final Neolithic (FN) phase in Greece. The activities may well have been separated by brief episodes of abandonment.

The FCP 5 pots, while exhibiting many stylistic similarities to sites around the Aegean and beyond, appear for the most part to have been made locally. The selection of style or technique of finishing the surfaces seems less the mark of a particular group, as was the case in FCP 4, than an adjustment for a particular occasion—perhaps the natural outgrowth of the imitation of each other's styles that had begun in FCP 4.

The potters appear to have worked quickly, with little concern for structure and strength of the pot. Most pots were left without decoration, although many had plastic elements—tabs, handles, lugs, piecrust rims, and finger-impressed rope bands. For the minority of decorated vessels, considerable attention was given to the visual effect, some of the most striking of which were apparently achieved after firing. Minimal firings produced pots that were relatively fragile and easily subject to wear and breakage. Post-firing decoration would have been relatively fragile and short-lived as well. Shapes are almost exclusively open—bowls that would have displayed contents. Damaged vessels were, at least occasionally, superficially mended before or after firing with clay, Lime, and perhaps other "glues." Some pots, of various sizes, were given multiple coats of whitewash. White Lime was also used to decorate ceramics, and perhaps in other, non-ceramic contexts.

Although weathered sediments and C-14 dates point to a long hiatus between the end of FCP 4 and the beginning of FCP 5, a number of ceramic features suggest some degree of cultural continuity between the phases. Post-firing decoration in white Lime and bright red pigments first appear at Franchthi in FCP 4, on the strange four-legged rhyta with their apparent connection to the Dalmatian Danilo culture. Ceramic objects related to the rhyta occur also in FCP 5. The use of post-firing pigments which continues in FCP 5 is extended to include other ceramic containers, figurines (Talalay 1993:FC 4, FC 41, FC 88, FC 112), and perhaps spindle whorls. Small rim tabs, first appearing in FCP 4, become more common and elaborate in FCP 5. Horned handles, generally associated with Final Neolithic ceramics, occur in FCP 4 first in Andesite ware, and then in Lime plus Iron. Calcium carbonate, perhaps from calcined Lime in FCP 4, and almost certainly in FCP 5, may have been used even more extensively than the poorly preserved remains document. That these elements survived not only many generations, but major changes in the rest of the ceramic tradition, suggests they carried some particular association or symbolic meaning.[5] Even the occasional use of pedestals on "crusted" pots, in a ceramic tradition that otherwise eschews ring bases entirely, may echo earlier times and meanings.

Many of the generically identified varieties and features of FCP 5 occur throughout the phase and are common at most excavated Final Neolithic sites. None of the known sites has sufficient depth and quantities of material to suggest it was occupied for the entire phase. All the known sites cannot have been occupied at the same time. It is difficult to establish secure temporal relations among known Final Neolithic sites,[6] but the absence of the Heavy Burnished variety in the earlier subphases at Franchthi provides a starting point for the southern Argolid.

Pullen reports Final Neolithic pottery from a total of 36 sites in the southern Argolid, in addition to Franchthi, although only three produced more than five Final Neolithic sherds (Pullen 1995:7). He reports a few sherds with traces of red and white pigments, some identified as "crusted" (1995:10), but these occur throughout the Franchthi FCP 5 deposits. No examples of "rolled rims"[7] or shouldered bowls, the equivalent of Franchthi's Heavy Burnished variety, were recognized from the survey (Pullen 1995:10).[8] That might suggest that most of the Final Neolithic sites found by the survey pre-date the Heavy Burnished variety. On the other hand, none of the published Final Neolithic sherds, nor any of those I saw years ago in Kiladha from the survey, closely resembles material in the stratified FCP 5 assemblage. A few solid knobs (e.g., Runnels et al. 1995: Fig. 4 nos. 53–56) occur in unstratified surface deposits inside the cave, presumably later than anything in the stratified deposits and possibly post-Neolithic. Other features of the survey sherds—e.g., sharp edges and slashes on applied bands, and sharp neat incisions—are suggestive of later ceramics. Pullen notes that it was often difficult to distinguish Final Neolithic from Early Helladic, and that only two sites that produced Final Neolithic sherds lacked Early Helladic material as well (1995:10). I suspect that most, and perhaps all, of the sites identified in the Southern Argolid Survey post-date the latest stratified FCP 5 material at Franchthi.[9]

EXPLAINING THE PATTERNS

I concluded my study of the earlier Neolithic pottery from Franchthi by noting that the abandonment of the site after FCP 2.5 may only have been the final response to problems that had been building for generations and that affected the larger Neolithic community throughout southern Greece. I also suggested optimistically that the hindsight provided by the present study might help in determining whether the problems faced during FCP 2 had been instigated by internal or external social and political conflict or by environmental and economic stresses. Having now examined the details of the later Neolithic record at Franchthi, I still cannot identify the precise problems that caused strife within the Middle Neolithic communities. Probably all of the elements noted played a role (below). Whatever their specific causes, the struggles of the Middle Neolithic Urfirnis-producing society and their final resolutions certainly provided the impetus for the new social and economic groupings and behaviors of the later Neolithic. My attempt at explaining the patterns evident in the later Neolithic begins, therefore, with FCP 2.

After nearly 1500 years of consistent development and regular, if not continuous occupation in FCP 1 and FCP 2, what happened to the final group of FCP 2 occupants of the cave, and their contemporaries all around the Peloponnese, whose families had been making and using Urfirnis for generation upon generation? At some sites (e.g., Corinth) Urfirnis may have continued in production for a while alongside newly introduced traditions that gradually replaced it. That situation, however, has yet to be demonstrated at any site, was not the case at Franchthi, and does not, in any event, explain why or how Urfirnis gave way to other traditions after its long and successful dominance.

The end of the Urfirnis ceramic tradition can perhaps be explained by reference to social changes. My analyses of the earlier Neolithic ceramics from Franchthi led me to suggest that, from the beginning of ceramic production in southern Greece, a restricted group of women made pottery as part of, and for use in, ceremonial and ritual occasions. Their role as shamans or social and physical healers granted them—and their pots—a degree of social power or influence (Vitelli 1993a:253–254; 1995:61–62).

By the Middle Neolithic, the groups living in the Peloponnese shared a ceramic tradition whose rules were closely adhered to by the potter/shamans over a large geographical area. Whatever the specific rationale for that common tradition, maintained over generations, the sharing itself implies a closeness among the groups—regular interaction, common interests, something that bound the scattered groups together socially (see also Cullen 1985:350–352).

Every social group experiences stresses and conflicts of varying degrees of severity. Some may be initiated by nonhuman forces, e.g., environmental factors, such as rising sea levels, which may have dramatically reduced the availability of agricultural land and access to fresh water (van Andel and Sutton 1987:44, Jameson et al. 1994:204 and *passim*). Even such external threats, however, induce a social response. Environmental conditions and related economic pressures may have spurred the social alliance among the groups in the first place, encouraging each group to assist the others in times of crop failure or comparable hardship (Halstead 1989:73). If a group is to survive, means must be found to respond to stresses and to choose among different ideas of appropriate responses.

Apparently the Middle Neolithic groups were successful at negotiating responses to conflict for many generations. The shaman/potters may have played a primary role in such negotiations, making fruitful and effective use of their rituals. Perhaps, by the middle of the fifth millennium, the environmental and economic strains were too much to overcome with the social arrangements that had to that point been effective. Perhaps other, purely social difficulties prompted the split. Whatever the reason(s), the Middle Neolithic alliances ceased to function in the same ways at the end of the phase. Their ceramic tradition that had been a material symbol of the close relationships among the groups no longer had that role. Indeed, it would have been a symbol of the past, something that newly independent groups might well have discarded precisely for that reason. Although unanticipated, my explanation of the role of pots and potters in the earlier Neolithic makes it relatively easy to explain the abandonment of the style in social terms.

More difficult to explain is what happened to the population that lived throughout the region during the earlier Neolithic, that survived and apparently thrived for centuries, but essentially disappeared in the Late Neolithic. Franchthi, which remains the only excavated Late Neolithic site in southern Greece with documented stratified deposits, provides useful information about the Late Neolithic ceramic sequence and has contributed to our models of increasing exploitation of the sea and long-distance exchange, as well as an apparent increase in pastoralism. But in fact, even Franchthi, one of the few "major sites," was apparently occupied for only a brief part of the Late Neolithic. How can we rationalize the evidence for more far-reaching intergroup contacts, a richer inventory of artifacts, and an increase in pastoralism with a landscape essentially devoid of people?

It is unlikely that the entire Middle Neolithic population died, or that they climbed onto boats and sailed off into the sunset, never to be seen again, although some may have gone north and contributed to the increase in Late Neolithic settlements evident in Thessaly (e.g., Halstead 1989:75). The relatively brief stays by small groups that are documented during the Late Neolithic at Franchthi do not make sense as brief colonizing efforts (by whom?) that apparently failed, given the long hiatuses between occupations and the continuing absence of remains elsewhere in the southern Argolid. But if the people were still there, why can we not find them?

Years ago, Rutter pointed out that certain cultural phases have "low [ceramic] visibility" and "may appear to be poorly represented in a survey report due to the failure to isolate and recognize its ceramic output among the small and battered fragments of pottery recovered in the typical survey" (Rutter 1983:137). He cites as reasons for such low visibility that a phase may be poorly known because few if any sites of the phase have been excavated, or that the repertoire includes few distinctive shapes and little or no decoration. While the Final Neolithic, as he suggested, might be expected, on those grounds, to have "low visibility" in archaeological surveys, in fact, many Final Neolithic sites have been identified by the Peloponnesian survey teams. It is the Late Neolithic in southern Greece that qualifies as a phase with "low visibility." The Late Neolithic pottery is, however, reasonably well known from excavated, if unstratified, sites and the repertoire includes distinctive shapes and decorative techniques and styles. Still it remains largely invisible.

Nevertheless Rutter may be essentially correct. I think we must consider the possibility that the Late Neolithic people used the distinctive pottery we have come to recognize them by only for special occasions, at special sites. In their daily lives they either used no pottery at all, or not the distinctive pottery we find at the excavated sites. If that was the case, their presence in the larger archaeological landscape would, as Rutter pointed out, have very low visibility.[10] Only when they gathered for special occasions that called for the production and use of finer pots would their activities have resulted in the ceramic remains by which we recognize the Late Neolithic.

When this possibility first occurred to me, it was more an expression of my frustration in trying to understand the evidence of the later Neolithic than a serious suggestion. As I worked my way through the evidence at Franchthi and elsewhere, however, it kept resurfacing as an explanation that fits the evidence better than any other. I now propose it with all seriousness.

At Franchthi, it may have been the rising sea level and the diminished availability of good agricultural land or some related problem that first encouraged the group to split up into smaller units and move inland and into the hills. A focus on pastoralism has been inferred from the increased use of upland caves in the later Neolithic and a strong dominance of sheep and goat in faunal remains (e.g., Johnson 1996b:284–85; Demoule and Perlès 1993:389). For the potential role of ceramics in daily life, an emphasis on pastoralism might explain minimal use of pottery. Pots are bulky, heavy, and brittle—undesirable properties for people who move their base of operations regularly.[11] But relatively isolated groups of shepherds in the hills of the Argolid do not explain the evidence for increases in long-distance exchange, another innovation of the Late Neolithic.

In the Middle Neolithic, we have little evidence for exchange in ceramics beyond the immediate Urfirinis region, but other goods did travel. Perlès has shown that obsidian from Milos was acquired throughout the region from specialist itinerant knappers, who presumably traveled to Milos to acquire the raw materials, and then, from site to site, producing tools on demand (Perlès 1990b:35; Demoule and Perlès 1993:383). These adventuresome individuals provided an apparently valued product, but one that was not essential in any practical sense, for locally available raw materials could be, and were, worked locally into serviceable tools (Perlès 1990b:22, 1992:128). In addition to the shiny black rocks, the traveling knappers also, no doubt, brought news from other groups and lively stories of their adventures in far-off places unknown to most. Their visits must have been eagerly anticipated and were likely occasions for celebration. Whether originally members of the "Urfirnis group" or some other, more distantly based group, the services they provided must have assured their safe passage and warm welcome throughout the region. They may have carried messages or small quantities of supplies from one settlement to another, or been accompanied for part of their journey by residents of various settlements. They are likely, in that way, to have been agents of more than one kind of exchange moving in an essentially friendly landscape.

Changes in the lithic assemblages at the beginning of Late Neolithic in southern Greece accompany the changes in ceramics. Perlès notes that the percentage of obsidian increases sharply, and use of local resources becomes negligible. Standards of manufacture vary far more than in earlier phases. Provisionally, the evidence in Late Neolithic points to direct procurement of obsidian from the source (Perlès 1990b:36; Demoule and Perlès 1993:393). Whether because itinerant knappers could no longer anticipate safe passage through the region, or were members of a now-unfriendly group, or because social restrictions on who might travel were no longer effective, many more individuals began making the trip to and from Milos. The increase in seafaring surely contributed to the settlement of the Cyclades, to technical developments in boat-building (Jacobsen in press) and to the other increases in long-distance exchange and interaction that become manifest in a range of Late Neolithic artifacts, including the ceramics.

The initial adventures at long-distance seafaring may have been prompted by a desire for obsidian, a commodity the Middle Neolithic villagers had become accustomed to and may have imbued with symbolic significance. That such quests quickly provided opportunity for encounters with other groups and exchanges of many sorts was unavoidable.

I like to imagine that young adults, recalling the stories they had listened to intently as little children at the feet of the itinerant knapper, set out on quests, in search of a kind of Holy Grail, or undertaking a rite of passage into adulthood. Even without such fantasies, we can acknowledge that the trip to Milos and elsewhere must have been full of risk, as well as opportunity. Although perhaps more sophisticated than earlier craft, boats were surely small, with limited room for cargo and supplies. Sailors (with or without sails) must have had to beach at night, for water and probably food, and eventually in unfamiliar places potentially inhabited by unfriendly or strange people. Storms, rough seas, poor hunting, and accidents of many kinds could have added to and prolonged the adventure. The intended length of a trip could not have been precisely predicted nor its success assured. The outcome must have been disastrous on some occasions.

It is unlikely that entire villages or even families set out together on such a trip. Probably the adventurers were a small group of able-bodied young adults, in one or few boats. They would have left behind women with small children, and the less able-bodied and older members of the group. Marriage partners may well have been one of the exchanges eagerly and necessarily sought if relations within the region no longer encouraged intermarriage. Potters acquired by friendly exchange or capture along the northern coast may have been responsible for the similarity of FCP 3 pots to those in Thessaly.

Those who remained behind when the adventurers set out to sea would have been, in some senses, the more vulnerable members of the group. If boatloads of adventurers were setting out from many groups to "find their fortunes," it might well have been unwise to remain in open settlements on the coast, exposed to potential raids from the sea. Other groups from the formerly cooperative Middle Neolithic alliance might have attempted overland raids, a hostile taking of supplies that had once been freely shared. Combined with an environmental impetus to abandon former settlement sites, a concern for safety might have spurred a movement inland and up into locations that provided greater protection and opportunity to see approaching boats and strangers.

Those who did not go to sea may have farmed small plots, learning to conserve moisture in the soil with the use of an ard and developing the new farming techniques that appear in the later Neolithic (Johnson 1996b:273). Their herds may have proved more reliable sources of food and wealth, when bad weather or raiding groups spoiled the crops or forced a move to a new location. A growing emphasis on herding may have been related to a need to be relatively mobile and avoid detection by unwelcome intruders. Groups were probably small and scattered around the landscape. Pottery, largely used for ceremonial and ritual events in earlier times, would have been neither a necessary nor a desirable possession in the daily routine of the later Neolithic.

If people were living in small, scattered groups, they must necessarily have had times when they joined into larger groups, for "weddings and funerals," and for the general socializing that humans need. What the occasions were, how frequently they occurred, and how they were organized are probably beyond our ability to discover. The locations, however, were apparently sites such as Franchthi, where we find their ceremonial pottery and other remains of groups gathered with flocks, harvest produce, and other accoutrements, to feast and to participate in whatever their ceremonies and rituals celebrated.

Much of the pottery needed would have been specially made for the occasion. A few pots may have been brought back from distant places by the travelers, or contributed by foreigners present at the gathering. Wares such as the Low Lime of FCP 3, or Andesite Burnished of FCP 4, appear to have been made locally but share characteristics with pottery from, e.g., Thessaly. They may have been made by women who learned to make pots elsewhere; relocated as brides or booty, they made the necessary ceremonial pots in their new homes, using local materials to produce an approximation of the styles of their earlier experience.

Major gatherings were apparently infrequent, to judge from the remains at Franchthi,[12] which would be why the potters show signs of limited practice. Pottery-making may still have been restricted to relatively few women, but the numbers who knew something of the craft were surely greater than in the earlier Neolithic. The greater frequency and variety of shapes and quality in coarse wares during FCP 3 and FCP 4 may suggest that women with little skill or background nevertheless could make pots when the occasion called for it.[13] The mystique of production, which I have argued was central to the role of pots and potters in the early Neolithic, was largely gone by the Late Neolithic. The ceremonial attention and requirements were certainly on the pots, more than the producers. Women of varied backgrounds may have worked together to make pots they now saw and re-created only infrequently to supply the needs for a large ceremony. Such conditions would invite imitation and copying of elements once associated with a particular style or tradition, to produce the mix of traditions evident in the FCP 4 assemblage.

This scenario also implies that the Late Neolithic remains at Franchthi are not those of a permanent settlement, but of a site used intermittently for significant social gatherings. The cave may also have been used occasionally by shepherds who left little ceramic or other debris. Sheep and goat bones dominate the faunal assemblage. Cattle, rare in FCP 3 and 4 deposits, are less amenable than ovicaprids to the mobile existence I have postulated.

In spite of an apparently long break between the end of Late Neolithic and the earliest Final Neolithic activities at Franchthi, the ceramics suggest a degree of cultural continuity. The reworking and redeposition of cave sediments also suggest some similar activities went on in both phases. Although the decorated pots are a small proportion of the FCP 5.1 ceramic assemblage, their decoration—especially the post-firing versions—points to ceremonial uses.

Whether the cave became a place of more permanent settlement again in FCP 5.1 is harder to judge. The more widespread remains, extending onto Paralia, might point to relatively permanent occupation, as might the renewed presence of cattle bones, if in small quantities, among the faunal assemblage (Payne 1973:66, Phase G). The overall quantities of ceramics are somewhat greater than for the Late Neolithic occupations, and they are dominated by undecorated pots, some quite large and appropriate for storage (Johnson 1996b:284), although closed shapes are remarkably rare. Construction and firing do not suggest a concern for durability, as we might expect if the pots were intended to serve broader needs than those of relatively brief ceremonial occasions. On the other hand, after generations of producing only for infrequent ceremonial occasions, the basic understanding of ceramic processes, once so widespread and exceptional, may have been largely lost. Restrictions that limited pottery-making to relatively few women in earlier times may have disappeared, and pottery-making become a more general "woman's chore." More or all women making pottery, each working infrequently to provide pots for a growing but still limited number of functions, could explain the qualities observed in the FCP 5.1 assemblage.

Generations of women "exchanged" among geographically distant groups, occasionally making pots, copying and combining information, styles, and materials, may have led to the rather homogenized ceramic tradition that begins to be evident throughout much of the Aegean in the earlier Final Neolithic. While some forms of decoration—perhaps the incised, white painted, and polychrome varieties—may still have been associated primarily with particular groups or regions, others, such as the post-firing "crusted" varieties, seem to have developed associations with particular occasions rather than groups.

The appearance of the Heavy Burnished variety at Franchthi, and similarly thick-walled, slipped and well burnished, dark-fired pots in distinctive shapes at other sites over a broad geographical area in a later stage of Final Neolithic,[14] must mark another step in the significant cultural developments of the Final Neolithic. The Heavy Burnished pots were made in a number of distinctive, complex shapes that had been missing from the earlier FCP 5 repertoire. They were made by reasonably experienced, practiced potters, who followed a limiting set of rules. Pots that fall broadly into this category show subtle variations from site to site (judging from what is illustrated in publications and what I have seen first-hand), but share similarities sufficient to suggest a relationship something like that of the Middle Neolithic Urfirnis regional "alliance." The Final Neolithic ceramic region, however, was much larger, and part of a much more complex and complicated world. Whatever the cooperative arrangements among members of such an alliance, they must have been quite different from those of any Middle Neolithic alliance.

Given the distances involved, the relationships must have been established and maintained by sea. Boat-building technology had probably been developing throughout the later Neolithic, as more and more individuals spent more time at sea and ventured further from home. Opportunities to discover better raw materials, as well as techniques for constructing sturdier, larger, and/or faster craft must have been plentiful, and probably were actively sought out. The sudden appearance of large numbers of spindle whorls at Franchthi in FCP 5 indicates that the pastoralists were exploiting their animals for wool, and perhaps developing a local textile industry. As Jacobsen points out, this industry could have included weaving cloth for sails (Jacobsen in press), which are attested in Egypt and perhaps Mesopotamia by the fourth millennium BC (Casson 1971:12 n. 6; 22). Sails, especially if a new element in Aegean seafaring, would have presented a considerable advantage to those who had them, and may have created a market for those who could make them and, perhaps, provide training in their use. If not sails or a market for textiles, some comparable development seems likely at the base of the new "alliance" that brought a degree of cultural uniformity to such a broad geographical area.

The extent of cooperation and shared values within the area that also shared in a ceramic tradition remains to be explored, and I do not wish to overstate the case based primarily on ceramic analysis. Nevertheless, some relationship must be acknowledged to account for the similarities, as well as the differences in the ceramic assemblages.

An additional phenomenon of the Final Neolithic also bears notice in this context. The surveys that find only very limited remains from the Late Neolithic in the Peloponnese report increased quantities of pottery and sites for the Final Neolithic. Many if not all of the new Final Neolithic sites appear to belong to a late stage of the phase, largely post-dating the remains at Franchthi. If I am correct in suggesting that the Late Neolithic occupants of the Peloponnese are largely invisible because the times promoted activities that produced "low visibility" on the landscape, their increased visibility in the Final Neolithic may be exactly that. The numbers of new sites may not reflect a significant increase in population, but simply a more visible population.

I suggested that after the Middle Neolithic alliance broke down, small groups moved inland and up into the hills, perhaps motivated by a number of social, environmental, and economic concerns, but also in part, for safety. Keeping a low profile through limited modification of the natural surroundings, and eliminating obvious traces of their activities when they moved on, would have helped protect them from potential marauders, whether members of their former alliance or strangers arriving unexpectedly by sea. Along the way, they also increased the size of sheep and goat herds, and learned to exploit their secondary products, even as useful items for exchange with the new groups being encountered by their own fellows who went to sea. What may have begun as a form of piracy and adventure-seeking on the part of young sailors developed, during the course of the Late and early part of Final Neolithic, into a more stable form of interaction and exchange. People again found reasons to cooperate and share, to advertise their connections with each other, and to show their presence. Changes in the nature of their daily activities may have suggested new ways to use ceramic containers, and a more settled life encouraged their acquisition and use. By late in the Final Neolithic, people felt sufficiently secure to make their mark on a place, to become "visible" again.

Whether or not the scenario I have developed for the later Neolithic finds support as studies progress, it draws attention to the complexities of the later Neolithic evidence and times. Clearly there is more to the Neolithic picture than self-sufficient, egalitarian farmers and herders spread thinly across the valleys and hills of southern Greece. The millennia of the Neolithic—a very long time—saw energetic people, not afraid of taking risks, embracing change, at least when it was forced on them, and responding to changing circumstances with considerable creativity. A comparable effort on our part may bring broader understanding of and appreciation for the varied solutions they devised.

NOTES

1. I use the word "rules" as shorthand for the culturally accepted practices for the entire sequence of pottery production, from digging and preparing clay, the range of shapes, location and nature of decoration, through the firing, that would result in pots that a particular group considered appropriate.

2. The sherd is from the Kotena Cave (G-9), which produced many more Final Neolithic (133) than Late Neolithic sherds (4). The profile and fabric of the black carinated sherd might equally describe a Final Neolithic Heavy Burnished bowl.

3. Deposits of white calcrete, or caliche, are exposed today in coastal cliffs, sandwiched between layers of bright red clay, a few kilometers northwest of Franchthi. The caliche is sufficiently plastic that something like the "loaf" might have been modeled from it, without the need for burning Lime, although it tends to take on a pinkish color from the surrounding clay. The "loaf" includes small flecks of carbon, which might argue for burning of the constituent carbonates.

4. The two carinated dark burnished bowls (Pullen 1995:Fig. 1, nos. 6–7) look closer to FCP 5 Heavy Burnished bowls than to FCP 3 or 4 varieties. Little can be said about the polychrome sherd (no. 8), except to note that polychrome painting occurs also in FCP 5, contrary to Pullen's assumption (1995:7). The "Matt Painted" sherd (no. 10, Fig. 118) might equally be a piece of Urfirnis, other examples of which were also found at Didhima. The two remaining sherds, which present nothing truly diagnostic of Late Neolithic, would not be out of place in FCP 5.

5. I cannot help but think of the many elements of modern-day religious symbolism that have survived for many centuries amid repeated and extreme cultural changes.

6. Although the pattern of occupation Sampson describes for Skoteini Cave is similar to that at Franchthi, the ceramic styles and sequences are only vaguely similar (Sampson 1993:298–299 and *passim*). As Sampson points out, the sporadic nature of cave occupations in the Final Neolithic, coupled with the occupants' penchant for digging into and rearranging extant deposits, makes it difficult to isolate ceramic styles stratigraphically. Additionally, if multiple ceramic traditions were being transmitted from region to region through exchange of various sorts and took on new meanings in new places, the sequences of ceramic styles and traditions may have differed from site to site, depending on the particulars of recent exchanges.

7. Examples of the so-called KumTepe Ib rolled rims, lacking at Franchthi in the Heavy Burnished variety, occur at Lerna in that variety.

8. Although I suggested (above) that several carinated bowl fragments identified by Pullen as Late Neolithic might be Final Neolithic Heavy Burnished pieces.

9. A number of closed jars, a shape absent in the Franchthi assemblage, were recovered from the survey. The difference in occurrence may reflect a difference in site function as well as time.

10. Similarly, Halstead has suggested that the development of pastoralism in western Thessaly in the later Neolithic may have resulted in "small groups whose settlement traces are too ephemeral to be recognized in the current archaeological record" (1981:325).

11. The data that suggest pastoralism most strongly, however, come largely from the later Late Neolithic and especially, the Final Neolithic. A focus on pastoralism may have developed from, rather than come at the beginning of, the changes of Late Neolithic.

12. It is certainly possible that each stratum in FA accumulated, not during a single uninterrupted activity, but from a series of activities repeated over some years with brief absences separating each episode. The stratigraphic record would not necessarily capture such brief absences, especially given the amount of reworking of sediments evident within the later Neolithic deposits.

13. While the identification of various Final Neolithic pierced bowls as "cheese pots" may be in doubt, very porous coarse ware bowls of the later Neolithic might have served, without piercing, to absorb liquid from milk and to concentrate the fats for cheese and yoghurt.

14. Sampson refers to this phenomenon as the "internationalisation of the local styles throughout Late Neolithic IIb" (Sampson 1993:293).

DOCUMENT 1

"Franchthi Clay" (FC) Objects

This Document provides a brief listing of the inventoried "Franchthi Clay" (FC) objects—a few of which prove to be modeled from a calcium carbonate mixture—other than figurines (see Talalay 1993), pots or parts of pots, and ornaments (Miller in prep.) for which no further publication is currently planned. The listing is intended to inform colleagues of the range of materials and their availability for study. I have compiled the information from various sources, including my own observations of some pieces, but I have not verified all the information that is recorded in the excavation inventory books. When known to me, information about conservation treatment is included.

The entries consist largely of whorls and weights. All the specially formed whorls that were recovered are, to the best of my knowledge, included in this inventory. Numerous sherd disks, with and without holes drilled in the center, and in sizes ranging from 1 to 6 or 7 centimeters in diameter, were not inventoried; they are stored in bags with the other sherds according to excavation trench and unit (see Vitelli 1993a:41, 53, Pl. 4a). Following the FC number, the entries provide:

a preliminary identification of the object;
its excavation context (Trench:Unit)
maximum preserved dimensions in metres, with
- D. = diameter
- Th. = thickness
- Wt = weight
- L. = length
- W. = width; and

a brief description of the material and condition of the object.

FC 1 Spindle whorl, conical, central perforation.
A:2. D. 0.033, Th. 0.015.
Gritty reddish brown clay, burnished, orange to gray clouds. Chips missing.

FC 2 Spindle whorl, biconical, central perforation.
A:20. D. 0.0325, Th. 0.023.
Gritty reddish brown clay. Chipped and worn.

FC 3 Spindle whorl, conical, central perforation.
Surface find. D. 0.03, Th. 0.017.
Gritty red clay, black surfaces. Chipped edges.

FC 5 Spindle whorl, biconical, squat, central perforation.
A:22. D. 0.035, Th. 0.02.
Gritty clay, firing clouds. Chipped edges.

FC 6 Spindle whorl, conical, central perforation.
A:27. D. 0.037, Th. 0.014.
Gritty clay, firing clouds. Large chip from one edge.

FC 7 Spindle whorl, biconical, central perforation.
A:25. D. 0.039, Th. 0.026.
Gritty clay, burnished, firing clouds. Upper surface worn.

FC 9 Weight, spherical, central perforation.
G:9. D. 0.049, Th. 0.046, Wt 104 g, D. hole. 0.003–9.
Calcium carbonate with mixed pebbly inclusions, gray firing clouds. Surface badly cracked, possible string wear around perforation.

FC 10 Weight, spherical (slightly biconical), central perforation.
G:15. D. 0.05, Th. 0.048, Wt 110 g, D. hole. 0.005.
Calcium carbonate with angular red grit (flint?) to 4–5 mm, gray firing clouds. Cracks and

small chips from surface, possible string wear around perforation.

FC 13 Spindle whorl, biconical, central perforation.
A:40. D. 0.027, Th. 0.016.
Gritty clay, firing clouds. Chips from one edge of perforation.

FC 14 Spindle whorl, conical, central perforation.
A:40. D. 0.024, Th. 0.013.
Gritty clay, burnished, firing clouds. Chipped.

FC 15 Spindle whorl, biconical (rounded), central perforation.
A:40. D. 0.033, Th. 0.02.
Gritty clay, firing clouds. Complete.

FC 16 Spindle whorl, biconical (rounded), central perforation.
A:40. D. 0.035, Th. 0.025.
Gritty clay. Complete.

FC 17 Spindle whorl, biconical (rounded), central perforation.
A:40. D. 0.037, Th. 0.023.
Gritty clay. Complete.

FC 18 Spindle whorl, conical, central perforation.
A:40. D. 0.046, Th. 0.024.
Gritty clay, burnished, dark firing clouds. Chipped at lower edge and around perforation.

FC 19 Spindle whorl, conical, squat, central perforation.
A:40. D. 0.033, Th. 0.013.
Gritty clay, firing clouds. Complete.

FC 20 Spindle whorl, biconical, squat, central perforation.
A:40. D. 0.03, Th. 0.011.
Gritty clay, black firing clouds. Worn along edges.

FC 21 Spindle whorl, biconical, central perforation.
G:37. D. 0.026, Th. 0.015.
Gritty clay, black firing clouds. One side chipped.

FC 22 Spindle whorl, biconical, central perforation.
A:25. D. 0.038, Th.0.022.
Gritty clay, black firing clouds. Complete.

FC 23 Spindle whorl, conical (rounded), central perforation.
A:25. D. 0.04, Th. 0.019.
Gritty clay, black firing cloud. Complete.

FC 24 Spindle whorl, biconical (rounded), central perforation.
Surface find. D. 0.0275, Th. 0.017.
Gritty clay, burnished, fired black. Complete.

FC 25 Spindle whorl, conical, central perforation.
A:26. D. 0.0365, Th. 0.023.
Gritty clay, burnished, black firing clouds. Chipped along edge.

FC 26 Weight, spherical, central perforation.
A:16. D. 0.053, Th. 0.045, Wt 115 g, D. hole 0.006.
Calcium carbonate with pebbly inclusions.
Gray firing clouds. Surface badly cracked and worn.

FC 32 Spindle whorl, conical, central perforation.
FF1:10. D. 0.04, Th. 0.017.
Gritty clay, firing clouds. Small chip one side.

FC 33 Spindle whorl, biconical, squat, central perforation.
FF1:13. D. 0.038, Th. 0.019.
Gritty clay, firing clouds. Worn around edges.

FC 34 Spindle whorl, biconical, central perforation.
FF1:15. D. 0.036, Th. 0.027.
Gritty clay, firing clouds. Edges of perforation chipped and worn.

FC 35 Spindle whorl, biconical, central perforation.
F1:2. D. 0.031, Th. 0.019.
Gritty clay, black firing clouds. Half of surface rough and crumbling, other half well-preserved.

FC 36 Spindle whorl, biconical, central perforation.
FF1:11. D. 0.03, Th. 0.019.
Gritty clay, burnished, firing clouds. Worn at edges of perforation.

FC 37 Spindle whorl, conical, central perforation.
FF1:6. D. 0.034, Th. 0.02.
Gritty clay, firing clouds. Chips from edge of base and around perforation.

FC 38 Spindle whorl, biconical, central perforation.
FF1:23. D. 0.034, Th. 0.024.
Gritty clay, firing clouds. Fragmentary: broken vertically and mended. Ca. one quarter missing along broken edge.

FC 39 Weight, spherical, central perforation.
G1:8. D. 0.05, Th. 0.043, Wt 100 g, D. hole 0.005.
Calcium carbonate with plentiful 1–3 mm sand and shell inclusions, firing clouds.
Large chip missing on one side, whole surface pitted.

FC 40 Spindle whorl, conical, central perforation.
H:3. D. 0.034, Th. 0.016.
Gritty clay, firing clouds. Chips from surface edges and around perforation.

FC 43 Sling bullet (or figurine?), fragmentary.
G1:19. D. 0.03, Th. 0.038.
Calcium carbonate with white nonplastics under 1 mm and silver mica glitter, tan throughout. Slightly asymmetrical egg shape, broken on one side and at “top.” Breaks suggest it may be one buttock of a figurine, with upper body also missing. Alternatively, a sling bullet.

FC 44 Weight, spherical, central perforation.
G1:5. D. 0.051, Th. 0.047, Wt 60 g, D. hole ca. 0.006.
Calcium carbonate with pebbly inclusions, black firing clouds. Fragmentary: vertical half preserved.

FC 46 Spindle whorl or weight, rounded, central perforation.
G1:7. D. 0.029, Th. 0.009.
Gritty clay, firing clouds. Complete. Unusual shape for spindle whorl, but light for a fishing weight.

FC 47 Spindle whorl, conical, central perforation.

Surface find. D. 0.042, Th. 0.018.
Gritty clay, burnished, firing clouds.
Large chips missing from base.

FC 48 Spindle whorl, biconical, central perforation.
FA QSE:1. D. 0.035, Th. 0.026.
Gritty clay, burnished, firing clouds. Intact, small chip from one side.

FC 49 Spindle whorl, biconical, central perforation.
FA QSE:4. D. 0.035, Th. 0.027.
Gritty clay, burnished, firing clouds. Intact.

FC 50 Spindle whorl, biconical, central perforation.
FA QSE:9. D. 0.029, Th. 0.016.
Gritty clay, burnished, firing clouds. Intact, but chipped.

FC 51 Spindle whorl, biconical, squat, central perforation.
FA QSE:9. D. 0.032, Th. 0.014.
Gritty clay, dark firing clouds. Complete but very worn.

FC 53 Spindle whorl, biconical, central perforation.
FA QSE:21. D. 0.033, Th. 0.022.
Gritty clay, burnished, dark firing clouds. Chips around perforation and edges.

FC 55 Spindle whorl, biconical, central perforation.
FA QSE:33. D. 0.032, Th. 0.025.
Gritty clay, burnished, dark firing clouds. Fragmentary: most of one side missing.

FC 56 Spindle whorl, biconical, central perforation.
H1:20. D. 0.037, Th. 0.024.
Gritty clay, burnished, dark firing clouds. Chipped around edges and perforation.

FC 59 Spindle whorl, biconical, central perforation.
H1:21. D. 0.033, Th. 0.021.
Gritty clay, burnished, dark firing clouds. Chipped around edges and perforation.

FC 61 Spindle whorl, biconical, central perforation.
FA:36. D. 0.036, Th. 0.021.
Gritty clay, burnished, black firing clouds. Chipped around edges.

FC 62 Spindle whorl, squat, central perforation.
FA:37. D. 0.034, Th. 0.010.
Gritty, slightly micaceous clay, dark firing clouds. Complete.

FC 63 Spindle whorl, biconical, squat, central perforation.
FA:38. D. 0.032, Th. 0.013.
Gritty clay, black firing clouds. Complete.

FC 64 Spindle whorl, biconical, central perforation.
FA:28. D. 0.030, Th. 0.020.
Gritty clay, burnished, black and orange firing clouds. Intact but badly chipped on side.

FC 65 Spindle whorl, biconical, central perforation.
FA:29. D. 0.042, Th. 0.020.
Gritty clay, burnished, firing clouds. Fragmentary: missing large portions around perforation and one side.

FC 67 Spindle whorl, biconical, central perforation.
H1:44. D. 0.035, Th. 0.02.
Gritty clay, firing clouds. Fragmentary: badly chipped over most of surface.

FC 69 Spindle whorl, biconical, central perforation.
FA:42. D. 0.032, Th. 0.022.
Gritty clay, firing clouds. Intact but chipped around both ends of perforation.

FC 70 Spindle whorl, biconical, central perforation.
FA:41. D. 0.041, Th. 0.019. Very gritty clay, poorly fired, firing clouds. Complete.

FC 71 Spindle whorl, conical, central perforation.
FA:42. D. 0.038, Th. 0.024.
Gritty clay, black firing clouds. Chipped around circumference.

FC 72 Spindle whorl, biconical, central perforation.
FA:43. D. 0.037, Th. 0.023.
Gritty clay, firing clouds. Fragmentary: just slightly over half (vertical) preserved.

FC 73 Spindle whorl, conical, central perforation.
FA:43. D. 0.043, Th. 0.024.
Very gritty clay, firing clouds. Complete.

FC 74 Spindle whorl, biconical, central perforation.
FA:44. D. 0.032, Th. 0.023.
Gritty clay, firing clouds. Intact but chipped on edges.

FC 75 Spindle whorl, biconical, central perforation.
FA: surface. D. 0.029, Th. 0.018.
Gritty clay, firing clouds, complete..

FC 76 Spindle whorl, conical, central perforation.
FA: surface. D. 0.039. Th. 0.013. Very gritty clay, dark orange. Complete.

FC 77 Spindle whorl, biconical, central perforation.
FA:45. D. 0.031, Th. 0.025.
Gritty, micaceous clay, burnished, firing clouds. Complete.

FC 78 Spindle whorl, biconical, central perforation.
FA:45. D. 0.035, Th. 0.021.
Gritty, micaceous clay, burnished, firing clouds. Complete.

FC 79 Spindle whorl, biconical, central perforation.
FA:47A. D. 0.039, Th. 0.030.
Gritty, micaceous clay, burnished, firing clouds. Fragmentary: ca. one half (vertical) preserved.

FC 80 Spindle whorl, biconical, central perforation.
FA:51. D. 0.032, Th. 0.022.
Gritty clay, black firing cloud. Complete.

FC 81 Spindle whorl, conical, central perforation.
FA:51. D. 0.034, Th. 0.023.
Very gritty clay, burnished, firing clouds. Complete.

FC 82 Spindle whorl, conical, central perforation.
FA:51. D. 0.025, Th. 0.024.
Very gritty clay, burnished, firing clouds. Complete.

FC 83 Spindle whorl, biconical, central perforation.
FA:54A. D. 0.037, Th.0.018.
Gritty clay, firing clouds. Complete.

FC 84 Spindle whorl, biconical, central perforation.
FA:55B. D. 0.034, Th. 0.021.
Gritty clay, firing clouds. Complete.

FC 85 Spindle whorl, biconical, central perforation.
FA:55C. D. 0.029, Th. 0.021.
Gritty clay, burnished, firing clouds. Missing about a (vertical) third.

FC 87 Weight? with two perforations.
H1:68. L. 0.042, W. 0.063, Th. 0.025.
Gritty, micaceous clay, fired hard, gray firing clouds. In plan, a rough hemisphere, in section, oval. One face slightly convex and abraded, the other worn to nearly flat. Sides and bottom are rounded. The "top" seems to have had two projecting flanges with a shallow groove between them. It appears that a shaft could have sat in the groove, and been fastened to the object through the string holes. Possibly used as a weight.

FC 89 Spindle whorl, biconical, central perforation.
FA:34. D. 0.038, Th. 0.021.
Gritty clay, burnished, firing clouds. Complete.

FC 90 Spindle whorl, biconical, central perforation.
FA:58. D. 0.032, Th. 0.020.
Gritty clay, firing clouds. Complete.

FC 91 Spindle whorl, biconical, squat, central perforation.
FAN:59. D. 0.039, Th. 0.010.
Gritty clay, firing clouds. Complete.

FC 92 Spindle whorl, biconical, central perforation.
FAN:59. D. 0.034, Th. 0.022.
Gritty clay, burnished, firing clouds. Complete.

FC 93 Spindle whorl, biconical, central perforation.
FAN:60. D.0.032, Th. 0.022.
Gritty clay, burnished, firing clouds. Intact, with chips around one end of perforation.

FC 94 Spindle whorl, conical, central perforation.
FAN:60. D. 0.029, Th. 0.020. Very gritty clay, burnished, dark firing clouds. Complete.

FC 95 Spindle whorl, conical, central perforation.
FAN:63. D. 0.042, Th. 0.020.
Gritty clay, firing clouds. Complete. Was broken through center, now mended. Small chips from edge and along break.

FC 96 Spindle whorl, biconical, central perforation.
FAN:83. D. 0.032, Th. 0.022.
Very gritty clay, burnished, firing clouds. Intact, but chipped along edges.

FC 99 Spindle whorl, biconical, central perforation.
H1B:73. D. 0.038, Th. 0.023.
Gritty clay, black core, light surfaces. Fragmentary: vertical half preserved.

FC 100 Spindle whorl, conical, central perforation.
H1B:76. D. 0.035, Th. 0.022.
Gritty clay, firing clouds. Intact, chipped at bottom.

FC 102 Amorphous lump of unbaked "clay."
H1B:73. L. 0.037, W. 0.033, Th. 0.012.
Calcium carbonate with sandy pebbles to 2 mm and flecks of charcoal. Gray-tan clouds. Probably intact, possibly water-deposited sediment, or a stopper.

FC 103 Spindle whorl, biconical, central perforation.
FAS:61. D. 0.032, Th. 0.023.
Gritty clay, burnished, firing clouds. Intact, chipped along circumference.

FC 104 Spindle whorl, conical, central perforation.
FAS:61. D. 0.039, Th. 0.019.
Gritty clay, fired gray on all surfaces. Intact, a few chips along circumference.

FC 105 Spindle whorl, biconical, central perforation.
FAS:64. D. 0.037, Th. 0.020.
Gritty clay, burnished, light tan. Intact, chips along circumference.

FC 106 Spindle whorl, biconical, central perforation.
FAS:67. D. 0.031, Th. 0.021.
Gritty clay, burnished, gray firing clouds. Intact, with chips along circumference.

FC 108 Spindle whorl, biconical, central perforation.
FAS:68. D. 0.034, Th. 0.016.
Gritty clay, burnished, firing clouds. Complete.

FC 109 Spindle whorl, biconical, central perforation.
FAS:69. D. 0.034, Th. 0.020.
Gritty clay, firing clouds. Intact, chipped around perforation.

FC 110 Spindle whorl, conical, central perforation.
FAS:69. D. 0.032, Th. 0.019.
Gritty clay, burnished, firing clouds. Intact, chipped around perforation.

FC 111 Spindle whorl, biconical, central perforation.
FAS:70. D. 0.031, Th. 0.024.
Gritty clay, burnished, firing clouds. Intact, chipped around perforation.

FC 113 Spindle whorl, biconical, central perforation.
FAS:72. D. 0.037, Th. 0.022.
Gritty clay, firing clouds. Complete, slightly off-center perforation.

FC 115 Spindle whorl (?), central perforation.
FAS:74. D. 0.026, L. 0.033, Th. 0.020.
Gritty clay, burnished, firing clouds. Fragmentary: broken at "top" and three areas around sides. Object appears to have been re-used. It may originally have been the handle of a scoop, subsequently drilled for use as a whorl.

FC 116 Pendant (?).
H2A:69. W. 0.031, L. 0.041. Th. 0.008.
Calcium carbonate, micaceous, powdery red flecks on surface. Appears water-worn. Roughly oval in shape, with two flat, but uneven surfaces, two drilled holes at top: one hole drilled through from both sides, other also drilled from both sides but the two depressions do not meet. Fragmentary: drilling appears to have broken off corner of piece. Object was coated with fugitive red powder when excavated. Consolidated with Atlacol.

FC 119 Sherd disc, central perforation.
Q5N:11. L. 0.043, W. 0.028, Th. 0.006.
FCP 1–2 No Lime ware. Fragmentary: roughly one quarter of a disc ground from sherd (two joined fragments), central hole drilled from both sides. Possibly used as a spindle whorl.

FC 120 Pellet of unknown material, spherical.
H1A:190. D. 0.015.
Soft reddish brown material, slight pressure from a fingernail creates a dent. Reacts moderately to hydrochloric acid. Spherical

pellet, slightly convex and polished on one face, more convex on other. Complete, pitted. Possibly bone. Consolidated with Atlacol.

FC 121 Spindle whorl, conical, central perforation.
Q5N:19. D. 0.032, Th. 0.015.
Gritty clay, red slip, burnished, firing clouds. Complete, although heavily worn.

FC 123 Daub with impression of wattle.
H2:Scarp. W. 0.046, L. 0.067, Th. 0.041.
Sherd and stone inclusions, including slivers of obsidian; orange surface with reed impressions. Reed appears to be of type commonly seen in southern Argolid today, particularly near Hermione and Thermisi. Daub disintegrates in hydrochloric acid.

FC 125 Spindle whorl, conical, central perforation.
A:13. D. 0.032, Th. 0.019.
Gritty clay, burnished, firing clouds. Chipped and worn around edges and base.

FC 126 Spindle whorl, biconical, central perforation.
A:13. D. 0.036, Th. 0.023.
Gritty clay, firing clouds. Several chips missing.

FC 136 Mud plaster (?) fragment.
Q5N:80. L. 0.027, W. 0.021, Th. 0.019.
Clay and/or calcium carbonate mix with plentiful sand inclusions and impressions of vegetal fibers. One side flattened as though had been attached to something. Similar samples found in Q5N:80, 83, 89.

FC 137 Pellet of baked clay, spherical.
Q5S:27. D. 0.009.
Micaceous, Lime-free clay, firing clouds. Complete: small sphere of baked clay, surface pitted and abraded.

FC 138 Spindle whorl, biconical, central perforation.
L5NE:2. D. 0.034, Th. 0.019.
Gritty clay, firing clouds.
Large chips missing.

FC 139 Spindle whorl, conical, central perforation.
L5NE:3. D. 0.046, Th. 0.020, Wt 30 g.
Gritty clay, firing clouds. Chipped around edges, pitted. Cleaned in hydrochloric acid.

FC 140 Spindle whorl, biconical, central perforation.
L5NE:6. D. 0.032, Th. 0.018, Wt 15 g.
Gritty clay, firing clouds. Intact, chipped around perforation, one face heavily weathered. Cleaned in hydrochloric acid.

FC 141 Spindle whorl, central perforation.
L5NE:7. D. 0.038, Th. 0.018, Wt 20 g.
Gritty clay, firing clouds. Fragmentary: horizontal half preserved, chipped. Cleaned in hydrochloric acid.

FC 142 Spindle whorl, biconical, central perforation.
L5NE:7. D. 0.036, Th. 0.022, Wt 20 g.
Gritty clay, firing clouds. Intact, chipped on edges and around perforation. Cleaned in hydrochloric acid.

FC 143 Weight, perforated horizontally across upper third.
L5NE:3. D. 0.034, Th. 0.022, Wt 20 g.
Lime and sandy grit to 2 mm, firing clouds. Intact, chipped around perforation. Cleaned in hydrochloric acid.

FC 144 Spindle whorl, discoidal, central perforation.
L5NE:3. D. 0.037, Th. 0.012, Wt 10 g.
Gritty clay, burnished, firing clouds. Fragmentary: restored from three fragments, missing large chip. Cleaned in hydrochloric acid.

FC 145 Spindle whorl, biconical, central perforation.
L5NE:11. D. 0.036, Th. 0.021, Wt 20 g.
Gritty clay, burnished, firing clouds. Intact, battered around edges. Cleaned in hydrochloric acid.

FC 146 Spindle whorl, discoidal, central perforation.
L5NE:11. D. 0.041, Th. 0.022, Wt 30 g.
Gritty clay, black inclusions, firing clouds. Intact, one large chip missing. Cleaned in hydrochloric acid.

FC 147 Spindle whorl, biconical, central perforation.
L5NE:13. D. 0.039, Th. 0.020, Wt 25 g.
Gritty clay, burnished, firing clouds. Complete. Cleaned in hydrochloric acid.

FC 148 Spindle whorl, conical, central perforation.
L5NE:13. D. 0.040, Th. 0.015, Wt 20 g.
Gritty clay, firing clouds. Intact, missing chips from edges. Cleaned in hydrochloric acid.

FC 149 Spindle whorl, discoidal, central perforation.
L5NE:15. D. 0.032, Th. 0.013, Wt 15 g.
Gritty clay, firing clouds. Complete. Cleaned in hydrochloric acid.

FC 150 Spindle whorl, central perforation.
L5NE:15. D. 0.038, Th. 0.015, Wt 15 g.
Gritty clay, red. Fragmentary: horizontal half preserved, badly chipped. Cleaned in hydrochloric acid.

FC 151 Spindle whorl, discoidal, central perforation.
L5NE:17. D. 0.035, Th. 0.014, Wt 21 g.
Gritty clay, firing clouds. Intact, missing large chip, worn around edges.

FC 152 Spindle whorl, conical, central perforation.
L5NE:17. D. 0.036, Th. 0.018, Wt 23 g.
Sandy grit, firing clouds. Intact, chipped on one side and around perforation; worn along edges.

FC 153 Spindle whorl, biconical, central perforation.
L5NE:19. D. 0.036, Th. 0.018, Wt 22 g.
Gritty clay, firing clouds. Intact but badly chipped around edges and perforation.

FC 154 Spindle whorl, central perforation.
L5NE:29. L. 0.027, Th. 0.019.
Gritty clay, firing clouds. Fragment: roughly one quarter of a squat, conical whorl.

FC 155 Spindle whorl, conical, central perforation.
L5NE:30. D. 0.041, Th. 0.016, Wt 25 g.
Gritty clay, gray firing clouds. Intact, chipped around edges. Cleaned in hydrochloric acid.

FC 157 Sherd disc, unperforated.
Q5S:84. D. 0.021, Th. 0.004.

Waterworn Urf, mended from two sherds. Flat, roughly circular clay disk.

FC 164 Sherd disc, unperforated.
H2A:177. D. 0.011, Th. 0.004.
Ungritted ware, black. Sherd rounded by grinding edges.

FC 165 Sherd disc, unperforated.
L5NE:48. D. 0.037, Th. 0.008.
FCP 1–2 Lime ware, chipped and ground to disc shape.

FC 166 Sherd disc, perforated.
L5NE:45. D. 0.036, Th. 0.007.
FCP 1–2 Andesite sherd. Fragmentary: roughly half of a disc, chipped to rough disc shape and pierced by drilling from exterior.

FC 168 Carbonate ball, spherical.
Q5S:158. D. 0.015.
Light pink calcium carbonate, mica glitter. Intact.

FC 173 Spindle whorl, discoidal, central perforation.
O5:3. D. 0.034, Th. 0.013, Wt 9 g.
Gritty clay, firing clouds. Fragment: roughly half of formed whorl.

FC 174 Spindle whorl or bead.
O5:5. D. 0.019, Th. 0.016, Wt 5 g.
Finely gritted clay, possible vegetal inclusions, Lime, firing clouds. Complete.

FC 179 Sherd disc.
P5:32. D. 0.036, Th. 0.007, Wt 11 g.
Monochrome Urf sherd, edges rounded by grinding.

FC 182 Sherd disc.
Q4:72. D. 0.035, Th. 0.0063, Wt 5.95 g.
FCP 1 Lime ware. Fragmentary: slightly more than half a disc with the beginning of a drill hole that apparently broke the sherd before it was completed.

FC 183 Sherd disc, perforated.
Q4:84. D. 0.026, Th. 0.006, Wt 4.1 g.
Monochrome Urf sherd, chipped into a rough disc, hole drilled in center.

FC 184 Sherd disc.
Q4:81. D. 0.027, Th. 0.005, Wt 4.4 g.
FCP 1–2 Lime ware sherd shaped by grinding edges to form a disc.

FC 185 Sherd disc.
Q6N:32. D. 0.044, Th. 0.005, Wt 13.3 g.
FCP 1–2 Andesite ware sherd roughly shaped into a disc.

FC 187 Sherd disc, perforated.
Q5S:185. D. 0.034, Th. 0.006, Wt 5 g.
Fragmentary sherd disc with edge of drilled hole at center.

FC 188 Sherd disc, perforated.
Q5S:186. D. 0.04, Th. 0.009, Wt 8.2 g.
FCP 1 Lime ware. Fragmentary sherd disc formed by chipping, with traces of drilled hole near center.

FC 189 Sherd disc, perforated.
Q5S:187. D. 0.033, Th. 0.004, Wt 3.6 g.
FCP 1 Lime ware. Fragmentary sherd disc with drilled hole near center.

FC 192 Whorl or weight, central perforation.
Q4:118. D. 0.034, Th. 0.0202, Wt 13 g.
Small sandy grits, possibly red painted, burnished, firing clouds. Fragmentary: roughly half of a formed whorl or weight with a hole pierced before firing at center.

FC 193 Fragmentary object of calcium carbonate.
Q6N:53. Th. 0.030, W. 0.032, Th. 0.026.
Yellowish matrix with mixed sand and shell grit; dissolves in hydrochloric acid. The object was molded with wet fingers, has a rounded corner, but gives no indication of original shape or function.

FC 197 Spindle whorl, biconical, central perforation.
H Terrace:4. D. 0.033, Th. 0.017, Wt 20 g.
Gritty clay, firing clouds. Intact, chipped along edges and perforation.

FC 198 Spindle whorl, biconical, central perforation.
H Terrace:14. D. 0.031, Th. 0.015, Wt 14.3 g.
Gritty clay, firing clouds. Intact, chipped on edges.

FC 199 Spindle whorl, conical, central perforation.
H Terrace:12. D. 0.033, Th. 0.009, Wt 12.3 g.
Gritty clay, firing clouds. Intact, chipped around edges and perforation.

FC 200 Spindle whorl, biconical, central perforation.
A:10. D. 0.030, Th. 0.017, Wt 14.8 g.
Gritty clay, firing clouds. Fragmentary: missing several large chips around edges..

FC 201 Spindle whorl, conical, central perforation.
F:3. D. 0.025, Th. 0.012, Wt 4.5 g.
Gritty clay, gray firing clouds. Roughly half (vertical) preserved.

FC 205 Sherd disc, perforated.
P5:180. D. 0.036, Th. 0.007.
FCP 1–2 Lime ware sherd, with tail of lug, shaped into a rough disc, central hole drilled from both sides.

FC 206 Spindle whorl, conical, central perforation.
L5:60. D. 0.035, Th. 0.016.
Gritty clay, gray firing cloud. Intact, large chip missing from one side.

FC 207 Spindle whorl, biconical, central perforation.
L5:65. D. 0.027, Th. 0.021.
Gritty clay, possibly slipped, burnished, fired black. Slightly chipped around edges and perforation.

FC 215 Spindle whorl, biconical, central perforation.
H1:Surface. D. 0.029, Th. 0.023.
Gritty clay, firing clouds. Just under one vertical half preserved.

DOCUMENT 2

Post-Neolithic Franchthi

James A. Dengate

Although the work in the Franchthi Cave concentrated on the remains from the Neolithic and earlier periods, the post-Neolithic human activities in the cave had a significant impact on the excavations and their results. Evidence of these activities was encountered throughout the site and consisted mainly of pottery sherds and a scattering of metal objects. At least one modern burial was excavated (see Cullen and Cook forthcoming). On Paralia, post-Neolithic remains were recovered from surface units in all of the trenches (see Table 10), but there were no indications of significant disturbance of Neolithic deposits. Inside the cave, however, it is clear that massive digging occurred prior to the archaeological excavations, disrupting much of the Neolithic stratigraphy (above, Chapter 2). A significant collection of post-Neolithic remains was recovered in the surface collection from the diving done in the pool at the back of the cave, undertaken to determine the extent of possible prehistoric remains in that area.

This report catalogues the post-Neolithic inventoried objects from the cave, pool, and Paralia. It includes, first, ten inventoried ceramic pieces, followed by ten metal objects.[1] References to Jacobsen and Farrand (1987) direct the reader to plans and sections that provide contextual information for the objects. Following the catalogue, I provide a brief discussion of the underwater exploration I conducted for the project in 1973 in the pool and the rear of the cave along with a summary of the context of the post-Neolithic finds from the front of the cave and on Paralia. All dates are BC unless otherwise stated.

CATALOGUE

Clay

The post-Neolithic clay objects were made on a fast wheel or with a mold. Some of the fabrics are labeled "Argive?" indicating that they are similar to those found in the excavations at Argos, at the Argive Heraeum, at Mycenae, at Tiryns, at Asine, and at nearby Halieis. While we cannot be certain where these objects were made, they appear to have been manufactured in the Argolid, possibly locally.[2]

The miniature pots #2 and #3 are Corinthian. Although #2 is very worn, the horizontal zigzag in the handle zone clearly places it among miniature kotylai ranging from the late 6th through the 5th century. (See Stillwell and Benson 1984:310 and compare no. 1689:Pl. 67.) The second miniature kotyle, #3, appears to belong to a type that was a common offering in the area. Several have been found on the Halieis acropolis (Dengate forthcoming); two were found outside burials in the Halieis necropolis and one inside a grave dated to the mid 5th century (HP 3107 in Rafn forthcoming). See also the two fragments from Paralia, PQ5:10 and O5:7 recorded on Table 10. The type seems to be late in the series of Corinthian miniature kotylai. (Closely comparable is Stillwell and Benson 1984:310, no. 1699, Pl. 67.)

#1 Black-glazed stemless cup (?) rim and handle.
FP 200=18488. H. pres. 0.029, est. D. rim 0.11, Th. 0.004 m. Reddish-yellow clay (7.5YR 7/6), dull black glaze, thin and chipped. Pool, unit 1. Jacobsen and Farrand 1987:Pl. 2.
Nearly straight rim, horizontal handle, round in section, attached on upper body and tilted up. Profile of body appears to have been shallow. This compares closely to a stemless cup from a grave group at Halieis containing pottery belonging primarily to the late 5th–first half of the 4th century (Dengate 1976:319, no. 183, Pl. 79). A similar cup (HP 222) was found on the Halieis acropolis in a 4th-century context (Dengate forthcoming). Argive?

#2 Miniature kotyle.
FP 201=18489. H. 0.033, D. rim 0.042 m. Reddish yellow clay (7.5YR 8/6), black to red glaze, very worn. Handles and part of body missing. Pool, unit 1. Jacobsen and Farrand 1987:Pl. 2.
Horizontal zigzags around rim. Glaze on lower body and underside. Underside slightly recessed between resting surface and center. The treatment of the underside compares closely to Pemberton 1989:175, no. 567, Pl. 52. Corinthian.

#3 Miniature kotyle (Pl. 9d).
FP 146=16643. H. 0.016, est. D. rim 0.028 m. Very pale brown clay (10YR 8/3), reddish-brown glaze. H1:37. Jacobsen and Farrand 1987:Pl. 13.
Shallow body, large handles. Thick, vertical bars around rim framed by band below, band around middle. Interior and underside glazed. Corinthian.

#4 Miniature kotyle.
FP 203=18491. H. pres. 0.012, D. base 0.02 m. Pink (7.5YR 8/4) to reddish yellow (5YR 7/6) clay. Pool, unit 1. Jacobsen and Farrand 1987:Pl. 2.
Base and lower half of body preserved. Trace of reddish glaze inside. Corinthian?

#5 Kalathiskos (Pl. 9a).
FP 174=16671. H. 0.043, est. D. rim 0.062 m. Gritty, light yellowish brown clay (10YR 6/4), trace of white. H2A: cleaning, perhaps associated with unit 18. Jacobsen and Farrand 1987:Pl. 26.
Nearly cylindrical profile, beveled toward base. Underside slightly concave. Horizontal rim has been broken almost entirely away, probably to form a small scoop with lug handle.[3] The shape is close to Pemberton 1989:173, no. 547, Pl. 51, dated to the later 4th century. Argive?

#6 Lopas rim fragment.
FP 204=18492. H. pres. 0.026, max. Th. 0.003 m. Gritty, reddish yellow clay (5YR 6/6), fired gray in places. Pool, unit 1. Jacobsen and Farrand 1987:Pl. 2.
Part of rim and stub of handle preserved. Thin, wide inner flange. The profile is similar to Sparkes and Talcott 1970:373, no. 1962, fig. 18, from a context ca. 400–350, but too little is preserved for exact comparison. Argive?

#7 Lopas rim fragment.
FP 202=18490. H. pres. 0.025, max. Th. 0.009 m. Gritty, light red clay (2.5YR 6/8), gray at core. Pool, unit 1. Jacobsen and Farrand 1987:Pl. 2.
Concave rim bulging toward junction with body. Trace of inner flange? Lopas fragments of the same fabric have been found at Halieis. See Rudolph 1974:151, A.39, fig. 12, dated to the first half of the 5th century or later. Argive?

#8 Terracotta female protome head (Pl. 9b).
FC 171=17693. H. pres. 0.043, W. pres. 0.041 m. Reddish yellow clay (5YR 6/6). Pool, unit 1. Jacobsen and Farrand 1987:Pl. 2.
Badly preserved; mended from many small fragments.[4] Moldmade head with concave back. Low polos with hole pierced at center top. Hair appears to have been drawn back from center and massed over temples. This compares closely to Papaspyridi-Karouzou 1933–35:33, fig. 16, right, and Dengate 1976:323, nos. 203 and 204, Pl. 82, from burials dated to the mid 5th century. Argive?

#9 Terracotta female protome head.
FC 172=17694. H. pres. 0.043, W. pres. 0.038 m. Reddish yellow clay (5YR 7/6). Pool, unit 1. Jacobsen and Farrand 1987:Pl. 2.
Compare #8.

#10 Lamp handle.
FP 208=18496. H. pres. 0.043, L. pres. 0.025 m. Reddish yellow clay (7.5YR 6/6) with some small inclusions. Pool, unit 3. Jacobsen and Farrand 1987:Pl. 2.
Unglazed pierced handle with two grooves on the front. Handle extends toward lamp base. Probably Broneer Type XXVII, 2nd–3rd century AC (Broneer 1930:90–102; Perlzweig 1961:7–8). The coarseness of the clay, however, suggests that this may be a local imitation. Argive?

Metal

#11 Bronze coin. Valentinian II, Theodosius I, Arcadius, or Honorius, AD 383–408, AE 4.
FV 348=18366=HN 1973-3.[5] D. 0.011 m. Wt 0.61 g. Die position ⊖. Paralia O5:5N. Jacobsen and Farrand 1987:Pl. 46.
Very worn and corroded bronze coin with legends and mint mark obscured. Obverse:

Bust of emperor right. Reverse: [SALVS REI PVBLICAE] Victory to left, trophy on shoulder, dragging captive. Buttrey (1981:117–18) notes the large numbers of these excavated at Athens, Corinth, Sardis, and Antioch, a total of 2800. This is a much larger number in comparison with other issues of small denomination Roman bronzes. According to Buttrey, the issues of Honorius, the only ones continuing to be struck as late as AD 402–408, are rare compared to those struck earlier, suggesting that #11 is earlier.

#12 Bronze coin. Zeno, AD 474–491, AE nummus.
FV 524=17883=HN 1976-4. D. 0.011 m. Wt 0.55 g. Die position ↗. Paralia QR:4. Jacobsen and Farrand 1987:Pls. 51 and 70.
Very worn and corroded bronze coin with legends and mint mark (if ever present) obscured. Obverse: Bust of emperor right, pearl diademed. Reverse: Monogram of Zeno, number 4 of Carson, Hill, and Kent 1965:110.

#13 Bronze coin. Anastasius I, AD 491–518, AE nummus.
FV 523=17880=HN 1976-3. D. 0.008 m. Wt 0.50 g. Die position ↑. Paralia Q/R:2. Jacobsen and Farrand 1987:Pls. 51 and 70.
Very worn and corroded bronze coin with legends and mint mark (if ever present) obscured. Obverse: Bust of emperor right, pearl diademed. Reverse: Partially preserved monogram of Anastasius (more than enough is preserved to distinguish it from the A on the reverse of the nummi of Justinian I). Compare Bellinger 1966:11, no. 15.

#14 Bronze coin. Justin II, AD 576–577, half follis from the mint of Thessalonica
FV 391=17435=HN 1974-2. D. 0.20 m. Wt 5.15 g. Die position ↓. Paralia O5:4. Jacobsen and Farrand 1987:Pl. 47.
Somewhat worn and corroded bronze coin. Obverse: DN IVS[TI]NVS PP [AV], Justin and Sophia facing, enthroned. Reverse: K; to left, ANNO; to right, XII; above, cross between phi and lunate sigma; below, TES. Compare Bellinger 1966:225, no. 84.

#15 Copper coin. Modern Greek AD 1895. Five lepta.
FV 398=17431=HN 1974-1. D. 0.017 m. Wt 1.95 g. Die position ↓. Paralia P5:3. Jacobsen and Farrand 1987:Pl. 48.
Slightly worn and corroded light-copper coin. Read with a traditional, non-phonetic transliteration of the katharevousa Greek: Obverse: BASILEION THS ELLADOS, crown below L BORREL, A, 1895. Reverse: LEPTA, 5, in olive wreath.

#16 Bronze sheet. Reinforcement (Pl. 9c).
FV 204=18034. L. 0.035, W. 0.009, Th. 0.003 m. Paralia Q5S:12. Jacobsen and Farrand 1987:Pl. 50 (but the unit did not extend to the drawn edge of this section).
Pierced and corroded bronze sheet cut into diamond shape, slightly bent and worn on each of the narrow sides of the hole. This is a common Archaic and Classical shape of a reinforcement used to attach something to bronze or to join two pieces of bronze.[6] These are often found with a bronze rivet or nail in them. An earlier or later date, or other use such as a toggle pin, cannot be ruled out by this identification.

Bronze sheet fragments like the following three are more common from the Archaic through the Byzantine or Ottoman periods than from earlier Bronze or Iron Age contexts. Such thin sheets were hammered, cut, and formed into a great variety of decorative supports and sheathing for buildings, furniture, tools, hardware, horse trappings, clothing, armor, jewelry, and votive objects. This variety of uses precludes any specific identification of mere fragments. These have not been analyzed and might be copper without any addition of tin, lead, etc., to make them classifiable as bronze. But they are normally called bronze because the softness of pure copper sheets would not be appropriate for the potential uses identified above.

#17 Bronze sheet, pierced, with two preserved edges.
FV 577=18487. L. 0.019, W. 0.017, Th. 0.005 m. H2B:6. Jacobsen and Farrand 1987:Pl. 30 (unit did not extend to the scarp).
Corroded and mended sheet fragment once pierced by typical square-sectioned bronze nail or rivet of at least the Archaic through Hellenistic periods.

#18 Five fragments of bronze sheet.
FV 25 A–E=16356. Largest A: L. 0.028, W. 0.017, Th. 0.001 m. H1:37. Jacobsen and Farrand 1987:Pls. 13 and 14.
Corroded and mended non-joining sheet fragments without preserved edges.

#19 Fragment of bronze sheet.
FV 26=16357. L. 0.019, W. 0.017, Th. 0.005 m. H1:40. Jacobsen and Farrand 1987:Pls. 13 and 14.
Corroded and mended sheet fragment without preserved edges. It may have originally been part of #18.

#20 Bronze or copper drip or slag fragment.
FV 576=18444. L. 0.008, W. 0.006 m. Paralia L5:55, >5 Residue. Jacobsen and Farrand 1987:Pl. 44.
Corroded with one side smooth and the other pitted.

CONTEXTS

Pool

The cave is about 150 m in length, but more than two-thirds of it is filled with the massive breakdown of the roof (Jacobsen and Farrand 1987:2 and 6; Fig. 8a).[7] The pool, located at the southeastern end of the cave, is about 35 m. roughly E–W and, at its widest, about 5 m roughly N–S (Pl. 4a). It narrows to about 1.5 m near the center to form two parts, a larger southern area almost 25 m N–S and a smaller northern section more than 15 m N–S (see the plan in Jacobsen and Farrand 1987:Pl. 2). In this plan, the undisturbed water in the pool is about 1 m below the Greek Mean Sea Level Datum. This is about the same as that found at sea level in front of Paralia. (See Cooper 1987:13–14; on June 13, 1976, when the bay was still, the sea level was –1.247 MSL relative to Corinth MSL.) The back part of the cave is filled with rubble whose elevation descends steeply from a high of 31.9 m immediately below the largest of the two windows down to that of the pool at the southwestern end. Jacobsen (1979:279 and Pl. 181a illustrating part of this rubble) provides a preliminary report on the 1974 investigations of an area located near the southeast corner of the cave below the east end of the smaller, higher window—this is marked "1974" on Jacobsen and Farrand (1987:Pl. 2). Here there were some apparently undisturbed sediments that may date a major collapse in the roof of the cave (Farrand forthcoming). The sherds from this work were predominantly Final Neolithic.

The smaller window of the cave breakdown opens slightly more than 5 m to the southwest of the southern end of the pool. Neither it nor the larger window, more than 50 m from the northern end of the pool to the northwest, brings much daylight into the area. A huge number of bats sleep in this part of the cave during the day—many were disturbed by our flashlights and swarmed around us as we investigated the darker regions. Their droppings form a thin layer covered with a growth (moss, algae, or lichens?) that provides a green, iridescent glow as one looks upwards toward either window. Rain coming through the windows apparently washes this away in the area immediately around them. But where this layer is found, it makes the jagged rock surface very slippery which further inhibits access to the pool. The large rubble fragments are so loosely packed that the droppings or other soil seldom collect between them.

The breakdown from the collapse(s) of the cave ceiling is so varied and massive here that constant climbing is necessary to move around. But during visits to the pool sherds were noted along its edge.[8] During the shallow water archaeological exploration of the inundated remains at nearby Halieis, the idea was conceived of exploring the pool farther in order to determine the extent of the artifacts, their dates, and the size of the cavern below the surface of the pool and possibly to determine more about the date of the ceiling collapse(s). I use the term "cavern" throughout when referring to the underwater cave beneath the surface of the pool to differentiate it from the rest of the cave, which, except for the pool, is all above sea level.

In spite of the difficult working conditions imposed by the collapse of the cave ceiling, on July 24 and August 12, 1973, a team of diver/archaeologists from the Halieis excavations investigated the pool. Thomas Jacobsen published the preliminary report of the work (1979:268 and 273). Hooka equipment, including a compressor, tank, and 30 m hoses as well as the diver's mask, snorkel, regulator, wetsuit, and underwater flashlights, was carried from the boat dock below the northeast entrance to the cave. The distance was about 200 m in a straight line, but in reality it was much more in order to twist around and follow the easiest path through the massive rubble up from sea level to a height at least 30 m above and back down to sea level at the pool. The weight of the equipment, especially the compressor, and the steepness of the ascent and descent slowed the progress. Often the equipment had to be handed up or down from one climber to the next, both of whose footing on the rocks was very precarious. Transporting the equipment from the dock to the pool took between an hour and a half and two hours depending on the amount of rest time needed. On the return trip, the finds added additional weight.

An exploratory dive was made during the afternoon of July 24. Standing at the edge of the pool, it was not possible to determine how far back from the edge of the cave the pool cavern extended. But that first dive indicated a much greater extent than we had expected and revealed many sherds on the bottom of the pool. We had thought it likely that the pool was simply a small part at the rear of the cave, now below sea level, that otherwise was like the rest of the sediments and rock falls in the cave. These sloped down as they approached the wall of the cave (compare the slope of the surface and deposits in Trenches G and G-1 excavated against the cave wall in Jacobsen and Farrand 1987:Pl. 21). The first dive proved that this was not the case with the pool.

A full day's work occurred on August 12 with arrival at the dock about 7 a.m. and departure from it shortly after 6 p.m. Artifacts were collected from the bottom of the visible pool by snorkeling. During the first dive of the day, two divers laid down a line about 50 m long out from near the edge of the pool to a maximum depth of about 45 feet registered on the diver's depth gauge.[9] A second dive explored along this line, taking photographs and sherding at the 5 m intervals marked on it. A final dive concluded the sherding and exploration. This brief investigation identified evidence of human activity in the pool from the artifacts collected from its bottom. In addition it determined that the pool extended well below the visible surface where it intersects the eastern wall of the cave and much beyond the end of the 50 m line and 45-foot depth reached by the divers.

There is a narrow, interrupted pebble beach along the edge of the pool that continues for up to half a meter below the water level. Then the bottom drops as one nears the overhang of the cave wall. The subsurface ceiling of the pool cavern is at first narrow enough for the diver to easily touch it while swimming beneath it. But as the bottom continues to descend, the ceiling incline decreases and a large undersea cavern opens up. As one enters this, the angle of the bottom descends less sharply. The water in the pool was clear and still; hand-held underwater lights were used, but the darkness made the visibility very poor—divers could see little more than a meter beyond the light source. The fine silt comprising the bottom quickly obscured what visibility there was as the diver moved about. This was not a problem while the slope of the pool bottom was steep, but as the slope declined the layer of silt thickened. No current was detected, suggesting that the pool was not spring fed nor disturbed by wave action from the open sea. The ceiling was covered with a soft, silt-like layer. This and larger limestone fragments readily broke from the ceiling when touched; even the diver's bubbles were sufficient to dislodge fragments from the ceiling. Under the silt-like layer, the ceiling of the cavern was very soft limestone in contrast to the hard, solid walls of the cave above. As the diver descended beneath the surface of the pool, there was a blurring of vision caused by a distinctive change in the water at about one-third of a meter below the surface. We attributed this to a separate layer of colder, fresher water on top of the warmer, saltier water below.[10]

For the first 10 meters from the beach edge the bottom of the pool consisted of small, rough limestone chips and pebbles and water-logged wood fragments lying on and under the silt. Artifacts were concentrated near the mouth of the pool; they decreased in quantity with the depth of the water and ceased entirely after about 20 m from the pool edge (Pl. 8b). Most of the artifacts were potsherds (228 were recorded—including eleven that were inventoried plus one modern glass and FB 481, a worked antler fragment that is likely not post-Neolithic). Those identified were primarily Final Neolithic (e.g., Fig. 75a, FP 205) with a few Middle Neolithic Urfirnis (FP 206 and 207, not illustrated). The sherds, often poorly preserved, were divided into two groups: handmade, and wheel- or mold-made. There were 61 of the latter (including the eight inventoried and catalogued above). This is about 28% of the total that are clearly post-Neolithic. Those that were identifiable included some possible Bronze Age; most were Archaic, Classical or Hellenistic, and Late Roman to Early Byzantine. Much of the Archaic and Classical or Hellenistic were typical of the kinds of sherds commonly found in sanctuary deposits (although of course many are also found in domestic debris). The dates of the sherds represented are similar to the post-Neolithic material from the excavations in the cave. There only a few sherds per unit might be identifiably wheel- or mold-made.

The distinctively votive material from the pool #2, #4, #8, and #9 and, from the cave, #3 and #5—suggests that both might have been the site of a cult. Sacred caves, springs, and pools are well known from Classical Greek religious practice. But the votive objects in the pool and the cave are probably to be associated with similar material found on the Franchthi headland at the nearby Mases temple (Site C17 in Runnels and Munn 1994:469 and Dengate 1974). This site is a relatively easy, generally level, walk of about 15 minutes following modern shepherds' paths from the end of the terrace toward the larger window of the cave. The end of the temple terrace nearer to the cave terminates in a wide path that slowly narrows after it leaves the terrace. This suggests that the temple builders planned the path to continue toward the cave—there was nothing else at the end of the rocky Franchthi headland. From the temple terrace level, the climb to the window and into the cave is not difficult and can be done in less than five minutes. In the second century AC, Pausanias (2.36.1–3), whose description of the Southern Argolid is translated and commented on in Appendix D of Jameson, Runnels, and van Andel (1994: 573–80), departed from the Mases *polis* site (C11 in Runnels and Munn 1994:466–67) toward Navplion without mentioning the temple terrace on the Franchthi headland, probably in ruins and forgotten by his time. He would likely have mentioned the cave/pool had he known of a cult or myth associated with it or if local informants had called it sacred. Nevertheless, during the Archaic and Classical or Hellenistic periods both the cave and the pool may have acquired votives because the people of Mases associated them with some local cult or myth.[11] But the significant locus of cult activity on the Franchthi headland remained at the Mases temple site.

Through time the collapse(s) of the cavern ceiling and the changes in the level of the sea have certainly affected the size and bottom of the pool and whatever artifacts can now be collected there—nothing we collected can in any way be considered stratified but merely to have tumbled down the slope of the pool bottom. Nor can we be sure of how long the pool existed, the elevation of the water, and when it became connected to the sea. (For the ancient variations in the level of the sea near the Franchthi headland and the southern Argolid, see van Andel and Sutton 1987:31–54, Jameson, Runnels, and van Andel 1994:194–213, and the references cited by them.) After the two days of diving, there was no further exploration of the pool. The dangers to divers from working in the the dark, enclosed, and unstable pool cavern and the difficulty of access to the pool area at the very back of the cave led instead to more intensive work in the sea near Paralia—the results of which are described in Gifford and Bottema (1990).

Cave

The massive post-Neolithic digging in the cave, encountered during the excavations, is discussed above (Chapter 2; see also Vitelli 1993a:33, especially p. 34, note 12). Compared to the almost 28% post-Neolithic sherds from the pool noted above, there were probably at the most about 1% in the disturbed portions of the cave. Excavation records indicate only a few wheel- or mold-made sherds for deposits with several hundred sherds identifiably Neolithic. The types and the amounts of each type of the post-Neolithic sherds identified, however, correspond roughly to those from the sites near and on the Franchthi headland recorded in the survey of the Southern Argolid (Jameson, Runnels, and van Andel 1994:Pocket Map 2, C11, C17, C38–41, C42, C45, F4, and F12). The datable sherds from the survey sites range from the Bronze Age through Modern (Runnels and Munn 1994:469, 473–77, and 508–10). Details for the Bronze and Iron Age material are now available in Runnels, Pullen, and Langdon (1995). The similar sherds found at Franchthi probably reflect visits to the cave by nearby inhabitants of the Franchthi headland. Clearly this was for cult purposes, as noted above for the pool. In addition, some of the post-Neolithic remains might have come from shepherding, analogous to the cave's modern use. (See the description of its environment and modern use by van Andel and Sutton 1987.)

Paralia

The post-Neolithic stabilization and soil formation of Paralia are described by Wilkinson and Duhon (1990:78 and 155–57). The post-Neolithic finds derive from surface units. The coins are the most datable and significant finds, probably lost by local shepherds and/or visitors to the cave. The clustering of Late Roman and Early Byzantine dates is similar to the coins and other occupation debris from site C17 below the Mases temple terrace (Runnels and Munn 1994:469) and from the Late Roman and Early Byzantine occupation at Halieis (Rudolph 1979). The large number of sites of this period in the southern Argolid and the reasons for them are given in Jameson, Runnels, and van Andel (1994:400–404).

CONCLUSION

Although the post-Neolithic remains from the Franchthi cave, pool, and Paralia are meager, they suggest cult usage at least from the Archaic through the Hellenistic periods, if not earlier or even later. If we could only fill the many obvious gaps, post-Neolithic activity, combined with the ceremonial use of the cave in the Neolithic suggested by Vitelli (above, Chapter 6, and 1993:216–17), may represent a remarkably long tradition of human cult activity at the Franchthi cave and headland. In addition the post-Neolithic objects suggest the projection of the current use of the cave by shepherds, at least intermittently, back perhaps as far as the Bronze Age. While statistically the post-Neolithic items are not significant, they do lend support to the picture of the Southern Argolid as described by Jameson, Runnels, and van Andel (1994:325–414)—Fifty Thousand Years of Coevolution of Landscape and Human Settlement.

NOTES

1. Inventoried objects were organized in an alphanumeric system prefaced by the letter F for Franchthi and by a letter for material, B = Bone, P = Pottery, S = Stone, V = Various (other materials), followed by a sequential number within each category. The number given after the equal sign is the sequential inventory number of the Navplion Archaeological Museum required by the Greek authorities because the inventoried objects are stored in the Franchthi excavation storage room in the Leonardo Annex to the Navplion Archaeological Museum.

2. On local ware, see the discussion of "Eastern Peloponnesian" by Rudolph 1974:127.

3. Ancient votive objects are seldom reworked before or after deposition.

4. The few terracottas recovered from the now-submerged sanctuary of Apollo at Halieis are also poorly preserved (for the preliminary report on the excavations, see Jameson 1974).

5. The Franchthi excavation coins have been stored with the much larger number of coins from Halieis. To keep them in order among the coins from Halieis, they were assigned to the alphanumeric series HN = Halieis Numismatics, followed by the year the coin was found and its number sequence within that year. This was also done for the coins from the Southern Argolid Survey through 1972. All these coins are stored by HN number in the Halieis excavation storage room in the Leonardo Annex to the Navplion Archaeological Museum.

6. I am grateful to N. Kalligas and L. Weier Krystallis for this information.

7. The geology and geomorphology of the cave and the Franchthi headland are treated by Vitaliano 1987a and 1987b, and Wilkinson and Duhon 1990:3–14. See also Farrand forthcoming.

8. These visits include surveying to draw the plan of the cave by Marian Holland McAllister in 1967–68 when the elevation of the pool was taken.

9. I use feet for the measurements taken from the depth gauge to avoid any confusion with elevations taken with a transit. One foot equals 0.305 m.

10. The worldwide average chlorine content of the sea is about 19 milligrams per milliliter of water, with the average for the Mediterranean somewhat higher (pers. comm. Riley Schaeffer, Indiana University Chemistry Department, 1973). Schaeffer's analysis of water samples from the pool showed that sample number 1, taken from the pool surface, had 6.7 mg of Cl/ml; from a depth of ±5 feet, number 2 had 15.3 mg of Cl/ml and number 7 had 12.2 mg of Cl/ml; from a depth of ±15 feet, number 3 had 10.7 mg of Cl/ml, number 8 had 12.6 mg of Cl/ml, number 9 had 13.4 mg of Cl/ml, number 10 had 11.7 mg Cl/ml, and number 15 had 13.5 mg Cl/ml. This indicates that fresher water was concentrated near the surface. Whether these results have any implications about the direct connection of the water in the pool with that of the open sea is unclear. There is obviously some connection between the sea and the pool cavern because at least two eels, apparently the common moray, inhabited the pool. No other sea life was observed in the pool. On the salinity of the Aegean, see van Andel and Sutton 1987:44–53, Jameson, Runnels, and van Andel 1994:210–12, and references cited there.

11. Even #10 might be an early Roman period votive, but lamps would have been needed, in any case, for moving about in the dark pool area.

BIBLIOGRAPHY

Alram-Stern, Eva
1996 *Die Ägäische Frühzeit*. 2. Serie. *Forschungsbericht 1975–1993*. 1. Band. *Das Neolithikum in Griechenland*. Verlag der Österreichischen Akademie der Wissenschaften, Wien.

Andreou, Stelios, Michael Fotiadis, and Kostas Kotsakis
1996 Review of Aegean Prehistory V: The Neolithic and Bronze Age of Northern Greece. *American Journal of Archaeology* 100:537–597.

Aurenche, Olivier and Claudine Maréchal
1985 Note sur la fabrication actuelle du plâtre à Qdeir (Syrie). *Cahiers de l'Euphrate* 4:221–226.

Barbour, Jane and Simiyu Wandibba (editors)
1989 *Kenyan Pots and Potters*. Oxford University Press, in association with the Kenya Museum Society, Nairobi.

Barley, Nigel
1994 *Smashing Pots. Works of Clay from Africa*. Smithsonian Institution Press. Washington, D. C.

Bellinger, Alfred R.
1966 *Catalogue of the Byzantine Coins in the Dumbarton Oaks Collection and the Whittemore Collection*. Vol. 1, *Anastasius I to Maurice, 491–602*. Dumbarton Oaks, Washington, D. C.

Bentley, Francis
1971 Poisons, Pigments and Metallurgy. *Antiquity* 45:138–140.

Betancourt, Philip P.
1984 *East Cretan White-on-Dark Ware*. University Museum Monograph 51. The University Museum, University of Pennsylvania, Philadelphia, PA.

Blegen, Carl W.
1930 Gonia. *Metropolitan Museum Studies* 3 (Part 1):55–80.

Boardman, John
1981, 1982 *Excavations in Chios 1938–1955. Prehistoric Emporio and Ayio Gala, I, II*. Annual of the British School at Athens, Supplements 15, 16. Thames and Hudson, London.

Boardman, John, and John Hayes
1973 *Excavations at Tocra, 1963–1965. The Late Archaic Deposits II and Later Deposits*. Annual of the British School at Athens, Supplement 10. Thames and Hudson, London.

Broneer, Oscar
1930 *Terracotta Lamps. Corinth*. Vol. 4, part 2. The American School of Classical Studies at Athens, Cambridge, MA.

Broodbank, Cyprian
1992 The Neolithic Labyrinth: Social Change at Knossos before the Bronze Age. *Journal of Mediterranean Archaeology* 5:39–75.

Bunzel, Ruth L.
1972 *The Pueblo Potter. A Study of Creative Imagination in Primitive Art*. Reprinted by Dover Publications, New York. Originally published 1929, Columbia University Press, New York.

Buttrey, T. V.
1981 II. The Roman Coins. In *Greek, Roman and Islamic Coins from Sardis*, edited by T. V. Buttrey, Ann Johnston, Kenneth M. MacKenzie, and Michael L. Bates, pp. 90–203, Archaeological Exploration of Sardis, Monograph 7. Harvard University Press, Cambridge, MA.

Carson, R. A. G., P. V. Hill, and J. P. C. Kent
1965 *Late Roman Bronze Coinage, A.D. 324–498*. Spink & Son, London.

Casson, Lionel
1971 *Ships and Seamanship in the Ancient World*. Princeton University Press, Princeton, NJ.

Chapman, John
1981 *The Vinca Culture of South-East Europe. Studies in Chronology, Economy and Society*, I, II. BAR International Series 117, Oxford.

Cherry, John F., Jack L. Davis, Anne Demitrack, Eleni Mantzourani, Thomas F. Strasser, and Lauren E. Talalay
1988 Archaeological Survey in an Artifact-Rich Landscape: A Middle Neolithic Example from Nemea, Greece. *American Journal of Archaeology* 92:159–176.

Coleman, John E.
1977 *Kephala. A Late Neolithic Settlement and Cemetery. Keos*. Vol. 1. American School of Classical Studies, Princeton, NJ.

de Contenson, Henri, and Liliane Courtois
1982 Redécouverte d'une technologie néolithique: les vaiselles blanches. *La Recherche* 13:778–779.

Cooper, Fredrick A.
1987 The Engineering Survey, in Jacobsen and Farrand 1987:10–14.

Cullen, Tracey
1985 *A Measure of Interaction among Neolithic Communities: Design Elements of Greek Urfirnis Pottery*. Ph.D dissertation, Program in Classical Archaeology, Indiana University, Bloomington. University Microfilms, Ann Arbor, MI.
In preparation Scattered Human Bone at Franchthi Cave: Remnants of Ritual or Refuse?

Cullen, Tracey, and Della Collins Cook
Forthcoming *Burial Practices and Human Biology*

at Franchthi Cave. Excavations at Franchthi Cave, Greece, fasc. 14. Indiana University Press, Indianapolis and Bloomington, IN.

Demoule, Jean-Paul, K. Gallis, and L. Manolakakis

1988 Transition entre les cultures nèolithiques de Sesklo et de Dimini: les catégories céramiques. *Bulletin de Correspondence Hellénique* 112:1–58.

Demoule, Jean Paul and Catherine Perlès

1993 The Greek Neolithic: A New Review. *Journal of World Prehistory* 7(4):355–416.

Dengate, Christina F.

1976 [1980] A Group of Graves Excavated at Halieis. *Archaiologikon Deltion* 31.1:274–324.

Forthcoming The Pottery, in *Halieis* 1: *The Acropolis*. Indiana University Press, Bloomington and Indianapolis, IN.

Dengate, James A.

1974 The Archaic Temple at Mases. *Archaeological Institute of America, Abstracts of Papers*, Archaeological Institute of America, New York, p. 22

Diamant, Steven R.

1974 *The Later Village Farming Stage in Southern Greece*. Ph.D dissertation, Classical Archaeology, University of Pennsylvania. University Microfilms, Ann Arbor, MI.

Dousougli-Zachou, Angelika

1989 Aria: eine spätneolithische Siedlung in der Argolis. Unpublished manuscript.

Edson, Gary

1979 *Mexican Market Pottery*. Watson-Guptil Publications, New York.

Elster, Ernestine S.

1986 Tripods, Plastic Vessels, and Stands: A Fragmentary Collection of Social Ceramics. In *Excavations at Sitagroi. A Prehistoric Village in Northeast Greece*, Vol. 1, edited by Colin Renfrew, Marija Gimbutas, and Ernestine S. Elster, pp. 303–344. Monumenta Archaeologica 13. Institute of Archaeology, University of California, Los Angeles, CA.

Evans, J. D.

1964 Excavations in the Neolithic Settlement at Knossos, 1957–60. Part I. *Annual of the British School of Archaeology at Athens* 59:132–240.

Evans, J. D. and Colin Renfrew

1968 *Excavations at Saliagos near Antiparos*. Annual of the British School of Archaeology at Athens, Supplement 5. Thames and Hudson, London.

Farrand, William R.

1993 Discontinuity in the Stratigraphic Record: Snapshots from Franchthi Cave. In *Formation Processes in Archaeological Context*, edited by Paul Goldberg, David T. Nash, Michael D. Petraglia, pp. 85–96. Monographs in World Archaeology No. 17, Prehistory Press, Madison, WI.

Farrand, William R.

Forthcoming *Stratigraphy, Sedimentology and Chronology of Franchthi Cave*. Excavations at Franchthi Cave, Greece, fasc. 12. Indiana University Press, Bloomington and Indianapolis, IN.

Frierman, J. D.

1971 Lime Burning as the Precursor of Fired Ceramics. *Israel Exploration Journal* 21:212–216.

Gallis, Kostas J.

1982 *Kavsis nekron apo ti neolithiki epohi sti Thessalia*. Ekdosi Tamiou Arheologikon Poron kai Apallotrioseon, Athens.

1987 Die stratigraphische Einordnung der Larisa-Kultur: eine Richtigstellung. *Praehistorische Zeitschrift* 62:147–163.

1992 *Atlas proistorikon ikismon tis anatolikis Thessalikis pediadas*. Ekdosi Eterias Istorikon Erevnon Thessalias, Larisa.

Gifford, John A., and Sytze Bottema

1990 Part II: The Offshore Investigations, in Wilkinson and Duhon 1990:85–138.

Gourdin, W. H. and W. D. Kingery

1975 The Beginnings of Pyrotechnology: Neolithic and Egyptian Lime Plaster. *Journal of Field Archaeology* 2:133–150.

Grimshaw, Rex W.

1971 *The Chemistry and Physics of Clays and Allied Ceramic Materials*. Fourth Edition, Revised. John Wiley and Sons, New York.

Hadjianastasiou, Olga

1986 A Late Neolithic Settlement at Grotta, Naxos. In *Problems in Greek Prehistory. Papers Presented at the Centenary Conference of the British School of Archaeology at Athens, Manchester, April 1986*. Edited by E.B. French and K.A. Wardle, pp. 11–20. Bristol Classical Press, Bristol.

Hadzipouliou, Elissavet

1989 Neolithiki keramiki apo tin Aria Argolidos. *Arheologikon Deltion* 36(1981):139–168.

Halstead, Paul

1981 Counting Sheep in Neolithic and Bronze Age Greece. In *Patterns of the Past. Studies in Honour of David Clarke*, edited by Ian Hodder, Glynn Isaac and Norman Hammond, pp.307–339. Cambridge University Press, Cambridge.

1989 The Economy has a Normal Surplus: Economic Stability and Social Change among Early Farming Communities of Thessaly, Greece. In *Bad Year Economics: Cultural Responses to Risk and Uncertainty*, edited by Paul Halstead and John O'Shea, pp. 68–80. Cambridge University Press, Cambridge.

Hansen, Julie M.

1991 *The Palaeoethnobotany of Franchthi Cave*. Excavations at Franchthi Cave, Greece, fasc. 7. Indiana University Press, Bloomington and Indianapolis, IN.

Hauptmann, H.

1981 *Die deutschen Ausgrabungen auf der Otzaki-Magula in Thessalien* III. *Das späte Neolithikum und das Chalkolithikum*. Rudolph Habelt Verlag, Bonn.

Hauptmann, H. and V. Milojcic

1969 *Die Funde der frühen Dimini-Zeit aus der Arapi-Magula Thessalien*. Beiträge zur Ur- und Frügeschichtlichen Archäologie des Mittelmeerkulturraumes, für das Institut für Ur- und Frühgeschichte der Universität Heidelberg. Band 9. Rudolf Habelt Verlag. Bonn.

Heurtley, W. A.
1939 *Prehistoric Macedonia*. Cambridge University Press, Cambridge.

Hill, J. N. and R. K. Evans
1972 A Model for Classification and Typology. In *Models in Archaeology*, edited by David L. Clarke, pp. 231–273. Methuen, London.

Holmberg, Erik J.
1964 The Appearance of Neolithic Black Burnished Ware in Mainland Greece. *American Journal of Archaeology* 68:343–348.

Immerwahr, Sara Anderson
1971 *The Neolithic and Bronze Ages. The Athenian Agora*. Vol. 13. American School of Classical Studies at Athens, Princeton, NJ.

Jacobsen, T. W.
1969 Excavations at Porto Cheli and Vicinity, Preliminary Report, II: The Franchthi Cave, 1967–1968. *Hesperia* 38(3):343–381.
1973a Excavations in the Franchthi Cave, 1969–1971, Part I. *Hesperia* 42(1):45–88.
1973b Excavations in the Franchthi Cave, 1969–1971. Part II. *Hesperia* 42(3):253–283.
1979 Excavations in the Franchthi Cave, 1973–1974. *Archaiologikon Deltion (Khronika)* 29.2:268–82.
In press Maritime Mobility in the Prehistoric Aegean. *Tropis V. Fifth International Symposium on Ship Construction in Antiquity, September 1993, Nauplion, Greece*, edited by Harry Tzalas. Hellenic Institute for the Preservation of Nautical Tradition.

Jacobsen, T. W. and W. R. Farrand
1987 *Franchthi Cave and Paralia. Maps, Plans, and Sections.* Excavations at Franchthi Cave, Greece, fasc. 1. Indiana University Press, Bloomington and Indianapolis, IN.

Jameson, Michael H.
1974 The Excavation of a Drowned Greek Temple. *Scientific American* 231, no. 4 (October):110–19.

Jameson, Michael H., Curtis N. Runnels, and Tjeerd H. van Andel
1994 *A Greek Countryside. The Southern Argolid from Prehistory to the Present Day.* Stanford University Press, Stanford, CA.

Johnson, Mats
1996a The Berbati-Limnes Archaeological Survey. The Neolithic Period. In *The Berbati-Limnes Archaeological Survey 1988–1990*, edited by Berit Wells in collaboration with Curtis Runnels, pp.37–73. Skrifter Utgivna av Svenska Institutet I Athen, 4°, 54. Acta Instituti Atheniensis Regni Sueciae, Series in 4°, 54, Stockholm.
1996b Water, Animals and Agricultural Technology: a Study of Settlement Patterns and Economic Change in Neolithic Southern Greece. *Oxford Journal of Archaeology* 15(3):267–295.

Jones, R. E.
1986 *Greek and Cypriot Pottery. A Review of Scientific Studies*. Fitch Laboratory Occasional Paper 1, The British School at Athens, Athens.

Kalogirou, Alexandra
1994 *Production and Consumption of Pottery in Kitrini Limni, West Macedonia, Greece, 4500 BC–3500 BC*. Ph.D. dissertation, Program in Classical Archaeology, Indiana University. University Microfilms, Ann Arbor, MI.
1995 Greek Neolithic "Cheese Pots:" A Reevaluation of the Evidence. Paper presented at the 60th Meetings of the Society for American Archaeology, Minneapolis, MN.

Keighley, Jenifer Marriot
1986 The Pottery of Phases I and II. In *Excavations at Sitagroi. A Prehistoric Village in Northeast Greece*. Vol. 1, edited by Colin Renfrew, Marija Gimbutas, and Ernestine S. Elster, pp. 345–392. Monumenta Archaeologica 13. Institute of Archaeology, University of California, Los Angeles, CA.

Lambert, Nicole
1981 *La Grotte Préhistorique de Kitsos (Attique), Missions 1968–1978. Tomes 1, 2. L'occupation néolithique, Les vestiges des temps paléolithiques, de l'antiquité et de l'histoire récent.* Recherche sur les grandes civilisations. Synthèse no. 7. Editions A. D. P. F. Ecole Francaise d'Athènes.

Lavezzi, John C.
1973 Prehistoric Investigations at Corinth 1968–1970. Ph.D. dissertation, Department of Art, University of Chicago, IL.
1978 Prehistoric Investigations at Corinth. *Hesperia* 47:402–451.

Lawrence, W. G.
1972 *Ceramic Science for the Potter*. Chilton Book Company, Radnor, PA.

Noble, Joseph Veach
1988 *The Techniques of Painted Attic Pottery*. Revised Edition. Thames and Hudson, London and New York.

Novak, G.
1959 Problems and Chronology in the Finds in the Cave of Grabak, *Archaeologica Iugoslavica* 3:11–39.

Papaspiridi-Karouzou, Semnis
1933–35 [1938] Anaskaphi taphon tou Argous, *Archaiologikon Deltion* 15:16–53.

Papathanassopoulos, George A. (editor)
1996 *Neolithic Culture in Greece*. Nicholas P. Goulandris Foundation, Museum of Cycladic Art, Athens.

Payne, Sebastian
1973 Animal Bones. In T. W. Jacobsen, Excavations in the Franchthi Cave, 1969–1971, Part I. *Hesperia* 42(1):45–88, pp. 59–66.
1975 Faunal Change at Franchthi Cave from 20,000 BC to 3,000 BC. In *Archaeozoological Studies*, edited by A. T. Clason, pp. 120–131. North-Holland and American Elsevier, Amsterdam.

Pemberton, Elizabeth G.
1989 *The Sanctuary of Demeter and Kore. The Greek Pottery. Corinth*. Vol. 18, part 1. The American School of Classical Studies at Athens, Princeton, NJ.

Périnet, G. and L. Courtois
1983 Evaluation des températures de cuisson de céramiques et de vaisselles blanches néolithiques de Syrie. *Bulletin de la Société Préhistorique Francaise* 80:157–160.

Perlès, Catherine
1987 *Les industries lithiques taillées de Franchthi (Argolide, Grèce)*. Vol. 1, *Présentation générale et industries paléolithiques*. Excavations at Franchthi Cave, Greece, fasc. 3. Indiana University Press, Bloomington and Indianapolis, IN.
1990a *Les industries lithiques taillées de Franchthi (Argolide, Grèce)* Vol. 2, *Les industries du Mésolithique et du Néolithique initial*. Excavations at Franchthi Cave, Greece, fasc. 5. Indiana University Press, Bloomington and Indianapolis, IN.
1990b L'outillage de pierre taillée Néolithique en Grèce: approvisionnement et exploration des matières premières. *Bulletin de Correspondence Hellénique* 114(1):1–42.
1992 Systems of Exchange and Organization of Production in Neolithic Greece. *Journal of Mediterranean Archaeology* 5:115–164.

Perlzweig, Judith
1961 *Lamps of the Roman Period. The Athenian Agora*. Vol. 7. The American School of Classical Studies at Athens, Princeton, NJ.

Peterson, Susan.
1984 *Lucy M. Lewis. American Indian Potter*. Kodansha International, Tokyo, NY, San Francisco.

Phelps, William Walter
1975 The Neolithic Sequence in Southern Greece. Ph.D. dissertation, University of London.

Pluciennik, Mark Z.
1997 Historical, Geographical and Anthropological Imaginations: Early Ceramics in Southern Italy. In *Not so Much a Pot, more a Way of Life. Current Approaches to Artefact Analysis in Archaeology*, edited by C. G. Cumberpatch and P. W. Blinkhorn, pp. 37–56. Oxbow Monograph 83. Oxbow Books, Oxford.

Pullen, Daniel J.
1995 The Pottery of the Neolithic, Early Helladic I, and Early Helladic II Periods, in Runnels, Pullen, and Langdon 1995:6–42.

Rafn, Birgitta
Forthcoming *The Halieis Necropolis*. Indiana University Press, Bloomington and Indianapolis, IN.

Renfrew, Colin, Marija Gimbutas, and Ernestine S. Elster (editors)
1986 *Excavations at Sitagroi. A Prehistoric Village in Northeast Greece*. Vol. 1. Monumenta Archaeologica 13. Institute of Archaeology, University of California, Los Angeles, CA.

Rice, Prudence M.
1987 *Pottery Analysis. A Sourcebook*. Univeristy of Chicago Press, Chicago, IL, and London.

Ridley, Cressida, and K. A. Wardle
1979 Rescue Excavations at Servia 1971–73: A Preliminary Report. *Annual of the British School at Athens* 74:185–230.

Riegger, Hal
1972 *Primitive Pottery*. Van Nostrand Reinhold Company, New York.

Roebuck, Carl
1951 *The Asklepieion and Lerna. Corinth*. Vol. 14. The American School of Classical Studies at Athens, Princeton, NJ.

Rose, Mark
Forthcoming *Fish and Fishing at Franchthi Cave, Greece* (provisional title). Excavations at Franchthi Cave, Greece, fasc. 13. Indiana University Press, Bloomington and Indianapolis, IN.

Rudolph, Wolf W.
1974 Excavations at Porto Cheli and Vicinity, Preliminary Report, III: Excavations at Metochi 1970. *Hesperia* 43:105–31.
1979 Excavations at Porto Cheli and Vicinity, Preliminary Report, V: The Early Byzantine Remains. *Hesperia* 48:284–324.

Runnels, Curtis N.
1980 *A Diachronic Study and Economic Analysis of Millstones from the Argolid, Greece*. Ph.D. dissertation, Program in Classical Archaeology, Indiana University, Bloomington. University Microfilms, Ann Arbor, MI.

Runnels, Curtis N. and Mark H. Munn
1994 A Register of Sites. Appendix A, in Jameson, Runnels, and van Andel 1994:415–538.

Runnels, Curtis, Daniel J. Pullen, and Susan Langdon (editors)
1995 *Artifact and Assemblage. The Finds from a Regional Survey of the Southern Argolid, Greece*. Vol. 1. *The Prehistoric and Early Iron Age Pottery and the Lithic Artifacts*. Stanford University Press, Stanford, CA.

Rutter, Jeremy B.
1983 Some Thoughts on the Analysis of Ceramic Data Generated by Site Surveys. In *Archaeological Survey in the Mediterranean Area,* edited by Donald R. Keller and David W. Rupp, pp. 137–142. BAR International Series 155, Oxford.

Rye, Owen S. and Clifford Evans
1976 *Traditional Pottery Techniques of Pakistan: Field and Laboratory Studies*. Smithsonian Contributions to Anthropology 21. Smithsonian Institution, Washington, D. C.

Sampson, Adamantios
1980 *I Neolithiki ke i protoelladiki I stin Evia*. Etairia Evoikon Spoudon. Athens.
1993 *Skotini, Tharrounia. To Spileo, o Ikismos ke to nekrotafio*. Athens. [No publisher given.]
1997 *To Spilaio ton Limnon sta Kastria Kalavriton*. Eteria Peloponnisiakon Spoudon, Ar. 7, Athens.

Schneider, Gerwulf, Heinz Kroll, Kostas Gallis, and Jean-Paul Demoule
1994 Production and Circulation of Neolithic Thessalian Pottery: Chemical and Mineralogical Analyses. In *La Thessalie. Quinze années de recherches archéologiques, 1975–1990. Bilans et Perspectives. Actes du colloque International Lyon, 17–22 Avril 1990*, pp. 61–70.

Ministère Grec de la Culture, Athens.
Shackleton, Judith C.
1988 *Marine Molluscan Remains from Franchthi Cave.* Excavations at Franchthi Cave, Greece, fasc. 4. Indiana University Press, Bloomington and Indianapolis, IN.
Shepard, Anna O.
1968 *Ceramics for the Archaeologist.* Publication 609. Carnegie Institution of Washington, Washington, DC.
Skibo, James M.
1992 *Pottery Function. A Use-Alteration Perspective.* Plenum Press, New York and London.
Smith, Jill Carrington
1977 Appendix 2: Cloth and Mat Impressions. In *Kephala. A Late Neolithic Settlement and Cemetery. Keos.* Vol. 1, by John E. Coleman, pp. 114–127. American School of Classical Studies, Princeton, NJ.
Sparkes, Brian A., and Lucy Talcott
1970 *Black and Plain Pottery of the 6th, 5th and 4th Centures B.C. The Athenian Agora.* Vol. 12. The American School of Classical Studies at Athens, Princeton, NJ.
Sperling, Jerome K.
1976 Kum Tepe in the Troad, Trial Excavation, 1934. *Hesperia* 45:305–364.
Stecher, Paul G., Martha Windholz, Dolores S. Leahy (editors)
1968 *The Merck Index. An Encyclopedia of Chemicals and Drugs.* Eighth Edition. Merck, Rahway, NJ.
Stillwell, A. N., and J. L. Benson
1984 *The Potters' Quarter. The Pottery. Corinth.* Vol. 15, part 3. The American School of Classical Studies at Athens, Princeton, NJ.
Talalay, Lauren E.
1993 *Deities, Dolls, and Devices. Neolithic Figurines from Franchthi Cave, Greece.* Excavations at Franchthi Cave, Greece, fasc. 9. Indiana University Press, Bloomington and Indianapolis, IN.
Thuesen, I. and R. Gwozdz
1982 Lime Plaster in Neolithic Hama, Syria. A Preliminary Report. *Paléorient* 8/2:99–103.
Touchais, Gilles
1980 La Céramique Néolithique de l'Aspis. *Études Argiennes*, Supplément 6. *Bulletin de Correspondance Hellénique* pp. 1–40.
Treuil, René
1983 *Le Néolithique et le Bronze Ancien Égéens. Les problèmes stratigraphiques et chronologiques, les techniques, les hommes.* École Française d'Athènes, Athens.
Tringham, Ruth and Dusan Krstic (editors)
1990 *Selevac. A Neolithic Village in Yugoslavia.* Monumenta Archaeologica 15, Institute of Archaeology, University of California, Los Angeles, CA.
van Andel, Tjeerd H., and Susan B. Sutton
1987 *Landscape and People of the Franchthi Region.* Excavations at Franchthi Cave, Greece, fasc. 2. Indiana University Press, Bloomington and Indianapolis, IN .
Vitaliano, Charles J.
1987a The Geological Survey, in Jacobsen and Farrand 1987:14–15.
1987b Geological History, in van Andel and Sutton 1987:12–17.
Vitelli, Karen D.
1993a *Franchthi Neolithic Pottery.* Vol. 1. *Classification and Ceramic Phases 1 and 2.* Excavations at Franchthi Cave, Greece, fasc. 8. Indiana University Press, Bloomington and Indianapolis, IN.
1993b Power to the Potters. Comment on Perlès' 'Systems of Exchange and Organization of Production in Neolithic Greece' [JMA 5:115–64], *Journal of Mediterranean Archaeology* 6(2):247–257.
1994 Experimental Approaches to Thessalian Neolithic Ceramics: Gray Ware and Ceramic Color, in *La Thessalie. Quinze années de recherches archéologiques, 1975–1990. Bilans et Perspectives. Actes du colloque International Lyon, 17–22 Avril 1990*, pp. 143–148. Ministère Grec de la Culture, Athens.
1995 Pots, Potters, and the Shaping of Greek Neolithic Society. *In The Emergence of Pottery. Technology and Innovation in Ancient Societies*, edited by William K. Barnett and John W. Hoopes, pp. 55–63. Smithsonian Institution Press, Washington, DC, and London.
1997 Inferring Firing Procedures from Sherds: Early Greek Kilns. In *Prehistory and History of Ceramic Kilns,* edited by Prudence M. Rice and W.D. Kingery, pp.21–40. American Ceramics Society, Westerville, OH.
In press "Looking Up" at Greek Neolithic Pottery. In *Pottery and People: a Dynamic Interaction*, edited by James Skibo and Gary Feinman. University of Utah Press, Salt Lake City, UT.
Forthcoming *Lerna I and II. The Neolithic Pottery.* The American School of Classical Studies at Athens, Princeton, NJ.
Wace, A.J.B., and M.S.Thompson
1912 *Prehistoric Thessaly.* Cambridge University Press, Cambridge.
Walter, Hans and Florens Felten
1981 *Alt-Agina III, 1. Die vorgeschichtliche Stadt: Befestigungen, Hauser, Funde.* Verlag P. von Zabern, Mainz.
Walter, Hans and Hans-Joachim Weisshaar
1993 Alt-Agina. Die Prähistorische Innenstadt westlich des Apollontemples. *Archäologischer Anzeiger*:293–297.
Weinberg, Saul S.
1965 Ceramics and the Supernatural: Cult and Burial Evidence in the Aegean World, in *Ceramics and Man*, edited by Frederick R. Matson, pp. 187–201. Aldine Publishing Company, Chicago, IL.
Weisshaar, Hans-Joachim
1989 *Die deutschen Ausgrabungen auf der Pevkakia-*

Magula in Thessalien, 1. Das späte Neolithikum und das Chalkolithikum. Rudolf Habelt Verlag, Bonn.

Whitaker, Irwin and Emily Whitaker
1978 *A Potter's Mexico*. University of New Mexico Press, Albuquerque, NM.

Whitbread, I. K.
1986 The Characterization of Argillaceous Inclusions in Ceramic Thin Sections. *Archaeometry* 28 (1):79–88.

Whitney-Desautels, Nancy
Forthcoming *Franchthi Cave Riverine and Terrestrial Molluscs*. Excavations at Franchthi Cave, Greece, fasc. 11. Indiana University Press, Bloomington and Indianapolis, IN.

Wilkinson, T. J., and Susan Duhon
1990 *Franchthi Paralia: The Sediments, Stratigraphy, and Offshore Investigations*. Excavations at Franchthi Cave, Greece, fasc. 6. Indiana University Press, Bloomington and Indianapolis, IN.

INDEX

Tables

Conventions and Abbreviations of Tables 1–8, the Frequency Tables

Each table records a single sequence of superimposed units in a corner of Trench FAN or FAS (the deepest unit shown at the bottom of the table), the location of which is indicated in the table heading. The sequences are recorded on the section drawing (Fig. 86) and on the schematic sections in Jacobsen and Farrand (1987:Pls. 31–32).

Unit	the number assigned to the unit during excavation
Total grams	total weight in grams of all sherds from the unit
% residue	the percentage of the total sherd weight comprised of residue
Grams w/o residue	total weight in grams of sherds in the unit with the weight of the residue subtracted

EN	all Early Neolithic wares and varieties combined
Urfs	all Middle Neolithic Urf varieties combined

For ware and variety abbreviations see Table 1.1

Fr#	Fr###:inventory numbers assigned to human bones recovered in the unit. Numbers are those assigned by Cullen and Cook (Forthcoming)

numbers	the numbers in each column record the percentage (calculated by weight) of the variety in the total unit sample after the residue was removed.
•	the variety is present in the unit as less than 1%
blank	the variety is absent from the unit
P	the variety is present

Table 1. FAS NW. Relative Frequencies

unit	total grams	% resi-due	grams without residue	EN	Urfs	Lo Li	Li Co	Mn Pt	Poly	Li Fe	And B	Ugr Mn	Gray B	NoLi Co	Cal Co	FN Ruff	FN Fine	Fr #
61S	1460	9	1330		1	•				2	1					80	16	
63S	505	6	475													72	28	
67S	1308	15	1108		3					4	•					75	18	
68S	1945	8	1785		2											84	14	
69S	3221	14	2781		3					3	1				1	82	11	Fr 148
70S	3210	23	2480		4	1				•	•					77	18	Fr 154
71S	3725	32	2545		10			•		2	•					72	16	Fr 132
74S	5280	40	3180		2					7					1	71	19	
76S	8021	39	4921		12	•			•	14	1		•		2	54	18	Fr 153, 431
81S	3685	26	2735		4					15					10	62	8	Fr 27
82S	3110	30	2165		5				•	45	3	•		5	20	18	3	Fr 28, 430
83S	2425	16	2025	•	4					48	7		1		15	10	13	Fr 135
93S	2624	15	2229		10					53	9	•	2	20	6			
97S	305	16	255							86	14							
98S	2439	18	2009	•	12	7		1	•	53	3	1	8	13				Fr 126
102S	782	19	632		14	13		2		56	2		3	9				
103S	2007	19	1627		20	18	6	1		37	3	1	6	7				
109S	3216	27	2336	1	26	11	7	1	•	42	1	•	3	9				
111S	2000	6	1880		21	27	6	9	•	31	5							
113S	429	26	319	2	47	22	6		17	3								
114S	326	28	234	14	36	35	11	6										Fr 131
115S	2534	26	1874		48	34	16	1	1									Fr 29a, 29, 144
116S	14765	18	12075	1	39	40	7	1	4				•					Fr 145–147a, b, 283, 432
117S	20630	14	17730	9	91	•												Fr 139–142
120S	5461	12	4831	21	79													

Table 2. FAS SW. Relative Frequencies

unit	total grams	% residue	grams without residue	EN	Urfs	Lo Li	Li Co	Mn Pt	Poly	Li Fe	And B	Ugr Mn	Gray B	NoLi Co	Cal Co	FN Ruff	FN Fine	Fr #
60S	ca. 25																	
63S	505	6	475													72	28	
67S	1308	15	1108		3					4	•					75	18	
68S	1945	8	1785		2											84	14	
69S	3221	14	2781		3					3	1				1	82	11	Fr 148
70S	3210	23	2480		4	1				•	•					77	18	Fr 154
71S	3725	32	2545		10			•		2	•					72	16	Fr 132
73S	3936	30	2736		3	1				2						58	36	Fr 136
78S	1263	27	918		8				2	7						80	4	
81S	3685	26	2735		4					15					10	62	8	Fr 27
82S	3110	30	2165		5				1	45	3	•		5	20	18	3	Fr 28, 430
83S	2425	16	2025	•	4					48	7		1		15	10	13	Fr 135
90S	3586	17	2986		1	1				49	7	•	•	12	29			
92S	1055	11	940		1					66	4				22			
94S	1412	20	1132	3	5	1				49	4	•	1	24	13			Fr 156
101S	441	24	336		25	5				48	3	3	1	14				Fr 138
103S	2007	19	1627		20	18	6	1		37	3	1	6	7				
109S	3216	27	2336	1	26	11	7	1	•	42	1	•	3	9				
111S	2000	6	1880		21	27	6	9	•	31	5							
113S	429	26	319	2	47	22	6		17	3								
115S	2534	26	1874		48	34	16	1	1									Fr 29, 29a,144
116S	14765	18	12075	1	39	40	7	1	4									Fr 145–147a, b, 283, 432
117S	20630	14	17730	9	91	•												Fr 139–142

Table 3. FAS NE. Relative Frequencies

unit	total grams	% residue	grams without residue	EN	Urfs	Lo Li	Li Co	Mn Pt	Poly	Li Fe	And B	Ugr Mn	Gray B	NoLi Co	Cal Co	FN Ruff	FN Fine	Fr #
59S	1018	20	818	2	9			8		4						70	9	
61S	1460	9	1330		1	•				2	1					80	16	
64S	401	7	371		2	.										81	18	
65S missing																		Fr 45
66S	2322	13	2012		•					•						88	12	
72S	2440	18	2005		8				•	1						72	19	
74S	5280	40	3180		2					7					1	71	19	
75S	855	42	495		12					9						67	12	
76S	8021	39	4921		12	•			•	14	1		•		2	54	18	Fr 153, 431
82S	3110	30	2165		5				1	45	3		•	5	20	18	3	Fr 28, 430
85S	2030	24	1550		1					53	3		•	15	28			
86S	1135	13	990		3					39	4			26	25	2		
89S	1918	15	1638		4	1				47	7	1	•	13	27			
90S	3586	17	2986		1	1				49	7	•	•	12	29			
93S	2624	15	2229		10					53	9	•	2	20	6			
95S	325	35	210		22					26		2	7	29	7			
99S	907	21	717	5	32	8			3	35	3	4		1	8			
104S	693	9	628	3	10	14	6	1		31	11		5	19				
110S	275	15	235		79	19				9								
111S	2000	6	1880		21	27	6	9	•	31	5							
112S	1270	11	1125		26	15	20			38								Fr 127, 434
114S	326	28	234	14	36	33	11	6										Fr 131
115S	2534	26	1874		48	34	16	1	1									Fr 29a, 29, 144
116S	14765	18	12075	1	39	40	7	1	4				•					Fr 145–147a, b, 283, 432
117S	20630	14	17730	9	91	•												Fr 139–142

Table 4. FAS SE. Relative Frequencies

uunit	total grams	% residue	grams without residue	EN	Urfs	Lo Li	Li Co	Mn Pt	Poly	Li Fe	And B	Ugr Mn	Gray B	NoLi Co	Cal Co	FN Ruff	FN Fine	Fr #
61S	1460	9	1330		1	•				2	1					80	16	
63S	505	6	475													72	28	
67S	1308	15	1108		3	.				4	•					75	18	
68S	1945	8	1785		2											84	14	
72S	2440	18	2005		8				•	1						72	19	
74S	5280	40	3180		2					7					1	71	19	
75S	855	42	495		12					9						67	12	
76S	8021	39	4921		12	•			•	14	1		•		2	54	18	Fr 153, 431
77S	1454	34	954		9					7						72	12	
82S	3110	30	2165		5				1	45	3		•	5	20	18	3	Fr 28, 430
88S	1105	9	1005		4					45	6			23	21			
89S	1918	15	1638		4	1				47	7	1	•	13	27			
93S	2624	15	2229		10					53	9	•	2	20	6			
96S	334	30	234		9					51	6	15	4	15	•			
100S	603	23	463		19	9		2		58	9	2		2				
104S	693	9	628	3	10	14	6	1		31	11		5	19				
108S	478	20	383		19	9				37	7	1		27				
109S	3216	27	2336	1	26	11	7	1	•	42	1	•	3	9				
111S	2000	6	1880		21	27	6	9	•	31	5							
112S	1270	11	1125		26	15	20			38								Fr 127, 434
115S	2534	26	1874		48	34	16	1	1									Fr 29, 29a, 144
116S	14765	18	12075	1	39	40	7	1	4				•					Fr145–147a, b, 283, 432
117S	20630	14	17730	9	91	•												Fr 139–142
118S	3298	10	2954	9	91	•												
119S	1052	13	919	17	83													

Table 5. FAN NW. Relative Frequencies

Note: In units 114N and 119N the missing % are undiagnostic.

unit	total grams	% resi-due	grams without residue	EN	Urfs	Lo Li	Li Co	Mn Pt	Poly	Li Fe	And B	Ugr Mn	Gray B	NoLi Co	Cal Co	FN Ruff	FN Fine	Fr #
59N	2296	•	2289		3	1										85	11	
60N missing																		
61N	1477	•	1475		5	•										85	9	
62N missing																		
63N	1067	2	1043		3					•					1	82	14	
64N	1322	3	1276		7	•				5						61	25	
70N	691	9	632		8	•				4						81	7	
71N missing																		
75N	427	19	347		12				1	16	1					56	13	
79N	560	11	499		3					35					10	43	9	
82N	605	8	555		3					45	1			5	17	16	13	Fr 443
85N	139		139													P	P	
87N	1205	12	1055		8					57	7	2	13	1	3	9		
97N	129			P	P					P		P						
99N	583	16	488		15			3		67			3	8	4			
108N	598	25	451		32	2	4		7	42	3	4	3	3				
110N	1117	22	872	3	28	22	13	3		29	1							
111N	1634	14	1399	3	41	35	8	3		7	5	•						Fr 442
112N	1689	18	1385	2	40	43	7	•	2									Fr 120+121, 210+440–441
114N	3655	5	3470	3	28	57	5	1	1									
117N	6472	9	5907	1	26	45	26		2									
118N	978	28	708	9	77	14												
119N	1256	27	916	7	36	4		4	2	•								
120N	7331		7331	9	89	1												Fr 206, 211
121N	15546	7	14491	4	95	•												

Table 6. FAN SW. Relative Frequencies

Note: In units 109N, 115N, and 119N the missing % are undiagnostic.

unit	total grams	% residue	grams without residue	EN	Urfs	Lo Li	Li Co	Mn Pt	Poly	Li Fe	And B	Ugr Mn	Gray B	NoLi Co	Cal Co	FN Ruff	FN Fine	Fr #
59N	2296	•	2289		3	1										85	11	
60N missing																		
61N	1477	•	1475		5	•										85	9	
63N	1067	2	1043		3					•					1	82	14	
64N	1322	3	1276		7	•				5						61	25	
66N	2722	1	2689		14	2				1						75	8	
70N	691	9	632		8	•				4						81	7	
74N	566	7	526		6					13						30	51	
78N	632	13	552		9					3	1					43	43	
81N	1417	8	1308		9					47	1			6	6	12	19	Fr 203
84N	1564	9	1421		9	1				29	2		•	40	18		•	
88N	2465	11	2190		7					36	4		1	27	9	12	4	
89N	970	19	790		6					56	11	1	1	20	5			
90N	1020	15	870		7	5				42	9		1	14	16		6	
94N	1015	11	900		7	2		3		42	17	4	6	19	•			
95N	862	15	732		9	3				55	17	1	8	5	1			
96N	448	30	313		15	3				61	3	10	3	6				
98N	555	20	445	1	14	2		8		54	2	7	11					
109N	1975	6	1848		27	7	4	1		35	3	•	3	18				
110N	1117	22	872	3	28	22	13	3		29	1							
111N	1634	14	1399	3	41	35	8	3		7	5	•						Fr 442
113N	626	23	480	2	48	40	11		1									Fr 189
115N	2994	21	2364	3	34	46	10		3									
116N	1243	10	1123	6	18	64	12		•									
119N	1256	27	916	7	36	4		4	2	•								
120N	7331		7331	9	89	1												Fr 206, 211
121N	15546	7	14491	4	95	•												
122N	10157	12	8937	4	96													Fr 207

Table 7. FAN NE. Relative Frequencies

Note: In units 103N, 114N, and 119N the missing % are undiagnostic.

unit	total grams	% resi-due	grams without residue	EN	Urfs	Lo Li	Li Co	Mn Pt	Poly	Li Fe	And B	Ugr Mn	Gray B	NoLi Co	Cal Co	FN Ruff	FN Fine	Fr #
59N	2296	•	2289		3	1										85	11	
60N missing																		
61N	1477	•	1475		5	•										85	9	
63N	1067	2	1043		3					•					1	82	14	
64N	1322	3	1276		7	•				5						61	25	
66N	2722	1	2689		14	2				1						75	8	
69N	1486	2	1451	4	7											74	16	
73N	1222	13	1067		3					9	•					50	38	
76N	700	7	649		10					13						69	9	
80N	1221	2	1197		2					10	•					76	11	
83N	935	3	909		12											74	14	
90N	1020	15	870		7	5				42	9		1	14	16		6	
94N	1015	11	900		7	2		3		42	17	4	6	19	•			
95N	862	15	732		9	3				55	17	1	8	5	1			
100N	626	8	576	3	6	3			3	85								
101N	2375	14	2045	•	22	6	16	•	2	30	•	1	•	21				
103N	1173	9	1063		31	15	8	4	3	32	1	1						
105N	1022	22	802	5	38	23	6	2		19	6	1						
106N	565	23	435	3	42	38	3	4		9								
107N	456	28	328	2	55	26	12	6				1						
111N	1634	14	1399	3	41	35	8	2		7	5	•						Fr 442
114N	3655	5	3470	3	28	57	5	1	1									
117N	6472	9	5907	•	26	45	26		2									
118N	978	28	708	9	77	14												
119N	1256	27	916	7	36	4		4	4	•								
120N	7331		7331	9	89	1												Fr 206, 211
121N	15546	7	14491	4	95	•												
122N	10157	12	8937	4	96													Fr 207

Table 8. FAN SE. Relative Frequencies

Note: in units 103N, 114N, and 119N the missing % are undiagnostic.

unit	total grams	% residue	grams without residue	EN	Urfs	Lo Li	Li Co	Mn Pt	Poly	Li Fe	And B	Ugr Mn	Gray B	NoLi Co	Cal Co	FN Ruff	FN Fine	Fr #
59N	2296	•	2289		3	1										85	11	
61N	1477	•	1475		5	•										85	9	
63N	1067	2	1043		3					•					1	82	14	
64N	1322	3	1276		7	•				5						61	25	
67N	246	2	242		6					9						70	15	
72N	275	5	261		3					31						43	23	
73N	1222	13	1067		3					9						50	38	
76N	700	7	649		10					13						69	9	
80N	1221	2	1197		2					10						76	11	
83N	935	3	909		12											74	14	
92N	370	3	361		2					34				63				
94N	1015	11	900		7	2		3		42	17	4	6	19	•			
95N	862	15	732		9	3				55	17	1	8	5	1			
100N	626	8	576	3	7	3			3	85								
101N	2375	14	2045	•	22	6	16	•	2	30	•	1	•	21				
103N	1173	9	1063		31	15	8	4	3	32	1	1						
105N	1022	22	802	5	38	28	6	2		19	6	1						
106N	565	23	435	4	42	38	3	4		9								
107N	456	28	328	2	55	26	12	6					2					
111N	1634	14	1399	3	41	35	8	3		7	5	•						Fr 442 (Fr 441)
112N	1689	18	1385	2	40	43	7	•	2									Fr 120+121, 210+440+441
114N	3655	5	3470	3	28	57	5	1	1									
116N	1243	10	1123	6	18	64	12		•									
117N	6472	9	5907	1	26	45	26		2									
118N	978	28	708	9	77	14												
119N	1256	27	916	7	36	4		4	2	•								
120N	7331		7331	9	89	1												Fr 206, 211
121N	15546	7	14491	4	95	•												
122N	10157	12	8937	4	96													Fr 207

Table 9. C-14 dates from Franchthi relevant to FCP 3 through 5.

Note: Measurements have been calibrated to two standard deviations (2 sigmas) and rounded off.

phase	sample number	context	radiocarbon age BP	calibrated date calBC	calBC 6000	calBC 5500	calBC 5000	calBC 4500	calBC 4000	calBC 3500
FCP 2	I-6128	FAN:120	6855±190	6090–5420						
FCP 3	P-1662	FAN:114	6690±80	5720–5480						
FCP 4	P-1921	FAS:102	8410±90	NA						
FCP 4	P-1661	FAN:97	6160±70	5240–4905						
FCP 4	P-1630	FAN:89	6110±90	5240–4805						
FCP 4	P-1920	FAS:83	6170±60	5240–4940						
FCP 5	P-1660	FAS:72	5260+60	4310–3970						
FCP 5	P-1659	FA:39	5160±80	4230–3790						

Table 10. Distribution of FCP 5 pottery on Paralia.

Trench: Unit	Sure FN	Probable FN	Possible FN	Post-Neo.	Comments
QR5:5		x			Flat bottom.
QR5:6		x		x	Rope band, possible HB with white paint.
QR5:7		x		x	Red lumps; EBA.
QR5:8	x			x	Ca. 10 red lumps, 1 Red on White, possible HB carination; EH II.
QR5:9			x		Several possible FN.
Q5S:71			x		2 possible FN.
Q5S:72			x		2 possible FN.
Q5S:75	x				Worn rope band.
Q5S:91	x				Rope band.
Q5S:114		x		x	Red lumps; Roman grooved?
Q5S:115		x		x	Red lumps; wheel made.
Q5S:117		x		?	Red lump.
Q5S:115		x			Strap handle, red lumps. Soft.
Q5S:120			x		Several possible FN.
Q5S:130	x			?	Rope band, lumps; possible wheel-made.
Q5S:131			x		Undiagnostic, possible FN.
Q5S:148			x		Creamy white slip.
Q5N:4	x			x	Red lumps; modern glass and wheel-made.
Q5N:5	x				Black cores, horned handle.
Q5N:6		x			Red lumps.
Q5N:8		x			Black cores, grass impression.
Q5N:10	x				Hollow foot, red lump, possible PB with white Lime on int.
Q5N:12			x		Possibly with grass impression.
Q5N:17		x			Red lump.
Q5N:19	x				Red lumps, possible rope band, whorl (FC 121).
Q5N:35			x		Possible FN.
Q5N:36			x		Possible FN.
Q5N:38			x		Possible FN.
Q4:1		x		x	Red lumps; recent wheel-made.
Q4:2		x		x	Red lumps; recent wheel-made.
Q4:3	x				FCP 5.2 red PB, soft pink fabric like L5 polychrome.
Q4:6			x		Several possible FN.
Q4:10		x	x		Red lumps, awful condition.
Q4:16		x			Lime-rich powder coating red lumps.
Q4:17		x			Red lumps.
Q4:25		x			Red lumps.
Q4:36		x			4–5 Red lumps.
Q4:38	x				Red lumps, HB handle.
Q4:39	x				Red lumps, rope band.
Q4:40			x		Red lumps, very worn.
Q4:107			x		Several possible FN.
Q4:113		x		x	Red lumps possible; black glaze, lamp fragment.
Q4:117		x		x	Cracked rim with lumpy lug.
Q4:118	x				Red handle lump with horn.
Q4:119		x			Red lumps.
Q4:120			x		Possible FN.
Q6N:1			x		14 lumps possible FN.
Q6N:5			x		Possible FN lumps.
Q6N:6			x		1 possible FN.
Q6NE:4-10			x		A few possible FN lumps.
PQ5:4			x	x	Red lumps; black glaze.
PQ5:5	x				Red (powder) "crust."
PQ5:6	x				Joins red powder in PQ5:5.
PQ5:7		x			Red lumps.

Trench: Unit	Sure FN	Probable FN	Possible FN	Post-Neo.	Comments
PQ5:8		x			Red lumps with black cores.
PQ5:9		x			Red lumps.
PQ5:10		x		x	Red lumps; miniature kotyle handle.
PQ5:12			x		Undiagnostic, possible FN.
PQ5:14		x			Handle with relief band.
PQ5:16			x		Undiagnostic, possible FN.
PQ5:36			x	x	Modern glass.
PQ5:37			x	x	Possible FN or later.
PQ5:38			x	x	Very badly weathered.
PQ5:39			x		Possible red lump.
P5:5			x	?	Very worn.
P5:9		x		x	Red lumps; wheelmade.
P5:17		x		?	Red lumps, very worn.
P5:22	x	x		?	Rope band, red lumps ca. 440 g FN sherd.
P5:29	x	x			Rope band; Lime-rich smear; strutted loop handle.
P5:30			x		Uncertain, worn sherds.
P5:37	x				Rope band, 8–9 possible FN.
P5:43			x		Residue size undiagnostic.
P5:56		x			Rounded knob.
P5:42			x		Whole unit soft and dissolving.
O5:2			x	x	Red lump; black glaze.
O5:3		x		x	Rope band with possible white crust.
O5:4	x			x	Elephant lug, HB lug; black glaze.
O5:6			x	x	Possible FN; molded cup frag.
O5:7			x	x	Possible FN; miniature kotyle.
O5:8	x				Soft pink fabric with red powder, black cores on lumps.
O5:9			x	x	Red lumps; wheel made.
O5:10		x		?	Red lumps.
O5:11	x				Rope band, ca. 500 g red lumps.
O5:12		x			Red lumps; soft pink fabric.
O5:14	x				Rope band, red lumps.
O5:15			x		Possible FN.
O5:16	x				Horned strap handle, piecrust rim, soft pink strap stump .
O5:17	x				Rope band, soft pink strap handle frag.
O5:18		x			Creamy white slip, 8 red lumps.
O5:19			x		Several possible FN.
O5:20		x			Red lumps.
O5:23		x		x	Red lumps; rope band of overlapping disks (BA?); black glaze.
O5:24			x		Small red lumps.
O5:25		x			FC 176 (FN figurine).
O5:43			x		1 possible FN.
O5NE:1			x		2 possible FN.
O5NE:2		x			9 probable FN.
O5NE:3		x		x	1 probable FN; black glaze.
O5NE:4		x			4 probable FN coarse.
O5NE:6			x		7 possible FN.
O5NE:11	x				2 possible FN PB; FP 197.
O5N:4	x				Rope band.

Plans

Plan 1. Cave trenches.

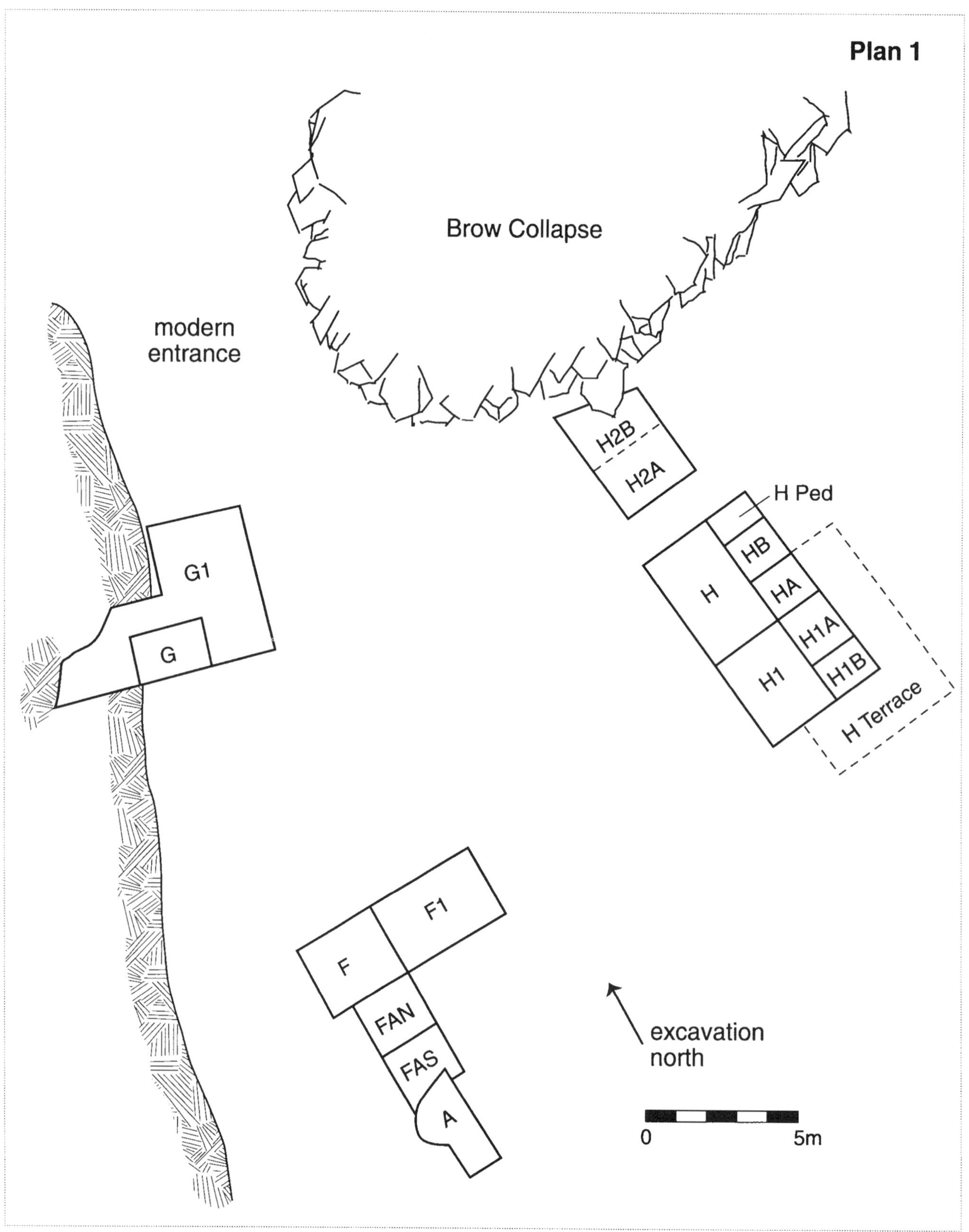

Plan 2. Trenches A–FA–FF1.

Note: Dashed lines indicate limits of Trench A after removal of surface units that also removed portions of eventual trench FAS.

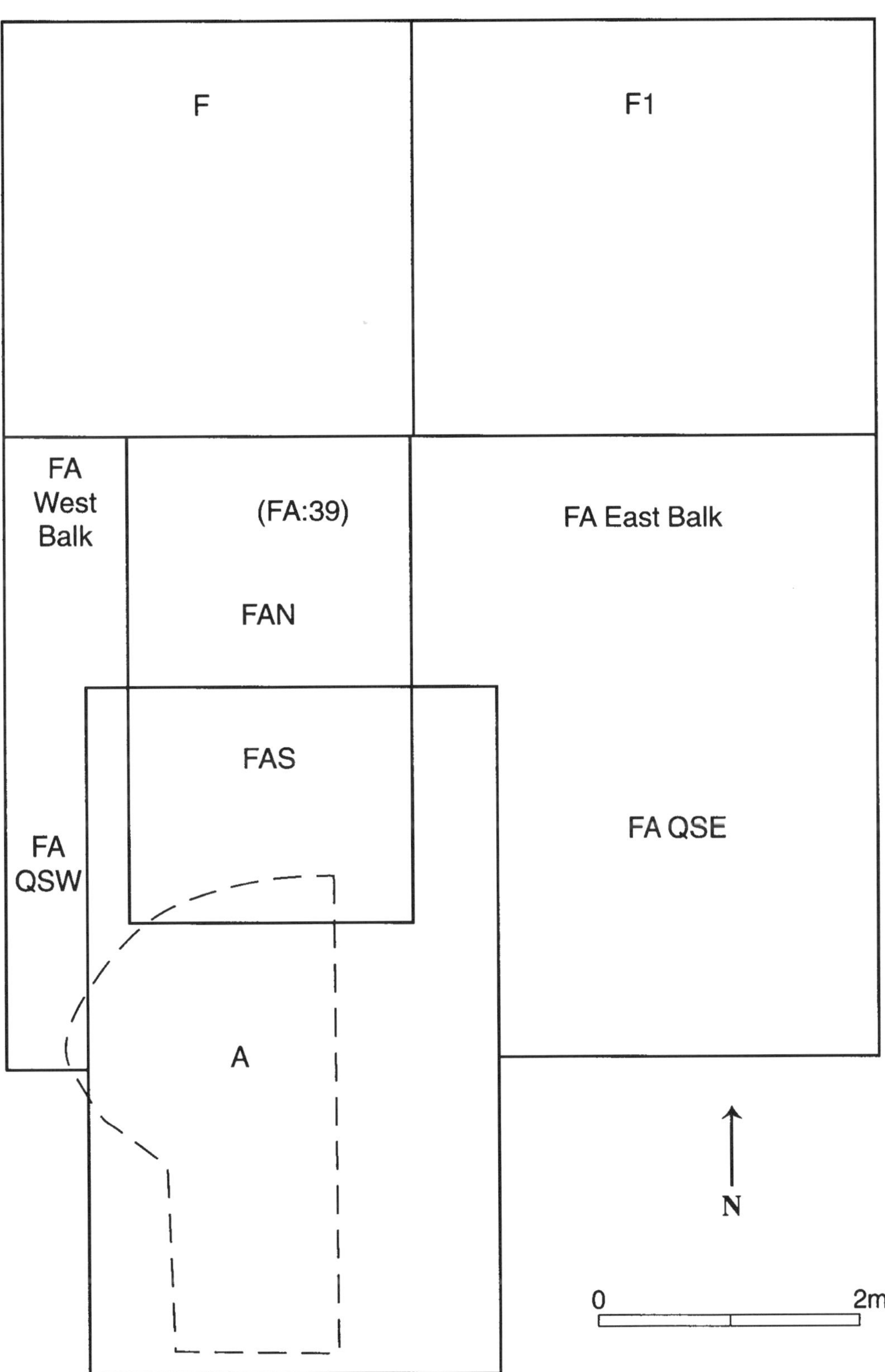

Plan 3. FCP 5 remains on Paralia, with enlargement of Trench L5.

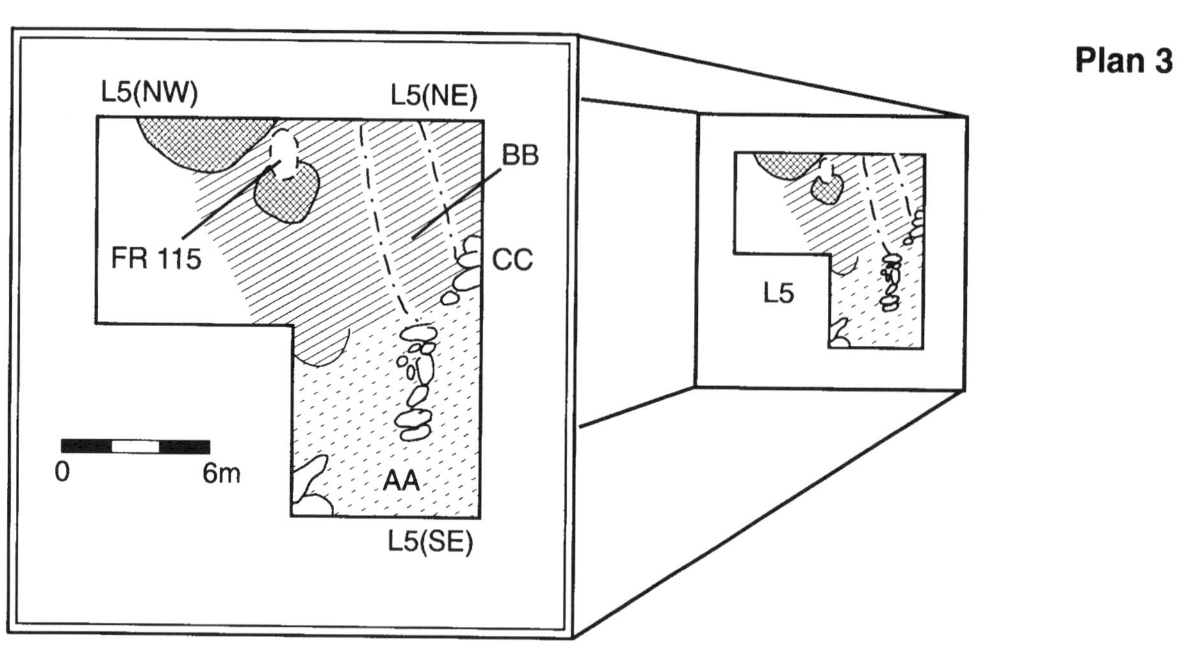

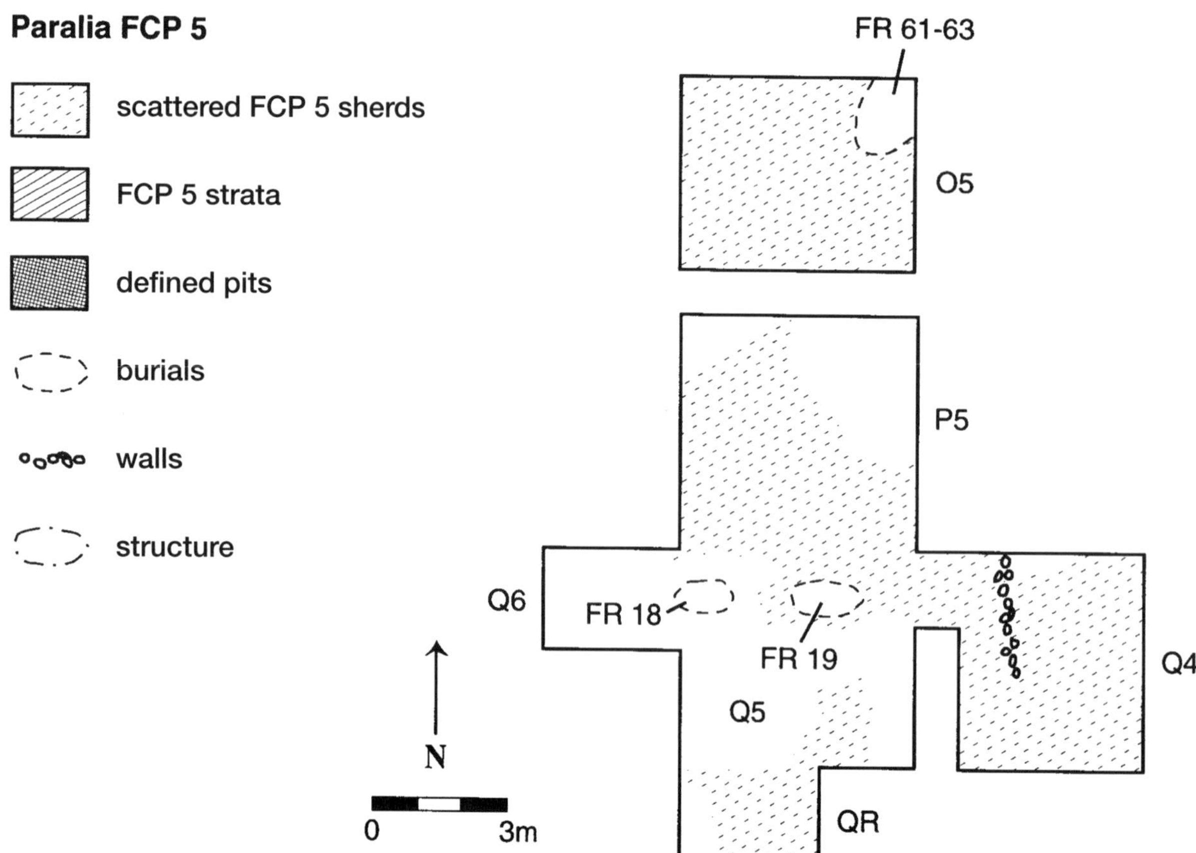

Figures

Abbreviations and Codes used in Captions for Figures

Nonplastics

L	Lime, unspecified calcium carbonates that react in HCl
R	Red, unspecified mineral, possibly grog
D	Dark, unspecified mineral, possibly grog
MG	Mixed grits, unspecified minerals of variable colors, textures
S	Sand, probably quartz, variable colors, shapes
B	Biotite, black or gold mica
H	Hornblende
H+B+F	andesite matrix implied
F	Feldspar
Q	Quartz

a	angular
r	rounded
m	many
f	few
<1, 2, 3	nonplastics smaller than number of mm indicated
1, 2, 3	number of mm = maximum size of most nonplastics

Major headings

FP##	Franchthi Pottery, inventory number
FC##	Franchthi Clay, inventory number
FPSC##	Franchthi Pottery Study Collection, assigned number
E, ext	exterior
I, int	interior
U	underside (of bases, bottoms, handles)
C	core
0.00	diameter, in meters

Potters' procedures

scrp(d)	scrape(d)
smth(d)	smoothe(d)
brnsh(d)	burnished
PB	pattern burnished
pt(d)	paint(ed)
patt	pattern

Colors, conditions

H#	hardness, Mohs' scale
brwn	brown
blk	black
pops	Lime pops
RIP	restored in plaster

General abbreviations

surf(s)	surface(s)
irreg	irregular
w/	with
vert	vertical
hor	horizontal
asym	asymmetrical
bot	bottom
max	maximum (diameter)
th	thickness
poss	possibly, possible
prob	probably, probable
car	carination
+	links joining sherds from different units
, and	links non-joining sherds from different units

Figure 1 FCP 3 Low Lime Burnished variety

a. FAN:118 LoLiB 0.10–11, irreg 14 joined, 10+ non-joining E:scrpd, smthd, brnshd, dull gray w/ a few blk glossy areas, matte granular gray pt, disappears in places w/o trace. I:scrpd, brnshd, pitted, greenish-blk (5Y5/1). H:3–4.

b. FAS:115 LoLiB MG<1 0.14–15, irreg E, I:hor brnsh, striated troughs, slight crackling, blk surfs, granular gray pt. H:5–6.

c. FAN:119 LoLiB fLMG<1 0.12 E:brnshd,blk, small red cloud, many scratches, some crackling. I:smthd, no brnsh, clear traces red slip. C:dark gray-green. H:3, 5 where brnshd.

d. FAN:105 LoLiB fLMG, mica glitter 0.13 E, I:well scrpd, brnshd, blk. C:gray. H:2–3.

e. FAN:117 LoLiB fLMG<1 0.15 E:well scrpd, brnshd, glossy, waxy, blk , trace of matte white line, isolated, no trace of additional pt.

f. FAS:115 LoLiB LMG<1 0.16 joint E, I:scrpd, brnshd, streaky dark gray. C:light gray. Worn. H:2–3.

g. FAS:116 LoLiB LMG<1 0.19 car E:brnshd, dark gray, granular gray pt, hole through lug is brnshd nearly closed one side. I:scribbly brnsh. C:light gray. H:5–6.

h. FAS:116+115 LoLiB LMG<1 0.13 max E:scrpd, brnshd, impressed, then final brnsh except around dimples, glossy blk. I:scrpd, scribbly brnsh, pitted. C:light gray. H:2–3.

i. FAN:117 LoLiB LMG<1 0.16 shoulder E:scrpd, brnshd, blk, crackling, groove at neck. I:scrpd, once brnshd, now worn w/ tiny pits. C:light gray. H:2–3.

j. FAS:115 LoLiB LMG<1 0.21 neck E:scrpd, brnshd, blk, crackling, relief donut. I:scrpd, brnshd, pitted, gray. C:light gray. H:2–3.

k. FAN:112 LoLiB MG<1, mica glitter 0.16 neck E:scrpd, brnshd, was glossy blk but worn, granular gray pt. I:scrpd, brnshd hor, worn and pitted at bott, light gray. C:light gray. H:2–3.

l. FAN:105 LoLiB LMG<1, mica glitter 0.17 E, I:scrpd, brnshd, dark gray ext, light int. C:light gray. H:2–3.

m. FAN:112 LoLiB LMG<1rR 0.20 E:scrpd, PB glossy blk. I:scrpd, brnshd glossy blk for 2 cm below rim, below is brnshd gray, no gloss, pitted at bott. H:2–3 int, 4 ext.

n. FAN:114 LoLiB LMG<1 0.19 E:scrpd, erased gray patt: smeared light gray on glossy blk near rim. I: blk (slip) just at rim, gray below with minimal brnsh. H:2–3.

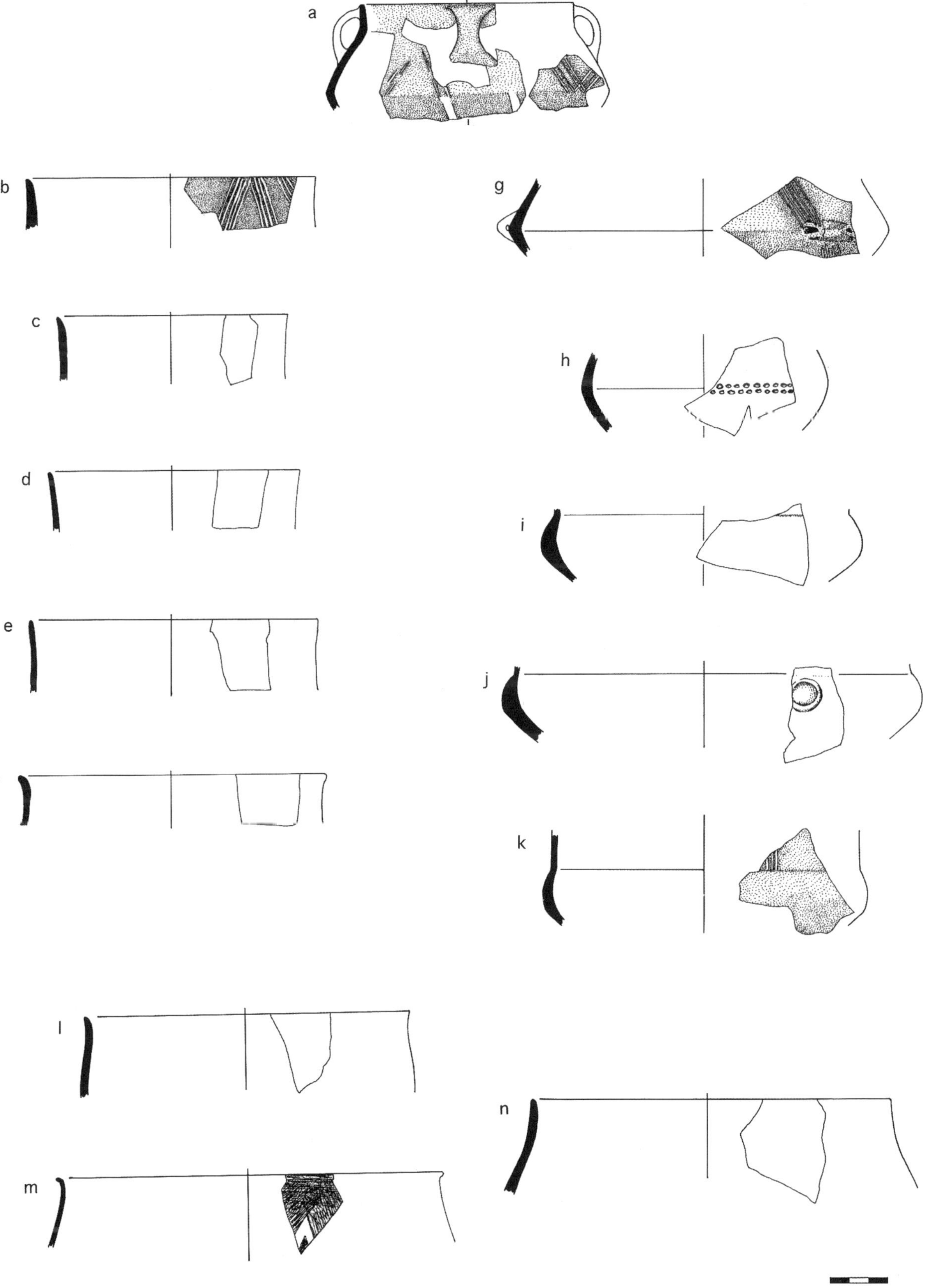
a
b
c
d
e
f
g
h
i
j
k
l
m
n

Figure 2 FCP 3 Low Lime Burnished variety

a. FAS:116 and "neighboring units" FP 242 LoLiB LMG1 0.14–15 irreg at joint, 0.33 max RIP E:scrpd, slipped, brnshd, waxy blk where reduced, streaky red slip visible in oxidized clouds. I:scrpd, lightly brnshd. Slip extends just to edge of collar joint. Three drill holes in lower half. H:2–3.

b. FAS:117 (most)+116S+114N+56 LoLiB LMG1rRDf4, tend to fall out leaving rounded depressions 0.18 joint, 0.095 irreg bott many dozens non-joining, 2 w/ partial drill holes E:well scrpd, regular even surface, poss slip, brnshd, color varies red, tan, glossy blk. I:scrpd, brnshd except under shoulder, no signs wear. U:scrpd, brnshd. H:2–3.

Figure 2

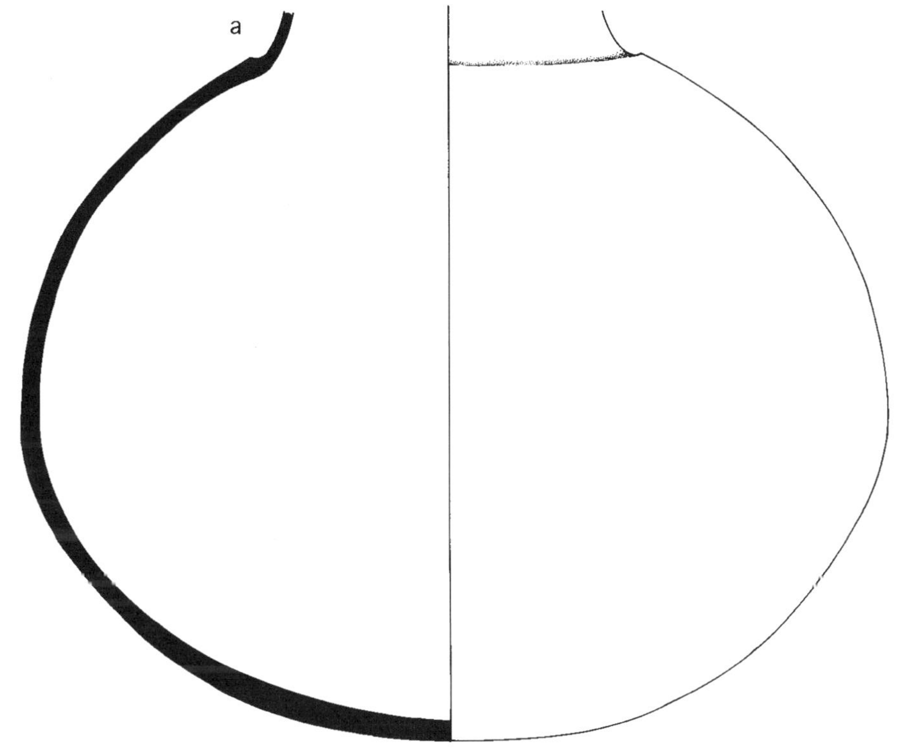

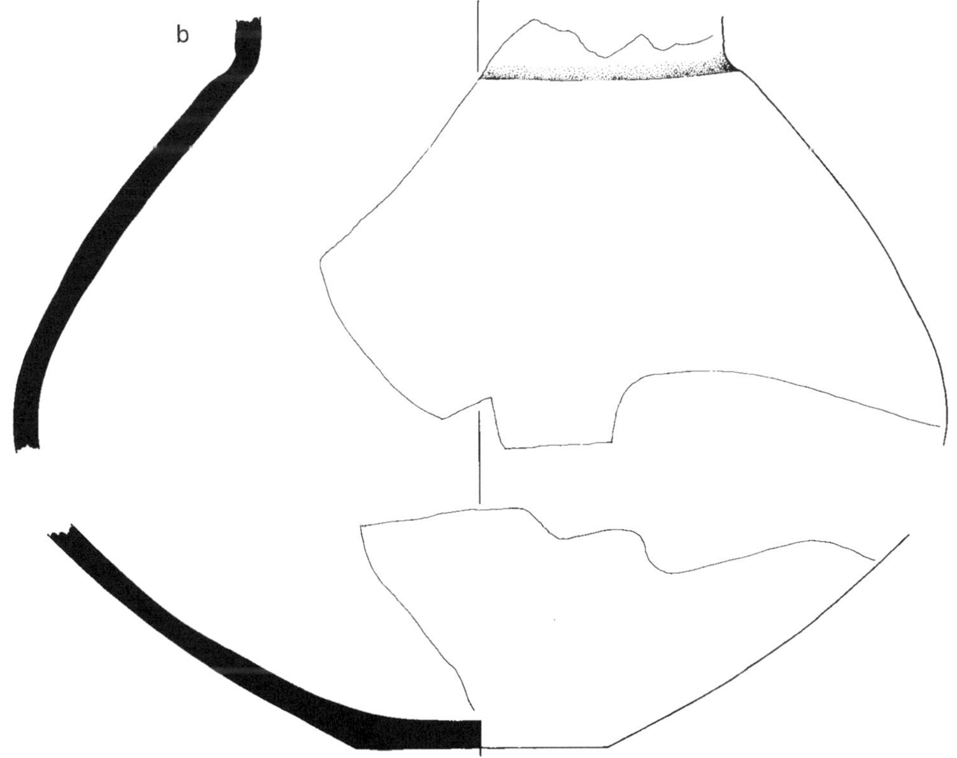

Figure 3 FCP 3 Low Lime Burnished variety

a. FAS:117 LoLiB LMG1r R2 0.18 E:lumpy, poorly scrpd, brnshd, blk. I:scrpd, smthd, gray. C:uniform light gray. H:2–3.

b. FAS:116+116N+A Lot 16 FP 241 LMGrR1–2 Lime prominent on bott where burned, barely visible elsewhere 0.27 max, 0.085 bott E:well scrpd, smthd, brnshd, patt in broad strokes of stacked chevrons on one side, more random patt on other; firing clouds all around, pt varies blk to red; 2 pairs of drill holes, plus two holes missing their pair. I:scrpd, wet smthd, but missed a spot, very bott has several strokes of brnsh; carbon sooting on int bott in irreg patt, penetrates core to variable depths, sandwich core in places. Burned after breaking: 2 sherds are pale pink, heavily worn, color changes sharply along join to main body.

c. FAS:116+118N, 6 joining LoLiB LMG1 0.30 max E:scrpd, red pt, brnshd, traces ptd vertical lines fired red, largely worn off. I:scrpd, smthd. C:uniform light 2.5YR 6/8. H:2–3.

d. FAN:116 LoLiB LMG2 0.10–12 bott E, I:scrpd, smthd, brnshd, fired to 7.5YR 6/6. I:heavily charred with blk extending deeper into core on wall than on bott, thus presumably from use in sherd form. Found sitting upside down on "hearth." H:3.

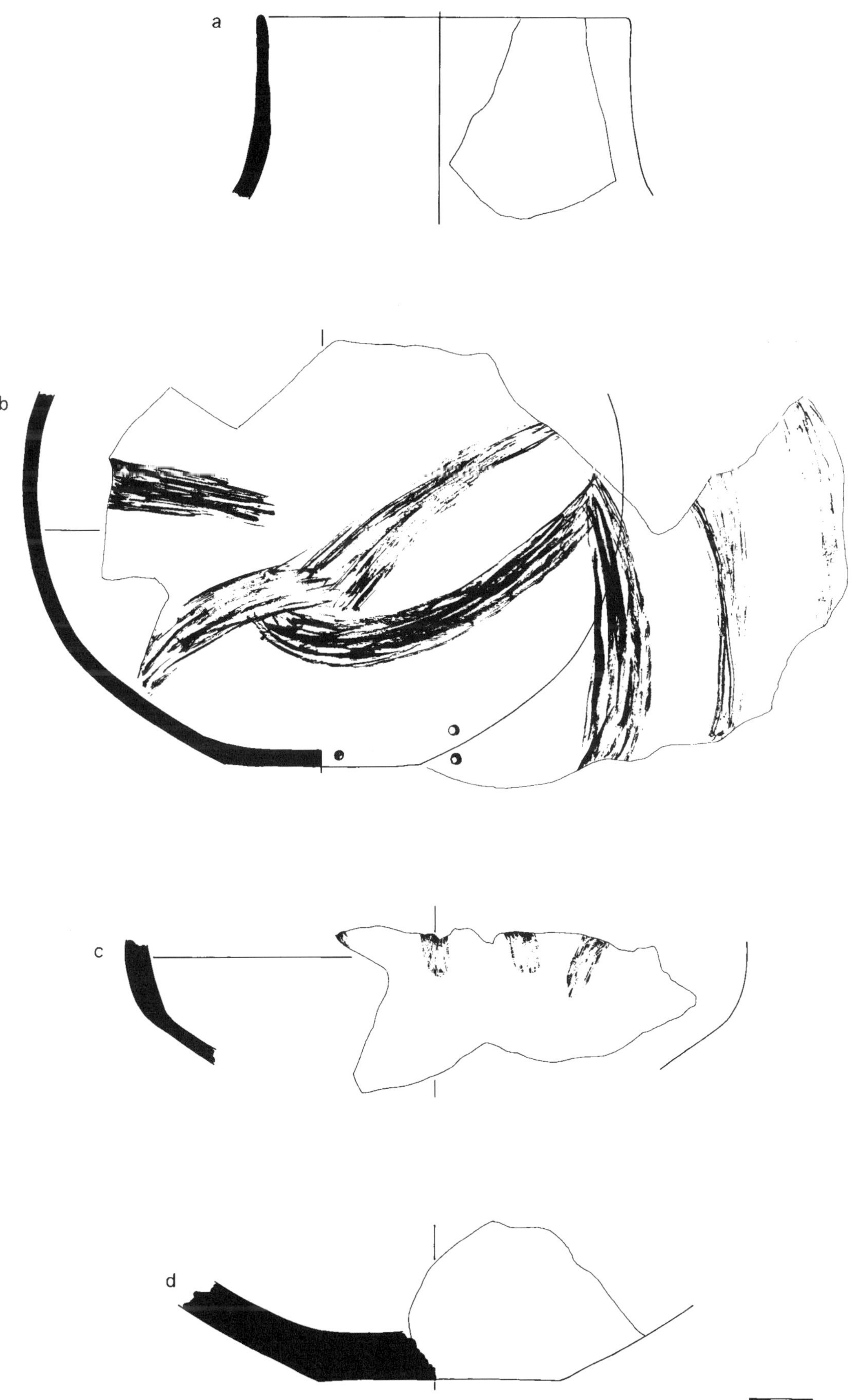
a
b
c
d

Figure 4 FCP 3 Low Lime Burnished variety

a. FAS:111 LoLiB LMG1 0.27 E:scrpd, waxy brnsh, fired red, flaking. C:uniform light red. H:2.

b. FAN:109 LoLiB L<1rR1f9 0.33 E:scrpd, slipped, brnshd hor, uniform light red (2.5YR 6/8). I:slipped just inside rim, light brnsh, streaky red. H:2–3 fabric, 4–5 pt.

c. FAN:117 LoLiB aLMG<1 0.38–40, irreg 2 fragments, one of 8 sherds, one of 6 E:scrpd, slipped, brnshd glossy blk w/ small clouds, clear troughs, flaking. I:scrpd, slipped, brnshd. C:uniform light. H:2–3.

d. FAS:116 LoLiB LSMG1 0.16 E, I:scrpd, poss slip, brnshd, clear troughs, fired red (7.5YR 7/6). C:uniform light (5YR 7/6), jagged breaks. H:2–3.

e. FAN:114 LoLiB mLMG<1 0.12 E:scrpd, smthd, brnshd, blk cloud at heel and tip handle. I:scrpd, smthd, brnshd only along rim. H:2–3.

f. FAN:114 LoLiB LMG<1 0.20–22, irreg E:surf almost completely pecked away, specks of waxy brnsh, blk. I:scrpd but slightly lumpy, brnshd hor. H:2–3.

g. FAN:115 LoLiB LMG<1 0.20 car E, I:scrpd, smthd, brnshd, red. H:3.

h. FAN:110 LoLiB mrRfL1 0.19 base E:scrpd, smthd, brnshd, red pt (2.5YR 5/8) on light (2.5YR 6/8). I:roughly scrpd. H:2–3.

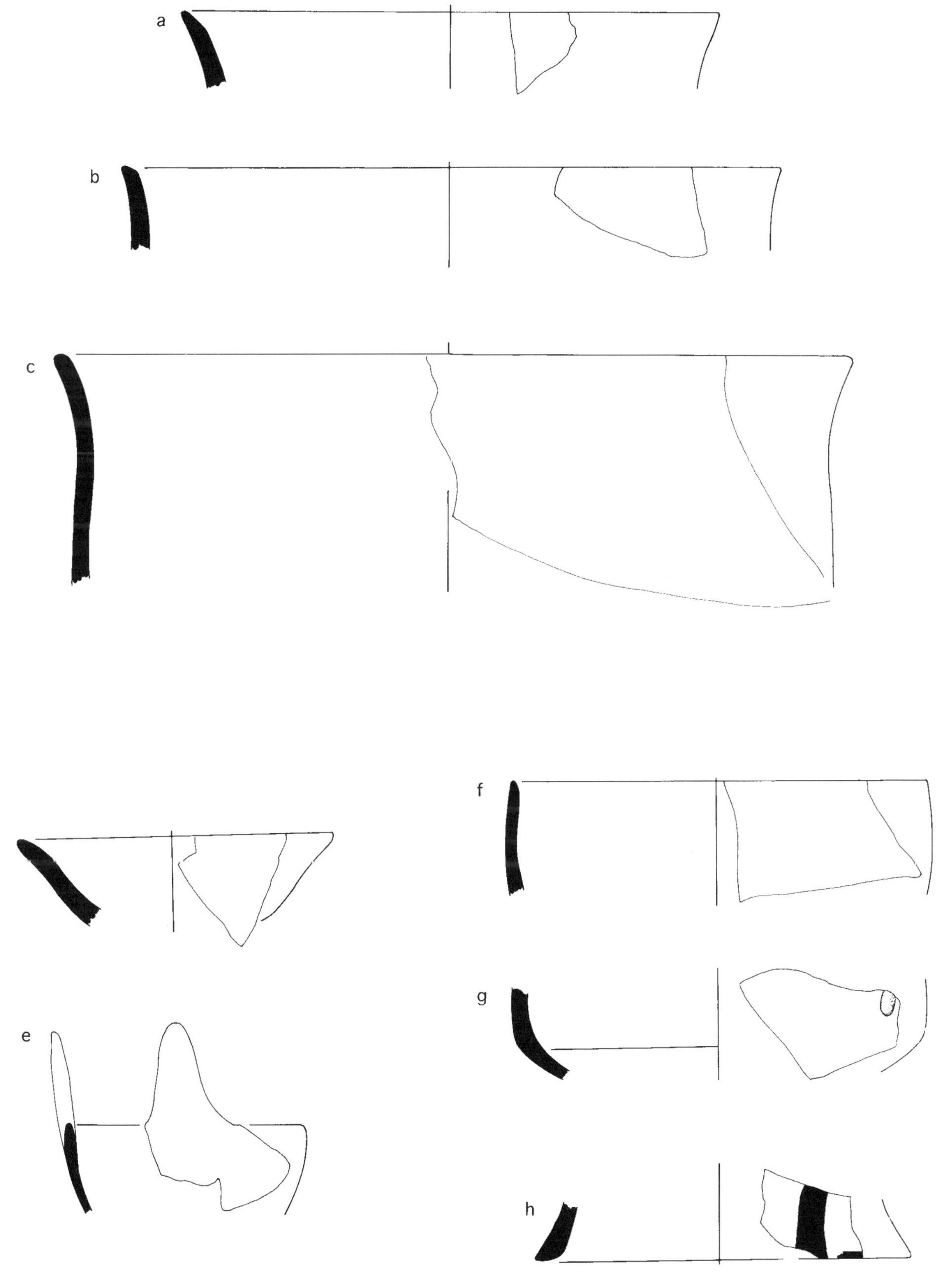
a
b
c
d
e
f
g
h

Figure 5 FCP 3 Low Lime Burnished variety

a. FAN:115 LoLiB LMG1 0.20 E:scrpd, smthd, poss slip, brnshd, glossy dark gray, granular gray pt in relief above car, thinner below, no relief. Pt scratches off with fingernail. I:scrpd, smthd, slipped, brnshd for 2 cm inside rim, pale gray. Sharp edges. H:3–4.

b. FAN:114 and FA:55D LoLiB fLMG<1, mica glitter 0.18–0.22, irreg E:scrpd, smthd, impressions along car, brnshd, gray w/ blk clouds. I:same, pale gray. C:light gray. Sharp edges. H:3.

c. FAS:116+115 LoLiB fLMG<1, mica glitter 0.21 E:scrpd, smthd, impressions along car, brnshd, dark gray w/ blk clouds. I:same, lighter gray. C:light gray. Sharp edges. H:3.

d. FAS:113 LoLiB LMG<1 0.22 E:scrpd, smthd, brnshd, glossy blk, flaking. I:same, clear hor troughs, lighter gray. H:2–3 int, 3–4 ext.

e. FAS:105 LoLiB fLMG<1 0.20 E:scrpd, smthd, brnshd, worn, blk. I:scrpd only, gray. C:light gray. H:2–3.

f. FAN:117+FAS:112+113S+FF1:20 FP 247 LoLiB LMG<1 0.25 E:scrpd, smthd, brnshd, glossy blk; th granular pale gray pt, lumpy lug pierced through body of pot. I:scrpd, smthd, brnshd, no luster. Brwn-blk stain over much of int as though something burned in pot. Rim slightly worn on ext, hole drilled near rim from int. H:3 ext, 7 over stain. Pl. 1b.

g. FAN:119+116N+114N+117S+116S+115S+3 unstratified FP 240 LoLiB LMG<1 0.23, irreg 11 sherds join, almost half of pot preserved E:scrpd, smthd, poss slip, PB, brnsh missed an area on bottom near lug; PB strokes are gray on paler gray ground, in between patt is darker glossy blk, flaking. I:scrpd, smthd, brnshd. C:uniform light gray. Pierced hole in lug barely 1mm diam. H:5–6.

h. FAN:117 LoLiB LMG1 0.22 car E:well scrpd, smthd, brnshd, dark gray. I:same, worn and pitted, flaking at bott. C:gray-blk. Jagged edges. H:3.

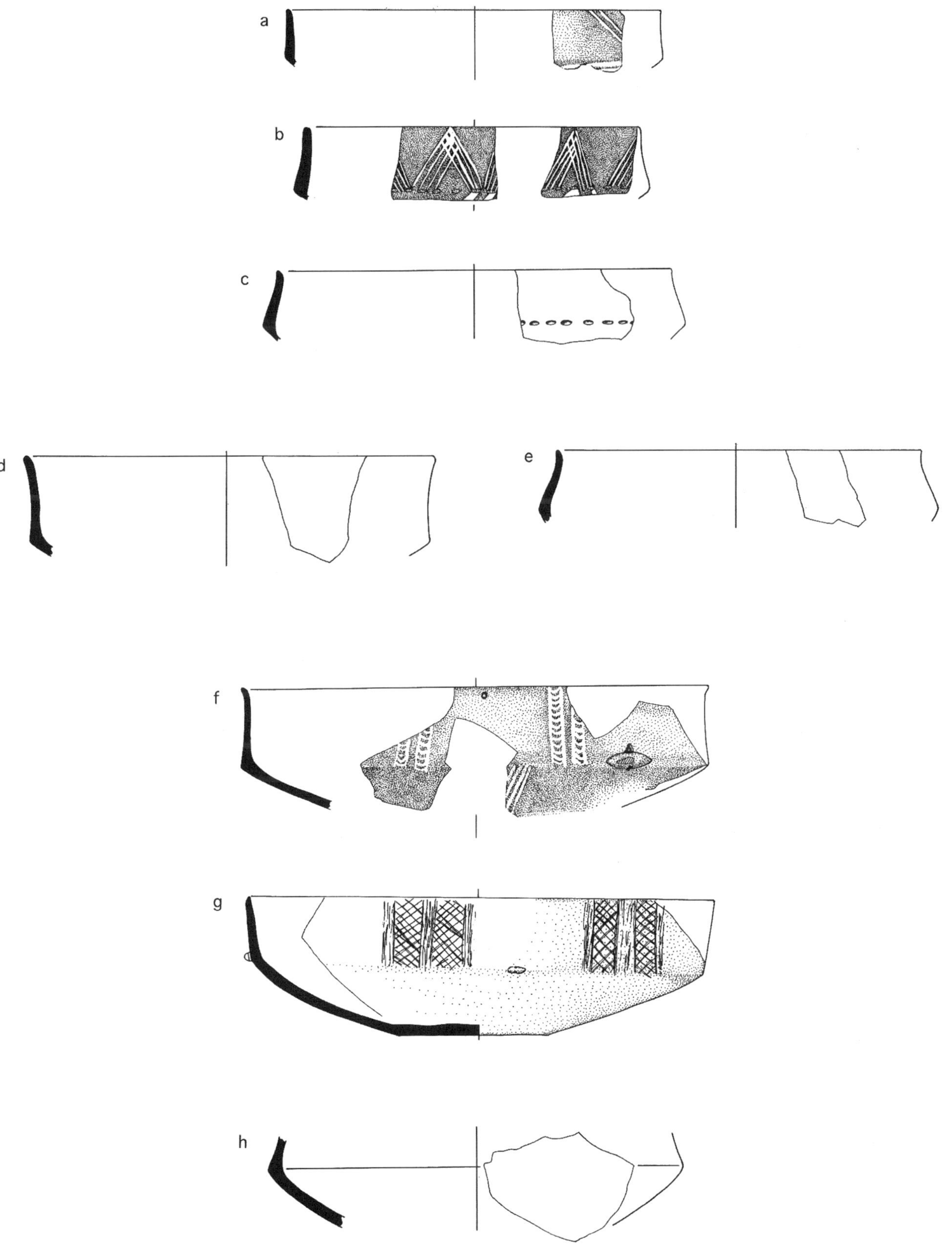
a
b
c
d
e
f
g
h

Figure 6 FCP 3 Low Lime Burnished variety

a. FAN:111 LoLiB MG1 0.16 E, I:scrpd, smthd, applied pellet, brnshd, clear troughs, dark gray. C:gray. H:3–4.

b. FAS:116 LoLiB LMG<1 0.20 E, I:scrpd, smthd, applied pellet, brnshd, blk. C:gray. H:2–3.

c. FAS:116S LoLiB DMG<1 0.20, irreg 3 joining sherds E, I:scrpd, smthd, applied pellet, brnshd except in crease, clear troughs, blk, glossy. C:gray green. Clear coil joint 2 cm below rim. H:3.

d. FAN:117 LoLiB LMG1 0.25 E:scrpd, smthd, applied pellet in very low relief, trace of a second, brnshd, very worn. I:scrpd, smthd, trace of red slip, brnshd, very worn. H:2–3.

e. FAS:116+FA:56+unstratified LoLiB LMG<1 0.075 bott Almost complete bottom preserved E:scrpd, smthd, brnshd, clear troughs, greenish-gray. I:scrpd, smthd, brnshd but very worn and pitted at bott, greenish-gray. H:2–3.

f. FAS:116 LoLiB LMG<1, mica flecks 0.065 bott E:scrpd, smthd, well brnshd, clear troughs, dark gray. I:scrpd, smthd, brnshd, pitted, gray. U:brnshd, slight wear at edge. H:2–3.

g. FAN:117 LoLiB rMG1 0.065 bott E:scrpd, smthd, well brnshd, blk, hole drilled from ext. I:scrpd, smthd, brnshd, gray, extremely worn and pitted bott. H:2–3.

h. FAS:116 LoLiB LMG1, 4mm pebble in break 0.07 E:scrpd, smthd, poss slip, brnshd, glossy blk, flaking. I:apparently burned, brwn-blk stain, flaking. U:scrpd, smthd, poss slip, brnshd, flaking, very worn. H:2–3.

i. FAN:114 LoLiB LMG1 Body sherd E:scrpd, smthd, poss slip, brnshd, glossy blk, granular pale gray pt.

j. FAS:116 LoLiB LMG1 0.08 E:scrpd, smthd, slipped, brnshd, waxy blk. I:scrpd, smthd, red slip at rim, roughly brnshd, red-brwn. Trace of smooth edge within break of "handle" suggests handle was pierced. H:2–3.

k. FAN:117 LoLiB LMG<1 0.10–0.11, irreg E:scrpd, smthd, slipped, PB, both pattern and ground are dark gray, worn, pattern barely visible. I:scrpd, smthd, slipped at rim, brnshd, greenish-gray. Rim worn and chipped. H:2–3.

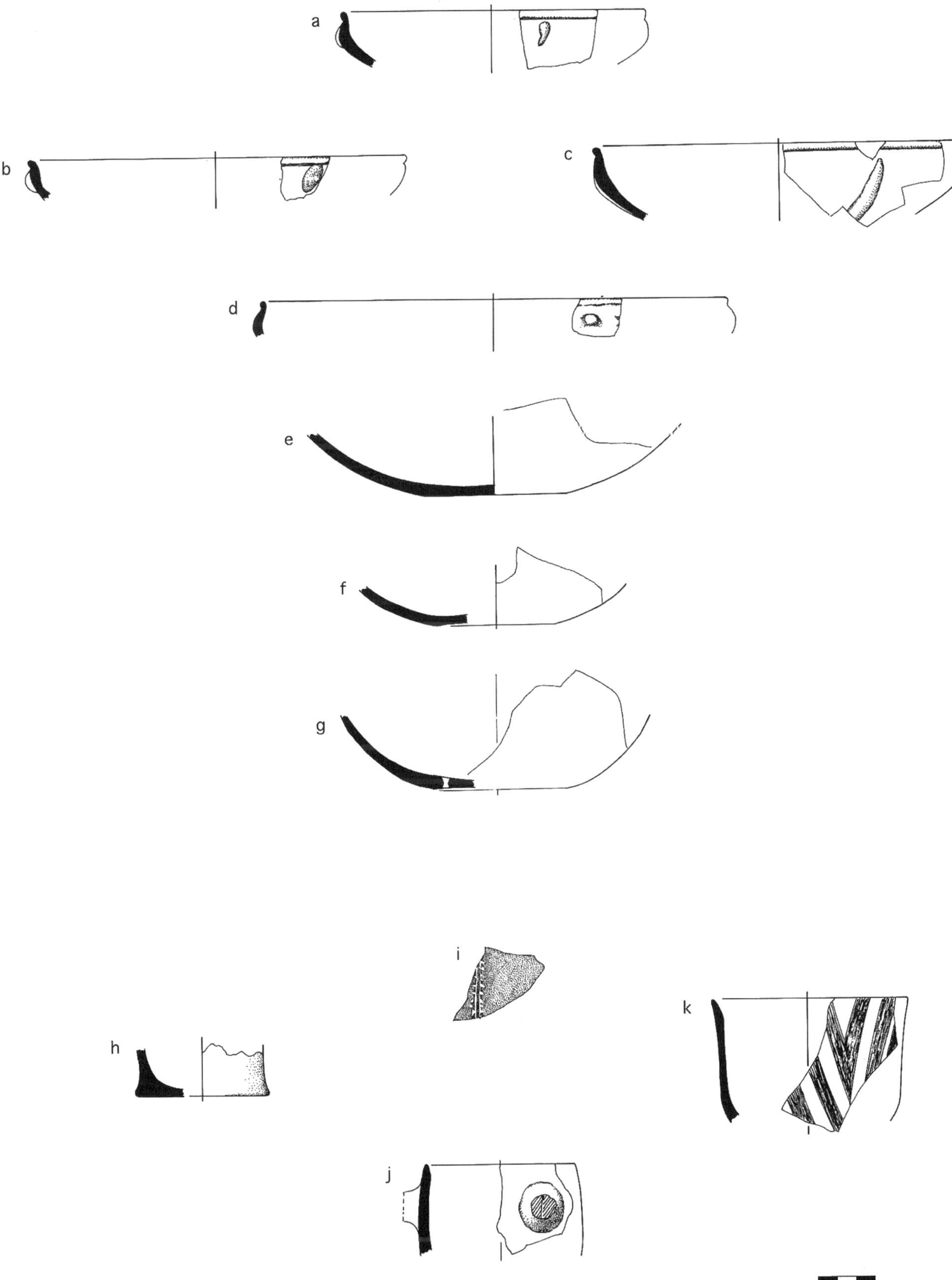
a
b
c
d
e
f
g
h
i
j
k

Figure 7 FCP 3 Low Lime Burnished variety

a. (1) FAS:114 LoLiB LMG1 no measurable curve E:scrpd, smthd, brnshd, glossy blk with line of oxidation following break. I:scrpd, smthd, brnshd, light gray. (2)FAN:114 LoLiB LMG1 0.36–0.37, irreg E:well scrpd, smthd, brnshd, blk. I:scrpd, smthd, rim rolled to interior, light gray. H:2–3.

b. FAN:103 LoLiB MDG<1 0.30 E:scrpd, smthd, brnshd, clear troughs, blk. I:same, brwnish-green. H:5–6.

c. FAN:112+112S LoLiB rMG1 0.10 base Half of pedestal preserved E, I:scrpd, smthd, slipped, brnshd, glossy blk, flaking. U:scrpd, roughly smthd. H:2–3.

d. FAN:119 LoLiB LMG<1f2–3 0.25 E:scrpd but lumpy, smthd, slipped, irreg brnshd, blk with light cloud. I:scrpd, smthd, slipped red inside rim, brnshd, light, very pitted. H:2–3.

e. FAN:115 LoLiB SMG<1 0.30–0.32, irreg E:scrpd, smthd, slipped, brnshd, color changes w/ drips on ext from light at rim to blk below. I:scrpd, smthd, slipped, brnshd. H:2–3.

f. FAN:117 LoLiB LMG1 0.11 base E:scrpd, smthd, slipped red-blk, brnshd, glossy blk. I:scrpd, smthd, slipped, brnshd, gray, pitted. U:lumpy, unscrpd, brnshd, blk. H:2–3

Figure 7

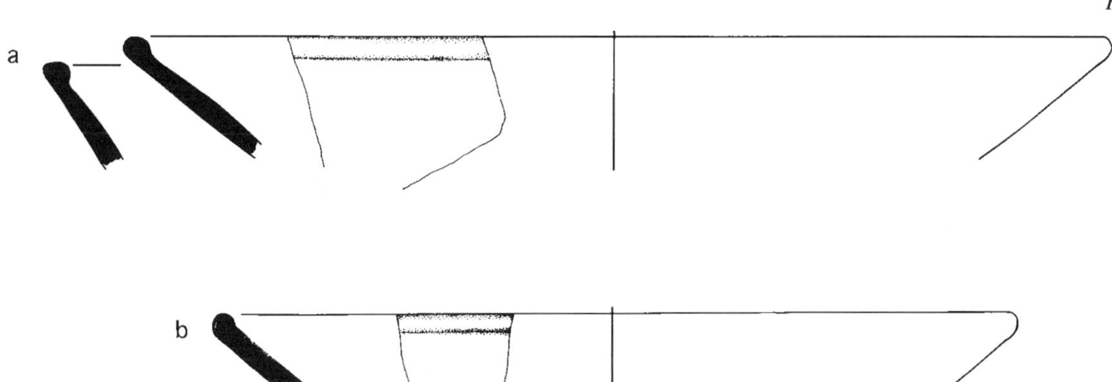

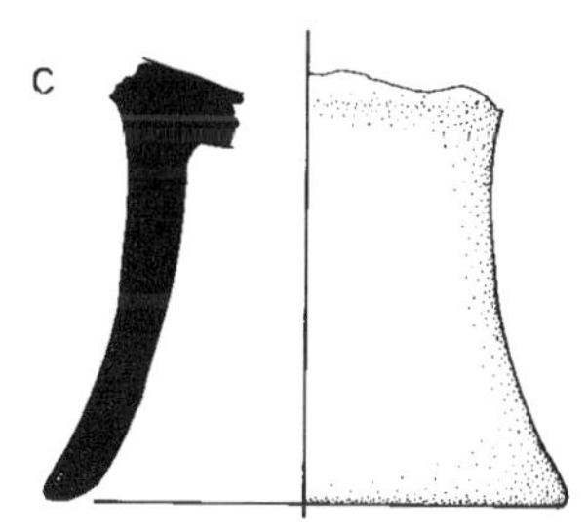

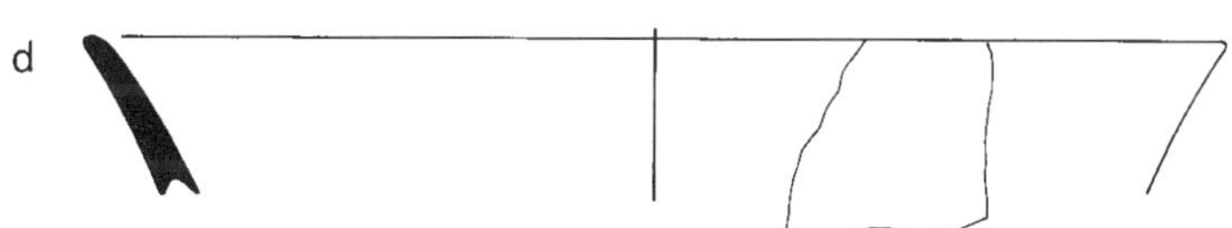

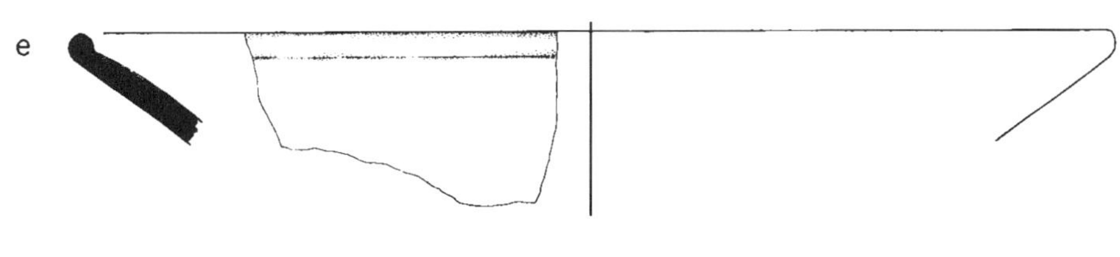

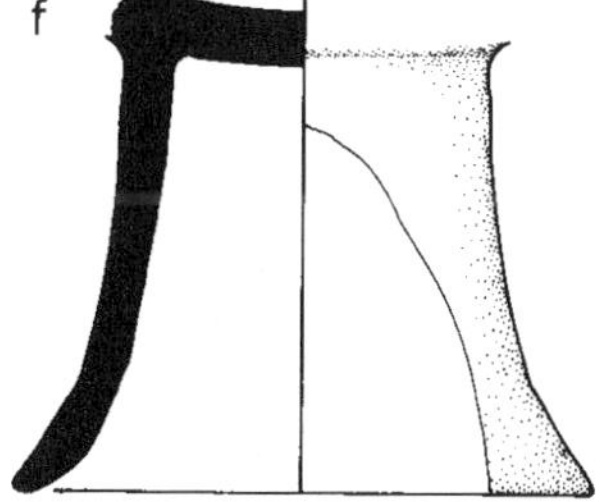

Figure 8 FCP 3 Low Lime Burnished variety from poor contexts

a. A Lot 16 LoLiB LMG<1 0.185 E:scrpd, smthd, slipped, brnshd, waxy blk, very worn. I:scrpd, smthd, hor brnshd, gray.

b. A Lot 16 LoLiB LMG<1 0.020 E:scrpd, smthd, brnshd, impressed along car in very regular even dents w/ something delicate, perhaps a seed, gray, not waxy. I:scrpd, smthd, brnshd, milky gray. Sharp edges. H:5–6.

c. G1:4 LoLiB LMG<1 0.18 E, I: scrpd, smthd, brnshd, not waxy, gray w/ milky bloom, very worn.

d. G1:4 LoLiB LMG<1 0.125 joint E:scrpd, smthd, slipped, brnshd, glossy, waxy blk, worn. I: scrpd, smthd, brnshd, gray.

e. Unstratified LoLiB FPSC 152 aWrD1 that fall out 0.09 E:scrpd but lumpy, smthd, poss slip, brnshd, waxy blk but quite worn, incisions filled w/ white Lime, chip off lip and lower edge one side suggest poss handle, poss asym. I:scrpd, brnshd at rim, dark gray. C:dark gray.

f. A Lot 16 LoLiB LMG<1, mica glitter 0.065, irreg E:prob brnshd, uniformly dark gray, surfaces very worn, incised. I:brnshd, very worn. H:5.

g. FAS:116 LoLiB LMG<1 body sherd E:scrpd, smthd, brnshd, incised, white Lime fill, dark gray, very worn. I: scrpd, smthd, brnshd, gray, very worn.

h. A Lot 16 LoLiB LMG<1 0.30 max E:scrpd, smthd, faint vertical flutes created by brnshd, not waxy, gray. I:worn, no original surface preserved, soft pale gray. C:dark gray to ext, light to int.

i. G1:4 LoLiB LMGrR1 that fall out 0.23 max E:scrpd, smthd, brnshd, granular gray pt, worn, dark gray. I:scrpd, light gray.

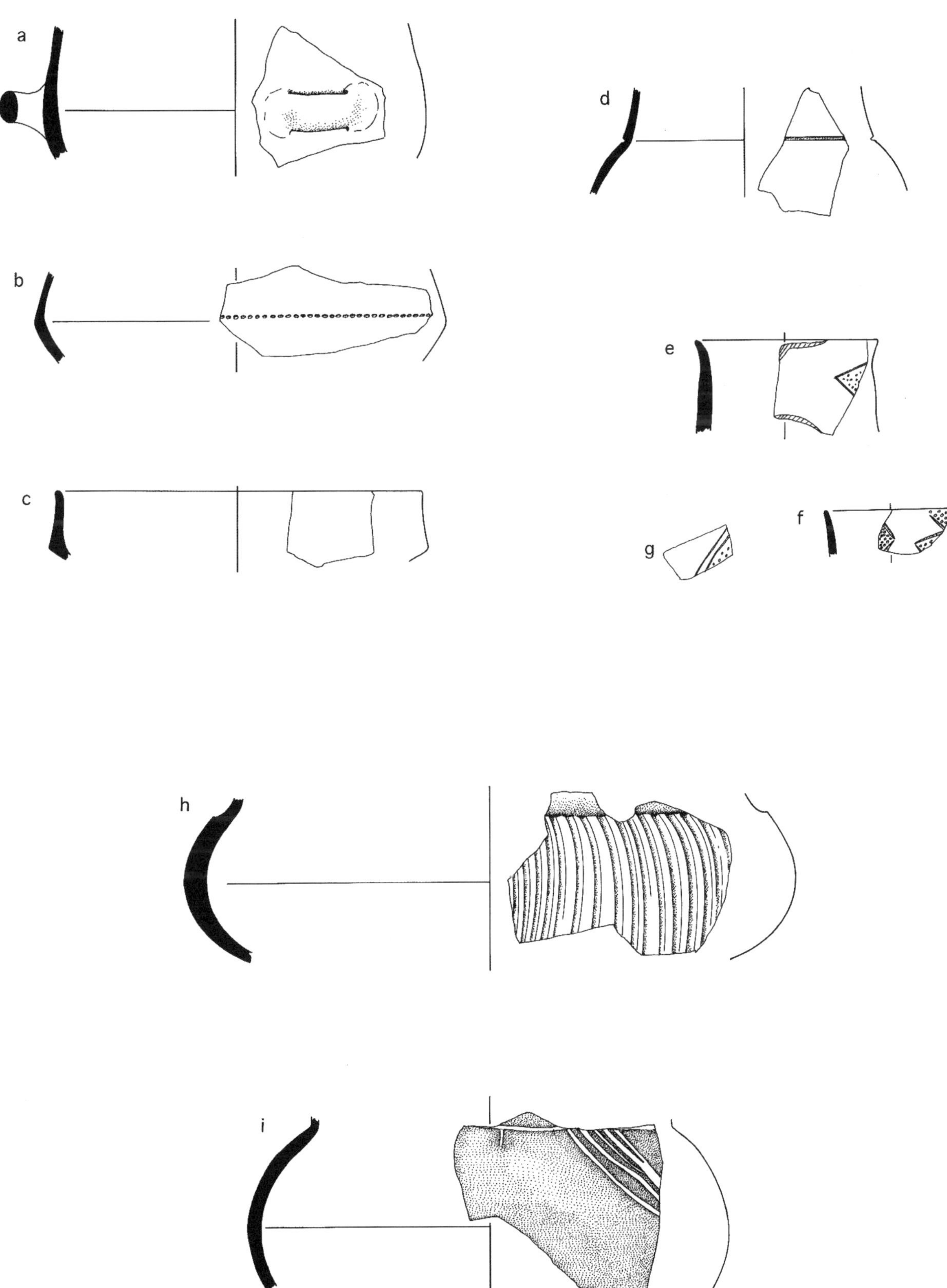
a
b
c
d
e
f
g
h
i

Figure 9 FCP 3 Low Lime Burnished variety from poor contexts

a. A Lot 16 LoLiB LMG<1 0.32 joint 2 non-joining E:original surf gone, can still feel brnsh, patt lines are neat depressions, dots random and variable sizes, traces Lime fill in neck groove, pale gray. C:pale gray.

b. A:34 (Lot 16) FP 31 LoLiB mLMG1rRf2–3 0.31 joint E:scrpd, smthd, brnshd, impressed dots, Lime fill, blk. I:scrpd, lightly brnshd. Jacobsen 1973b:Pl. 50d.

c. FA:56 FPSC 219 LoLiB SMG1fL 0.46 joint E:scrpd, smthd, very neat lines and dots incised in damp clay, brnsh nearly closed some holes; most is glossy blk but 2 sherds on left burned after breaking to pale gray. I:scrpd, brnshd while damp, no gloss, dark gray. C:dark gray (10YR 4–5/1).

d. G1:5 LoLiB DMG<1 0.44 joint, 0.56 max E:scrpd, prob applied ridges, smthd, brnshd, granular gray pt, blk. I:scrpd, smthd, brnshd, light gray, pale cloud one side. C:light gray H:2–3.

Figure 9

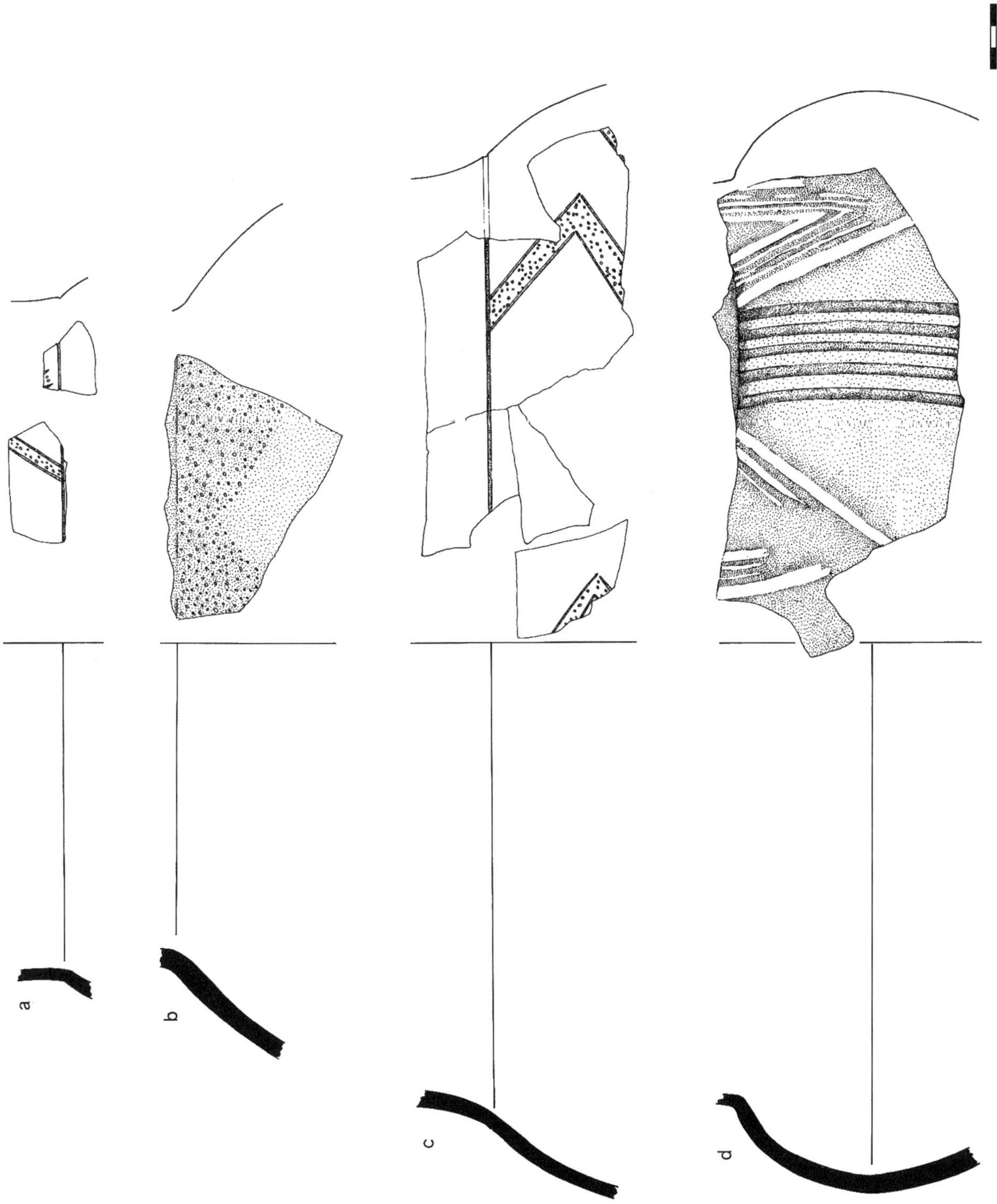

Figure 10 FCP 3 Low Lime Burnished variety

a. A:31+32+33+34 FP 55 LoLiB LMG1–2rRD2–3 that fall out 0.36 rim, 0.52 max RIP (broken) half of rim continuously preserved, 3/4 of neck below rim, 4 small areas of body, including joint E:scrpd, not smthd, poss slipped, brnshd several times, shallow narrow troughs, granular gray pt applied w/ brush: lines feathery at ends; dashed lines indicate places where pt was erased and patt moved to left, prob to coordinate w/ lower body. Three sets of vertical lines preserved on neck. I:scrpd below joint, brnshd neck, better near rim, very pitted, gray. C:gray to brwnish-gray. Rim is uneven horizontally and vertically. H:1–2. Fragments of similar pots from FAN:117, A Lot 16, H1:71, H1B:76, G1:4. FP 29, FP 30 (A:34), not illustrated, possibly non-joining from FP 55. Pl. 2a.

Figure 10

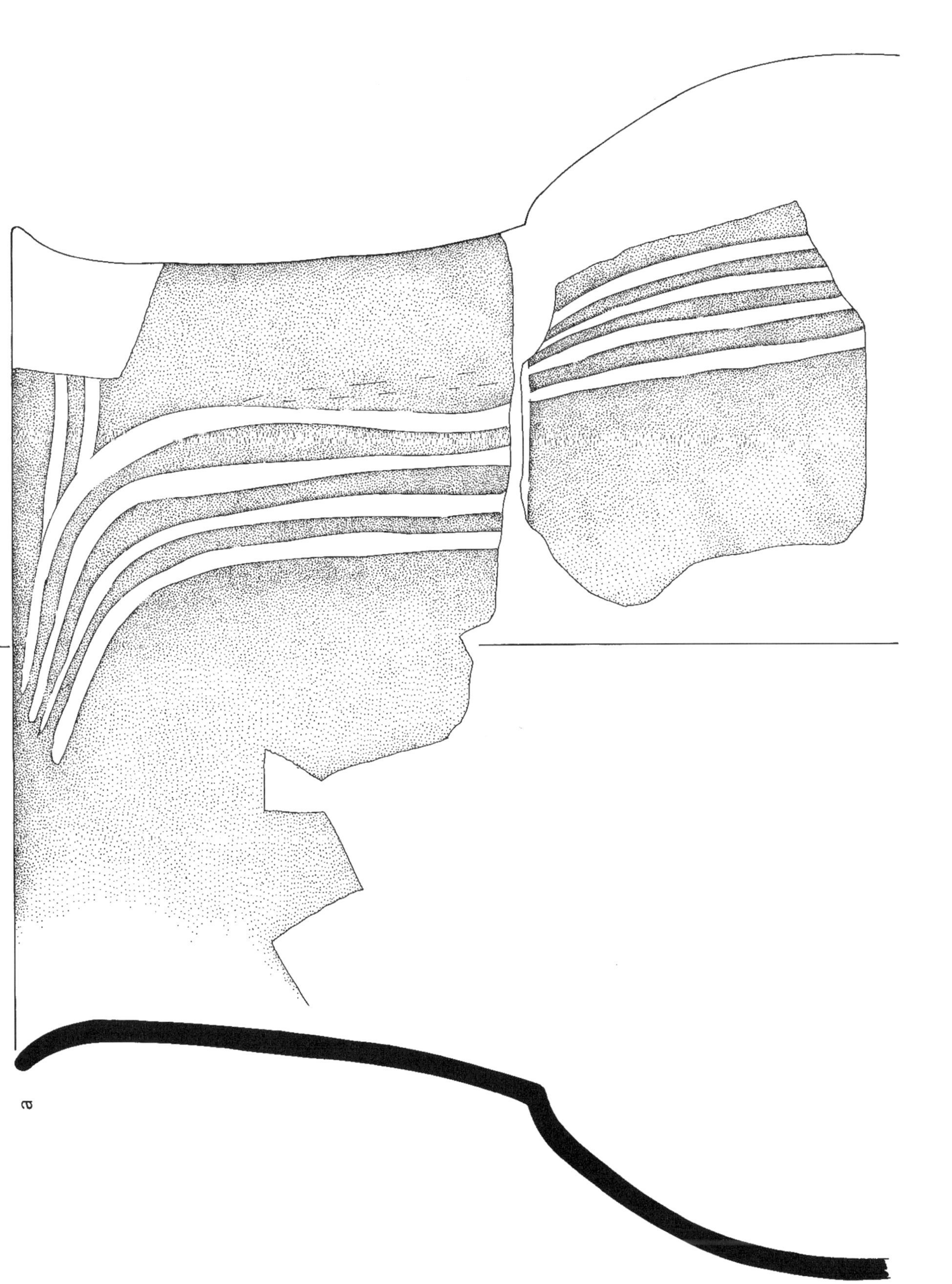

Figure 11 FCP 3 Low Lime Burnished, Lime Coarse varieties

a. FF1:22 LoLiB LMG1, mica glitter 0.15 E:scrpd, smthd, well brnshd, granular pt, no traces of patt beyond what drawn, gray w/ creamy bloom. I:scrpd, smthd, brnshd, no gloss, pitted, bott peeling off in layers. C:uniform gray. H:2–3.

b. FF1:22 LoLiB LMG<1 0.22 E:scrpd, smthd, poss slipped, brnshd, striated troughs, blk where brnshd, dull gray in between gives scribbly effect, dull gray granular pt. I:scrpd, smthd, hor brnsh, blk at rim, greenish-gray below w/ creamy bloom, 1 mm pits. Drill hole from exterior. H:2–3.

c. FF1:22 LoLiB LMG<1, mica glitter 0.14 E:scrpd, smthd, brnshd, light gray (10YR 5/0). I:scrpd, smthd, brnshd, lighter greenish-gray. H:2–3.

d. FF1:22 LoLiB SLMG1, rR that sparkle 0.06 E:scrpd, smthd, brnshd, brwn (5YR 7/6), applied lugs. I:scrpd, smthd, brnshd. C:red.

e. FF1:25 FP 258 LoLiB L<1 0.30, irreg 4 joining sherds give < one quarter of pot E:scrpd, smthd, brnshd, glossy dark gray. I:scrpd, smthd, brnshd, gray (10YR 4/1) w/ lighter subsurfs, pitted toward bott. H:3.

f. FF1:20 LoLiB DMG1 0.06 joint Complete joint preserved E:scrpd, smthd, brnshd, gray-blk w/ creamy bloom. I:worn, no original surf. U:scrpd, smthd. C:blue-gray.

g. FF1:22 LiCo L1R5 that sparkles, mica glitter 0.405 E:building surf, smthd w/o scrping, mottled red to gray. I:well scrpd at bott, less on upper walls, brnshd or worn smooth at bott, yellowish-gray. C:gray. Coil joint in break.

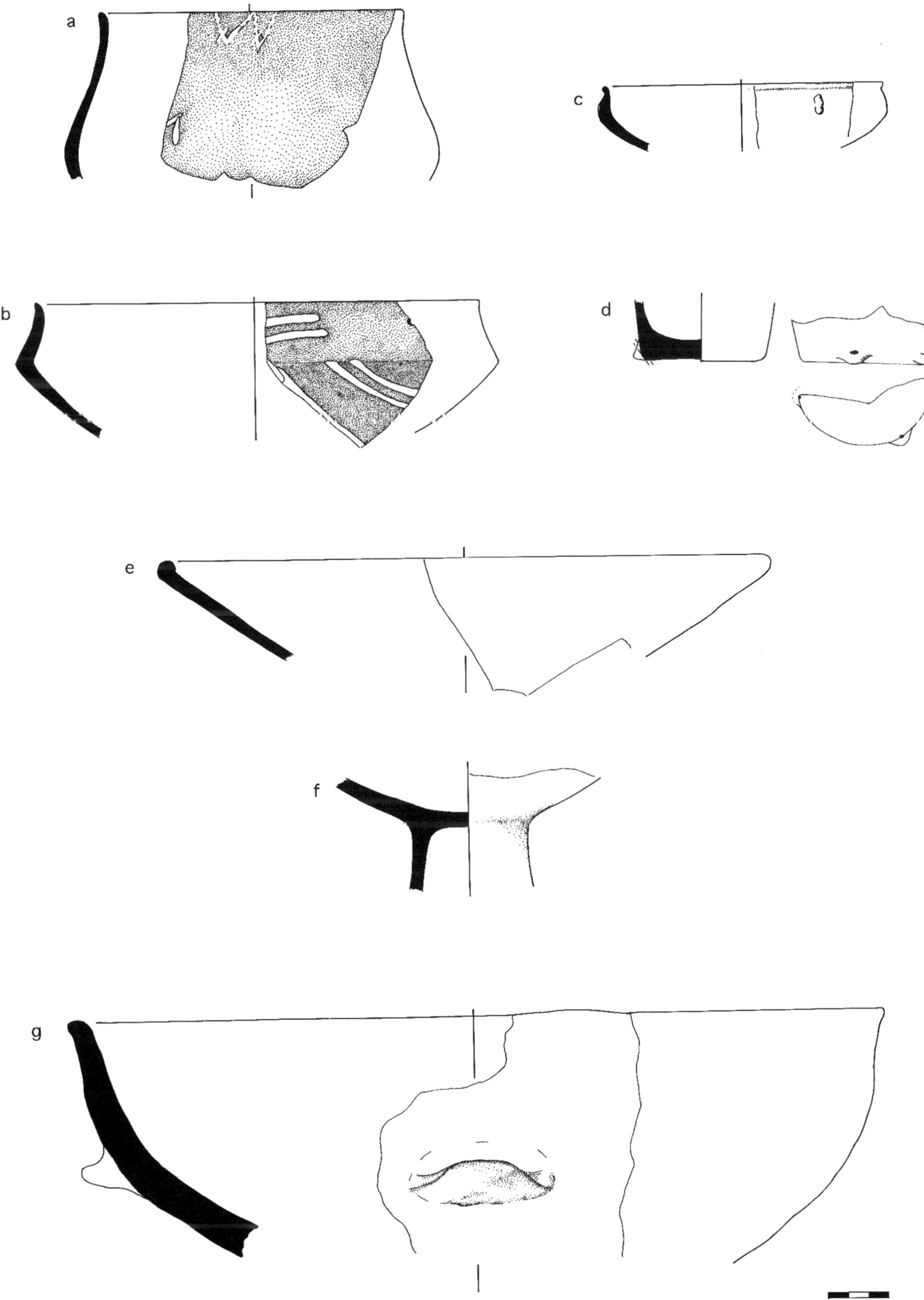
a
b
c
d
e
f
g

Figure 12 FCP 3 Polychrome varieties

a. FAN:120+FF1:30 FP 257 Black MnO on Red FeO LMG, pops 1–2 0.10 E:scrpd, smthd, FeO slip, patt in MnO, sloppy strokes, both pts dull and flaking; 2 handle scars preserved. I:slip extends just inside rim. C:uniform light (5YR 7/4). H:2–3.

b. FAS:116 FP 184 Black MnO on Red FeO PowderyL1R<1, mica glitter 0.155 max E:scrpd, smthd, FeO slip, flaking around lug scar, blk MnO pt, thick, dull, flaking. I:scrpd only, very red-fired clay (2.5YR 5–6/8). C:uniform light.

c. FAS:116+115S+114N+FF1:20+22+A Lot 16 and non-joining, poss same pot: FAN:112, FF1:21, 25, 26, 98S Poly L1D<1 0.36 max E:scrpd, smthd, patt in MnO dark, maroon, FeO light, red-orange-white, brnshd and smeared patt lines; clouds of orange-white and greenish-gray penetrate subsurfs. Piece badly over-fired or burned, vitrified. I:scrpd, smthd, brnshd; greenish ground, orange where brnshd. C:blue-gray, jagged edges.

d. FAS:113 Poly fRDG<1 0.20, irreg E, I:scrpd but lumpy, smthd, pt in FeO, MnO , brnshd. C:thin gray center, pink subsurfs and surfs. H:4–5.

e. FAN:114 Poly mL<2, rRD1 No measurable curve, but large E, I:scrpd, smthd, brnshd, ptd patt in FeO and MnO, white bloom to ground where brnshd, pitted and worn , esp int. Th:4–5mm. H:4–5.

f. FAN:117+115N Poly LD1rRD<1 No measurable curve, but large 6 non-joining E:scrpd, smthd, ptd patt in FeO, crackling, and granular MnO, sloppy execution, brnsh scribbly. I:scrpd, damp brnshd. C:uniform light. Over-fired or burned. H:3–4.

g. FAN:115+112N+114S+56A+FF1:11 FP 243 Poly 0.24 L<1, pops, powdery, rR that fall out, biotite flecks 10 sherds joined into 6 pieces E:scrpd, smthd, brnshd damp, ptd in FeO, slight relief, crackling, and MnO, flaking, both pts brnshd, no clouds. I:scrpd, smthd, brnshd, clear troughs. C:thin gray center. H:4–5.

h. FAS:116 (2), FAN:116, FA:55B (2), A Lot 16 FP 162 Poly mLR1, powdery L<3 0.22 max 6 sherds, one suggests a collar E:scrpd, smthd, brnshd, ptd patt in granular, matte FeO and MnO, and white, not Lime, flaking. I:scrpd, brnshd. C:uniform, striking red-orange fabric (2.5YR 6/8). Pl. 3a.

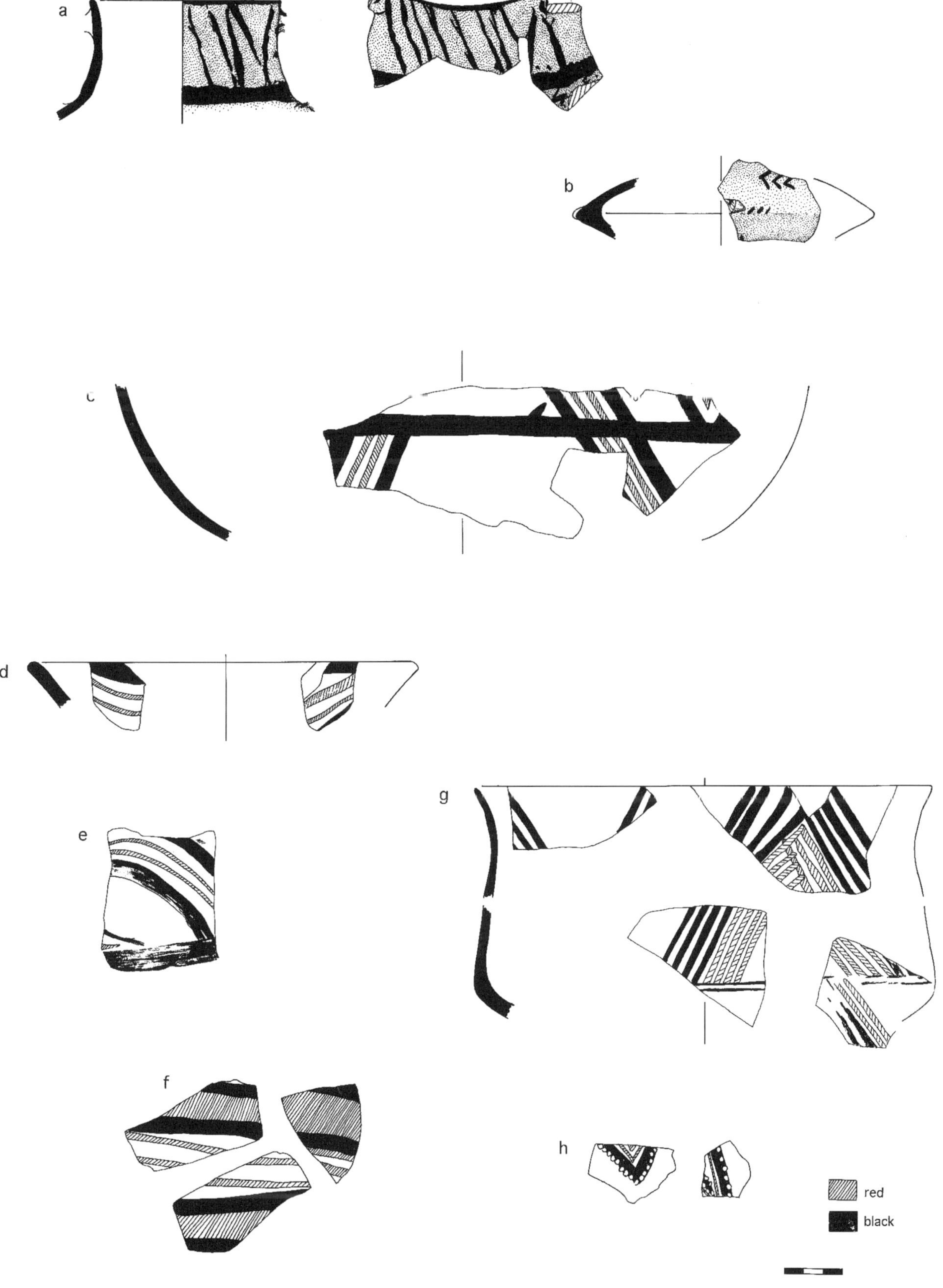
a
b
c
d
e
f
g
h
red
black

Figure 13 FCP 3 Unusual and potentially intrusive pieces

a. FAS:116 FP 181 White? On FeO Slip LR2R3 that sparkles 0.20 E:scrpd. smthd, FeO slip, ptd patt is completely gone, ghost lines evident in interruption of brnsh. I:scrpd, smthd, FeO slip, brnshd, very worn at bott, slightly gray at center bott, th car w/ scar of poss lug, rim curves out directly above scar. H:3–4.

b. FAS:116 FP 183 GrayB DMG<1fL 0.13 E:scrpd, applied ridges, tooled grooves, well brnshd, creamy bloom, pale gray. I:scrpd, smthd, brnshd, pale gray. C: uniform light gray, surfs blue-gray (2.5Y 4–6/0). Sharp edges. H:3–4.

c. FAN:113 Red on Blk? LMG2 0.24 max E, I: scrpd, smthd, slip fired blk, ptd lines fired red-brwn, flaking, all brnshd. Jagged, raspy edges. H:2–3.

d. FAS:116+A Lot 16 FP 273 MnO Ptd L1, some pops and pits 2 0.13 11 sherds, joining and not E:well scrpd, smthd, MnO pt, brnshd to good gloss, purple. I:scrpd, smthd, brnshd. Several sherds over-fired/burned, excessive pops, voids and slits in breaks, surfs greenish-gray (10YR 5–6/1–2 to yellowish (10YR 7/4). Poss same pot as OES sample #43, which is entirely oxidized, w/o pops.

e. FAS:116+A Lot 16 MnO Ptd LR1 0.22 E:scrpd, smthd, granular brwn MnO pt, brnshd, flaking, ground yellowish-pink with creamy areas. over-fired/burned. I:scrpd, brnshd at joint. C:blue-gray. H:6.

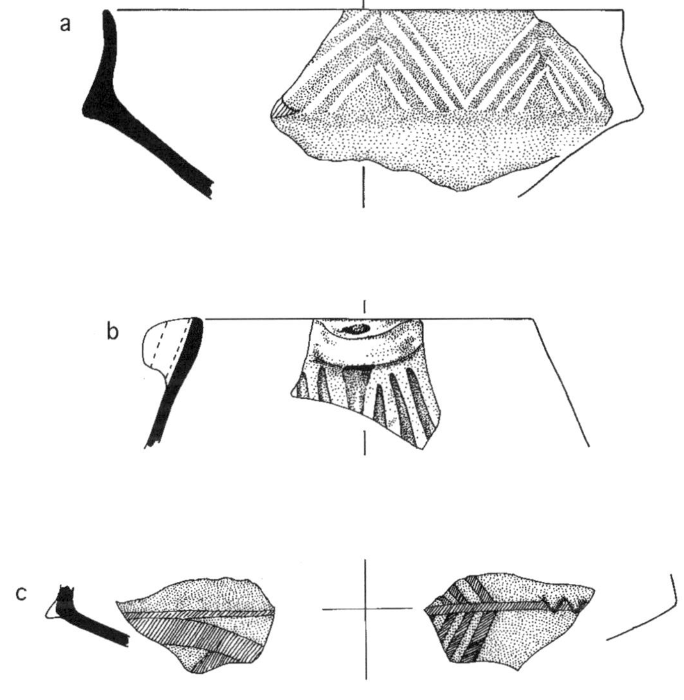
a
b
c

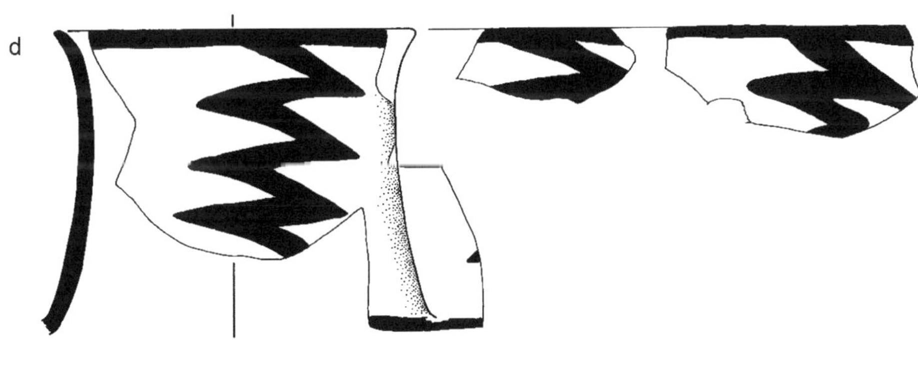
d

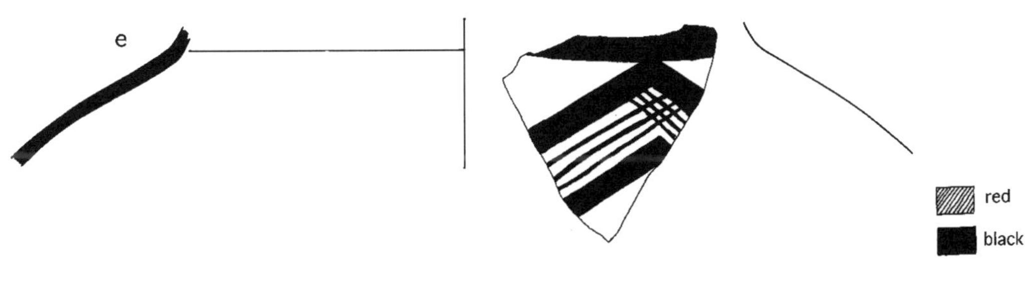
e
red
black

Figure 14 Polychrome varieties from poor contexts

a. G1:5 FP 256 Poly mLMG<1, f pops 0.26 max E:scrpd, smthd, alternating ptd patt lines in FeO red and MnO blk, brnshd, sloppy FeO red filling between patts. I:scrpd, smthd, brnshd, sloppy FeO slip, applied in hor strokes. Pale ground, small cloud on ext. H:2–3.

b. G1:4 Poly mL1–2RD<1, f3 0.30 max 5 joining E:scrpd, brnshd, ptd patt in FeO and MnO, thick, crackling, some pops. I:scrpd, brnshd. C:pink, surfs tan (7.5YR 7/4), dark cloud on ext. H:2–3.

c. FF1:19 Poly LrR1, mica glitter 0.11 joint E, I:scrpd, smthd, brnshd, ptd patt in FeO not brnshd, and MnO, brnshd. C:uniform pale yellow, surfs same.

d. A:30+A:32 FP 56 Poly mR<1, mica glitter 0.065 joint E:well scrpd, regular surfs, even th, smthd, faint fingerprints in wet clay, ptd patt in FeO and MnO, brnshd, worn. I: same but any brnsh has worn off, wear evident at bott where red grits prominent. U:heavy gouges from attachment process; break suggests ground down to new edge, sits at angle slightly off center, wear centered to this angle, rather than to center of bowl. H:2–3.

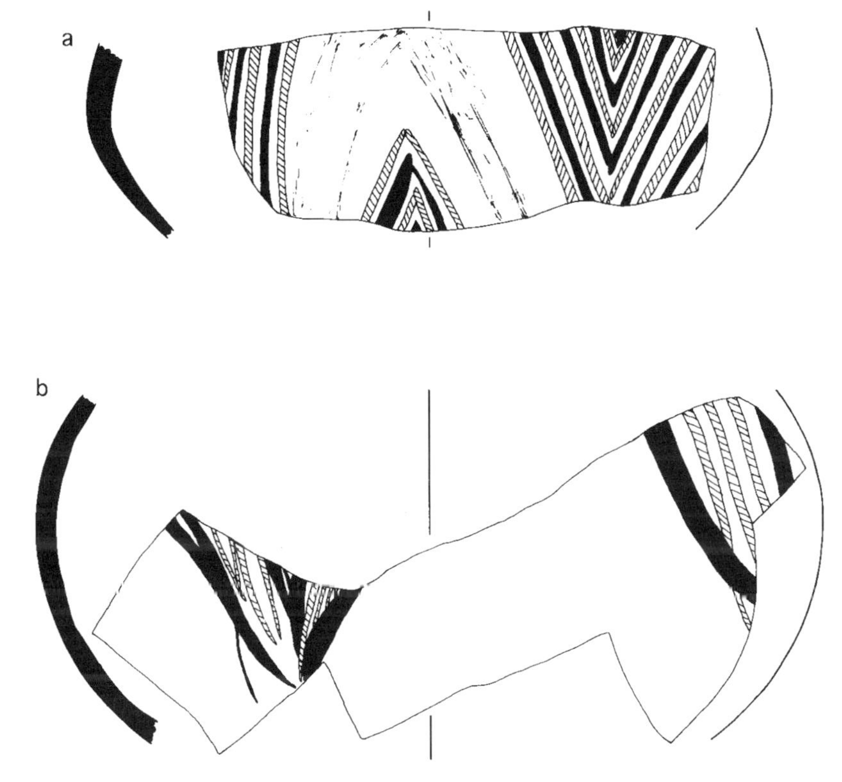

a
b

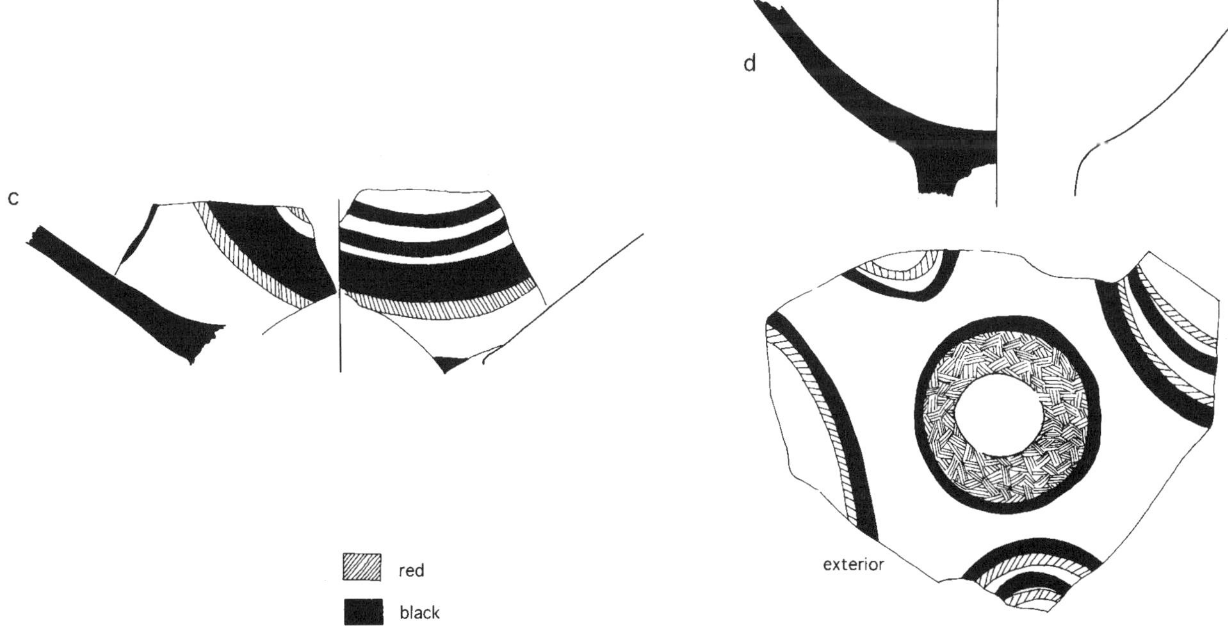

c
d
red
black
exterior

Figure 15 FCP 3 Lime Coarse variety

a. FAN:117 LiCo Lf7RD3–4 0.18, irreg E, I: scrpd, wet smthd w/ finger, crackling at rim, tan surfs, blk cloud around lug. C:uniform red. H:2–3.

b. FAN:117 (8) and FAN:117+A Lot 16 (5) Powdery L6–7 at surf, L5–6MG1–2 in breaks 0.18–0.20, irreg 5 rim sherds, w/o lug (not illustrated) E:scrpd, damp brnshd, deep troughs, FeO slip, 10R 5–6/6 w/ blk clouds. I:scrpd, brnshd, red slip inside rim, 7.5YR 5–6/4. Core red-gray. H:2–3. Pl. 2b.

c. FAN:115+114N+111N LiCo PowderyL2RDMG3 0.31 max E:lumpy, brnshd, FeO slip. I:scrpd, brnshd, drips of red pt . Sherd colors vary from pink (2.5YR 6/6–8) to pale yellowish (7.5YR 8/2), color changes coincide w/ breaks: post-breakage exposure to fire. H:2–3.

d. FF1:24+25 (5) and FF1:24+22 (6 non-joining, not illustrated) FP 261 LiCo L3MG1 pops 2 0.25, irreg ca. half of pot E:minimally scrpd, wet smthd, yellowish-tan w/ blk and red clouds. I:scrpd, damp brnshd. C:gray. Irreg surf and curves in all dimensions. C:gray, surfs vary pink to yellowish, dark clouds. H:2–3.

e. FAN:117 LiCo mMG3 0.07 bott E:scrpd, rough. I:scrpd, worn to smth sandy subsurf; one sherd is pink, joins yellow-tan sherd: post-breakage exposure to fire. H:2–3.

f. FAN:119 LiCo rR, DMG2 0.32 E, I:barely scrpd, quite lumpy, striations from wet finger smthing. C:gray, subsurfs reddish. H:2–3.

Figure 15

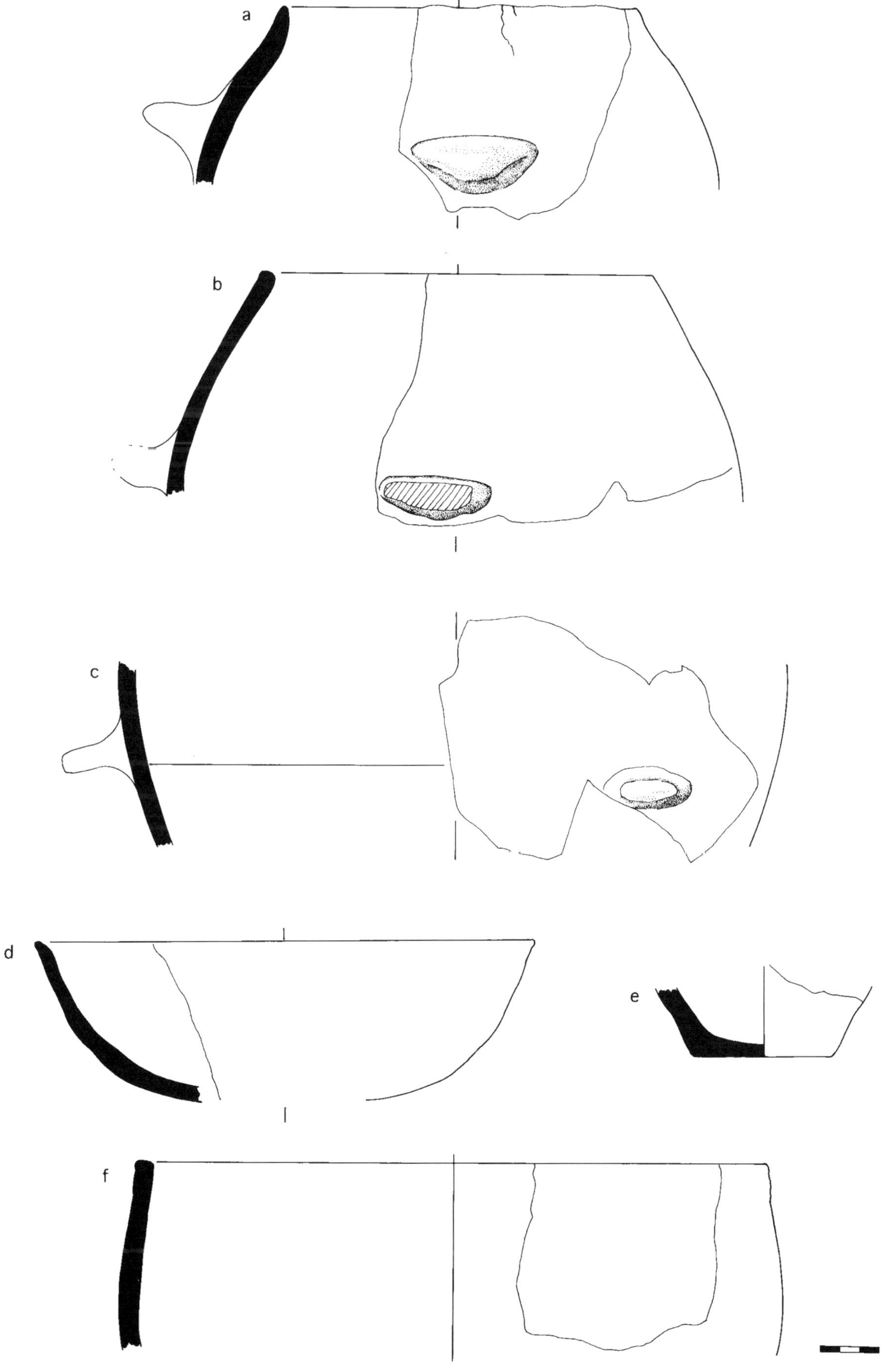

Figure 16 FCP 4.1 Andesite Burnished variety

a. FAS:103 AndB HBF1 0.17 max E:scrpd, smthd, slipped, brnshd deep waxy blk, ptd patt prob in granular white, now ghost in interrupted brnsh. I:scrpd, smthd, slipped, brnshd, little gloss.

b. FAN:105 AndB HBF1 0.25 E, I:scrpd, smthd, slipped, brnshd hor then vert, blk surfs. Jagged edges. H:2–3.

c. FAS:104 AndB HBF1 0.20 max E:scrpd, smthd, slipped, brnshd, blk, ptd patt in granular gray-white, no reaction in HCl. I:scrpd, smthd, brnshd. Broken at car.

d. FAN:108 AndB HBF1 0.13 E:scrpd, smthd, slipped, brnshd, blk with red tinge. I:scrpd, brnshd just inside rim, grayish-brwn. C:gray, subsurfs red. H:2–3.

e. FAS:104 AndB HBF1 0.14 E, I:scrpd, smthd, poss slip, brnshd, patt ptd in thin granular grayish white, no reaction in HCl.

f. FAN:108 AndB HBF<1 0.04 bott E, U:scrpd, smthd, poss slip, brnshd and PB, blk. I:scrpd, smthd, poss slip, brnshd, no gloss, brwn. C:light red. H:2–3.

g. FAS:102 AndB rDBF1 0.20 max E, I:scrpd, smthd, poss slip, brnshd, blk. C:dark gray. "Rim" is not finished, perhaps a thin collar was attached.

h. FAN:101+FAS:104 AndB HFB1 0.28 E:scrpd, smthd, poss slip, hor brnsh, red (2.5YR 4/6). I:same, mottled gray-blk to red-brwn, PB below thick rim fold. C:reddish-tan. Jagged edges. H:3–4.

i. FAN:109 AndB HFB1–2, 4 mm L pebble in break 0.26 E:surf worn away, gray-brwn. I:scrpd, smthd, prob slip, brnshd, gray w/ red clouds. C:reddish-tan. Crumbly edges. H:2–3.

j. FAN:105 AndB HFB1 0.23 E, I:scrpd, smthd, prob slip, brnshd, clear troughs, grayish-blk w/ reddish green clouds. I:worn, drill hole from int. H:2–3.

k. FAS:97 AndB HFB1 0.22 E, I:scrpd, smthd, prob slip, brnshd hor in, shallow troughs, vert brnsh ext, poss in PB, surfs blk, some gloss. C:reddish-brwn. H:2–3.

l. FAN:109 AndB HFB<1, fF2 0.30 E, I:scrpd, smthd, prob slip, brnshd, glossy blk, light cloud on ext rim. H:2–3.

m. FAN:111 AndB HFB1,f2 0.30 E, I:scrpd, smthd, clear slip, red in places, brnshd, troughs, no gloss, slight flaking. H:2–3.

n. FAS:111 AndB HFB1 0.38–0.40, irreg E:scrpd, smthd, brnsh scribbly, blk. I:scrpd, smthd, prob slip, brnshd, glossy blk. H:2–3.

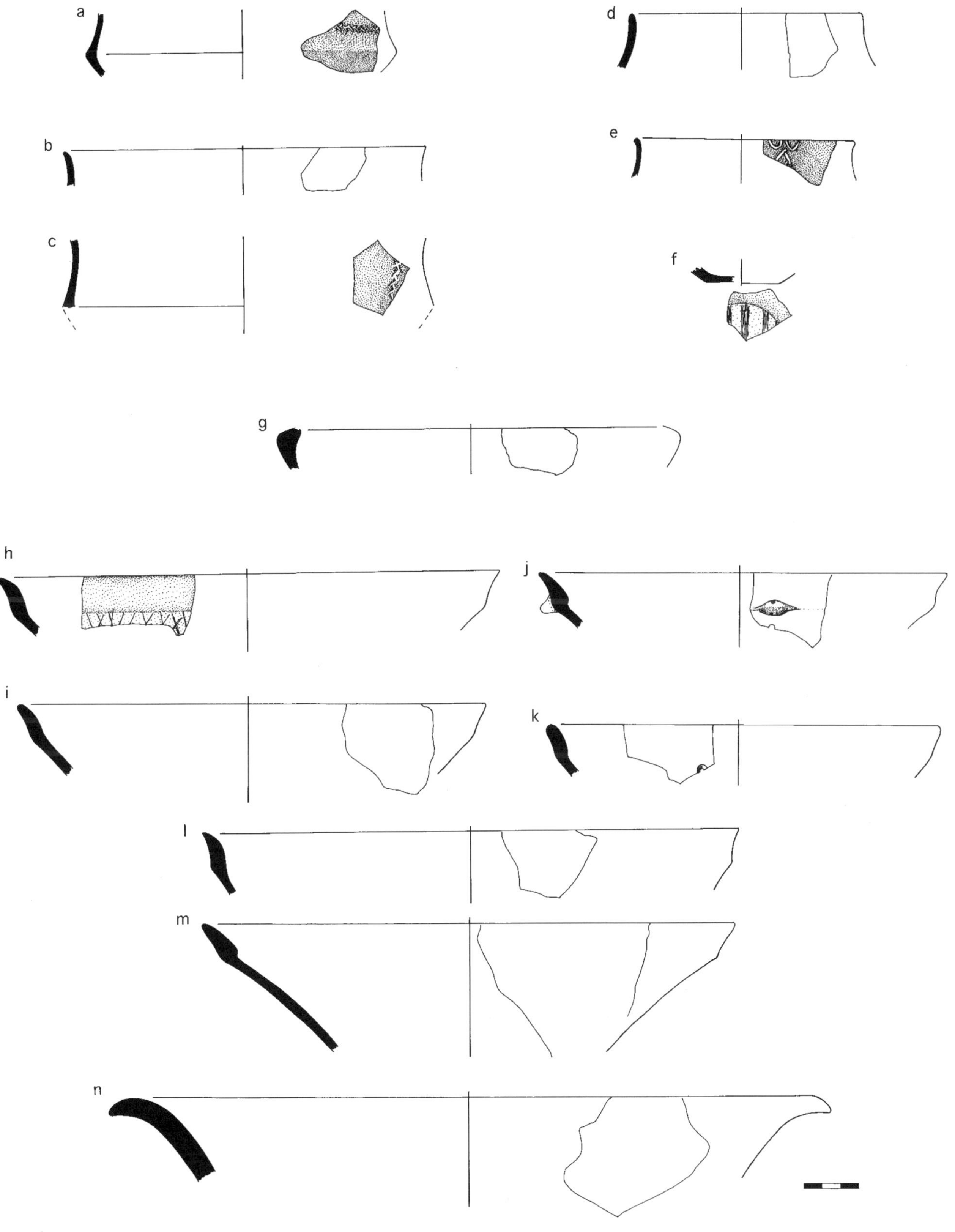
a
b
c
d
e
f
g
h
i
j
k
l
m
n

Figure 17 FCP 4.1 Ungritted Manganese Painted variety

a. FAN:101 UgrMn fD<1, Lpops1 0.13 E:scrpd, smthd, patt ptd in granular MnO, brnshd. I:scrpd, worn. Trace of handle or lug at edge. H:2–3.

b. FAS:105 UgrMn fD<1 0.16 max E:scrpd, smthd, patt in granular MnO pt, prob brnshd. I:scrpd, smthd.

c. FAN:96 UgrMn fD<1, 3 mm L pebble at surf 0.17 E: scrpd, patt in powdery MnO, brnshd, flaking. I:scrpd, brnshd. C:uniform light, surfs pale gray (10YR 6–7/1–2). H:2–3 int, 4–5 ext.

d. FAN:108 UgrMn fDL<1 0.04–0.05, irreg E:scrpd, smthd, brnshd, patt ptd in MnO, prob brnshd. I:scrpd, finger smthd. Drill hole from ext. H:2–3.

e. FAS:105+FF1:18 UgrMn RDL<1 0.14 E:scrpd, smthd, brnshd, deep narrow troughs, patt ptd in th granular brwn-blk MnO on greenish surf. I:scrpd. C:pink. Well preserved, looks new. H:2–3.

f. FAN:103+FF1:18 UgrMn fDL<1 0.10–0.11, irreg E:scrpd, smthd, patt ptd in brwn MnO, th at rim, largely flaked off elsewhere leaving pale ghostly lines, brnsh has smeared pt slightly. I:scrpd, wet smthd. U handle:wet smthd. C:pale, and surfs (2.5Y 8/2). H:2–3.

g. FAN:102 FP 252 UgrMn fDL<1 0.10 E:scrpd, smthd, patt ptd in brwn-blk MnO (5YR 5/1) where th, pale ghostly line where gone, brnshd. I:scrpd. C:pale (5YR 8/4), surfs greenish (2.5Y 7/2). H:2–3 int, 4–5 ext. Jacobsen 1973b:Pl. 51a.

h. FAN:109 UgrMn fWD<1,fL1 0.09, irreg E:scrpd, smthd, patt ptd in brwn MnO, pale gray ghost where flaked off, prob brnshd, tiny bubbles and pits on surf. I:scrpd, finger smthd. C:greenish yellow. H:1–2 int, 2–3 ext.

i. FAS:101 UgrMn LD1 0.20 max E:scrpd, smthd, patt ptd in velvety brwn MnO, pale brwn ghost where gone, brnshd, clear troughs, no smearing of pt. I:scrpd. C:pink. H:5.

j. FAS:96 UgrMn fLD1 0.28 max E:scrpd, smthd, patt ptd in MnO, scratches off easily. I:scrpd. H:5.

k. FAS:98 UgrMn fDL<1 0.30 E:scrpd, smthd, patt ptd in MnO. I:scrpd.

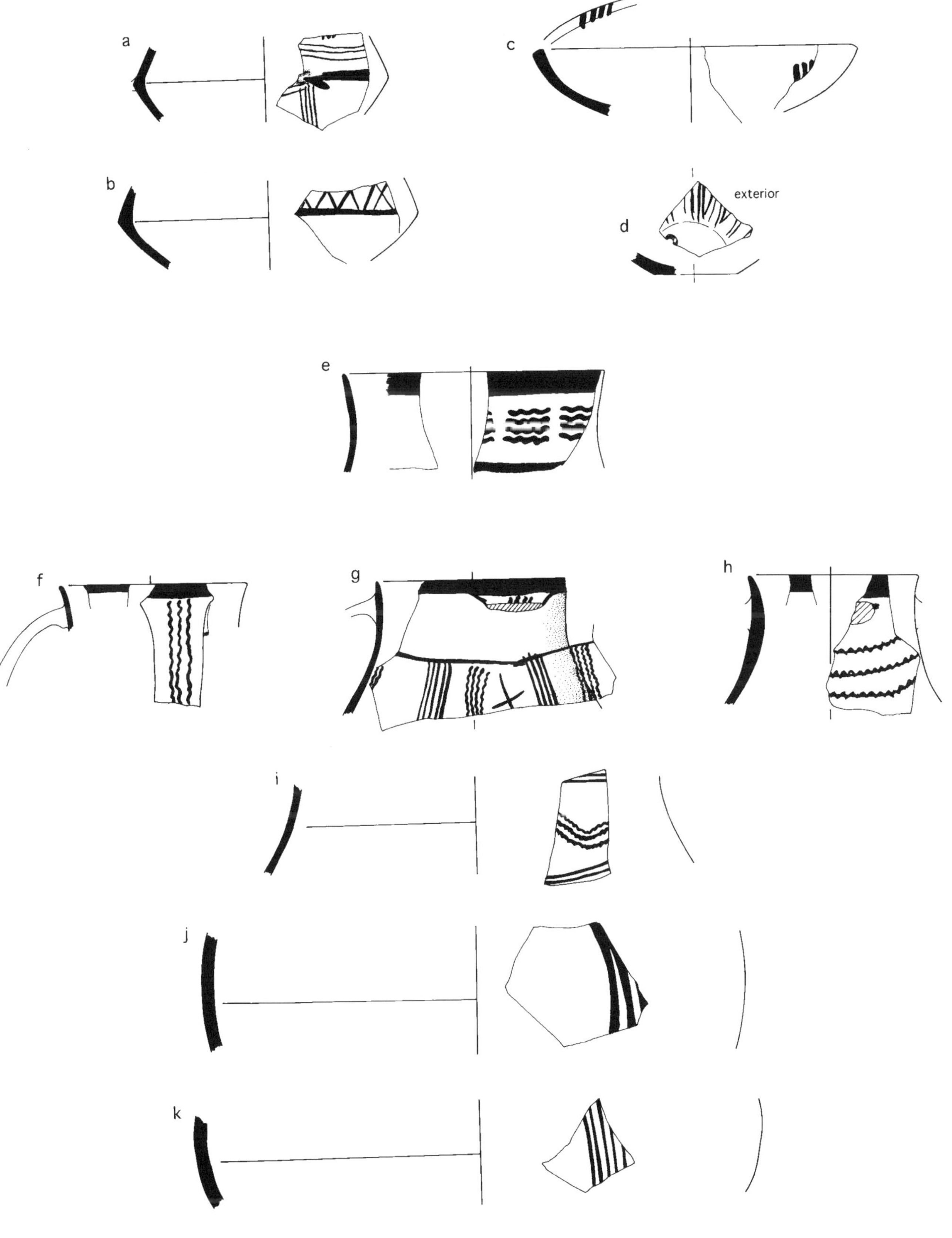
a
c
b
exterior
d
e
f
g
h
i
j
k
black

Figure 18 FCP 3 or 4.1 Manganese Painted and Polychrome varieties

a. FAN:110 MnPtd LRD<1, mica glitter 0.23 E, I:scrpd, smthd, damp brnshd, patt ptd in MnO, reddish gray, scratches up brwn powder. Bott int slightly worn. C:uniform. Sharp edges. H:2–3.

b. FAN:103 MnPtd L1, some pops,MG1 0.30 E:scrpd, smthd, brnshd, no gloss. I:scrpd, smthd, patt ptd in MnO, brwn-blk, brnshd. Jagged edges. H:3–4. Jacobsen 1973b:Pl. 51a.

c. FAS:103+110N MnPtd LS<1, gold and silver mica glitter no measurable curve, hint of joint at top E:scrpd, smthd, patt ptd in MnO in relief, scratches off leaving ghost, brnshd. I:scrpd, feels sandy. Th:3–4.

d. FAN:98 MnPtd RDL1 0.04 joint Just under half of pedestal preserved E:scrpd, smthd, brnshd, patt ptd in blk, prob MnO, flakes off to leave a ghost, surf gray. I:worn smth, no original surf. C:gray. Ped may have been hollowed out from nearly solid lump of clay:heavy gouges on underside.

e. FAN:103 and 100N Poly LRD<1 0.20 joint E:scrpd, smthd, brnshd, patt ptd in FeO and MnO, prob brnshd. I:scrpd, worn, sandy feel, many rounded pits to 1mm H:3–4.

f. FAN:103 Poly LR<1, mica glitter 0.23 E:scrpd, smthd, patt ptd in FeO and MnO, brnshd. I:scrpd, wet smthd. C:blue gray, surfs pale tan. H:2–3.

Figure 18

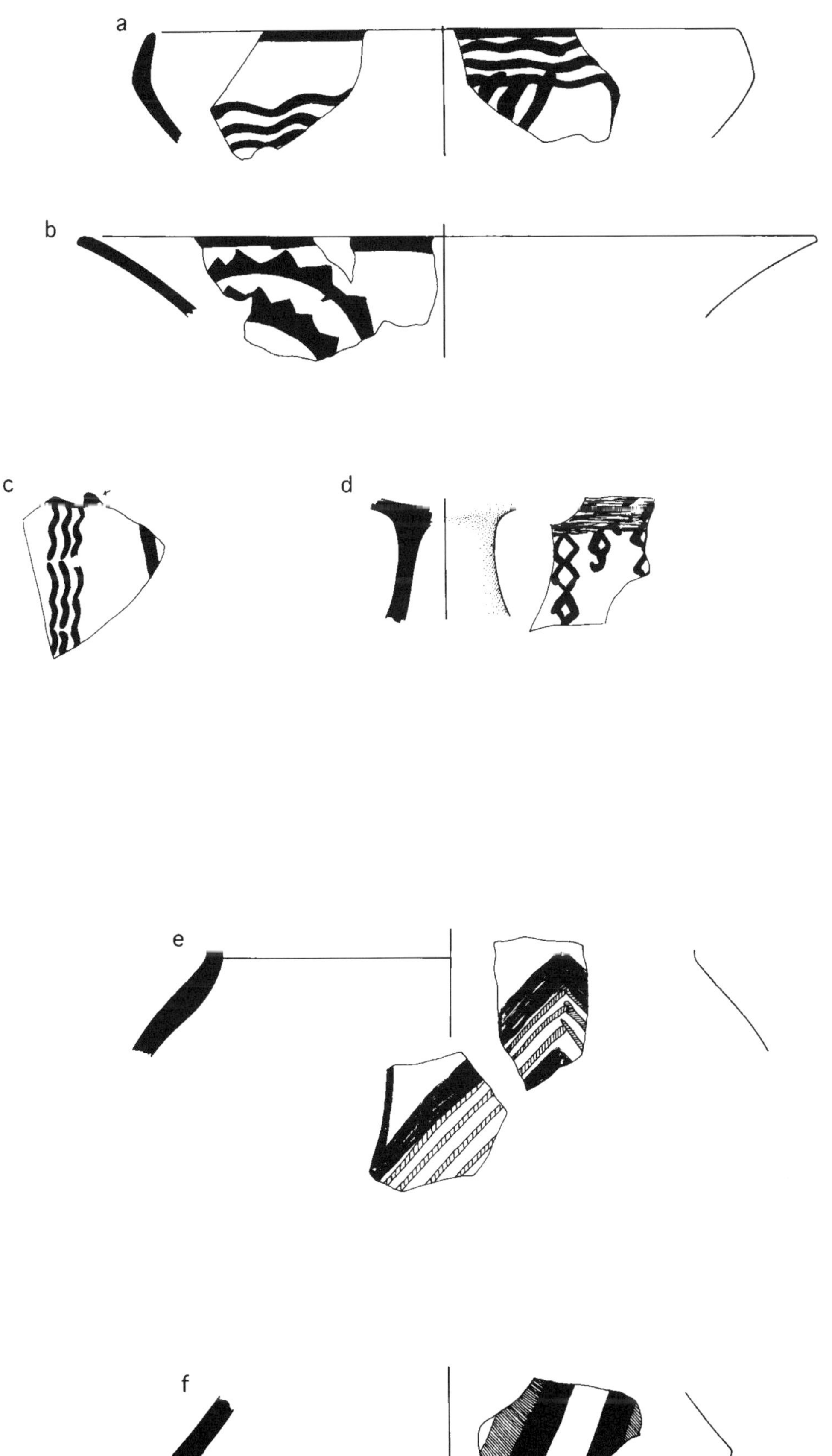

Figure 19 FCP 4.1 Gray Burnished variety

a. FAS:103 GrayB LMG<1, pops2, mica glitter 0.18 E:scrpd, smthd, brnshd. I:scrpd, brnshd at rim. C:uniform pale gray, same as surfs. H:4.

b. FAS:109 GrayB LMG<1 0.12 E:scrpd, smthd, brnshd, 2 small holes below rim pierced before firing. I:scrpd, smthd, brnshd. H:4.

c. FAS:103 GrayB LMG<1, mica glitter 0.17 joint E:scrpd, smthd, brnshd. I:scrpd, finger smthd, pitted at bott. C:uniform pale gray. H:2–3.

d. FAN:103 GrayB MG<1 0.06 E:scrpd, smthd, brnshd, troughs. I:scrpd, traces of red pigment caught in cracks, do not appear to have been fired, poss from use. Core light gray (7.5YR 7/0), surfs 10YR 5/2. Breaks look virtified, layers visible within breaks, large blister in bott. H:4–5.

e. FAS:98 GrayB DL<1 0.25 E, I:scrpd, smthd, brnshd, blue-gray surfs. C:reddish. Edge of lug preserved. H:5.

f. FAS:98 GrayB D1fL 0.25 E, I:scrpd, smthd, brnshd, dark gray surfs. C:reddish. Ext has delicate post-firing scratches/doodles. H:5.

g. FAS:103 GrayB LMG<1 0.25 E, I:scrpd, smthd, brnshd, blk ext, gray int. C:gray. H:3 int, 6 ext.

h. FAS:98 GrayB fDL<1 0.27 E:scprd but still lumpy, smthd, brnshd. I:scrpd, smthd, brnshd more thoroughly than ext, worn near bott, a few pits in bott have traces of powdery red pigment, prob from use. H:6.

i. FAS:107 GrayB LMG<1, mica glitter 0.32 E, I:scrpd, smthd, brnshd, surfs light gray, lighter int than ext. C:lighter gray. H:2–3.

j. FAN:109 GrayB GMG<1, tiny voids, flecks silver mica 0.20 base E:scrpd, smthd, damp brnshd, clear troughs. I:barely scrpd, except lightly brnshd at lip, poss coil joint at top of break. H:2–3.

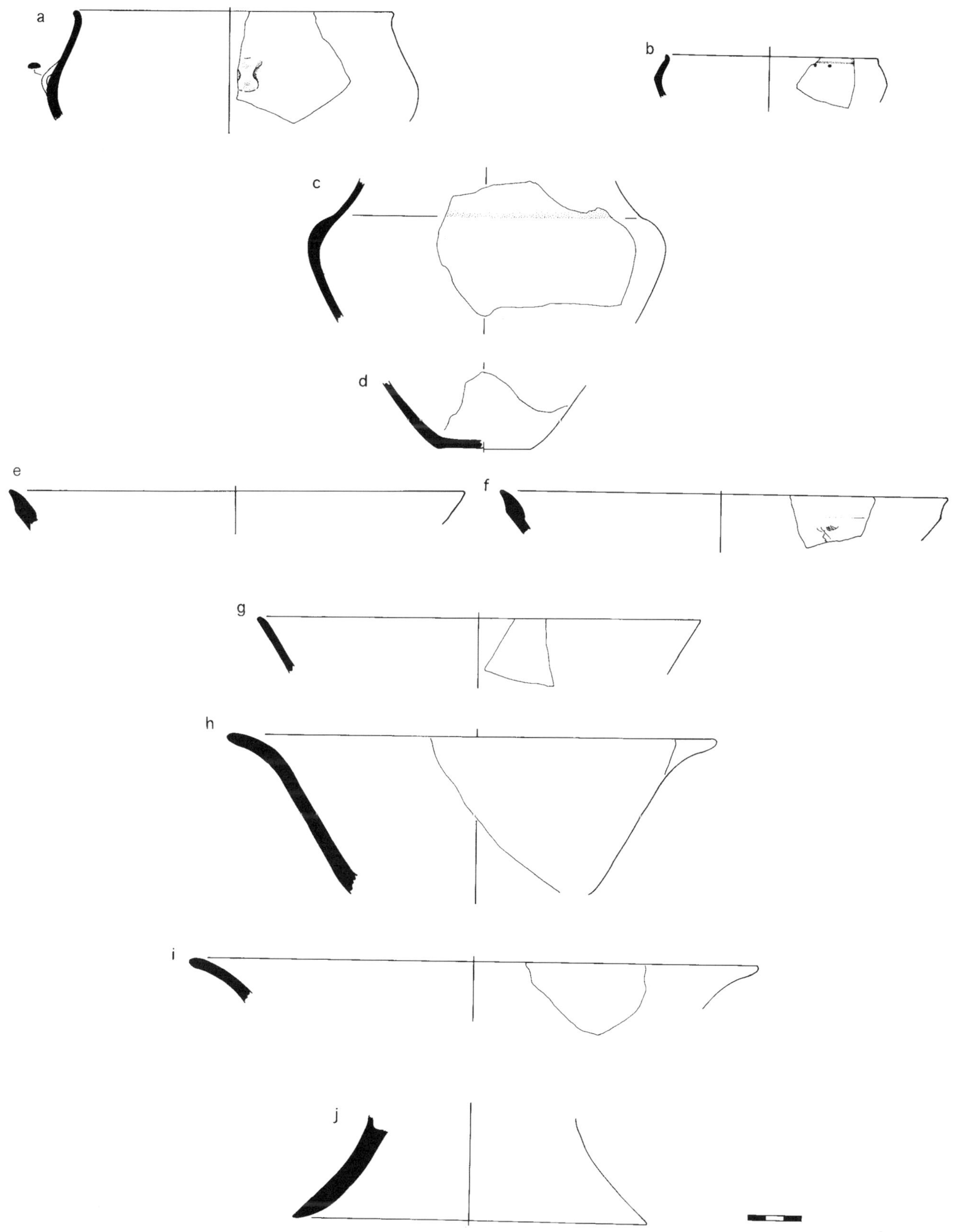
a
b
c
d
e
f
g
h
i
j

Figure 20 FCP 4.1 Lime plus Iron Pattern Painted variety

a. FAN:102 FP 249 LiFe L2–3aRD1, pops 0.07–0.08, irreg/asym E:scrpd to uniform th but surf lumpy, smthd, damp brnshd, FeO pt, dark gray on dirty gray-green ground. I:scrpd, wet smthd inside rim, pitted. Jagged edges. H:4–5. Pl. 4c.

b. FAN:110 LiFe mLRD<1 0.08 E:scrpd, brnshd except under handle, patt in FeO, red at rim to brwn on handle. I:scrpd, brnshd. C:uniform. H:2–3.

c. FAN:101 LiFe LMG1, pops E:scrpd, brnshd, pt in FeO barely visible orange. I:scrpd, brnshd, worn smth. C:slightly gray, surfs tan. H:2–3.

d. FAS:104 LiFe mLMG<1, pops 0.11 E:scrpd, smthd, minimal brnsh, patt ptd in FeO, grainy blk, reddish in places. I:scrpd, minimal brnsh. C:uniform, surfs tan. H:2–3.

e. FAS:103 LiFe LMG2 0.12 E:scrpd, slight brnsh, patt in Feo, very dilute, barely visible reddish on tan. I:scrpd, stripe at rim. H:4.

f. FAS:103 FC 118 LiFe Figurine LMG1, pops 2–3 Patt in granular FeO pt, blk on tan, except yellowish cloud under buttocks. Talalay 1993:18, Pl .1 (negative reversed).

g. FAN:110 FC107 Calcium carbonate "loaf" Treated w/ atlacol R2–3 embedded within, and flecks of carbon in one end, few pebbles to 5 mm, more white than 10YR 8/3. Many fingerprints on surfs suggest molding of wet paste. Traces of red pt on one short end and one concave side.

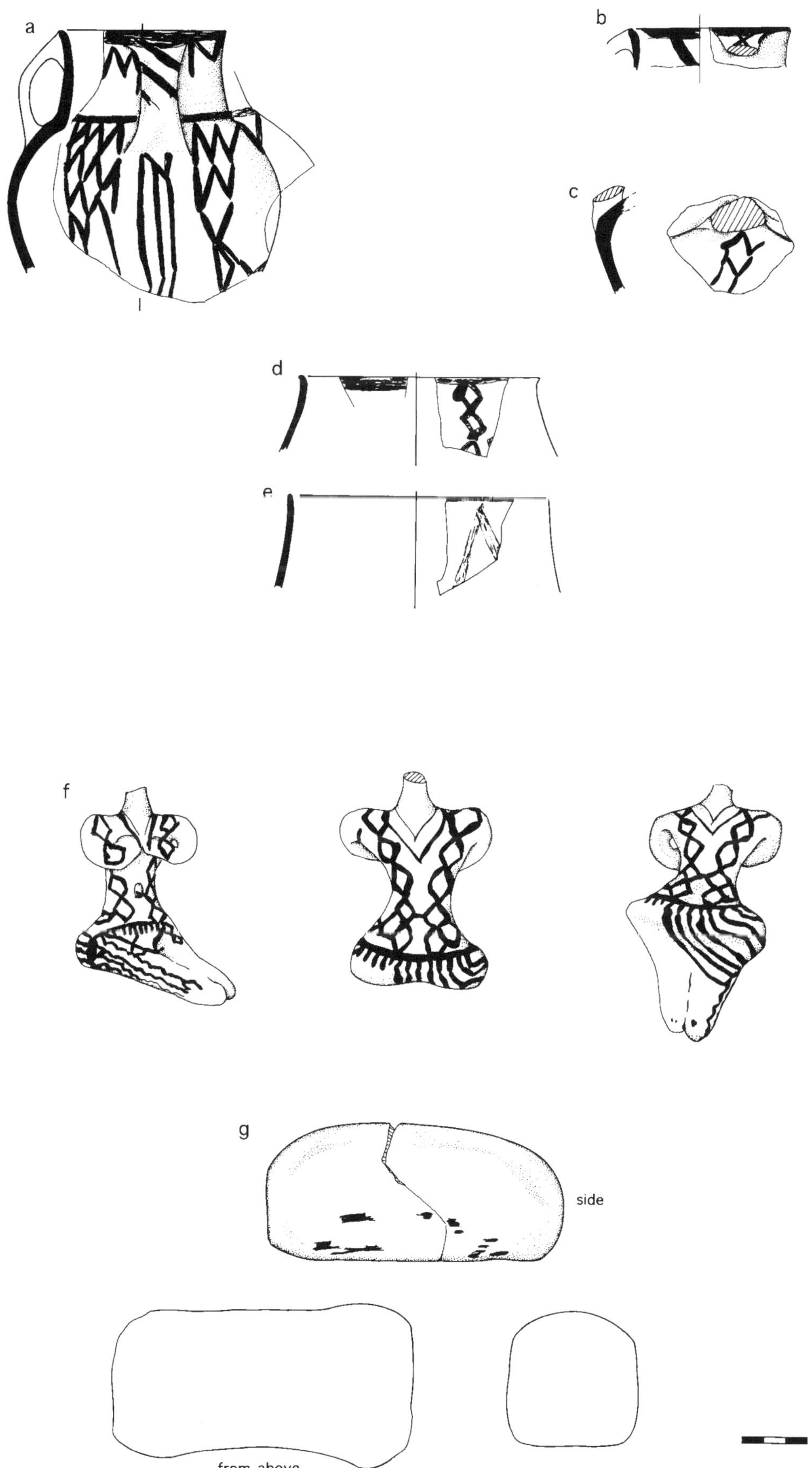
a
b
c
d
e
f
g
side
from above

Figure 21 FCP 4.1 Lime plus Iron Pattern Painted variety

a. FAS:90+91S+94S+97S+88N+A Lot 14 LiFe LMG<1 0.13 Nearly entire collar with two strap handles from rim preserved E:scrpd, smthd, patt ptd in FeO red on tan. Handle applied to scrpd and smthd surf.

b. FAS:109 LiFe fLmR<1 0.16 E:scrpd, smthd, brnshd, patt ptd in FeO, crackly red on pinkish-tan. I:scrpd, wet smthd. C:gray. H:2–3.

c. FAN:101 LiFe LMG1, pops 2–3 0.25 E:scrpd, damp brnshd, patt ptd in FeO, dull brwn-blk on tan. I:scrpd, wet smthd. C: light. H:4–5.

d. FAS:98 LiFe LMG<1 0.23 E:scrpd, smthd, slight brnsh, patt in FeO, red, on pinkish surfs. I:scrpd, smthd. C:uniform light. Rim folded in and poorly melded. H:2–3.

e. FAN:110+101N and FAS:109 LiFe LD<1, mica glitter, f pops 0.26 E:well scrpd to even th, brnshd, broad shallow troughs, patt in FeO dull red on tan surfs, cloud on shoulder. I:scrpd, brnshd at rim. Hole drilled from ext. Non-joining sherds are slightly reduced:post-breakage exposure to fire. H:2–3 int, 3–4 ext.

f. FAS:100 LiFe L3MG<1 0.43 max E:scrpd, smthd, patt in streaky dull blk FeO pt on whitish surf. I:scrpd, deep gouges, pinkish surf.

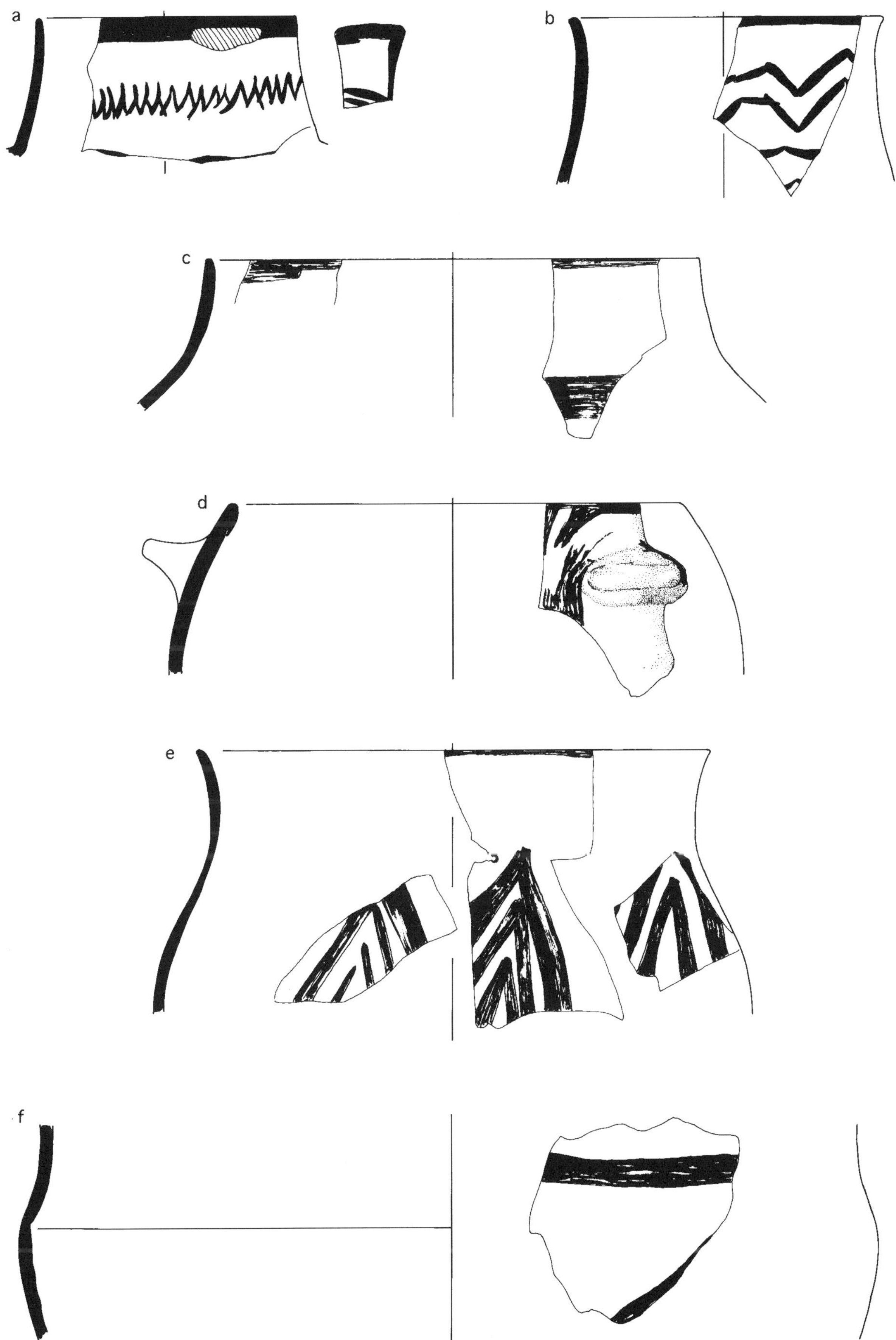
a
b
c
d
e
f

Figure 22 FCP 4.1 Lime plus Iron Pattern Painted variety

a. FAN:110 FP 250 LiFe L3RD1, pops 0.19, irreg 3 sherds preserve just under half of pot E:prob scrpd but lumpy, smthd, minimal brnsh, irreg th and lip. I:scrpd, smthd, brnshd, patt ptd in granular FeO, sloppy short lines, red on gray surfs. C:gray center, pinkish subsurfs. Sharp edges, prob virtified. H:4–5. Pl. 4a.

b. FAN:96 LiFe LR<1, mica glitter, pops 1 0.06 bott E:scrpd, finger smthd, patt in FeO, reddish gray on tan. I:scrpd, smthd, brnshd, patt in FeO, reddish-gray. H:2–3.

c. FAN:101 FAS:104 LiFe mLD<1, mica glitter, pops 1 0.13 E:scrpd, smthd, brnshd, patt in FeO, brwn-blk on tan surfs, 2 holes drilled from int. C:uniform. Sharp edges. H:5–6.

d. FAN:96 LiFe LMG1, pops 1–2 0.17–0.18, irreg E, I:scrpd, smthd, brnshd, patt in FeO blk on rim, red-brwn int, on tan. H:3–4.

e. FAN:102 LiFe LMG<1, gold and silver mica glitter, f pops 0.19 E:scrpd, smthd, brnshd, patt in FeO, red-orange on tan. I:scrpd, brnshd, troughs, bott worn. C:gray where thick, surfs tan. H:2–3.

f. FAS:96 LiFe mLRMG<1 0.25 E:scprd, smthd, brnshd, patt in FeO, red on tan. I:scrpd, smthd, brnshd. C:gray. H:2–3.

g. FAN:109 LiFe LmrR2 0.24, irreg E:scrpd, smthd, hor brnsh, slipped w/ FeO, red, crackling and dull, blk clouds. I: same,blk at rim, then red, then blk below, pt wearing off in places. H:3–5.

h. FAS:108 LiFe LR1 0.28–0.35, irreg E, I:scrpd, smthd, brnshd, patt in FeO, blk on tan. H:2–3.

i. FAN:101 LiFe rRL1, pops 1 0.20 max E:scrpd, smthd, brnshd, patt in FeO, very pale pink on pink, hard to make out patt. I:scrpd, brnshd, pitted, worn. H:3–5.

j. FAN:102 LiFe LMG1 0.20 E:scrpd, smthd, BO, patt in FeO, dark gray on gray surf. H:6–7.

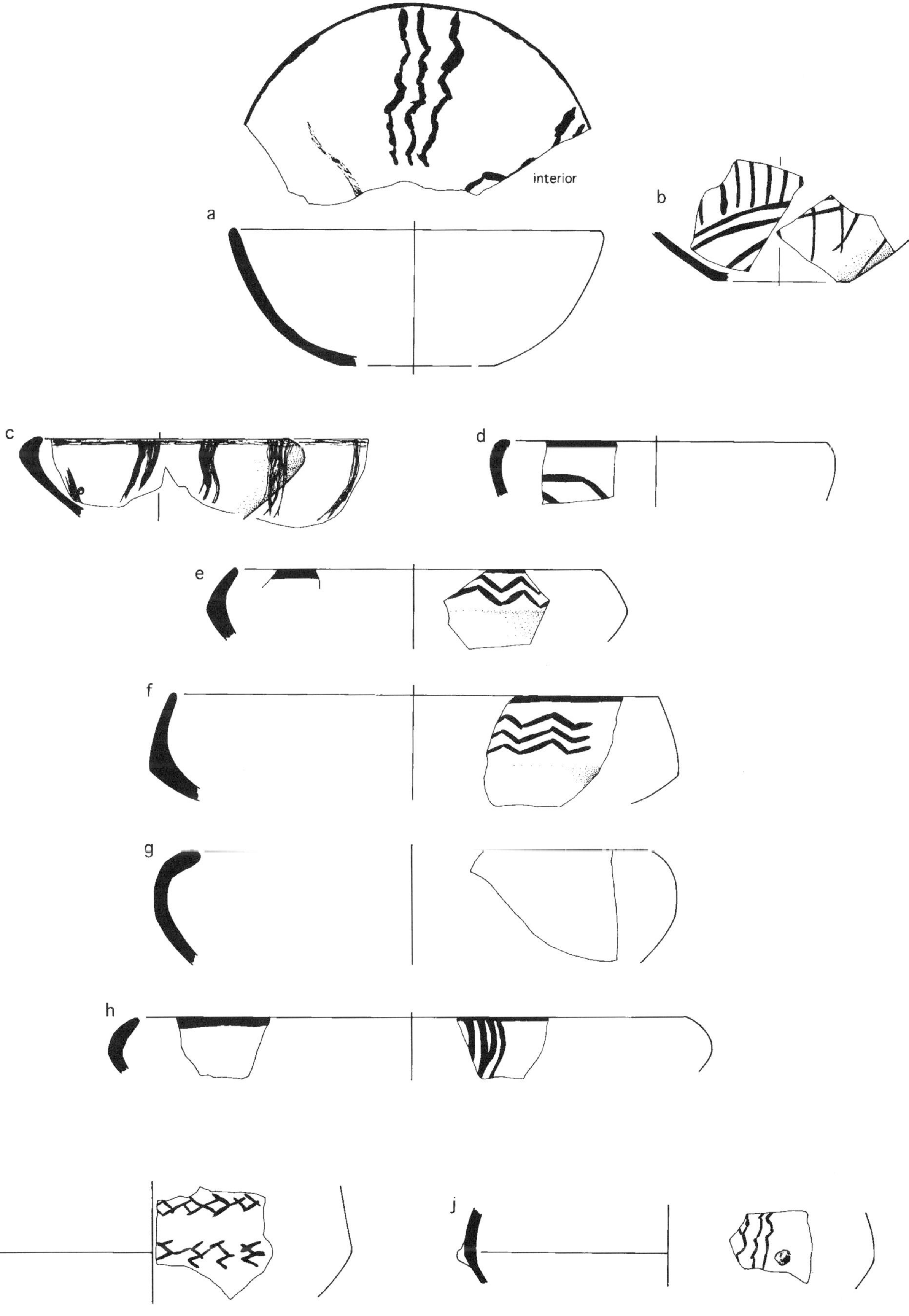
interior
a
b
c
d
e
f
g
h
i
j

Figure 23 FCP 4.1 Lime plus Iron Pattern Painted variety

a. FAN:101 LiFe LMG<1, mica glitter, f pops 0.34 E:scrpd, smthd, brnshd less well than int. I:scrpd, smthd, brnshd, patt in FeO, brwn-blk on light gray-brwn. H:4–5.

b. FAN:103+FAS:112 LiFe LrRD1, mica glitter 0.32 E, I:scrpd, smthd, brnshd, few troughs, patt in FeO, reddish-gray on tan surf. Ext pt very pale and streaky. H:3–4.

c. FAN:110 LiFe LRD1, pops 1–2 0.25, irreg E, I:scrpd, smthd, damp brnshd, clear troughs, patt in FeO red to blk, clouds. Th varies, although well scrpd. C:gray, subsurfs and surfs pale pink. H:2–3.

d. FAN:105 LiFe LMG1 0.14 E:scrpd, smthd, prob brnshd, patt in FeO, blk on pale gray. I:roughly scrpd, brnshd inside lip. Sharp edges, prob vitrified. H:6–7.

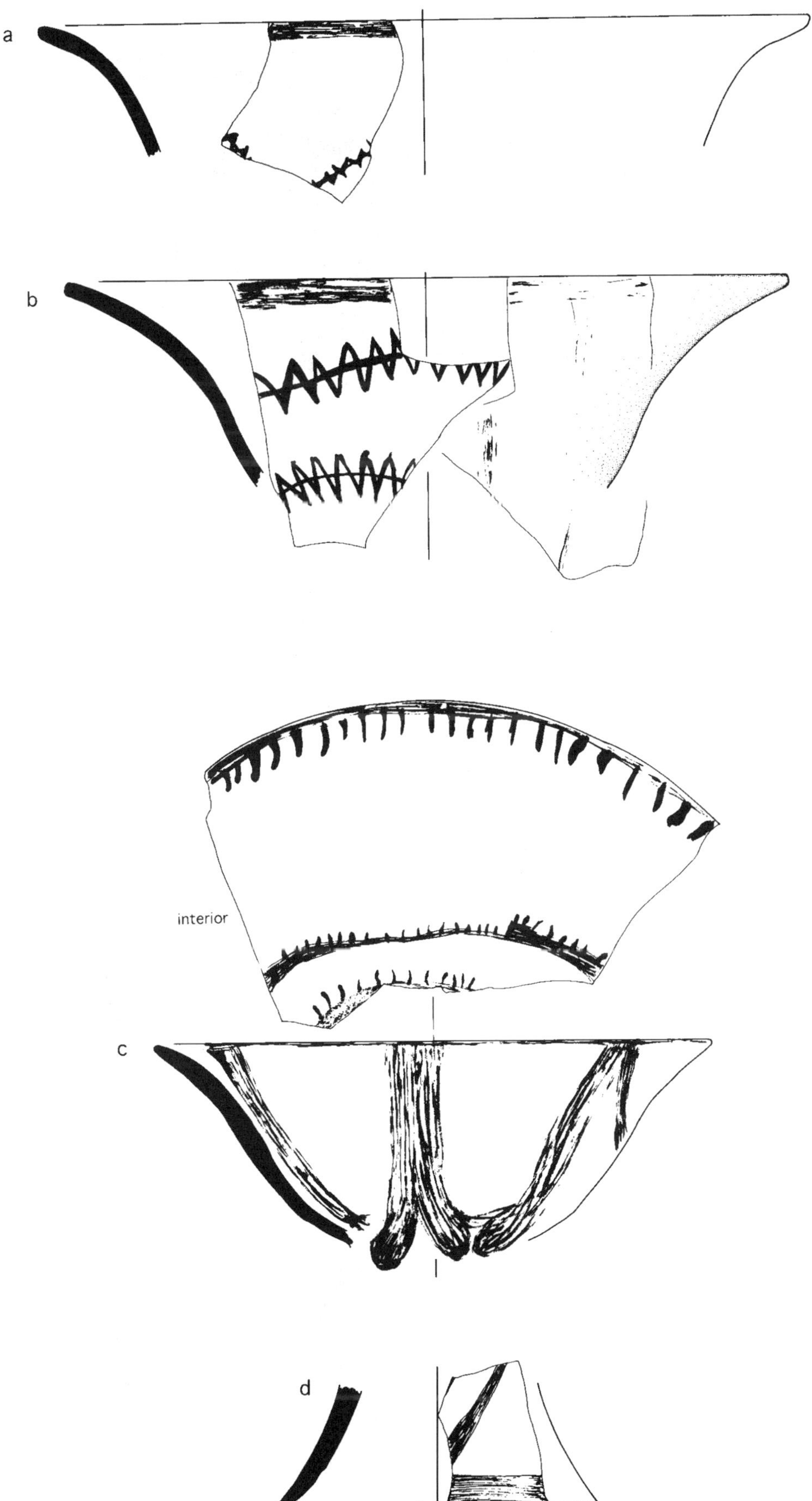
a
b
interior
c
d

Figure 24 FCP 4.1 Lime plus Iron Pattern Painted variety

a. FAS:107 LiFe LMG1, mica glitter, pops 1 0.15 E:scrpd, smthd, brnshd, no troughs, patt in FeO, blk on tan surfs. I:scrpd, smthd, brnshd, clear troughs. H:5–7.

b. FAN:102 LiFe LMG1, silver and gold mica glitter, pops 1 0.26 E, I:scrpd, smthd, brnshd, patt in FeO, blk on tan surfs, light cloud at lip on int. C:gray. H:4–5.

c. FAN:96 LiFe LMG1, pops 1 0.22 E, I:scrpd, smthd, brnshd, patt in FeO, sloppy, brwn-blk on light gray surfs. C:reddish. H:2–3.

d. FAS:107 LiFe mL,fMG<1, pops 1–2 0.26 E, I:scrpd, smthd, brnshd, patt in FeO, brwn-blk, runny, slight luster, dirty greenish-gray surfs, light cloud on ext. H:6.

e. FAS:105+104S+99S LiFe LMG<1, pops 1 0.32 E, I:scrpd, smthd, brnshd, patt in FeO blk, gray surfs. Core:gray, lighter subsurfs. H:7.

f. FAS:103 LiFe LMG1 0.35 E, I:scrpd, smthd, brnshd, patt in FeO, one sherd is pale orange on tan, other brwn-blk on gray; both flaking, worn int bott. C:gray. H:2–3.

g. FAS:98 LiFe LMG1, pops 1–2 0.26 E, I: scrpd, smthd, brnshd, patt in FeO, red to blk on yellowish-tan to pink surfs. Poss ptd mark on ext. H:5–6.

h. FAN:98 LiFe LMG1, pops 1–2 0.16 E:scrpd, smthd, brnshd, patt in FeO, blk on light gray. C:gray. H:4–5.

i. FAS:107 LiFe LMG1 0.14 E:scrpd, smthd, brnshd, patt in FeO, brwn-blk on tan. I:scrpd, brnshd at lip. C:gray where th, rest is deep red. H:7.

j. FAN:102 LiFe LMG<1, f pops 0.12 E:scrpd, smthd, damp brnshd, FeO pt, brwn-gray on tan surf. I:scrpd, drying cracks from pressure. H:3–4.

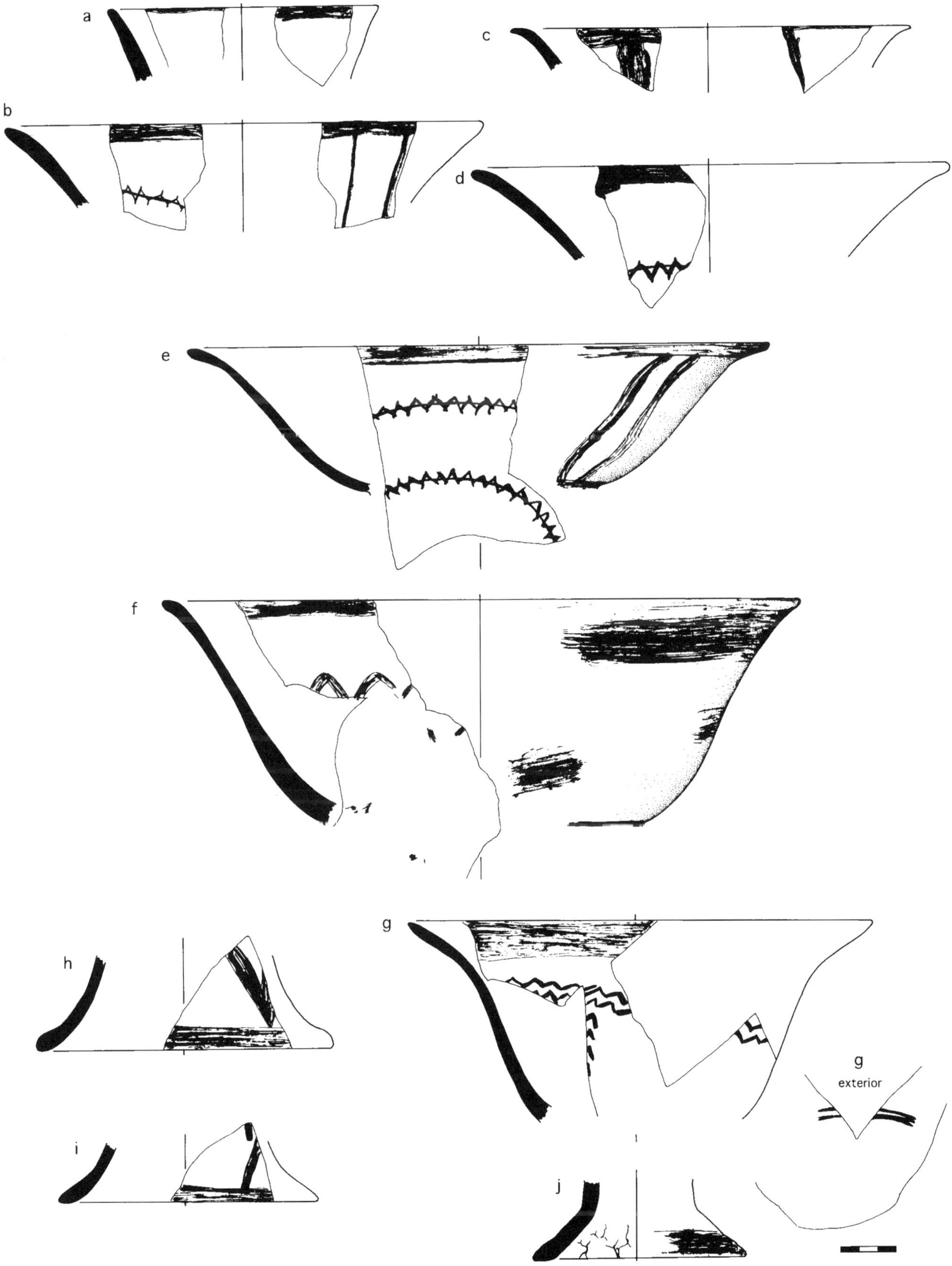
a
b
c
d
e
f
g
h
i
j
g
exterior

Figure 25 FCP 4.1 No Lime Coarse variety

a. FAS:105 NoLiCo RQ1–2 0.14 E, I:well scrpd, wet smthd. C:red-brwn, darker surfs. Jagged edges. H:2–3.

b. FAN:101 NoLiCo MG1, f2, silver and gold mica glitter, blk flecks 0.17 E, I:roughly scrpd, scribbly brnsh, troughs ext. C:light gray-brwn. Jagged edges w/ vertical slits. H:2–3.

c. FAN:109 NoLiCo aRD2, flecks of mica 0.24 E. I:scrpd to regular th, finger smthd. C:dark gray center, subsurfs and surfs red. Crumbly edges. H:2–3.

d. FAS:107 NoLiCo RMG3–4 0.25 E, I:scrpd, better int, wet smthd, uniform th. C:slightly redder to ext, surfs gray-brwn. H:2–3.

e. FAS:109 NoLiCo R1 0.25 E, I:scrpd, finger smthd. C:blk, subsurfs and surfs brick red, dark cloud ext rim. H:1–2.

f. FAS:107 NoLiCo mR1–2,f3 0.24 E, I:scrpd, finger smthd, still lumpy ext. C:brick red to brwnish, surfs same, blk clouds ext around lug. H:2–3.

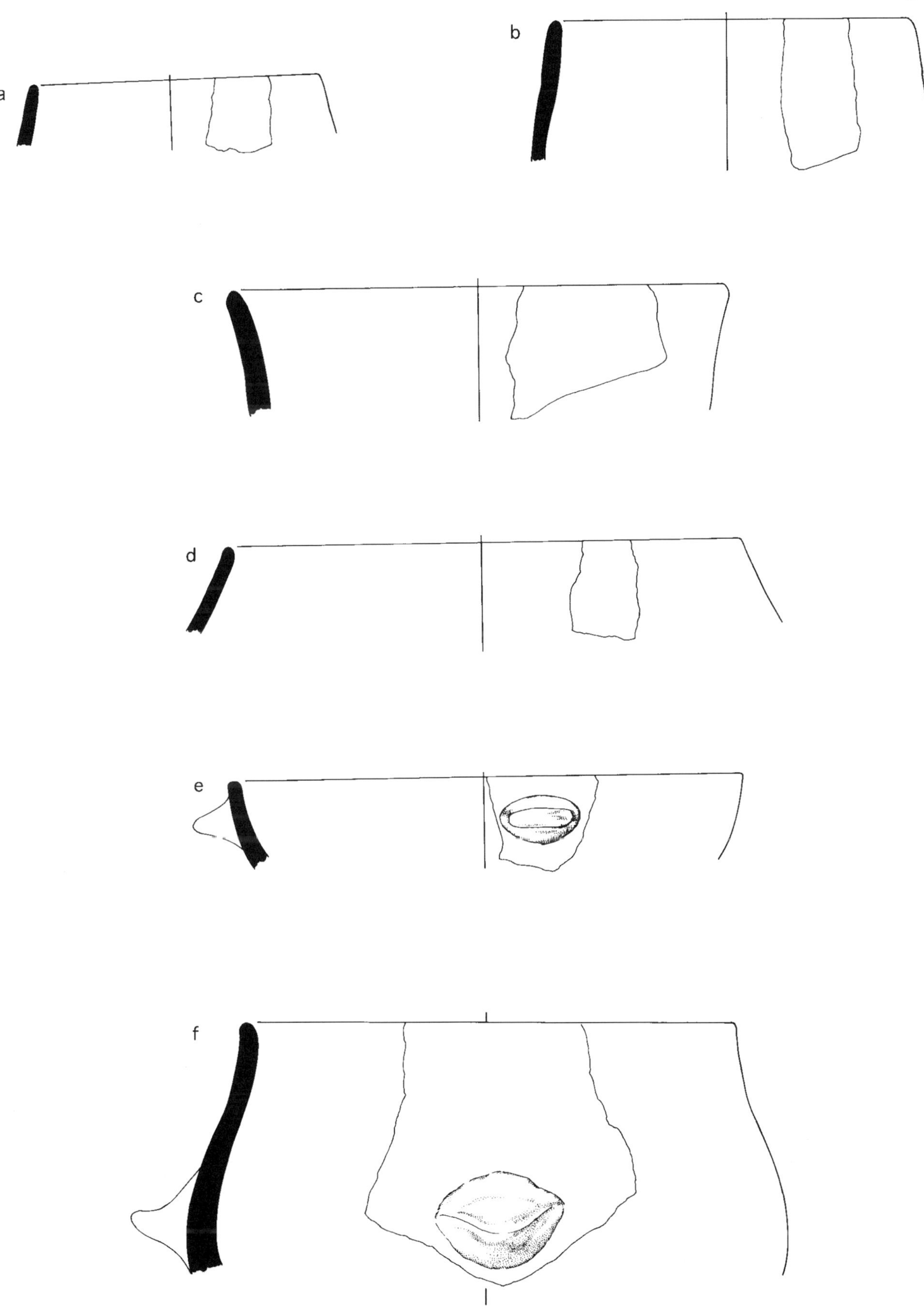
a
b
c
d
e
f

Figure 26 FCP 4.2 Andesite Burnished variety

a. FAS:94 AndB HBF1 0.10 E:scrpd, smthd, slipped, PB, blk, trace of pellet or handle and of joint. I:scrpd, smthd, brnshd at rim only. C:red. H:2–3.

b. FAS:84 AndB HBF1 0.10 E:scrpd, smthd, slipped, brnshd, blk. I: scrpd, smthd, brnshd at rim only, blk. H:2–3.

c. FAS:88 AndB HBF1 0.10 E, I:scrpd but lumpy, smthd, slipped, brnshd, blk, clear finished rim with handle extending above it, poss traces white Lime in ext joint. H:2–3.

d. FAN:94 AndB HBF1 0.15 E:scrpd but lumpy, finger smthd, PB, reddish-gray w/ greenish tinge. C:reddish-brwn. Jagged edges. H:2–3.

e. FAS:93 AndB HBF1 0.14 E:scrpd, smthd, slipped, brnshd, scribbly below car, blk, trace of pellet at left edge car. I:scrpd, wet smthd, gray. H:2–3.

f. FAS:84 AndB HBF1 0.18 E:scrpd, smthd, slipped, brnshd, blk. I:scrpd, wet smthd. H:2–3.

g. FAS:84 AndB HBF1 0.20 car E:scrpd, smthd, slipped, brnshd, blk. I:scrpd, wet smthd. H:2–3.

h. FAS:90(3)+91S+93S FP 253 AndB HBF<1 0.20, irreg E:scrpd, smthd, slipped, brnshd, waxy blk where well preserved, most worn w/ only scribbly vert brnsh troughs, blk w/ creamy bloom or misfired slip in depressions, 2 pellets at car and scars of 2 more. I:scrpd, especially well under shoulder, rest lumpy, finger depressions from pinching, surf chipped off bott, dark gray. U:scrpd. C:light grey-brwn. H:3 int, 5–6 ext.

i. FAS:95+94N FP 254 AndB HBF1, f2 0.10 E:scrpd, smthd, slipped, brnshd, blk waxy, granular greyish-white pt, no reaction in HCl. I:scrpd, smthd, slipped and brnshd at rim. U handle: smthd. C:reddish-brwn w/ thin gray center. H:2–4.

j. FAS:93 AndB HFB1 0.20 E, I:scrpd, smthd, slipped, brnshd on top handle, brwnish-pink, traces poss white Lime. H:4–5.

k. FAS:91 AndB HBF1 0.21 max E:scrpd, smthd, slipped, brnshd, stump of strap handle at car turning up towards rim. I:scrpd, wet smthd. H:3–4.

l. FAS:91 AndB HBF1 0.16 car E:scrpd, smthd, slipped, brnshd, int handle wet smthd, ext worn. I:scrpd, wet smthd. H:2–3.

m. FAS:91 AndB HBF1 E:scrpd, smthd, slipped, brnshd, small flattened pellet applied at narrow portion of handle. I:scrpd, wet smthd.

n. FAS:91 AndB HBF1 E:scrpd, smthd, slipped, brnshd, waxy gloss, red (2.5YR 5/8), crackling and flaking, flattened pellet at narrow part of handle. I:scrpd, wet smthd.

o. FAN:94 AndB H<1BF2 0.15 joint E:scrpd, smthd, PB above joint, grayish-green, traces of pellet or handle on shoulder. I:scrpd, smthd. H:2–3.

p. FAS:91 AndB H<1BF1, sliver mica flecks1 0.17, car E, I:scrpd, smthd, poss slipped, brnshd, greenish-orange ext, blk int. C:blue-gray. H:2–3.

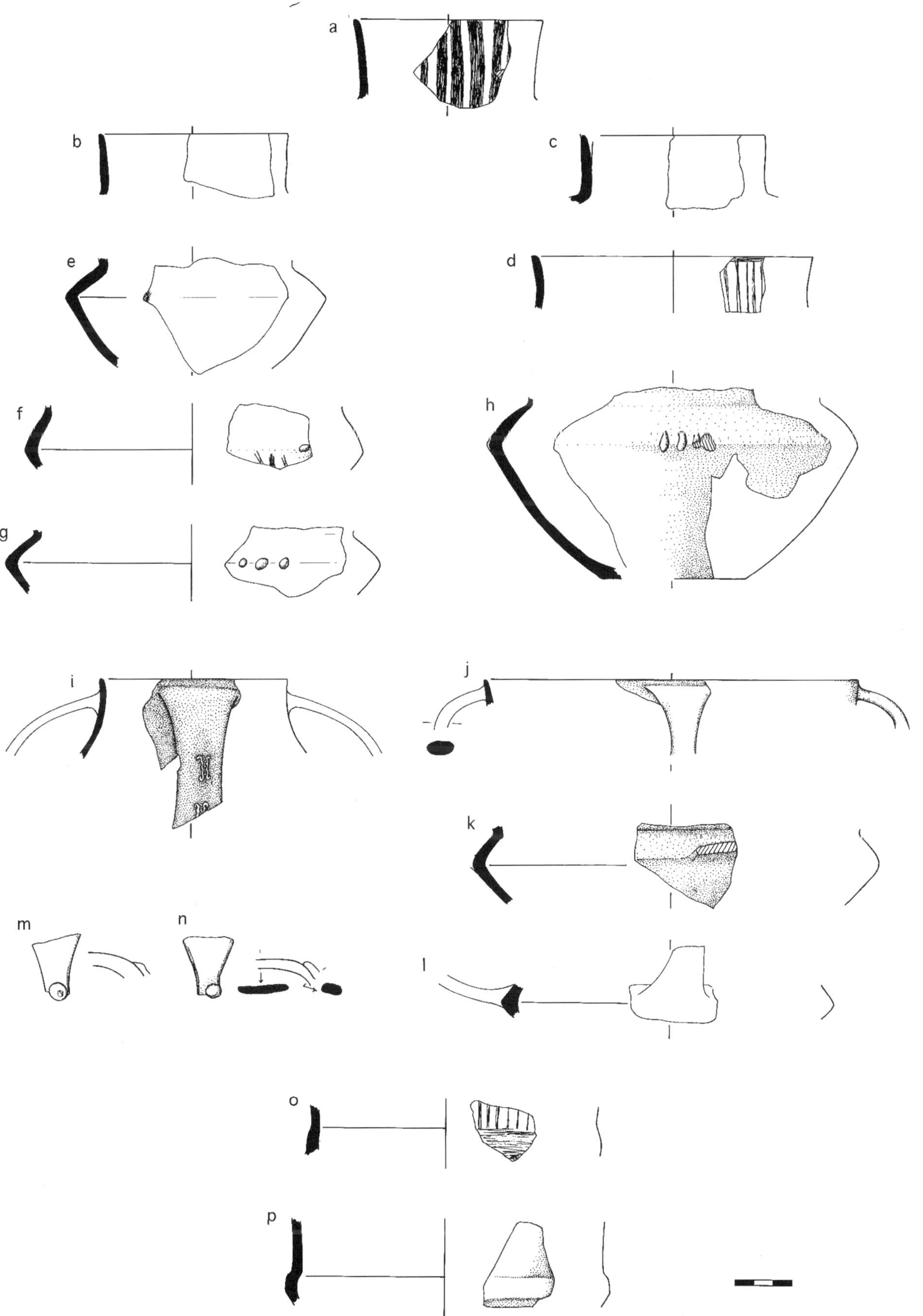
a
b
c
e
d
f
h
g
i
j
k
m
n
l
o
p

Figure 27 FCP 4.2 Andesite Burnished variety

a. FAS:93 AndB HBF1 0.24 All surfs gone, but traces of brnshd blk int and ext. H:2–3.

b. FAN:94 AndB H<1BF1 0.20 E:scrpd, smthd, slipped, brnshd, poss PB, waxy, blk w/ red-yellow clouds. I:scrpd, smthd, slipped, brnshd, blk. C:reddish-brwn. H:2–3.

c. FAS:88 AndB HBF1 0.17 E, I:scrpd, smthd, slipped, brnshd, blk. C:gray. H:2–3.

d. FAS:93 AndB HBF1 0.30–0.31, irreg E:scrpd but lumpy, smthd, slipped, brnshd, blk w/ red grains of slip in unburnished grooves, trace of applied pellet at edge. I:scrpd, smthd, slipped, brnshd, blk at rim, rest slightly oxidized. C:gray. H:4–5.

e. FAS:90 AndB HBF<1 0.32 E, I:scrpd, smthd, slipped, brnshd, blk. H:2–3.

f. FAS:84 AndB HBF1 0.25–0.26, irreg E, I:scrpd, smthd, slipped, brnshd, then final brnsh leaving reserved band at int and ext rim, final brnsh is glossy, blk at rim, oxidized below int and ext. H:2–3.

g. FAS:91 AndB HBF1 0.08 joint E:scrpd, smthd, slipped, brnshd, glossy blk. I:scrpd, finger smthd, worn and pitted, blk. U:scrpd, smthd, blk. H:3.

h. FAS:91 AndB HBF1 0.13 E:scrpd, smthd, slipped, PB, blk. I:scrpd, gray. H:2–3.

i. FAS:91 AndB HBF1 0.10 E:scrpd, smthd, slipped, brnshd, blk. I:scrpd. H:2–3.

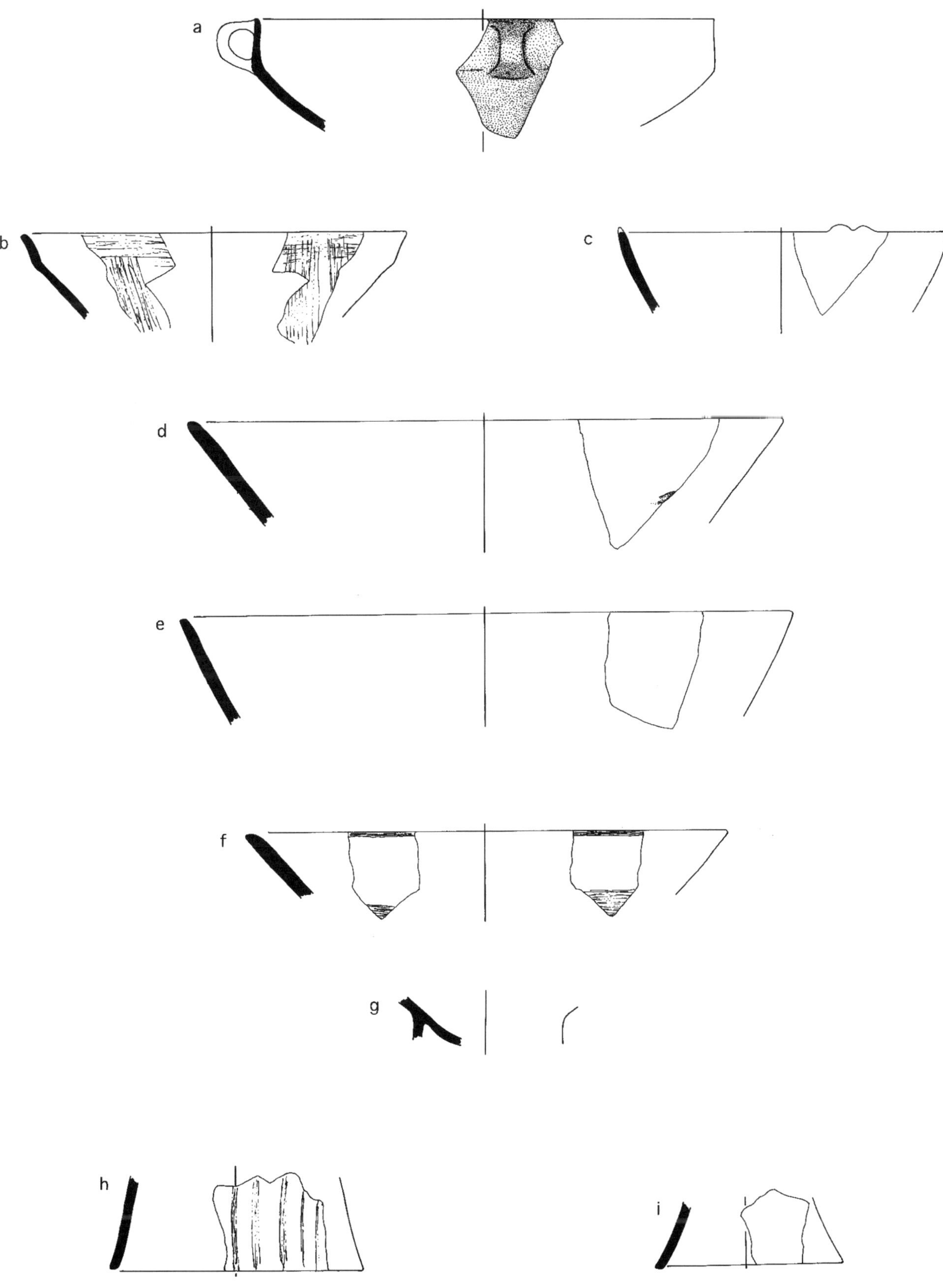
a
b
c
d
e
f
g
h
i

Figure 28 FCP 4 Rhyta from all contexts

a. G:2 FP 44 AndB H<1B2F1 E, I:scrpd, smthd, slipped, brnshd, glossy blk w/ reddish tinge, patt on one side:deeply incised V, white ptd zigzag below incision, traces red powder around incisions and along ridge of handle, traces white Lime on ridge. H:3–4.

b. FF1:13 FPSC 145 AndB HBF1 Top:scrpd, slipped, brnshd, red. U:scrpd, slipped, red, trace of joint one end.

c. FAN:94 AndB HBF1 Top:scrpd, slipped, brnshd, waxy blk, patt in red and white Lime powder. U:scrpd, smthd, slipped, red. C:brwnish-gray. H:2–3.

d Unstratified AndB HBF<1, 3mm pebble in break E:scrpd, smthd, slipped, brnshd, gray, incised line at joint, poss white Lime fill. I:scrpd, wet smthd, traces of red powder. C:gray.

e. A Lot 16 AndB HBF1 E:scrpd, smthd, brnshd, blk, patt in dull grainy white, with rusty red powder on top, no reaction in HCl ; other side of leg is only wet smthd, blk. I:scrpd, wet smthd, blk. C:red.

f. A:46 FP 38 AndB MG<1aD2B2 E:scrpd, slipped, scribbly brnsh, waxy blk, patt in powdery white grains, no reaction in HCl, traces red powder, 2 legs and part of third preserved, legs separated by incised Vs, on "front" incised dots within V. I:scrpd, finger smthd, large drip of red pt, scratches off with fingernail.

g. FAN:95 FP 166 AndB HBF1 Leg molded in one piece, clay smeared on to attach to body, broken at top. E:scprd, smthd, poss slip, brnshd, glossy blk w/ red tinge, patt in white pt, partly Lime, flecks orange powder. I:scrpd, wet smthd, blk. C:pale gray.

h. FF1:18 FP 170 NoLi WD<1 ca. 0.15 at mouth E:scrpd, smthd, brnshd, blk, no gloss, underside of handle and top of rim coated w/ red powder (7.5R 4/6), slight groove at handle joint w/ red stripe around it and incised line w/ fringe, incisions filled with white powder that does not react in HCl. I:well scrpd, dark gray. H:3–4.

i. FAS:98 FP 179 maDR5–6, fL<1, L pebble 6 E:scrpd, smthd, red pigment on front, side of legs, and just inside rim, brnshd, powdery where not brnshd but appears fired on, varies red-blk-brwn, incised after brnshd, no apparent fill in lines. I:scrpd, wet smthd, blk, poss charred. C:gray, subsurfs brwn, surfs mottled. H:2–3.

j. A:40 FP 32 GrayB MDG<1 E:scrpd, smthd, incised patt, brnshd except around patt, faint traces red powder and white Lime around incisions, pale gray. I:scrpd, smthd, brnshd, pale gray.

k. FAN:99 NoLime WD1, f2 E:scrpd, smthd, brnshd, incised patt, line at joint filled w/ white Lime, traces red powder in incisions. I:scrpd, smthd, traces red powder.

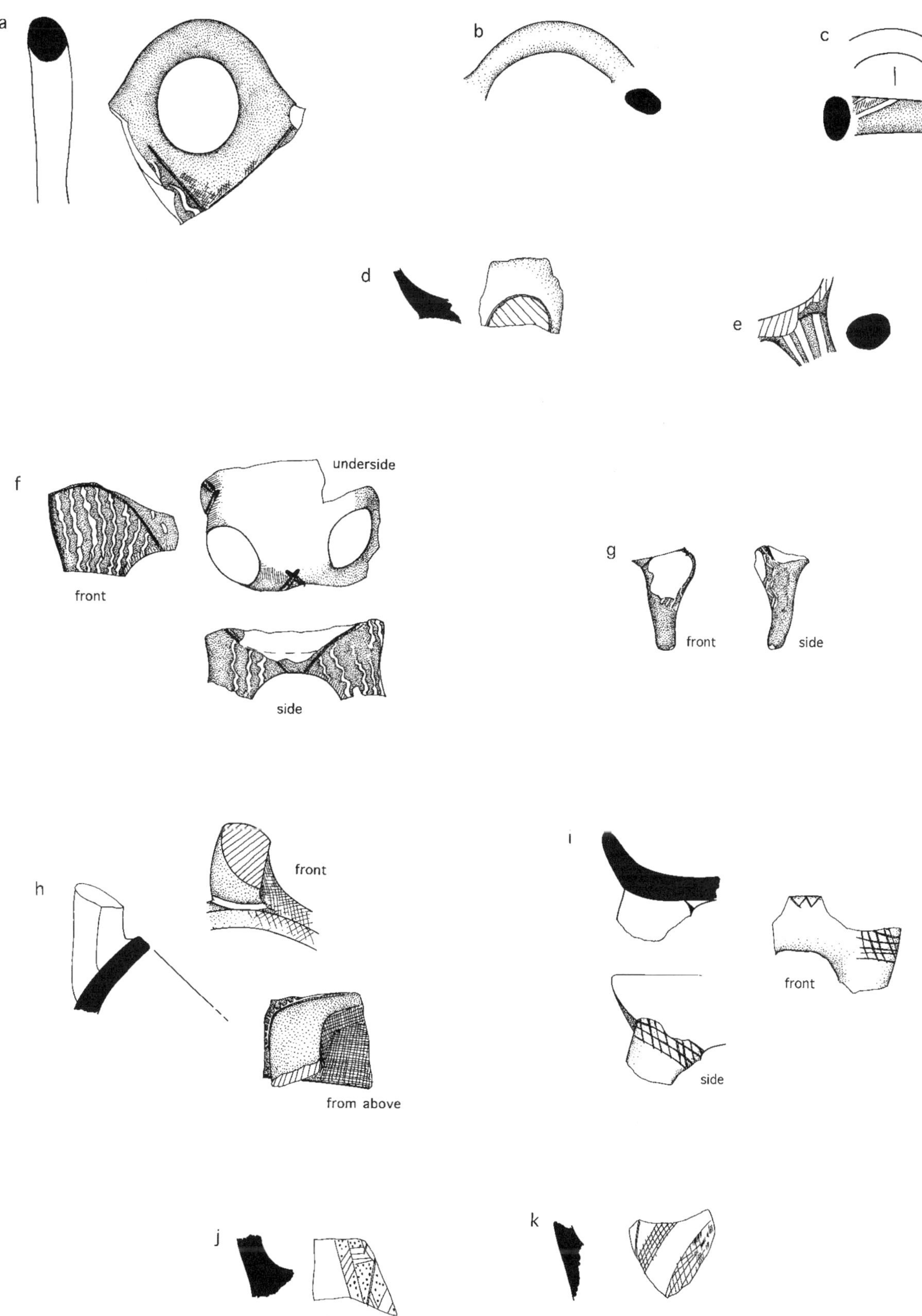
a
b
c
d
e
f
front
underside
side
g
front
side
h
front
from above
i
front
side
j
k

Figure 29 FCP 4.2 Ungritted Manganese and Gray Burnished varieties

a. FAS:99 UgrMn f tiny MG<1, fL 0.18 E, I:scrpd, smthd, prob brnshd, patt in brwn-blk MnO on tip of rim. H:2–3.

b. FAN:95 UgrMn D<1, fL 0.10 E:scrpd, smthd, patt in brwn-blk MnO on greenish surf, brnshd. I:scrpd. C:uniform pale pink. H:2–3.

c. FAN:94+90N+87N UgrMn D<1, fL, FeO pebble in break 3 0.25 E:scrpd, patt in brwn-blk MnO, brnshd, pale yellow surfs. I:scrpd, support clay added at joint and bott break. H:2–3.

d. FAS:91 GrayB LD<1 0.25 E, I:scrpd, smthd, brnshd, pale gray. C:pale gray. H:4.

e. FAN:95 GrayB fL, MG1 0.08 bott E, I:scrpd, smthd, prob brnshd, pale gray. H:5–6.

f. FAN:95 GrayB MG<1, mica glitter 0.25 E, I:scrpd, smthd, brnshd, clear troughs, breaks worn, 1 hole drilled from interior just below rim fold, another unfinished within rim fold. H:2–3.

g. FAN:87(2)+95N(2) GrayB fLD<1 0.095 bott E:scrpd, smthd, brnshd, light gray. I:scrpd, scraps of clay from scraping still clinging to int. H:2–3.

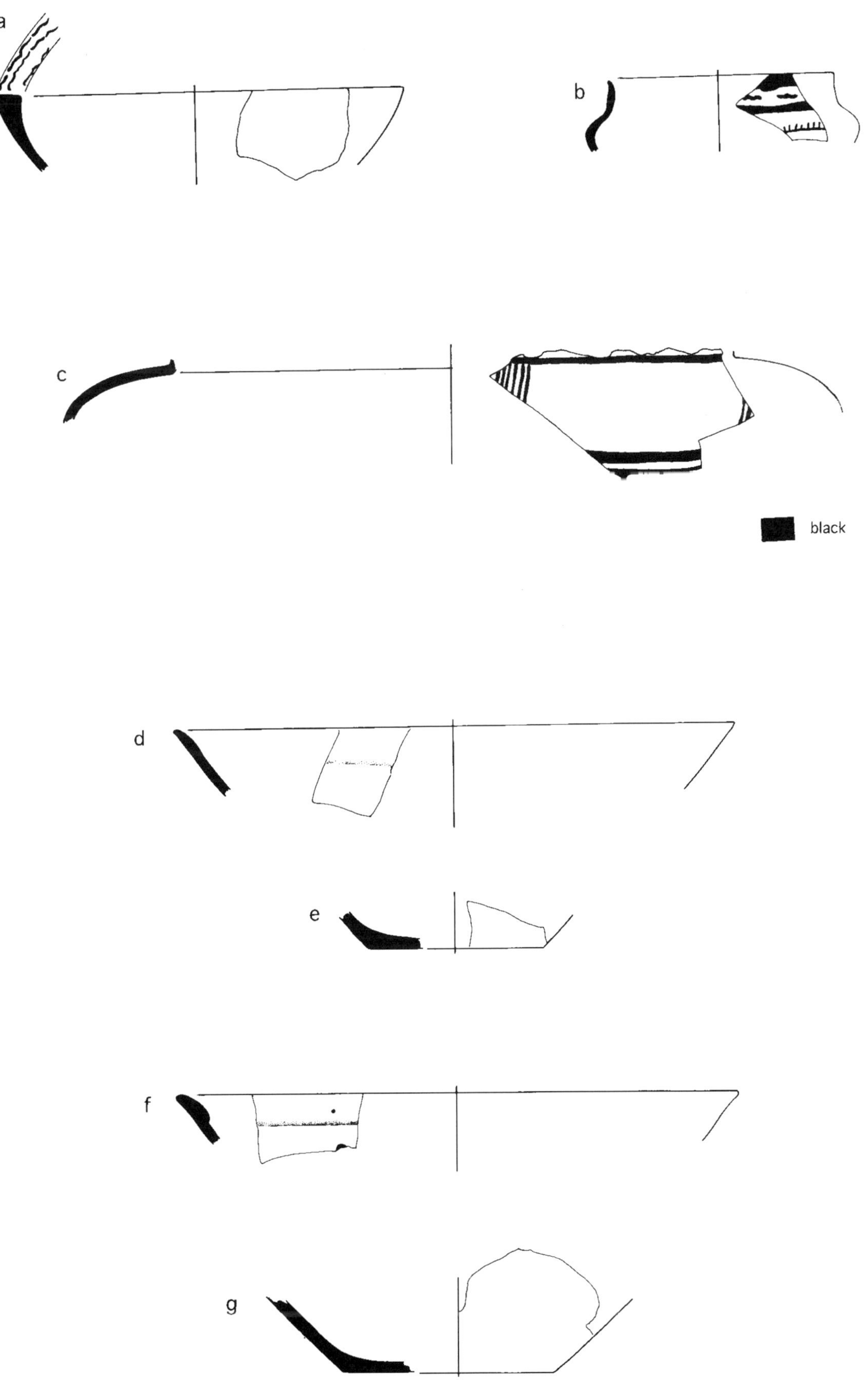
a
b
c
black
d
e
f
g

Figure 30 FCP 4.2 Lime plus Iron Pattern Painted variety

a. FAS:93 LiFe LMG1, pops 2 0.10 E:scrpd, prob smthd, patt in FeO, dark gray, gray surfs. I:scrpd, gray. H:6–7.

b. FAS:84 LiFe LMG1 0.09 E:scrpd but lumpy, brnshd, patt in FeO, blk, gray surfs, drill hole from ext. I:scrpd, light brnsh. H:5–6.

c. FAS:99 LiFe L1, pops 1 0.13 E:scrpd, brnshd, patt in FeO, dark gray, gray surfs. I:scrpd. H:6.

d. FAS:91 LiFe LMG1, pops 2–3 0.23 max E:scrpd, light brnshd, patt in FeO reddish-gray to grayish-brwn, on greenish-tan surfs. I:scrpd. H:6–8.

e. FAS:92 LiFe LMG1, pops 2–3 0.27 neck E:scrpd, light brnshd, patt in FeO, grayish-red, tan surfs. I:scrpd, grayish-tan. C:gray. H:5–6.

f. FAS:92 LiFe LDG1, pops 0.26 E:scrpd, smthd, patt in FeO reddish-gray, greenish-tan surfs. I:scrpd diagonally, gouges from grit. Handle has void in center of core from rolling or folding, vitrified. H:5–6.

g. FAS:89 LiFe LMG1, f pops 1 0.28 E:scrpd, lightly brnshd, patt in FeO reddish gray, surfs gray w/ light cloud. I:scrpd dry. C:gray. H:4–5.

h. FAN:89 LiFe LMG1 0.34 E:scrpd, smthd, patt in FeO gray, surfs gray, patt nearly invisible. H:7.

i. FAS:84 LiFe LRMG1–2 0.45 E:scrpd, smthd, patt in FeO looks muddy white against dark gray surf. I:scrpd. C:red, gray subsurfs. H:5.

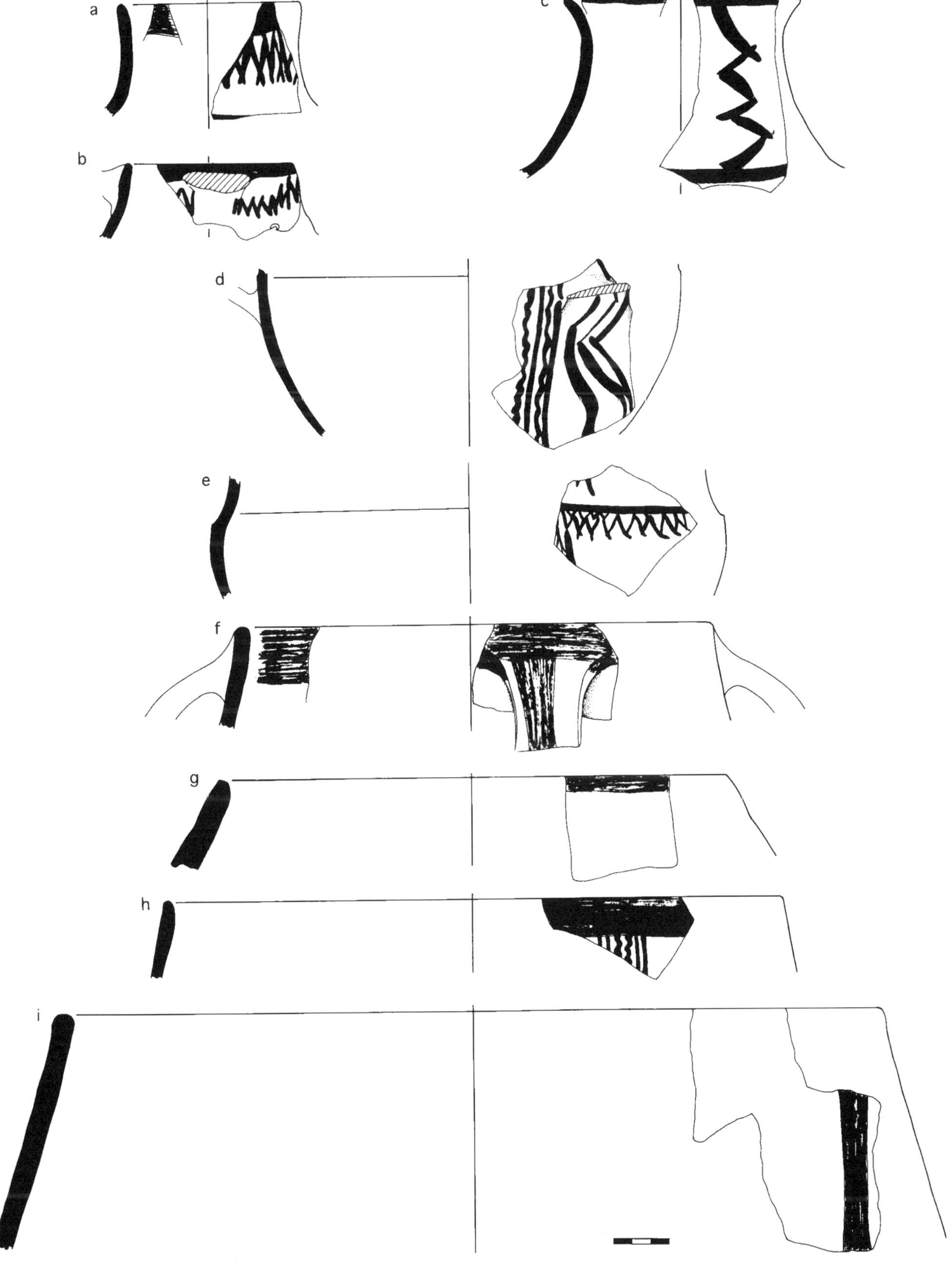
a
b
c
d
e
f
g
h
i

Figure 31 FCP 4.2 Lime plus Iron Pattern Painted variety

a. FAN:94 LiFe LMG1, pops 2 0.16 E:scrpd, smthd, patt in FeO red, surfs yellowish-tan. I:scrpd, pinkish. Sharp edges. H:2–3.

b. FAS:94 LiFe LMG1 0.18 E:scrpd, smthd, patt in FeO, reddish-gray, surfs tan. Looks as though collar broke off and pot finished as a bowl.

c. FAS:90 LiFe LMG1 0.18 E:scrpd, smthd, patt in FeO orange, nearly invisible under handle, surfs tan. I:scrpd, smthd, greenish-orange. C:gray. H:5.

d. FAS:91 LiFe LMG1, pops 2 0.19 E:scrpd but lumpy, smthd, few strokes brnsh at rim and base of handle, patt in FeO reddish-gray, tan surfs, handle barely attached at lower end. I:scrpd, well smthd. C:gray. H:3–4.

e. FAS:91+93S(3) LiFe RD1, seed impressions, pops 1–3 0.28 E:scrpd, light brnsh, patt in FeO red-orange, tan surfs. I:scrpd, lightly brnshd, tan. C:gray. Jagged edges. H:2–3.

f. FAS:84 LiFe LRD1, pops 1 0.11 E:scrpd, wet smthd, light brnsh, patt in FeO red, surfs greenish-tan. I:scrpd, wet smthd. C:gray, vitrified.

g. FAS:84 LiFe LDR<1 0.14 E:scrpd, light brnsh, patt in FeO blk, barely visible, grayish-tan surfs. I:scrpd, light brnsh. C:blue-gray. Sharp edges, raspy.

h. FAS:84 LiFe LMG1 0.21 E:scrpd, light brnsh, patt in FeO orangish-gray, tan surfs, patt nearly invisible. I:scrpd, smthd, FeO red stripe on rim, large hole drilled from both sides.

i. FAS:89 LiFe fL, RD1 0.30 E:scrpd, lumpy, smthd, light brnsh, patt in FeO reddish-gray, tan surfs w/ blk cloud at rim. I:well scrpd, lightly brnshd. C:gray. H:4.

j. FAS:93 LiFe RD1, pops 1 0.32 E:scrpd, wet smthd, minimal brnsh, patt in FeO. I:scrpd, smthd. C:gray.

k. FAS:91 LiFe RD1, pops 1–2 0.22 E:scrpd, smthd, light brnsh, patt in FeO dull reddish-gray, grayish surfs. I:scrpd, wet smthd. C:light gray. H:2–3.

l. FAN:95 LiFe LMG1 0.06 max Pinch pot or part of hollow figurine E:scrpd, light brnsh, patt in FeO reddish, gray surfs. I:scrpd. C:gray. H:2–3.

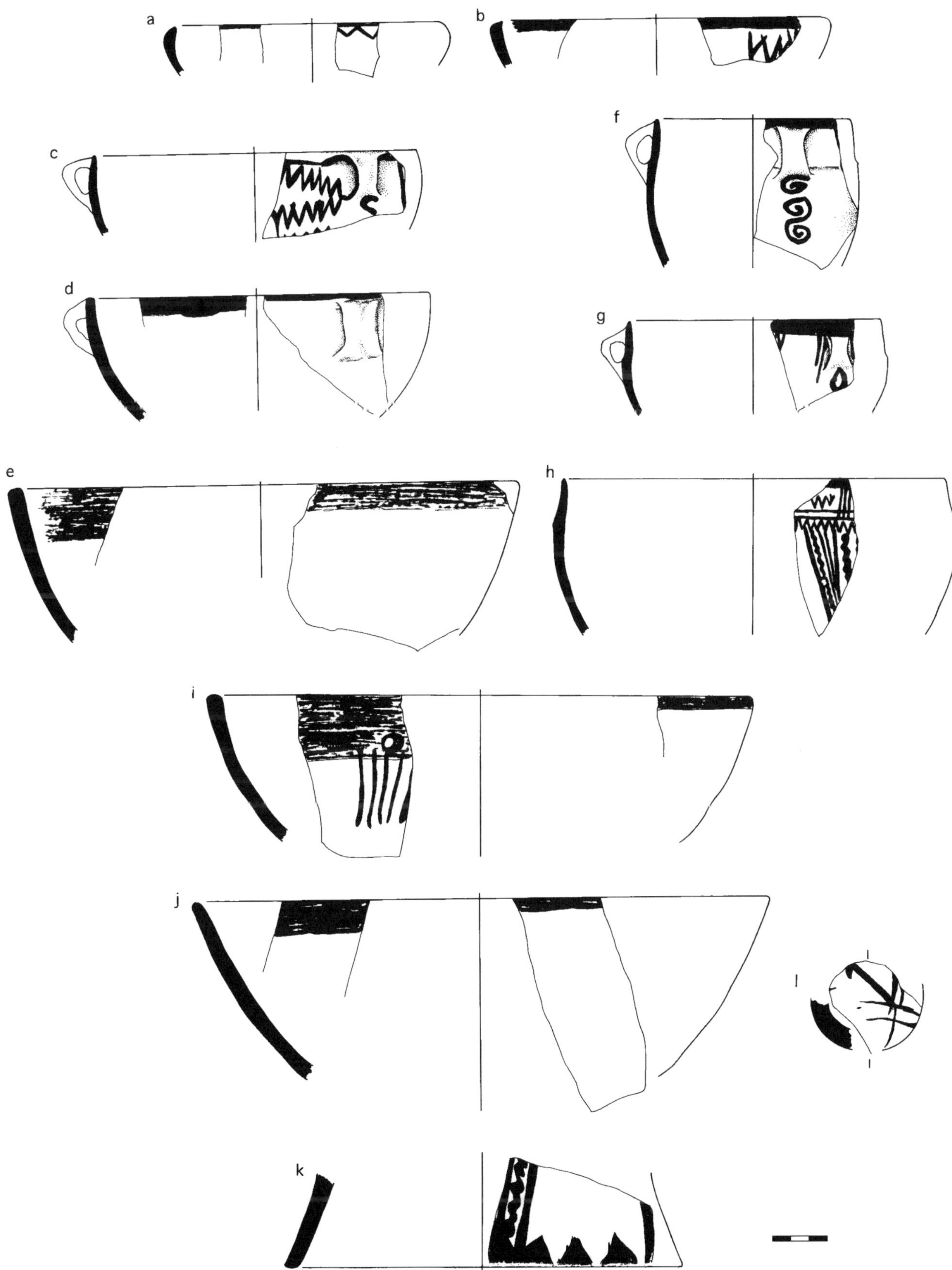
a
b
c
f
d
g
e
h
i
j
l
k

Figure 32 FCP 4.2 Low Lime Coarse and Calcite Coarse varieties

a. FAS:88 NoLiCo R3–4 0.16 E, I:scrpd but pebble grit gives lumpy appearance, damp brnshd, slight crazing int, mottled gray surfs. C:gray, reddish-brwn subsurfs. H:2–3.

b. FAS:91+90S+89S+88S+84S+82S+86N NoLiCo mD1 0.17 E, I:scrpd, finger smthd, pierced w/ multiple holes 0.5 cm below rim. C:gray, lighter surfs. Sherds from 88S and 84S burned after broke. H:2–3.

c. FAN:89 NoLiCo R1–2, oatmeal quality 0.15 E, I:scrpd, smthd, gray w/ reddish clouds. Rim nicked. H:2–3.

d. FAS:90 NoLiCo R1–2,L1, oatmeal quality 0.23 E, I:scrpd, light brnsh, dark w/ light cloud. H:2–3.

e. FAS:91 NoLiCo aRD4 0.30 E:scrpd, smthd, light brnsh, brwnish surfs, slight crackling. I:scrpd. C:dark gray, lighter subsurfs. H:4.

f. FAS:89 NoLiCo mR3–4, oatmeal quality 0.32 E, I:scrpd, smthd, brwnish-red ext, deep red int. H:2–3.

g. FAS:89 NoLiCo aRD2–3, oatmeal quality 0.31–32, irreg E, I:scrpd, smthd, uniform gray-blk. H:2–3.

h. FAN:86 CalCo C2R1–2 0.21 E, I:scrpd, smthd, dry brnshd, uniform tan. H:2–3.

i. FAS:92 CalCo C5 0.255 E, I:scrpd, wet smthd, ext light brnsh. H:2–3.

j. FAS:91 CalCo C1–2, pops 0.28 E, I:scrpd, smthd, light brnsh. C:gray, surfs gray, red cloud at rim. H:2–3.

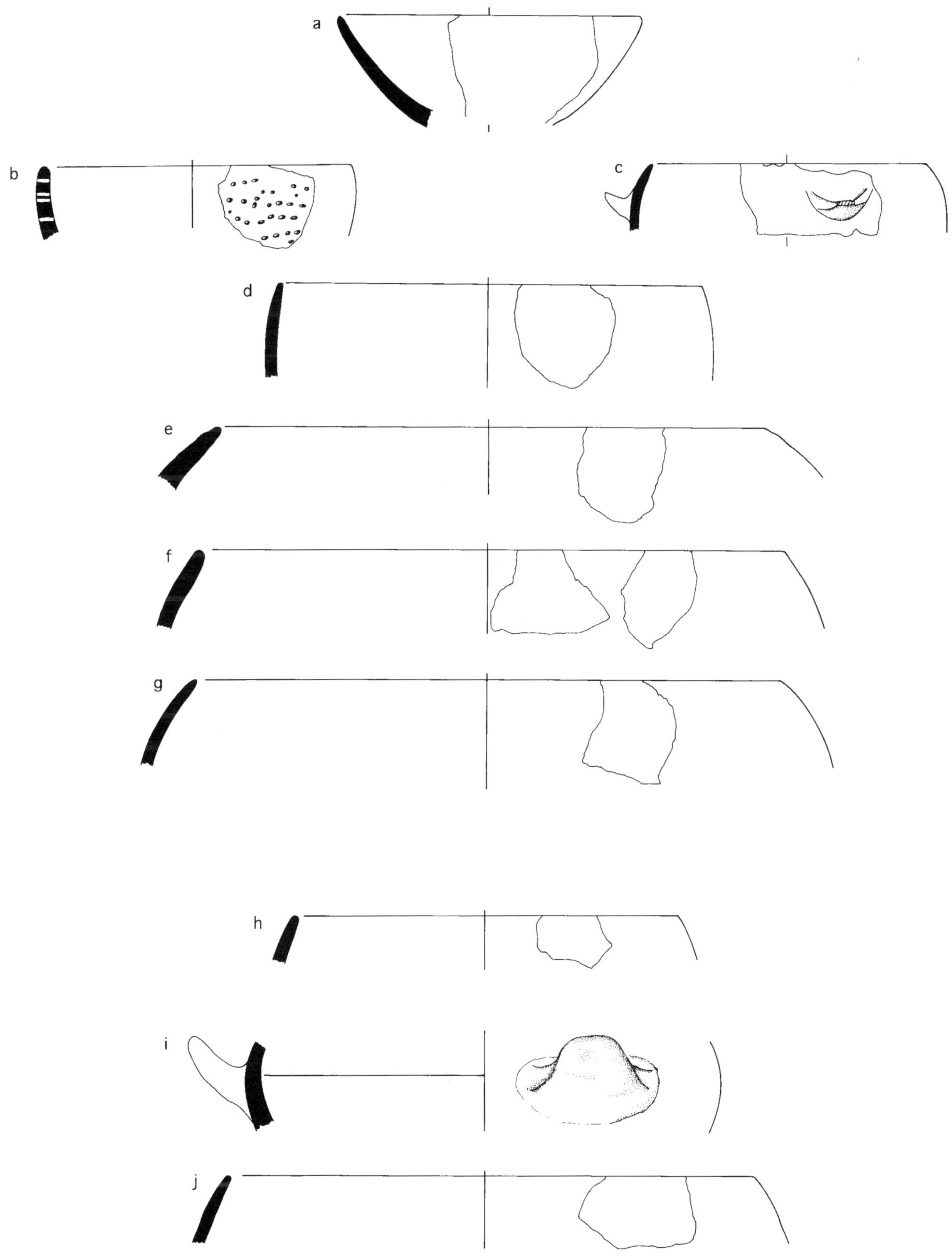
a
b
c
d
e
f
g
h
i
j

Figure 33 FCP 4.3 Andesite Burnished and No Lime Coarse varieties

a. FAS:83 AndB HBF1 0.14 E:scrpd, smthd, slipped, PB, reddish-blk, trace of handle below rim. I:scrpd, smthd, brnshd at rim. C:blue-gray. H:2–3.

b. FAN:86 AndB MDGB1–2 0.19 max E:scrpd, smthd, slipped, brnshd, waxy gray-green w/ reddish tinge, flaking. I:scrpd, smthd, lightly brnshd, dark gray. Jagged edges, sandy feel. H:2–3.

c. FAS:83 AndB HBF1 Top:scrpd, smthd, slipped, brnshd, blk w/ reddish tinge. U:scrpd, smthd, traces red slip not brnshd. Faint trace of white Lime on top of handle.

d. FAN:84 AndB HBF<1 0.22 E, I:scrpd, smthd, slipped, brnshd, waxy blk, 1 hole pierced pre-firing, start of another that does not penetrate. Tab is only on ext half of rim. C:brwn. H:2–3.

e. FAS:76 AndB HBF<1 0.22 E:scrpd, smthd, slipped, brnshd, worn, blk w/ reddish tinge, tail of lug or handle. I:missing original surf. C:gray, ext subsurf darker, poss burned. H:2–4.

f. FAS:83 AndB HB1 0.075 joint ca. half of joint preserved E, I:scrpd, smthd, slipped, brnshd, blk, PB int, traces of cutouts in ped. U:roughly scrpd. H:3–4.

g. FAS:83 AndB HBF1 0.18 E:scrpd, smthd, slipped, brnshd, grayish-green. I:scrpd, finger smthd, gray. C:reddish-brwn. H:2–3.

h. FAN:84 AndB HB1 0.30, irreg E:scrpd, smthd, slipped, brnshd, strip detached below rim from finger smthd surf, dark brwn. I:scrpd, slipped, damp brnsh. C:dark brwn. H:2–3.

i. FAS:81 NoLiCo R1–3 0.22 E:scrpd, smthd, light brnsh, pinkish. I:scrpd. H:2–3.

j. FAS:85 NoLiCo RD1–2, oatmeal quality 0.20 E:scrpd, smthd, light brnsh, dark surfs w/ light cloud at rim, trace of poss lug or handle. I:scrpd, wet smthd. Jagged edges. H:2–3.

k. FAS:83 NoLiCo SMG1, several FeO pebbles 5 0.30 E:scrpd, lumpy, smthd, lightly brnshd at rim, mottled grays. I:well scrpd, finger smthd. C:light yellow-brwn. H:2–3.

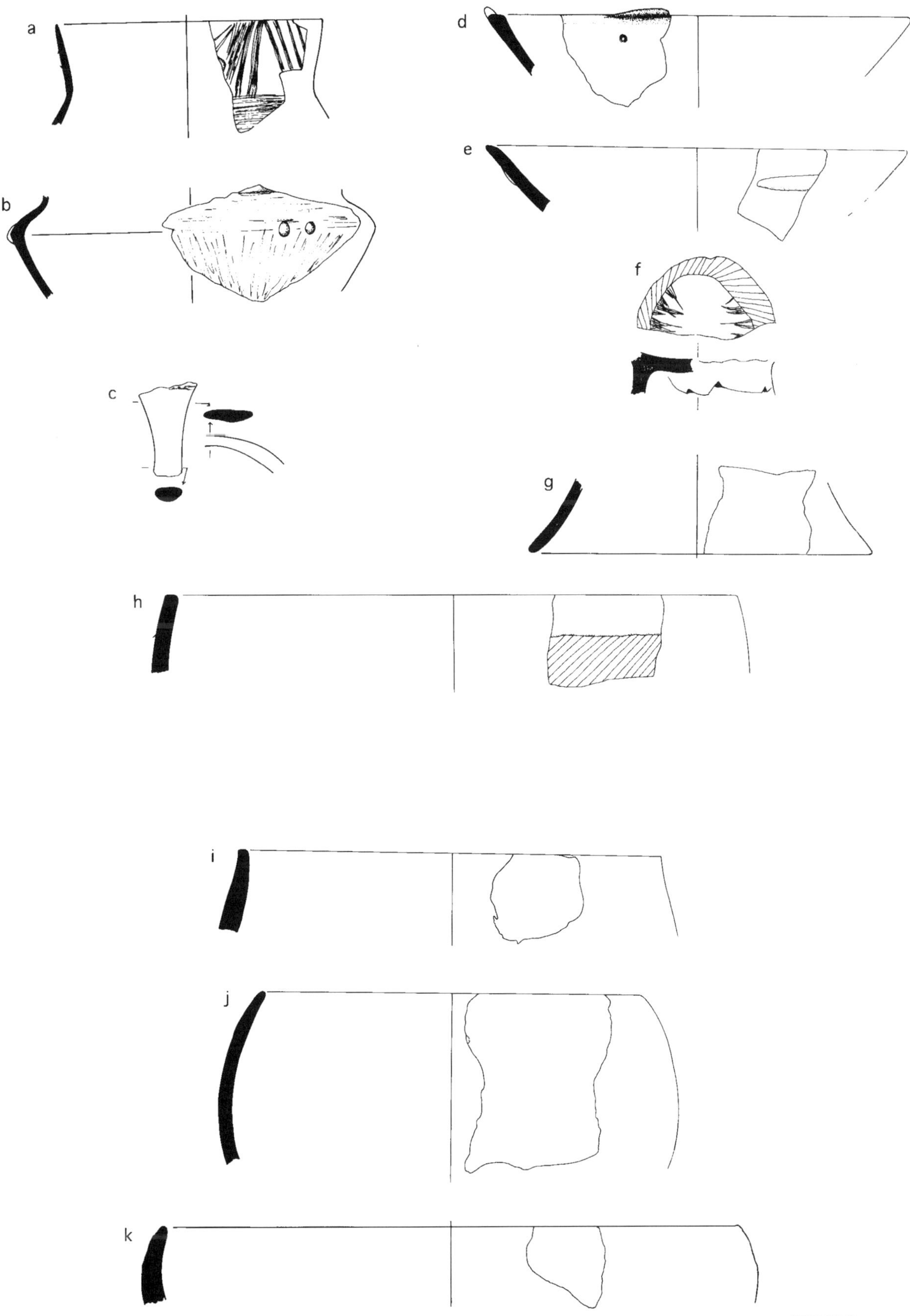
a
b
c
d
e
f
g
h
i
j
k

Figure 34 FCP 4.3 Lime plus Iron Pattern Painted and Plain varieties

a. FAS:81 LiFe LMG1, pops 2 0.10 E, I:scrpd, smthd, patt in FeO dull gray, tan surfs 2 holes pierced before firing, slightly asym.

b. FAS:86 LiFe RMG1–2 0.12 E, I:scrpd but lumpy, smthd, brnshd, tan surfs. H:2–3.

c. FAS:81 LiFe LRD1–2 0.13 each bowl E, I:scrpd, smthd, brnshd, pinkish-tan surfs. H:2–3.

d. FAN:87 FP 259 LiFe mrR1fl<1 0.07 7 sherds mended E, I:scrpd, smthd, light brnsh, worn int breaks layered. C:pink, surfs same. H:3–4.

e. FAS:83 LiFe rR,L1, pops 0.07 E:scrpd, smthd, patt in FeO pale orange, tan surfs. I:scrpd, smthd. H:2–3.

f. FAS:76 LiFe LMG1 0.06 E:scrpd but lumpy, smthd, clay smeared over cracked rim before patt in FeO, patt barely visible, surf worn and pitted. I:scrpd. H:3.

g. FAS:82 LiFe RD<1, L1, pops 0.14 E:scrpd, smthd, patt in FeO, pale reddish-gray, surfs tan. I:scrpd, extreme pitting, no original surfs preserved. Jagged edges. H:2–3.

h. FAS:83 FA Pot 40 LiFe LD1, many pops, powdery lime and holes 0.10 E:not scrpd, lumpy, smthd, patt in FeO, dark gray, gray surfs, patt visible only when wet, thickening at rim and shoulder for handle. I:smthd, lumpy, support clay under shoulder. C:dark gray, vitrified, poss burned. Raspy edges. H:5–6.

i. FAS:83 LiFe LMG1, pops 0.22 E:scrpd, finger smthd, patt in FeO grey with reddish tinge, surfs gray, prob burned. I:scrpd. C:gray, very sharp edges. H:4.

j. FAS:81 LiFe LR1–2 Top, U: smthd, brnshd, neat horn on top C:deep blue-gray, creamy pink subsurfs and surfs H:2–3.

k. FAS:83 FA Pot 41 LiFe ca. half of rim preserved LMG1–2, pops 0.10 E:scrpd, smthd, patt in FeO, sloppy blk, gray-green surfs, patt difficult to see. I:scrpd, grayish-brwn. H:5–6.

l. FAS:84 LiFe mLR1, pops Strap handle detached at joint one end, broken at other, smthd, patt in FeO, brnshd, orange pt, tan surfs.

m. FAS:83 LiFe fLMG1 0.40 max E:scrpd, smthd, brnshd, patt in FeO, blk, red in clouds, surfs tan. I:scrpd, wet smthd, int and edges covered with yellow and brwn stain. C:dark, vitrified. H:5–6.

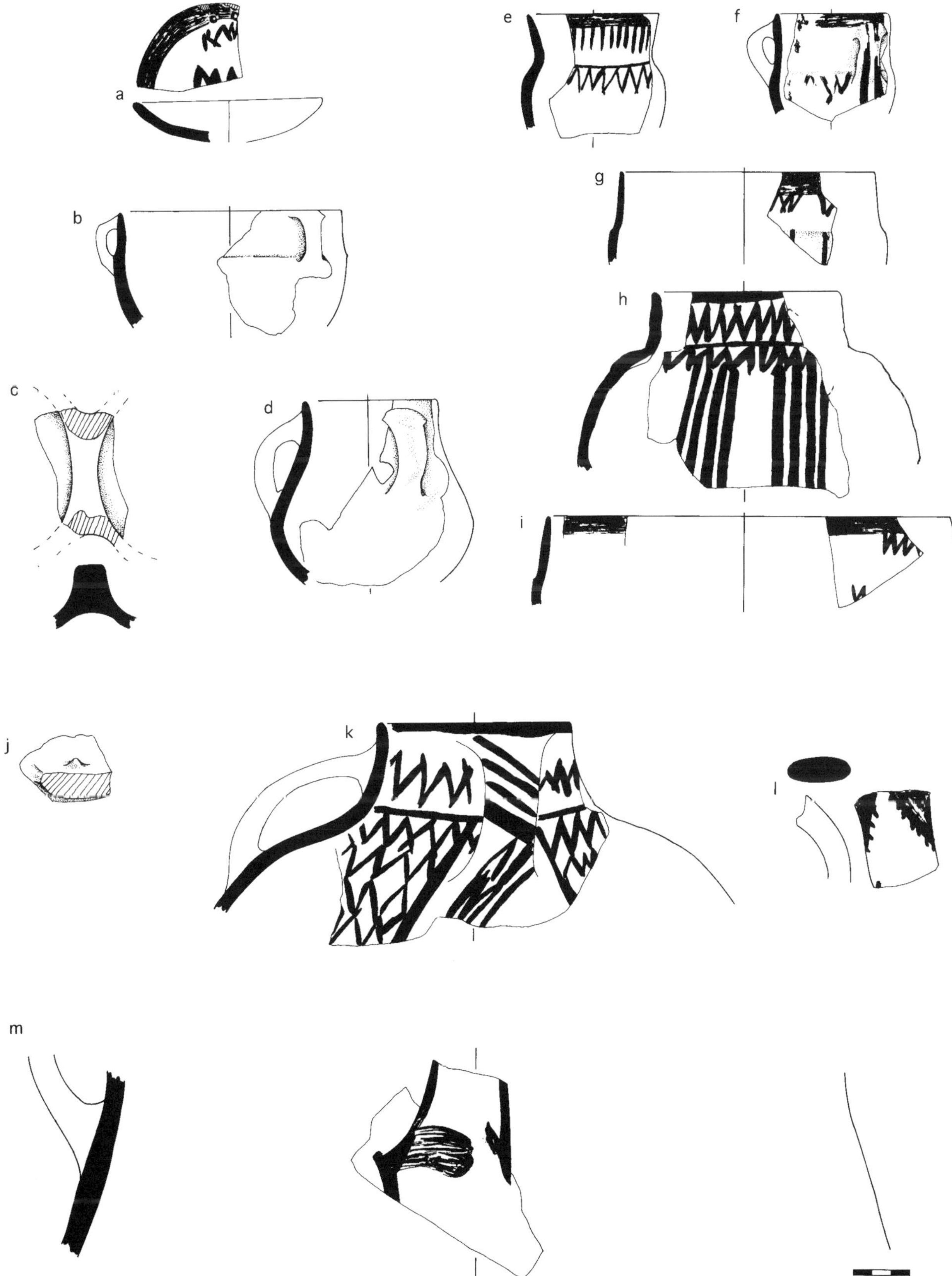
a
b
c
d
e
f
g
h
i
j
k
l
m

Figure 35 Andesite Burnished variety from poor contexts

a. Unstratified AndB H<1BD, silver mica glitter 0.18 joint E:scrpd, smthd, poss slipped, brnshd, ghost of patt on neck, poss below, pale gray. I:scrpd, brnshd at rim, darker gray. H:3–5.

b. FF1:15 FPSC 149 AndB HBF1 0.13 car E:scrpd, smthd, slipped, brnshd blk, waxy gloss, neat patt in granular grayish-white, slight wear. I:scrpd, slipped, brnshd, blk waxy, no gloss. C:gray at center, red subsurfs.

c. A Lot 14 AndB HBF1 0.12 E:scrpd, smthd, slipped, brnshd, blk at joint, red cloud below, detached at joint. I:scrpd, gray. C:gray. Worn down to new edge after broke.

d. FF1:19 AndB 0.16 E:scrpd, smthd, slipped, brnshd, waxy blk. I:same w/ single PB stroke.

e. FF1:15 AndB HBF1 0.16 E, I:scrpd, smthd, slipped, brnshd, worn, ext poss reused for scraping:covered w/ vert scratches.

f. A Lot 14 AndB HBF1 0.22 E, I:scrpd, smthd, slipped, brnshd, was waxy blk w/ reddish tinge, most original surf gone, small worn pellet on handle C:gray at center, reddish brwn subsurfs.

g. A Lot 15 AndB HFB1 0.085 max E:scrpd, smthd, slipped, brnshd blk. I:scrpd. Car w/ applied spout, pierced before firing through spout and wall.

h. G1:8+10+11+FF1:24 FP 110 AndB HBF1, pebble 5 0.30 RIP ca. 1/6 of pot w/ full profile preserved E:scrpd, smthd, slipped, brnshd hor, shallow troughs, waxy blk w/ reddish tinge. I:scrpd, smthd, slipped, PB began by bisecting from rim to rim, 2–3 strokes per line, red (10R 6/8) over much of int w/ blk tinges. H:3–4. Pl. 3b.

i. Unstratified FPSC 153 AndB HBF1 0.29 E:scrpd hor, grooves evident, smthd, slipped, scribbly vert brnsh, nearly PB effect, blk-red-tan, red grains of pigment visible where not brnshd. I:scrpd, smthd, slipped, brnshd, worn esp at bott near joint. C:reddish-brwn. H:3–4.

j. A Lot 14 AndB HBF1 0.34 E, I:scrpd, smthd, slipped, brnshd, worn, only flecks of original surf, gray-reddish-blk, large drill hole from int, applied pellet on ext.

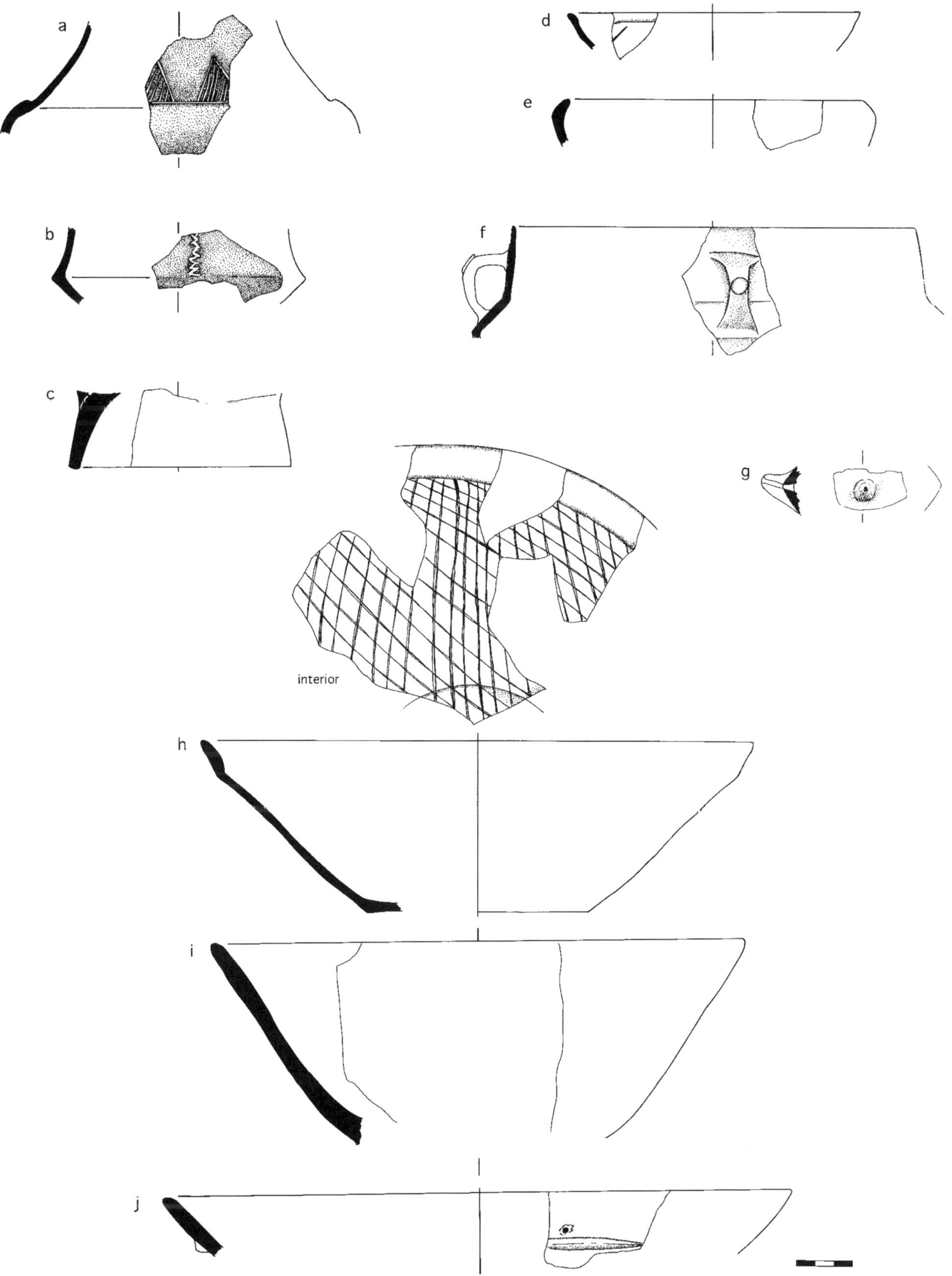
a
b
c
d
e
f
g
interior
h
i
j

Figure 36 Ungritted Manganese Painted variety from poor contexts

a. FF1:19 UgrMn D<1,voids 0.15 E:scrpd, smthd, patt in th powdery MnO, brwn-blk, prob brnshd, yellow surfs. I:scrpd below MnO stripe at rim. C:yellow, pink subsurfs.

b. A Lot 16 UgrMn no clear grits 0.18 E:scrpd, smthd, patt in MnO, brwn blk where th, most is pale silvery ghost, prob brnshd. I:scrpd, 1 cm MnO stripe at rim.

c. A Lot 16 UgrMn fD<1, slits and voids 0.20 E:scrpd, smthd, patt in fine lines of MnO, brwn-blk, surfs yellow-green. I:scrpd, smthd.

d. A:11 FPSC 184 UgrMn fD<1 0.10, bent E:scrpd, smthd, patt in th MnO, except on bott edge handle where silvery ghosts, greenish surfs. I:scrpd, MnO stripe at rim.

e. A:10 UgrMn fFeO2 0.18 neck E:scrpd, smthd, patt in MnO, brwn-blk, brnshd. I:scrpd. C:pink, yellow subsurfs and surfs, poss vitrified.

f. FF1:23 FPSC 183 UgrMn fD<1 0.12 E:scrpd, smthd, patt in MnO, blk, surfs so pale greenish-white looks like plaster. One side of rim thicker than other.

g. FF1:15 UgrMn fL<1, poss seed hole penetrates whole th 0.16 max Mended w/ gomma lacca, re-broken E:scrpd, smthd, patt in MnO, blk, powdery, no trace where gone, brnshd, surfs yellow. I:scrpd, yellow surfs. C:blue at center, yellow subsurfs.

h. A:10 FPSC 188 UgrMn fDL<1, fD1–2 0.13 max E:scrpd, smthd, patt in MnO, brwn-blk, th in spots, elsewhere silvery ghost, brnshd, surfs yellowish-green. I:scrpd, yellowish-green. C:blue gray center, pink subsurfs.

i. FF1:20 UgrMn LR nodules1, mica glitter 0.15 max E:scrpd, smthd, patt in MnO, brwn-blk, prob brnshd, yellowish-pink surfs. I:scrpd. C:blue center, yellowish-pink subsurfs. Thicker than most Ugr, slightly asym near handle scar.

j. FF1:18 UgrMn fLD1 0.19 max E:scrpd, smthd, patt in MnO, brwn-blk, prob brnshd, flaking, surf pinkish. I:scrpd, pinkish. C:blue where th.

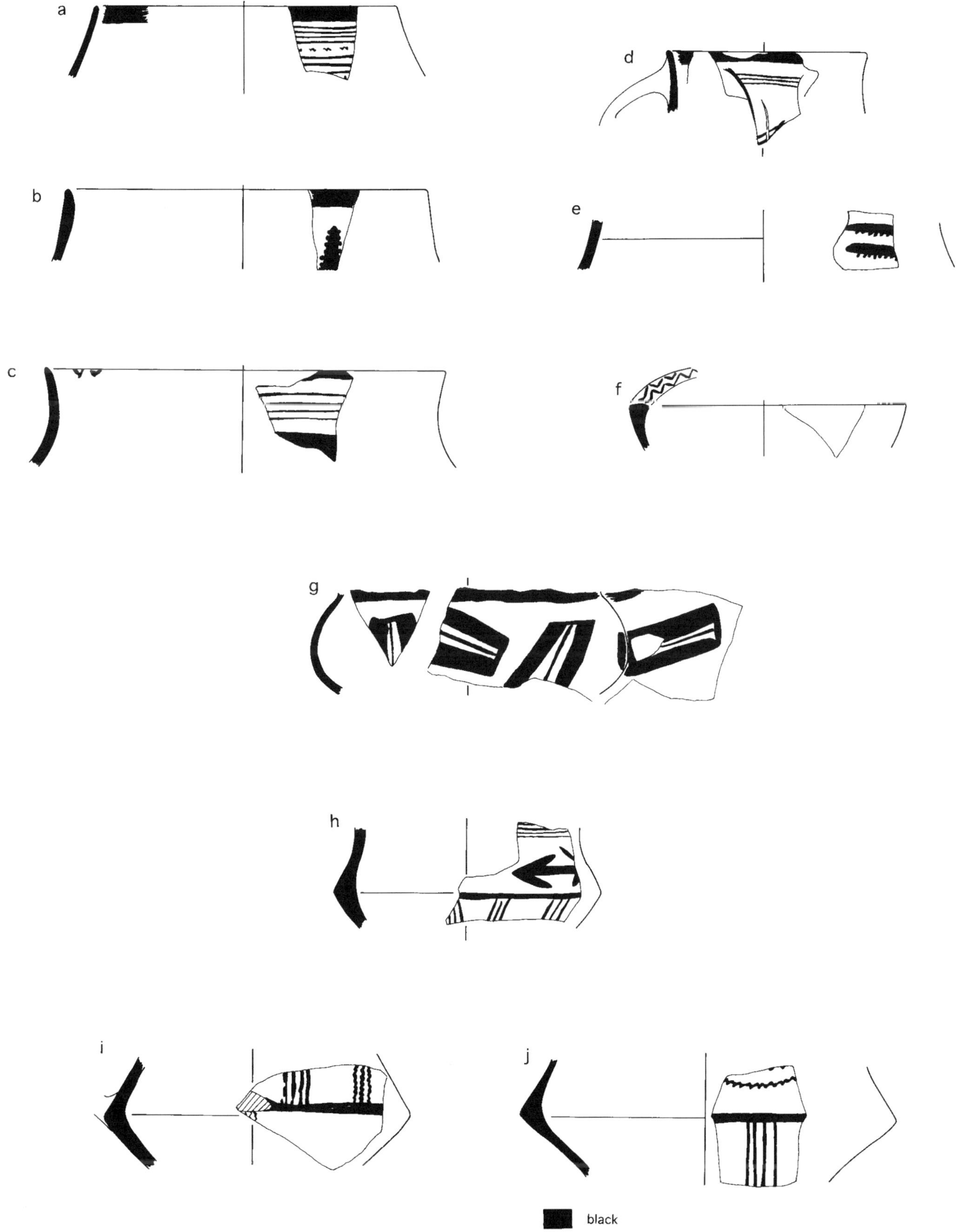
a
b
c
d
e
f
g
h
i
j
black

Figure 37 Manganese Painted varieties from poor contexts

a. A Lot 16 MnPtd LMG<1, silver mica glitter 0.18 E:scrpd, smthd, patt in MnO, brwn-blk, surfs pinkish. I:scrpd, prob brnshd, yellowish surfs. C:yellowish. Sharp edges. H:4–5.

b. Unstratified FPSC 186 MnPtd L1–2, B<1, mica glitter 0.20–0.21, irreg E:scrpd, smthd, patt in MnO, blk, prob brnshd, surfs pinkish. I:scrpd, MnO stripe on rim, brnshd, pinkish. C:light gray, poss vitrified.

c. Unstratified FPSC 185 MnPtd LDMG1, mica glitter 0.16, irreg E, I:scrpd, smthd, patt in MnO (poss blk-fired FeO), blk, brnshd, pinkish surf, harder than most.

d. A Lot 16 MnPtd fLrR that fall out 0.20 E:scrpd, smthd, patt in MnO, brwn blk, prob brnshd, surfs tan. I:scrpd only (poss pedestal), hole drilled largely from int, finished on ext. C:light gray center. H:2–3.

e. A:30 FP 64 MnPtd mLR<1 0.19 max E:scrpd, smthd, patt in granular MnO, gray, brnshd, pale tan surfs. I:scrpd, smthd, brnshd. H:3–4.

f. G1:5 MnPtd LMG1, pops, pits 3 0.30 E:scrpd but still lumpy, smthd, patt in MnO, brwn-blk but largely gone, brnshd, pitted, edge of joint preserved. I:scrpd, smthd, patt in MnO, ghost only, barely visible patt, heavily pitted.

g. A Lot 16 MnPtd mLMG1, mica glitter, pops, pits1 0.09 joint E:scrpd, smthd, patt in MnO, gray, neat lines, brnshd but no troughs except in joint and around cutout. I:scrpd, smthd, worn free of original surf but traces MnO patt remain. U:scrpd, neat tooling marks at joint. H:5–6.

h. FA QSE+EB:43 FPSC 187 MnPtd LMG1–2, mica glitter 0.35 max E:scrpd, smthd, patt in MnO, gray, flaking, brnshd, yellowish. I:scrpd, poss wear, yellowish. C:gray center, pinkish subsurfs, yellowish surfs. Sandy edges. H:3–4.

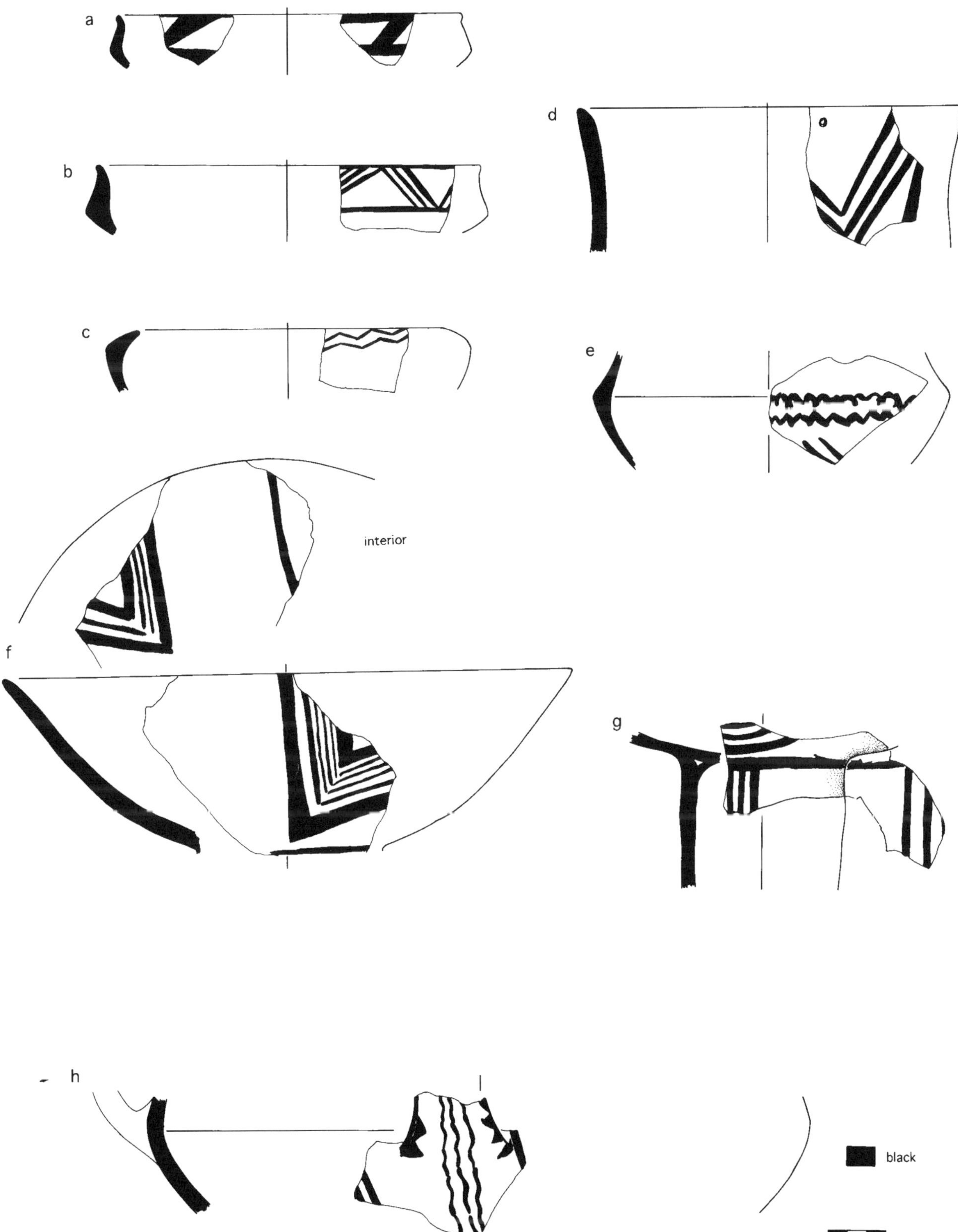
a
b
c
d
e
interior
f
g
h
black

Figure 38 Gray Burnished variety from poor contexts

a. A Lot 14 GrayB fL1 0.10 E, I:scrpd, smthd, brnshd, light gray surfs, v. small handle. C:lighter gray. Sharp edges. H:4–5.

b. Unstratified GrayB fD, if any 0.14 E, I:scrpd, smthd, brnshd several times, glossy gray. C:same gray as surfs. H:4–6.

c. A Lot 16 GrayB MG<1 0.13 4 joining E:scrpd, smthd, brnshd, gray. I:scrpd, darker gray. C:uniform gray. H:5–6.

d. A Lot 16 FP 73 GrayB LMG<1 0.16 max E:scrpd, smthd, applied knobs on belly, patt ghosts on neck and joint, trace of white pt in slight groove at joint, gray, crack at neck joint as though scrpd too thin. I:scrpd, poss brnshd, very light gray, bott to max diam is heavily worn, strange crack or hole in bott. C:same gray as ext. Sharp edges. H:3–4.

e. A Lot 14 GrayB fL<1 0.17 max E, I:scrpd, smthd, brnshd, light gray. C:lighter gray. Sharp edges, poss vitrified. H:4–5.

f. A Lot 14 GrayB fLD<1, voids 0.25, irreg E: scrpd, smthd, brnshd, gray. I:scrpd, smthd, depressions in neat row along interior of lip, brnshd. C:lighter gray.

g. Unstratified GrayB mLD<1 0.30, irreg E, I:scrpd, smthd, brnshd, worn on int, gray, slightly lighter on int. C:greenish-gray. H:2–3.

h. A:11 GrayB fMG1 0.20 E, I:scrpd, smthd, brnshd, completely uniform gray surfs and core. H:2–3.

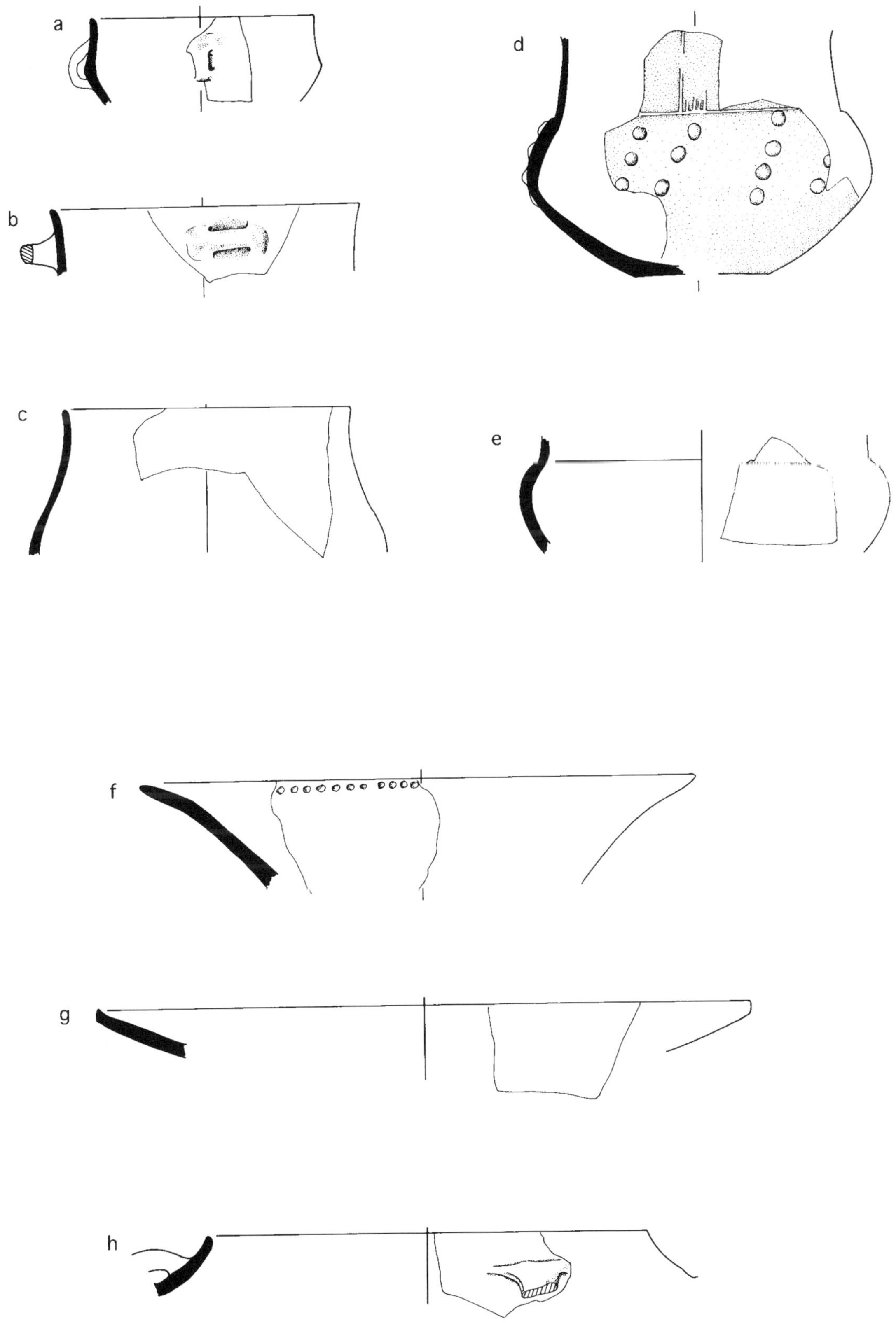
a
b
c
d
e
f
g
h

Figure 39 Lime plus Iron Pattern Painted variety from poor contexts

a. A:16 FP 72 LiFe LRD1, pops 3 0.20 E:scrpd, smthd, cursory brnsh, patt in FeO, blk, reddish at rim, surfs gray green to tan. Handle detached from unscrpd surf, hole drilled from ext below rim. I:scrpd, smears of mend clay below drill hole suggest cracked before firing, rim folded to int. C:gray, int surf pink. Wear on int edges suggests used in sherd form. H:2–3.

b. A:16 LiFe rD2, L<1 0.14 neck E:scrpd, smthd, patt inFeO, reddish, pinkish surfs. I:scrpd. C:gray to int half, pinkish tan subsurf on int. H:2–3.

c. A:14 LiFe mL2, powdery E, I:smthd, patt in FeO, red-blk, surfs light, small horn near top of handle.

d. A:30 FP 57 LiFe LMG1, pops 2–3 0.42–0.44 max E:scrpd, smthd, damp brnshd, patt in FeO, red-gray, surfs tan w/ blk and red clouds. I:scrpd, deep gouges, gray. H:2–3.

a
b
c
d

Figure 40 Lime plus Iron Pattern Painted variety from poor contexts

a. A:14 FP 71 LiFe LrR1, pops 2, especially on int 0.18 E:scrpd, smthd, patt in FeO, pale red, crackling and flaking, surfs tan. I:scrpd, smthd, light damp brnshd, troughs clear. Sharp edges, poss vitrified. H:5.

b. A:14+15 FP 70 LiFe LrR1, pops 2, 1 cm R in break 0.19 Poss same pot as FP 71, above E:scrpd, smthd, damp brnshd, patt in FeO red-gray, dull, crackling, surfs tan, shoulder ridge very irreg. I:scrpd, smthd, damp brnshd, clear troughs, tan surf w/ patch of orange in over-fired/burned area at rim. H:6. Jacobsen 1973b:Pl. 51a; 1969:Pl. 98a.

c. FF1:11 FPSC 155 LiFe LD1, irreg distributed, pits 1–2 0.20, irreg E:scrpd, smthd, damp brnshd, patt in FeO, pale orange barely visible on pinkish surf. I:scrpd, smthd, brnshd, greenish-gray at bott. C:blue-gray to int, pink to ext.

d. FF1:11 FPSC 154 LiFe LDMG1–2 0.16, irreg 5 joining E:scrpd, smthd, damp brnshd, patt in FeO, dusty reddish-gray, pt thicker and more clear on left, runnier and thinner as move to right, surfs tan, heavily pitted. I:scrpd, damp brnshd, worn. C:gray at center. Pl. 5a.

e. Unstratified LiFe fL1 E, I:smthd, patt in FeO, red-blk, tan surfs, small applied horn, one end detached at joint, quality of clay suggests attached very wet. C:blue-gray, surfs tan. H:6.

f. A Lot 14 LiFe mL2, pits 0.16, irreg or asym E:scrpd but lumpy, smthd, patt in FeO, dull blk, crackling, greyish-tan surfs, poss scar of asym ring base, detached from smthd surf, taller and w/ sharper curve on right. I:scrpd more evenly, smthd, light brnsh, stripe at rim, tabs uneven and lumpy. C:gray-green at center, light subsurfs, grayish surfs.

g. FA QSE+EB:34 FP 144 LiFe LRD1–2, f pops 0.12 E:lumpy, damp brnshd, clear troughs. I:scrpd, damp brnshd, patt in FeO, red-orange to gray, clouds/burned: end of handle is greenish-gray, surfs pinkish to gray. C:gray. Jagged edges. H:4–6.

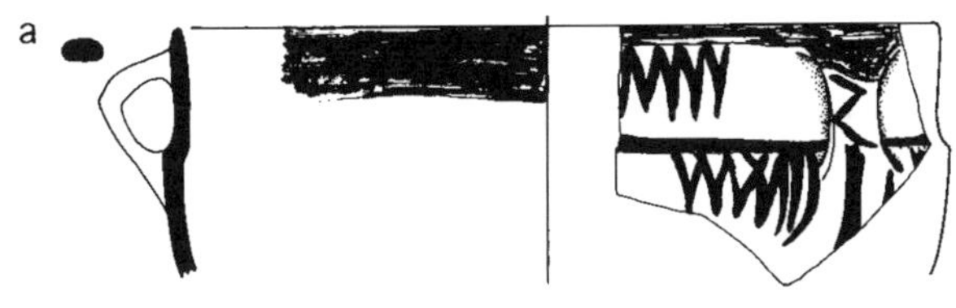
a

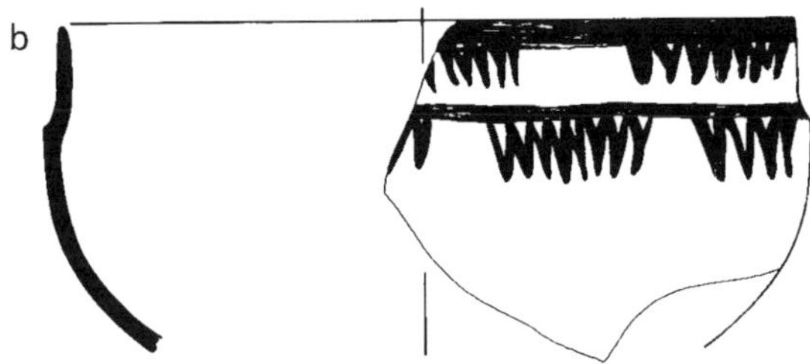
b

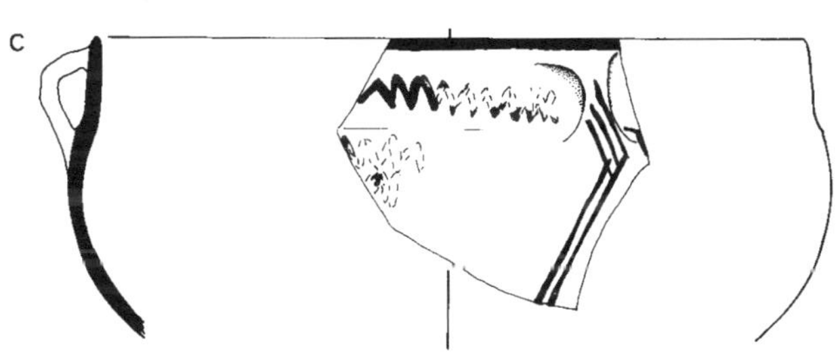
c

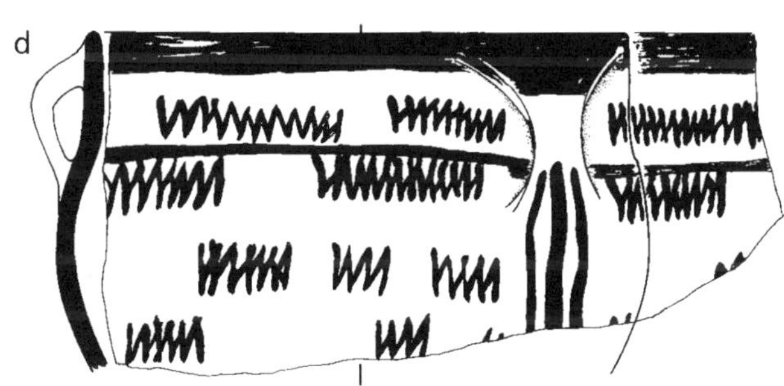
d

e

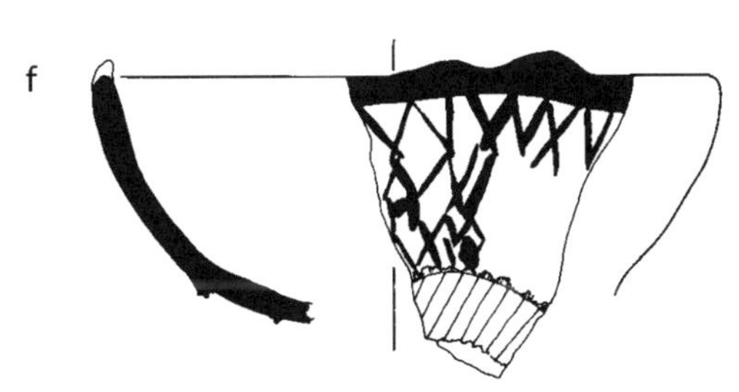
f

g

Figure 41 Lime plus Iron Pattern Painted variety from poor contexts

a. A Lot 16 LiFe LR1 pops 1 0.10.12, irreg E:scrpd, smthd, brnshd, patt in FeO, red, surfs tan, protrusion above rim is more substantial than a pellet, rim curves out at break. I:scrpd, smthd, brnshd, tan. C:gray. H:2–3.

b. G:11 LiFe LMG<1 0.16 E:scrpd, smthd, patt in FeO, blk, brnshd, slight luster, tan surfs. I:scrpd, smthd, brnshd but less well than ext.

c. A Lot 15 LiFe LMG1 pops 2 0.16, irreg E:scrpd, smthd, damp brnshd, patt in FeO, red to blk, surfs yellowish tan. I:scrpd, smthd, damp brnshd. C:red. H:3–4.

d. A:31 FP 60 LiFe LMG1 pops 2 0.22 E:scrpd, smthd, brnshd, patt in FeO, brwn where thin, blk where thick, surfs light grayish-tan, two relief pellets on rim. I:scrpd, smthd, dry brnshd, grayish-tan. C:grayish-green, voids, slightly vitrified. H:4–6.

e. A Lot 16 FP 75 LiFe LRD1, mica glitter, pops 2 0.25–30, irreg E:scrpd, smthd, tan w/ cloud. I:scrpd, smthd, patt in FeO, gray-blk to reddish gray, brnshd, surfs tan, small pellet on rim. C:gray where th. H:2–3.

f. FF1:11 FP 109 LiFe LRD1–2, pits 0.15–0.16, irreg/asym RIP Almost complete E:lumpy, smthd, patt in FeO, very pale red, barely visible, patt repeats 4 time. I:scrpd, smthd, light brnsh, worn at bott, several sherds burned after broke, stripe at rim is red on burned gray sherds, invisible on light/oxidized sherds. Lip is wavy and uneven, light car not present all the way around. H:2–3.

g. A Lot 16 FPSC 159 LiFe LSMG1 pops 2–3 0.17–0.18, irreg 5 joining, complete profile preserved E:scrpd but lumpy, smthd, patt in FeO, dark gray, crackling, surfs gray-green. I:scrpd, smthd. Bott is off center, not flat. C:lighter gray. H:4–5.

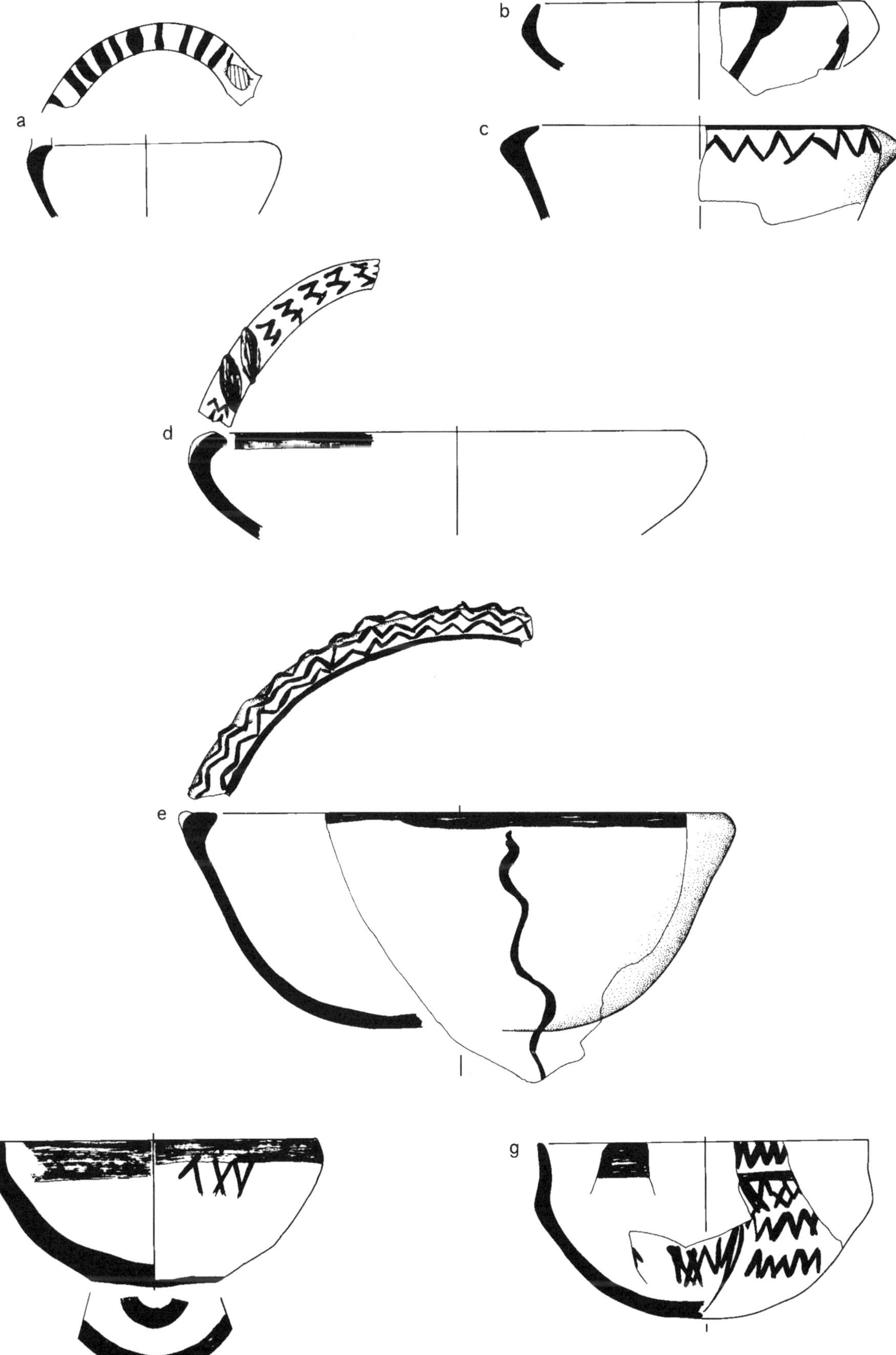
a
b
c
d
e
f
g

Figure 42 Lime plus Iron Pattern Painted variety from poor contexts

a. A:15 LiFe LR1 pops 1–2 0.36 4 joining E:lumpy, wet smthd, pink surfs, cloud one side. I:scrpd, smthd, damp brnshd, patt in FeO, irreg lines w/ trailers, reddish, crackling, worn away in spots, hor stress crack int. C:uniform light. Profile and th vary. H:2–3.

b. A:30 FP 4 LiFe LRD1 pits 2 0.35 E:scrpd, smthd, patt in FeO, red, surfs tan, traces of cutouts in ped, very th walls, stripe around joint made w/ 5 overlapping strokes. I:scrpd, smthd, slipped over entire int, red, crackled, soot stains. H:2–3

c. FF1:20 LiFe LMG1, pops 2 0.29 E, I:scrpd, smthd, poss brnshd, patt in FeO, blk-brwn, slight luster, surfs greenish-gray. C:uniform light.

d. FF1:11 LiFe LRD1 pits1–2 0.08 joint E:scrpd, smthd, lightly brnshd, patt in FeO, dull red-orange, surfs pale pink. I:scrpd, smthd, damp brnshd, broad streaky red stripe in FeO, surf greenish-gray, center bowl worn, stress crack through wall. U:rough, poss mend clay around stress crack, pale gray w/ splotch of crackling red pt, finger groove along joint, below is lumpy w/ finger impressions from pinching.

e. Unstratified LiFe LMG1 pops 1 0.06 joint E:scrpd, smthd, damp brnshd, patt in FeO, dark, slight luster. I:worn smth, pitted, orange-greenish-gray surf. U:clay added and smeared to secure joint. H:6.

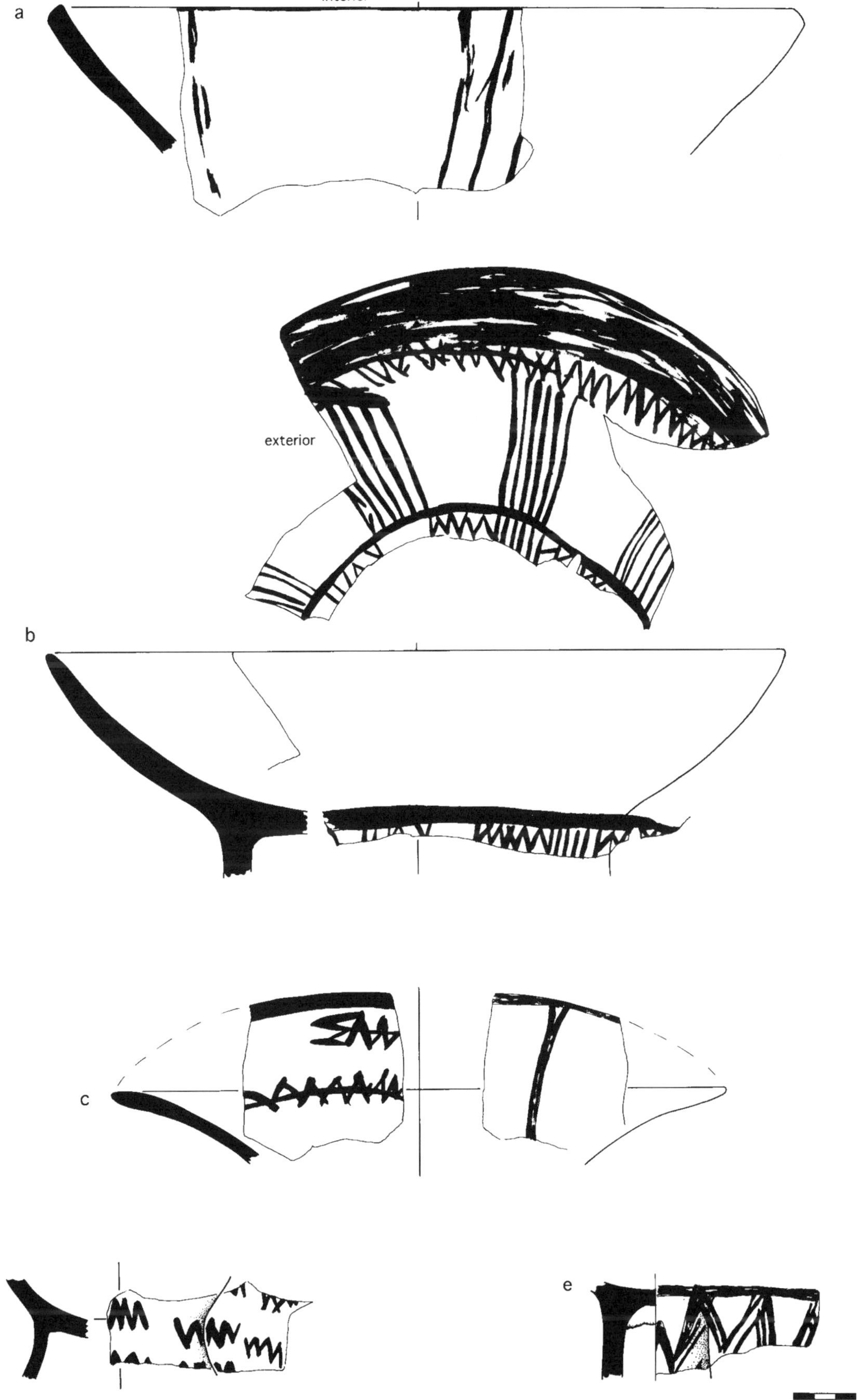
interior
a
exterior
b
c
d
e

Figure 43 FCP 5.1a Cave assorted surface Finishes

a. FAS:76 fL,RMG<1, 1rR4 0.24 E, I:scrpd, wet smthd, a few scribbly brnsh strokes, pinkish tan surfs. C:blk. H:2–3.

b. FAS:76 mSMG1,fl 0.20–0.25, irreg E:lumpy, poss seed impressions. I:well scrpd, uniformly gray-green. Pumicy edges. H:2–3.

c. FAS:76 LDMG2 pops 0.21 E:scrpd, poss slip, lightly brnshd, crackling, mottled surfs. I:well scrpd. C:dark gray. H:3–4.

d. FAS:79 LR1, blk voids from vegetal inclusions 0.37 E:scrpd, smthd, few damp scribbles up to handle, 2 applied bands added after handle, finger impressed, red surfs (5YR5/6). I:scrpd, hor scribbly damp brnsh. H:2–3.

e. FAS:76 maMG1–2, fL, mica glitter 0.35 E:scrpd, wet smthd, patt in FeO, dull red, crackling, surfs reddish w/ clouds, grassy impression on surf. I:most of surface missing, brwnish-gray. C:blue-gray. H:2–3.

f. FAS:76 aDR2MG1, fL 0.38–0.40, irreg E:scrpd, smthd, damp brnshd, red surfs. I:scrpd, wet smthd, light brnshd, pitted from grit pulling out H:2–3.

g. FAN:73 DMG1 0.45 E:scrpd, smthd, applied bands, gray surfs w/ light cloud I:scrpd, smthd, very even surf, red. C:dark gray. H:2–3.

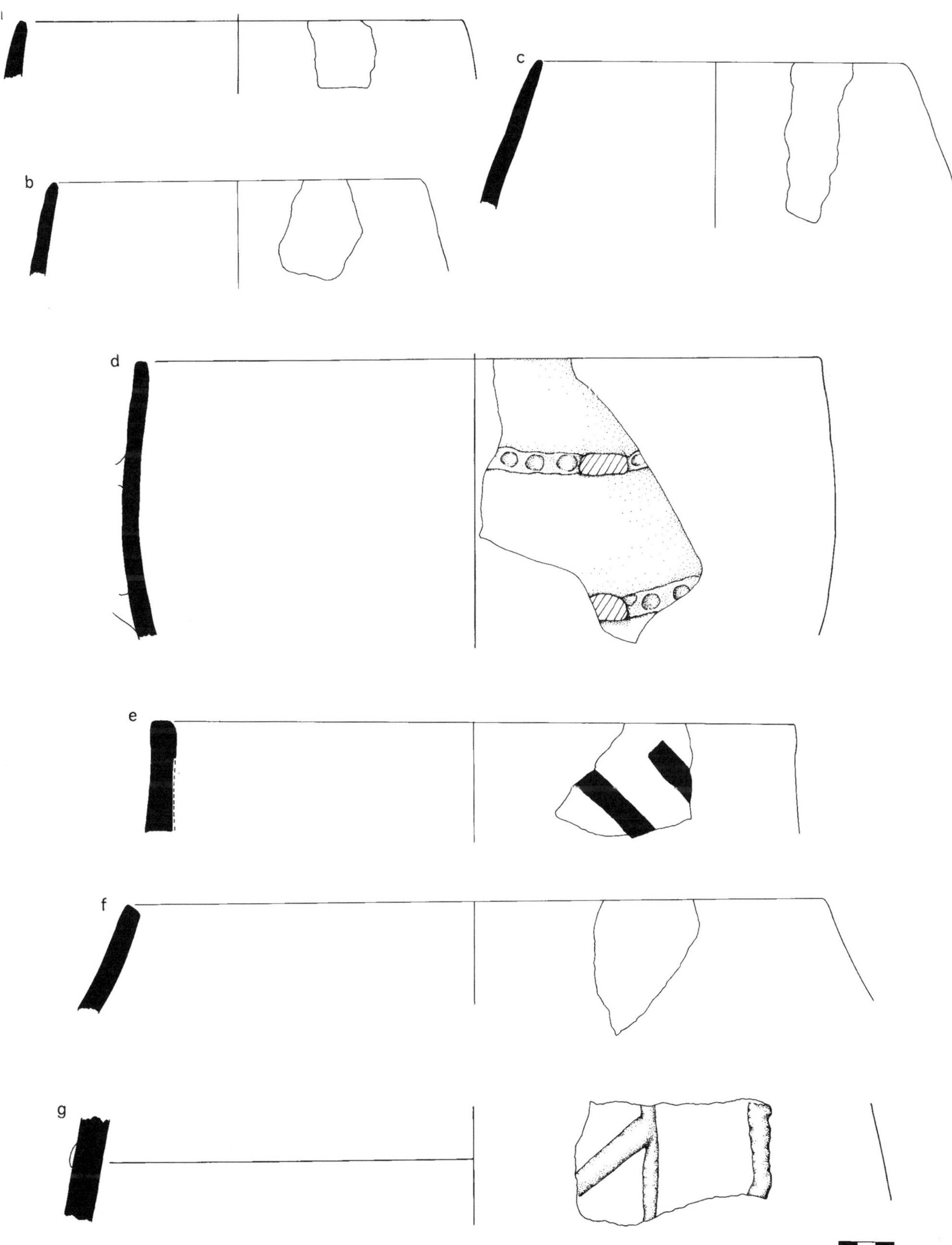

b
c
d
e
f
g

Figure 44 FCP 5.1a Cave assorted surface finishes

a. FAS:76 White mRD<1 0.19 E, I:scrpd, smthd, poss light brnsh, surfs grayish-white (10YR 8/2), both surfs crackling slightly. H:2–3.

b. FAS:76 fL, RD1 0.19 E, I:scrpd, smthd, damp brnshd, clear troughs, pale tan surfs, traces bluish-red powder (7.5R 5/8) both surfs, poss patt ext. C:blue-gray center, red-brwn subsurfs. H:2–3.

c. FAS:79 RDMG<1 0.21 E:scrpd, slipped, PB, red. I:scrpd, slipped, hor brnsh. H:2–3.

d. FAS:82 fL1–2 0.19 E:scrpd, slipped, PB, dark gray, arc on rim suggests area between two tabs, traces red powder. I:scrpd, smthd, PB, very pale, traces red powder. C:dark gray to ext, pale to int. H:2–3.

e. FAS:79 fL, DMG1–2, 4 mm piece of sherd (poss grog), 5mm L near rim 0.21 E:scrpd, smthd, shallow troughs, faint traces two red crackling hor stripes, blk surf. I:well scrpd, trace red pt, mostly worn off, lightly brnshd, light piecrust rim w/ traces red pt in depressions. C:dark gray. H:3–4.

f. FAS:76 MG<1fL, L pebble 2mm, pits on surfs from vegetal inclusions 0.14 E, I:scrpd, smthd, few strokes of dry brnshd, better on int than ext , mottled grays and brwns. C:dark gray. H:2–3.

g. FAN:73 rRWG1 0.21 E, I:scrpd, cursory damp brnshd. Tan ext w/ blk cloud at rim, more pink int, traces red powder (10R 6/6) on int, edge of handle or lug. C:dark gray. H:2–3.

h. FAS:76 maDR1, f<1L 0.24–0.25, irreg E, I:scrpd thin walls and regular, smthd, lightly brnshd, pink surfs w/ creamy quality ext, brwn int, traces red, poss white Lime powder int. C:blk, light subsurfs. Jagged edges. H:2–3.

i. FAS:77+FAN:70 aLD1, frR3–4, holes on surfs from vegetal/grass inclusions 0.32, irreg E, I:scrpd, wet smthd, lightly brnshd, better int than ext, int blk w/ light cloud at rim, ext striped from clouds:blk at rim, orange below, then gray. H:2–3.

j. FAS:79 LRMG1 0.30, irreg and lumpy E, I:poss scrpd int, not ext, damp brnshd both, gray-brwn surfs, piecrust ridges made w/ tip of long fingernails. Red grains give red glow to whole when wet. C:blk. H:2–3.

k. FAN:73 fL,MG1 0.31 irreg E, I:scrpd but lumpy, smthd, few strokes brnshd, mottled grays and brwns, lighter ext. H:2–3.

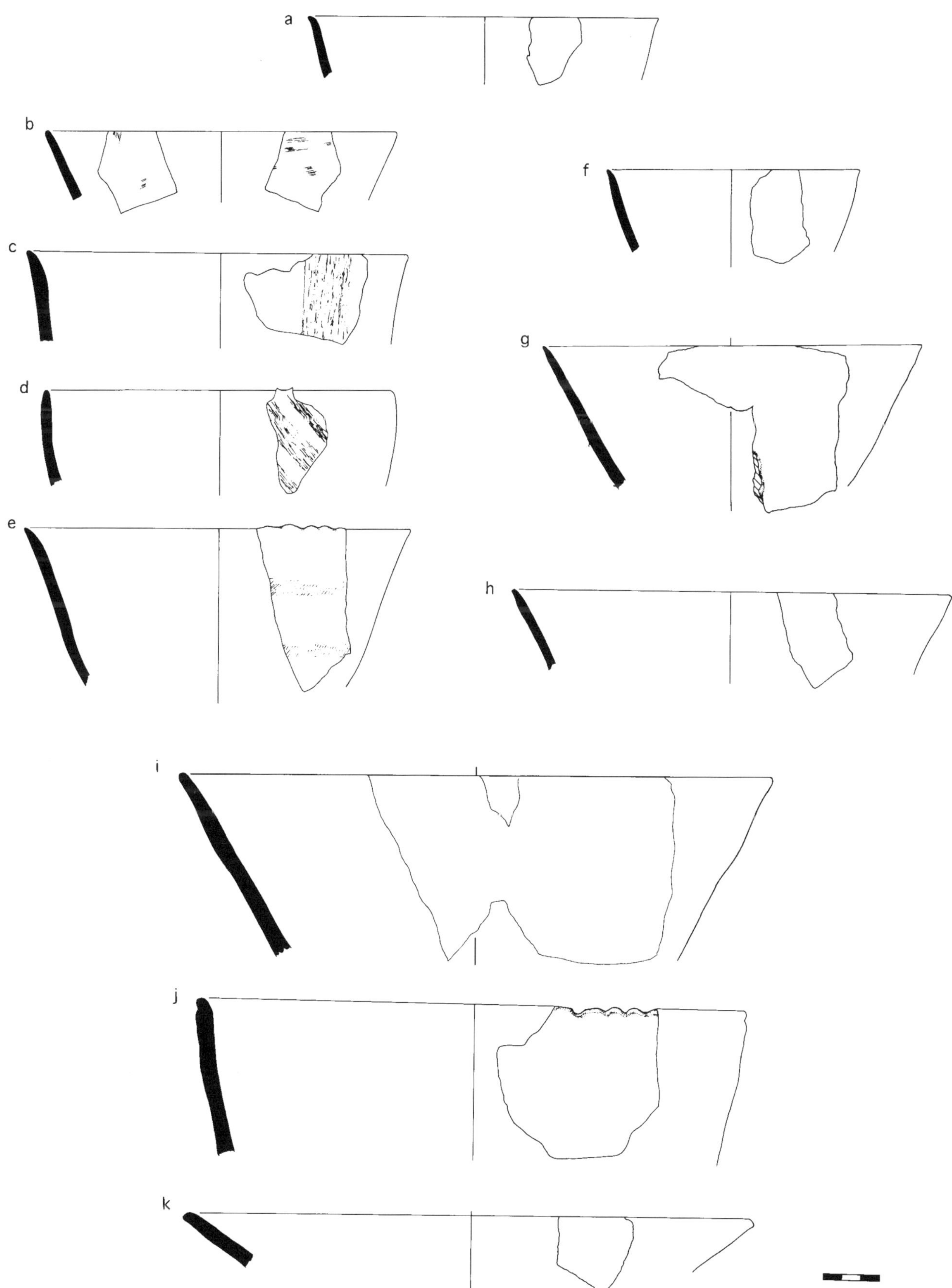
a
b
c
d
e
f
g
h
i
j
k

Figure 45 FCP 5.1a Cave assorted surface finishes

a. FAS:82 Poly MG<1, silver mica glitter 0.13 4 non-joining, 2 illustrated E:scrpd, wet smthd, brnshd, patt in MnO at rim, dull gray, in FeO below, dull red, light surfs. I:scrpd, wet smthd, patt in MnO, dull gray, few strokes brnshd. C:gray int, reddish ext. H:2–3.

b. FAS:75 Poly LmG1 pops 0.16 E, I:scrpd but lumpy, brnshd, ghost lines from MnO patt.

c. FAS:76 (1), 78S (2) Poly aRL3, mica glitter Body sherds E:scrpd but lumpy, patt in MnO, gray and FeO watery brwn. I:scrpd. Sharp edges. H:4–5.

d. FAN:84 Incised LMG1 0.15 E:scrpd, finger smthd, incised, dark surfs. I:scrpd, smthd, dark surfs.

e. FAS:76 MG<1 0.24 irreg E:scrpd, smthd, brnshd, waxy, incised after brnshd, gray. I:scrpd, smthd, brnshd, gray. C:uniform gray.

f. FAS:77 mD<1, L2 0.17 max E, I:scrpd, wet smthd. H:2–3.

g. FAS:76 RW1, D<1 E:scrpd, poss slip, red, brnshd, flaking, surfs brwnish-gray, hole pierced before firing, prob a tab. I:scrpd, smthd, brick red. C:light gray. H:2–3.

h. FAS:76 aDMG5, fL 0.27 max E:scrpd, lumpy, smthd, light brnshd. I:scrpd, smthd. H:3–4.

i. FAS:76 mRD2, f8–9, fL E:smthd, fugitive red pt/powder, surely post-firing, rusty, dissolves in water, was preserved by heavy encrustation of cave Lime.

j. FAS:77 RMG2–3 0.14 E:scrpd, smthd, slipped, red, base broken and ground down to new edge, deep red surfs and fabric. I:scrpd, finger smthd. U:scrpd, smthd. H:2–3.

k. FAS:79 RMG1–2, unevenly dispersed 0.025 bott E, I:scrpd, smthd, brnshd, red. C:gray. H:2–3.

l. FAS:82 LMG1 0.12 bott E:scrpd, smthd, lightly brnshd, blk. I:scpd, smthd, coated w/ red powder, poss from use as pigment pot since unusual fabric for decoration w/ red powder. Jagged edges. H:3–4.

m. FAS:79 WR1 0.12 E, I, U:scrpd, smthd, brnshd, blk-dark brwn. H:2–3.

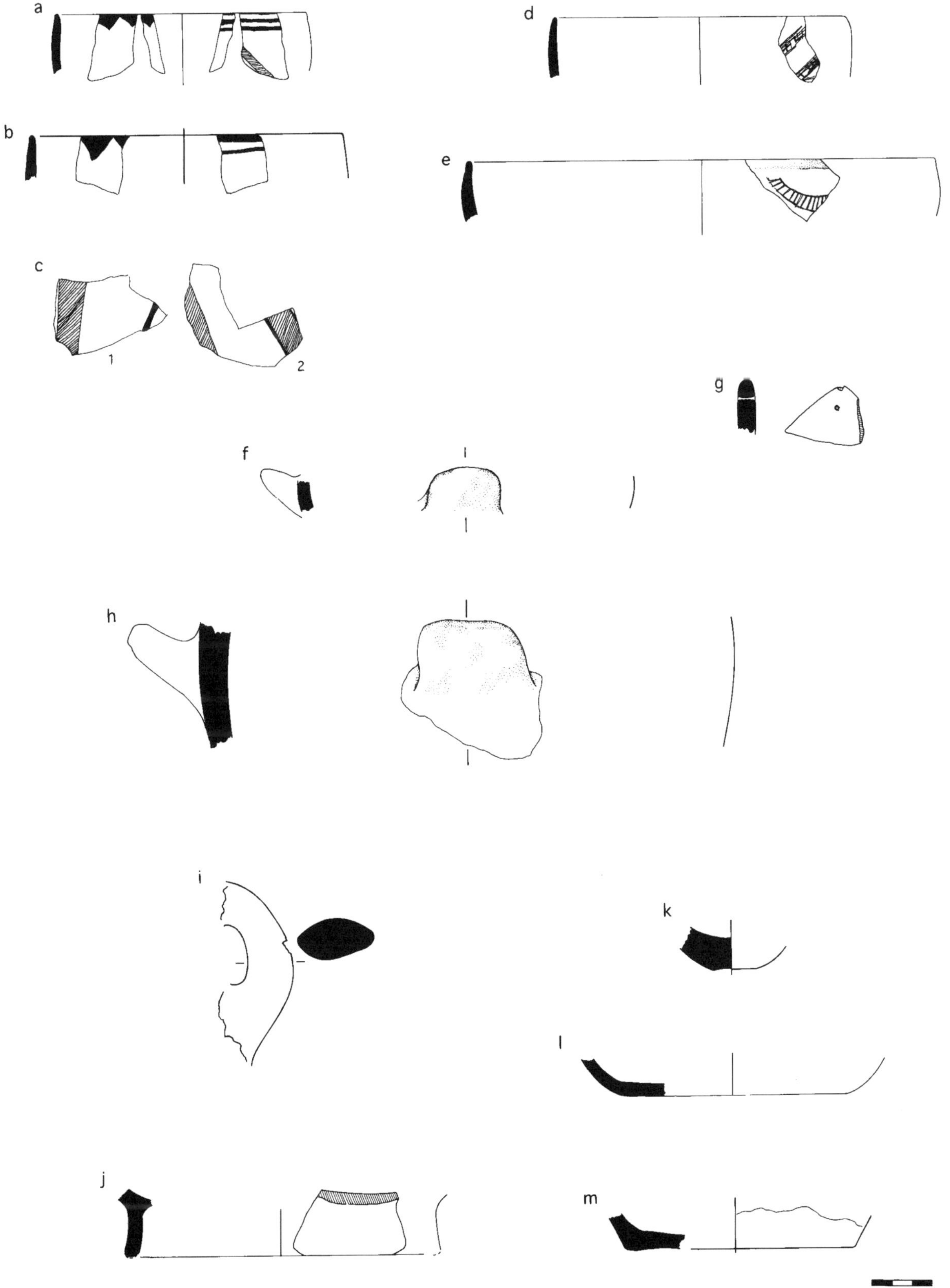
a
b
c
1
2
d
e
g
f
h
i
k
l
j
m

Figure 46 FCP 5.1b Cave assorted surface finishes

a. FAN:67 mL<1, R1 0.19 irreg E:scrpd vert, damp brnshd, mottled grays. I:scrpd hor, damp brnshd. Pumicy edges. H:3–4.

b. FAS:59 MG1, vegetal holes 0.18 E, I:scrpd lightly, gray surfs. C:gray. H:2–3.

c. FAS:73 aMG1, frR2 0.22 E, I:scrpd with jagged tool, poss white pt at lip. C:gray. H:2–3.

d. FAS:67 LD1pops 4 0.25 E:bldg surf, pink. I:hor scrpd, vert brnshd. C:gray. H:2–3.

e. FAS:73 LMG1 0.24 E:scrpd, brnshd. I:scrpd. C:gray, surfs same, H:2–3.

f. FAS:61 LMG1 pops 2 0.26 E:scrpd, damp brnshd, piecrust rim. I:scprd, brnshd at rim, mottled reds-brwns both surfs. C:gray. H:2–3.

g. FAN:64(1)+63N(3) RD1 0.26 E:scrpd, applied band, finger impressed, lightly brnshd except band, deep troughs. I:scrpd, smthd, brnshd, mottled surfs. C:light gray. H:2–3.

h. FAS:72 LR1–2 0.39 E:scrpd, smthd, lightly brnshd, tan. I:scrpd. H:2–3.

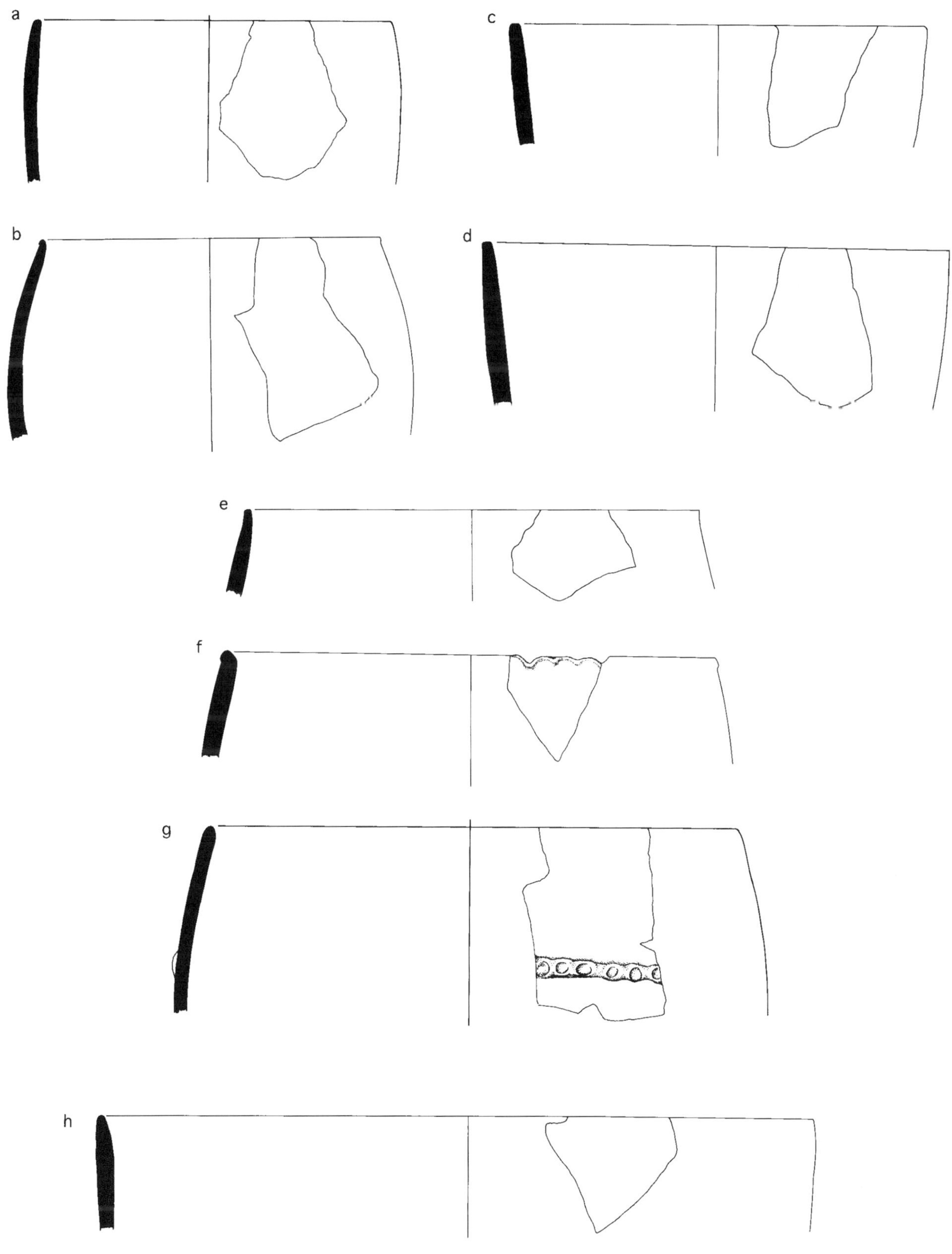
a
b
c
d
e
f
g
h

Figure 47 FCP 5.1b Cave assorted surface fsinishes

a. FAS:73 fMG<1 E:scrpd, cursory damp brnsh. I:scrpd, reddish surfs. C:gray. H:2–3.

b. FAS:71 fMG<1 E:scrpd, smthd, gray surfs. I:scrpd, smthd, lightly brnshd, reddish brwn surf. C:gray. H:2–3.

c. FAS:73 mRD1, several big holes from seed impressions 0.285 max E:scrpd, wet smthd, poss white pt on handle. I:scrpd, wet smthd, hor brnsh. H:2–3.

d. FAS:71 LR1 0.32 max E:scrpd, smthd, tan w/ dark clouds. I:scrpd, smthd, lightly brnshd. H:2–3.

e. FAN:64(2)+65N(1) LRD1 0.32 max E:scrpd wet, smthd, light vert brnsh, pinkish-tan w/ gray clouds. I:scrpd, smthd, damp hor brnsh, pinkish-tan surfs, splashed w/ pigment that has fired yellowish-green. C:gray. H:2–3.

f. FAS:73 RMG1, mica glitter 0.10 bott E, I:scrpd, wet smthd, mottled red-blk surfs. C:dark. Pumicy edges. H:2–3.

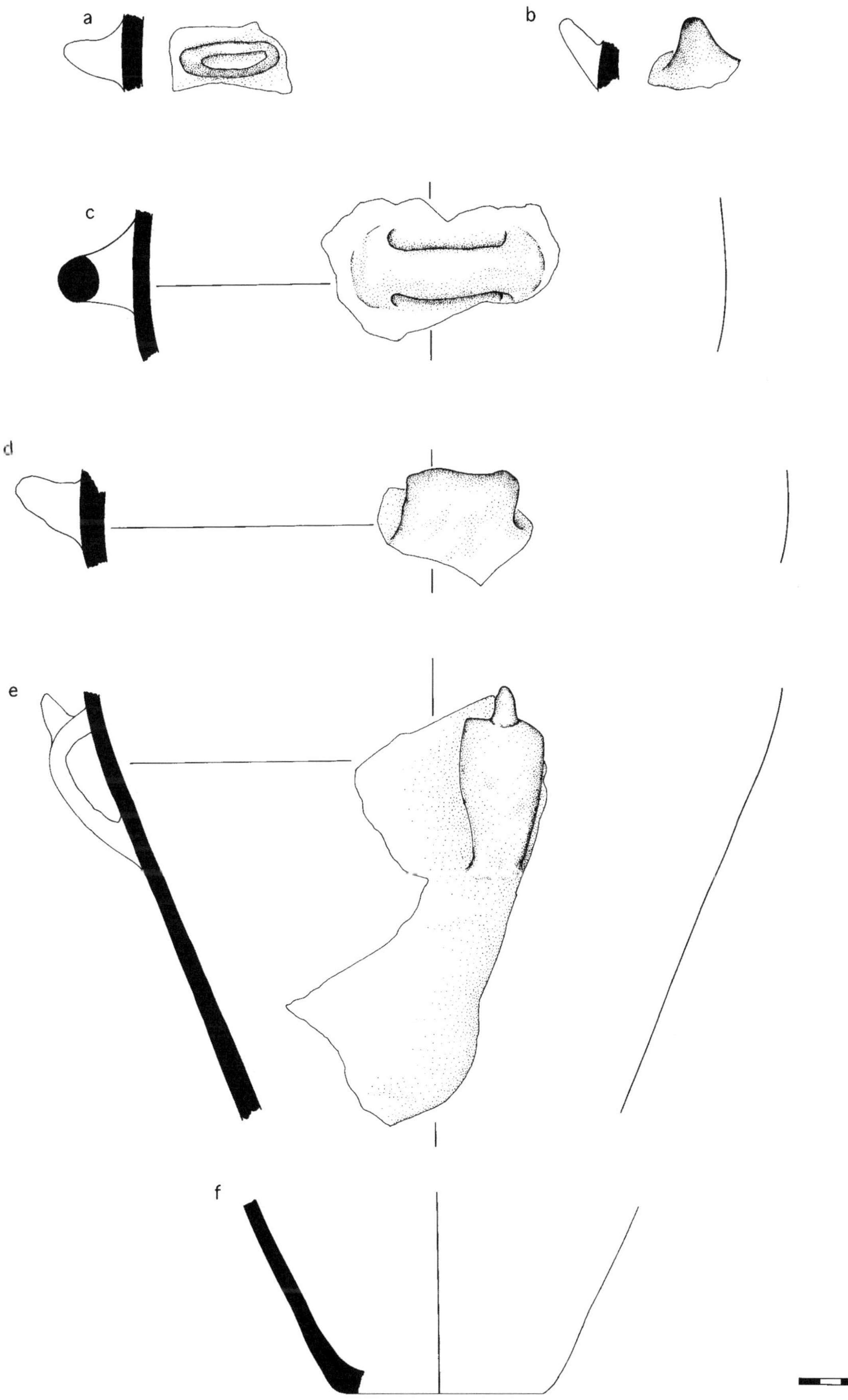
a
b
c
d
e
f

Figure 48 FCP 5.1b Cave assorted surface finishes

a. FAN:65 fLR1 0.12 E:scrpd, smthd, lightly brnshd, pinkish tan. I:smthd. H:2–3.

b. FAS:73 LMG<1 0.10 E, I:smthd, few strokes of brnshd, poss coat of slip, reddish, holes poked below rim from int, edge of another hole near bott, mend clay near rim, right edge blocks one hole, uniform brick red surfs. C:blk. H:2–3.

c. FAS:61 fLMG1 0.055 joint E, I:bldg surfs, 5 oval holes poked through lower wall of bowl, only 3 clearly penetrate, pinkish surfs. C:gray. H:3–4.

d. FAS:61 LMG1 E, I:bldg surfs, handle added over rim, thick attachment clay masks diameter, prob small bowl. H:3.

e. FAN:65 fL1 0.10 E, I:bldg surfs, pinkish surfs. C:pinkish. H:2–3.

f. FAS:69 LRMG1 0.15 E:scrpd, brnshd below handle only, prob bent from pressure of handle attachment, grayish-brwn surfs. I:scrpd, lightly brnshd. C:blk, H:2–3.

g. FAS:73 fLmMG<1 0.18 E, I:scrpd, smthd, pink. C:gray. H:2–3.

h. FAS:73 LR1 pops int 0.20 E, I:scrpd, damp brnshd, clear troughs, mottled grays-brwns. C:blk. H:2–3.

i. FAN:64 mDRL<1 0.10 E, I:scrpd, wet smthd, ext surf largely missing, mottled pink to gray surfs. C:gray. H:2–3.

j. FAS:66 LMG<1 0.18 E:scrpd, smthd, damp brnshd at rim, small clump of Lime on lower body may suggest crust. I:scrpd, smthd, damp brnshd at rim only, red surfs. C:gray. H:2–3.

k. FAS:66+FAN:63 LRMG<1, f1 0.09 bott E:scrpd but lumpy, smthd, damp vert brnshd, yellow-brwn surfs. I:scrpd, smthd, damp brnshd, pink surfs. C:blk. H:2–3.

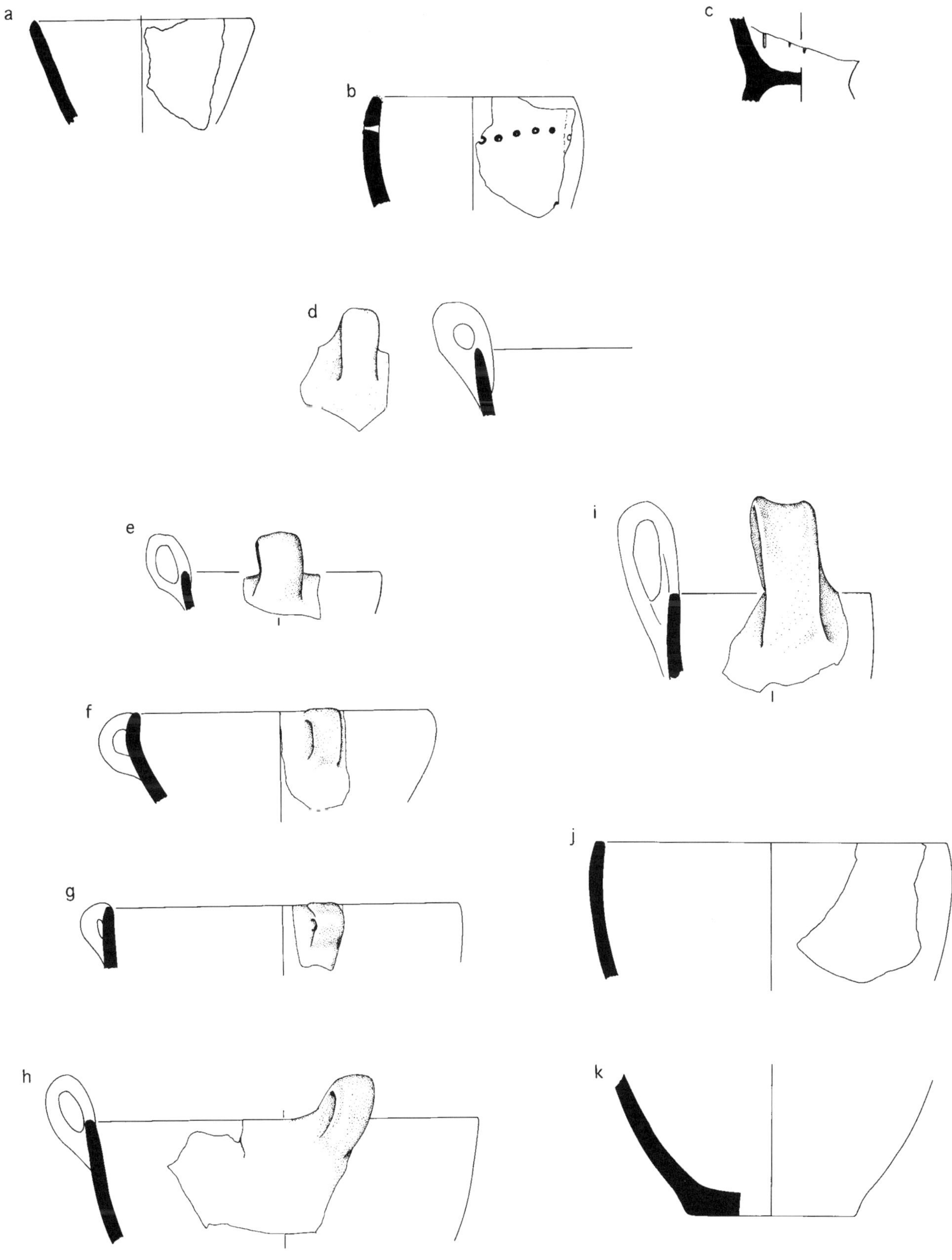
a
b
c
d
e
f
g
h
i
j
k

Figure 49 FCP 5.1b Cave assorted surface finishes

a. FAS:68 LMG1, some mica glitter 0.18 E, I:scrpd, smthd, cursory damp brnshd, red, worn. C:red. H:2–3.

b. FAS:70 LMG1 pops 0.24, warped in both directions E:smthd, lumpy, light brnshd, dull gray surfs. I:scrpd, lightly brnshd, pink surfs. H:2–3.

c. FAN:63 aRLMG1 pops, voids 0.25 E:scrpd, finger smthd, blk, crackling. I:scrpd, smthd, damp brnshd, blk w/ lighter clouds. C:gray. H:2–3.

d. FAS:67 (4)+68S (2) aRSMG1 0.30 E, I:scrpd, smthd, poss slipped (scratching produces powder), dry brnshd, blk w/ reddish tinge. H:2–3.

e. FAS:74 LMG1 0.28 E, I:scrpd, smthd, poss slip, dry brnshd, reddish surfs, hole drilled from ext, second hole started from int, does not penetrate. C:dark. H:2–3.

f. FAS:63 RD2 0.20 E, I:scrpd, smthd, poss slipped, brnshd, blk w/ reddish tinge, worn along rim. C:gray. H:2–3.

g. FAS:66 LRMG1 0.32 E:scrpd, very fine white Lime powder clings to parts of ext, not crystally like crust. I:scrpd, wet smthd. C:gray. H:2–3.

h. FAS:71 LR1, holes from vegetal inclusions 0.41 E, I:scrpd, smthd, slipped while standing on rim, slip stops abruptly at tip of lip, damp brnshd, poss traces white Lime powder on ext , brwnish-gray surfs w/ white bloom on ext. H:2–3.

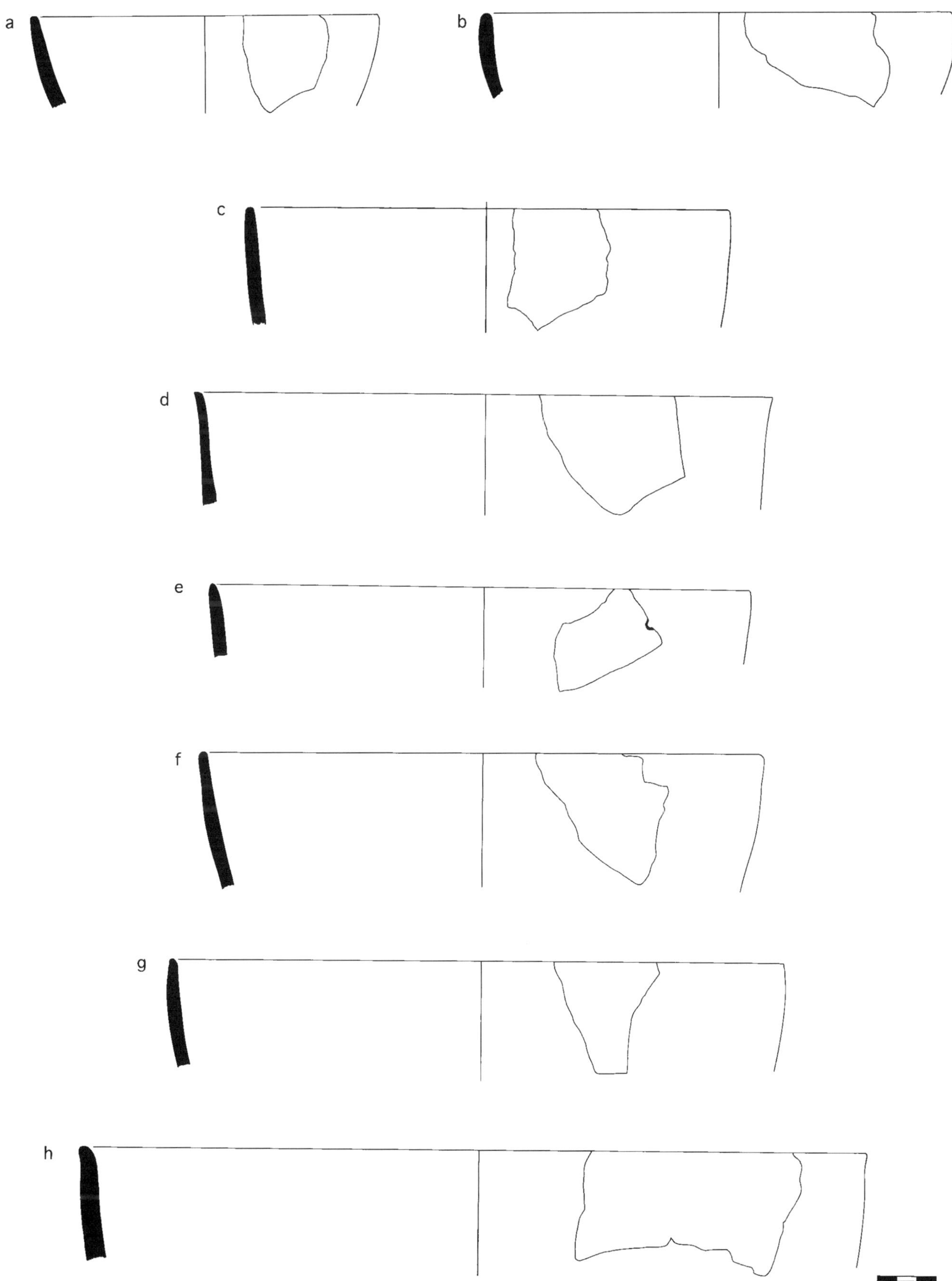
a
b
c
d
e
f
g
h

Figure 50 FCP 5.1b Cave assorted surface finishes

a. FAN:69 D1fL3–4 0.18 E, I:scrpd but lumpy, dry brnshd, light gray. H:2–3.

b. FAN:69 LMG1 pops 0.10 E, I:scrpd, wet smthd, gray, friable, finger depressions from pinching. Pumicy edges. H:3–4.

c. FAS:70 LMG1, holes from vegetal inclusions 0.24 E:scrpd, smthd, slipped, brnshd, blk, crackling, tab at rim. I:scrpd, slip at rim only, blk, rest of surf tan. H:3–4.

d. FAN:64 LRMG<1 0.38 E:scrpd, smthd, applied band impressed w/ dots, poss slip, damp sloppy brnsh, blk, crackling. I:scrpd, smthd, hor brnshd, reddish brwn. H:4–5.

e. FAN:69 maD1 0.44 E, I:scrpd, smthd, lightly brnshd, brwn-blk, traces of red powder. H:2–3.

f. FAN:64 maLRD<1 0.42 E:scrpd, smthd, damp brnshd, pinkish-gray to dark gray. I:scrpd, wet smthd, tan. C:gray ext, tan int. H:2–3.

g. FAS:73 LRMG1, holes from vegetal inclusions 0.25–0.26, irreg E:lumpy, lightly brnshd, light w/ dark clouds. I:scrpd w/ gouges, mottled, bott thickness varies substantially. H:2–3.

h. FAS:68 fL1 0.12 bott E, I, U:scrpd, smthd, damp vertical brnsh, mottled. C:gray. H:3.

i. FAN:64 fLRD1 0.20 bott E, I:scrpd, barely smthd, pink surfs. C:gray. H:2–3.

j. FAS:76 mRD1–2, fL 0.10 bott E:scrpd, smthd, few strokes brnsh, grayish-brwn. I:scrpd, well-smthd, reddish-brwn. U:poss faint mat impression. C:reddish-brwn. H:2–3.

k. FAS:69 fLMG<1, f pebbles 3, pops ext 0.11 bott E, I:scrpd, smthd, damp brnshd, blk int, yellow-tan ext. Entire bott preserved, broken along coil joint except for short portion of wall that forms tab-like extension.

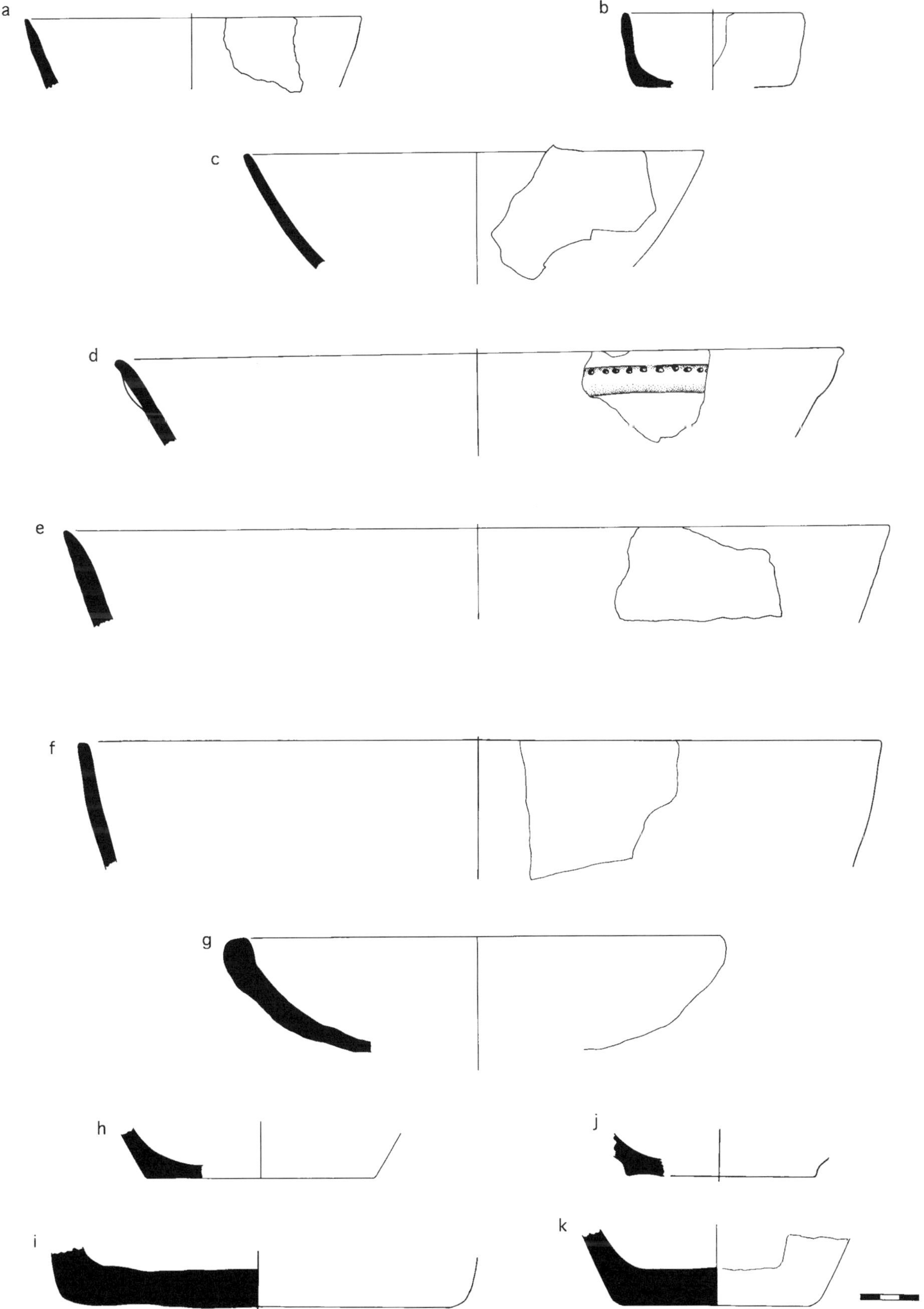
a
b
c
d
e
f
g
h
j
i
k

Figure 51 FCP 5.1b Cave crusted varieties

a. FAS:73 FP 176 White Crust mWR<1 0.17–0.18 irreg E:scrpd, smthd, th white Lime crust, tan to gray surf under crust, one side of bott much thinner than other. I:scrpd, smthd, red tinges but no pigment grains visible. Nicks along rim. H:3–4.

b. FAN:64 White Crust RrDMG1–2 0.08 base E:scrpd, smthd, thick white Lime crust in groove of joint. Detached at joint. H:2–3.

c. FAS:72 FP 160 White Crust Ptd RDW<1 0.15 E:scrpd, poss brnshd under crust, surf removed w/ crust, brwn, coated w/ thick, powdery white Lime, sugar-like, traces red pt at rim and below. I:scrpd, smthd, faint traces of orange powder, surfs pinkish. C:gray. Jagged breaks. H:3.

d. FAS:69 White Crust LMG<1 0.17 E:scrpd, smthd, brwn, coated w/ thick white Lime crust, traces red pt. I:scrpd, smthd, traces red powder at rim only, light tan surfs. C:gray. H:2–3.

e. FAS:68 LMG<1 0.13 E:scrpd, damp smthd, gray-blk, looks as though should have been crusted, but no trace. I:scrpd, smthd, tan. H:2–3.

f. FAS:69 RMG<1 0.14 E, I:scrpd, roughly smthd, mottled, surf looks like should have been crusted, no traces: large L pebble in break suggests may have broken before received crust. C:gray. H:2–3.

g. FAS:63 White Crust LMG<1 0.18 E:scrpd, prob smthd, coated w/ thick white Lime crust, traces red at rim. I:scrpd, smthd, traces pinkish-red powder. H:2–3.

h. FAN:67 White Crust tiny aMG<1, round voids 0.18 E:scrpd, prob smthd, tan, coated w/ white Lime powder. I:scprd, smthd, red powdery stripe at rim, tan surfs. C:thin gray at center. H:2–3.

i. FAS:67 White Crust MG<1, faR3 0.25 E:scrpd, finger smthd, tan, trace white Lime crust. I:scrpd, smthd, tan, traces red powder. C:light. H:2–3.

j. FAS:64 FP 158a–c Crusted LRMG1, flecks of gold mica 0.25 max non-joining E:scrpd, smthd, looks like has layer of red powder, w/ white Lime on top, then patt lines in grayish Lime, which dissolves in HCl leaving red powder showing through. I:scrpd, smthd, red powder (10R 6/8). C:blk. H:2–3.

k. FAS:68 Crusted MG<1 0.16 pedestal E:scrpd, smthd, pinkish surfs w/ apparently, multiple layers of red powder on white Lime, on red powder on white Lime, no discernable patt. I:bldg surf, blk. C:blk. H:2–3.

l. FAS:68 White Crust aRMG1 0.18 pedestal E:finger smthd, lumpy, lightly brnshd, tan, traces of thick white Lime crust. I: smthd, tan. C:gray center. H:2–3.

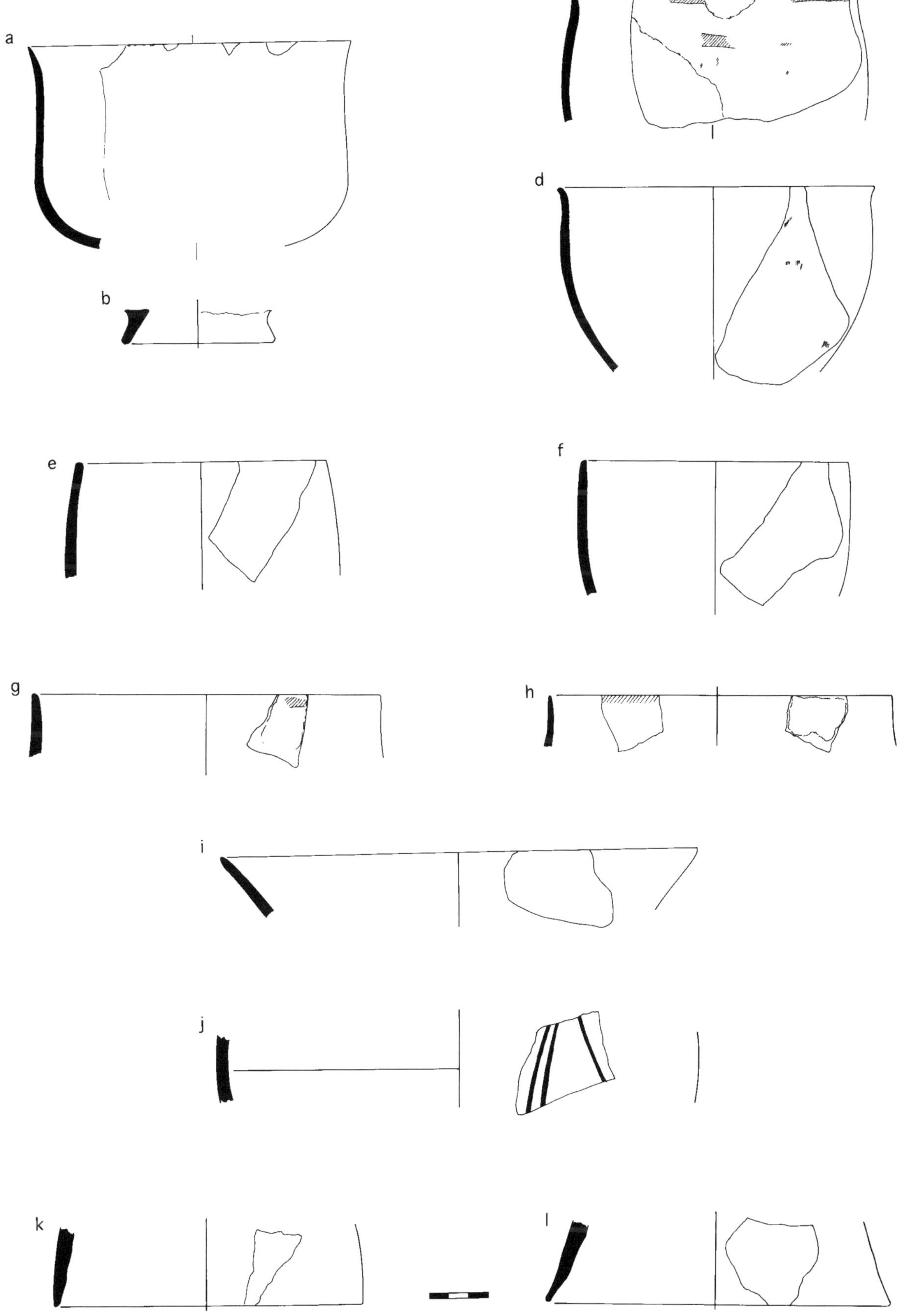
a
b
c
d
e
f
g
h
i
j
k
l

Figure 52 FCP 5.1b Cave White Painted decoration

a. FAS:73 WhitePtd MG1–2 0.09 E:barely scrpd, lumpy, smthd, faint traces white ptd patt, reacts in HCl, tan surfs, thickening at break suggests handle. I:scrpd, smthd, worn, crystally clumps of red pigment in bott, reacts slightly in HCl, poss used as pigment pot. H:2–3.

b. FAS:66 WhitePtd LMG<1 0.18 E:scrpd, finger smthd, poss red pt, white ptd stripe at rim, edge of handle or pellet. I:scrpd, finger smthd. H:2–3.

c. FAS:66+67S+68S WhitePtd LR1–2 0.12 E:scrpd, smthd, pink, white pt, reacts slightly in acid. H:2–3.

d. FAS:74 WhitePtd LMG<1 0.19 E:scrpd, damp brnshd, reddish surfs, white ptd. I:scrpd, damp brnshd. C:dark gray. H:2–3.

e. FAS:69 WhitePtd LMG<1 0.18 E:scrpd, wet smthd, damp brnshd, reddish surfs, traces white pt. I:scrpd, smthd, reddish. C:gray. H:2–3.

f. FAS:71 WhitePtd RMG1 0.16 E:scrpd, damp brnshd, poss white pt, grayish-white surfs. I:scrpd, smthd, poss red powder, reddish-brwn. C:gray. H:2–3.

g. FAS:69(5)+70S(9)+71S(1)+73S(8) FP 229 WhitePtd LRMG1, holes from vegetal inclusions, several pebbles 7–8 0.25 E:scrpd, wet smthd, gray surfs, patt in white pt, not Lime, crackling, fades out on some sherds, whole is cindery, burned, warped and bent flat in one place. I:scrpd, wet smthd, gray (FP 34, A:40, not illustrated, prob from same pot). H:3–4.

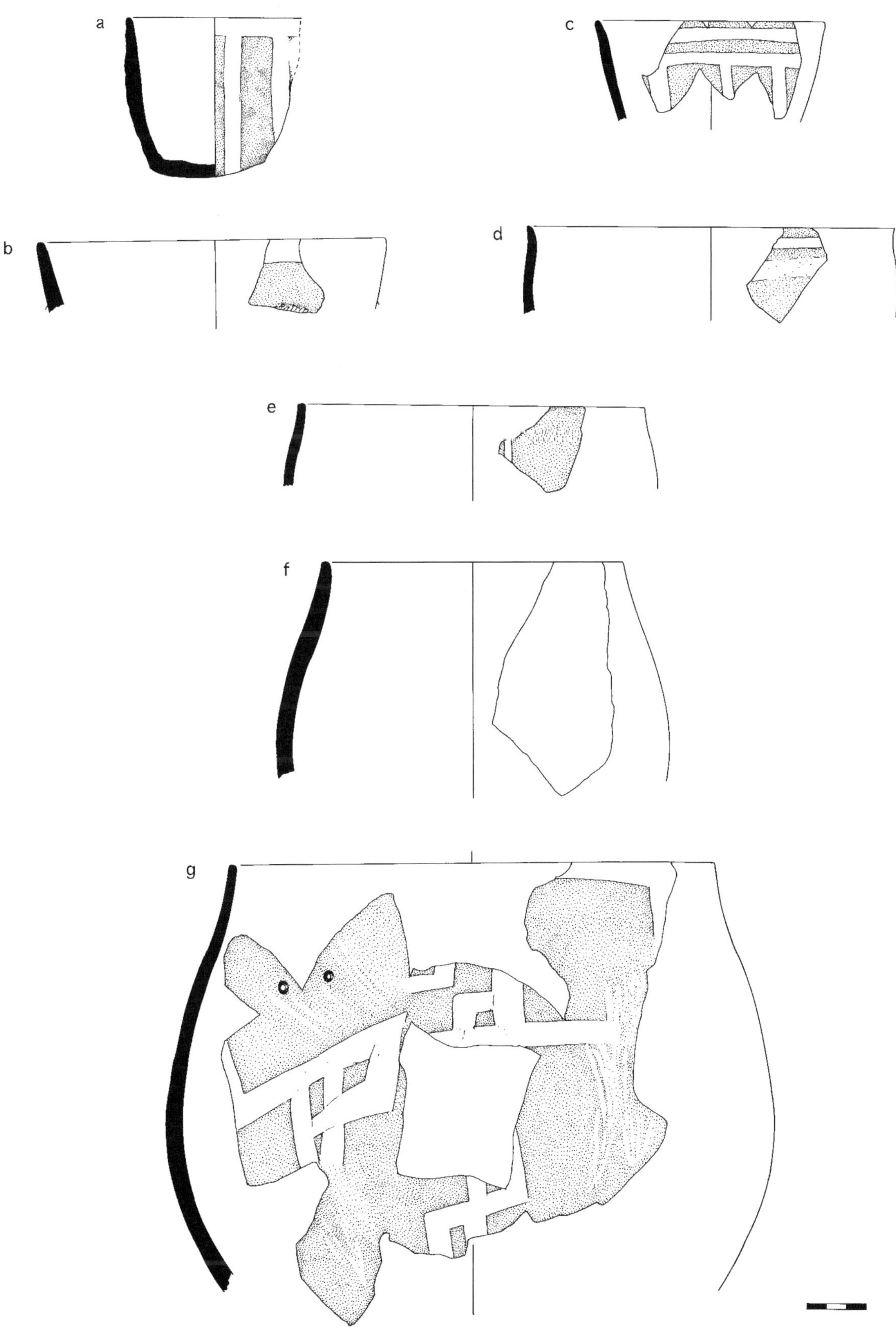
a
b
c
d
e
f
g

Figure 53 FCP 5.1b Cave Red on White Painted and Incised decoration

a. FAS:70 Red and White Crust? LRMG1–2 0.26 E:scrpd, smthd, ptd lines in FeO, red to blk, traces white Lime crust (stippling). I:scrpd, smthd, slipped, red, orange on gray ground. C:gray, subsurfs red. H:2–3.

b. FAS:71 Red on WhitePtd LMG<1, m voids 0.22 scrpd, whitish surfs w/ traces red pt, brnshd. I:scrpd, creamy ground w/ orange tint. C:gray. H:2–3.

c. FAN:64 Red on WhitePtd DR>1 0.20 E, I:scrpd, white slip, mostly gone, traces red pt, brnshd, flaking, no reaction in HCl, surfs tan to gray. C:red. H:2–3.

d. FAS:69+70S Red on WhitePtd MG<1 0.18 E:scrpd but lumpy, slipped in white pt, Lime-rich but not pure Lime, patt in FeO, red, if brnshd now worn, tan surfs, suggestion of handle or lug at lower edge. I:scrpd, traces red and white pt, brnshd, tan surfs. C:blk. H:2–3.

e. FAS:74 Red on WhitePtd DMG1, f2, poss grog 0.16 max E:scrpd, white slipped, patt in FeO, red, brnshd removed or smeared much of white slip, flaking away to scrpd surf. I:well-scrpd, thick red pt, brnshd, flaking. C:blue-gray, subsurfs orange. H:2–3.

f. FAS:74 Red on White Ptd LD1, f3–4 no measurable curve E:scrpd, creamy white slip w/ blk cloud, patt in thick red pt, brnshd. I:scrpd, creamy slip, brnshd, traces red pt, worn. C:blue-gray, pink subsurfs.

g. FAS:74 Red and White Ptd DMG<1, f1 0.26 E:scrpd, patt of red and white stripes, neither reacts in HCl, no brnsh, when wet, white appears applied over the red. I:scrpd, slipped in red pt, crackling. C:gray.

h. FAS:74 Incised LRMG1–2 0.31 E:scrpd, smthd, incised or impressed with tool that produced a double line, dry brnshd below rim fold, grayish surfs. I:scrpd, well smthd, pink. C:gray. H:2–3.

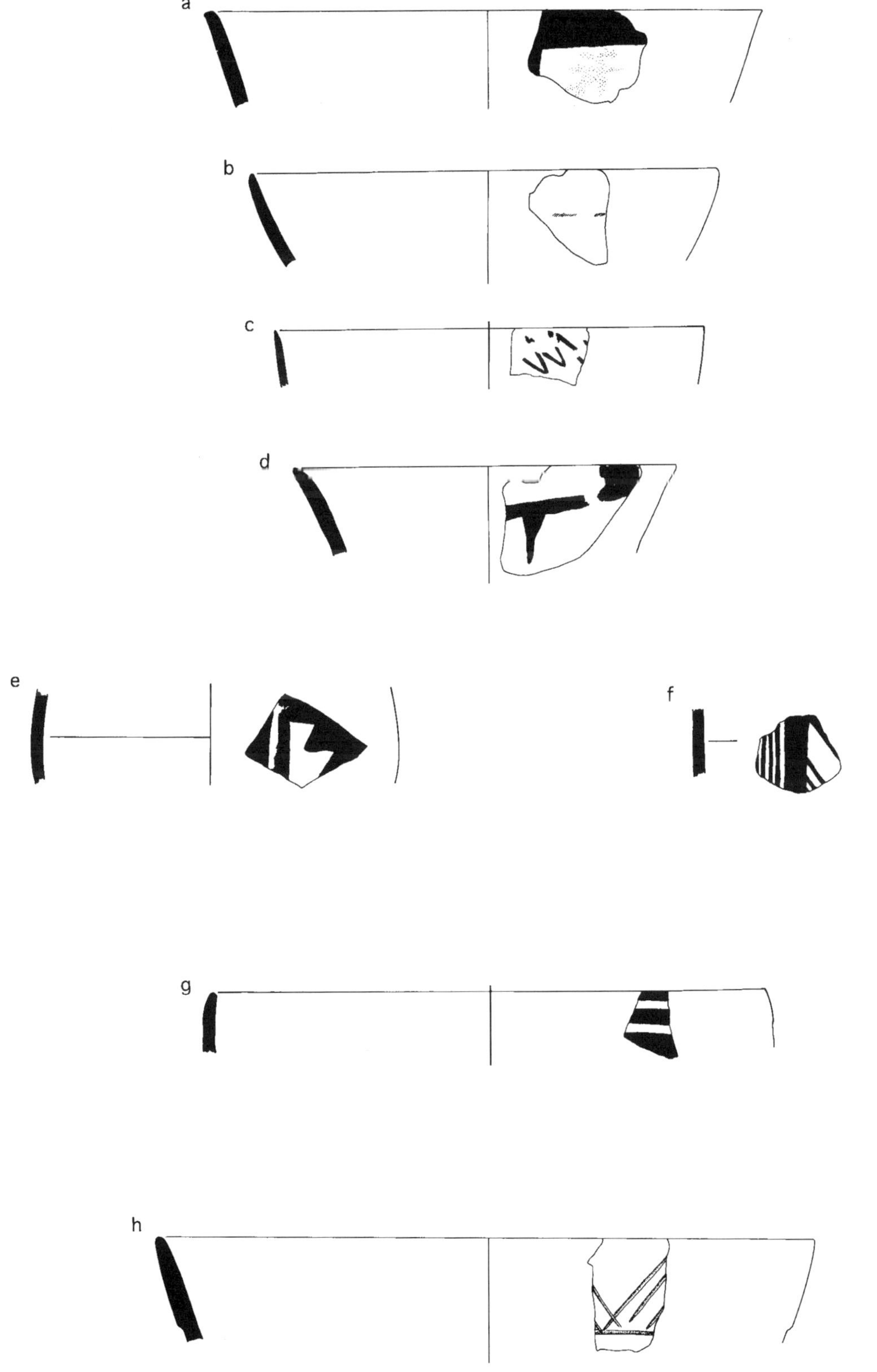
a
b
c
d
e
f
g
h

Figure 54 FCP 5.1b Cave assorted surface sinishes

a. FAS:72 FP 161 L1, DR<1 0.23 E:scrpd, smthd, brnshd except reserved area at rim, traces white Lime and red powder in reserved area, glossy blk-red surfs. I:scrpd, well-smthd, traces red powder, blk surfs. C:blk at center, red-brwn subsurfs. H:2–3. Jacobsen 1973b:Pl. 52a.

b. FAS:68(3)+70S(1) FP 228 LMG1, pebble 3, mica glitter 0.16 E:lumpy, brnshd except reserved at rim, traces white Lime in reserved band, orange powder (ca. 10R 6/8) on brnshd just below reserved band, blk surfs. I:scrpd, wet smthd, coated w/ red powder, gray surfs. Thickness varies, flat side prob accidental, hint of base joint. H:2–3.

c. FAS:71 R<1L2 0.12 E:scrpd, brnshd except band at rim, brick red surfs. I:scrpd, lightly brnshd at rim, red surfs. C:blk. H:2–3.

d. FAS:63 MG1 0.11 base E:scrpd, smthd, band at tip has traces of thick white Lime crust and red powder. I:scrpd. H:2–3.

e. FAS:68 MG1 0.15 inside handle E, I:smthd, pink to tan surfs, orange powder. H:2–3.

f. FAN:64 RDMG, L1–2 0.10 E, I:scrpd, smeared roughly, traces orange powder. I:scrpd, rusty red powder. H:2–3.

g. FAS:74 DMG1 0.24 E, I:scrpd, brnshd, powdery pink (7.5YR 6/6) pigment in cracks, hole drilled from ext, traces red pigment in hole. H:2–3.

h. FAS:66 DMG<1 0.28 E, I:scrpd, brnshd, traces pink powder int and under rim fold on ext, surfs blk to tan. H:2–3.

i. FAS:71 PattBurnished MG<1, pits 0.20 E:scrpd, slipped, orange, PB. I: scrpd, slipped, brnshd. C:gray, pink subsurfs. H:2–3.

j. FAN:70 PattBurnished fLRMG<1 0.30 E:scrpd, smthd, poss slipped, PB, 2–3 strokes per line w/ pointed tool, pink surfs. I:scrpd, smthd, poss slipped, brnshd. C:gray. Pumicy edges. H:3.

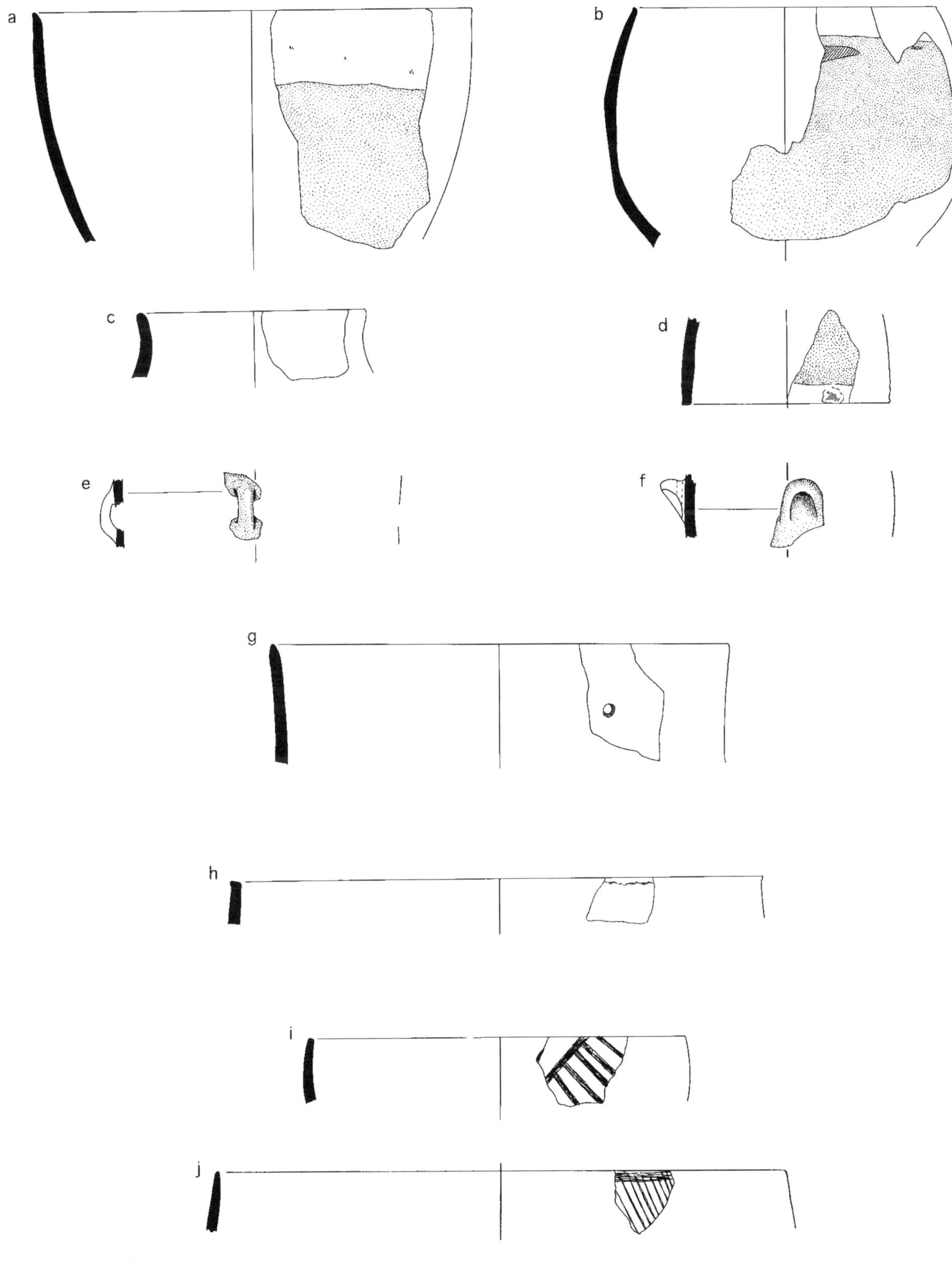
a
b
c
d
e
f
g
h
i
j

Figure 55 FCP 5.1c Cave assorted surface finishes

a. FAN:60 LMG1 0.22 E, I:scrpd, rim tip flattened, tan surfs. H:2–3.

b. FAN:59 LMG<1, pebble3–4, holes from grassy stems int 0.18 E, I: scrpd but lumpy ext, damp brnshd, hole drilled below rim from ext. H:2–3.

c. FAN:60 RDG1, 1 mm pits from vegetal inclusions 0.25 E:bldg surf, gray. I:lightly scrpd, smthd, light gray, piecrust rim impressed w/ small half moons, not fingernail, in very wet clay. C:gray. H:2–3.

d. FAN:60 LMG<1, fR2–3 pops 0.25–0.30, irreg E, I:scrpd, raspy surfs, greenish-tan ext, gray int, piecrust rim, profile varies around sherd, quite warped, burned. H:2–3.

e. FAN:60 fLMG<1 0.30 max E:scrpd, damp brnshd vert, except handle, smthd only, pink w blk clouds. I:scrpd, hor brnsh damp, incomplete. H:2–3.

f. FAN:60 LMG1–2, f pops 0.08–0.10 bott, irreg E, I:scrpd, lumpy ext, damp brnshd, red w/ blk clouds ext, gray int. H:2–3.

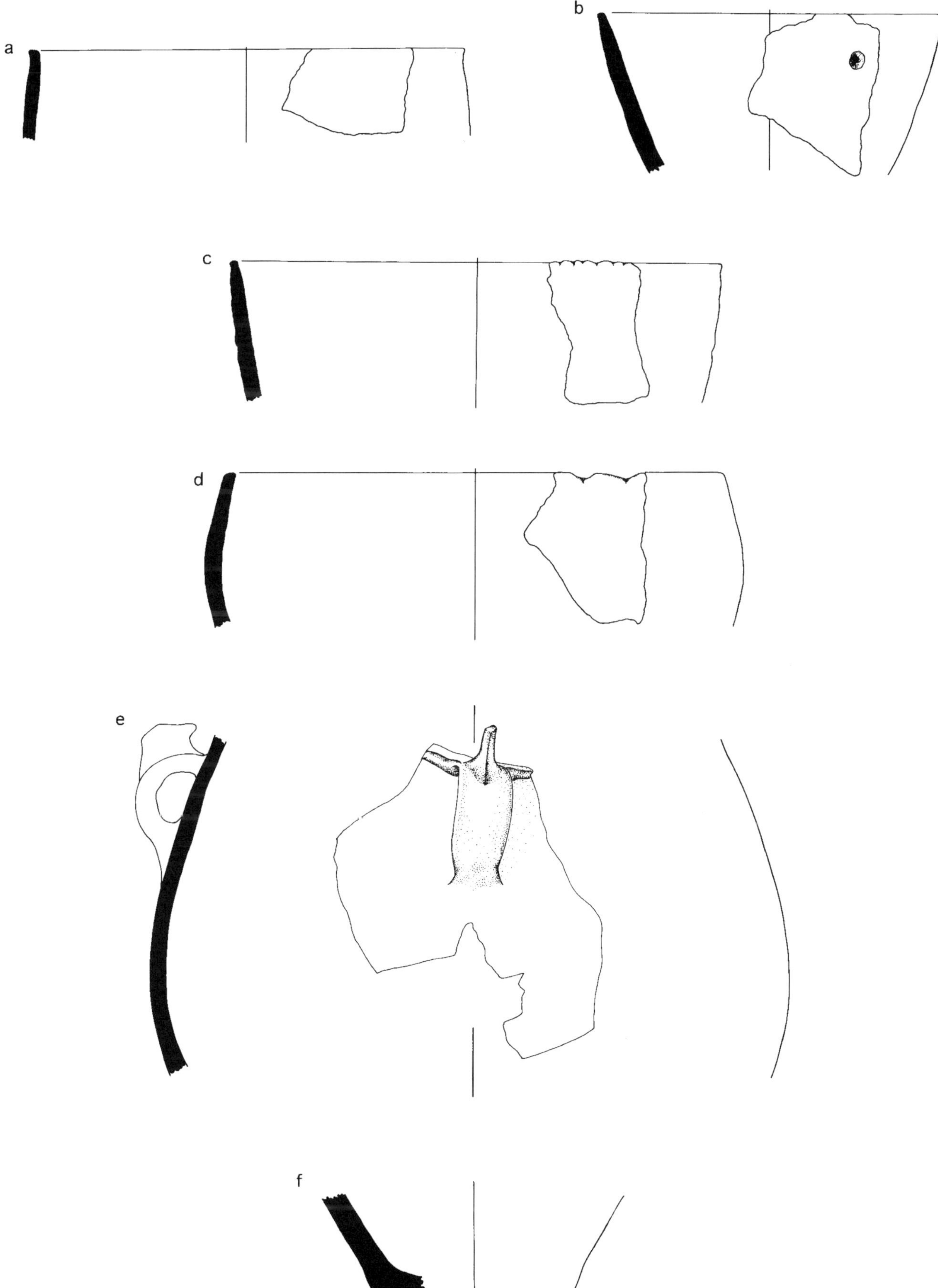
a
b
c
d
e
f

Figure 56 FCP 5.1c Cave assorted surface finishes

a. FAN:59 WhitePtd LMG<1 0.10 E:scrpd, damp smthd, white pt at rim, tan surfs. I:scrpd, damp brnshd, tan surfs. H:2–3.

b. FAN:60 WhitePtd LR1, f pops 0.23 E:scrpd, damp brnshd, patt in powdery white Lime pt at rim, flecks only below, tan surfs w/ dark cloud. I:scrpd, finger smthd. H:2–3.

c. FAN:60 Poly LMG<1 0.14 E:scrpd, brnshd at rim, white pt in rim band and 2 vertical lines, 2 dull red lines, brnshd, flaking, 2 blk lines poss same pigment as red, gray surfs. I:scrpd, brnshd band at rim, gray surfs. H:2–3.

d. FAN:59 LRMG<1 0.21 E:scrpd, smthd, brnshd except reserved band at rim filled w/ powdery red (10R 5/8) and, below, powdery white Lime, blk surfs. I:scrpd, smthd, red powder, gray surfs. C:gray, subsurfs pink. H:3–5.

e. FAN:61 LMG<1 0.13 E, I:scrpd, lightly smthd, pink surfs, depression on side suggests handle removed before firing. H:2–3.

f. FAN:61 LMG<1, gold mica flecks 0.09, oval E:scrpd, pink surfs, coated w/ powdery white Lime w/ traces orange powder on top, from above rim angles suggest a spout. I:scrpd, traces orange powder, pink surfs. C:blk. H:2–3.

g. FAN:59 LMG<1 0.12 E, I:scrpd, damp brnshd. H:2–3.

h. FAN:61 LMG<1 0.16 max E:scrpd, pink surfs, traces powdery white Lime, 2 vertical holes pierced through crescent lug, poss same pot as Fig. 56f. I:scrpd, traces orange powder. H:2–3.

i. FAN:59 fLMG<1 0.16 pedestal E:scrpd, smthd, slipped, red, granular, tails of PB scribbly lines, red to brwn surfs, fingernail scratch produces orange powder. I:scrpd, smthd, slipped near tip, red surfs. C:gray. H:2–3.

j. FAN:61 LR1 0.08 bott E:scrpd, powdery white Lime w/ traces rusty orange powder. I:scrpd, smthd, faint traces red powder, pink surfs. C:dark gray. H:2–3.

k. FAN:59 LRMG<1 0.08 bott E:scrpd, curls of clay on bott edge, light vert brnsh, traces red and white pt, unclear if a patt or overall slip. I:scrpd, smthd, brnshd, pinkish surfs. C:gray. H:2–3.

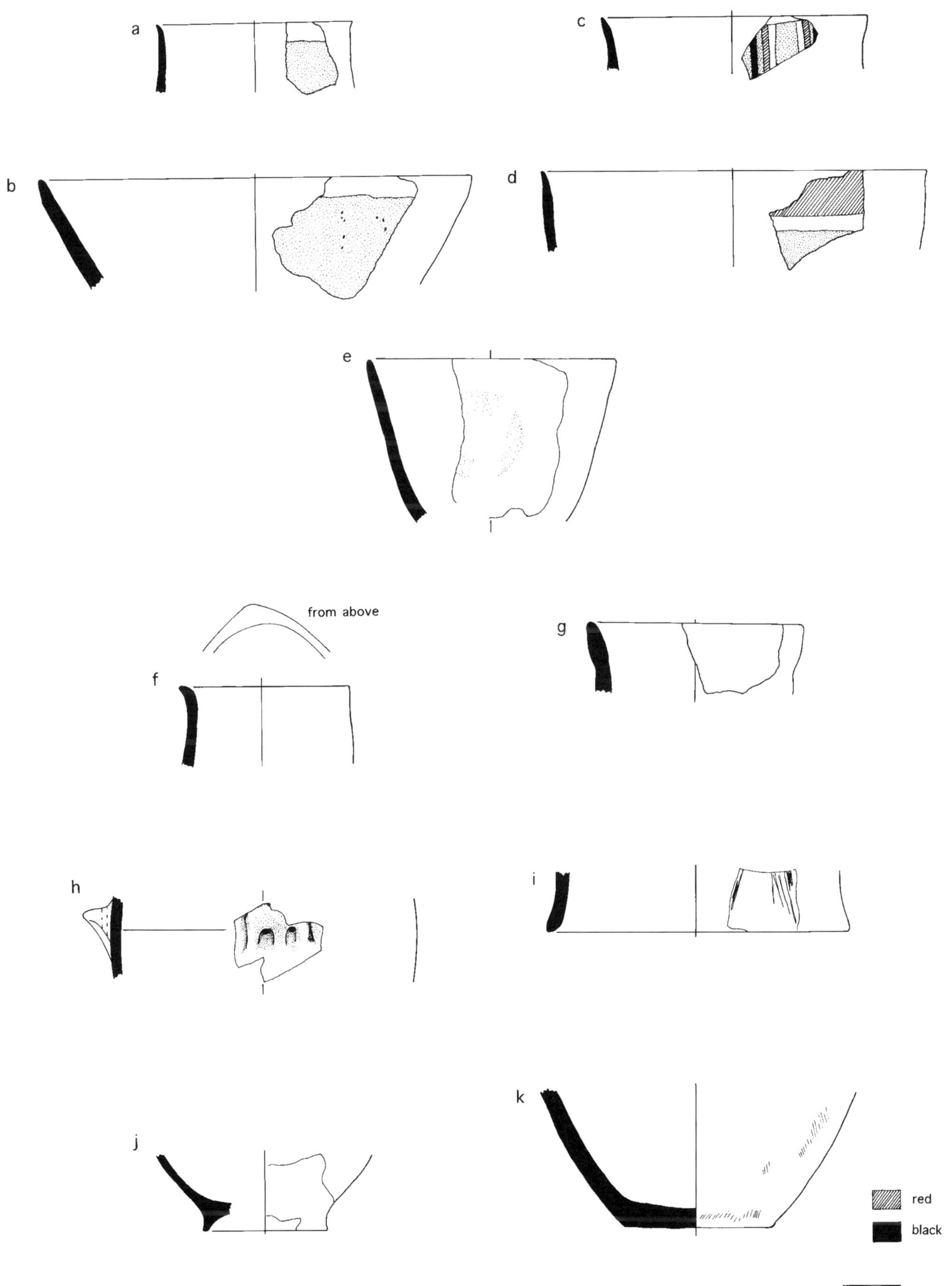
a
b
c
d
e
from above
f
g
h
i
j
k
red
black

Figure 57 FCP 5 Cave Rhyta

a. FAS:68 LRMG1, f2 E, I:flat strap w/ depression along one broken edge, traces orange powder both surfs, pink. C:gray. H:2–3.

b. FAS:72 LMG1 pops E, I:large flat strap, no curvature, scrpd, smthd, poss slipped, pink surfs, brnshd ext, less well int, one hole drilled from ext penetrates, second is incomplete, third in break. C:gray. H:2–3.

c. FAS:76 FP 178 LrRMG1–2 E:scrpd, smthd, prob slipped, brnshd, incised and punctate, filled w/ white Lime, surfs pink to tan. C:blk. H:2–3.

d. FA QSW+WB:31 FPSC 233 WaR4–5 E:smthd, incised or impressed w/ rows of deep herringbone patt, red surfs, prob one side of handle. C:blk. H:5.

e. FA QSW+WB:34 FPSC 230 MDG3 E:smthd, neatly incised or impressed w/ rows deep herringbone patt, heavily encrusted w/ cave Lime, burned gray-red. C:gray. H:4–5.

f. FA QSW+WB:40 LMG1 E:bldg surfs, red-gray surfs. C:gray. H:3–4.

g. FA QSE+EB:43 FPSC 125 LMG1, f2 E:smthd, less well on flat side, red surfs w/ gray clouds. C:blue-gray. H:3.

h. FAS:73 mR1–2 0.26 E:scrpd, wet smthd, poss red slip, poorly attached coil may be start of base, at sharp angle to rim. I:scrpd, wet smthd, poss red slip, worn and rolled. H:2–3.

i. FAS:68 fLR1 E, I:bldg smthd, pink surfs, hollow foot. H:2–3.

j. FA QSW+WB:29 mLRMG1–3, f5, pink stone that sparkles E:no original surf, brwn surfs w/ blk cloud, solid conical leg. H:2–3.

k. FA QSW+WB:29 LMG1–2 E:smthd, mottled reds-yellows, very crumbly, heavily encrusted w/ cave Lime, solid foot. H:2–3.

l. FA QSE+EB FPSC 138 SMG1 E:smthd, pale pink surfs, heavily encrusted w/ cave Lime, edges of toes chipped, hollow foot. C:gray. H:2–3.

m. A:13 aDMG<1R3–4 fL, pits E:finger smthd, tan, solid leg w/ bent knee. C:uniform light. H:2–3.

Figure 57

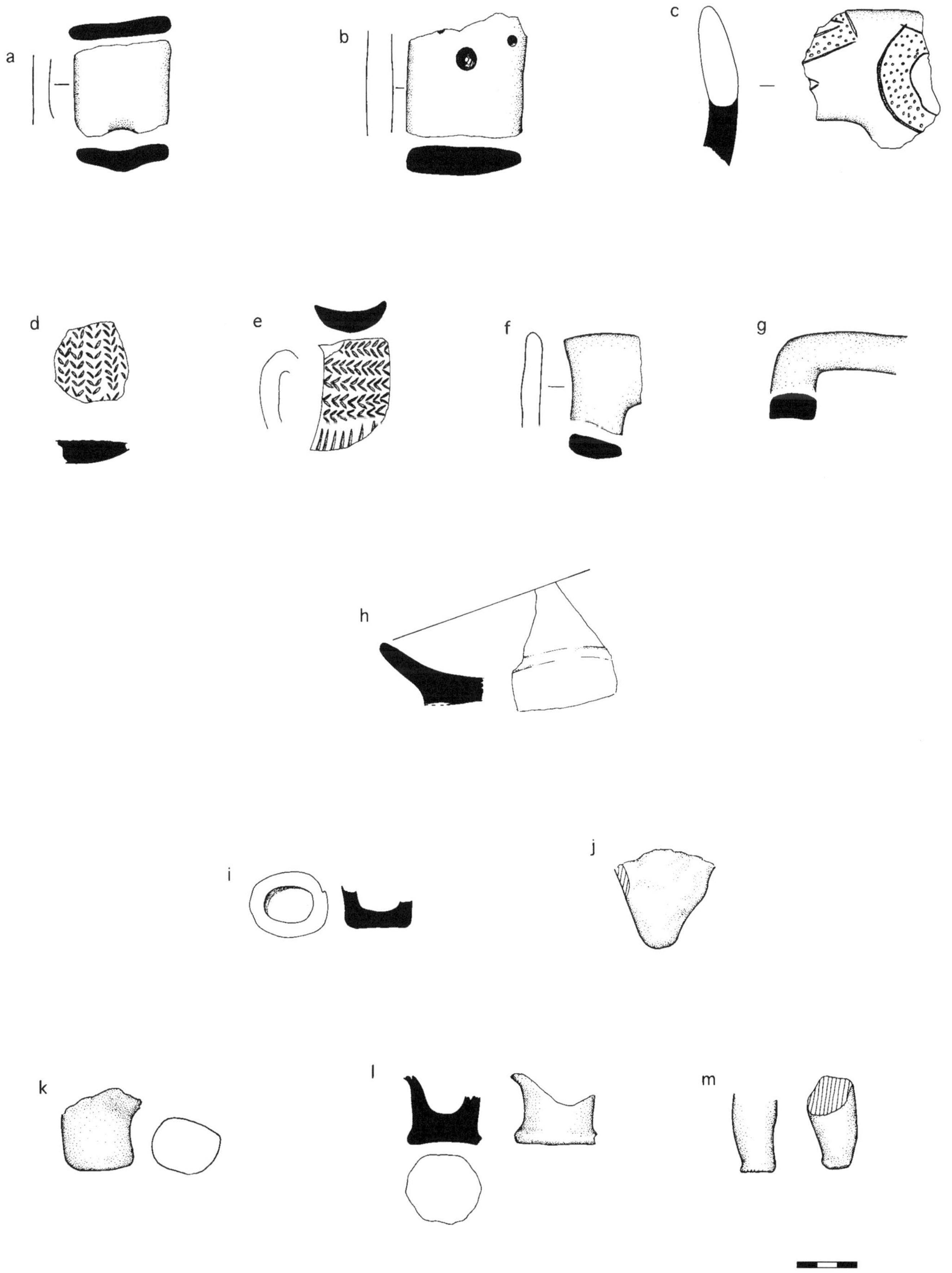

Figure 58 FCP 5.1 L5 assorted surface finishes

a. L5NE:24+27NE RSMG1 0.08 E, I:bldg surfs, largely gone, crumbly, barely fired, brick red surfs, part of int spalled. C:gray. H:1–2, crumbles at touch.

b. L5NE:13 LRMG1 0.10–0.11 irreg E, I:scrpd, smthd but most of ext gone, pink w/ small gray cloud. H:1–2.

c. L5(NW):66 fDMG<1, f2 0.08–0.09, irreg E, I:bldg surf, irreg lumpy rim, hole pierced below rim pre-firing, grayish-tan surfs. H:2–3.

d. L5NE:23 LRMG1 0.14 E, I:scrpd but lumpy, smthd, better int, red surfs. C:red. H:1–2.

e. L5NE:17 mL1, R2–3 on bott 0.15 E, I:bldg surfs, slightly smth int, red surfs. C:blk. H:1–2.

f. L5NE:6 LRMG3 0.19 E, I:barely scrpd, smthd int, lumpy, mottled yellow-pink-gray, trace of pellet. C:gray. H:1–2.

g. L5NE:13 SRLMG<1, f2–3 0.16–0.22 irreg E:bldg surf, pink. I:smthd, pink, cracked along bott but did not quite break. C:gray center. H:2–3.

h. L5NE:8 LRMG1 0.24 irreg E, I:bldg surf, smthd, red surfs. C:red. H:1–2.

i. L5(NW):66 fR<1, aW5 at surf 0.22 E:bldg surf, slightly smthd, blk surfs, large rim tab w/ pre-firing oval hole, 2 holes drilled post-firing, 1 entirely from ext, 1 from both sides, half of third hole in break. I:scrpd, wet smthd, lightly brnshd. C:blk. H:2–3.

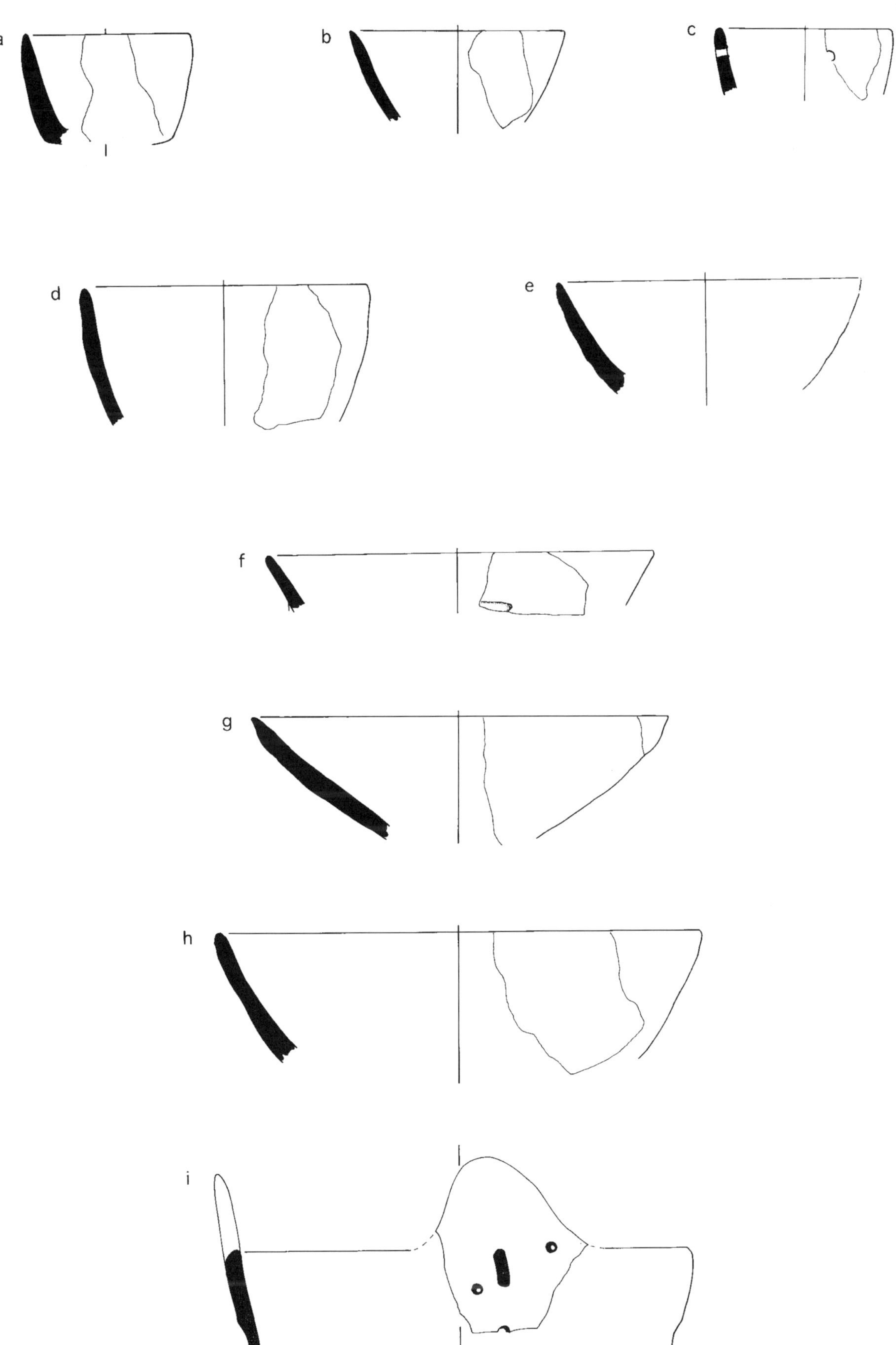
a
b
c
d
e
f
g
h
i

Figure 59 FCP 5.1 L5 assorted surface finishes

a. L5(NW):65 FP 219 SMG<1 0.06 3 joining, complete profile E, I:bldg surfs, finger depressions from pinching, pale red w/ dark clouds, darker int. C:gray center. H:1–2.

b. L5NE:15, non joining L5NE:3, 7, 11, 21 FP 220 SRMG<1 0.06–0.07 irreg complete profile preserved E, I:bldg surfs, lumpy pinch pot, asym, oval-rectangular holes poked before firing from ext, broken along line of holes, red surfs. C:gray. H:1–2.

c. L5NE:17 RLMG<1, mica glitter 0.15 E, I:bldg surf, slightly smthd, tab rim, brick red surfs. H:2–3.

d. L5NE:7 LMG1 0.10–0.12 irreg E, I:bldg surfs, lumpy, tan surfs. H:1–2.

e. L5NE:29 LMG1 0.19 E, I:scrpd but lumpy, few strokes brnshd, reddish-tan surfs, red cloud ext, milky white substance in rough areas, not affected by HCl. H:2–3.

f. L5NE:19 LRMG1, f2 0.25 E, I:scrpd, few strokes brnshd int, red w/ gray clouds, 2 sherds w/ incomplete crack through body. C:red. H:2–3.

g. L5NE:13 LRMG1, f2 0.23 E, I:bldg surfs, dark red surfs. C:gray center. H:1–2.

h. L5NE:23 LRMG1 0.30 E, I:bldg surf ext, smthd int, red surfs w/ gray clouds. C:gray at center. H:2–3.

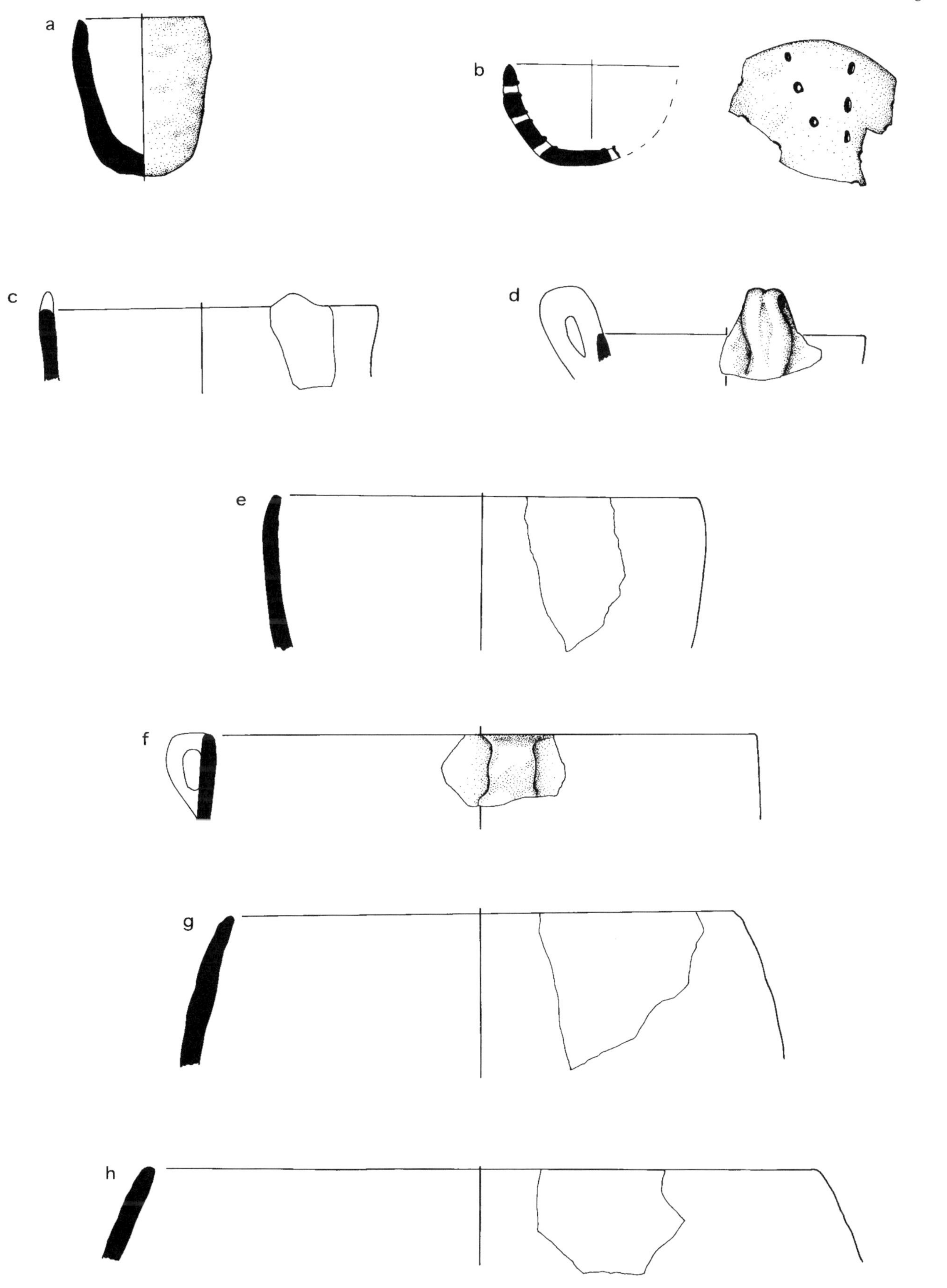
a
b
c
d
e
f
g
h

Figure 60 FCP 5.1 L5 assorted surface finishes

a. L5(NW):66 fRLMG<1 0.12 E, I:scrpd, few strokes brnsh ext, brwn-blk surfs, prob burned. Jagged edges. H:2–3.

b. L5NE:23 LRMG<1 0.18 E:scrpd, smthd, slipped, brnshd, blk surfs w/ yellow-orange clouds, crackling. I:scrpd, smthd, grayish-tan surfs. H:2–3.

c. L5NE:18 LRMG1, mica glitter 0.10 E, I:scrpd but lumpy, lightly damp brnshd, tan to gray surfs. Jagged edges. H:2–3.

d. L5NE:25 LRMG1 0.26 E, I:scrpd, slipped, brnshd, dark red surfs, int slip is thick, fingernail scratches up red powder. C:gray. H:1–2.

e. L5NE:3 LMG<1 0.28 E, I:scrpd, slipped, brnshd, gray surfs. C:gray. H:2.

f. L5NE:18 LRMG1 0.23 E:lumpy, brnshd, red surfs. I:scrpd, red surfs. C:gray. H:2–3.

g. L5NE:6 LRMG1, f2 0.28 E, I:lightly scrpd, few strokes brnsh, especially on int bott, red surfs. C:gray. H:1–2.

h. L5NE:7 LRMG2, hole from lost pebble inclusions 0.16 bott E:smthd, poss slip, red, brnshd. I:scrpd, smthd. H:1–2.

i. L5NE:23 LRMG1, f 3–5 0.15, bott E, I:scrpd but lumpy ext, poss slip, lightly brnshd, crackled, gray-tan ext, red int, traces white pt or encrustation. C:dark brwn. H:2–3.

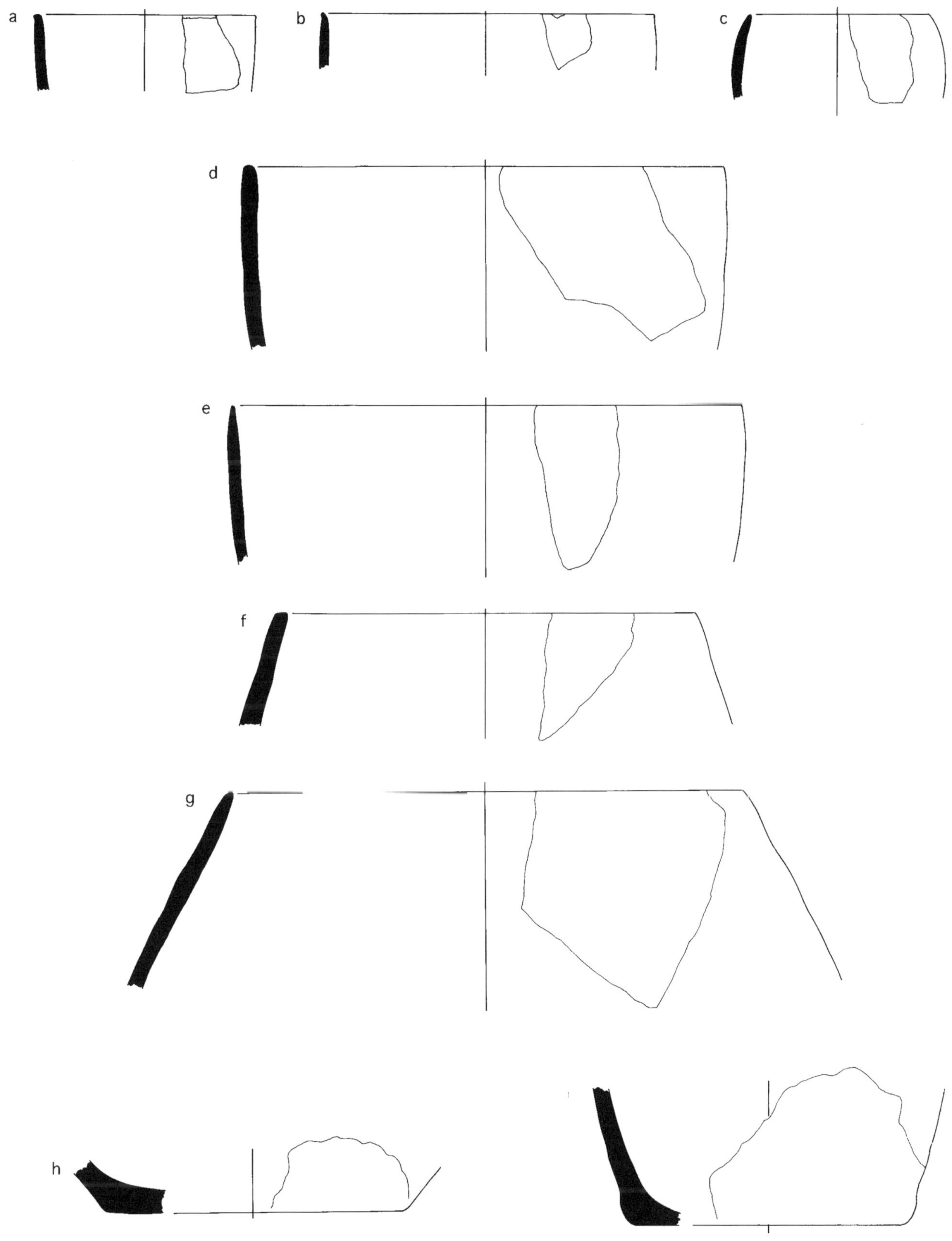

a
b
c
d
e
f
g
h

Figure 61 FCP 5.1 L5 assorted surface finishes

a. L5NE:17 LMG<1 0.21 E:scrpd but lumpy, poss slip, brnshd, crackling, gray surfs, poss burned. I:scrpd, smthd, gray surfs. C:gray. H:2–3.

b. L5(NW):64 fLRMG1–2 0.045 bott E, I:scrpd, smthd, lightly brnshd, gray-brwn surfs. C:gray. H:2–3.

c. L5(NW):64 aRWD<1 0.18 E, I:scrpd, poss brnshd, dark gray surfs, small red clouds. Raspy edges. H:2–3.

d. L5NE:13+15NE FP 222 LRMG1, f2–3 0.14–0.18, nearly oval 15 join, over half of upper body preserved E:lumpy, smthd, brnshd, red to blk surfs ext, brwn-blk int, Lime pebble in bott edge. C:red. H:2–3.

e. L5NE:19+23NE, non-joining 7NE, 11NE FP218 LSMG1, f2–3 0.21 E, I:scrpd but lumpy, poss slip, cursory damp brnsh, poss white pt, but no clear lines, brwn-blk surfs. C:gray center. Sharp edges. H:2–3.

f. L5(NW):65 fMG, frR2–3 0.08 bott E, U:scrpd, prob slipped, damp brnshd, blk, waxy, trace of handle stump, thin wall one side of bott that prob broke in firing. I:scrpd, damp brnshd, deep red center bott, rest surfs brwn. C:reddish-brwn. H:2–3.

g. L5NE:6 LRMG1 0.25 E, I:scrpd, smthd, lightly brnshd, brwn-blk surfs, burned. C:brwn-blk. H:1–2.

h. L5NE:13 FP 221 LRMG2–3, f pops 0.26 6 joining, rim and 2 handle scars preserved E, I:scrpd, smthd, brnshd, poss white pt, crackled and spalled, much original surf missing, dark surfs. C:dark gray. H:1–2.

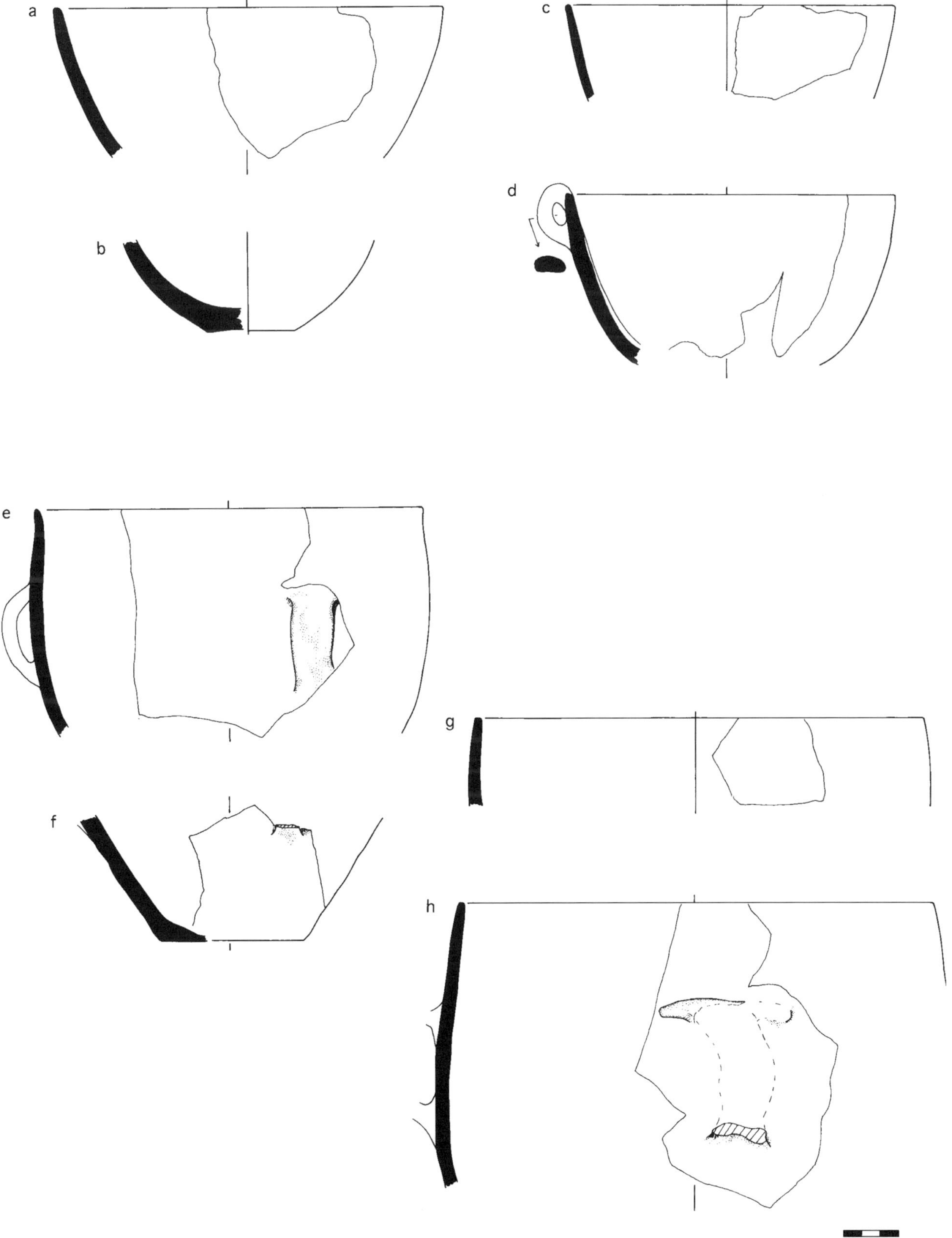
a
b
c
d
e
f
g
h

Figure 62 FCP 5.1 L5 assorted surface finishes

a. L5NE:2 LMG1–2 0.30 E, I:lumpy, wet smthd better on int, reddish-gray surfs, body sherd broken along coil joints, spalled at bott. H:2–3.

b. L5NE:6 LMG<1 0.32 E, I:scrpd, damp brnshd, piecrust rim w/ shallow indentations made with finger tip and short nails, red to gray-brwn. C:dark gray. H:1–2.

c. L5NE:3 LRMG<1, f3–4 6 joining E:lumpy, wet smthd, blk to greenish-white. I:scrpd, well smthd, red surfs, very lumpy rim. H:2.

d. L5(NW):62(1)+65NW(2)+66NW(1) SRMG<2 0.50 slightly warped Many joining and not E:bldg surf, rim folded to ext 5 cm, uneven, mottled red-brwn-blk-yellow surfs. I:scrpd, smthd, brnshd parallel to rim, tan surfs. C:red. Sharp edges, raspy. H:2–3.

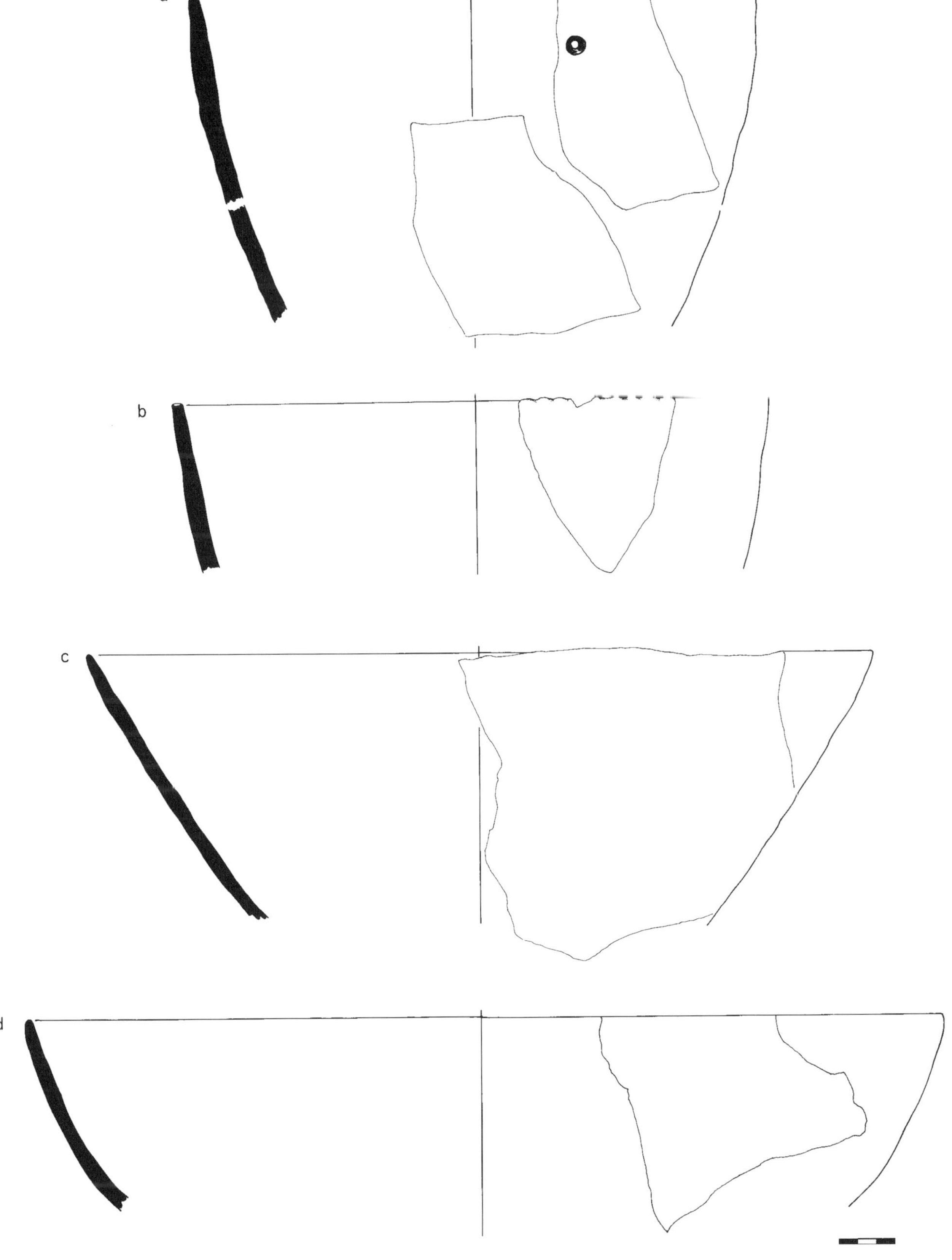
a
b
c
d

Figure 63 FCP 5.1 L5 assorted surface finishes

a. L5NE:15 (most)+18NE+19NE (rim, total 26 sherds), non-joining body sherds 7NE+15NE+18NE+19NE FP 226 mS1faRL1–2 0.37 E:well scrpd, smthd, cursory brnsh, red surfs w/ dark cloud, piecrust rim impressed w/ finger tips, applied band on body, impressed w/ finger tips. I:scrpd, smthd, crackling and worn, greenish surfs, spalled on int of body sherd. H:1–2.

b. L5NE:5 LMG<1 0.40–0.42 E, I:scrpd, smthd, light damp brnsh, brick red surfs, piecrust rim. Bott broken along coil joint. H:2–3.

c. L5NE:7+11NE LMG1f2 0.40 E, I:scrpd, smthd, brick red surfs. C:blk. H:1–2.

d. L5NE:10 aRLMG1 0.14–0.18 irreg E, U:lumpy, coil attached to ext of bottom disc, barely smthd, left to dry in situ, dark gray surfs. I:lightly smthd, reddish-gray surfs. H:2–3.

e. L5NE:13 LRMG1 0.11 bott E, I:lumpy, smthd, uneven wall thickness, red-gray surfs. H:2–3.

f. L5NE:11 LRMG<1, f2 0.26 bott E, I:coil attached to edge of disc that was resting on rough surf, along ext joint traces of pinkish Lime-rich clay, deep red surfs. C:gray. H:1–2.

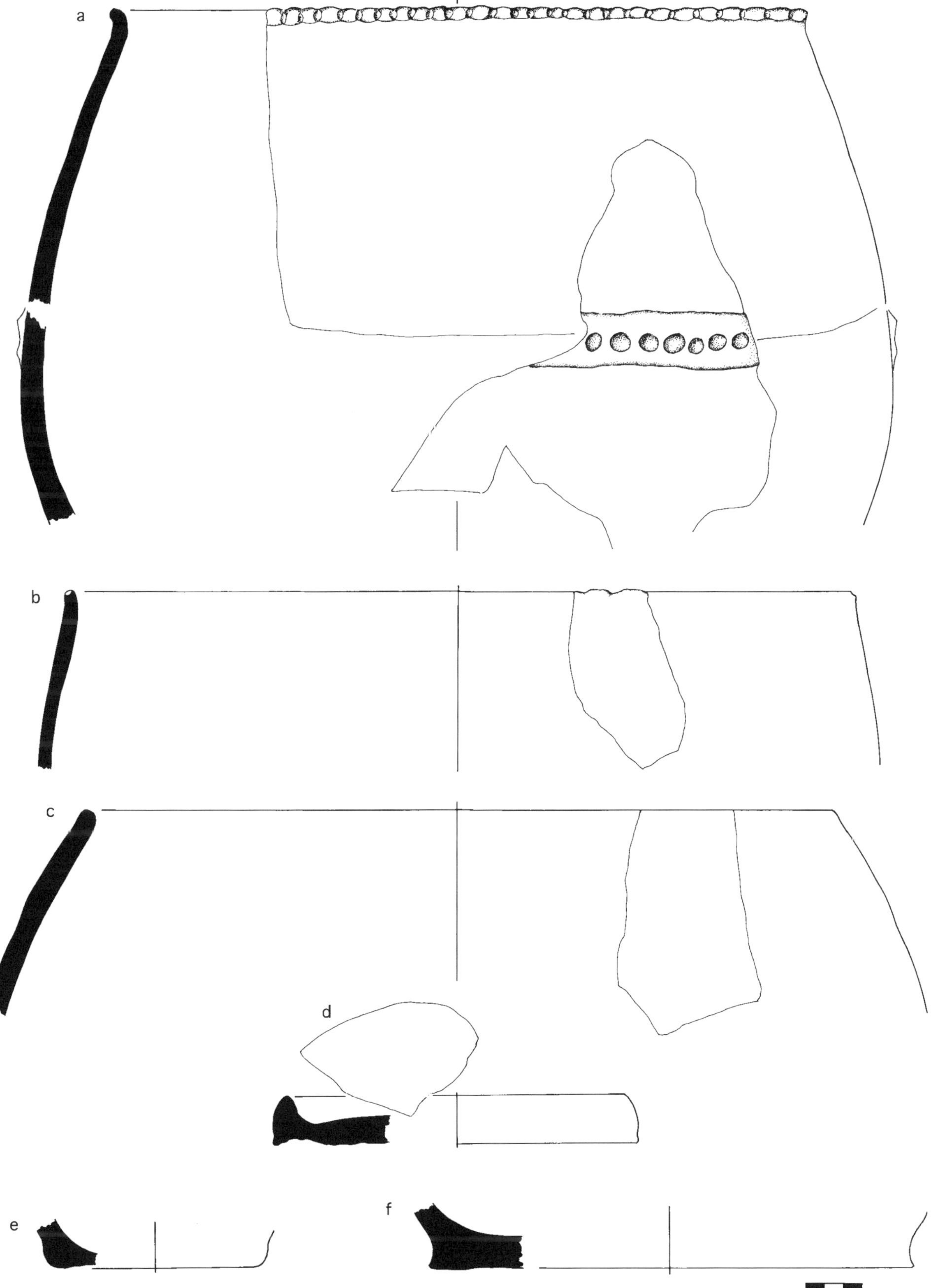
a
b
c
d
e
f

Figure 64 FCP 5.1 L5 Crusted variety

a. L5NE:13+3(2) a.1, L5(NW)61+63, a.2 FP 223 LSMG<1, pebble 2 in break 0.16 prob treated w/ PVA when excavated E:scrpd, finger smthd, 2 mm-thick crust of white Lime, patt in red pt; on a.2 also clear blk pt. I:scrpd, smthd, troughs from damp brnsh, pink surfs (a.1), brwn (a.2), traces red powder. C:blk. Pl. 6a.

b. L5(NW):60 (5 and 1 non-joining) b.1–2, L5NE:23(3) b.3 0.14 prob treated w/ PVA when excavated E:scrpd, smthd and roughened, 2 mm-thick white Lime crust, patt in red pt, 1 sherd charred after breaking, crust powdery white, tan surfs. I:scrpd, smthd, faint traces red powder. C:dark.

c. L5NE:32 5 joining DMG<1, frR2 0.18 prob treated w/ PVA when excavated E:scrpd, wet smthd, 1 mm-thick white Lime crust, patt in red pt, trace of blk outline. I:scrpd, wet smthd, traces red powder.

d. L5NE:20 (5)+23NE (1) and non-joining 18NE SRMG<1 0.18 prob treated w/ PVA when excavated E:scrpd, smthd, mottled surfs, white Lime crust, unclear patt in red pt. I:scrpd, smthd, traces red powder. C:blk.

e. L5NE:18+19NE fSDMG<1 0.17 irreg prob treated w/ PVA when excavated E:scrpd, smthd, tan surfs, white Lime crust, patt in red and blk pt. I:scrpd, smthd, no traces powder. C:tan.

f. L5(NW):65 SDLMG<1 0.15 E:scrpd, smthd, pinkish-brwn surfs, 2–3 mm white Lime crust, very granular crystals. I:scrpd, smthd, red pt, poss white pt. C:gray. H:2–3.

g. L5NE:19 RLMG<1, blk spots poss from organic inclusions 0.12 E:scrpd, smthd,pink surfs, clump of powdery white Lime crust. I:scrpd, smthd, pink surfs. C:gray. H:1–2.

h. L5NE:18 or 19 SMG<1 0.14 max treated w/ PVA when excavated E:scrpd, smthd, red surfs, thick white Lime crust, patt in red (10R 6/8) and blk powdery pt. I:scrpd, damp brnshd, reddish surfs, wall thickness varies. H:1–2.

i. L5NE:19, 2 joining 0.16 max, 0.035 bott E:scrpd, finger smthd, reddish-brwn, mottled surfs, traces 1 mm-th white Lime crust, traces red pt. I:scrpd, wet smthd, traces red powder, gray-brwn surfs, wall thickness varies, bulge above dimple. H:1–2.

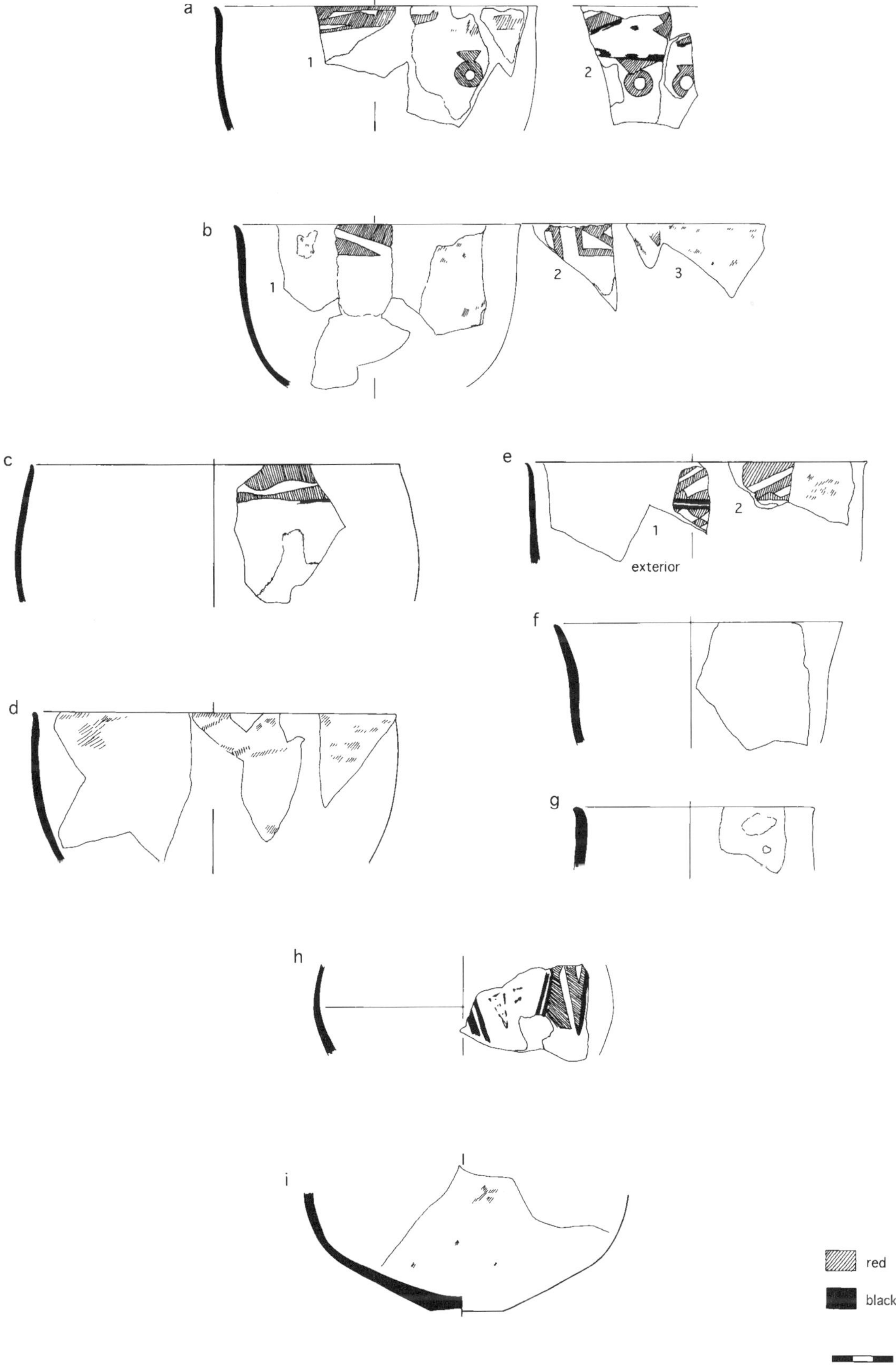
a
1
2
b
1
2
3
c
e
1
2
exterior
f
d
g
h
i
red
black

Figure 65 FCP 5.1 L5 White Painted decoration

a. L5(NW):65+66 FP 225 fSRMG<1, straw-like impressions, several L2 in breaks 0.12 15 joining preserve two-thirds of cup E:scrpd, damp brnshd, patt in white pt, no reaction in HCl, 4 groups of 3 lines each, mottled red-brwn-gray surfs. I:scrpd, finger smthd, finger groove around bott, center bott sags. H:2–3.

b. L5(NW):65+66NW FP 217 LMG<1 0.12 4 joining preserve complete profile E:scrpd, smthd, poss slipped, lightly brnshd, ghost patt in interruption of brnsh, mottled surfs red-tan-gray. I:scrpd, smthd, poss slipped, brnshd, lumpy rim, wall thickness varies, center bott thin and sagging. C:gray. H:2–3.

c. L5NE:19 FP 198 LMG1–2, powdery 0.20, warped E:scrpd, smthd, patt in white pt, damp brnshd, dark gray surfs, burned and warped, pt looks blk in places, crackling and crawling. I:scrpd, smthd, damp brnshd, dark gray surfs. C:gray. H:2–3. Pl. 6b.

d. L5NE:7 LRMG1 0.24 E:scrpd, smthd, poss brnshd, traces white pt, red surfs, tab at rim. I:scrpd, smthd, red surfs. H:1–2.

e. L5NE:23 RLMG1 0.26 max E:scrpd, smthd, poss brnshd, patt in white pt, disappears in HCl, blk surfs on 2 sherds, red on others. I:scrpd, smthd, few strokes of brnsh, red surfs on all sherds.

f. L5NE:21 LRMG<1, f2 0.30 E:scrpd, smthd, poss slipped, brnshd, patt in white pt, red surfs. I:scrpd, smthd, pale red surfs. C:gray. H:1–2.

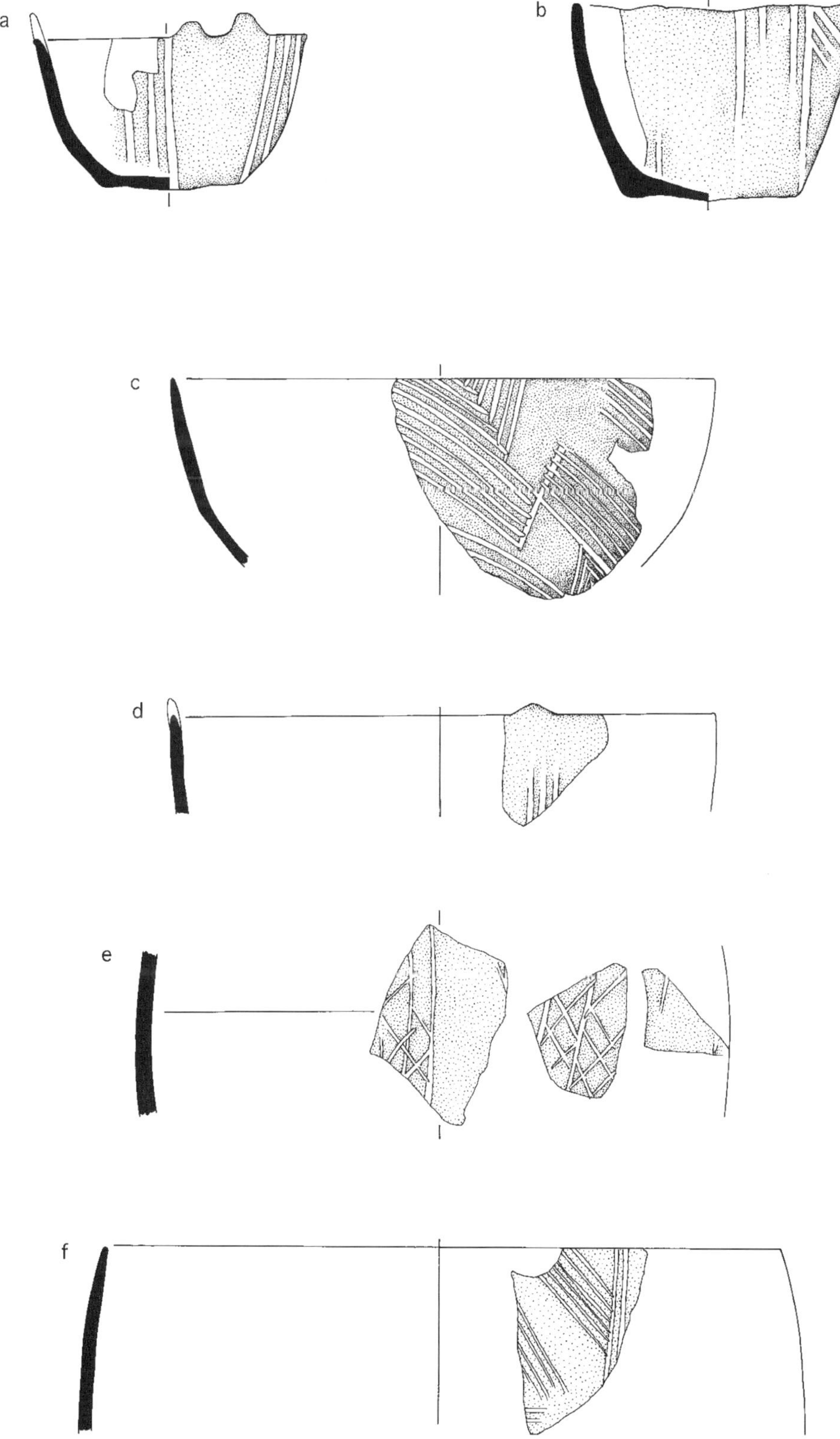
a
b
c
d
e
f

Figure 66 FCP 5.1 L5 Polychrome and other painted decoration

a. L5NE:2+3NE FP 224 RDLMG<1 0.30 max 15 joining, 16 non-joining w/ no trace of patt, prob treated w/ PVA E:scrpd, smthd, damp brnshd, prob white slip, largely gone, patt of broad areas red pt outlined in blk, barely visible, pale pink surfs, small gray clouds, hole drilled from ext. I:scrpd, smthd, light brnsh at neck, grayish to yellowish-white surfs, spall on same break as drill hole, edges badly worn. C:deep gray, light subsurfs. H:1–2.

b. L5NE:23 RDLMG<1 0.30 max E:scrpd, smthd, flecks of red pt on white pt. I:scrpd, smthd, drips of red pt, pale pink surfs. C:gray. H:1–2.

c. L5(NW):58 aRLMG<1 0.22 Treated w/ PVA E:scrpd, smthd,patt in white pt and red (2.5YR 5/8) pt, unclear which was applied first, no reaction in HCl, yellowish-gray surfs. C:dark gray. H:2–3.

d. L5NE:17 LRMG<1 0.24 E:scrpd, smthd, traces of white encrustation or Lime pt, few flecks of powdery red pt, pale surfs. I:scrpd, damp brnshd, traces red powder, pale surfs. C:blk. H:1–2.

e. L5NE:17 LRMG<1 0.20 E:scrpd, damp brnshd, slipped w/ creamy white pt, traces red pt, pink surfs. I:scrpd, traces red (10R 5/8)pt, brnshd. C:gray. H:1–2.

f. L5NE:21 RLMG1, f2 0.19 E:scrpd, wet smthd, hint of white slip, traces of red pt. I:scrpd, smthd, red slipped. C:gray center. H:1–2.

g. L5NE:23 LMG1 0.12 base E:rough at lip, smthd above, poss white creamy slip, traces red pt. I:scrpd, wet smthd, pink surfs. C:gray. H:2–3.

h. L5NE:19 LRMG1 0.09 bott Almost complete bott preserved E:scrpd, smthd, prob white slip, flecks of red pt, brnshd, mottled surfs. I, U:scrpd, smthd, 2 drill holes, one each on opposite sides of wall.

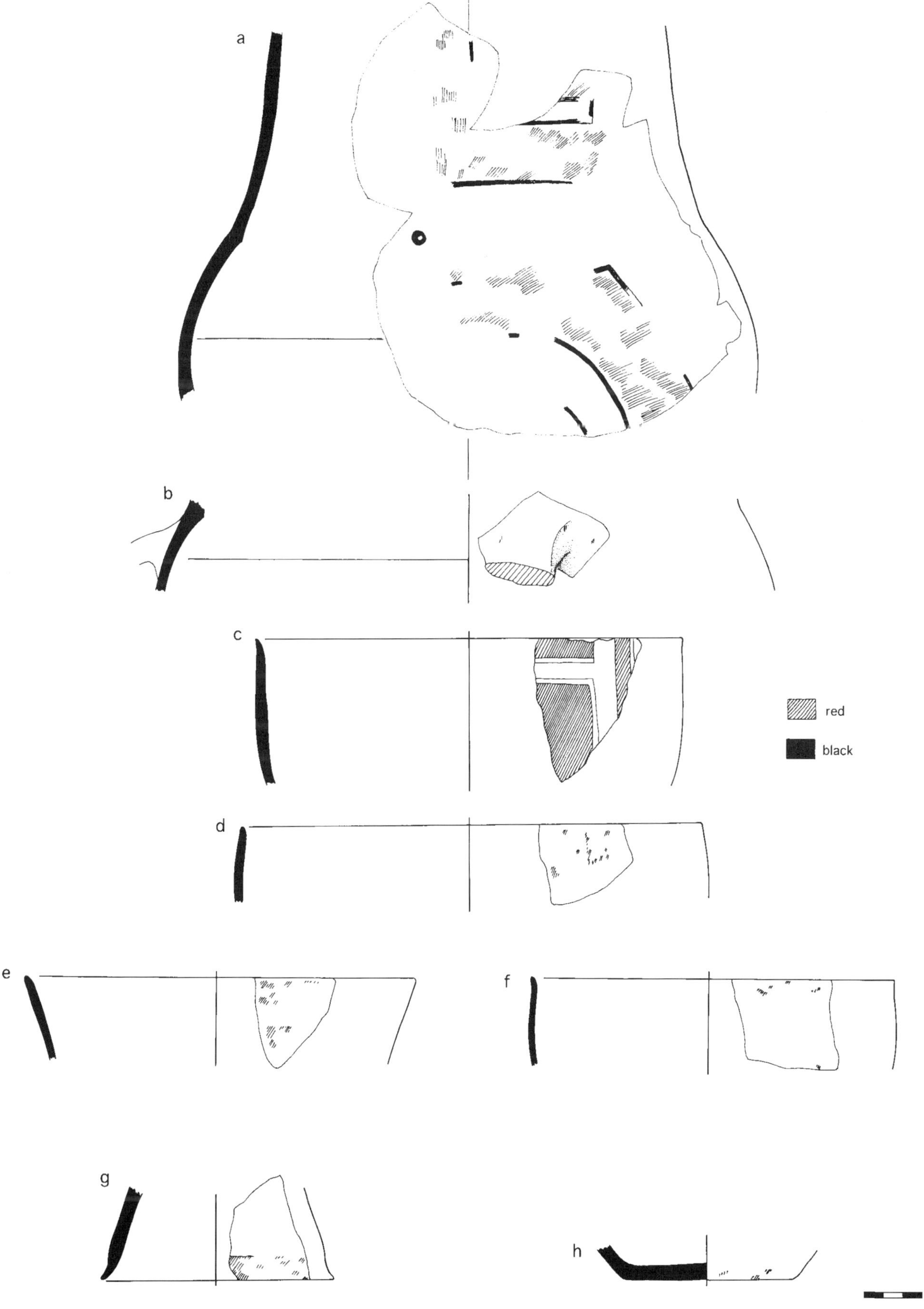
a
b
c
d
e
f
g
h
red
black

Figure 67 FCP 5.1 L5 assorted surface finishes

a. L5NE:17 RMG<1, gold mica glitter 0.12 E:scrpd, smthd, brnshd, trace of poss white slip or encrustation, orange (2.5YR 5/6) pigment that looks unfired, although surfs dark gray and burned. I:scrpd, smthd, traces red-orange pigment, dark gray. C:dark gray. H:2–3.

b. L5NE:6 LMG1 0.14 E, I:scrpd, smthd better int than ext, red slipped, light brnsh. H:1–2.

c. L5NE:23 LRMG1 0.15 E, I:scrpd, wet smthd, poss slip, red, cursory brnsh, dark red surfs. C:gray. H:2–3.

d. L5NE:18 LRMG1 0.18 E:scrpd but lumpy, smthd, slipped, red, few strokes brnsh. I:scrpd but lumpy, smthd, pink surfs. C:dark gray. H:2–3.

e. L5NE:11+6NE LRMG1 0.20, irreg E:lumpy, smthd, white encrustation that might be Lime crust, pink surfs w/ yellow and gray clouds. I:smthd, traces red pt, mottled surfs. C:gray. H:1–2.

f. L5(NW):65 aRDMG<1, pebble 4 in break 0.25 E, I:scrpd, smthd, poss slip, red, brnshd, very friable. C:dark gray. H:2–3.

g. L5NE:10 LRMG<1 0.24 E, I:scrpd, smthd damp w/ pebble, some of ext looks intentionally roughened, no traces of crusting, tan surfs w/ yellow-gray cloud ext. C:gray. H:2.

h. L5(NW):65+66NW+67NW LMG1, pops 0.10 bott 5 joining E:scrpd, smthd, poss slipped, brnshd, patch of encrustation treated w/ PVA, has flecks of carbon in it, gray to pale yellowish surfs. I:scrpd, smthd, dark surfs, sherds from 65NW burned blk int, light ext. H:2–3.

i. O5NE:11 FP 197 (prob FCP 5.2) SRDW<1 0.12 Missing several rim sherds and small body sherd E:scrpd, smthd, slipped, pinkish-red, powdery when excavated, consolidated w/ PVA, poss brnsh, very worn, yellowish-tan surfs w/ gray clouds. I:scrpd, smthd, traces pinkish-red pigment, int rim beveled and old breaks worn smth. C:gray. H:2–3.

j. L5(NW):79, 80NW, 88NW, 89NW, 92NW PB SMG1, fL<1 0.18 E, I:well scrpd, even wall thickness, smthd, slipped, PB, greasy, waxy blk, bott sherds worn, rim not. C:red. H:1–2.

k. L5NE:2 SMG<1, mica glitter 0.15 max E:scrpd, wet smthd, incised, pink surfs. I:scrpd, smthd, pink surfs. C:gray. H:2–3.

l. L5NE:3 SRMG<1 0.20 E:scrpd, smthd, narrow shaky incisions, gray surfs w. pink area, prob burned, scar of pellet or handle. I:scrpd, damp brnshd, grayish-tan. C:gray. H:1–2.

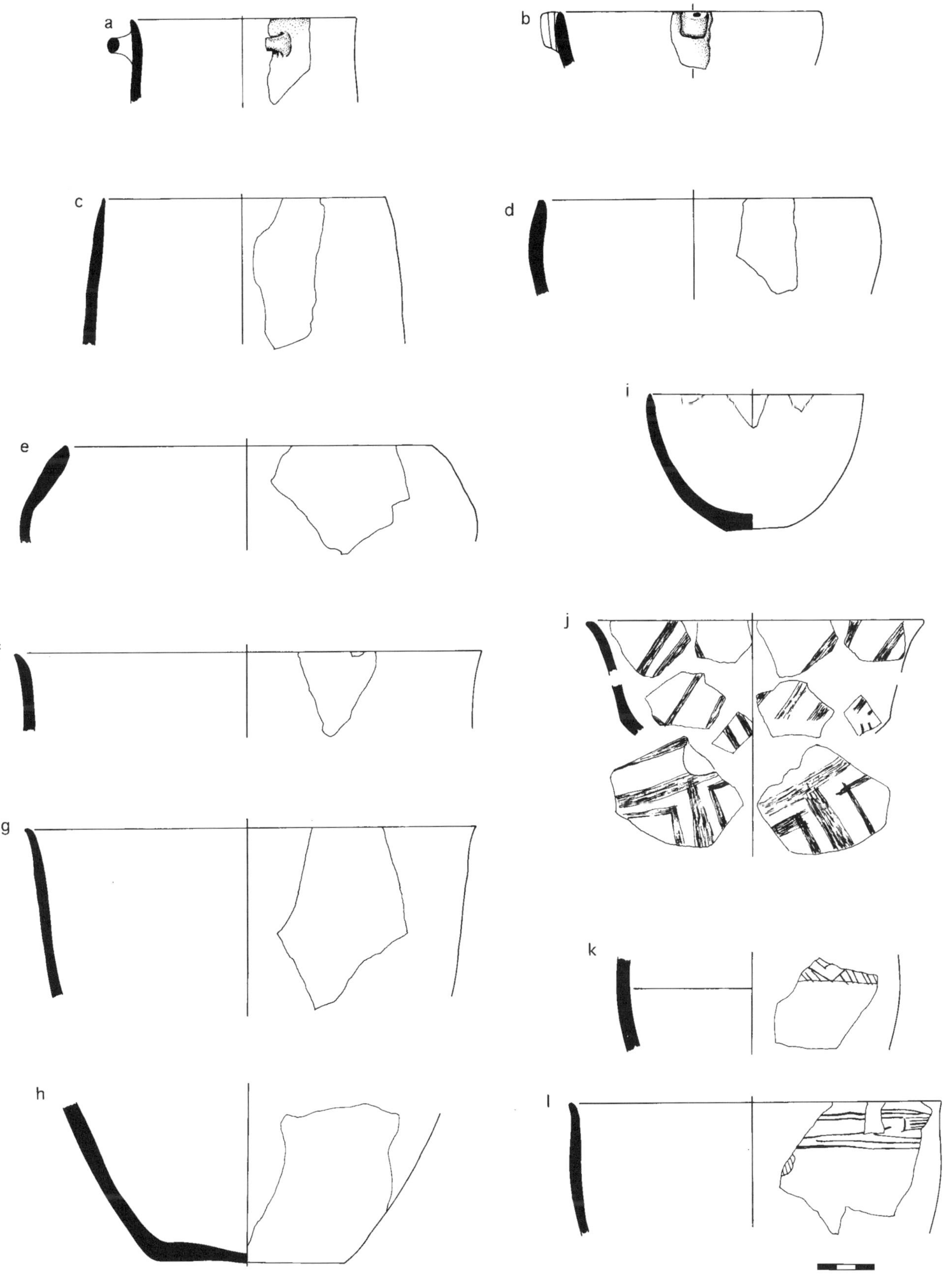
a
b
c
d
e
f
g
h
i
j
k
l

Figure 68 FCP 5.1 L5 assorted surface finishes

a. L5NE:7 LRMG1 0.16, irreg E:scrpd, brnshd, pink surfs, lumpy rim. I:scrpd, few strokes brnsh, pink surfs. H:1–2.

b. L5NE:6 LRMG<1 0.22 E, I:scrpd, brnshd, pink surfs. C:dark gray. H:1–2.

c. L5NE:13 mRMG<1 0.08 E, I:scrpd, brnshd, pink surfs, flecks red pt, worn. C:dark gray. H:1–2.

d. L5NE:19 LRDMG<1 0.10–0.11, irreg E:scrpd, smthd, poss white slip, poss brnsh, pink surfs, poss red pt, worn. I:scrpd, smthd, poss slip, red surfs, poss brnsh. C:gray center. H:2–3.

e. L5NE:6 SLRMG<1 2 handles, each w/ applied horn, surely from same pot but no body sherds in units E, I:scrpd, smthd, traces red pt on all surfs, one detached at both joints, other detached at one joint, broken at other end. C:dark gray. H:1–2.

f. L5NE:11 LRMG<1 0.12–0.13 max E, I:smthd, traces red pt all surfs, pale pink fabric. C:gray. H:1–2.

g. L5NE:11 LRMG<1 0.23 neck E:scrpd, smthd, traces red pt, pale pink fabric. I:scrpd, traces drips of red pt at neck, support clay added under shoulder. H:1–2.

h. L5NE:11 LRMG1, f2 greenish (talc?) 0.28 max E:scrpd, smthd, pale pink surfs, poss creamy white slip, traces red pigment. I:scrpd, slipped, red (2.5YR 5/8). C:gray. H:1–2.

i. L5NE:8 FP 227a(1), b(2) fRDLMG<1 0.13 (1), 0.15 (2) E, I:scrpd thin, smthd, traces red pt on all surfs, lightly brnshd, pale pink fabric, gray clouds. C:gray. H:1–2.

Figure 68

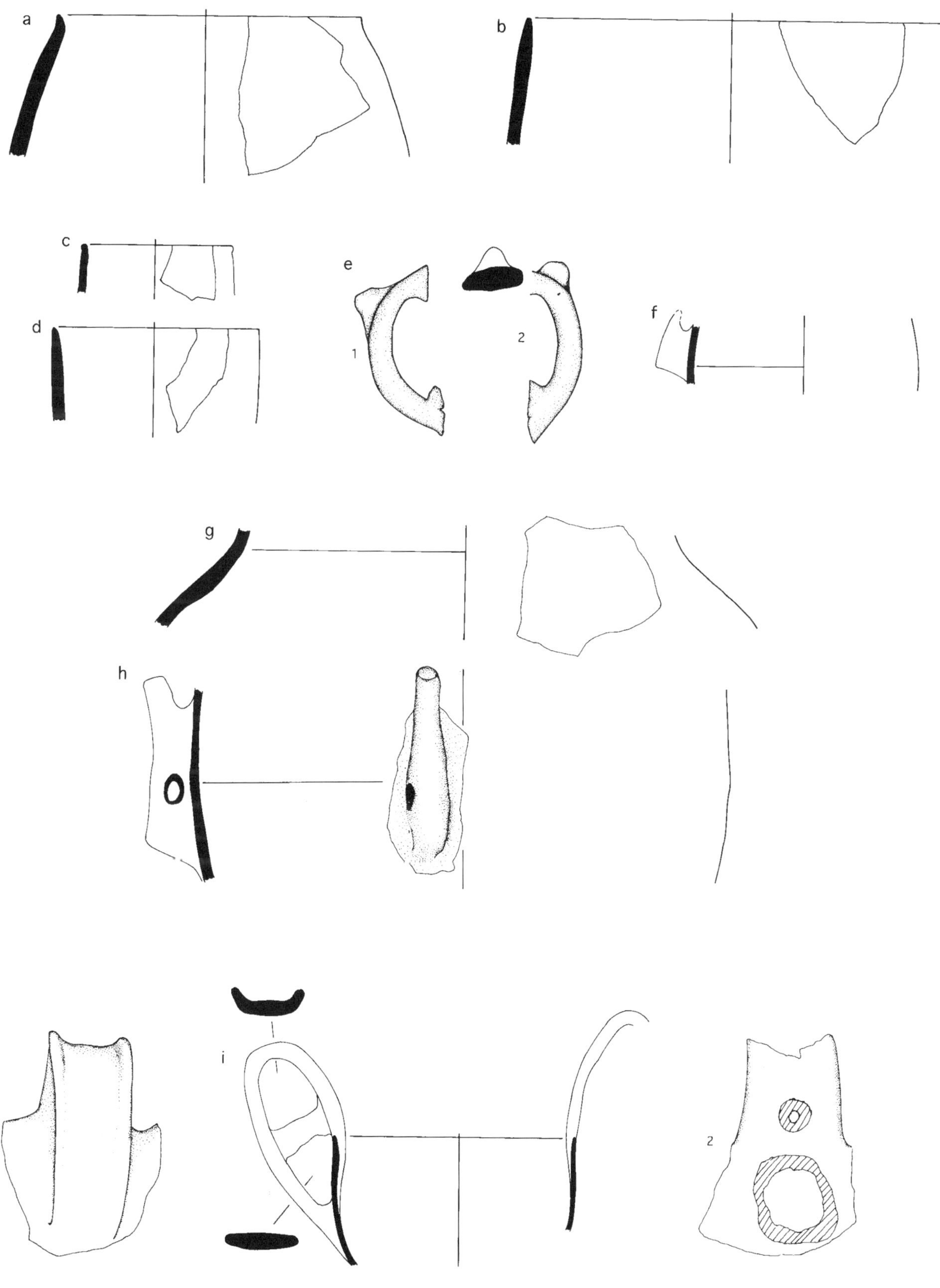

Figure 69 FCP 5.2 Heavy Burnished variety from poor contexts

a. G1:3 FP 118, display HB LR2–3 0.09 RIP 2 large frags, each w/ rim and double lug E:scrpd but lumpy, slipped, well brnshd, mottled surfs tan-gray, side not illustrated has 2 lugs, pierced separately. I:bldg surf, wet smthd collar, incompletely joined coil, support clay added under shoulder, gray surfs.

b. FA QSW+WB:29 HB RWLMG2–3 0.12, irreg E, I:scrpd, slipped, brnshd, waxy but worn, brwn surfs, red cloud at ext rim. C:blk to brwn. H:4.

c. Unstratified FP 266 HB aRDMG2 0.13 E:scrpd, slipped, brnshd, waxy, glossy, blk w/ red clouds on one lug, opposite rim. I:smthd, red pt to joint, brnshd just at rim, grayish-tan surfs. C:blk, pink subsurf int. H:4–6.

d. A:40 (Lot 12) HB DMG1 0.18 joint E:scrpd, prob slipped, brnshd, grayish-brwn w/ red clouds, patt looks blk, prob was white ptd, barely visible. I:scrpd, brnshd brwn. C:dark w/ light subsurfs. H:4.

e. FA QSE+EB:35 FPSC 218 HB LMG1 0.18 max E, I:scrpd, slipped, brnshd, blk surfs w/ creamy and reddish tinges, ridge around body swells to droopy lug w/ double vert piercing. C:blk. H:4.

f. FA QSW+WB:29 FPSC 207 HB LDMG2 0.30 E:scrpd, slipped, brnshd, was waxy, glossy, worn, patt in dull white-brwn pt, brwn-blk surfs. I:scrpd, slipped, brnshd, dark surfs. C:blk. H:3.

g. A:40 (Lot 12) HB aRDMG1, voids 0.31 E, I:scrpd, slipped, brnshd hor, dark brwn-blk surfs w/ reddish tinge, patt barely visible in white/blk pt ext. C:gray. H:2–3.

h. A Lot 13 HB DMG1 0.36 irreg E, I:scrpd, slipped, brnshd, red-orange-blk surfs. C:gray. H:2–3.

i. A:40 (Lot 12) HB aRMG1–2, voids 0.35 max E, I:scrpd, slipped, brnshd, waxy, patt in thin white pt ext, dark gray surfs. C:dark gray. H:2–3.

j. A:2 FP 6 HB mDRSMG<1, voids 0.22 E:scrpd, slipped, brnshd, brwn-reddish-brwn U:scrpd, slipped, brnshd, impressed or incised patt, yellow-brwn surfs w/ dark clouds. I:scrpd, smthd, blk surfs, worn along int curve and bott. C:dark gray. H:4.

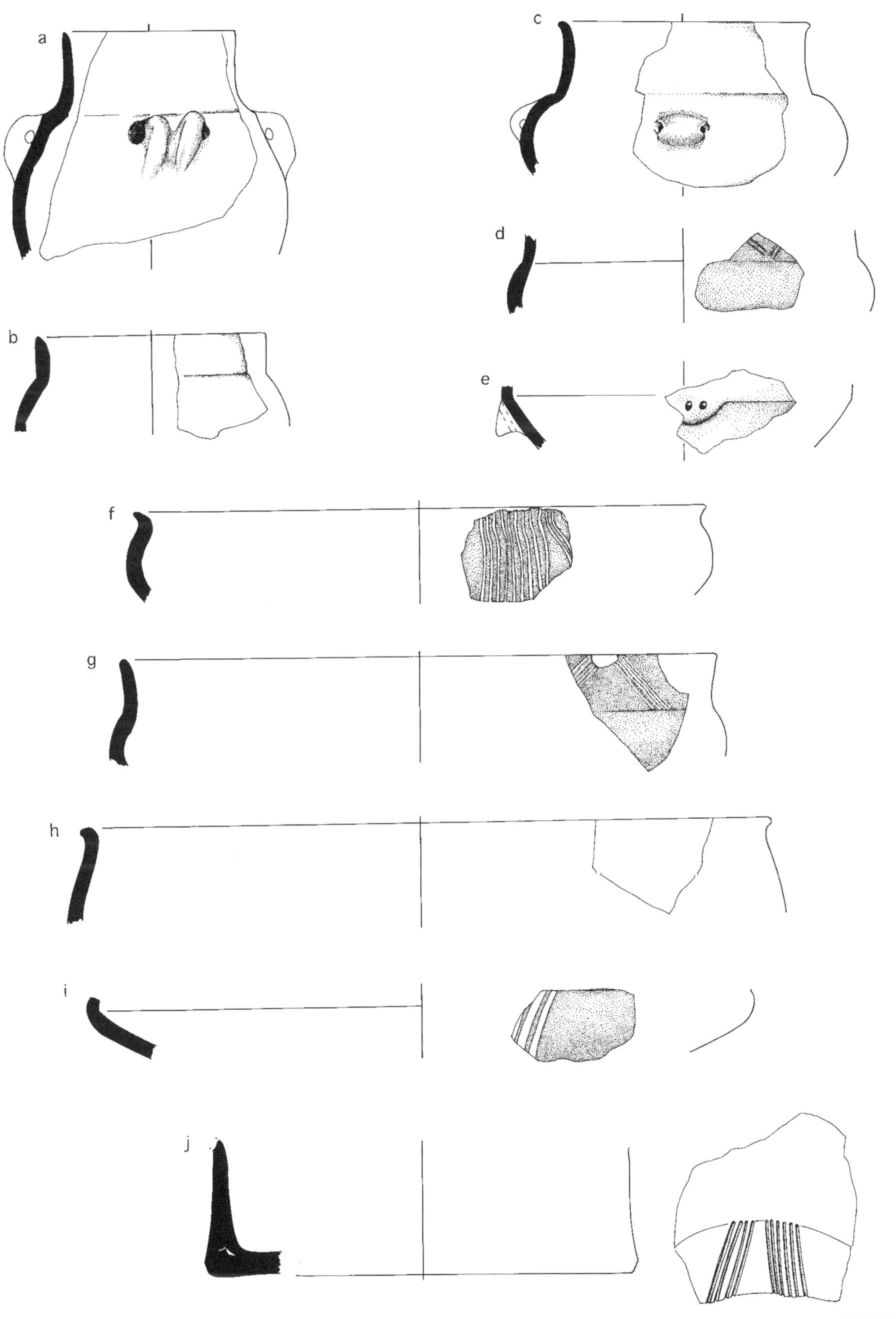
a
b
c
d
e
f
g
h
i
j

Figure 70 FCP 5.2 Heavy Burnished variety from poor contexts

a. A:24 (Lot 13) HB SMG<1, f1 0.19 E, I:scrpd, smthd, prob slipped, brnshd, creamy orange ext, gray cloud at car, crackling ext, burned or high-fired. Raspy, sharp edges. H:4–5.

b. FA QSE+EB:43+45EB FP 267 HB DMG1, fL 0.22–0.23 irreg E, I:scrpd, slipped, brnshd, waxy, glossy, blk w/ dark brwn clouds ext, blk int, overlapping coils evident in break. C:dark gray. H:4–5.

c. A:40 (Lot 12) HB aDSMG1 0.19 E, I:scrpd, slipped, brnshd, waxy, blk surfs, several 2 mm diameter red clouds. C:blk. H:2–3.

d. FA QSW+WB:33B FPSC 210 HB DMG<1 0.22 E, I:scrpd, slipped, brnshd, dark w/ creamy reddish tinge. C:dark gray. H:3.

e. A:40 (Lot 12) FP 33 HB SMG1 0.24 E:scrpd, slipped, brnshd, waxy, glossy, reddish at rim, gray-brwn below, patt in white pt, no reaction in HCl. I:scrpd, slipped, brnshd, grayish-green surfs. C:gray w/ light int subsurf. H:2–3.

f. FA QSW:34 HB LRDMG2 0.29 E, I:scrpd, slipped, brnshd, waxy but worn, dark gray surfs w/ creamy tinge, int bott worn, slits w/in breaks suggest overlapping coils. C:dark gray H:3.

g. Unstratified HB RDMG1, f2 FPSC 214 0.31 E,I:scrpd, slipped, brnshd, blk surfs, hor tube lug very thin, horizontal piercing cuts through body wall, overlapped coils in break C:gray-green. H:4.

h. FA QSW:27 FPSC 212 HB LRDMG2 0.26 or more, bent by pressure from lug E, I:scrpd, slipped, brnshd, much original surf worn away, blk surfs w/ pink powder from slip or poss crusting around lug ext, flecks of white Lime ext. C:blk. H:3–4.

i. FA QSW:27 FPSC 215 HB aWDMG2 0.23, irreg E, I:scrpd, smthd, slipped, brnshd, waxy, mottled bluish-gray-brwn-red ext, gray int, applied pellet/lug ext. C:blue-gray w/ orange streaks. H:3–5.

j. FA QSW+WB:40 FPSC 211 HB aDRMG<1,fL 0.18 E:scrpd, slipped, brnshd, dark surfs, heavy vert tube lug made from spiraling coil, pierced, very worn, poss burned. I:scrpd, smthd, few strokes brnsh, traces red powder. C:blk. H:3.

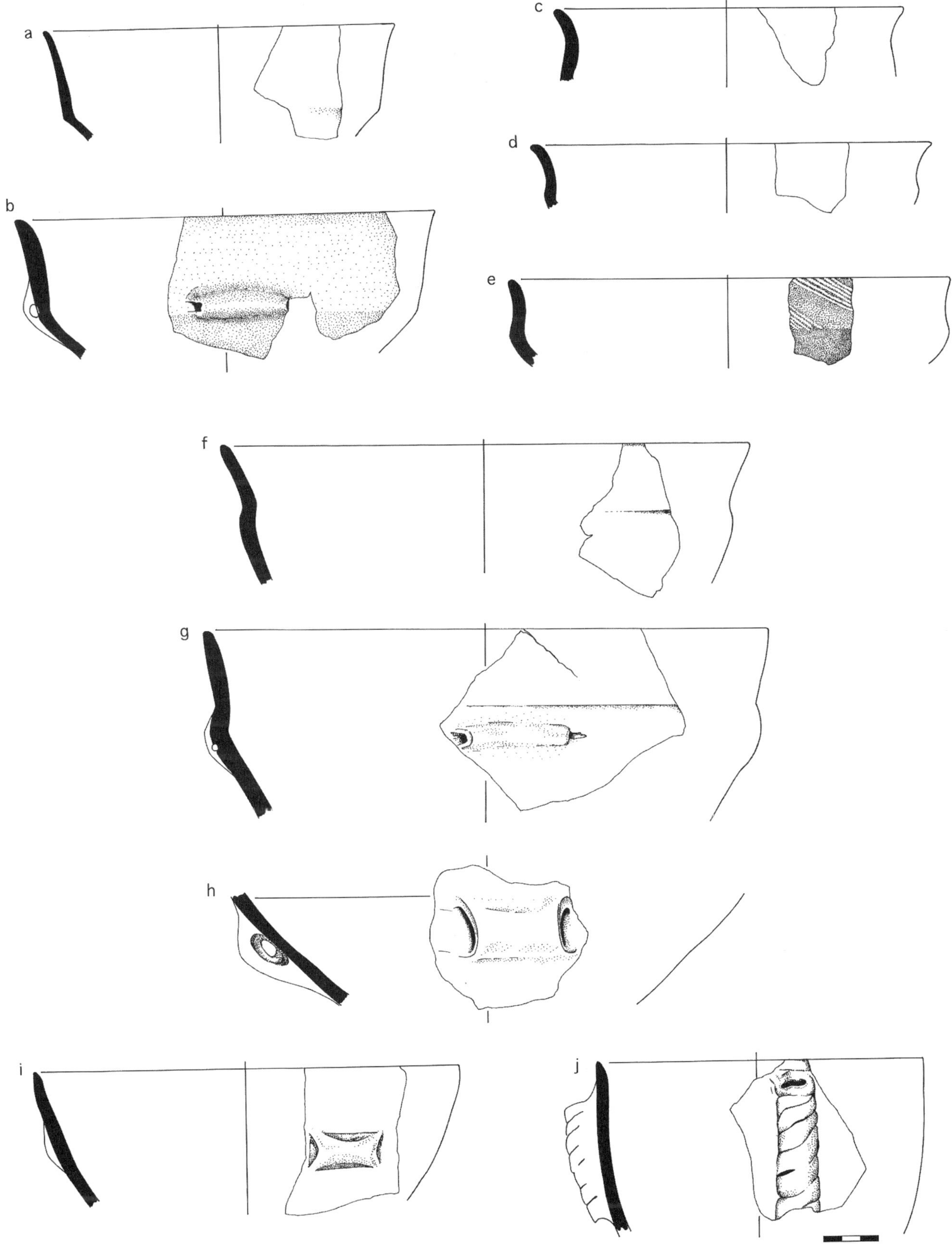
a
b
c
d
e
f
g
h
i
j

Figure 71 FCP5.2 Polychrome and Powdery decoration from poor contexts

a. FA QSE+EB:34 FP 145 PB aDMG<1 0.25 E:scrpd, smthd, slipped, red, PB w/ reserved band at rim, traces orange powder in reserved band. I:scrpd, smthd, surfs tan-gray, traces red-orange powder, does not react in HCl. C:light gray-green. H:2–3. Pl. 6c.

b. H1:51 FP 147 PB mDMG<1 0.17 E:scrpd, slipped, PB w/ reserved band at rim, traces orange powder in reserved band, grayish-brwn surfs. I:scrpd, smthd, traces orange powder, gray-brwn surfs. C:gray w/ lighter subsurfs. H:2–3.

c. A:23 (Lot 13) PB DrRMG<1, f2, voids 0.22 E:scrpd, smthd, slipped, PB w/ reserved band at rim, traces orange powder in reserved band, brwnish-gray surfs. I:scrpd, smthd, brnshd. C:brwnish-gray. H:2–3.

d. A:40 (Lot 12) PB DRMG1 0.18 bott E:scrpd, smthd, poss slipped, PB or solid brnsh w/ worn areas, dark surfs. I:scrpd, smthd, traces red powder. H:2–3.

e. FA QSW+WB:45 FP 152 Poly Powder DMG<1, frR2 0.13 treated w/ PVA E:scrpd, smthd, brnshd, blk surfs, patt in powdery white Lime and orange (2.5YR 6/8) pt. I:scrpd, smthd, clear traces powdery red pigment (7.5YR 3/8). C:light gray. H:3.

f. A:40 (Lot 12) FP 37 SMG<1, rR that fall out 0.20 E:scrpd, smthd, thin white slip, no reaction in HCl, brnshd, patt in red-orange powder, dark gray surfs below patt. I:scrpd, finger smthd, traces red powder, dark gray surfs. C:red center, gray subsurfs. H:2–3.

g. FA:55C DMG<1 0.14 E:scrpd, smthd, brnshd, dark surfs, patt in white Lime and red-orange powder. I:scrpd, smthd, red-orange powder, light surfs. C:gray. H:2–3.

h. Unstratified rRDMG<1 E:scrpd, smthd, traces glossy brnsh ext, red surfs. I:scrpd, wet smthd, few strokes brnsh, dull red surfs. H:2–3.

i. FA QSW+WB:31 FP 171 aDRMG1, fL E:scrpd, smthd, patt in red-orange, dull, crackling, and white pt, no reaction in HCl, light surfs. I:smthd, light surfs, three holes drilled from both sides, start of fourth, unfinished. C:dark gray. H:2–3.

j. A:40 (Lot 12) FP 46 fSWMG1 0.055 E:scrpd, smthd, coated w/ pale pink powder, traces white Lime powder, tan surfs. I:bldg surf, smthd as built, tan surfs. C:gray. H:2–3.

k. A Lot 13 SRMG<1 0.20 E:scrpd, smthd, damp brnshd, reddish glow to surfs, poss from red powder. I:scrpd, smthd, lightly brnshd, poss reserved area at rim, traces orange powder in reserved band. C:dark gray center, red subsurfs. H:2–3.

l. FA:58 FP 155 LMG<1, f2 E:unscrpd, smthd, creamy white Lime pt, patt in powdery orange, no longer clear, brnshd but flaking,pinkish-tan surfs. I:bldg surf, strut scar, upper end (as drawn) has traces of joint, lower finished in series of "toes." C:gray.

m. A:22 FP 8 SRMG<1 0.09 joint E, I:scrpd, brnshd, traces red-orange powder, pink surfs. U:bldg surf, smeared, crackling, pre-firing pin hole through base, pink surfs. C:blk, pink subsurfs.

n. A Lot 13 SRMG<1, voids 0.08 bot E:scrpd, smthd, bright orange powder, traces cutout edges. I:scrpd, dark red fingerprint. C:dark. H:2–3.

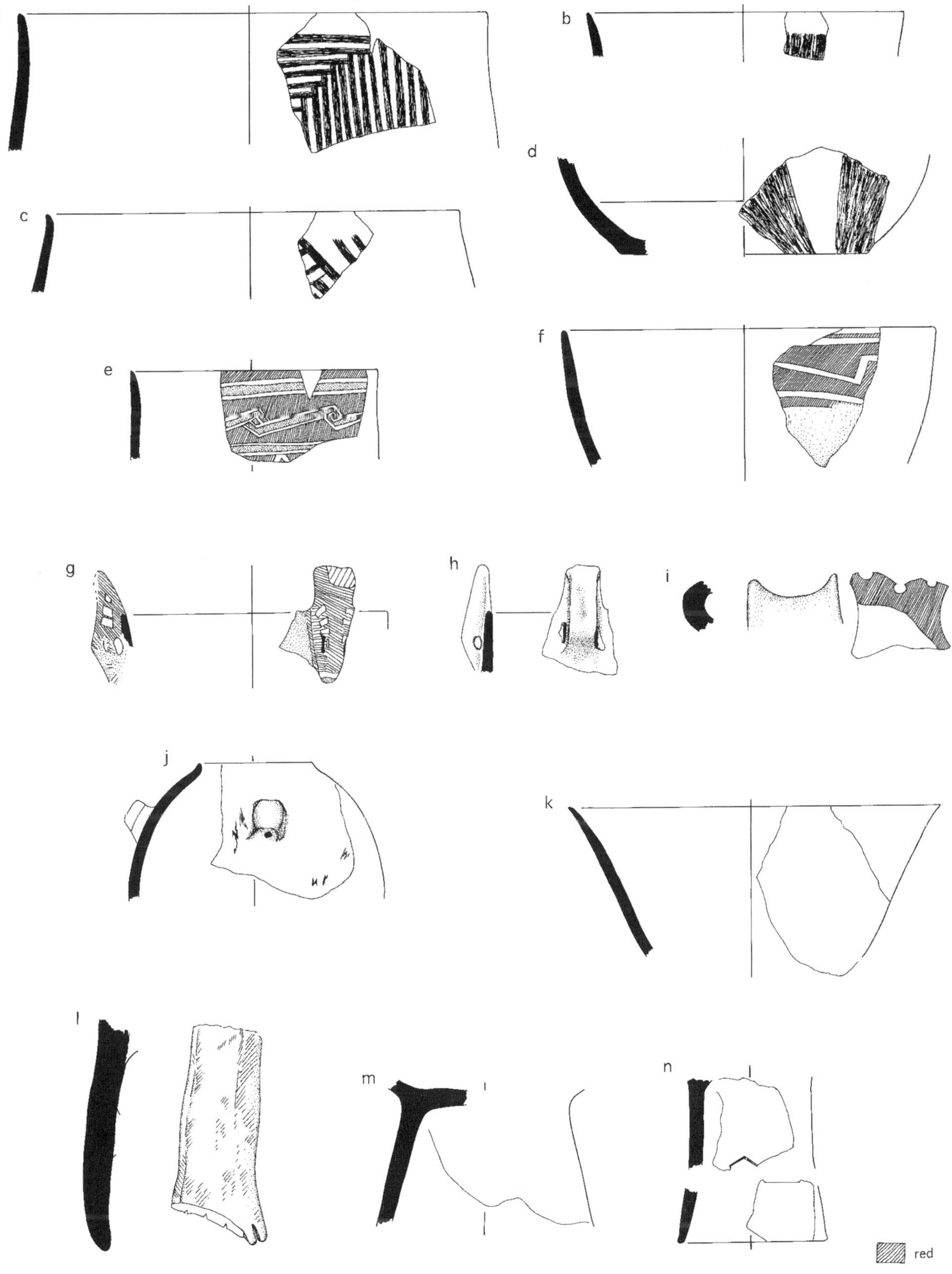
a
b
c
d
e
f
g
h
i
j
k
l
m
n
red

Figure 72 FCP 5 assorted painted decoration from poor contexts

a. G1:3 Red on White LRMG1 0.12 E:scrpd, white slip, patt in red, brnshd, flaking, light surfs. I:scrpd, traces red pt. C:gray. H:2–3.

b. A:25 (lot 13) Red on White 0.18 neck E:scrpd, smthd, white slip, patt in red, flaking, pink surfs. I:scrpd, smthd, white slip, flaking, pink surfs. C:gray center, pink subsurfs.

c. A:25 (Lot 13) Red on White LRMD<1 0.18 E:scrpd, white seems clay ground, color extends to subsurf, patt in red, tooling suggests base. I:scrpd, red-gray pt. C:gray.

d. G:38 FP 36 Red on White LMG<1 E, I:scrpd, smthd, brnshd, brwn surf, white slip where not brnshd, brnsh turns to yellow-brwn, patt in red, brnshd, glossy, flaking, thick 6–7 mm. C:gray. H:2–3.

e. H1:16 FPSC 202 Red on White DWMG<1 E, I:scrpd, smthd, white slip, patt in red, brnshd, waxy, flaking.

f. FF1:6 FP 90 Red on White RDMG<1, f1 E:scrpd, smthd, white slip, patt in red, well brnshd, flaking, pink surfs, gray cloud in "white" slip, red fired orange in cloud. I:scrpd, smthd, brnshd, flecks of white and red, thick 7–8 mm. C:gray, light subsurfs.

g. H1A:78 FP 173 LRMG<1, f2, pink sparkling stone 0.05–0.06 E:well-modeled, missing right eyeball, smthd, brnshd, white Lime once coated entire ext, flecks of red pt, poss brnshd, tan surfs. I:scrpd, trace of red-brwn stripe at top, brwn surfs. C:gray-brwn, light subsurfs. Talalay 1993 Pl. 8b, Jacobsen 1973b:Pl. 50a–b.

h. FA QSW+WB:31 fRDW<1, voids 0.25 max E, I:scrpd, smthd, white-fired fabric or white slip, patt in pinkish-red, outlined in blk, brnshd, poss burned, poss vitrified. C:dark.

i. FA WB:30 FPSC 200 PolyPtd mWMG1 0.30 E:scrpd, smthd, patt in MnO, blk, brnshd, and FeO, red, dull, crackling, pink surfs. I:scrpd, smthd, clear hor troughs, patt in MnO, blk, thick in places. C:blue, vitrified, pink subsurfs.

j. FA:50.2 FP 216 Poly SMG<1, fW1–2, silver mica glitter 0.19–0.20, irreg E:scrpd, smthd, patt in MnO, faint gray ghosts, and FeO, red, flaking, lightly brnshd, red-brwn surfs. I:scrpd but lumpy, smthd, patt in MnO, light brnsh, yellow-brwn surfs. C:blue-gray to int, poss vitrified/burned.

k. A:40 MnPtd soft R, poss grog, fL1 no curve E:scrpd, smthd, patt in MnO, gray ghost, pale surfs. I:surf missing. C:pale.

l. A:40 MnPtd fDMG, m voids 0.20 E, I:scrpd, smthd, patt in MnO, gray ghost, greenish surfs, rim fold to ext left rough. C:greenish ext, pink int.

m. A Lot 13 MnPtd fD,m voids 0.17 E, I:scrpd, smthd, creamy white surfs ext, penetrates to subsurfs, int reddish, patt in MnO, blk, prob brnshd, worn. C:pink, creamy subsurf ext.

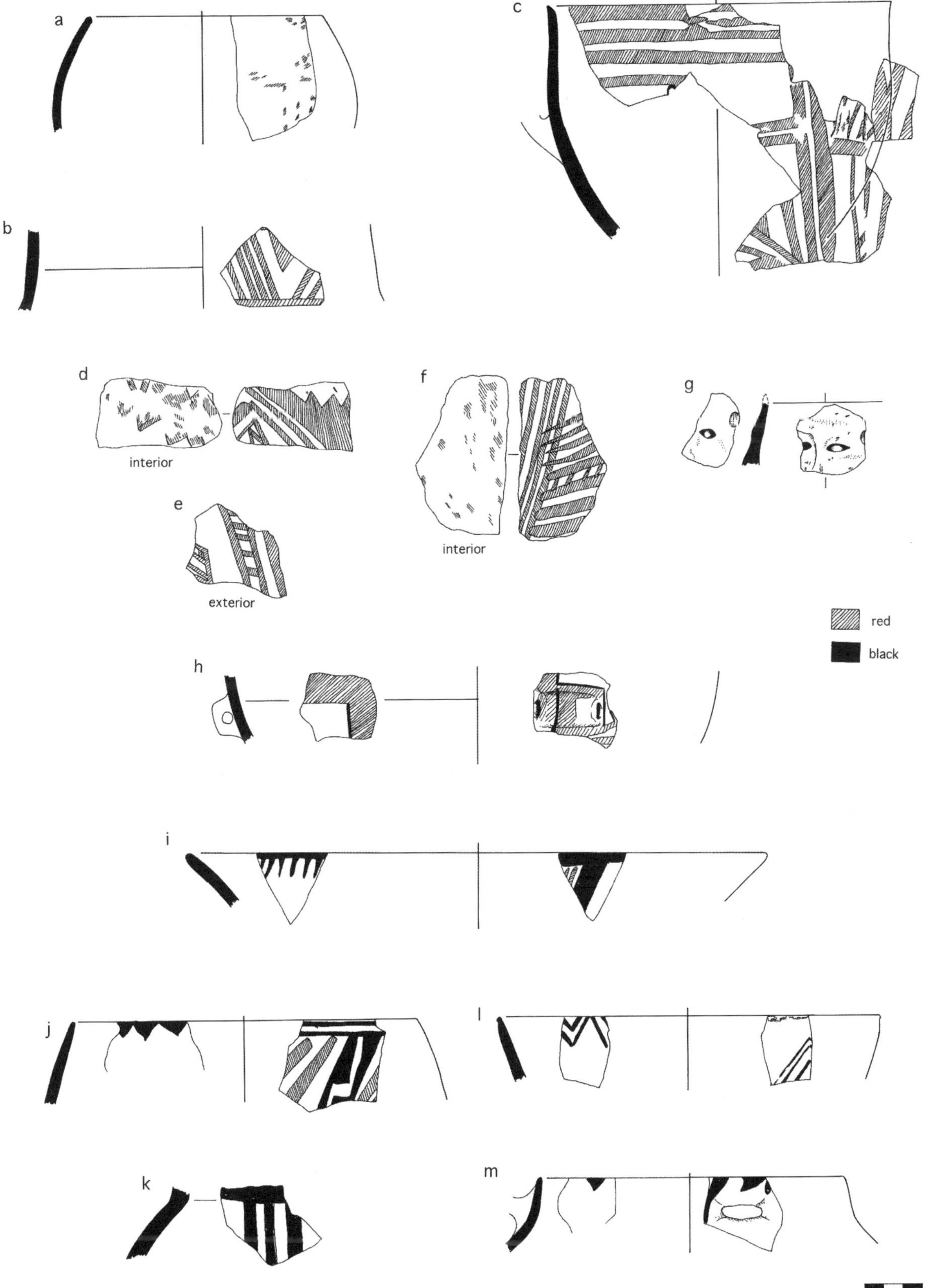
a
b
c
d
interior
e
exterior
f
interior
g
red
black
h
i
j
l
k
m

Figure 73 FCP 5 assorted surface finishes from poor contexts

a. A Lot 13 mDMG1, fR3–4 no curve E, I:bldg surf, smthd, tan to pink surfs, two holes poked below rim before firing. C:uniform light. H:2–3.

1. Lerna L.1149, RIP Restored vessel from Final Neolithic pits at Lerna, shown here 1/6 actual size. Possible shape from which sherds in Fig.73a–b derive.

b. FA WB:29 LMG2–3, grassy impressions 0.28–0.30, irreg E, I:bldg surfs w/ deep scrping marks parallel to rim, two holes poked below rim before firing, brwn surfs. C:brwnish-blk, crumbly. H:3

c. A:11 LMG2–3 0.52 max E, I:scrpd, troughs from scrpg, very irreg surfs, horn on handle modeled in wet clay, pink w/ dark clouds. C:dark gray. H:1–3.

d. A:23 (Lot 13) rRDMG1–2fL 0.15 slightly oval 5 joining E:rim, walls made from single coil attached to ext edge of bottom disc, joint evident on bott, pinched together, scalloped joint, piecrust rim, red surfs w/ gray clouds or sooting. I:smthd but lumpy, finger depressions, grayish surfs. U:faint circular impressions of mat, slightly smeared over, easier to feel than see. C:gray, light subsurfs. H:2–3.

e. FA QSE:9 mSLMG1–2 0.18–0.19 irreg E, I:bldg surfs, tan surfs, faint impression of woven mat w/ curves concentric w/ base. C:gray. H:3. Pl. 7b.

f. A:23 (Lot 13) fLDMG1, holes from vegetal inclusions 3–4 0.085, irreg E, I:walls attached as 2 slabs to ext edge of flat bott disc, bldg surfs, lightly brnshd int, reddish-tan surfs, dark cloud ext bott and int, poss sooting. C:gray, light subsurfs. H:2–3.

Figure 73

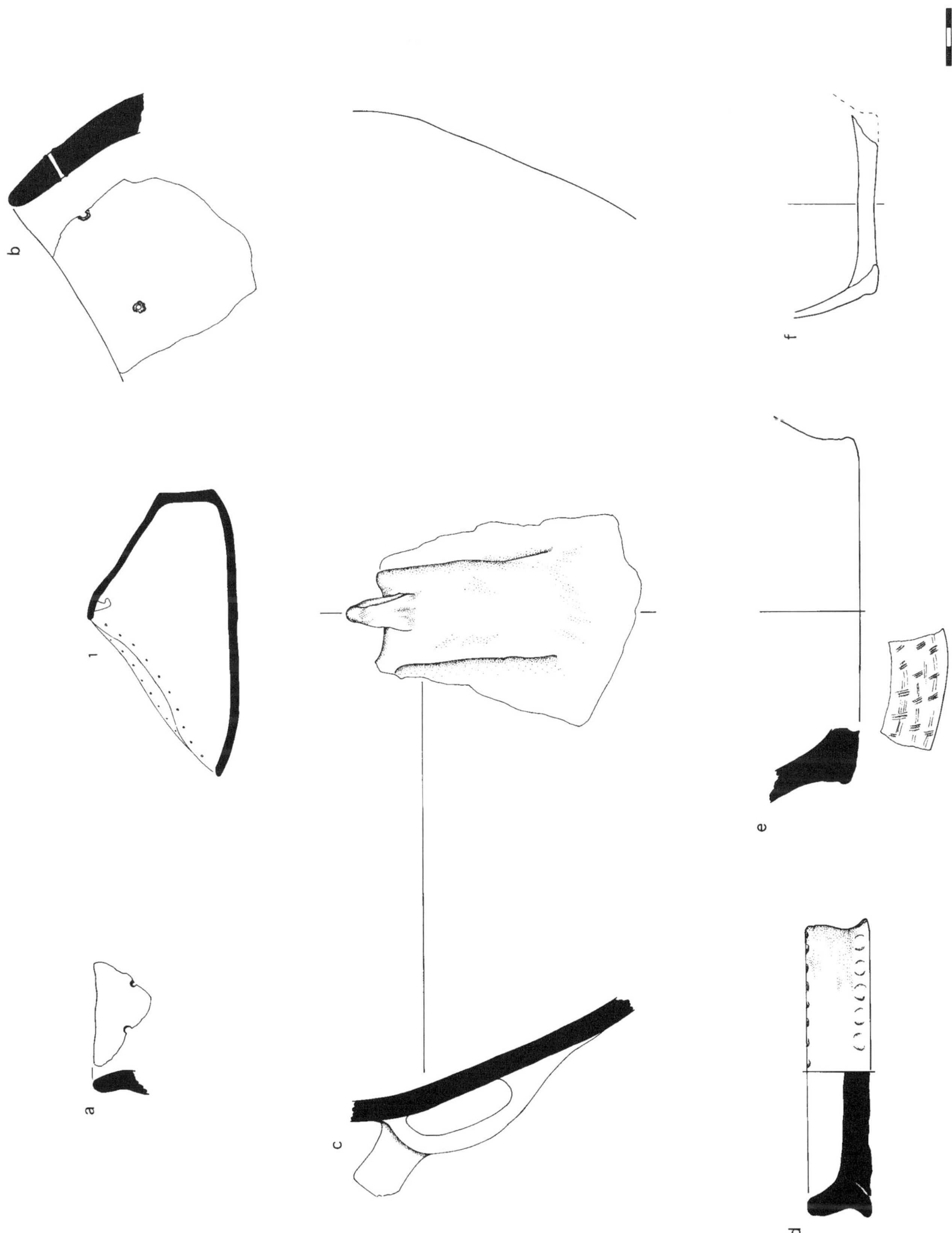

Figure 74 FCP 5 assorted surface finishes from poor contexts

a. A Lot 13 FP 74 LRMG1–2, impressions of short vegetal stalks 0.10 RIP E, I:finger smthd, tan to pink surfs. H:2–3.

b. FF1:15 LMG1–2 0.14 E, I:scrpd, finger smthd, tan surfs, traces 5 holes poked before firing through bott.

c. FA QSW+WB:33B maRW2–3 0.24 E:scrpd, smthd, red surfs w/ gray clouds. I:scrpd, red surfs, poss coil joint at lower edge. C:varies red-blk. H:4.

d. A:40 FP 39 MG<1, frR3 0.055 E, I:clay for walls smeared onto flat bott disc, small accidental hole in bott, v. crude, bldg surfs, traces red pt ext, scratching w/ fingernail turns to orange powder (10R 6/8), traces white Lime ext, three holes poked on each side before firing, two pairs aligned, third is not, brwn w/blk cloud. H:2–3.

e. A:11 RDW1 E:most original surf gone, pink surfs. I:scrpd, pink surfs. C:gray w/ pink subsurfs.

f. FF1:20 FP 168 mLMG1, f5 no measurable curve E:scrpd, wet smthd, applied strips in relief cover surf except at bott, a few detached at joint. I:scrpd, spalled, red-brwn surfs, wall thickness 1.7 cm. C:gray at center. Jacobsen 1973b:Pl. 51b.

g. FA QSE+EB:43 LSMG1–2 E, I:bldg surfs, loop handle detached from rim at joint, brwnish-gray surfs, poss burned.

h. A:40 FP 45 LMG1–2 E, I:bldg surfs, lightly smthd, few strokes brnsh, pinkish-tan surfs, mottled, two ears on top of handle give zoomorphic effect. C:dark gray. H:2–3.

i. A:11 maDWMG1 E, I:smthd, pinkish surfs w. dark cloud, 2 pre-firing holes, one in each arc of prob tab. C:gray. H:2–3.

j. A:11 fDMG<1 E, I:smthd, dark brwn surfs, coated w/ orange powder (10R 6/8). C:gray center. H:2–3.

k. Unstratified LRMG1 E:smthd, applied relief strip w/ higher relief forming crescent lug, pierced vertically before firing, lightly brnshd, reddish-gray surfs. I:scrpd, reddish-gray surfs. C:gray. H:2–3.

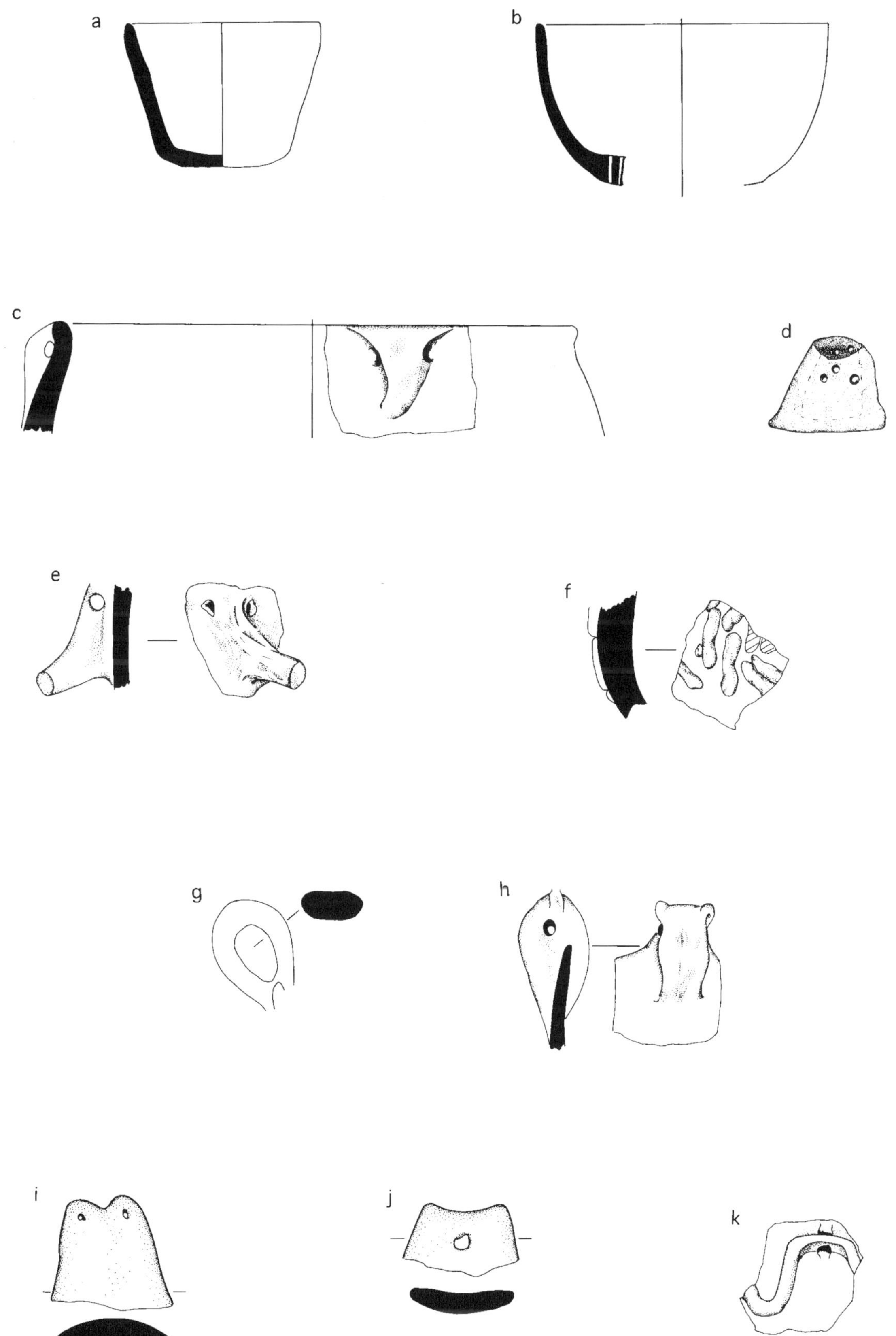
a
b
c
d
e
f
g
h
i
j
k

Figure 75 FCP 5 assorted surface finishes from poor contexts

a. Pool FP 205 HB LSMG1, f2 0.31 E:scrpd, smthd, brnshd below rim ridge, sloppy incised or impressed patt on rim ridge, all surfs crackling, surfs mottled red to gray. I:scrpd, smthd, brnshd, crackling, mottled surfs. C:varies light to gray.

b. A Lot 13 HB rRMG1 0.33 E:scrpd, smthd, brnshd, less well on ext, deep incisions on rim ridge ext, pinkish-brwn surfs, lighter int, blk clouds at rim. C:gray.

c. FA WB:30 LRD<1–2, fL4 0.34, irreg E:scrpd, wet smthd, applied relief band at rim, impressions of finger tips in very wet clay, reddish surfs. I:scrpd, cursory brnsh, mottled gray surfs. C:gray. H:3.

d. A Lot 13 poss EH rlMG2 0.36 E, I:scrpd, wet smthd, applied relief band ext w/ neat finger tip impressions in nearly dry clay creating series of rectangular relief ridges, blkish-red surfs. C:gray.

e. A Lot 13 DMG1–2, holes from vegetal inclusions 2 0.20 E:scrpd wet, light brnshd ext below handle, poss trace of red pt, pinkish-tan surfs, grayer at rim. I:scrpd wet, pinkish-tan surfs. C:gray to int.

f. A:40 mSMG1 0.24 max E, I:scrpd, smthd, pink surfs ext, 2 diagonal lines incised, then 2 hor, dark brwn surfs int. C:gray to brwn.

g. A:20 fLW1–2D<1 0.13 E:scrpd, wet smthd, deep but wobbly incisions, tan surfs. I:wet smthd better than ext, blk surfs. C:gray.

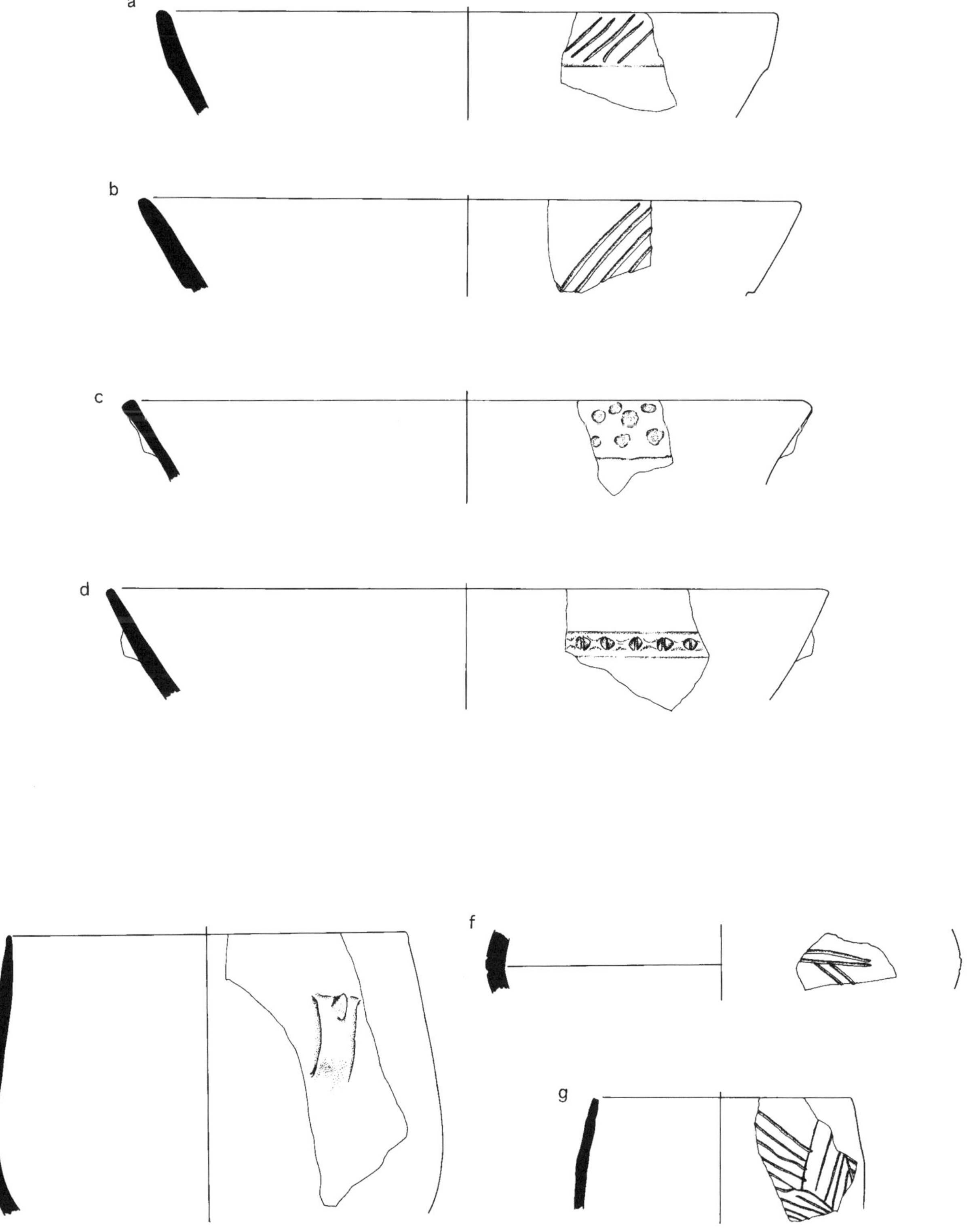
a
b
c
d
e
f
g

Figure 76

FCP 3 range of vessel shapes, all varieties.
Restorations are hypothetical.

Figure 77

FCP 4.1 range of vessel shapes, all varieties.
Restorations are hypothetical.

Figure 78

FCP 4.2 range of vessel shapes, all varieties.
Restorations are hypothetical.

Figure 79

FCP 4.3 range of vessel shapes, all varieties.
Restorations are hypothetical.

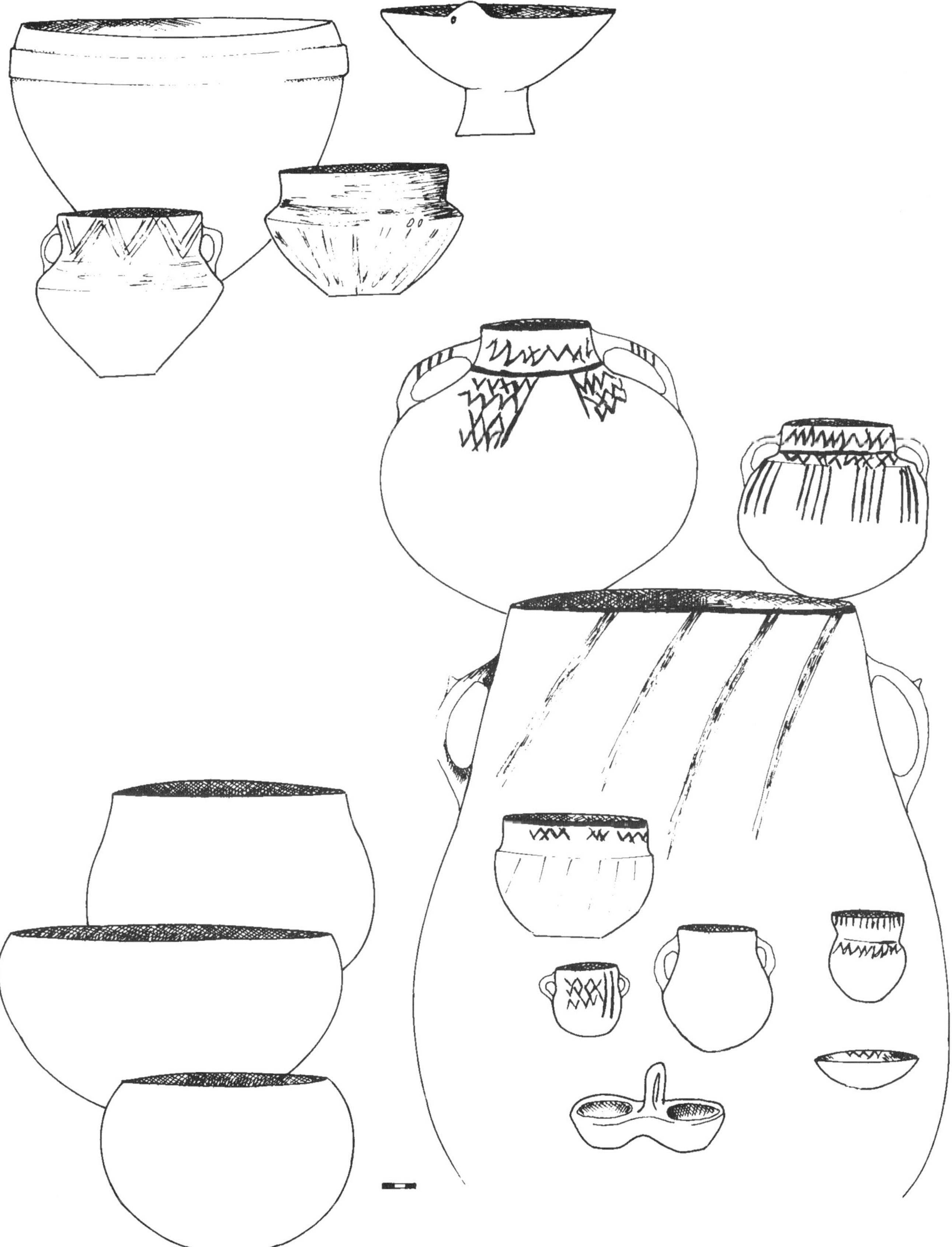

Figure 80

FCP 5.1a range of vessel shapes, all varieties.
Restorations are hypothetical.

Figure 81 FCP 5.1b range of vessel shapes, all varieties. Restorations are hypothetical.

Figure 82

FCP 5.1c range of vessel shapes, all varieties.
Restorations are hypothetical.

Figure 83 FCP 5.1 L5 range of vessel shapes, undecorated surfaces. Restorations are hypothetical.

Figure 84 FCP 5.1 L5 range of vessel shapes, elaborated surfaces. Restorations are hypothetical.

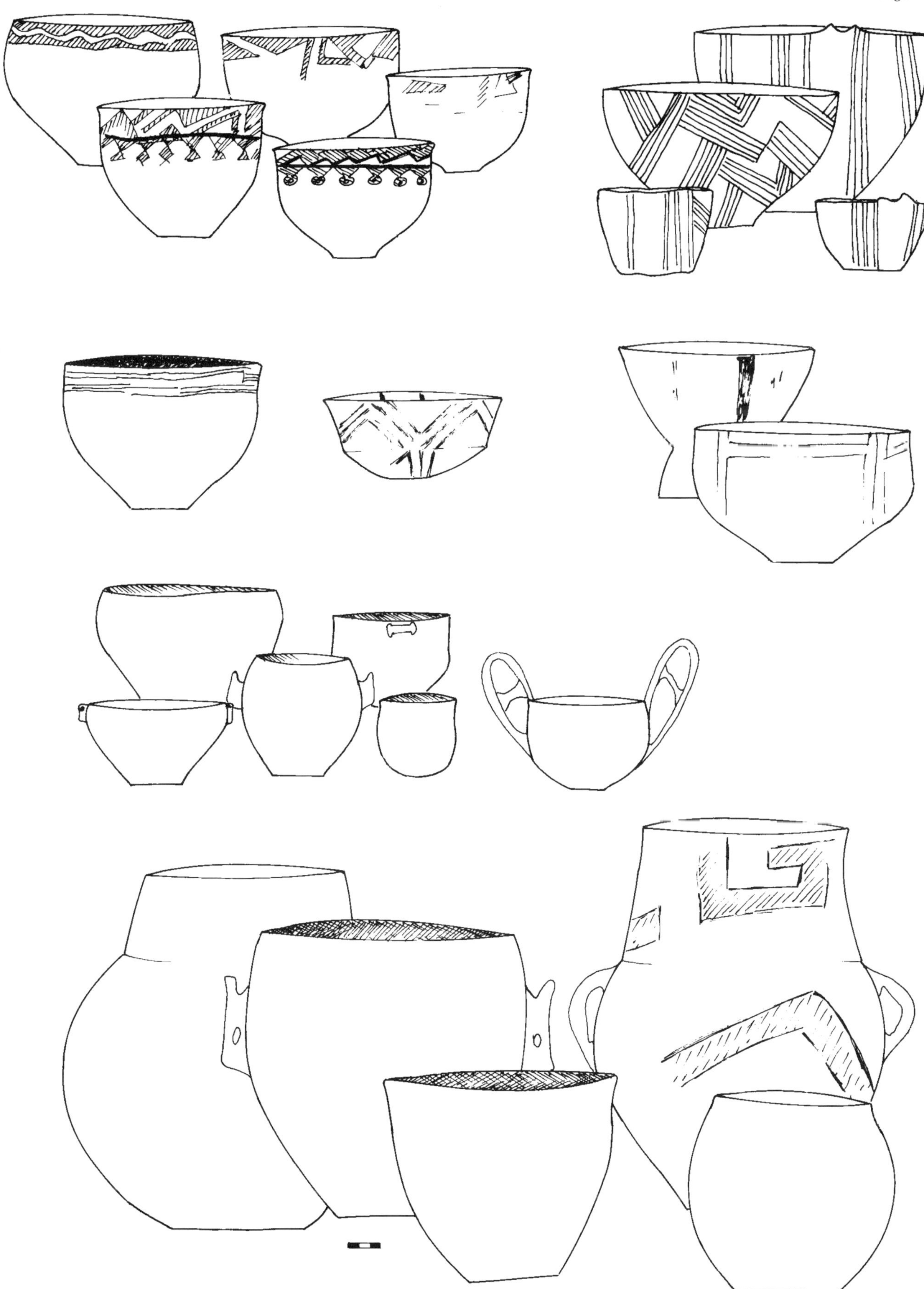

Figure 85

FCP 5.2 range of vessel shapes, all varieties.
Restorations are hypothetical.

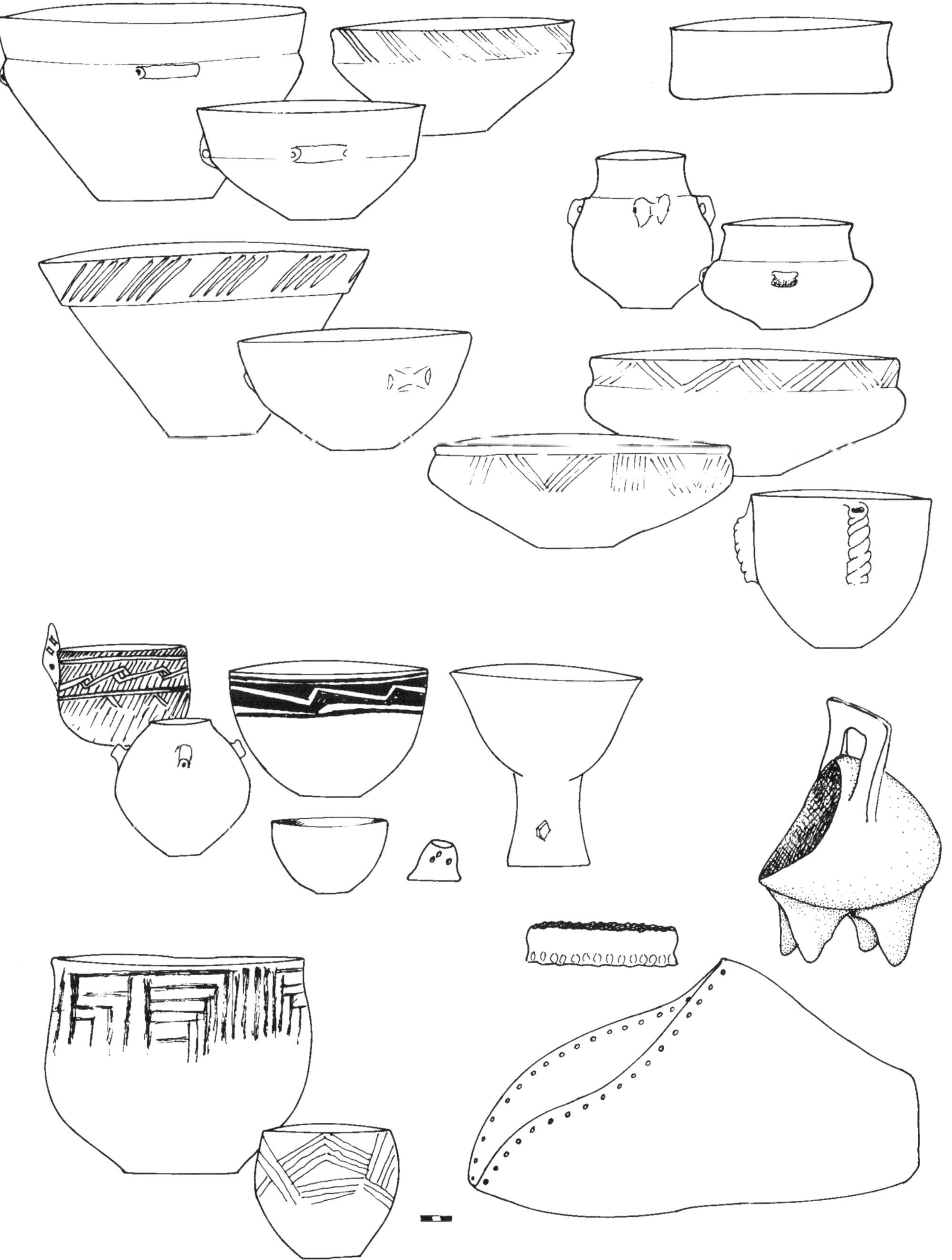

Figure 86

FA West Section, Neolithic strata.
The lower portion, not reproduced here, is of older date.
From Jacobsen and Farrand:Pl. 7.

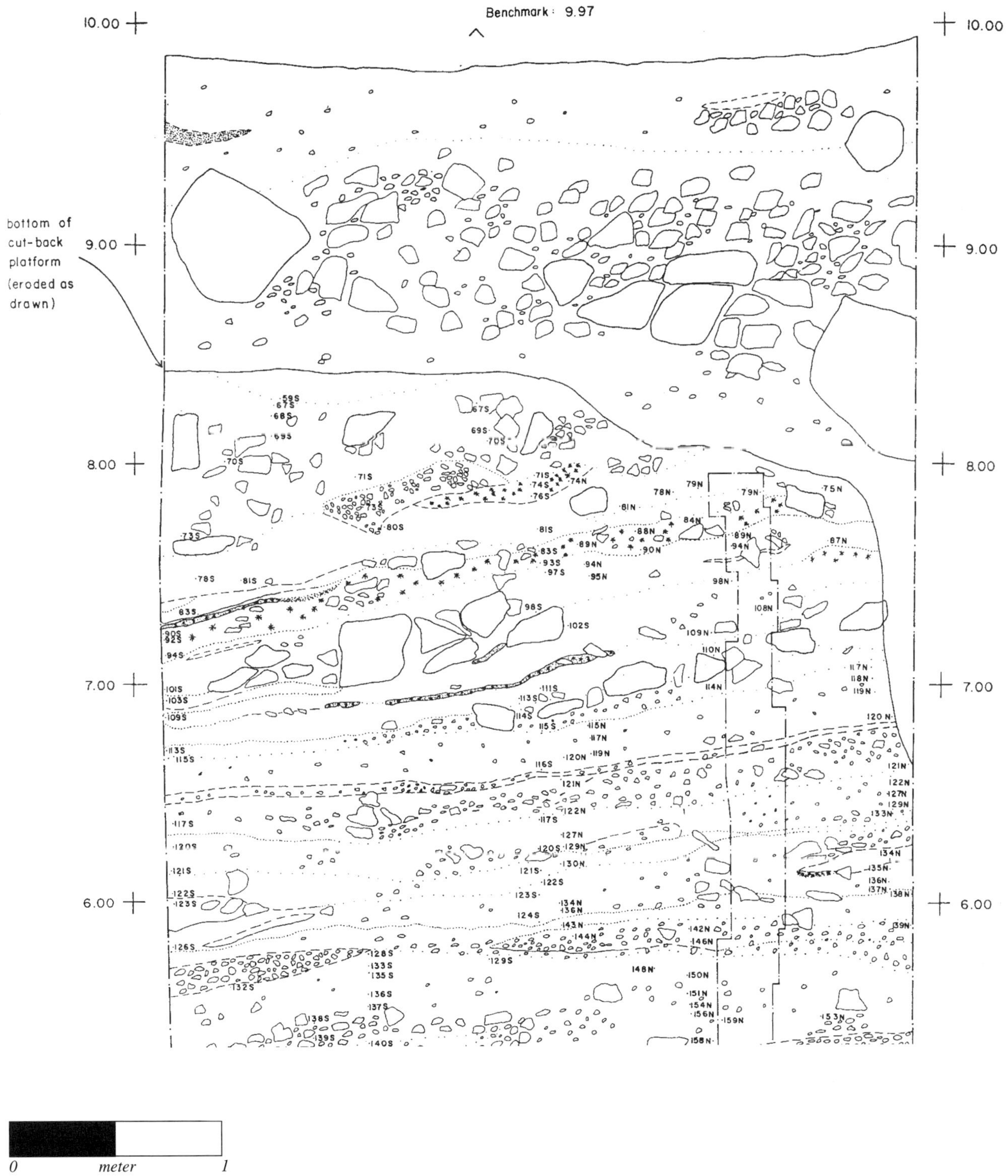

10.00 Benchmark: 9.97 10.00

bottom of cut-back platform (eroded as drawn)

9.00 9.00

8.00 8.00

7.00 7.00

6.00 6.00

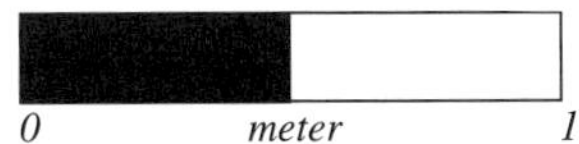

Franchthi FA West
D. J. Pullen 1979, 1985

Elevations in meters above sea level

Plates

Plate 1a. "Three-burner hearth" in FAS:91 (FCP 4.2) from the southeast. Trench A is visible in lower left, Trench FAN (plastic-covered) and FF1 (deep sounding) in upper right.
Photo by excavator.

Plate 1b. FCP 3 LoLiB carinated bowl, Fig. 5f: lighter sherds to right of rim sherd with drill hole may have been burned after breaking. See figure for scale. Photo by Reg. Heron.

Plate 2a. Close-up of neck of very large FCP 3 LoLiB jar, Fig. 10: erased pattern lines visible to right of replacement lines. NB: feathered ends of brush strokes.

See figure for scale. Photo by Reg Heron.

Plate 2b. FCP 3 LiCo sherds, Fig. 15b, with variable size and distribution of powdery Lime grits.

See figure for scale. Photo by Reg Heron.

Plate 3a. FCP 3 non-joining Poly sherds, Fig. 12h. See figure for scale. Photo by Reg Heron.

Plate 3b. FCP 4 AndB bowl with PB interior, Fig. 35h. See figure for scale. Photo by Reg Heron.

Plate 4a. Interior and, Plate 4b, exterior of FCP 4.1 LiFe bowl with Lime pops, sloppy decoration, and irregular rim, Fig. 22a.

See figure for scale. Photos by Reg Heron.

Plate 4c. FCP 4.1 LiFe small jar: firing resulted in dark gray pattern on lighter gray background, both marred by Lime pops, Fig. 20a.

See figure for scale. Photo by Reg Heron.

Plate 5a. FCP 4 LiFe bowl with floating zigzag patterns, Fig. 40d. See figure for scale. Photo by Reg Heron.

Plate 5b. FCP 5 sherds with multiple coats of a mixture of Lime, clay, and vegetal tempering "smeared" over the exterior, including over rope band, after firing. Photo by Reg Heron.

Plate 5c. Four examples of FCP 5 "smears": Lime-rich clay fired onto pot in original or subsequent fire. Sherd on upper left includes "smear" over applied rope band and handle. Photo by Reg Heron.

Plate 6a. FCP 5.1 Poly Crusted sherds, Fig. 64a. See figure for scale. Photo by Reg Heron.

Plate 6b. FCP 5.1 burned White Ptd rim, Fig. 65c. See figure for scale. Photo by Reg Heron.

Plate 6c. FCP 5.2 PB sherd with reserved rim, Fig. 71a. See figure for scale. Photo by Reg Heron.

Plate 7c (opposite).

Left: FCP 5 bottom sherd impressed with "twill matting with 'warp' of paired strands and 'weft' of triplets, forming a 3 x 2 broken twill. No strand shows any sign of twisting" (J. Carrington-Smith, inventory notebook, FP 151, H1:53, MPL 0.06 m).

Right: FCP 5 bottom sherd with impression of short, grassy fibers in apparently random arrangement, i.e., not a mat. FP 150, FA:44, MPL. 0.05 m.

Photos by Reg Heron.

Plate 7a. FCP 5.1 bottom sherd with the impression of a circular mat. Impression does not continue up sides, which retain the building surface , FP 232, MPL 0.12 m.
Photo by Reg Heron.

Plate 7b. FCP 5 bottom sherd with faint traces of impression of woven mat, Fig. 73e. See figure for scale. Photo by Reg. Heron.

Plate 8a. The Pool (flash photograph).

Plate 8b. Surface of the Pool near its edge showing sherds, wood, and limestone chips (underwater photograph).

Plate 9a. Kalathiskos, post-Neolithic object #5.
Height 0.043 m.

Plate 9b. Terracotta female protome head, post-Neolithic object #8.
Present height 0.043 m.

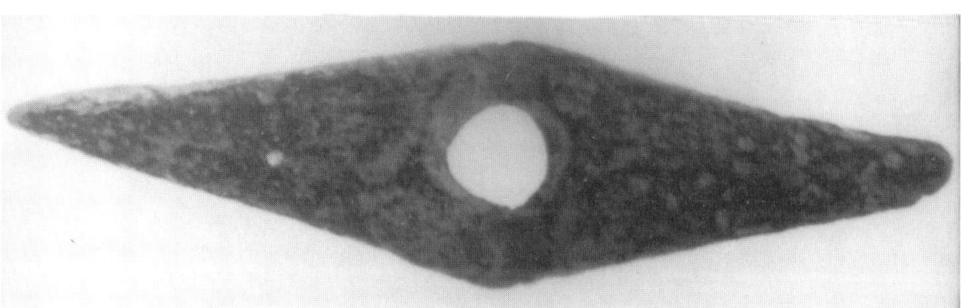

Plate 9c. Bronze sheet, post-Neolithic object #16.
Length 0.035 m.

Plate 9d. Corinthian miniature kotyle, post-Neolithic object #3.
Height 0.016 m.